DATE DUE

AP 26 00		

DEMCO 38-296

THE
THIRD
CHIMPANZEE

THE THIRD CHIMPANZEE

The Evolution and Future

OF THE

Human Animal

JARED DIAMOND

HarperCollins*Publishers*

HarperCollins books may be purchased for educational, business, or sales promotional use. For information, please call or write: Special Markets Department, HarperCollins Publishers, Inc., 10 East 53rd Street, New York, NY 10022. Telephone: (212) 207-7528; Fax: (212) 207-7222.

FIRST EDITION

Designed by Ruth Kolbert

LIBRARY OF CONGRESS CATALOGING-IN-PUBLICATION DATA
Diamond, Jared M.
  The third chimpanzee : the evolution and future of the human animal / Jared Diamond. — 1st ed.
    p. cm.
  Includes bibliographical references and index.
  ISBN 0-06-018307-1 (cloth)
  1. Human evolution.   2. Social evolution.   3. Man—Influence on nature.   I. Title.
GN281.D53   1992
573.2—dc20
                                                              91-50455

92 93 94 95 96 AC/HC 10 9 8 7 6 5 4 3 2 1

Dedicated to my sons
Max and Joshua,
to help them understand
where we came from
and where we may be heading

THEME

*How the human species changed, within a short time,
from just another species of big mammal
to a world conqueror;
and how we acquired the capacity
to reverse all that progress overnight*

CONTENTS

Contents

Prologue

IT's OBVIOUS THAT humans are unlike all animals. It's also obvious that we're a species of big mammal, down to the minutest details of our anatomy and our molecules. That contradiction is the most fascinating feature of the human species. It's familiar, but we still have difficulty grasping how it came to be and what it means.

On the one hand, between us and all other species lies a seemingly unbridgeable gulf that we acknowledge by defining a category called "animals." It implies that we consider centipedes, chimpanzees, and clams to share decisive features with each other but not with us, and to lack features restricted to us. Among those unique characteristics of ours, we talk, write, and build complex machines. We depend on tools, not on our bare hands, to make a living. Most of us wear clothes and enjoy art, and many of us believe in a religion. We are distributed over the whole Earth, command much of its energy and production, and are beginning to expand into the ocean depths and into Space. We're also unique in darker behaviors, including genocide, delight in torture, addiction to toxic drugs, and extermination of other species by the thousands. While a few animal species have one or two of these behaviors in rudimentary form (like tool use), we still far eclipse animals in even those respects.

Thus, for practical and legal purposes, humans aren't considered animals. When Darwin proposed in 1859 that we had evolved from apes, it's no wonder that most people initially regarded his theory as absurd and continued to insist that we had been separately created by God. Many people, including a quarter of all American college graduates, still hold to that belief today.

But, on the other hand, we obviously are animals, with the usual animal body parts, molecules, and genes. It's even clear what particular type of animal we are. Externally, we're so similar to chimpanzees that eighteenth-century anatomists who believed in divine creation could already recognize our affinities. Just imagine taking some normal people, stripping off their clothes, taking away all their other possessions, depriving them of the power of speech, and reducing them to grunting, without changing their anatomy at all. Put them in a cage in the zoo next to the chimp cages, and let the rest of us clothed and talking people visit the zoo. Those speechless caged people would be seen for what we all really are: chimps that have little hair and walk upright. A zoologist from Outer Space would immediately classify us as just a third species of chimpanzee, along with the pygmy chimp of Zaire and the common chimp of the rest of tropical Africa.

Molecular genetic studies of the last half-dozen years have shown that we continue to share over 98 percent of our genetic program with the other two chimps. The overall genetic distance between us and chimps is even smaller than the distance between such closely related bird species as red-eyed and white-eyed vireos. Thus, we still carry most of our old biological baggage with us. Since Darwin's time, fossilized bones of hundreds of creatures variously intermediate between apes and modern humans have been discovered, making it impossible for a reasonable person to deny the overwhelming evidence. What once seemed absurd—our evolution from apes—actually happened.

Yet the discoveries of many missing links have only made the problem more fascinating, without fully solving it. The few bits of new baggage we acquired—the 2 percent difference between our genes and those of chimps—must have been responsible for all of our seemingly unique properties. We underwent some small changes

with big consequences rather quickly and recently in our evolutionary history. In fact, as recently as a hundred thousand years ago that
zoologist from Outer Space would have viewed us as just one more
species of big mammal. Granted, we had a couple of curious behaviors, notably our control of fire and our dependence on tools. But
those behaviors would have seemed no more curious to the extraterrestrial visitor than would the behaviors of beavers and bowerbirds.
Somehow, within a few tens of thousands of years—a period that is
almost infinitely long when measured against one person's memory
but is only a tiny fraction of our species' separate history—we had
begun to demonstrate the qualities that make us unique and fragile.

What were those few key ingredients that made us human? Since
our unique properties appeared so recently and involved so few
changes, those properties or at least their precursors must already be
present in animals. What are those animal precursors of art and
language, of genocide and drug abuse?

OUR UNIQUE QUALITIES have been responsible for our present biological success as a species. No other large animal is native to all the
continents, or breeds in all habitats from deserts and the Arctic to
tropical rainforests. No large wild animal rivals us in numbers. But
among our unique qualities are two that now jeopardize our existence: our propensities to kill each other and to destroy our environment. Of course, both propensities occur in other species: lions and
many other animals kill their own kind, while elephants and others
damage their environment. However, these propensities are much
more threatening in us than in other animals because of our technological power and exploding numbers.

There's nothing new about prophecies to the effect that the world's
end is near if we don't repent. What's new is that this prophecy is
now likely to come true, for two obvious reasons. First, nuclear
weapons give us the means to wipe ourselves out quickly; no humans
possessed this means before. Second, we already appropriate about 40
percent of the Earth's net productivity (i.e., the net energy captured
from sunlight). With the world's human population now doubling
every forty-one years, we soon shall reach the biological limit to
growth, at which point we shall have to start fighting each other in
dead earnest for a share of the world's fixed pie of resources. In

addition, given the present rate at which we are exterminating species, most of the world's species will become extinct or endangered within the next century, but we depend on many species for our own life support.

Why rehearse these familiar depressing facts? And why try to trace the animal origins of our destructive qualities? If they really are part of our evolutionary heritage, that seems to say that they are genetically fixed and hence unchangeable.

In fact, our situation is not hopeless. Perhaps the urge to murder strangers or sexual rivals is innate in us. But that still hasn't prevented human societies from attempting to thwart those instincts, and from succeeding in sparing most people the fate of being murdered. Even taking two world wars into account, proportionately far fewer people have died violent deaths in twentieth-century industrialized states than in Stone Age tribal societies. Many modern populations enjoy longer life spans than did humans of the past. Environmentalists don't always lose in battles with developers and destroyers. Even some genetic infirmities, such as phenylketonuria and juvenile-onset diabetes, can now be mitigated or cured.

My purpose in rehearsing our situation is to help us avoid repeating our mistakes—to use knowledge of our past and our propensities in order to change our behavior. That's the hope behind the dedication of this book. My twin sons were born in 1987 and will reach my present age in the year 2041. What we are doing now is shaping their world.

It is not the goal of this book to propose specific solutions to our predicament, because the solutions we should adopt are already clear in broad outline. Some of those solutions include halting population growth, limiting or eliminating nuclear weapons, developing peaceful means for solving international disputes, reducing our impact on the environment, and preserving species and natural habitats. Many excellent books make detailed proposals for how to carry out these policies. Some of these policies are being implemented in some cases now; we "just" need to implement them consistently. If we all became convinced today that they were essential, we would already know enough to start carrying them out tomorrow.

Instead, what is lacking is the necessary political will. Through this book I seek to foster that will, by tracing our history as a species. Our problems have deep roots tracing back to our animal ancestry. They have been growing for a long time with our growing power and numbers, and are now steeply accelerating. We can convince ourselves of the inevitable outcome of our current shortsighted practices just by examining the many past societies that destroyed themselves by destroying their own resource base, despite having less potent means of self-destruction than ours. Political historians justify the study of individual states and rulers by the resulting opportunity to learn from the past. That justification applies even more to the study of our history as a species, because the lessons of that study are simpler and clearer.

A VOLUME that ranges over such a broad canvas as this one has to be selective. Every reader is bound to find some absolutely crucial favorite subjects omitted, some other subjects pursued in inordinate detail. So that you won't feel you were misled, I'll lay out at the start my own particular interests, and where they come from.

My father is a physician, my mother a musician with a gift for languages. Whenever I was asked as a child about my career plans, my response was that I wanted to be a doctor like my father. By my last year in college, that goal had become gently transformed into the related goal of medical research. And so I trained in physiology, the area in which I now teach and do research at the University of California Medical School in Los Angeles.

However, at the age of seven I had also become interested in bird-watching, and I had been fortunate to go to a school that let me delve into languages and history. After I got my Ph.D., the prospect of devoting the rest of my life to the single professional interest of physiology began to look increasingly oppressive. At that point, a happy constellation of events and people gave me the chance to spend a summer in the highlands of New Guinea. Ostensibly, the purpose of my trip was to measure nesting success of New Guinea birds, a project that collapsed dismally within a few weeks when I found myself unable to locate even a single bird nest in the jungle. Yet the real purpose of the trip succeeded completely: to indulge my thirst for adventure and bird-watching in one of the wildest remaining parts of the world. What I saw then of New Guinea's fabulous birds, including its bowerbirds and birds of paradise, led me to develop a parallel second career, in bird ecology, evolution, and biogeography. Since then, I've returned to New Guinea and neighboring Pacific islands a dozen times to pursue my bird research.

But I found it hard to work in New Guinea amid the accelerating destruction of the birds and forests that I loved, without getting involved in conservation biology. So I began to combine my academic research with practical work as a consultant for governments, by applying what I knew about animal distributions to designing national park systems and surveying proposed national parks. It was also hard to work in New Guinea, where languages replace each other every twenty miles, and where learning bird names in each local language proved to be the key to tapping New Guineans' encyclopedic knowledge of their birds, without returning to my earlier interest in languages. Most of all, it was hard to study the evolution and extinction of bird species without wanting to understand the evolution and possible extinction of *Homo sapiens,* by far the most interesting species of all. That interest, too, was especially hard to ignore in New Guinea, with its enormous human diversity.

Those are the paths by which I came to be interested in the particular aspects of humans that are emphasized in this book. Numerous excellent books by anthropologists and archaeologists already discuss human evolution in terms of tools and bones, which this book can therefore summarize briefly. However, those other volumes devote much less space to my particular interests of the human life cycle, human geography, human impacts on the environment, and humans as animals. Those subjects are as central to human evolution as are the more traditional subjects involving tools and bones.

I believe that what may at first seem to be a plethora of examples drawn from New Guinea is appropriate. Granted, New Guinea is just one island, located in a particular part of the world (the tropical Pacific), and hardly providing a random cross-section of modern humanity. But New Guinea harbors a much bigger slice of humanity than you would at first guess from its area. About a thousand of the world's approximately five thousand languages are spoken only in New Guinea. Much of the cultural diversity that survives in the modern world is contained within New Guinea. All highland peoples in New Guinea's mountainous interior were Stone Age farmers until very recently, while many lowland groups were nomadic hunter-gatherers and fishermen practicing somewhat casual agriculture. Local xenophobia was extreme, cultural diversity correspondingly so, and travel outside of one's tribal territory would have been suicidal. Many of the New Guineans who have worked with me are deadly expert hunters who lived out their childhood in the days of stone tools and xenophobia. Thus, New Guinea is as good a model as we have left today of what much of the rest of the human world was once like.

THE STORY of our rise and fall divides itself into five natural parts. In the first part I'll follow us from several million years ago until just before agriculture's appearance ten thousand years ago. These two chapters deal with the evidence of bones, tools, and genes—the evidence that is preserved in the archaeological and biochemical record, and that gives us our most direct information about how we have changed. Fossilized bones and tools can often be dated, permitting us to deduce in addition just when we changed. We'll examine the basis of the conclusion that we're still 98 percent chimps in our genes, and we'll try to figure out what difference of 2 percent was responsible for our great leap forward.

The second part deals with changes in the human life cycle, which were as essential to the development of language and art as were the skeletal changes discussed in Part One. It's restating the obvious to mention that we feed our children after the age of weaning, instead of leaving them to find food on their own; that most adult men and women associate in couples; that most fathers as well as mothers care for their children; that many people live long enough to experience grandchildren; and that women undergo menopause. To us, these traits are the norm, but by the standards of our closest animal relatives they are bizarre. They constitute major changes from our ancestral condition, though they don't fossilize and so we don't know when they arose. For that reason they receive much briefer treatment in books on human paleontology than do our changes in brain size and pelvis. But they were crucial to our uniquely human cultural development, and merit equal attention.

With Parts One and Two thus having surveyed the biological underpinnings of our cultural flowering, Part Three proceeds to consider the cultural traits that we consider as distinguishing us from animals. Those that come first to mind are the ones of which we are proudest: language, art, technology, and agriculture, the hallmarks of our rise. Yet our distinguishing cultural traits also include black marks on our record, such as abuse of toxic chemicals. While one can debate whether all these hallmarks rank as uniquely human, they at least constitute huge advances on animal precursors. But animal precursors there must have been, since these traits flowered only recently on an evolutionary time scale. What were those precursors? Was their flowering inevitable in the history of life on Earth? For example, so inevitable that we suspect there to be many other planets out in Space, inhabited by creatures as advanced as we are?

Besides chemical abuse, our black traits include two so serious that they may lead to our fall. Part Four considers the first of these: our propensity for xenophobic killing of other human groups. This trait has direct animal precursors—namely, the contests between competing individuals and groups that, in many species besides our own, may be resolved by murder. We've merely used our technological prowess to improve our killing power. In Part Four we'll consider the xenophobia and extreme isolation that marked the human condition before the rise of political states began to make us more homogeneous culturally. We'll see how technology, culture, and geography affected the outcome of two of the most familiar historical sets of contests between human groups. We'll then survey the worldwide recorded history of xenophobic mass murder. This is a painful subject, but here above all is an example of how our refusal to face up to our history condemns us to repeat past mistakes on a more dangerous scale.

The other black trait that now threatens our survival is our accelerating assault on our environment. This behavior too has its direct animal precursors. Animal populations that for one reason or another escaped control by predators and parasites have in some cases also escaped their own internal controls on their numbers, multiplied until they damaged their resource base, and occasionally eaten their way into extinction. Such a risk applies with special force to humans, because predation on us is now negligible, no habitat is beyond our influence, and our power to kill individual animals and destroy habitats is unprecedented.

Unfortunately, many people still cling to the Rousseauian fantasy that this behavior did not appear in us until the Industrial Revolution, before which we lived in harmony with Nature. If that were true, we would have nothing to learn from the past except how virtuous we once were and how evil we have now become. Part Five seeks to dismantle this fantasy by facing up to our long history of environmental mismanagement. In Part Five as in Part Four, the emphasis is on recognizing that our present situation is not novel, except in degree. The experiment of trying to manage a human society while mismanaging its environment has already been run many times, and the outcome is there for us to learn from.

This book concludes with an epilogue that traces our rise from animal status. It also traces the acceleration in our means to bring about our fall. I wouldn't have written this book if I had thought that the risk was remote, but I also wouldn't have written it if I had considered us doomed. Lest any readers get so discouraged by our track record and present predicament that they overlook this message, I point out the hopeful signs and the ways in which we can learn from the past.

PART ONE

JUST ANOTHER SPECIES OF BIG MAMMAL

The clues about when, why, and in what ways we ceased to be just another species of big mammal come from three types of evidence. Part One considers some of the traditional evidence from archaeology, which studies fossil bones and preserved tools, plus newer evidence from molecular biology.

One basic question concerns just how extensive the genetic differences between us and chimps are. That is, do our genes differ by 10, 50, or 99 percent from chimpanzee genes? Merely eyeballing humans and chimps or counting up visible traits wouldn't be any help, because many genetic changes have no visible effects at all, while other changes have sweeping effects. For example, the visible differences between breeds of dogs such as Great Danes and Pekinese are far greater than those between chimps and us. Yet all dog breeds are interfertile, breed with each other (insofar as it's mechanically feasible) when given the opportunity, and belong to the same species. To a naïve observer, a glance at Great Danes and Pekinese would have suggested them to be genetically much further apart than chimps are from humans. Those visible differences among dog breeds in size, proportions, and hair color depend on relatively few genes, which have negligible consequences for reproductive biology.

How, then, can we estimate our genetic distance from chimps? This problem has been solved only within the past half-dozen years, by molecular biologists. The answer is not just intellectually surprising but may also have some practical ethical implications for how we treat chimps. We'll see that gene differences between us and chimps, although large compared to those among living human populations or among breeds of dogs, are still small compared to differences among many other familiar pairs of related species. Evidently, changes in only a small percentage of the chimpanzee genetic program had enormous consequences for our behavior. It has also proved possible to work out a calibration between genetic distance and elapsed time, and thereby to get an approximate answer to the question of when we and chimps split apart from our common ancestor. That turns out to be somewhere around seven million years ago, give or take a few million years.

While these molecular biological results yield overall measures of genetic distance and elapsed time, they tell us nothing about how specifically we differ from chimps, and when those specific differences appeared. Hence we'll go on to consider what more can be learned from bones and tools left by creatures variously intermediate between our apelike ancestor and modern humans. The changes in bones constitute the traditional subject matter of physical anthropology. Especially important were our increase in brain size, skeletal changes associated with walking upright, and decreases in skull thickness, tooth size, and jaw muscles.

Our large brain was surely prerequisite for the development of human language and innovativeness. One might therefore expect the fossil record to show a close parallel between increased brain size and sophistication of tools. In fact, the parallel is not at all close. This proves to be the greatest surprise and puzzle of human evolution. Stone tools remained very crude for hundreds of thousands of years after we had undergone most of our expansion of brain size. As recently as forty thousand years ago, Neanderthals had brains even larger than those of modern humans, yet their tools show no signs of innovativeness and art. Neanderthals were still just another species of big mammal. Even for tens of thousands of years after some other human populations had achieved virtually modern skeletal anatomy, their tools remained as boring as those of Neanderthals.

These paradoxes sharpen the conclusion drawn from the evidence of molecular biology. Within that modest percentage of difference between our genes and chimpanzee genes, there must have been an even smaller percentage not involved in the shapes of our bones but responsible for the distinctively human attributes of innovation, art, and complex tools. At least in Europe, those attributes appeared unexpectedly suddenly, at the time of the replacement of Neanderthals by Cro-Magnons. That is the time when we finally ceased to be just another species of big mammal. At the end of Part One I'll speculate about what those few changes were that triggered our steep rise to human status.

CHAPTER I

A Tale of
Three Chimps

THE NEXT TIME YOU VISIT A ZOO, MAKE A POINT OF WALKING PAST the ape cages. Imagine that the apes had lost most of their hair, and imagine a cage nearby holding some unfortunate people who had no clothes and couldn't speak but were otherwise normal. Now try guessing how similar those apes are to us in their genes. For instance, would you guess that a chimpanzee shares 10 percent, 50 percent, or 99 percent of its genetic program with humans?

Then ask yourself why those apes are on exhibit in cages, and why other apes are being used for medical experiments, while it's not permissible to do either of those things to humans. Suppose it turned out that chimp genes were 99.9 percent identical to our genes, and that the important differences between humans and chimps were due to just a few genes. Would you still think it's okay to put chimps in cages and to experiment on them? Consider those unfortunate mentally defective people who have much less capacity to solve problems, to care for themselves, to communicate, to engage in social relationships, and to feel pain than do apes. What is the logic that forbids medical experiments on those people, but not on apes?

You might answer that apes are "animals," while humans are humans, and that's enough. An ethical code for treating humans shouldn't be extended to an "animal," no matter how similar its genes are to ours, and no matter what its capacity for social relationships or feeling pain. That's an arbitrary but at least self-consistent answer that can't be lightly dismissed. In that case, learning more about our ancestral relationships won't have any ethical consequences, but it will still satisfy our intellectual curiosity to understand where we come from. Every human society has felt a deep need to make sense of its origins, and has answered that need with its own story of the Creation. The Tale of Three Chimps is the Creation Story of our time.

FOR CENTURIES it's been clear approximately where we fit into the animal kingdom. We are obviously mammals, the group of animals characterized by having hair, nursing their young, and other features. Among mammals we are obviously primates, the group of mammals including monkeys and apes. We share with other primates numerous traits lacking in most other mammals, such as flat fingernails and toenails rather than claws, hands for gripping, a thumb that can be opposed to the other four fingers, and a penis that hangs free rather than being attached to the abdomen. Already by the second century A.D., the Greek physician Galen deduced our approximate place in nature correctly when he dissected various animals and found that a monkey was "most similar to man in viscera, muscles, arteries, veins, nerves, and in the form of bones."

It's also easy to place us within the primates, among which we are obviously more similar to apes (the gibbons, orangutan, gorilla, and chimpanzees) than to monkeys. To name only one of the most visible signs, monkeys sport tails, which we lack along with apes. It's also clear that gibbons, with their small size and very long arms, are the most distinctive apes, and that orangutans, chimpanzees, gorillas, and humans are all more closely related to each other than any is to gibbons. But to go further with our relationships proves unexpectedly difficult. It has provoked an intense scientific debate, which revolves around three questions:

What is the detailed family tree of relationships among humans, the living apes, and extinct ancestral apes? For example, which of the living apes is our closest relative?

When did we and that closest living relative, whichever ape it is, last share a common ancestor?

What fraction of our genetic program do we share with that closest living relative?

At first, it would seem natural to assume that comparative anatomy had already solved the first of those three questions. We look especially like chimpanzees and gorillas, but differ from them in obvious features like our larger brains, upright posture, and much less body hair, as well as in many subtler points. However, on closer examination these anatomical facts aren't decisive. Depending on what anatomical characters one considers most important and how one interprets them, biologists differ as to whether we are most closely related to the orangutan (the minority view), with chimps and gorillas having branched off our family tree before we split off from orangutans, or whether we are instead closest to chimps and gorillas (the majority view), with the ancestors of orangutans having gone their separate way earlier.

Within the majority, most biologists have thought that gorillas and chimps are more like each other than either is like us, implying that we branched off before the gorillas and chimps diverged from each other. This conclusion reflects the commonsense view that chimps and gorillas can be lumped in a category termed "apes," while we're something different. However, it's also conceivable that we look distinct only because chimps and gorillas haven't changed much since we shared a common ancestor with them, while we were changing greatly in a few important and highly visible features like upright posture and brain size. In that case, humans might be most similar to gorillas, or humans might be most similar to chimps, or humans and gorillas and chimps might be roughly equidistant from each other in overall genetic makeup.

Thus, anatomists have continued to argue about the first question, the details of our family tree. Whichever tree one prefers, anatomical studies by themselves tell us nothing about the second and third questions, our time of divergence and genetic distance from apes. Perhaps, however, fossil evidence might in principle solve the questions of the correct ancestral tree and of dating, though not the question of genetic distance. That is, if we had abundant fossils, we might hope to find a series of dated protohuman fossils and another series of dated protochimp fossils converging on a common ancestor around ten million years ago, converging in turn on a series of protogorilla fossils twelve million years ago. Unfortunately, that hope for insight from the fossil record has also been frustrated, because almost no ape fossils of any sort have been found for the crucial relevant period between five and fourteen million years ago in Africa.

THE SOLUTION to these questions about our origins came from an unexpected direction: molecular biology as applied to bird taxonomy. About thirty years ago, molecular biologists began to realize that the chemicals of which plants and animals are composed might provide "clocks" by which to measure genetic distances and to date times of evolutionary divergence. The idea is as follows. Suppose there is some class of molecules that occurs in all species, and whose particular structure in each species is genetically determined. Suppose further that that structure changes slowly over the course of millions of years because of genetic mutations, and that the rate of change is the same in all species. Two species derived from a common ancestor would start off with identical forms of the molecule, which they inherited from that ancestor. But mutations would then occur independently and produce structural changes between the molecules of the two species. Thus, the two species' versions of the molecule would gradually diverge in structure. If we knew how many structural changes occur on the average every million years, we could then use the present difference in the molecule's structure between any two related animal species as a clock, to calculate how much time had passed since the species shared a common ancestor.

For instance, suppose one knew from fossil evidence that lions and tigers diverged five million years ago. Suppose the molecule in lions was 99 percent identical in structure to the corresponding molecule in tigers and differed only by 1 percent. If one then took a pair of species of unknown fossil history and found that the molecule differed by 3 percent between those two species, the molecular clock would say that they had diverged three times five million, or fifteen million, years ago.

Neat as this scheme sounds on paper, testing whether it succeeds in practice has cost biologists much effort. Four things had to be done before molecular clocks could-be applied: scientists had to find the best molecule; find a quick way of measuring changes in its structure; prove that the clock runs steady (i.e., that the molecule's structure really does evolve at the same rate among all species that one is studying); and measure what that rate is.

Molecular biologists solved the first two of these problems by around 1970. The best molecule proved to be deoxyribonucleic acid (abbreviated DNA), the famous substance whose structure James Watson and Francis Crick showed to consist of a double helix, thereby revolutionizing the study of genetics. DNA is made up of two complementary and extremely long chains, each made up of four types of small molecules whose sequence within the chain carries all the genetic information transmitted from parents to offspring. A quick method of measuring changes in DNA structure is to mix the DNA from two species, then measure by how many degrees of temperature the melting point of the mixed (hybrid) DNA is reduced below the melting point of pure DNA from a single species. The method is generally referred to as DNA hybridization. As it turns out, a melting point lowered by one degree centigrade (abbreviated: $\Delta T = 1°C$) means that the DNAs of the two species differ by roughly 1 percent.

In the 1970s most molecular biologists and most taxonomists had little interest in each other's work. Among the few taxonomists who appreciated the potential power of the new DNA hybridization technique was Charles Sibley, an ornithologist then serving as Professor of Ornithology and Director at Yale's Peabody Museum of Natural History. Bird taxonomy is a difficult field because of the severe anatomical constraints imposed by flight. There are only so many ways to design a bird capable, say, of catching insects in midair, with the result that birds of similar habits tend to have very similar anatomies, whatever their ancestry. For example, American vultures look and behave much like Old World vultures, but biologists have come to realize that the former are related to storks, the latter to hawks, and that their resemblances result from their common life-style. Frustrated by the shortcomings of traditional methods for deciphering bird relationships, Sibley and Jon Ahlquist turned in 1973 to the DNA clock, in the most massive application to date of the methods of molecular biology to taxonomy. Not until 1980 were Sibley and Ahlquist ready to begin publishing their results, which eventually came to encompass applying the DNA clock to about seventeen hundred bird species—nearly one-fifth of all living birds.

While Sibley's and Ahlquist's achievement was a monumental one, it initially caused much controversy because so few other scientists possessed the mixture of expertises required to understand it. Here are typical reactions I heard from my scientist friends:

"I'm sick of hearing about that stuff. I no longer pay attention to anything those guys write." (An anatomist.)

"Their methods are okay, but why would anyone want to do something so boring as all that bird taxonomy?" (A molecular biologist.)

"Interesting, but their conclusions need a lot of testing by other methods before we can believe them." (An evolutionary biologist.)

"Their results are the Revealed Truth, and you better believe it." (A geneticist.)

My own assessment is that the last view will prove to be the most nearly correct one. The principles on which the DNA clock rests are unassailable; the methods used by Sibley and Ahlquist are state-of-the-art; and the internal consistency of their genetic distance measures from over eighteen thousand hybrid pairs of bird DNA testifies to the validity of their results.

Just as Darwin had the good sense to marshal his evidence for variation in barnacles before discussing the explosive subject of human variation, Sibley and Ahlquist similarly stuck to birds for most of the first decade of their work with the DNA clock. Not until 1984 did they publish their first conclusions from applying the same DNA methods to human origins, and they refined their conclusions in later papers. Their study was based on DNA from humans and from all of our closest relatives: the common chimpanzee, pygmy chimpanzee, gorilla, orangutan, two species of gibbons, and seven species of Old World monkeys. Figure 1 summarizes the results.

As any anatomist would have predicted, the biggest genetic difference, expressed in a big DNA melting-point lowering, is between monkey DNA and the DNA of humans or of any ape. This simply puts a number on what everybody has agreed ever since apes first became known to science: that humans and apes are more closely related to each other than either are to monkeys. The actual number

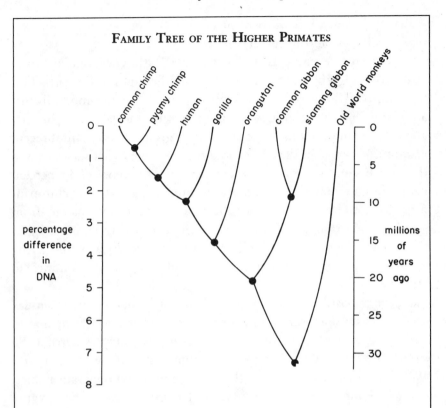

FAMILY TREE OF THE HIGHER PRIMATES

Figure 1. Trace back each pair of modern higher primates
to the black dot connecting them. The numbers to the left
then give the percentage difference between the DNAs of
those modern primates, while the numbers to the right
give the estimated number of millions of years ago since
they last shared a common ancestor. For example, the
common and pygmy chimps differ in about 0.7 percent of
their DNA and diverged around three million years ago;
we differ in 1.6 percent of our DNA from either chimp
and diverged from their common ancestor around seven
million years ago; and gorillas differ in about 2.3 percent of
their DNA from us or chimps and diverged from the
common ancestor leading to us and the two chimps around
ten million years ago.

is that monkeys share 93 percent of their DNA structure with humans and apes, and differ in 7 percent.

Equally unsurprising is the next-biggest difference, one of 5 percent between gibbon DNA and DNA of other apes or humans. This too confirms the accepted view that gibbons are the most distinct apes, and that our affinities are instead with gorillas, chimpanzees, and orangutans. Among those latter three groups of apes, most recent anatomists have considered the orangutan as somewhat separate, and that conclusion too fits the DNA evidence: a difference of 3.6 percent between orangutan DNA and that of humans, gorillas, or chimpanzees. Geography confirms that the latter three species parted from gibbons and orangutans quite some time ago: living and fossil gibbons and orangutans are confined to Southeast Asia, while living gorillas and chimpanzees plus early fossil humans are confined to Africa.

At the opposite extreme but equally unsurprising, the most similar DNAs are those of common chimpanzees and pygmy chimpanzees, which are 99.3 percent identical and differ by only 0.7 percent. So similar are these two chimp species in appearance that it was not until 1929 that anatomists even bothered to give them separate names. Chimps living on the equator in central Zaire rate the name "pygmy chimps" because they average slightly smaller (and have more slender builds and longer legs) than the widespread "common chimps" ranging across Africa just north of the equator. However, with the increased knowledge of chimp behavior acquired in recent years, it has become clear that the modest anatomical differences between pygmy and common chimps mask considerable differences in reproductive biology. Unlike common chimps but like us, pygmy chimps assume a wide variety of positions for copulation, including face to face; copulation can be initiated by either sex, not just by the male; females are sexually receptive for much of the month, not just for a briefer period in midmonth; and there are strong bonds among females or between males and females, not just among males. Evidently, those few genes (0.7 percent) differing between pygmy and common chimps have big consequences for sexual physiology and roles. That same theme—a small percentage of gene differences having big consequences—will recur later in this and the next chapter in regard to the gene differences between humans and chimps.

In all these cases that I've discussed so far, anatomical evidence of who just wanted an autograph to add to a collection. These letters were separated out and sent on to Gavin de Becker, a security expert we'd also hired, to be filed. The individuals were placed on a watch list. Mom did not want me to see these letters. Although I knew the people existed, I had no interest in reading the contents of their correspondence because I would only get scared for my life.

Once the piles of letters were made, I would sit for blocks of time and hammer out all the signatures. Mom said that every correspondence meant another loyal fan. In press lines or at appearances I signed every single fan's outstretched piece of paper or photo. She said they were all individuals and I must not alienate them. I posed for every paparazzo. I even signed the index cards from the "pros." The pros are the ones who ask for a nonpersonalized autograph, which they then sell. I was always the last to leave an event because Mom wanted me to personally engage with every single person taking pictures or asking for a poster to be signed. I admired her care for people's feelings, and because I also collected autographs myself, I understood how it felt to get passed over or denied. However, it was exhausting, and I do admit part of me wanted to avoid all of it.

Earlier on in my career, my mom and I had bought tickets to see the Academy Awards. Actors, celebrities, and presenters in the orchestra are invited, but there are additional seats, up in the mezzanine, that are open to the public for purchase. Mom and I were in California for some reason and, after years of watching the award show together on TV, had decided it would be exciting to attend in person.

We were seated way up high in the top balcony and I spotted Paul Newman. I jumped out of my seat and ran all the way down to the middle orchestra to ask Paul Newman for his autograph. He graciously declined, explaining that if he signed one for me, it would start a chain reaction and he would then have to sign everybody else's program. I was slightly hurt but remained what I thought was polite, and I said, "Oh, OK, then could you just wave up to my mom?"

He obliged and turned back up toward the balcony. He did a sweeping wave in the general direction of the mezzanine and had no idea whom he was addressing. It was very sweet but awkward, because when my mom saw to whom I was gesturing, she immediately ducked behind a seat. I think that she was actually embarrassed by the fact that I had asked him to wave to her, so she hid. She weirdly did not want to have the attention shifted to her. I thanked Mr. Newman and returned to the balcony.

Even though I remember being a bit sad he did not sign my book, I would fully appreciate the situation years later when I was forced to respond the same way to a fan. All it takes is one person at a restaurant or any crowded area and you could literally be signing autographs for an hour.

The funny part to the whole story was that years later, when I was invited to be a presenter at the Academy Awards, I still brought my autograph book. After the broadcast, the presenters and winners and Academy members were all seated on the stage to take a huge cast photo. I was in the middle, a bit to the right, and I spotted Paul Newman a few rows down. I passed my book and a pen down to him and asked for his autograph. I guess he knew that I'd be the only one in that crowd who would ask, and he kindly obliged. I was thrilled. I thanked him and chose not to try to remind him of my previous disappointment.

Mom made me so conscious of my fans that I began dreading being anywhere. There seemed to be no boundaries. I understood Mom's philosophy, but the sense of obligation and the fear of losing a fan's devotion were often too much for me to take. I could never say no.

Mom would not let me be disturbed when I ate, however, and would instead explain that I would take the photo or sign the autograph as soon as the meal was over. She explained to me that if they really wanted to, they would wait. She hated when people would say they were leaving — could I just sign it now?

She'd respond, "Well, I hope you enjoyed your meal, because she is not yet finished with hers. She will be happy to sign for you after she's done."

Sometimes the people would wait and sometimes they left disappointed. I felt tortured and unable to enjoy the meal knowing people were wishing I'd hurry, and when those impatient people left, I felt hurt that I wasn't worth the wait. Mom would joke that they were not my "biggest fans" after all. I know she was trying to make things easier, but the end result was that I could never relax.

Because of her hypervigilance toward my public, I felt as if the world owned me. It was the feeling that everybody wanted to take a piece.

I was offered *Endless Love,* and even though it was yet again another loss-of-innocence love story, the promise of working with Italian director Franco Zeffirelli made the project much more appealing. I had seen his film version of *Romeo and Juliet* and thought it was heartbreaking and beautiful. I had not worked with such an artist since Louis Malle. My mother and I both felt that this was going to be an important movie.

The story comes from a novel by Scott Spencer. Two teenagers, David and Jade, have an intensely romantic relationship as high school students. When Jade's grades suffer, her parents force the two of them to break up, resulting in David's breakdown, a criminal act, and much drama on both sides. The film shot in New York and on Long Island in the fall of 1980.

I am proud of my work in this film and attribute it all to Franco. He was tough, dramatic, and often insulting or drunk, but he expected your best and would not stop until he got it. He often made fun of my voice and sometimes made me cry by picking on me. But I felt he actually believed I had talent and could be better. In one scene without dialogue Franco wanted to see a certain expression on my face as I looked through a window at my scorned boyfriend. He wanted me to show love and longing and sadness, and so he told me to hum the theme song to *Romeo and Juliet* in my head while looking out. In doing this, I forgot about my face and did not try to project the emotion with an expression. I thought it was a brilliant trick and it helped me understand how much you can do by not trying too hard.

The actors in the film were all rather serious, accomplished actors with the exception of Martin Hewitt, who played David. Don Murray played my dad. I had seen him in *Bus Stop* with Marilyn Monroe. Shirley Knight played my mom and James Spader played my protective brother. They were all generous actors and I felt honestly supported. I'm not sure I took my job as seriously as they did, but I was very professional and learned from them about acting. Martin and I got along well and enjoyed working with one another.

We neither fell in love nor hated each other, and Franco did not force the issue. After experiencing such pressure during *The Blue Lagoon* to be in love, this opposite approach came as a relief. All we were required to do was *convince* people we were in love. This approach freed us both up to become actual friends. There were nude scenes, so just as on *The Blue Lagoon* I had a body double. Once again the heavier love scenes in the film were shot primarily between Martin and my double. This, too, helped keep our friendship intact.

Mom did not have to protect Martin in the same way that she felt she needed to protect Chris, but she made sure that Franco knew she was a person with whom to reckon, should a line be crossed.

I would like to add only one unfortunate truth: Both Chris Atkins and Martin Hewitt, my costar in *Endless Love,* hit career heights very quickly but would forever struggle as actors. Chris went on to develop a severe alcohol problem, and both of their careers took unexpected turns. It is harder, I believe, to become a "star" after your first movie, especially at an age when you are on the cusp of making one of your first monumental life choices. For instance, by the time the film was released, Chris had deferred college, put his sports-medicine degree on indefinite hold, and had bought a red Ferrari. Later, a manager later screwed him out of most of his money.

Both these men have recovered and have

matured into wonderful and kind people. Chris has never lost his sweetness and openness. I have yet to witness any underlying anger. Martin maintains a chip on his shoulder in my opinion but was always a sensitive young man and fine actor. For me, even though I achieved fame at a younger age, I was guarded by my mother and allowed to face celebrity in a surprisingly nurturing environment. Even if my talent may not have been protected, I somehow was. Mom's drinking was way more damaging to me than fame.

Her protection didn't stop with me. She insisted on trying to protect my costars whenever she could. She looked out for young Tom Cruise, who had been handchosen by Franco to play a bare-chested boy with a short but memorable scene shot in Central Park.

Years later Tom would recall how kind my mother had been to him during the shoot. We were sitting alone in my living room in LA, and Tom had come to personally apologize to me for attacking me on the *Today Show* for my use of antidepressants to treat postpartum depression. He said my mom had made it a point to look after him on the set of *Endless Love* and he'd "never forgotten it." Even though Tom only appeared in one scene, he said he was surprised by Mom's kindness toward him and always remembered it. Tom apologized to my mother as well, saying that he did not know why he chose to attack me "of all people." He added that he basically felt cornered and I was the "scapegoat."

Mom and Franco were both big, drinking, theatrical personalities who liked being dramatic and in control. He would tease her and give her a hard time about staying out of his way, and she would challenge him perpetually but never overtly interfere. They were like two proud peacocks splaying their colorful tails and puffing out their chests. Each of them owned part of the film; my mother possessed me, and Franco controlled all the rest. Both sides were needed for the film to be made. I believe she once again felt I was in good hands by working with a European filmmaker.

I clearly remember how mad and upset I was when, three months after wrapping this film, we were called back to reshoot the ending. It hadn't been emotional enough and Franco wanted more. The ending was kept the same, but Franco wanted a more powerful, more emotional breakdown by my character. In a conflicted, angst-ridden final scene, the two lovers heartbreakingly say good-bye. Franco wanted to show the buildup of pain, irreparable loss, and sadness that the arbitrary separation of these two lovers had generated.

Somehow, Franco got me to connect to the character and really cry. There was a famous story that the press picked up where he said he pinched my toe in order to get me to express ecstasy, but that was not true. It was actually in this scene that I remember him pinching me, and it was because he wanted me to connect with pain as well as sadness. It didn't hurt, but I got the message. It remains one of the best scenes I have ever done on film. I was raw and honest and tired and I was directed.

It was during my high school years that Mom decided she wanted to get her eyes done. She consulted with Dr. Sherrell Aston about an eye lift. Her top lids were drooping slightly, and her theory was that if you got such work done in your earlier years, it was less obvious. Your skin had more elasticity and therefore healed better. The doctor agreed but suggested that she also get a slight face-lift. Mom agreed but said that, so help her God, if she came out of surgery with her bottom lids looking pulled down she would "break every bone in his hands."

She made him swear he would not give her bug eyes and that her lids, when closed, would completely meet in a clean line. He assured her she could wear makeup in a week.

"Yeah, if you want to look like a friggin' *clown*," she said. "Forget makeup — just make sure my eyes close or I'll come after you!"

Even though she was joking (sort of), Mom was scared about her eyes being too taut and skeleton-like. She had seen some actress or news anchor whose bottom lids looked as if they were being pulled down by invisible strings with tiny lead weights at the ends. Mom was terrified of a similar result. She had always been savvy about plastic surgery — she could pick out a nose job from miles away and could often even name the doctor whose work it had been.

Well, anyway, she got the surgery. Afterward she developed some kind of infection that traveled down her neck and she had to stay in the hospital for a few extra days.

One of the horrible nurses tried to get Mom to give her a tip when her shift was over. The woman began rummaging through Mom's closet for her purse to get her money and to get her own tip. I guess Mom was getting scared and upset and obviously, because of medication, did not have her wits about her. She called me in New Jersey sounding upset and a bit panicked. The large Jamaican woman spoke little English but seemed to be raising her voice, trying to get my mother to understand that she had to leave and wanted a tip.

Mom put me on the phone with this crazy nurse and I threatened to get her fired if she did not leave my mother's room that instant. I called our part-time driver to take me into the city to settle everything. I had my license but did not feel comfortable driving into Manhattan. By the time I got there the woman was gone (angry and without a tip) and Mom was doped up and chatty but more relaxed. I made arrangements for a different nurse and remained near Mom while I completed my homework. I kept my schoolbooks with me at all times because I never knew when I might be called to work or find I had some spare time to study. Mom had a small drainage tube coming from an insertion in her neck and connected to a little plastic bag. It was meant to drain the fluid from the infection. Mom called it her "purse." Every now and then she would loudly say, "I should have given her this purse and told her to fuck off!" She was obviously uncomfortable and in pain, but I was sure glad she still had her humor.

However, I was trying to do my French homework, and she would not shut up about any of it. I could not really follow all her jabbering and really needed to get my work done. I patiently suggested she shut her eyes for a bit and take a nap. I would be right there by the window and would not leave without telling her. She quieted a bit and I began, once again, to study. At one point I glanced up at her and was shocked that even though she had stopped babbling, she was sneakily peeking out at me! I couldn't believe that she could not resist spying on me. Did she not trust me to stay?

I jumped up, went to her bed frustrated, and said, "Mom! I'm right here; I'm not leaving, close your eyes and rest!"

Well, she had actually been asleep, and after being startled awake, she growled, "They arrrrrre clooosed!"

Oh boy, I thought. Her eyes were swollen and could not yet close all the way, and it looked as if she was squinting through them. I prayed for the doctor's sake for that to be the actual truth. I apologized for waking her, told her she was fine, and got her to settle again. But it was a laugh we had for years to come. It was always laughter that maintained our deep bond. It was the truth in our connection. The sound of Mom's sober laughter was like music and medicine to me.

While she was in the hospital recovering, it was one of the best times for me. My aunt Lila was living with us in the house in Haworth, so I was not alone, but this was the first time since Mom went to rehab that I could be calm knowing she was alive and not drinking. I could relax. I had peace of mind and a regular schedule.

It was around my sophomore year in high school that I was approached to do the infamous Calvin Klein commercials. Mom and I knew Richard Avedon and his creative team, and she was friends with Carl Rosen, who ran Calvin. We were going to do a series of commercials all playing on the word *Calvin* or on famous sayings or songs and their connection to the concept of genes and jeans. There was a great deal of excitement surrounding the whole campaign. No one had ever attempted this approach in advertising. It was also groundbreaking to have still photographers directing the actual TV commercials.

We were also going to be the first brand

to advertise in movie theatres before the coming attractions. We filmed a minute-long uncut shot of me describing Darwin's survival-of-the-fittest law while undoing my hair and loosening my blouse. I memorized the minute-long definition of genes and the concept of natural selection. The funny thing is that the idea that the commercial would show in movie theatres was rejected because the agency said, "The day will never come when brands will be allowed to advertise in movie theatres." The spots were run only on TV instead. Today you can go to a showing of a movie twenty minutes after the scheduled time, because of how long the advertising spots are before the show.

For a different spot, I was supposed to laugh hysterically and try to get across some messaging. I was so nervous that I would sound fake and that I would not be able to actually crack up on camera. Crying felt easier than laughing to me and I was extremely stressed about it. The sound department gave me a set of earphones and they had prepared a bunch of jokes to tell me to get me to laugh.

The jokes were not really that funny and it wasn't working. But then, all of a sudden, I heard my stepsister Diana's voice in the

287

earphones. She was recounting some of our favorite inside jokes. I couldn't believe my ears and was so happy she was there, and I got a case of the giggles. It was a "cut and print," and Mom was thanked for her innovative surprise.

We filmed many different spots for this campaign and they were all unique and fun and amazingly clever. They all had smart historical, sociological, political, and biological references. The only one, however, that will forever haunt us, was one in which a colloquial phrase was grossly taken out of context.

Now, in hindsight, it is possible that somebody in the writers' room had an inkling that there might be different ways the statement could be interpreted, but I maintain that I was never aware of the double entendre. It would hurt me to think that the creative team was trying to exploit my innocence, and I uphold the belief that their intention was not as crude and juvenile as was the interpretation. I am, of course, speaking about the famous "Nothing comes between me and my Calvins" line.

I think there are a number of misunderstandings about this. First of all, the actual line involved a rhetorical question, not a statement about ejaculation. The line actually was: "Do you want to know what comes between me and my Calvins? Nothing."

The second misunderstanding is about the tone and meaning. In no way did I think I was saying something controversial or sexual. This was just another spot in which I was affirming how much I loved my blue jeans. I had used a similar expression often, and it had always been meant as a declaration of my love for something: "Nothing comes between me and my mom." "Nothing comes between me and by favorite doll, Blabby."

It never occurred to me it could mean that I wasn't wearing underwear. Or that the spelling of the word *come* was really meant to be *cum*. I swear I don't believe my mother read into it that way, either. We just thought of it as another well-conceived commercial. We filmed a number of spots in all and didn't think about it again.

But when the spots began to air, they were incredibly popular and controversial. My mother and I had been away in Europe, where I was working for *Harper's Bazaar Italia* shooting the collection, and returned to an onslaught of media attention. The commercial was pulled from the air and I was ambushed by questions as to the "true meaning" of my words. It was ridiculous and insane. Mom was attacked for allowing me to verbalize such smut, and I was once again perceived as both a Lolita and an abused daughter.

We laughed it off at first, but the controversy continued. At times I felt compelled to try to explain, but this proved useless. The press wanted to hear what they wanted to hear. Just as they had after *Pretty Baby* and *The Blue Lagoon,* they wanted to assail my mother and me with criticism and judgment. This one incorrectly quoted line would usurp all positive attention surrounding this innovative, landmark ad campaign.

Nobody talked about how brilliantly the references to history, literature, music, religion, and science had played into advertising blue jeans. Nobody commented on how I had memorized a minute-long monologue and what a brilliant play on words "survival of the fittest" actually was. (Although I would go on to get an A on a pop quiz in school because I wrote out a very in-depth answer to the question "What are genes?" So I guess all wasn't lost.)

This proved to be yet another example of the press preferring a sordid story to a creative one. I was not immune to criticism, but I was getting familiar with a certain amount of controversy surrounding almost everything I did.

Mom capped it all off once again with her "Fuck 'em" attitude. "You know what you meant. Are you proud of the commercials?"

"Yes."

"So fuck 'em."

And that was usually Mom's attitude about these types of things. I don't know if she was actually hurt, angry, or regretful, but if she was, she'd never let me know.

I am not sure if my mom knew how conflicting the images of me she was projecting were. When I was young I was looked at as a provocative young woman, yet I became the virginal "America's sweetheart." I went from doing movies like *Pretty Baby* and *Endless Love* to working with George Burns and Bob Hope and having a doll made in my likeness.

The body of the doll actually had to be altered to honestly represent my flatter chest. Most dolls by the same company take their template body and just change the heads. My mom contractually made the factory create a new mold of the body with a smaller chest. The fifties' big pointy boobs did not represent a teenager. Mom insisted.

This was all very weird for me. Not only is it strange to have a doll made of you, but

291

to then also have it be publicly known that the boobs had been shaved off did not make me any more comfortable in high school. To be called a beautiful doll was too outrageous for me to bear, but it was fun to help design her fashionable leggings and long sweaters, as well as her prom dress, which was a copy of a McCall's pattern I had modeled and Lisa and I both actually wore to our junior prom.

Mom even had the Brooke Shields Glamour Center (a head with hair you could style) sent back to the factory three times because the cleft in the chin was not right.

All the while, I was being photographed looking much older on the covers of major fashion magazines and doing ads like the controversial Calvin commercials. There were such polarized views of me concurrently being disseminated that it is no wonder I wasn't the only one confused.

During this time period I began to more frequently get invited to and attend parties at Manhattan clubs. Excursions to Studio 54 were always connected to some event. It might have been a Warhol party, a Calvin Klein launch, or a film premiere. I had been on the cover of *Interview* magazine and had become friendly with Andy. I would always go at the beginning of the night and the event. The paparazzi would line up outside on either side of the infamous red rope, and the crowds waited to be selected for entry.

My mother would get so mad at me because I never wanted to get out of the car and go in first. When we arrived at the club, I always cringed inside once I saw the mob. I'd wade through the throngs of people to reach the rope, which would suddenly be dramatically lifted, like a magician pulling off a cape to reveal the rabbit in the hat. I would apologize to those waiting as I was ushered ahead of them. The flashes blinding me helped mask the looks of rejection from the crowd.

Even though I loathed the feeling of waltzing right past everyone, once inside I could fully relax. Even today I can easily picture the long corridor that led into the club, with dark red carpet stretching the distance and red-painted walls. There was always a moment after the mayhem of the outside, when the doors closed behind you and you were temporarily free from photographers, fans, and disgruntled, rejected, and desperate people. When all you'd hear was the faint thump of the music and the promise of a good time. You'd get a feeling in your stomach, like right before a roller coaster takes its stomach-flipping descent.

I would quicken my pace a bit in anticipation of going through the main door. I was probably going to see famous people and I was going to hear all my favorite songs. Even though I was a celebrity myself at this time, I was always a bit starstruck by the people I'd see inside. There was always somebody famous to say hello to and take some photos with. Whether it was Calvin Klein, Diane von Furstenberg, Bianca Jagger, Cornelia Guest, or Debbie Harry, Steve Rubell corralled them all and took very good care of us.

I must admit, I had no issue with special treatment once inside the club. Sitting inside the club was always easier than getting in because people were busy dancing and having fun and were not focused only on people coming in. On any given night it was dark enough to feel anonymous, and there was a roped-off VIP area I could use. There was always some group laughing and drinking on couches placed a bit higher than all the other seating areas. I was relieved to be seated there, not because I felt superior, but because I felt protected from drunk, intrusive, and usually stoned clubbers.

I would usually sit to take a few photos with people in this area and then it was all about the music for me. Mom rarely danced but stayed with our stuff and drank and chatted. Once it was time to dance, my heart would actually pound a bit faster and I'd look to my mom with an excited expression. She was happy. I would immediately ask my mom if I could go dance. All I wanted to do was dance, and I would dance with anybody who would dance with me. People hardly ever interrupted me when I was dancing.

I don't remember much of Mom at Studio 54 since I hardly ever sat with her for any length of time. The minute I'd get permission, I'd be gone. I would basically stay on the dance floor, dancing and sweating the entire time. I felt freedom and anonymity amid the throngs of dancers. I always found a good gay dancer to be my partner and I would not stop dancing until I heard two songs in a row that I did not like.

Mom never posed for any of the photos. I assume she knew either she'd be cut out or I'd run the risk of not making it to Page Six in the *Post* the next day if pictured only with her instead of being flanked by famous people.

I always loved it when Andy Warhol was there because he was incredibly sweet to me and I could always make him laugh. He often had his camera and would click from all different angles but never look in the viewfinder and through the lens. I never saw the photos after they were developed.

I would leave by 11:00 or 11:30 if a party was during the week or stay until midnight if it was on a weekend. I don't recall Mom making any drunk scenes while we were at Studio 54. For me it was a fun place to go, even if Mom was drinking, because I was distracted by dancing. I'd dance. I'd sweat. I'd go home. I don't remember signing autographs at the club, either. It was as if dancing created a force field around me.

I'm sure there was plenty of drug use going on around me, but I never noticed. Steve must have put some kind of word out to his employees or something, because even though people always asked me about the drugs during the 54 days, I never saw any. The infamous "little cloth bag of pills" was never in my eyeline. I was like a mascot or somebody's kid sister. I don't know if people were scared that my mother was there, or if they just tried to shield me from the darker side of nightclub life, but I was basically exempt. Mom never smoked or used drugs. Alcohol was her sole vice.

I don't believe it was all about age, either. We all saw how poor Tatum O'Neal and

Drew Barrymore were not able to dodge the substance-abuse bullet. They both had eccentric mothers, but they didn't have the experience that I had of choosing to become the sole caretaker at such a young age. I was friendly with both these young ladies, but I never went out with them back then. We remain friends to this day.

For many years, I thought I avoided addiction because my mom was an addict. But I believe there were other factors at hand that contributed to my safety. Part of it was just who I was — the spirit they could all see. Part of it was my mom, and another part was people's desire to protect me. This last part may be a naïve assumption, but I can honestly say I never felt preyed upon or tempted.

This period in the eighties had a fast and furious pace. Although I wasn't personally experiencing a carefree life filled with promiscuous sex and rampant drug use, I was engaged in my own personal high-energy race. I was burning my candle from both ends, but instead of its being a negative thing, I was met with success. I was working extremely hard at school with four or five hours of homework per night, and I was either filming or modeling the other hours. I did not need a great deal of sleep and I drove myself harder than anybody else did. I believe it was during these years that I began to be a perfectionist. I saw how much I could get accomplished and how I could have two equally full lives. I felt motivated by it all. It worked for me.

During high school, my mom's drinking escalated. She did not try to hide it or curtail it. It was as if we were back to the time before rehab. It was simply a consistent factor in our lives and I still tried everything I could think of to get her to stop.

Sometimes after a particularly bad night, she might stop for a few days, but it never lasted. We fought a great deal about it, but it never seemed to have an impact. Even when Mom started an evening attempting to curtail her drinking, she'd end the night switching to vodka and getting angry. She never actually passed out and would never allow anybody else to drive us home. I never took over as the driver, strangely. I was insecure about my driving and believed her driving drunk was better than my driving sober.

I am not sure how she managed it, but Mom rarely lost her control in front of the press. My honesty about her rehabilitation was what alerted the public to her struggles.

We both did press for various projects after her stay in rehab and spoke openly about her drinking. After publicly claiming that I had loved my mother so much that I had asked her to go to rehab, I felt that I could not now say she was drinking again. It felt like such a failure. The story was just too good to refute. I adored my mother and she adored me and this young daughter was mature enough to save her own mom from the jaws of alcohol and everything had turned out well. The truth was just too sad to admit. I felt terrible upholding what was now a lie. This dilemma would only get worse.

I buried myself in my schoolwork but we often had ugly outbursts that ended in tears. I remember once screaming at my mother during a particularly bad evening. It was the angriest I'd ever been. I remember wanting to say something — anything — to hurt her. I had a vague memory of the name of a boy. As if there was a baby before me, or some child named "baby somebody." The mentions I recalled were usually in conjunction with a reference to this boy in one of Auntie Lila's prayers. The word *angel* was often used. I never knew whom they were talking about and was too scared to come out and ask. Instead, I waited until I needed to pull out the big guns and I fired.

I once blurted, "Well, maybe if you had taken care of me the way you took care of Baby John, then I wouldn't be here, either, and I wouldn't have to live with your drinking!"

Well, she turned on a dime, and with instant, steely cold sobriety she glared at me.

"Don't you *ever* mention that name *ever* again."

I stopped cold and saw how deeply I had cut her. I felt empowered knowing what I held in my arsenal. But, like intervention, you don't get too many opportunities to use such tactics. I would never again use this partial information in anger, and I would only find out the truth when she was on her deathbed, and not by her tongue.

High school basically continued with bouts of her getting drunk and then stopping for a day. There was not one major moment or birthday celebration during which she could remain sober. I learned how to plan my joy. I would front-load my birthdays with breakfast activities or plan to be with her for only the beginning of an event. Then I would go off to be with friends and know that that would be the last I would see of my mother's real facial expressions.

She still managed to get up every morning and get me to school. She was never the kind of drunk who passed out at the dinner or party or who stayed in bed all day with a hangover. She slept little, drank a lot, and had found a way to continue through each day. Plane rides were the worst, however, because even if she'd start off the flight with soda, she would end highly inebriated and needing help off the plane. This was before *TMZ* waited at the airports for celebrities, and I could usually get her through baggage claim and into a waiting car without too much fuss.

She had her drinking down to a science and switched up her methods whenever she needed to do so. Sometimes it was red wine at dinner and an endless slide into a boozy, sad, wanting-to-sing-soprano drunkenness. Then there was the "I'm only drinking diet soda" (a.k.a. rum and Coke) at parties where people knew her issue. She had bartenders all over New Jersey who knew what it really meant when she ordered her Diet Coke.

Then there was her new favorite: vodka bottles hidden all over the house and garage. She hid bottles everywhere and sometimes even forgot where she had hidden them. I'd find empty bottles in cowboy boots, behind cereal boxes, in purses at the back of her closet, and wedged in between folded sweaters.

There were times when I thought I had gotten her into the car and out of the house drink-free. But just after the engine was started, she'd tsk and say she forgot something in the house. She would put the car in park and run inside to retrieve some item and make a quick pit stop for a slug of something. I'd demand to smell her breath and she'd either already have a mint at the ready or perform her go-to open-mouth, held-breath move.

She'd smirk as if it were all on her own terms. She claimed she could drink socially and I guess that was not a lie. She was like a girl who claims, with all honesty, that she did not "sleep with" a certain boy because, in fact, they had had sex all night. Mom could *absolutely* drink socially. She drank and was social. She could just as easily drink while out and then go home and finish off half a bottle of vodka while getting ready for bed.

I ran out of ways of asking her to quit. Tears didn't work, rage didn't work, pleas when sober didn't work, and letters didn't work. Other people tried and I prayed.

On the day of graduation I decided to finally get drunk myself. I was at my friend Diane Coleman's party and we were all in the pool. I wanted to show my friends that I could be "cool" and drink like they all did. I took the screw top off a bottle of Riunite and opened up the back of my throat. I poured as much as I could down my open gullet while standing in waist-deep, cool water and enjoyed the gasps and applause.

I then looked around and knew I was going to be sick. I called my mother from the guest bathroom on the house portable phone and asked her to come get me right then. I hung up, groaned, and called her right back. Why hadn't she come yet? It had been a long time. She chuckled and I knew she was actually sober. She said to stay calm and Mama would come and get me as soon as possible. I felt too sick to even be embarrassed and I went home. In the car I sat in the backseat and put my forehead on the headrest in front of me.

"Are you mad at me, Mom?"

And she actually came out with "No . . . I'm just disappointed."

I was unaware of the cliché and she was unaware that she was a hypocrite. Her rules didn't apply to her. Unlike me, obviously, she could handle drinking.

Preteen Mom with her
beloved sister, Louise.

Mom at the age when she'd sneak
into the "movin' pictures."

Mom the majorette. One of the
only times she followed the rules.

Mom while she was working at
Krueger Brewing Company.

Mom and her legs getting pinned.

Mom and Sal out on the town.

The "gams" that Mom was proud of.

Mom with some adoring sailors.

Mom out with one of her
many attractive suitors.

Mom making sure we notice
her favorite asset.

One of the only photos I have of Mom pregnant and wearing a wedding ring. Look how my dad is lovingly gazing at her.

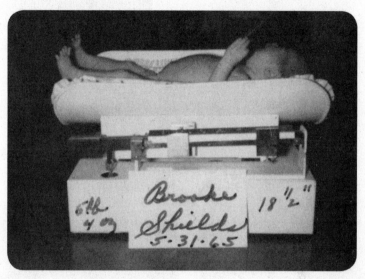

I was two months premature and weighed only five pounds, four ounces.

Mom walking me into the beach club. Notice my diaper-only-clad body and hot dog with no bun.

Dad taking me on the same path. Notice the neat outfit and no hot dog. Dad was a smoker.

Chic Mom and me on the street where I met Greta Garbo.

Daddy and me at his Fifty-Second Street apartment. My baggy cloth diaper was Dad's doing.

Mom and me on
Southampton Beach.

One of my favorite pictures of me with my dad. I loved
to make him laugh by doing imitations.

"Hold still, Brookie."

Matching camel coats in front of
my favorite store, Woolworth's.

The Kennedy look-alikes,
Frank and Didi Shields.

Mom and true love Antonio
Rius in Brazil. I did not like
sharing my mommy.

Mom's birthday at our
Seventy-Third Street
apartment.

Teri Terrific shows off her bone structure on
a flight to New Orleans.

I struck this pose every time I said trick or treat.

Mom with Chris Atkins in front of our
bure on the Turtle Island location of *The
Blue Lagoon.* Mom wore only blue jeans.

Mom and me in 1996.

Mom's famous laugh with best friend and collaborator John Holland on *The Brooke Book*.

Us at a barbecue. Mom holding her ever-present inhaler.

On my wedding day
to Chris.

Lara Porzak

Happy Mom and Dad at
the lunch I missed before
my wedding.

Lara Porzak

Lara Porzak

Mom's beautiful smile on the
veranda during the rehearsal for
the ceremony.

Surprise dinner party for Mom's seventieth birthday at our California house.

Mom, Lila, and me in our favorite New York City photo booth on the Upper East Side.

Mom being silly on Thanksgiving with a doomed turkey.

My favorite picture of
Rowan kissing her mama.
She peed on me a second
later.

Two of my favorite baby dolls,
Rowan and Blabby.

Easter—Toots and Rowan.

Chris, Rowan, and myself in our backyard, Grier in the oven.

Lara Porzak

Elizabeth Messina

Grier eating my face and me loving every minute of it.

My real-life doll.

Ladies who lunch.

Delicious kisses from my Gdawg.

Mom with her two dogs, Blabby and Donut. See if you can find both. . . .

Me and my ladies.

Winter in Southampton.

■ ■ ■ ■

PART THREE

■ ■ ■ ■

I hope you will see that I can't ask you to change, but I hope you let me change. . . . It's like pruning a tree or rerooting plants so that they all keep growing.
            — *Letter from Brooke to Teri*

CHAPTER TEN:
REMEMBER THE HULA-HOOP

I had always known that I wanted to go to a school like Princeton. I had a romantic view of what I thought a college experience would be like, and it included old architecture and ivy on the walls. There would be wise-looking professors and students carrying books. I pictured a big, old campus and autumn leaves. I didn't focus on my future education as much as I thought about the entire experience of college life.

My dad had gone to the University of Pennsylvania, where he rowed crew. But he never mentioned my going to an Ivy League college and did not keep tabs on my application plans. My mother had never gone to college at all, so she was entirely unfamiliar with the process. Both my parents were supportive but didn't press me to follow any particular path.

It was a given that I was going to go to college, but what I studied and where I went felt entirely up to me. When my parents divorced, they'd come up with the idea that my father would support my education until I graduated from college. I was earning my own living by this time and therefore was able to pay for myself, but my father insisted on holding up his end of the deal.

I had always assumed I would find a college not too far from home. Despite the fact that my mother's drinking was getting worse and worse, the idea of escape never entered my mind. I wanted to be near my home and near my mom, and I wanted to find a school that did not require a plane to get me back to visit. I was so attached to my mother that I did not want to leave her. I was also attached to saving her. Subconsciously I also wanted to remain near enough to rescue her if need be.

I thought I had as good a chance as anybody to go to a good school. I had brought my grade point average up rather steadily over my four difficult years at Dwight-Englewood, I was a cheerleader, and I had an impressive extracurricular résumé. My life experience was rather eclectic by this point and I was committed to various charitable organizations. I approached the admissions adviser at my school and informed him that I was thinking of going to a school like Princeton but was also look-ing at Vassar, Trinity, and Brown.

Right off the bat, he insinuated that I should probably just forget about Prince-ton, because although I was finishing with strong grades, I had not taken enough AP courses, my SATs were not high enough (I just broke 1000), and I didn't play sports. He reiterated how hard it was to get ac-cepted to a school like Princeton and that I should concentrate on schools that were less selective. He was the college adviser, so I accepted and heeded his advice. I figured he must have known what he was talking about.

I began collecting applications and mak-ing arrangements to visit and interview at various schools. I put the Princeton applica-tion aside and kept the others to fill out once I had visited their campuses. I visited Trinity with a friend who was an undergrad, and John Kennedy Jr. gave me a tour of Brown. We spent the day together on cam-pus, and I told him the sugar-cube story, carefully omitting the part about my marry-ing him. I had a huge crush on John and remembered nothing about the school.

Each university was special in different ways, but they all felt a bit far from home for my comfort. I decided I could be happy anywhere as long as I was getting a college degree and rashly decided that I would just apply to Vassar early-decision and be done with the trauma of it all. I went to see the campus and didn't feel at all as if it was the place for me. It neither had the old-school, ivy-covered charm nor fit the image I had in my mind, but by then my choices felt limited. I submitted the early-decision application and got word back almost immediately. Of course they would love to have me attend their university. The admissions team was lovely and I could tell they would help make me feel at home there. But the fact that they were so eager to have me at their school made me wary. I was put off a bit because it felt as if they needed me more than I needed them.

I didn't have to commit for a while, so I decided to take some time to decide. In the meantime, I had forgotten that I had said yes to going to a Princeton football game with a friend of a friend who was a junior there. It was too late to cancel because he had tickets to the game and plans to show me the fun part of the school. We were going to hear the a capella singing group the Tigertones sing under one of Princeton's echoing arches in what was called an "arch sing." This was just a few days before applications were due, and I hadn't even looked at my Princeton application since my college adviser's discouraging words.

Well, I got onto the beautiful campus and I was awestruck. The architecture was stunning and the gargoyles atop the massive library seemed alive. There was actually ivy growing up the walls that had witnessed the education of Woodrow Wilson, F. Scott Fitzgerald, and Jimmy Stewart, just to name a few. The atmosphere made me giddy. The campus was exactly what I'd dreamt about all these years. Surrounded by academia, I could feel an excitement for knowledge. I met up with my friend, who introduced me around and gave me some insider's information on what it was really like to go to Princeton.

I thought about my adviser's advice, but I was slowly getting a different picture from these students. Maybe he was wrong about what Princeton wanted? Maybe he had just wanted to protect me from what he thought would be rejection based on my fame?

It was time for the game, and as I sat in the bleachers, my heart started to pound. I was so comfortable with these people, who were unassuming and seemingly unfazed by my professional persona. They were extraordinarily genuine and smart, but not affected. I felt at ease and accepted. I absolutely had to be a student at this university. The only way to ensure that I would not get in was to not apply. That was no longer an option.

Halftime arrived and I practically took off running. I explained that I hadn't yet even applied to Princeton and that the application was due in the mail by Monday. I needed to go home and get it done.

I went home and fished around on my rolltop desk for the folder with the orange and black shield and began feverishly filling out the pages. My mom was concerned that I hadn't had a good time, but when she realized what I was doing, she just let me complete my task. I was so focused on my mission that I did not notice whether she had been drinking.

I worked throughout the rest of the weekend and had the application completed and postmarked on Monday. I went into high school that day and told nobody except my adviser. I told him I loved the school and wanted to take my chances before saying yes to Vassar. I don't remember his reaction, but it must have involved one or two raised eyebrows.

I guess it was my mother who called the Princeton admissions board to set up an interview for me. Mom had never pushed me to go to college, but it was always presumed I would. She supported my decision to apply to Princeton and wanted me to be happy. We also never discussed purposely taking time off from my career. It was just assumed that I would attend college as I had attended high school and continue to work on my breaks.

Mom got me an interview and drove me out to the university on her own. I think she was more nervous than I was, but shockingly she did not drink that day. She sat in the waiting area while I went in for my interview, and she whispered, "Just be yourself, darling."

During the interview the dean of admissions asked me why I wanted to go to college and why Princeton. It was not a trick question but rather an attempt to address a curiosity shared by the press and the public. Why bother going to university when I already had a full-blown career?

I explained I had worked my whole life and needed to expand my mind and my personal experiences. I was very realistic about how unique my life had been but how much I craved education as well as a conventional scholastic experience. I don't think I was as articulate as this sounds, but he claimed I was disarmingly "down to earth, and surprisingly unaffected."

I explained that I realized my SATs were not stellar but that I had worked hard to improve my GPA and that I was very serious about attending university. Even though this Princeton admissions officer had alluded to the fact that their school really was looking at students as whole entities, rather than just walking SAT scores, I worried that he was just being kind. It was really a very informal interview that stressed the diversity of the university and the commitment to excellence. This last part sounded a gong in my head and I said a prayer in my brain. I made a quiet promise that if I was allowed into this school, I, too, would commit myself fully to the same "excellence." I went back home and to school to wait for the verdict.

The next few weeks I felt as if I was waiting for a crush to call. Mom and I kept passing the phone, which hung on the sidewall of the kitchen pantry, a tiny room that was under the stairs, where you had to sit on a small chair so as not to hit your head. We both would randomly lift up the receiver to see if we still had a dial tone.

These weeks were some of the most excruciating ones of my life. Vassar was getting anxious for a response and I had heard nothing from my real first choice. What made it even worse was that a friend — who had better SATs and was also a legacy — didn't get accepted. I felt terrible for her and believed that if she had gotten rejected then I obviously had no chance. By this time it was known around high school that I had decided to apply to Princeton.

Well, the days kept going by and everybody in the high school had heard about colleges except for me. Everyone who had applied to Princeton from my school had gotten rejected and I still had heard nothing. Something had to be wrong.

I moped, I cried, and I fretted. I still don't remember if Mom was drinking or not. She seemed pretty present for this drama. It always amazed me the moments she chose to show up and those when she could not. In this case she seemed shockingly cognizant of the importance of this situation. This was my future and consequently hers as well.

Finally, Mom secretly called the head of admissions and apologized, but said that every single child applying to colleges had heard about their fate except her daughter. Could he shed some light on what was happening?

She stopped him before he gave her the news and said that she did not want to be the first to know. To this day this remains one of the most important moments in my life. Mom was standing up for me in an important and unselfish way. She was being a mom. She took the determination she had had her whole life to help me, even though it meant that she would eventually have to let me go. She physically and emotionally stepped aside and let me have the big moment for myself. It impressed me that she was willing to sacrifice like this. And it's interesting that I interpreted it as a sacrifice. Wasn't that a mom's job? Mom motioned me over to the phone and said the call was for me.

The admissions director explained what had happened. This was the last class he was to admit to Princeton because he was retiring, so he was taking everything very seriously. Somebody had leaked to the press that I had applied, and there had been an onslaught of press inquiries and controversy about my application. The school was faced with a complicated situation.

I was crushed and thought, *Oh God . . . they don't want to deal with me because I'm famous. Why did I apply to only one other school? I don't want to go to Vassar. But wait. . . . Hang on. . . . He's still talking. . . .*

He continued to say that he was currently

on vacation and had left Princeton with two letters in his hands. (The admissions office had called him on his vacation because my mother had been polite but quite insistent.) To ensure that another leak did not occur, the director had had his secretary print up both a letter of acceptance and a letter of rejection and seal them tight. His plan was to take both on vacation and personally post the one he intended to send by himself. Only he would know which one he sent. This was the reason for the delay, and I would be getting my letter of acceptance in the mail in the next few days. I had just heard the word *letter* — then he started sounding like the adults in *Peanuts* cartoons. I struggled to ask, "Oh, so in a few days I'll find out whether I got in or not?"

He must have wanted to run to the mailbox and switch the letters. This student didn't even know what the word *acceptance* meant!

"Oh no, you got in, Miss Shields; it's just that the letter is on its way. I am sorry for the delay, but it was necessary for all of us."

"Thank you, sir. Thank you very much."

I hung up the phone and screamed. I hugged Mom, whose eyes were welling with tears, not because I had gotten into an Ivy League school, but because I was so happy about it. I phoned my dad to tell him the good news and I could hear the pride in his voice.

The next day at school I didn't want to tell anybody. I eventually had to, but I played it down. I knew people would think I had just gotten in because I was famous, but I knew that this fact was actually a deterrent for universities for a myriad of reasons. I also knew that I was the right fit for Princeton. I loved every aspect of what the university stood for. They believed in hard work, excellence, and joy. These were things I sought after daily. Princeton did want well-rounded students who showed consistent improvements over the four years of high school and who had many extracurricular activities and varied tastes. Turns out the interview also had a big impact on their decision. One thing I was extremely comfortable doing was being interviewed and being honest.

I had been accepted to Princeton University, the academic institution of my dreams. I glowed instead of gloated, and for the rest of the year, I had an overwhelming sensation that I was really going to be OK in the world.

I had no idea of the feelings I would have when I actually went away. But more on that in a minute. On graduation day from Dwight-Englewood my mother and father beamed with pride. I had done it. I had graduated from high school during one of the busiest times of my career. Alex Hayley was the class speaker, thanks to my mother. Mom and I had befriended Alex Haley after he'd expressed his interest in charting my genealogy. He had invited my mother and me to a festival in Tennessee. And we had all truly bonded. I think my mother was actually a bit in love with him. He was a kind and gentle soul who really warmed to my mom. She made him laugh. Mom suggested that I ask him to speak at my graduation and he lovingly obliged.

Mom was able to stay sober during the ceremony but quickly began drinking at lunch. I remember being relieved that my father left before she got sloppy. I hated the thought of him ever thinking any less of my mom. The idea of Mom embarrassing herself in front of my father killed me, but for the most part, she kept it together, and at least for a moment we were a happy family.

Mom and I had taken a vacation every summer to one new place that I usually chose. In the past we had always had a lot of fun. My inspirations usually came out of a movie

I had seen, and it was true that the reality often didn't match up with my fantasy. I once wanted to go to the isle in Scotland that had a magical red telephone booth. We went to the spot and realized the booth had been a prop, only placed there for the film.

Another time we went to a remote city in Italy to learn how to marbleize paper. I had seen some movie about a woman leaving her urban life to find her soul in a remote Italian village. Mom and I thought marbleizing paper — like the paper we had seen at specialty stationery stores — would be fun. We arrived at the beautiful villa to learn about paints and oils, only to find out that the class was actually in bookbinding.

The summer before college, we went to the Greek island where the movie *Summer Lovers* had been shot. But of course, it looked nothing like the film in real life. You'd think that we, of all people, would have been able to foresee the fantasy aspect of moviemaking. But I guess we both wanted things to always be like they were in the movies.

In the past it hadn't mattered to me, because we always had fun, and kept busy, and laughed like hell at our insistent naïveté. Mom and I loved to travel and shop at local places and meet people and eat interesting foods. But this place, and at this age, it was different. Thankfully, it was only a week.

I had no idea what I was feeling. I was sad and mopey and bored. I had never actually felt boredom before. Mom remarked that nothing was wrong with me. I was just restless and bored and not used to relaxing. But that wasn't it. I was on the most romantic trip of my life, and I was holed up with my mother. I should have been on a trip with my girlfriends or on some type of adventure before the grind of college. This did not feel right. This place would have been perfect for a honeymoon, or a recluse, not a mother and daughter.

We finally returned home and the day came for me to go to my orientation week. The car was loaded with clothes and things I thought I might need to make my dorm room cozy, just like a home away from home. The drive was only an hour and a bit. Our driver, Dick, took the wheel, and Mom and I sat in the back and talked about how much fun it was all going to be.

Dick was a man my mother had hired as a handyman-driver a few years earlier. He often drove me to work appointments in the city and always to events so we would not have to hire a limo. We had a safe black Mercedes that he maintained, and he acted as somewhat of a caretaker for our home in Haworth. He also served as a huge safety net for my mother and was the main reason she wasn't either dead or arrested. It wouldn't be possible to count the number of times she was drunk in the backseat and we had to maneuver her to the house. To a certain extent he alleviated a great deal of my stress with regard to her safety. He also was the perfect addition to the enabling plan. She smartly eliminated the risk of being pulled over and I could be under the assumption that she was being responsible.

For many people, the threat of an impending car accident was enough to tell the person you loved that you wanted them to quit. That factor was eliminated from my arsenal and I just accepted Dick as a safety net for all of us. This was probably just another subconscious way for Mom to justify that her drinking did not have any adverse effects on our life. I was fed, clothed, housed, and would not have to be driven by a drunk driver. This by no means meant that she would never drive drunk. It just meant she was limiting the opportunities to do so.

Dick drove and when we hit the tree-lined road leading into the town, I felt nervous but excited. I looked up at the canopy of green and flickers of sunlight leaking through and I thought it was truly one of the calmest sights I had ever seen. The path opened at the end and you could see the majesty of ivy-clad buildings waiting to fill young minds.

I got my dorm-room assignment and went to drop my stuff off. The dorm consisted of three rooms. There were two bedrooms with a bunk bed and two dressers. The common living room had a couch and a big armchair. We would need to get more furniture. For now I brought clothes, linens, and electronics. I opened my room and was the third to arrive. The first two girls were a premed student from Texas and another student who was studying politics or medicine. They both chose their rooms. Both chose bottom bunks. I was next and chose the room closest to the front door. We all politely chatted and I began to get a sick feeling in my stomach. This was slowly becoming real. This was not a summer location where I could pretend to live an entirely new life. This was it. I was here, with these people, and we were going to actually live with each other, for the entire school year. It was actually happening.

What I had not factored into this new adjustment was the moment of my mother's departure. I hadn't really accepted the reality of her leaving me, especially with these strangers.

Princeton is divided into what they call "colleges." I was assigned to Mathey College, which contained Blair Arch. Blair was where I had heard the singing group perform. The architecture was all beautiful and the grounds richly green. I walked Mom to the entrance to the Mathey College archway and went with her to the car. I kissed both cheeks and hugged her good-bye. I planned on going home on the weekends, so I knew I would see her Friday. Mom was not crying and remained upbeat. This idea of going away to college was an entirely foreign concept for her, and my not living with her was borderline alien for both of us. I had spent vacations with my father and his family, and there was time during rehab when we were separated, but Mom and I had never honestly lived apart from one another. Remember, she was the one who nightly slept with me strapped to her chest.

I watched the black Mercedes getting smaller and smaller, and exhaled. Within an hour and a half I was on the phone with her, sobbing and asking her to come back and take me home. Our dorm phone's cord stretched just enough to make it to the floor of the entrance to my room. The other girls had all gone to the dining hall to check out dinner. They probably thought I was a snob or anorexic because I said I wasn't hungry.

I had waited till they were out of earshot and, like a husband sneaking a call to his mistress, quickly dialed my mother. She was just coming in the door when I explained to her that I had made a terrible mistake and wanted to come home immediately. I wasn't kidding.

"Oh, honey . . . you'll be fine. I promise. Try to get involved and go have some dinner, settle your things, and let's talk in the morning."

Sniff, sniff. "OK."

I never realized what a safety net my mother provided for me. And I use the term *safety net* fully aware of the irony. Even though in many ways I primarily took care of her, she was still there. Just knowing she was near was enough. It had gotten to the point that I almost didn't care that she was drunk, as long as she was near and alive. She still held the proverbial lifeline that I guess I had never intended on having cut.

For years, people attacked my mother for holding me down and for not allowing me my freedom. The press painted me as frustrated and bound. But the truth was, I didn't want freedom. Being bound was just fine. It was all I'd ever known, and it felt safe. I was not trying to escape.

It wasn't as if I wanted to return to the comforts and routines of a tranquil home life or a mom who baked and cleaned for me and held me softly underwing. I wanted to return to my mommy. I may have felt lonely when she drank, but a window of sobriety was never far away, and at least we were together.

I realized that this new situation — this whim I had to go to college — was not going to work for me. This pit in my gut was just not going away until everything returned to *normal.* Fine, I'd give it a fair amount of time to make it look as if I really gave it the old "college try" (the language seemed perfect for this scenario), and then this silliness could stop. The regular pattern of my life could peacefully resume.

I am shocked that it never occurred to me that I might feel homesick. I had dealt with scarier, more adult situations and had powered through much more dramatic scenes in life. I had suffered but survived. I had seen more, and was more adult, than any of these fresh young ones. I was mature. Or so I thought.

As the weeks went on, I realized how sheltered and immature I was in many ways. I wasn't mature enough to deal with passing the boys' dorms on the way to a bathroom consisting of communal sinks and multi-stalled showers. Everybody had these square garden buckets filled with their stuff and shower slippers and terry cloth robes. But it was all totally foreign to me. It wasn't as if I expected the Ritz or wanted an en suite toilet, but I had never even gone to sleep-away camp. A raft trip with a movie crew down the Colorado River did not constitute roughing it. To be fair, neither did this, but somehow I felt more uncomfortable and exposed here.

I managed to learn to deal with the living and showering arrangements, but I couldn't shake the sadness. My classes were great and I started to find a bit of a routine, but my life mostly revolved around studying and planning on seeing my mom. I did not extend myself much farther than the library and my dorm room.

The room itself began to be a war zone as well. My roommates would stay up incredibly late every night. It seemed that I was the only one who wasn't a vampire and who wasn't afraid to roam outside while it was daylight. I also decided to rent a small refrigerator, only to repeatedly find experiments growing inside and peanut butter–covered knives with stuck-on M&M's plastered on the top of the minifridge. This was not what I was used to, that's for sure.

In the beginning I had a very tough time finding a niche. The students were all being respectful about giving me my space, just like my first months of high school, but it meant I felt even more solitary. I thought nobody wanted to bother being my friend because I came with enough baggage to fill a cart. I believe the students thought they were doing the right thing. I don't think they realized that I did not want space or respect. I was terrified of space, and because I had never really had respect, I did not even know how to regard it as freedom. It felt irresponsible and unproductive. It was unfamiliar to me and grossly uncomfortable.

The paparazzi tried to sneak onto campus, dressed like what they thought college students looked like, and follow me around. The students were great and they alerted the school and me if anyone saw anybody suspicious. One photographer hid in a vent to photograph me walk to a class; another attempted to bribe a Mathey College freshman to take a camera into the showers and snap me in the nude. They would have been in for a surprise if they tried, because I had taken to showering in a one-piece bathing suit! My roommates asked whether I was on the swim team and I just said yes. I was pretty sure they were not fans of water sports and the secret would be safe.

Not one student took the bribes for information, and I established a rapport with campus security. I gave them my class schedule so they could be cognizant of my whereabouts without being obtrusive. I felt protected by the student body the most. It was not just about my safety, but also about my integrity, my freedom, and my personal growth. I was delighted. Who would have imagined that there were people out there who didn't wish to profit off of me?

But I didn't stop missing my mother. I fixed my class schedule so that I was most free on Fridays to go home and see my mother. I didn't think I wanted to give up going to Princeton and forfeit an education because I was "Mom-sick," but why was everybody else so seemingly settled in and happy?

Every night I would call Mom and fight back the tears. Her voice made me ache because I thought the feelings I had would last forever. Leaving Mom was something I had prepared to do when I threatened to live with my dad, but that was temporary. This felt different. I missed my house, my home, and the good parts of my mother.

For the first term, I spent most of my time in the library or driving back to Haworth. I would have Mom drive out every Wednesday to take me to dinner. We would either go have Indian food or go to a healthy diner in a club car that served things like veggie burgers. I was still a vegetarian at this time from a stint I had working at the San Diego Zoo during my senior year in high school. Many times I would actually cry during dinner. The only other time I had ever cried like this was when it was over a boy. It felt like a similar heartbreak, only not romantic. I was being forced to understand the feeling of being on my own. I was worried about my mother being alone and not properly looked after, but I was also just missing my house and my mommy.

I would always cry as she drove away. I'd bury my feelings until after my one Friday class (or sometimes as early as late Thursday night). Then I'd have Dick drive me straight home. Mom and I would go to the movies and eat Japanese food. I'd happily study in the car or at my rolltop desk. Sunday night, at about *60 Minutes* time, I started to feel heavyhearted once again. I resisted going to sleep, because I knew when I awoke Monday morning I would have to leave her and go away again.

Being away from Mom made me idealize her and her alcoholic behavior. I had learned how to navigate her drinking and to deal with every element of it, but the feeling of being released into a totally foreign way of life (and only possessing resources that worked in rare and unique circumstances) made me buckle emotionally. During this first term I was so antisocial and lonesome that I would have taken drunk, nasty Mom with all her insults over being without her.

I grappled with the idea of going home and commuting. I could get my courses done and still be home with Mom. Everything could go back to the way it was. One night at dinner I told Mom that it was time to quit. I couldn't do it emotionally. My studies were great, but I did not need or want the life part of college. I did not fit in.

Mom was calmer than I had ever known her to be, and her drinking at that time had curbed (temporarily) for some reason. She insisted that she knew me and that I knew me, too, and that if I quit the whole experience, I would never, ever forgive myself. High school had been a tough adjustment, and look how wonderfully that turned out. I had had a great high school experience and my best friend in the whole world, Lisa, I had met in ninth grade. I needed to give it my all this time as well, and just keep moving ahead.

She somehow kept encouraging me, even though I know it must have cut her up inside to know she was ensuring that I stay away. I realize that nothing would have made her happier than to have me back under the same roof.

She said, "Remember the Hula-Hoop, my darling."

"OK, Mom, I'll try."

And I did. But trying was tiring, and I felt a little bit like a failure and an ingrate. I tried out for dance companies and singing groups and did not get accepted. I had zero experience with anything musical but thought I could figure it out. It was also getting a bit more annoying with people trying to infiltrate the campus to get a glimpse of me. I kept my head down and went to class and the library, and I studied as if my life depended on it. And it did.

Then exam time came, and although I had never experienced something so intense, I was very prepared. No surprise, since I had spent none of my time socializing and all of it in the library.

Then a crazy thing happened. I took an early-level pysch course and the exam was a multiple-choice one. My grade would not be debatable. There were three hundred kids in the course and out of all of them, only four got A's. I was one of them.

I saw each student checking the grades posted on the bulletin board. The students would each look at their grade and then slide down to look at my name. I thought this was understandable, but it was still enraging. But this time I didn't mind, because they'd see my A.

Maybe the professors were not playing favorites or giving me any kind of break. Maybe I had actually studied my ass off to get through it.

After the class realized I'd earned such a good grade, people started to approach me more. Some kids asked me if I wanted to study with them, and others asked me to share my notes from class. I would have rewritten every page of notes if asked because I was so excited that people knew I was a serious student and not there expecting any special treatment. It was an academic icebreaker, and I took it.

As the year went on, the scholastic aspect was picking up and my social life was smoothing out a bit. I was making friends and decided to join a theatre group called the Triangle Club. I was no longer crying and Mom no longer had to visit me every Wednesday. I still enjoyed going home on the weekends because my roommate situation had not improved and our dorm was depressing. I was hardly in my room and could not wait to get out. But I was making friends and I had a better living situation planned for the next year.

I'd made it through the year. But at what cost? Mom very selflessly convinced me to stay at school instead of leave and go back home. Mom undoubtedly missed me, and her life lacked any focus.

At this point her drinking had become worse than ever. I couldn't do another intervention because she was too savvy. Addicts can see one coming miles away. In my opinion you get only one real impactful shot. I could no longer claim I would go live with my father, because I was already separated from her and she was, seemingly, in support of this separation. Mom still felt she did not have a problem with alcohol and claimed she could keep her drinking habits under control.

I was gone, but she knew it needed to happen, no matter the personal cost to her. She missed me unbearably because the day I left for school, our dynamic basically changed forever. Of course this would be traumatic for both of us.

But this was the first time that my mom put her pain and her deep fears aside to do the best thing for my future and me. She didn't want to live alone, or with anybody except me. This was the ultimate sacrifice for her and the first time she actually chose to physically let go. I will forever be grateful she would not let me quit.

"You're not a quitter, my darling."

Nobody would ever have guessed that Mom would have the strength to sacrifice herself for my benefit. She was always fighting for me and protecting me, but I was attached to her at the hip. Up until now, I hadn't wanted emancipation. But here I was, with the perfect opportunity to cut loose and rebel, and I was fighting it with all my might. We both profoundly knew that a shift was occurring, and neither one of us wanted to fully commit. It meant a breach of some kind. One we both never thought we'd see, but one we silently knew was inevitable. Yet without the change, we might not survive. (It would be just like *Grey Gardens.*) I would become Little Edie to her Big Edie, and although we would be tied to each other, our relationship would fester and love would turn to hate.

I wanted my mommy but I trusted that the outcome would most likely be better for me. Mom let me go and she did so as her ultimate sacrifice. I believe that this was a beginning to her end in many ways. In her mind, she was losing me. Now she had no impetus to not drink. I suppressed the guilt that I was leaving her. Sometimes when drunk she would glare at me, call me an ingrate, and coldly claim that she knew I would eventually leave her all alone.

I suspect she held the conviction that everybody she ever loved would leave her. Her father and her first fiancé — and a baby, I believed — and my father all disappeared from her life in one way or another. Why would I be any different? To her it was a self-fulfilling prophecy.

CHAPTER ELEVEN:
AMERICA'S SWEETHEART

During the years I was at Princeton, even though I worked very little, the press remained interested in everything from my class schedule to my romantic life. Ever since *Pretty Baby* I'd been the subject of all sorts of speculation — much of it unfair — and I don't think my mom reacted to the press in a systematic way, especially in regard to my sexuality and potential romantic relationships. Did she try to actively change my image from *Pretty Baby* and Calvin Klein model to an America's sweetheart saving her virginity until her wedding night? I don't think so.

The most poignant part of all was how disassociated I was with my own body. As a model, I was primarily a cover girl. I was labeled "The '80s Look" by *Time* magazine. People said I had the most beautiful face in the world.

Well, that seemed ridiculous to me. It

didn't register as true. "Most beautiful" was an arbitrary concept and I was afraid to buy into it. Because I shot cover after cover and never did runway, I simply avoided ever really thinking about my body and consequently my sexuality. I was a face first and I knew how to work that face according to the demand. I'd be shooting a cover for *Vogue,* and underneath the table I'd be wearing jeans and Top-Siders. I thought about my persona as existing only from the neck up. It was as if I was disconnected from my body from the neck down. So when I became the most celebrated virgin of our time it became even easier to not think about my body.

All my life, I'd been terrified of physical contact with boys. Perhaps it was because of the closeness and easy affection I shared with my mother; I didn't feel a void or a need for affection from boys.

I believe my mom wanted me to stay a virgin for as long as possible. I think she wanted to keep me her baby. I have to be honest: I'm a mother myself now, and I get it. I look at my girls and want them to be my delicious babies forever. I want to create designer chastity belts! The thought of them losing their virginity makes me cringe. Even the thought of them not letting me kiss them on their little rosebud lips makes me cry. I also hope and pray that their first experience is about love and trust and that they are not at all traumatized but feel free and safe.

When my mother did talk to me about sex growing up, it was brief and she didn't have to play the bad guy. She was raising me Catholic and it was the church that preached the sanctity of virginity and waiting till marriage. She was just the messenger. I also was so genuinely naïve and was kept so protected by my mother — Rapunzel in the tower — that intimacy with anybody seemed out of the question. I just didn't want to deal with any of it.

On top of all of that, my mom said I had a responsibility to my fans, who often wrote letters to me about pressure from boys and asking how I dealt with it. I would get hundreds of letters a month and most of them asked for autographs and advice.

Villard Books approached my mom and me and presented us the idea of my writing a book. Unlike *The Brooke Book,* which my mother had put together with a friend, the plan was that I'd take an active part in writing this second one. I had almost finished my first semester at Princeton and had become much more confident in my writing than I had been in high school. I was excited by the chance to tell the truth in my own words. The price was evidently right and Mom was happy with the contract.

The book was supposed to be an honest account of being a young woman during her first year of being away from home and going away to college. I was, of course, a famous young woman attending Princeton University, which was far from typical, but the book would integrate several universal themes.

I had taken many psychology courses by this time and felt I had a lot to say. I delved into the first chapter with excitement and clear self-awareness. The chapter was a heartfelt account of how scared and alone I felt my first semester away from my mom. I wrote about how strange it was being the only recognizable person on campus. It was humorous and vulnerable and focused on the complexities of trying to grow up.

My mom read it and was proud. I even showed my writing to a professor and he said he was impressed by the writing and my candor. He thought it would be a good book for young people. I handed in the first chapter and an introduction and awaited editorial notes.

To my dismay, the editor read it, trashed

the whole chapter, and hired a ghostwriter. They said something about it being faster and easier for me . . . blah blah blah. My mom thought that because of my heavy workload at school, it might actually be more convenient for me to meet with the ghostwriter and have the questions and conversations recorded, rather than having me pen the whole book. I remember thinking that if they were not interested in publishing the book I wanted to write, then I'd just have to give up on the tone I was trying to create. I had committed to the book, so I did not have much choice other than to just follow along with the new plan. It didn't occur to us to scrap the whole thing, because it was a job. We had a contract and it was money in the bank.

According to my mom, it would keep my name out there while I was at school and on hiatus from Hollywood. I am sure she had never thought to include an out clause in the contract should we be disappointed with content. Mom would have been satisfied with anything because it was all about me. I never read the contract and I doubt Mom read the fine print. I had no agent to help draw up or review anything. That was the way most of our deals were handled. We only thought about if the job would be interesting, pay well, and keep me in people's minds. It was a bonus if it fit into my school schedule. And that was about it.

I began by meeting with the ghostwriter on the weekends. Mom always left us alone to do the taped sessions. She said it was important that it was in my words.

When I started seeing the pages the ghostwriter was producing, I was appalled. All the deeper feelings and observations I made about this period of my life were overlooked. I hated the questions she was asking and kept trying to steer it all to a deeper level. The result, sadly, was a very silly book with short sentences about important things like the versatility of leg warmers. I gave up. I had bigger things with which to concern myself, such as surviving away from my mom and getting a degree.

Mom seemed unfazed by the vapid direction the book was taking and seemed to have no problem with its content. She hired the amazing Robert Risko to do illustrations and went about helping the publisher gather permissions from various photographers who would be featured in the book. I could tell she was happy to have a project and one that revolved around her finest creation: me. She liked being busy and necessary. She also seemed thrilled with the wholesome image that was being created by the book, which portrayed me as a hard-working, responsible, chaste America's sweetheart. I don't think my mom ever wanted to face the deeper side of all of it. Photos of me in leg warmers and a unitard, taking readers through a series of leg lifts and jumping jacks or describing packing the perfect weekend wardrobe, did not bother my mother one bit. She was satisfied with creating and upholding the sweet, untouchable, yet "normal" teenager image on the pages of a book ironically titled *On Your Own.*

One chapter of the book was dedicated to the idea of peer pressure and the subject of my virginity. I had agreed to divulge this truth because of a responsibility I felt to my female fans; I wanted to be a good role model. I admitted to being a virgin and expressed my plan to save myself for marriage.

I felt no shame in admitting that I was still a virgin at age nineteen. I had previously spoken out about the evils of drugs and smoking. Talking about the value of waiting until marriage to lose one's virginity didn't seem like a big deal. I also did not think it was going to cause such controversy. But I cringe now at the thought of my being so open, because there really was nothing off-limits with regard to my personal life. Looking back, I think it was actually sad that there was so much access to my life for press (and consequently the public). I mean, one of my orthodontist appointments was filmed! I guess it was all in attempts to paint me as a regular kid.

I did want to help however I could, though, and when you read the outpouring of admiration and respect from kids who wrote to me, it was easy to want to uphold my image in their eyes. I basically wanted to tell my young women fans that they need not fall prey to peer pressures regarding anything including their sexuality. My mom said it was important to include this in the book so my fans wouldn't feel alone. If Brooke Shields was a virgin, maybe it was OK for them to be as well.

Mom always impressed on me to lead by example. It became a torch I would happily carry. Mom had not lived her life that way, and I believe she used her sexuality slightly desperately and as an attempt to feel loved and accepted. The hypocrisy of it all would not become evident till decades later.

Here was my mother, an alcoholic who had lost a baby that she had conceived out of wedlock and had become an unmarried pregnant person a second time. Yet Mom was telling me to uphold the virtues of virginity and abstinence from all vices. I have recently wondered if it was all an attempt on my mom's part to counteract the overly sexual image with which I had been associated in my younger years. Was Mom now trying to dictate how the public viewed me? I believed my mom wanted me to be universally adored and untouchable. It is hard enough just dealing with being a teenager, let alone bearing the burden of the fate of young women everywhere.

In addition, because Mom and I had been so enmeshed, I wasn't able to have any romantic feelings without making her somehow a part of them. I told her everything and was constantly seeking her approval. There was little room for anybody else.

Looking as far back as my first "official" kiss, back in seventh grade at New Lincoln, my memories of it are not only that it was disturbing, but also that the first person I told was my mother. It was with a boy named Chris Serbagi at a friend's party. He asked me to go to a back room, and when I got there, he had set up the couch with pillows and had drawn the shades. He told me to lie down and he proceeded to slobber all over my face. (Maybe I should have made

Keith Carradine my first official kiss after all!) I was so grossed out and sad that this was the first kiss, which I had so eagerly anticipated. Not only was it not romantic or spontaneous as I had hoped it would be; it was tonguey and gross, too. We got busted and sent home by the mom of the house.

The next day, my mom was driving me to school in our black Jeep, as she often did, and her response after I recounted the horror was only to ask if I planned on doing it again. I told my mom "No!" and that was the end of it. It would have been nice if Mom had explained to me what a first could be like and how I could still have one with the right person. Instead, I then shut myself off to all boy kisses in general.

Basically my "relationships" had always been orchestrated by my mother in one way or another. She directed my romantic life sometimes subtly and sometimes not. She didn't focus on romance (never mind love), but instead wanted to associate me with names that connoted fame, money, and power. These were the relationships she supported, also because they were less attainable.

She loved that I had briefly dated John Travolta, Jimmy McNichol, Leif Garrett, Scott Baio, and John Kennedy. They were all on *Teen Beat* magazines and stars in their own right. She trusted I'd keep my vow of chastity and like the attention paid to me in these couplings. She genuinely loved Michael Jackson and said I was good for him as a supportive and honest friend.

My fame, my mother's choice to support certain romantic relationships more than others, and my increasingly complicated feelings about my virginity led to an enduring insecurity about my sexuality. The book's release the summer between my freshman and sophomore year didn't help. My virginity was the only thing anyone could talk about. In my opinion many things were wrong with the book, but the tour was fun. Mom and I went with Gavin and made the most out of every city we visited.

I had recently gone on *The Tonight Show* to promote *On Your Own* and Johnny had asked me with whom I would want to be stranded on a desert island. (Such an original question!) I said I had a crush on George Michael. Mom had decorated a denim shirt of mine with "WHAM" in glitter paint and Bedazzles. She glued pins and little pictures of George and surprised me with it to wear to his concert. I almost wore it on Carson.

As luck would have it, while in Chicago

on the book tour, we discovered we were staying at the same boutique hotel as George. Mom was enamored of the fact that he was famous, and she loved his voice. Mom had contacted George's publicist to say that I was staying in the same place and hoped to meet him if possible. He said he would love to take me to dinner but because of our being bothered by the press we should probably just arrange dinner at the hotel. I nearly fell on my face.

George decided to get food delivered to the private dining room on the rooftop. I arrived at the meal in colored jeans and a blouse. The table was beautifully set and all the foods I liked had been ordered. George said he had read some place that I liked to be healthy so he picked accordingly. There were flowers and candles and we talked nonstop. He complimented me on my blouse. When dinner was over, George walked me to my hotel room and said he wanted to see me again. He left without even trying to kiss me. I was so touched by what a real gentleman he was. (I wanted to yell, "Wait, please don't 'go go'!")

Back in my hotel bedroom Gavin and my mom had put CAUTION: POLICE LINE. DO NOT CROSS tape all over my bed. There were signs that said THIS MEANS YOU, GEORGE! I guess this was payback for my sign-hanging stunt down the hallway for Mom after her date with Woody Allen.

George and I managed to go on a few more dates in New York City that involved shopping or meals. He held my hand and even bought me a mauve cashmere sweater from Charivari on the Upper West Side. I thought he was a remarkable, respectful, and patient gentleman who was obviously aware of my hesitance regarding sex. Mom was thrilled. She said he had good taste and was sweetly old-fashioned. Nobody had ever been willing to move so slowly. It must be love.

On the night before I was to go back to Princeton for my sophomore year, George invited me to a party for Grace Jones. When we arrived at the club, Boy George ran up to us and started screaming about how he had heard the rumor but was happy to see us actually together. Before the evening got too late, my boyfriend George "carelessly" whispered into my ear, "Why don't we get out of here?"

We got into the limo and headed back to my home in New Jersey. As we were nearing the house, George put up the partition and turned to me. I thought, *Oh my God — I'm going to get to have my first time with George Michael in the back of the limo!* Forget Catholicism and the book. Forget my mother. God would understand! I gazed at George with puckered lips. He looked deep into my eyes and said, "I think we need to take a break. I need to concentrate on my career." WHAM!

I was devastated. Mom tried to comfort me and promised that I was going to be OK. She obviously didn't see him as a threat at any step of the way. Mom encouraged friendships with people like George Michael, Michael Jackson, and John Travolta, because I believe she was impressed by their genuinely sweet natures as well as their level of fame. These were the types of more gentle male friends who loved my mom and did not pose a threat to her.

I went back to my new place just off campus and cried myself to sleep for weeks. But my sophomore year went by and I finally got over George. I began dating, doing theatre, studying even harder, and was adjusting extremely well. I knew Mom was drinking, but I did not have to see it, and as long as I spoke to her before going to bed, I knew she was safe and fine.

During my junior year I met and fell madly in love with my first real love. I met Dean Cain, who was a football player at Princeton. He was a year behind me and we were instantly crazy about each other. I saw all his football games and he saw all my dance and theatre performances. We were a golden couple and everybody loved us together. I loved his family. His dad was a director and his mom was also somewhat of a blond bombshell who loved to laugh and hang out with the kids. She was an ex-model and always wore the current beach-babe fashion.

We got along wonderfully and she made me feel extremely accepted and like one of her children. He had a slightly older brother and an adorable little sister and they all lived in Malibu. Dean's parents were very California liberal and I was always a bit shocked whenever they had Dean and me stay in the same bedroom when I came to visit them, sometimes even giving us the best room in the house. This was such a contrast to how my mother always insisted Dean stay in a guest room. His family took me in as one of theirs and I fit in.

Dean's mom was always also a bit larger than life and a bit dramatic. She was never inappropriate but just loved to have a good time. Even though his dad was working hard and was very present, Dean was like the little man of the house from the time he was a baby. Maybe Dean just simply knew how to handle beautiful, flamboyant women who needed attention. But he was always very patient with my mom. Mom loved Dean at the start but began negating our relationship the longer it went on. She started to act disdainful and she would often blurt out or whisper under her breath, "Oh, it's just physical with you two!" I tried to overlook her comments because I really was in love and of course it was *not* physical. I was too bound to my virginity and to her!

Being with Dean was the best thing that

could have happened to me. It made such sense for us in so many ways. We shared the same sense of humor. He understood Hollywood from a personal perspective but was not yet an actor. He was not intimidated by my success or my fame, and he was a great dancer and fit in anywhere I took him. Everybody loved Dean and he was incredibly and painfully patient with me regarding sex. But it felt as if Mom was always lording over us, and I was self-conscious because the world assumed we were sleeping together. In truth, though, I was even more scared and shy with him because I was so in love. I had this fear that if I slept with him, I would want to run away.

Even when Mom wasn't around, I felt as if she was watching. We were in love and so incredibly attracted to one another in every way, that it would make sense that we were having sex. We were always holding hands and trying to find ways to be alone and kiss. But, poor guy, I made him wait and wait, and my mom kept track. She knew we were not sleeping together because she could pretty much guarantee that (like my first French kiss) I would tell her if we were. Still, I think Mom was actually threatened for the first time. But even though I really felt scared about sex and paranoid I was being watched by Mom and the world, Dean remained loving and patient.

We were almost the couple who got married after being college sweethearts. We did everything together and were well-known on campus. He was the first man (and the only one for a very long time) who really knew me and loved me. He even knew me better than my mother did because we had deep personal talks and he asked questions. He was witness to my struggles with my mom and he respected how much I loved her. I was honestly, truly, and purely in love. It made me the happiest person I had been in forever. And he loved me even more. He would have married me right out of college. He said he knew that I was it. He didn't need to keep looking. But he was a year behind me, and when I graduated, I was scared about our next year apart.

Even though being with Dean felt so right, I couldn't completely give myself to him — in any way — without my mother's approval. Her approval opened my world for me. I remember calling her to ask if I could drive up to Sierra Summit with Dean to go ski after I had graduated. She granted me permission and therefore I felt liberated.

First of all, I was twenty-one and still calling home for permission! But the second point, and the bigger one, is that I would have gone even if she had said no. But my enjoyment would have been dampened. I would have felt distanced from the ability to be free and have fun. But in this case, since Mom said I could go and have fun, I was liberated and free to enjoy myself.

It is fascinating how my mom's laugh could make me smile on the inside or how her being joyous could ease my mind and relax my hesitance immediately. And not just in person. Even from afar, I needed her to be accepting and condoning to let myself feel the same way.

When I was twenty-two, I finally lost my virginity. Dean and I had been together for what seemed like a lifetime. He was incredibly tolerant and admittedly long-suffering. I confess that I wish I had not made him wait as long as he did — for his sake and mine. I did not need him to prove anything to me, but I was still so bound and guilt-ridden by my mother. In retrospect, it was not fair to any of us, and all of this is still a regret of mine. Dean's and my relationship was exactly the kind that any parent would hope for. It was based on love and respect and should have been allowed the freedom to unfold.

Mom was unjustly judgmental of our romantic relationship and she feared it on a deeper level. I don't know if she would ever admit to it but this threat went beyond Catholicism. I believe she wanted me to stay hers alone. She believed in an absolute hold she had on me. And she prayed that I would never ever want to breach that bond in any way. And growing up, and having sex, would mean that I was leaving her. If I loved (and gave of myself to) another, I was no longer in her control. To her, losing control meant I did not love her.

When it finally happened, we were in Sun Valley, Idaho. Dean and I were in a bedroom upstairs and my mother was downstairs, drunk. In a strange way, it was her being drunk that freed me up. If she had not been drinking, I would have found it more difficult to follow through. But even though I knew she was totally out of it, the potential threat that she would hear us or walk in and shame me was crippling to me. Her drunkenness emboldened me, but it wasn't an act of rebellion as much as it was one of my own temporary autonomy.

The whole experience was beautiful. It was what you would wish for your daughter. It should have been what I had wished for myself, but in an instant, guilt slapped me in the face. Instead of giving in to what was a loving, and emotionally safe, relationship, and escaping into the most intimate and deserved moment, I began to cry deeply and silently. I didn't regret sharing this with Dean and felt so secure with him. But I deeply regretted being preoccupied and fearful and not allowing myself to enjoy how much we loved one another and how long we had been together.

I got so overwhelmed that I jumped out of my bed, which was a handmade pale-wood bed made from local trees and faced a window and a fireplace. It was very high and I actually kind of tumbled off it and started running. Out the window the moon and the stars burned so bright that you could practically read a book, but I saw none of the beauty. Instead I ran from the room and down a long hall as if I were being chased. I have no idea where I was going but it was probably to go sleep in another bed so my mother wouldn't find out.

I was buck naked, streaking down a hallway and running as if I had just stolen someone's wallet. What a sight! Dean leapt up and ran after me with the comforter in his arms. He threw it around me, grabbed me around my shoulders, and stopped me from running. He hugged me tight and quietly asked me where I was going. He then said the most amazing thing. He said, "Hey, stop running. Why are you running? Where are you going? I am not going anywhere. I am not going to leave you."

I was the one running and he was the one trying to take the responsibility. I was worried that once I slept with him I would become too vulnerable and would no longer own myself. I was afraid I was leaving my mother. As long as I kept that part of me untapped, I could remain emotionally closed. Being that exposed would destroy my escape route. I had always seen myself as alone, but with Mom. This meant I was possibly not alone. This meant I was attached to Dean and I feared that responsibility.

Even though I knew I had taken such a big step in committing to stay at Princeton, I remained entangled with my mother and our life. I didn't know where I began and where my mother ended, and that meant I didn't know how to fit Dean in.

I wish I had been more in touch with my own feelings about all of it, but I had my mother's voice in my head, the public's voice all around me in the press, and the shame of Catholicism in my heart. It wasn't so much about being a good Catholic as it was a promise I had made. I couldn't become a liar. And because the whole world knew I was a virgin, the whole world would know when I was not.

What should have been the beginning of a wonderful phase in my relationship with Dean turned out to be the beginning of the end. I regret the way I handled it. Without school and without virginity, I really was floating in a strange limbo. I suddenly did not know who or how to be around him. It all generated from a twisted sense of self. Dean never put pressure on me for anything, and he respected me in every way. I panicked. I was much better at arm's-length relationships. I was better with an exit-route strategy. I could not handle loving somebody more than my mom.

My fears had much more to do with my mother than they did with religion or public opinion. I knew Mom felt that if she protected my virginity, I could still remain her baby. She probably didn't have the confidence to not be threatened by someone I loved.

The moment I slept with Dean was the moment I left my mother. I chose him. I felt this and I am sure she did as well. I couldn't handle having made this symbolic decision. There really is no such thing as choosing between a parent and a love — but there kind of *is*. In a moment this intimate, you are choosing your partner over anybody else. It is a rite of passage, and this molting is terrifying and uncomfortable. It needs desire and commitment. I had buried my desire and I had misdirected my commitment.

Yes, Mom would always be my mother,

and yes, it was natural and right. But this was a severing of a cord that had become brittle. I would exert efforts at trying to re-attach said cord for many years to come.

I feel sad for these two young lovers. I feel sad for myself, and for him, and for us. I wish I had had the strength to revel in our relationship more, even from the very start. I gave it what I could, but I remained tethered. The leap was too much for me to handle.

Going to college was, in a way, an ending to the first major era of my career, and it was a closure to the first and longest chapter of my mom's and my relationship.

CHAPTER TWELVE:
I WISH I ONLY KNEW YOU
IN THE MORNINGS, MAMA

Even before my relationship with Dean became intimate — and before the life-changing trip to our mountain home — Mom remained in the swing of excessive drinking. By the beginning of my senior year she had progressively increased the amount she was drinking and began to mix the vodka, wine, and the rum and Diet Cokes. I was home less, and when I was, I was buried in homework and my thesis work. That and having fun with my now best friends as well as Dean. I loved him.

I begged her to stop. I'd say things such as "Can you at least try not getting drunk on the day of graduation?"

"I promise."

She had gotten so used to lying to me and to believing her own lies that the pattern just kept being repeated. I gave her one last request not to drink at my graduation. I should have specified *all day and also at the party.*

She managed to not drink before the actual ceremony. She was sober as I was walking up to the podium to accept my diploma: "cum laude, for French literature."

The honors were a nice surprise and might have been higher if I had gotten an A instead of an A-minus on part of my junior paper. Anyway, I walked up and hoped Mom was proud. I knew my dad was. I believe he just felt I earned and deserved it because of all my hard work. Dad left after lunch.

By the end of the day Mom had managed to smuggle alcohol in and either surreptitiously or openly drink it — I can't remember which. At the big graduation dinner Mom wanted to dance and I wanted to be as far away from her as I could be. I left her with Lila and my gay "godparents," Hank and Richard, who were my mom's friends from way back. They were the ones with the Fire Island house and the poodle who exposed the fact my mother wasn't wearing any underwear. At the dinner she had not done anything majorly embarrassing, but when she was drunk she cursed more and flirted more. I wanted out.

After I left the dinner, I went to Dean's

room and found him drunk after having just been punched in the lip. He had actually demanded a friend of his punch him. I have no idea why. I instantly felt as if I were surrounded by immaturity. I took my leave from him, too. I actually remember thinking at that moment that I was alone in a different way. I felt sad and disappointed in both my mom and Dean. Both of them felt out of my reach, and even though Dean did not have a problem with alcohol, alcohol had interfered with my enjoyment of this special day. But I forgave Dean.

College, which had been the focus of my life for four years, was over. I was about to start on a very scary, very unchartered path, and I would somehow have to navigate it.

After college, I basically moved more permanently into our townhouse on Sixty-Second Street. Up until then Haworth and Princeton had been where I lived. We had had the townhouse for a few years but only stayed there when necessary. But I wanted to live back in the city full-time, and I wanted to live alone. Mom stayed in New Jersey but would come and go as she wanted. But even though I liked living alone in the townhouse, I was constantly worried about my mother, just as I had been when I was at school. If we had lived in New York City only, I might have been less worried about Mom's drinking, because driving would have been less of an issue. Every time the phone rang later at night I was sure it was going to be the police. It was so strange because I did not want to be near her. But being away from her and not being able to monitor her was even more torturous. Dick, the driver, was only part-time by then because my work had diminished, and Mom always assumed she was OK to drive.

I did not have a movie lined up — or anything else professionally for that matter — but I was not yet concerned. I was enjoying being a graduate from Princeton University and I already had my vocation. Little did I know that it was all about to go horribly awry.

At this point in my career I did not have the luxury of not working and not earning. We had so much overhead. We had an office staff of five women, a handyman, a cleaning lady, and a part-time driver. We had four homes with mortgages and bills seemingly everywhere. We needed to make money, and much of the endorsements from the past — the doll, the hair dryers, the book, even the Brooke Jeans line — had all gone away. Great, I had a clean slate. What a luxury. Despite the financial pressures, I decided I had a degree and time and therefore would hone my craft.

I wanted to focus on myself as an artist. I started taking acting and dancing classes two and three times a day. I was still under the assumption that the jobs were going to keep flowing in. I was just going to be better in them because I was actually working on my acting ability. I was in an intense acting class that lasted for weeks and was six to eight hours long, including various exercises and scene work and two to four hours of meditation. We would spend the meditation portion lying on our back looking for a green light. People were crying all over the place and I felt incredibly alone. Basically this class was brainwashing and was incredibly unproductive for somebody like me. I needed to learn how to act, not how to get in touch with my "shadow side" while seeing the "green light" in my "mind's eye." It was a disaster because I became so stripped of any defenses during these exhausting, torturous techniques that I was mugged for the first time in my life. I had also basically stopped eating food, existing on fumes.

Mom and Lisa, my best friend from high school, drove into the city together one day and kidnapped me back from this pseudo-actor's religion. Lisa had graduated from Villanova and was working for a bank. She was still living at home and her house was not far from ours. Mom and Lisa talked often but mostly hung out only with each other when I was around. They usually drank together on movie sets or when I was nearby but working.

The two of them took me to a diner and

ordered me frozen yogurt with fruit and granola and said they just missed me. By the end of the meal I confessed to hating the class and realizing it was not where I wanted to be. Mom and Lisa said that I was starting to act weird and they were worried. Even though Mom did not show any signs of giving up drinking when aligned with my best friend, Lisa, she was able to help me become grounded again.

Mom and I were trying to scrounge up jobs for me to do. I assumed that when I graduated, my career would pick up where it had left off. I did not realize that it hadn't left off anywhere because I was really neither an actress nor a model. I had become a celebrity and an advertising icon. But these days I was an ad icon without any ads. Back when I worked for Calvin, he had not renewed my contract for a second year because the jeans were being too identified with me and less with the brand. I got dropped. I had gained twenty pounds in college, and the deal Mom and I had — she'd stop drinking and I'd stop snacking — she broke in a day. I wasn't getting my jobs but shitty commercials, mostly out of the country.

We decided a movie was needed.

I had filmed *Brenda Starr* the summer

between my junior and senior year at Princeton with the intention of its being released around the time I graduated. The movie was way ahead of its time and was brilliantly conceived. The movie had been my mother's idea. *Brenda Starr* had always been her favorite cartoon and she had been saying for years that she wanted me to play her in a film one day. She had optioned the rights at one point but was never able to set the project up. Our option ran out and Mom did not put more of our money into holding on to it. Finally, Mom found the original cartoonist, Dale Messick, and even got Delia Ephron to write the first draft, and Mom found some independent company to fund it.

The problem was it didn't have a studio behind it, and although the concept and the actors and the costumes and makeup and hair were incredible, the backers were questionable, and it got into terrible legal quicksand. The movie, although made before all the other cartoon and superhero movies, would not be released for three years, after a glut of blockbusters. It was doomed, but such a great idea. Mom had ideas like this and often seemed ahead of her time. She unfortunately was never able to parlay these trailblazing ideas into reality.

She never had a team or the big guns behind her. We were the scrappy insurgent group that would get slaughtered trying to defend our small territory.

Anyway, the plan of having a movie released after graduation was foiled and I would soon begin to realize in what dire straits my career lay.

Every day I would ask my mom, "Am I going to get a movie? Am I going to get to act again?"

"Of course, just be patient."

I kept asking, and I kept believing her words, but I was stagnating and I didn't know where to turn.

Something had to change. Mom and I knew a few people who worked with an ICM agent named Sam Cohn, and she set up a meeting to sit down with him. He was a big agent and had clients like Meryl Streep and Louis Malle. I remember hearing him say that he would only take me on if I ceased being a celebrity and committed to being an actress. That sounded wonderful to me. He wanted to represent me, but only if my mother stepped down.

Well, there was zero chance of my mother stepping down from anywhere and she was very angry that anyone would even ask.

Mom still had my utter support and I believed she would do whatever she thought best for my career. She refused and she made me walk away. I actually do feel that this was a pity because at the time it was a real opportunity that I was denied.

It's funny — I had forgotten all about this but was reminded of it recently by Lila, who said she begged my mother to reconsider. Mom got angry with her for trying to divide the two of us and for entrusting my career and my well-being to a total stranger.

Looking back at this now, I get a pang of regret. I start thinking about the what-ifs of it all and feel anger and sadness. For so many years I did not feel valid as an actress. Having been deprived of the opportunity to become a respected actress pains me.

But, thinking about it, I also see it as comforting — proof that I had actually always been seen as a valid talent. The endorsement from a big agent was very important and yet my mother denied me it. And I blindly believed in her, even at this older age.

I believe that if I had had an agent even earlier, there might have been more continuity in my work and a stronger focus on quality rather than popularity. But then maybe I would have never left the business to attend college. Maybe I would have done my coveted period movies and then never been heard from again. Maybe I would have never earned enough to be able to live as comfortably as I do. The piece I had to take away, even if it did not result in anything, was that an esteemed person in the film industry had faith in me as a talent. He had incredible taste and an impressive roster of clients and he wanted to add me to it. This I would take with me forever. But at the time, it was not enough to cause me to find the strength to "abandon" my mom. My instincts were secondary. I allowed her to make the decisions for me because I needed it and thought it was right. She had convinced me that nobody would have my best interests at heart as she did.

I had no idea that going away from the Hollywood game for years while getting an education would have such a negative effect. I also didn't realize that I had never really been in the Hollywood game. There wasn't even any footing to regain. Nobody knew what I was, myself included. Mom did not even think to ask me and didn't seem to care herself. We needed to make a living and keep our houses, and as long as I was well-known, I could earn. It did not matter how. We had no contacts with whom to reassociate. The connections my mom had were mostly with people of questionable integrity and talent. We thought the power of my face was enough. She had no idea that we had no groundwork on which to build. It was worse than starting from zero. It was like starting from negative ten.

I had no power at the box office. I was not the skinny, exotic woman-child I had once been. I had been marketed as a commodity that was obtainable to do whatever song and dance asked of me. I'd sell deodorant, dolls, hair dryers, shampoo, makeup, stockings, and socks — just about anything anybody asked. The last film of any quality I had acted in was *Endless Love* and that was already six years past. I hung out with people like Michael Jackson and Wayne Newton, my manager was practically pickled and useless, and I had no agency representation. Things were not looking promising for a career worthy of much respect. We were floundering.

All I knew at this point was that none of the choices we were making felt good. I thought they were bricks being laid. What I should have seen was that the bricks needed to be solid and not made out of sand. "Work begets work" has always been part of my mom's mantra and it had worked until now. But it should have been obvious to us all that shitty work begets shitty work and I was becoming trapped in a career path from which I might never recover.

The next few years featured creepy producers and shitty directors on independent films where my name procured the finances. They were bad movies without studio support and real low-rent talent at the helm. It was an extremely confusing and difficult time for me regarding my identity and my persona. Nothing was aligning.

I have no idea what Mom was doing to propel me toward anything except keeping my name out there. It still did not occur to her that we could use professional help. She did not want to share a percentage of the profits and resented giving 15 percent away to a person who did not get me the job in the first place. What I did not realize was that the jobs that she did get me were not the jobs I wanted anyway. It did not occur to my mom that there could have been a defined path if I wanted to be an actress. A path that included outside expertise and professional agents. I assume Mom contacted some old business connections, but what I remember from this time is *waiting*. I was trying to be patient by dancing and getting back in shape and by seeing films and by doing various less intense acting workshops.

Still, my patience was not paying off, and the Hula-Hoop had no need to be "remembered."

I got some horrible weight-loss campaign for a company in Japan in 1993. I needed to lose the stubborn twenty pounds that I had gained in college and had kept on for six years. I thought it would be a great way to get in shape and make money. Japan was still a world that wanted me.

Mom and I had been to Japan many times and we always had a good time. We'd travel with Gavin or someone from his team and we laughed our way through tatami-mat sleeping, geisha shows, and raku throwing pots. We pretended to eat the raw things we all secretly gathered in our napkins, and poured our whiskies into CEO's glasses. Gavin and I hardly drank alcohol, and getting the bosses drunk helped make the evenings shorter. I am sure Mom would have welcomed the pour, but neither Gavin nor I would let that happen. We made friends and money and I got to see another country. Diana, Lisa, and various buddies came with me on those trips.

This trip was different. It was not the heyday of my eighties experience, and the company I was representing was ambiguous and would later go bankrupt from fraud. The flight to Japan was long and while I was sleeping, my mother was drinking. She would usually start a trip off not even drinking in the lounge. But then we'd board and she'd plug into the steady drip of red wine in those dumb little doll-size glasses. She probably justified every new pour by exclaiming how small the glasses were.

While on the plane she must have struck up a conversation with two businessmen who worked for Nescafé. They no doubt recognized me. Every human being on the face of the earth seemed to be able to recognize me by this point despite the fact I wasn't really working.

We landed in Tokyo and went to the hotel to make that horrible decision whether to sleep for a while to combat jet lag. We had checked into our hotel suite and I had put on a hotel robe, when the doorbell rang. Mom had invited the two businessmen to meet me in our hotel room. I had not formally met them on the plane because I was asleep and Mom did not want to disturb me. She did not want to disturb me on the plane, but in the hotel, in a robe, jet-lagged

and disheveled, it was perfectly good business. I yelled that I did not want to come
out, only to see that the two men were
already in the sitting area.

I gave in and in a few moments I was out
there shaking hands and bowing and talking
about how much I loved their country.

"Oh yes, I drink coffee but I especially
enjoy the Japanese teahouses that we've seen
in Kyoto. Oh yes, I actually prefer Nescafé. . . . How did you know? Are you saying I could use some right now, you silly
you?"

I excused myself and tore the mask off in
my adjoining room. *Wow, I must be in bad
shape career-wise. That was gross. But this,
too, shall pass. Just wait it out, Brooke.*

Still, I did it. I got the Nescafé-
businessman gig and was flown to Paris to
shoot the commercial. How could it be that
despite the fact I'd acted in quality films
like *Pretty Baby* and *Endless Love* and box-
office hits like *The Blue Lagoon* — and also
had a degree from an Ivy League school —
I would still find myself in France doing a
Nescafé commercial that would be dubbed
in Japanese?

While in France, Mom would disappear
to have meetings in the lobby of the gorgeous hotel and would return just as din-

ners were starting or interviews conducted. We were there four days and I think she must have been inebriated the entire time. Again, she was basically safe because she was not driving and was more contained by her inability to speak French. I could forge ahead and complete the current job. It felt good to be working again and the shooting environment was similar to that in the States. The project was not something I was proud to endorse and something about it felt very wrong and a bit pathetic.

I wrapped the commercial and packed my bags. I warned my mother that we needed to pack up and be ready for the flight the next day. I went to bed and got up for early coffee in the glass-paned atrium restaurant. I had a book to read and kept my eye on the time. As we got closer to departure time, Mom still had not shown up. I knew she had come home but she was gone again. I had not slept a lot so she must have slept even less. I returned to her room and found out that, sure enough, she had not packed and didn't seem ready to get back to America. She had been out the whole night drinking and must have returned only for a short time.

I began getting the place packed up to go. When she finally stumbled in, I just stormed around the room throwing her stuff in bags and mumbling about how much I hated her. I had to get back to America. Staying another day was not an option. I had a bridal shower I was throwing with a friend for Lisa and had to get back to New York by that afternoon.

I stomped and screamed and accused her of being a loser and made big claims about what a fuck-up my mother was. How fucking pathetic she was and what an idiot I was to think that she could ever pull herself together. How I was never going to get any acting jobs but be relegated to selling fucking instant coffee! Not even real brewed coffee, but *instant.* I was throwing her stuff in bags and she just watched. I always either moped or stomped and slammed doors and raised my voice when Mom drank, but there was a panic in my gut this time. I had to get out of this hotel and France and away from her, and I could not handle another moment of any of it. I did not want her to be the reason our travel plans got screwed up.

She refused to listen but instead left the room, having not lifted a finger to prep for the trip. I yelled after her, "Be downstairs when the car gets here!"

Slam.

I finished getting everything thrown together and called a bellman to help get the bags into the car. I waited in the car in absolute embarrassment and disgust. I was disgusted at her. I was disgusted with myself for being so helpless and bound to this dynamic. When was I going to learn? Mom showed up at the last minute and I was seething inside at how pitiable my life was. We fought and her words were imbued with vitriol. I was an ingrate, she said, and why couldn't I be as talented an actress elsewhere as I was during the act of fury I was displaying? She said I had a fat ass and I did not appreciate anything.

She had been drinking all morning, either at the hotel bar or at some place nearby. When she had left the room earlier, she must have gone to get a few last-minute nips before the flight. The last few must have hit her while she was on the drive to the airport, and she actually passed out in the car. I can count on one hand the times Mom had ever passed out. She never even took naps. I watched her as the car stopped and the door was opened. She was still not wake. I made a weak attempt to stir her but realized I did not want her to awake at that moment. I got my bags and stormed off to check in. I purposely took her passport with me because I had gotten it from the room safe with the jewelry. I planned on leaving France with it in hand but did not have the guts to keep her ability to exit the country. At the very last second, I ran back to the car where she was still slumped over, and I threw the passport inside the slightly opened window.

"Mademoiselle, what should I do wif yur muzzer?"

"Je ne sais pas. . . . C'est comme tu veux. Merci." *I do not know. It is as you wish. Thank you.*

I boarded the Concorde flight to JFK airport. I sobbed the entire flight. The actress Amy Irving was on the same flight and asked if she could help. Ironically her mother, Priscilla Pointer, had been one of the acting coaches hired for me on *Just You and Me, Kid.* I told Amy that I had just left my mom passed out in a car at departures. She gave me a warm smile. Once again I had the feelings of survival and sadness mixed with a tad of freedom of not having to be on the trip with Mom.

We landed, and while in baggage claim, my new video camera was stolen right from under my nose. Mom managed to show up the next day at 11:00 A.M. at the shower as if nothing had happened. She breezed through the party with grandeur and a wrapped Hermès scarf and began the red wine all over again.

I should have held on to her passport.

Something had to shift. I could only think of shifting my mother's behavior, not my life. If I could just get her to stop drinking, my career would pick up again.

Lila and I researched treatment facilities together once again. Auntie Lila had moved away from Teri and from working at our company a few years prior and was now residing in her hometown of Tucson, Arizona. We both knew that it was bad with Mom, and even though I had much less leverage than the first time, we needed to try something. She'd never again fall for meeting us at a location with her bags secretly packed.

I put a call into Betty Ford herself. I explained my situation and she promised that if I could get my mother to go to the Betty Ford Center, she would have a bed ready for me. I would just have to get Mom to commit to going back into treatment. Lila knew an intervention specialist who flew in to places all over the country to help with interventions. We asked him to join Mom, Lila, and me in Haworth, New Jersey.

Mom saw us "interventing" a mile away.

383

She sat on our long, low, floral-upholstered couch and dug in. She said she would *never* again go to treatment and was insulted and disgusted by us all. She was angry and adamantly refused to go. She attacked me for trying to control her, and even when I was being soft, and loving, and saying this was necessary and good for us both, she just shook her head.

"If I want to stop, I'll stop."

I told her about Betty Ford and she blurted out something about not being an addict or in bad enough shape for a place like the Betty Ford clinic. She claimed she did not have a drinking problem. Well, she was right there! My mother never had a problem with her drinking. It was the rest of us who did. I even think she meant this double entendre herself. Another one of her little word manipulations.

"Fuck you. Fuck you both, Lila." She looked at the intervention specialist and said, "I don't give a shit who you are, but I want you out of my house."

"Your daughter asked me to come, Teri, to help her," he responded.

"Well, great, help her and get the fuck out of my life."

"But, Mom . . ."

"I began in this world alone, and I'll end

in this world alone. I don't need you, *Brooke,* to tell me how to live."

"But I really love you, Mom, and —"

"Yeah, and Peter really loved Jesus. Where did it get him?"

She had this cocky expression on her face as if she had just won. She would often say to me while I was growing up that one day I "would deny [her] like Peter." She sat there triumphant, seemingly pleased with the proof that I had denied her just like the apostle Peter did to Jesus when the pressure was on. It was crazy when she chose to pull out the religion card and how hypocritical she remained.

This attempt at an intervention was an abject failure. Money down the drain and a lost hot-commodity bed rejected. I called Mrs. Ford and apologized. I thanked her for the special treatment but said that my mom wouldn't be coming to the center. She told me that Mom would never get help until she wanted it for herself. I explained that it did not seem as if anything like that was ever going to happen. Mrs. Ford recommended that I never give up hope.

To this day, the ACOA kid in me thinks that if only Betty Ford's had been available the first time, maybe it would all somehow have been different.

I walked away in defeat and without any plan. I continued to live in New York City and go to events if asked. Mom proceeded as if nothing had ever transpired, but every now and then would throw the attempt up in my face to reinforce how I had failed and how she would never be outsmarted. She was a true addict.

I shot some interesting photos for *Paper* magazine and was kind of getting into the creative groups via the magazine. I did readings and performance pieces for fun makeup artists and was asked by the likes of Russell Simmons to join him on a panel to discuss what was in and what was out in our culture these days. I was hoping that maybe through my fabulous community of gay artistic friends I would find a niche and get back on top of things again.

It was during this time that I began to date Liam Neeson. He was a tall Irish actor and a drunk who was thirteen years my senior. He wooed me with his brogue, his poetry, and his shitty choice of cheap pinot grigio wine. I rebelled with him and poured myself into his rhythm. I would take dance classes all morning and then meet up with him at the bar at the Ritz-Carlton Hotel on Central Park South. We'd drink and talk to Norman, the bartender, and discuss literature and acting. We would daydream about our future. Norman was, and is, a living legend who looked out for me.

During those days, I existed on cheese and crackers and wine and the relationship. I was going to grow up and the Irish drinking actor was the perfect solution. I was so impressed with going out with a real movie star and I was so familiar with what it was like to live with an alcoholic who lived in dreamworlds. Liam and my mom were perfect for me. And, of course she took to him the way she did to all other tall, manly, gruff drunks. She flirted and welcomed him home. It did not get as creepy as it could have, since Liam hungered after any female attention, but none of it was healthy or real. I was struck by how it was somehow famil-iar. It was such a cliché and I could not see it.

We got serious enough after only three months, and I thought that this would get me away from my mother and earn me the respect I wanted so desperately. He was a real actor, and if he chose me, then I would be exposed to a higher caliber of the enter-tainment industry. I could finally be serious. He asked me to marry him but without a ring. I told Mom and she worried she would not be invited. That was her immediate response. Nothing about me, but about where she fit in instead. "Watch: When you get married, you probably won't even invite me!"

I told her I would always invite her for the rest of my life whether I wanted to or not. I added that even when she did show up for me, she was never really there anyway because she would be drunk. She brushed it off and said, "We'll see. . . ."

Who knows what she meant by that, but I pretended I was engaged. We spent a Christmas together and Mom suggested that I give Liam a copy of my brilliant book that had been crafted while I was at Princeton. She actually thought it was a clever idea just like her arranging for a Brooke doll to be delivered to John Travolta's hotel on his birthday. I inscribed the book with some mush about my days being in focus since he came into my life. The blurred handwriting was because of the steady flow of wine. I could not fight my mother's drinking, so why not throw responsibility away and join the booze brigade?

Everybody was staying slightly buzzed all day long and we were one big happy family.

Until I went to Italy for some job.

Liam had to fly to LA that night to check on a basement flood in his home. I told him to phone me when he arrived.

"Oh, it'll be late, darlin'."

"Well, I won't fall asleep until I know you are safe. And you did ask me to marry you, so you can tell me the plane was safe."

I never heard from him again.

When I got home I crawled back to Mommy. I was too weak and sad and scared and heartbroken. My mama would let me cry and tell me it would pass. We were living in this old Tudor-style house that was too big for two people and beginning to get run-down, and we had no future plans. The Grey Gardens tenure had actually begun. I was obviously incapable of living in the big world alone.

This time Mom did not try to talk me out of it. She happily let me get right back into some of the old routines. Who was the more pathetic one now? We were holding on to multiple properties and fostering dogs in attempts to find them homes. Strangely, people adopted them because they had been in my custody and because people are *crazy*. So maybe we differed from Little and Big Edie, in some ways, but the writing was on the wall for us to transform seemingly into a mother and daughter living alone in a festering relationship of enmeshment and fear. I cried a lot and tried to start every day anew.

I wish I only knew you in the mornings, Mama. . . .

It felt like I was back to the beginning. Even though I had gotten an education and I had done a great deal of work on myself to separate from her, I had been defeated yet again. I was right back in the thicket.

■ ■ ■ ■

PART FOUR

■ ■ ■ ■

She says things like how she hates me
and then in the next breath like a crazy
person says, "I love you more than life."
— *Brooke's diary*

CHAPTER THIRTEEN:
WE MET BY FAX

I survived my heartache from my whirlwind three months with the Irishman and a few more random crushes after that, but it was the last time I ran home to Mommy. I slowly and steadily eased back into living by myself in the city and did a lot of soul-searching.

I had gone to California to meet some filmmakers who were looking for an actress who would want to go live in South Africa for three months and film a movie about raising orphaned leopard cubs in the wild. The movie would be called *Running Wild*. I jumped at the offer. Going to live in a camp in the middle of the bush was just what I needed. Mom and I both traveled there, but after I got settled, Mom went back to America. Her asthma was bad and the dust and wildlife were doing a lot of damage. She was not well and was better off at home.

The movie was very mediocre but the experience was incredible. I lived in a tent

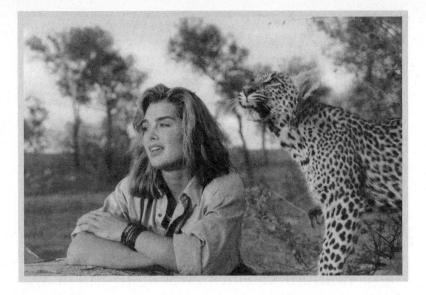

on stilts in the jungle and never needed to wear a watch. The experience was somewhat reminiscent of filming *The Blue Lagoon* because we were so isolated and were dictated primarily by the environment. But this time I was without my mother. We raised two leopard cubs and filmed them all the time. We were on a reserve park in the Eastern Transvaal and only left once in three months. I had very little downtime but I spent all of it writing letters and walking these letters to our makeshift offices, which had various information-transmitting devices.

A friend of mine from Los Angeles (Lyndie G, Kenny G's wife) had been gently pushing me to meet her friend Andre Agassi.

I was in no place to be in a relationship and had kept putting it off. While living in South Africa, I began thinking a lot about my life and what I wanted it to look like. I knew I needed to separate professionally from my mother so as to gain a sense of autonomy and career perspective. I also wanted to find a relationship with somebody not threatened by my celebrity and secure in his own profession. I still did not feel totally ready for a boyfriend or husband but I wanted to enjoy my solitude in this camp and settle my mind and my heart. I was always open to friendships and was enjoying those friends I had recently acquired on the film.

Lyndie wrote to me and gave me Andre's fax number, and said I should fax him, the only reliable and fast way to be in touch from the set. With thousands of miles between us, we began to communicate via long rambling faxes about life and God and the strange burden of fame and overpowering parents. Andre's father was, in my opinion, far worse than my mom ever was. He was the one who pushed his children to be professional tennis players and would throw away Andre's trophies if they were anything less than first place. My mom kept my Hula-Hoop trophy for twenty years. His dad had managed his career until Andre broke free and hired a manager. Andre and I both understood what it felt like to be famous and to have strong parents who controlled much of our lives.

We were similar in so many ways. Even though he was from Vegas and I was from Manhattan, we both still felt like little kids who had dealt with adult pressures and been given a great deal of responsibility at a young age. We both had begun very young and had been defined by others before developing our own sense of self-awareness. We had grown up in extraordinary circumstances and were desperate to find our place in the world. We were mirrors of one another, and we knew, somewhere deep inside, that we needed each other.

Every day on *Running Wild* I would wake very early before my call time and I would write my letter. Sometimes I had to finish it on the bumpy Jeep ride out to a far-off location and then give it to the cook to take to the office at base camp. I'd wait for Andre's faxes to come in and save them to read by myself at my favorite spot near the river. The people in the office would radio the set if a fax came in and everybody eagerly anticipated how happy I seemed when I got one. Let's just say I was pretty darn happy those three months.

It was like we were living in a different time. This was our carrier-pigeon romance. We poured ourselves into our faxes; they were like diaries in which we were able to explore who we were and who we wanted to be. We got to daydream and hope and cry and believe we could be deeply happy. My mom was nowhere near any of it and this freed my mind and my heart.

Both Andre and I were at a turning point in our lives when we met. He had just had wrist surgery and was not sure he would ever play tennis again, and I was desperately seeking to reclaim my floundering career. And we were falling in love by fax.

When the film wrapped and I went back to the United States, we began to talk on the phone and arranged to meet the next time I was in LA.

Back in New Jersey, Mom seemed to have settled into a drinking pattern consisting of binge drinking followed by a few days seemingly on the wagon before digging in again. Other times she'd maintain a low but constant hum of drunkenness throughout every day. What was different was that I was not living inside it and enveloped by it. I was preoccupied by it always, but the periodic distances — whether created by my being away on location or just by living in Manhattan and away from the dark Tudor house in Haworth — helped me stay afloat. Mom seemed to be happy about this kid Andre who was very famous and who, according to her, "obviously had a father worse than even me. Maybe you'll feel lucky, Brooke."

Mom and I flew out to LA to film some final city scenes for the movie, and stayed at a little bungalow we had bought a few years after Princeton. Andre came over to take me to dinner. He met Mom while wearing faded light jeans with serious holes in them, Nikes, and a T-shirt. His hair was vintage Andre hair, mostly blond with some brown bits and longer than even mine was at the time. I had no idea that he was wearing taped-on extensions but I would discover it much later, when he would tell me in an emotional and embarrassed admission. He looked like a rock star, complete with Oakley sunglasses and a cool sports car.

As he was walking away to get the door, Mom pointed to a specific hole in his jeans over his top left butt cheek. The hole had frayed and it was obvious he was either not wearing any underwear or wearing a thong. (I would later learn that it was a thong).

Mom secretly pointed to it and seemed to motion to me to touch it. Without even considering that this might have been rude and possibly premature, I put my index finger right on the skin peeking out through the material. He jumped and I said I just couldn't help it. Who the hell knows what he thought of that intro? What type of a mother tells her daughter to do that? And what type of a daughter obeys without considering the possible consequences? But later on he would comment on the fact that after spending some more time with me, he realized he was with a "real woman." If he thought I was a "real woman," I can only imagine the level of immaturity he had been used to in dating. The truth was that I was far from being a self-actualized woman. But compared to the way he felt and to those other famous people he had met, I guess it could seem like I had my life together.

His perception should have sent up a red flag, but alas, I was on a path I would not want to or be able to get off of for five years.

After the scene I had to shoot was completed, Andre flew me out to Las Vegas in his very own plane, where he'd grown up and still lived. I spent a very chaste first weekend with him in his gated community house on a golf course. All the houses looked alike and there was a Stepford-wives sensibility to the community. It was quiet and clean and surreal. This whole existence represented the antithesis of every aesthetic I had ever known and loved in New York City. It felt alien and wonderfully homogenized.

We drank champagne and talked endlessly about the similarities between our upbringings and about the crush of fame. We had both reached stardom at very young ages and had demonstrative parents. We were both highly publicized figures and were struggling with the demands of being in the public eye as well as dealing with the pressure of trying to grow up under the scrutiny of the press. We understood one another. We complained about how deeply dissatisfied we both were with our careers. His was from a lack of love for it and mine from a seemingly unrequited love from it. The air in Vegas at the beginning of fall was still and the temperature perfect. The sky was like a pastel watercolor and Andre exuded respect.

I expected nothing from him, and in this environment I felt safe. And for some reason, I was not considering my mom's feelings in any of it. He was a very gentle soul and seemingly calm and devoid of unnecessary drama. I actually felt more settled than I had in years. I thought we were becoming special to each other in a very unique way. It was not clouded by passion or fear but fueled by respect and fresh perspective. It felt like a safe respite from a life that had been beating me down. I felt like I'd finally found a relationship in which I felt totally understood. Even though we were actually just kids, we both possessed a level of self-awareness. We were somehow grounded and individually intent on self-improvement. Andre and I wanted to thrive, not just survive.

I also had a foot surgery planned and was not sure I would ever be able to dance the same again. After years of being in excruciating pain, I decided to get both bunions on my feet removed. The surgery was the next week and I knew that I'd be out of commission for a least three months. I hoped we would keep in touch but had no expectations. I did not anticipate more than the probable reversion back to the fax machine, but I was in for the shock of my life.

Andre knew when my surgery was and asked if I minded his coming to New York to visit. I had nothing to lose and said yes. It was the first time I had ever had major surgery and was actually a bit nervous. It was elective but so necessary to alleviate the chronic pain.

Mom was supposed to take me but got drunk the night before and I couldn't count on her. She got angry when she realized that Andre was going to visit. I can't remember if he brought me to surgery, but I do remember transferring my need to be taken care of onto Andre almost immediately when I realized Mom was drunk. It was a perfect position for both of us. I needed to be cared for and he needed to caretake. He did it sublimely.

After the operation, he and his trainer and close friend Gil Reyes loaded me up in the back of an SUV for the drive back to New Jersey. Once home they carried me and got me settled into my hospital bed that had been set up in the first-floor sunroom. It would be easier and quieter there than in New York City. I was groggy and exhausted and in no pain . . . yet. I could tell that Mom was deeply unsettled that Andre was around and that his main focus was caring for me. I knew she was thrown but I honestly was too exhausted and drugged up to address any of it. Nobody had ever shown me such interest and seeming commitment, and I am sure she felt threatened. I could tell she liked him because she didn't whisper behind his back to me but I could tell this was all getting a bit too close for her comfort. She seemed awkward and uncomfortable. Mom tried to regain control and kept insisting that Andre sleep in the guest room, but he kept refusing, saying that he would rather stay near me. He put the sofa cushions on the floor by my bed and he refused to leave. Mom was getting visibly angry and did not like anybody not doing as she said.

"Oh, you're that kind," she scoffed, and went into the kitchen.

I went in and out of sleep all through the night. If I shifted and a foot fell of its elevated position, Andre would jump up to right it. This vigilant attention left me in a daze. Nobody had ever taken care of me like this. Honestly it felt too good to be true but I did not fight it. I guess it was his version of strapping me to his chest and it felt good. The irony was that Mom chalked it up to control issues on Andre's part, and the competition for my loyalty began. I knew Mom would ultimately have been capable of tending to me, but I also knew she would be drinking throughout. I also had Lisa a few streets away. I was extremely vulnerable and scared and the pain was mounting.

At one point, Lisa came to visit and I

found myself trying to make light of the fact that she and my mother were in the kitchen getting drunk on Zima while I lay incapacitated and defenseless. Andre was appalled. I was broken and he was going to fix me. More writing on the wall that I should have seen, but the solid support felt intoxicating and I signed up with every ounce of my soul.

For the first time in my life, somebody stood up for what was best for me without any regard for, or disrespect of, my mother. Other boyfriends in the past either tried to ally me against my mother or were so threatened by her that they shrunk a bit around her. Those who thought they were going to be the ones to stand up to my mother and defend me were in over their heads, while the other, more intimidated ones lost my respect. There never seemed to be a loving happy medium. I couldn't strike it myself and needed somebody to help balance me.

With Andre I instantly felt a vicarious thrill. To me it seemed that he was never rude but simply forthright and steadfast. I could learn from him in how he dealt with things. He seemed straightforward and loving yet honest. There was no fight. He had come to support me and that was what he was going to do. It was a pretty funny sight

— Tennis Boy from Vegas sleeping on the floor on three square floral chintz pillows lined up vertically next to a hospital bed holding a girl whose both feet were broken and held together by pins, while her mother and best friend were getting hammered on shitty malt liquor in the nearby kitchen. Oh, the glamour. Andre and I actually had such a laugh that I never wanted him to leave my side. I was going to be safe. I was no longer alone.

In a few days Andre had to return home. But he had made his mark on my heart and I planned to visit him as soon as I could.

I healed rather quickly, as did Andre from a wrist surgery, and he began a first comeback in tennis. I started spending as much time with him as I could, which usually meant I would follow him around the country to watch him play tennis. I did my rehabilitation alongside him in his training sessions and we both soul-searched and trained our bodies and our minds. It was an evolution and a security I had never experienced.

I had the space to expand my thinking about my life and about my career. Andre supported my every dream and helped me see how I could make them actualities. I was away from my mother and living a totally new and different existence. I talked to Andre at length about my mother and her drinking and my staled career. I bared my insecurities to him and put my absolute, unfettered trust in him to guide me through. He said things like "I want your dreams to become my reality."

"What!"

"I wish you could see yourself the way I see you. You would really love what you see."

Oh, good Lord Jesus, where had this guy materialized from? He was too good to be real. And he would do incredibly thoughtful things like getting the LA house tented for termites when he heard we had a problem. He gave me books by Marianne Williamson and C. S. Lewis to read and thought *Men Are from Mars, Women Are from Venus* was a great way for the sexes to grow together. I did not question a thing he suggested. I just wanted to keep breathing in the fresh air of contentment.

I bared my heart about wanting to be an actress and feeling like a joke and a failure. I was out of shape and rejected and I didn't know how to turn my career around. He said that if I was serious about being an actress, I should be out in Los Angeles and I should get an agent. In order to do so I'd have to scale down propertywise and consolidate my finances. I'd have to sell and buy myself time to forge a new path and not be forced to take jobs just for the cash. And, most important, I'd have to leave my mother as my manager and establish myself financially and professionally separate from her and the debts. That last part I had come to know but hearing somebody else say it hit me like a Mack truck. I knew it was true, but the reality terrified me. It would kill her.

Andre said he would help, and I could use his office and lawyers to ease the transition. His manager and best friend since childhood, Perry Rogers, was controlling his life at this point. Perry had basically facilitated Andre's breakaway from his own father. I figured that since he had guided Andre through a similar disengagement, he must have all the answers. Plus, Agassi Enterprises was a huge operation with many on its payroll. There were trainers, doctors, massage therapists, secretaries, pilots, assistants, lawyers, ex-girlfriends, all being subsidized in one way or another. I was property-rich but had both an entangled relationship with a drunk business partner and a depleted cash flow. I was in no position to say no to the possibility of reclaiming my future. I felt empowered and scared but knew I needed to cause a huge shift in my life.

Andre helped me believe in myself and in my talent and in the possibility of future success. There were concrete steps that could and should be taken, and both Andre and Perry presented me with a game plan. I had never before understood any of the financial aspects of my life. Mom handled it all with an accountant and I never paid attention. These two guys, who were five years my junior, tried to educate me on what needed to happen financially and professionally, which aided personal growth as well. Andre was never as emotionally connected to his father as I was to my mom. I deeply loved my mom, whereas he remained ambivalent toward his dad and all he stood for. My emotional separation was going to be tougher for me than his was but the goal was the same. Andre suggested I investigate the possibility of obtaining an agent from an important agency in LA.

I went alone out to visit my mother in Haworth to tell her that I had thought a great deal about it and I had decided that I wanted to go out on my own as an actress and that if I failed, I wanted to fail on my own. I planned on trying to go back to William Morris and working once again with my old agent. I wanted to try my hand at a career my way and with a vetted professional team.

I explained to Mom that I felt we were becoming polarized as people because of her drinking and expressed my dissatisfaction with the way my career was going. I said I wanted to try to salvage the mother-daughter part of our lives. I told her the only way I thought that could happen would be for me to separate from her professionally. It was all too confused and becoming toxic. I added that I really wished she would quit drinking for once in her life.

"Don't you worry about my drinking. Have you talked to a lawyer?"

"No. I wanted to talk to you first."

It was true that I had not told our lawyers yet. I wanted to keep to my word about this being a personal decision and I wanted to show her respect by coming to her in person, and first. I was a bit hurt that she thought I had already contacted an actual lawyer but felt clean knowing I had not. The idea had not come from Perry or Andre — they were just helping with practical elements.

"Well then, do whatcha gotta do."

There was a hint of her thinking it bullshit that I wanted to save our personal relationship. I saw her smirk as if I were just using it as the excuse. She was a mix of hungover and still drinking, ingesting enough every time she left the room to have her senses dulled but her edges nicely sharpened. Most people soften their edges with alcohol. My mom's protruded and hardened with booze. I started to feel a sense of panic rising in my gut, and the moment she drove off to rehab, I felt guilty and I wanted to try to make it better for her. I did not realize that I could never have gotten her approval for something that was going to destroy the very foundation of all she thought she had built. But I wanted her approval nonetheless. I wanted to help give her security in this moment, so I stupidly threw in that I'd just split everything we had together in half and she would be fine. It was never going to be that easy. I had no idea how difficult it would all be financially and legally.

I left the house feeling vaguely concerned that it had all gone far too smoothly to be true. As it had been with rehab, I knew this was just the calm before the storm.

I had made sure I had been clear and unapologetic. I knew I could not want her approval on something that would devastate her. But I told her I loved her and wanted to repair our relationship and that without the pressure of the career we could start anew. But I think we both knew that this was only part of my plan, and maybe Mom sensed what she thought was the falseness of my approach.

I knew this is something I had to do. I desperately wanted a better relationship with her but was finally convinced that it was never going to happen as long as she was still drinking. The career part was true in the sense that I did want to learn independently from her. But I also knew I would have an agency at the ready. I did not want to eviscerate her, or undermine all she had done. I had a goal and I was not dishonest. I just tried not to be cruel in my delivery. I had to say I wanted to try on my own versus saying I was unhappy with the job she was doing. Both were true and I was leaving no matter what, so why not remain kind and generous in spirit? She was the one who would be left alone. I was not.

But even though she'd seemed calm about it, she wasn't buying any of it. I knew it. I got out of the house before I would want to back-pedal and apologize and ask her to tell me it was all OK with her and that I was making the right decision, and that I would end up getting work, right? And that maybe she was correct and I should just stay with her and we would figure it out?

I then called the William Morris Agency. I was humble and honest and said I had come to a place in my life where I needed a fresh start. I was separating from my manager-mother. Would I be able to sit and discuss the possibility of rejoining the agency?

I was given a bit of a scorned response that I played right into. I might not have known the business of entertainment, but I did know the business of people. Wasn't it all a game anyway? If my mother taught me anything, it was that it was all a game.

Bargaining and posturing was how the business was run, right? The only problem was that Mom would not bargain and she didn't consider her bravado false. But I'd learned from her mistakes as well. I had to find a way to make it their idea to represent me. I had to defer and slightly smooth their ego. After all, they had been scorned. I was sweet and humble, and even though I really was sincere, I played all the right cards on this call. After the agent seriously said his perfunctory "I'll have to run it by my colleagues to see if there is interest" line, I once again had representation.

I think Mom believed it was just a bluff and

that I was being manipulated and brain-washed by the Agassi team. I don't think she believed I would follow through on any of it. She would come to hate Perry with such venom in her veins that she would never accept him. She reveled in the fact that even Andre eventually fired Perry. Mom would never come to believe that this was a good move for any of us.

I explained the split to the lawyers Mom and I had been using for years, but I also informed them I would be using another team to handle the logistics. I couldn't afford the legal fees but Andre said he would help detangle the mess and help me get back on my feet. I took the charity for the first time in my entire life. I had no idea that once reality hit her, my mother would dig in her heels legally for quite some time and emotionally until her death.

I was offered a role replacing Rosie O'Donnell in the Broadway revival of *Grease* as the Pink Ladies leader, Rizzo. Andre and Perry and my "new" agent all thought it was an amazing idea and hoped that the quickest way to Hollywood was via old Broadway.

I was to go on tour for three weeks as a sort of break-in/rehearsal period with *Grease* so I could get used to the grueling schedule of doing eight shows a week and performing live in front of thousands of people. Right before I left I did something that I will never fully forgive myself for, but which was ultimately the only chance I had at survival. Soon there would be no turning back.

I had visited my mother right before leaving for the *Grease* tour. I had personally told the three employees at Brooke Shields and Co. Incorporated in Norwood, New Jersey, that some changes were being made and they would all be taken care of, but that I was scaling down and that after Friday they would not need to go into the office. I asked for their respect in not talking to my mom so as to give her time. I did not tell anybody of the other part of my plan. My mother went to the office on a pleasant Friday morning as if it was business as usual. She had gotten into the routine of going to the office practically every day, and this Friday was no different from any others. I had told her good-bye and left for tour in Cincinnati to be put into the company. I was busy and avoided phoning home for fear I would break down from nerves and guilt.

Perry had told me that the only way to have a clean break in a complicated relationship like ours was to be drastic. I had to take a stance and make everybody know I was serious. He was used to dealing with big corporations and a very discordant relationship like the one between Andre and his father. But Perry was insensitive to the layers of hurt that his tactics incited. He ruled by fear and by very false bravado and he loved reducing people in business so as to win.

He and Andre had convinced me that as with interventions or corporate takeovers, damage inevitably had to occur. But this was not supposed to be a hostile takeover. It was supposed to be a sensitive, but firm, declaration of my independence. Easier said than done.

I was relieved to trust Andre and his trusted friend and follow along, by proxy, with their plan and their team of bad cops. I always felt better as good cop anyway. Mom left the office on a Friday at about 6:00 P.M. The office was four floors completely filled with all my almost thirty years' worth of archives, film, TV and photo files, memorabilia, scripts, office equipment, collected antiques, and furniture. When Mom arrived back at the office on Monday morning, she put her key in the keyhole and opened the door to find a completely gutted space. Cowardly or not, over the weekend, while I was in an entirely other city, Perry had organized movers and trucks to come empty the space. It was devoid of all signs that any of us had ever been there. Everything — all the legal files, film reels, photos, wardrobe, art, and even my mom's personal desk and furniture — was loaded onto huge moving trucks and en route to Las Vegas.

Mom would never forgive me for what I had sanctioned. But I needed to go cold turkey. I would never have had the strength to do anything other than close my eyes and rip off the scab. The bleeding would not stop for decades.

I buried my head in the tour and avoided her attempts to call me. I stopped the credit cards and began the legal transactions to establish a new corporation, which would be based in Vegas. I got in touch with my mother and said that I would send her money on a monthly basis and that as soon as I returned from tour we should sit down to discuss how to divide all the various assets. I told her that doing what I did was the only way I knew how to do it, that I was sorry to do it to her but knew she would never have made the actual break possible, and that because of her drinking I could not trust her or her judgment. I did what I had to do. She kept reiterating that she knew Perry was the one who put me up to it and that I was being brainwashed. I refuted her claims and said that although Agassi Enterprises had assisted me, it was generated solely by me. She just kept spewing hate toward Perry. She did not blame Andre but kept her rage directed at his manager, Perry. This gutting of the office was the beginning of a deeper, more painful end. We never fully recovered.

Mom started telling anybody who would listen that her daughter had divorced her. She asked Lisa to come over to the house to start to go through my personal things. What she planned on doing with whatever she found I have no idea. Lisa refused, saying she did not feel comfortable doing so. She had recently moved our safe from upstairs in the house into the garage for some reason. Mom did things like that all the time. She hid precious things all over the place out of some kind of paranoia and then usually forgot where they were. She accused me of probably stealing all the jewelry as well. I told her I had not touched the jewelry. But I admit this sent up a warning signal to me. Much later on I finally did orchestrate a sneak into the garage to empty the safe of its contents.

After the office incident, I knew Mom would never willingly give me the jewelry we had bought together over the years. It had all been purchased with the money we both had earned, and even the stuff she had gotten before I was born was all left to me in her will. So, technically, my going into the garage with a girlfriend when I knew she was out was not stealing. My goal was not to keep everything for myself, but it was to prevent her from doing something potentially irresponsible, such as giving all the jewelry to a troubled young woman she had just met at the movie theatre or selling it to a guy she knew who knew a guy whose cousin was from Newark. I placed it all in a safe-deposit box until things settled down.

When I had my debut on Broadway three weeks later, I invited my mother to opening night. She was my mother. I was opening on Broadway for the first time in my life. I knew she would be proud and I was keeping to my word of wanting a mother-daughter relationship. I was not pretending. I wanted my mommy to "look at me, look at me. . . . Mom, watch. . . . Watch this."

She came to the dressing room a bit early, and in her hands she held my trophy from the Hula-Hoop contest twenty years prior. It was filled with fragrant lily of the valley — my birth flower and her favorite scent.

"You did it, kid."

"I love you, Mama."

Mom did not seem happy in life but she did seem a bit less angry. She was still hurt and I still felt bad for the way I handled it, but there was no going back. I really believed it had been the only way. I did hope that without her being my manager, our relationship would improve. I always seemed to forget that little, ever-present thing called addiction and still naïvely felt that this change would help. It would really only help me. I admit I did not expect her to change her views entirely and all of a sudden, but I was sure that once I felt more secure professionally, I would be more tolerant and compassionate. I would have more patience because I could not blame her for my career, and maybe she would affect me less. Neither one of us felt the need to apologize for anything. We all just had to wait and see.

Mom enjoyed the show and I got a standing ovation and a Theatre Guild award for outstanding newcomer on Broadway. The fastest way to Hollywood was via Broadway. Things were picking up for me professionally, and Andre and I were inseparable.

But as for my mother . . . she seemed to be aimless.

CHAPTER FOURTEEN:
MIA

Things were going well careerwise in late 1995. After my six-month run on Broadway I was offered a guest spot on the Super Bowl episode of the show *Friends.*

Andre visited the soundstage to watch me shoot my *Friends* scene. In the scene I played a crazed fan who begins licking Joey's fingers and throwing my head back with maniacal laughter.

As we were shooting the second pass of the same scene I saw movement out of the corner of my eye. Andre had stormed off the set. At cut I ran outside to find him and had to yell to him from the doorway so as not to get wet from the suddenly pouring sky. He said I made him look like a fool by licking Joey's fingers, and he got in his car and drove all the way back to Vegas.

Upon arrival he systematically smashed and destroyed every single trophy he had won, including Wimbledon and the US

Open, never mind all the others.

It took me three years to have them all replaced. I always believed his kids would one day want them. I hadn't thought of their being my kids at that point, but it was just a shame to waste the legacy. He probably threw them away, too, because I had them made.

But the *Friends* episode was ultimately a success, at least, and thanks to that one guest spot, I got the show *Suddenly Susan,* which ran for four seasons.

Suddenly Susan was the best thing that had happened in my career since being cast by Louis Malle in *Pretty Baby.* This was my real emancipation from my mother as a manager. This was all on my terms and with the help of an actual professional team. I was amazed at the support I had now. There were agents who said no for me. There were lawyers who negotiated better deals for me. I had never experienced the way the business should be run. I felt like I was getting away with something. I loved being able to say no and I loved being on a series on TV. I was in my element and I felt alive.

I wanted my mom to know I still wanted her to share the joy with me, but I also wanted the recognition for getting and carrying the show on my own. I never got to speak to her about it, but it was enough to know she thought I was funny. The bond that we always shared through comedy was shepherding me through what would be the next big phase in my career. I suspect that Mom felt a bit responsible for the possibility of this new turn because she always said I got my humor from her. I don't think it was selfishness on her part as much as pride for having nurtured and shared my sense of humor. It had amounted to something she could emotionally take part in. We were both still trying to define our relationship in the wake of the initial separation.

The actual separation of the business took years to complete because Mom would not agree to any way I offered to divide the properties and the various assets. She was becoming more sad and irrational and feared settling anything. I tried to tell her that she should sell off the Haworth and Sun Valley houses as well as the ranch in Montana and scale down.

She would agree to meet to discuss the issues, but then get drunk and either not show or leave in anger. I tried bringing in a mediator, but she refused to speak during our planned and paid-for meeting. It became a bizarre and frustrating situation that showed no signs of ever improving. I was so frustrated and exhausted by all of it and could not understand how I still managed to find myself on a hamster's wheel, getting nowhere with her. Meanwhile, Mom was drowning in sorrow and pickling her cortex more and more each day.

In many ways — both good and bad — I had basically allowed myself to be overtaken by Andre and his enterprise. It was such a relief to breathe for a change. He decided everything and planned everything and took care of everything. He was such a hero to so many that I could do my favorite thing; I would walk in slightly behind him into events or stadiums and enjoyed not having to be the center of attention for the first time in my life.

Our first few years together were amazing. I had never felt more taken care of and loved unconditionally in my entire life.

Once I was working again, I was incredibly happy. I loved performing in *Grease*, and Andre saw the show twenty-seven times. He loved it. He and Gil would stand in the back of the house and mime the dances, and the cast would send them secret messages from the stage. We were happy. Andre's game had begun yet another climb and he was feeling good about his road. He had begun slower and with qualifiers so as to regain his footing. I, too, was starting my career fresh and via a path that was undeniably the most difficult for me. We were an extremely famous couple and for the first time got to really share the burden. Because we were not in the same industry — and obviously not in competition — we could hold hands and jump into what we thought was real life together.

We were like little kids. We ate candy and huddled together like golden monkeys, with wide eyes and a giggle at the rest of the world. I always remembered what he said when we first met: "I want your dreams to be my realities." And it was happening.

Andre was loving and generous with my mother. He bought her a safer car and invited her whenever he could. He struck a very healthy balance, treating her with acceptance. He knew the sadness she caused me, but he also knew I loved her. He had the distance I would never have but would covet. He was a "reformed born-again Christian" who could name the origin of any quote from the Bible.

Mom hated Perry but could not reject Andre. I could tell from early on that she liked him. There was something about the essence of Vegas and his lack of formal education that rendered her less intimidated and less desperate. She also knew he was genuinely sweet and loyal and admired how he had built himself up in the world. I think she knew he helped me stay connected to her and saw herself being taken care of as well. Mom never really believed that I would completely abandon her. Now with Andre, she felt she would be protected somehow. I thought we'd all reached a happy place, and hopefully, it would last forever.

But, of course, there will be the inevitable bump in the road. One night while on hiatus from *Suddenly Susan,* I was in New York City and got a call from the emergency room at St. Vincent's Hospital. They had my mother there. She had taken a bad fall or had some kind of altercation that left her with an enormous hematoma on the side of her head. I rushed downtown and was terrified of what I'd find. She was so relieved to see me — weepy and oblivious to the fact that she looked like the Elephant Man.

As I was walking the corridor outside her bed's little pulled curtain, I looked up to see *Suddenly Susan* being aired on the TV up in the corner of the ward. There was a homeless man who had been beaten up and was off in his own area. He recognized me and said he wanted to give me a gift. I told him it was not necessary but that he should just take better care of himself. He insisted and he handed me a cardboard box with a turtle inside. He smiled a bloody smile and presented me with this gift as if he was one of the wise men following the North Star.

I thanked him and excused myself to check on my mother, who was starting to feel the pain of her bulbous, mushy, swelling mass of blood. I showed her the turtle and realized that it was in fact dead and stank up the whole area. The smell of the dead turtle and the sight of my mother's beaten-up head mixed with the one-liners being wittily emitted by my character on TV made me feel like puking all over the linoleum floor.

I excused myself to find the doctor and was relieved when he told me they wanted to keep Mom overnight for observation. I kissed my mom's good side and said I had to go home. She panicked, but I told her she should sleep. I waved bye to my homeless buddy and thanked him again for the turtle, promising to take good care of it. I waited until I got outside and out of view before I threw the box of dead turtle in a Dumpster. I walked a while and didn't even know how to feel.

Still, I told myself that things were going to keep getting better. I was doing comedy and I had found my home. My mom adored *Suddenly Susan* and watched it religiously. Even my dad, who never saw any of my movies (or if he did never told me), watched the show and loved it. Comedy was in my veins and it unified us all.

Suddenly Susan changed my life in another way. It gave me David Strickland. The day I met David, I knew I had met the brother I had never had. I really felt like his sister. I basically didn't need anybody as long as David was in my life. We were all at the first table read of the show, and right before beginning to read the script we were mingling around and chatting. I can't explain it properly, but we each simultaneously made a comment under our breath and it was the same comment. I heard him and he heard me and we both began to laugh. We were obviously on the same wavelength. I was four years older than he was and we even looked like we could be related. He understood me completely. He was the first person, since college, with whom I felt utterly myself. Even more than I did with Andre or Dean, to tell the truth, because it felt like blood.

David played Todd Stities, the music

reviewer at the show's magazine, *The Gate.* He became my best friend. By this point Lisa and I had become temporarily estranged because of Andre. Andre believed I needed to rid myself of any friend of mine who would choose to drink with my mother while I worked or was recuperating from surgery. Andre was very rigid and judgmental that way. All it would take was one meeting or one story and he could completely cut someone off from his life. I obeyed his wishes. Without Lisa in my life, there was a huge void. David overflowed it. It was love at first sight and a love not many would ever understand.

We loved each other on a level devoid of the complexity of a romantic relationship. People could not define it and we couldn't care less. We confided in one another about the deepest, darkest secrets we held and about our love lives and relationships. We gave each other sound and honest advice. We were connected and I hated being without him.

It was also meaningful that David was a recovering addict and he understood my mother deeply. He helped me and I helped him. David had been battling addiction practically his entire life. He had been diagnosed as bipolar at a later age and was struggling to live a balanced life. A fight he would never win.

Like most addicts, he was gorgeously and attractively intense. I was drawn to him like a moth to the flame. The difference, however, was that compared to my mother, this relationship was relatively stable and drama-free. He was actually feeling more contented and grounded by working on this show and by being with me, so much so that we all were able to take a bit of a breath. He was actively trying to lead a grounded and sober life. For the first time in my life I wasn't acting as the codependent. I consciously refused to fall into the same trap that I had with my mother. I insisted I not be that person in his life. And because we were never romantic, it was easier to enforce this healthier connection. During our short life together he was mostly clean. Mom, of course, adored David. I always wondered if she saw in him her lost baby boy. But we never spoke of it.

David and I worked together, worked out together, and had meals together. We helped each other in every way we could think of, and we laughed harder than I had ever laughed in my life. Not since Gavin had I found a partner to laugh at life with in this way. David and I understood how the other felt and thought. He knew me and I knew him with a depth that felt healthy.

Andre was not jealous of David. David understood Andre. Between David and Andre I was satisfied. My life and my circle was small but happy. David filled in the emotional and intellectual gaps and it all seemed to be a rather well-balanced, not overly dramatic life. We had the most connected and enjoyable platonic relationship any two people of the opposite sex could have. I was working, I had found a home in comedy, and life was great.

Andre and I got engaged and the wedding was stunning. I had wanted David to be my maid of honor but decided against it at the last minute. I chose to have a female bridal party only.

We had the ceremony in a boiling-hot, tiny chapel and had the reception where most of us were staying, the gorgeous Tuscan villa in Big Sur, California. While taking some photos before the actual wedding, Mom poked her head into the hallway from her room. I saw the look. I knew she would not do anything disruptive during the ceremony but it momentarily crushed me. I moved back to the opulent fantasy wedding and was determined to find the joy in the day. My dad cried in our photo together. I never got one with my mom. The wedding and reception went off without a problem, but I avoided Mom most of the night. I took photos with her table, then just danced. I'm sure she continued drinking but caused no scenes that I was aware of. That would come later.

The next day promised to be a fun and very relaxed event. We had a big western BBQ, and Mom arrived like the belle of the ball. She looked happy and radiant and entered with a grand air of fabulousness.

We were all departing. She was to take a ride down the coast with friends on their way to LA while Andre and I dropped off some relatives in LA and Vegas by plane before spending a mini honeymoon at a friend's house somewhere in Florida. I had hugged Mom good-bye in the driveway of the beautiful hotel nestled in the midst of beautiful Big Sur and said we'd talk later that day when we arrived in Florida.

I remember being in the back-bedroom cabin of the equally beautiful private plane that we were using to fly out of Carmel and suddenly being overcome with fear and sadness. Gavin came into the cabin and I looked him in the eye, unable to speak. I could not form a sentence. I kept shaking my head as if I had duct tape across my mouth.

It hit me all of a sudden — I knew I had made a mistake. I did not want to be married. I did not want to be married. I wanted to have the wedding because I wanted everyone I loved to be together. I loved Andre but was not sure I wanted to live the life we had been living. I wanted to be a bride, but I should not have been married yet.

When we landed in Vegas, I called to tell Mom we were safe, but she was nowhere to be found. I tried her friends but they said she never showed up to go on the drive. Mom had disappeared. She never left with her friends — they had waited and then departed without her. She was MIA for four days in Big Sur.

Mom being missing added to my anxiety about all of this being a terrible mistake. I felt stuck and hoped it was just because I felt like marriage meant leaving my mother more profoundly. Truthfully, however, I believed my professional life was finally opening up and I was entering a new phase and I wasn't ready to settle down. I had been so afraid that Andre would leave me if we didn't get married. I feared that if I had not said yes to his proposal he would have cut me off emotionally and it would have been over. I needed more time with him and I did love him, and I wanted the idea of being his wife.

My life and career were just beginning and I had wanted to know that I could have been OK alone before saying yes to marriage. I suddenly felt terrified and my mom was nowhere to be found. Gavin told me it would be fine and that it was just scary because it was new.

We finally arrived in Florida and walked into a house belonging to a business associate of Andre's. The place was a dilapidated seventies ranch house on the Intracoastal that had not been used in years. Yes, we would not be bothered, but that was because nobody would want to be anywhere near the place. There was really nothing to do and it was not relaxing or in any way honeymoon oriented. It felt run-down and I got even more depressed. I could not find my mother and I felt really lost instead of settled.

Mom finally resurfaced. I was told she had wandered around Big Sur drunk and alone. Apparently she believed either nobody would care or that it would serve them right to be worried — she could do anything she fucking well pleased. She was Teri Shields and she was born into this world alone and would leave it alone. She answered to no one.

The hopelessness and loneliness of the addict will never cease to amaze me. She hated being alone yet perpetually isolated herself in the alcohol. She ended up back home in New Jersey, and the cycle of my trying to keep tabs on her resumed yet again. Maybe I, too, was addicted.

Life on the show continued, and for the next two years Andre and I saw very little of one another. I was working so hard on the show and he was really working hard playing at various tennis tournaments. He alienated me when he lost and was on to the next tournament after he won. We did not experience much of our lives together and I had no idea we were really drifting apart. I then began to experience the other side to being an athlete's girlfriend and now wife: the side that gets shunned after a loss. Somehow I was made to feel it was my fault. I'd get the silent treatment or a projection of disdain that cut to my core. Sometimes he would not even look at me or speak to me when he lost but instead became even more isolated. In the past he had been more open, but he was changing drastically. It felt hateful at times, but I waited it out. Navigating someone else's moods was a task I knew all too well. This would be a piece of cake. I almost liked it, quite honestly. It was familiar and the hint of martyrdom was not a bad fit.

Overall, the marriage was just existing, but if it felt somehow not what it was supposed to be, it was easy to avoid dealing with it. I maintain that it was not due to a lack of love as much as it was a lack of life. David gave me advice. When I told him I thought I needed a relationship that had more mutual interests and desire for intellectual discourse and shared references, he said he worried I would regret my decision to move on. I wasn't saying I was some highbrow scholar whose intellect was being hindered or stunted. I was saying that it was becoming evident that Andre and I had less and less to talk about. Without an immediate trauma through which we needed to navigate, we floundered a bit. We had love, but it did not seem like that was enough. I always thought love was enough. But the truth was we were growing past one another. And I'm not sure if we individually enjoyed how the other liked to live.

I mentioned it to Mom on the phone one night and she made some snide comment about Perry. I said I was not married to Perry.

"Really? Are you sure about that, my dear?"

Wow. Every now and then, Mom came out with a zinger like this that made you realize how much she really did intuit. She was often not productive or helpful with her knowledge, but she had it in her arsenal, perpetually at the ready, just when it was needed.

It was at about this time that I adopted an older female pit bull. She had had litters of puppies and was older and slower and needing a home. Andre had said, "If you go get a dog, you are getting a dog for yourself only. Not for me."

Well, I'll show him, I thought.

David said I should focus on this dog. He grew up with dogs and would help. He said I had him and the dog and the show and my health, and my mother was relatively safe so life was not bad. He was right. What more did I need?

One day I took the dog into the gym on the Warner Bros. lot to meet my favorite staff members and she wandered away. I dropped the leash and knew she'd be fine. Soon a man brought her back to me, asking if she was mine. I was flustered and began explaining that she was, indeed, mine, because my husband had not wanted a dog but I had adopted her anyway. I must have said "my husband" twenty times. He must have been like, "I get it, you're married. I'm not hitting on you. I just thought the dog was lost."

I ran back to my dressing room and called my single girlfriend from college and told her I had met a guy she should go out with. "What's his name?"

"I have no idea."

I never got his name, but later learned it when he and David and I would work out in the gym together. He was a writer and had an amazing sense of humor. We all became friends. I didn't think anything more of it at the time — I was totally cut off from my feelings. I was not technically lonely, but I was not happy, either.

Andre and I were supposed to take my upcoming hiatus and go on a yacht trip that Andre had won at a charity auction. I dreaded going and thought it would be a mistake. He came to LA to take me out for sushi, and I said I didn't think the boat trip was a good idea because we would be pretending and we needed to figure some stuff out.

He said I would go with him to Vegas, then, and he could train. I did not want to go to Vegas, either. I would stay in LA. He looked at me and asked me if I thought we would ever want to go on vacation together again. My throat closed and the tears came out in hot, thick sheets of salty, blurry despair. I could not talk and needed to leave at once. As I left, I saw Liam Neeson sitting at one of the tables. I could not have cared less.

Andre and I drove home in silence and then he asked if I was happy. I told him no.

He did not say another word to me. He pulled in the driveway and disappeared upstairs. It was quiet and I began to panic. Suddenly I felt I was with my mother when she'd disappear and go guzzle from some hidden bottle of vodka or sneak out into the garage and take the car quietly out to drive to a bar. Sure enough, it was happening. He was leaving without a word.

Panic rising, I ran outside. His old convertible car was loaded and he was getting in the car to drive away. I begged him to talk to me. I explained that this was when a couple was supposed to fight, and scream, and sleep in separate beds, and cry and get back up and talk all night and get closer. Plus, it was starting to rain torrentially.

"Please don't do this. Don't drive away. Where are you going?"

"Home."

He drove off and I began to weep. The rain kept coming down and I was actually getting nervous for him. I knew the roads would be bad and this all felt so wrong. I would be lying if I said that I really wanted him to turn around and come back to make it all right, but I did not want to not try. I would never forgive myself if I did not try.

I called his cell repeatedly and he never picked up. I used to do the same thing with my mother, except we didn't have cell phones, so I would instead call her friends and restaurants and bars looking for her. I had slipped right back into all my old co-dependent habits.

Finally, Andre phoned from Barstow and said that the rain was so bad he had to stop. I half wanted him to come back, and I was also just so relieved he was not in an accident and had pulled over to spend the night.

I took an Ambien and went to bed. The next morning Andre called me and said he had something to tell me. My heart sank. I was instantly so scared, and I could feel my chest start to compress as if a vise was being tightened. I sat down in the window on a little window seat–like area in the kitchen.

He said he was about to tell me something he had never wanted to tell me because he had feared I would leave him. Then why tell me now? I thought. What was it? What had he been hiding? Had he had a child with his ex-girlfriend or somebody more recent for that matter? Was he sick? Was he having a long affair? Was he gay? All sorts of ideas flooded my brain.

I never could have guessed what he would say. He explained to me that for the whole first part of our relationship he had been addicted to crystal meth. I was shocked but immediately got hurt and insulted that he had not come to me at the time. I was the codependent queen! That was how I related to the world. I was the one who supported him unconditionally when he told me he was basically bald and had been wearing hairpieces most of his adult life. I took all of his innermost fears and had tried to quell them. Why should this have been any different? I would have been his biggest advocate and supporter in both the addiction and in his recovery.

"Why didn't you tell me?"

"I knew how difficult it was with your mother. I was afraid you would leave me."

I was really not sure what he wanted me

to do with this information. None of this was about giving or getting forgiveness, so I was unclear as to the tactic involved in suddenly disclosing such information. What was I supposed to do? He was already forgiven because I had never known about it, and he attested to quitting cold turkey before our marriage. He added that he was entirely clean and had been so for quite some time. He had managed to evade the USTA and pull some kind of a Lance Armstrong so he was able to stop and get drug tested and come out clear without the embarrassment.

I really couldn't have cared less about how it all affected his game or his reputation. I was trying to go back and remember the mood swings and chart the outbursts.

I feared our life together was not based in absolute truth. But it had felt that way early on, before the drugs. He had had his core confidants and his secrets, and then he had us as something different. I was relieved he was not gay and very relieved he had not fathered any kids I did not know about, but I questioned a lot. I also did not really care that he had had an addiction. Who cared if he had had an addiction? Many people have addictions, and he seemed to have gotten his life together by this point. He swore he quit before we were married but I don't think his book (the ironically titled *Open*) supports these details.

The way I remember it, I said I needed to think. He pleaded with me and said he would finally go to therapy and even resume couples therapy. We had gone briefly before getting married and were both so scared to be wed that we sought out this help.

I told him that we should both take a moment to collect our thoughts and suggested we talk in a week. I was going to have that hiatus and I would go to New York City, where I could go to therapy and get perspective. I called David and told him everything. He was going to be back east as well.

I called my mother to tell her that I was coming to New York instead of going on the boat trip. I did not have the energy to tell her that we were having problems. I was afraid of her response. I needed to have my own uninfluenced perspective.

I remember calling Andre during the next week and saying that we could not just throw away five years without somehow trying. I said we should try to get help and see what needed to be repaired. I'm sure I wasn't being completely honest with myself about wanting it to work, but I knew I would feel terrible to walk away after he said he would get therapy and he pleaded with me to try. I wanted to be sure I wasn't making a mistake. David had planted that seed and I needed to give it my best try in order to know.

"Why bother?" Andre said, interrupting me. "I don't see the need to delay the inevitable."

Was this what my mom had done to my dad?

Part of me was shocked and hurt that he didn't want to try, and part of me felt he was the more truthful of the two of us. I never discussed any of this with my mother. By this point I did not feel like I could go to her to get healthy advice regarding my relationships. I felt like my stomach had just been violently punched. I got so sad and knew I could never go back.

I went back to work and tried not to think about it and just be happy with the life we had had.

One night before a Monday table read I went out with some friends. I returned home to many messages from David's mother. I had gotten used to getting these calls and then helping locate him somewhere in Los Angeles. David had had a few slips since we met and had periodically gone on a tear or two. Because of my history and our closeness, as well as my connections to the world of security and addiction, I was very familiar with situations like this and I usually became involved. I would enlist Gavin, and David always ended up showing up some place. In every case I would be up all night sick with worry, and then he would eventually show up and be fine (or not so fine) but alive.

Tonight was the first time I did not jump on board the rescue mission. I knew I would see him the next day. We had had an event we were supposed to be going to, but because of my pending divorce, I did not feel like going out in public. The night before, David called and had suggested I join him and his soon-to-be fiancée. I had been helping David decide what type of engagement ring to get for his girlfriend.

I explained that I was not in the mood because of the recent developments in my marriage and that I did not wish to be a third wheel. I was sure his girlfriend would have preferred to be his date alone. I begged him instead to come over to my house that night for dessert, but he said his girlfriend was asleep because she had an early call the next day. I told him to stop by on the way home. That was the last I ever spoke to him.

David hung himself in a Las Vegas motel

sometime between when I last spoke to him and when I awoke the next day.

The next morning when the show's producers told me the news, something in me shut down, and I was never the same after that. I called my mom and sobbed to her. All she could do was say she was praying for him. My life was over as I knew it. I was ripped into two and no longer cared about Andre or my mother or the dog or my show or my career or any of it. I did not want to waste my time on anybody or anything I did not want in my life. I was finished being anywhere I did not want to be.

Nobody knew about the divorce (which took eight days to execute and nine minutes to file and be finished) just yet, and Andre and I went to the memorial as a couple. I was the only one not included in the memorial. His ex-girlfriend and his current girlfriend and his best male friend all had a part to play. I was not a party to any of it. I actually understood how I didn't fit in, but felt desperately sad in any case. I sat next to Andre, who generously paid for all the floral arrangements, and felt like I wasn't even there.

My one consolation would come later at David's family's get-together. His dad said that his life changed when he met me and he was happy for the first time in a long while.

"He looked at you like his sister."

Not long after David died, my stepsister, Diana, called me and told me that Dad had been diagnosed with stage-four prostate cancer. He would end up dying within two years of that phone call.

As if this wasn't enough, I had also been informed that I had had an irregular pap result and had a cervical dysplasia that was precancerous. I would have to have most of my cervix removed if I was to survive. I recalled a hurtful comment that Andre blurted out in anger: "Be thankful we never had kids because I would not have made this easy for you." He was referring to the divorce and the fact that if we had had children, there would have been a much bigger fight. But what if I had missed the opportunity to have children at all?

Too many things were hitting all at once and I wondered if this level of fear and sadness I was experiencing was enough to make a person just cease to exist. It was like my mother had written: "Does one start to slip from life this way, then suddenly it's over?" I had hit a real low, and for the first time in

447

my life, my mother had not been the cata-
lyst.

CHAPTER FIFTEEN: TOOTS

I did not want to continue on with *Suddenly Susan.* Without David it was a different show. The studio tried to revamp it to make it feel fresh. But the problem was that it hadn't been that broken and didn't need to be drastically fixed. It was never as good as it could be because of the focus of the writing, but people loved it and it could have endured if the cast had remained.

We did a farewell tribute to David in which my character goes all over the city trying to find his character, Todd. Along the way I learn how he impacted various people's lives and what a unique person he was. It was a fitting and beautiful tribute, but it did not bring David back. I would have done the show forever if David had been alive. But for various reasons the show was cancelled, and although I strongly missed doing a sitcom, I wasn't sorry. I was relieved to be away from everything that continuously reminded me of David.

I called Andre after I got the word that our divorce had all been filed and done with. I was driving in the Jeep that had been a gift from him and I called to ask, "So do I just take off my ring?"

"I guess so."

"OK, then."

I went to a bar where a friend from college was waitressing and I drank whatever they served me. I played with my thin platinum band in the booth and was very sad but felt like I was simply where I was. I called my mother to tell her it was over and she commented on it being fast. I could tell it was more important to be rid of Perry than it was sad for me to actually be divorced. Somehow I never thought I'd be. I had seen myself alone, even with a child, or married. But never divorced.

I could not admit it, but I was actually already falling in love with the guy I'd met when I was walking my pit bull. We had stayed in touch from working out with David in the Warner Bros. gym. He had eventually met the girlfriend with whom I was trying to set him up. Thankfully, they had not hit it off. I had kept him at a safe distance but believe subconsciously I'd wanted him close by. Nobody had yet known I was getting a divorce, and I needed time. I was dealing with too much with losing David, actually being divorced, and with my dad's diagnosis that I feared any relationship. Chris stayed around but had his own very busy life. He finally said that it was pretty clear he wanted to be more than friends but would rather be my friend than not have me in his life at all. But I had to tell him whether it would ever be possible. I told him yes but asked for his patience.

He did not pressure me but after a respectful amount of time finally said, "I'll wait, but I won't wait forever."

I leaned on him for support regarding my diagnosis and my dad's. I finally admitted that we were dating and I was falling in love. Andre had moved on, too, with my blessing. I helped Andre get dressed for his first date with Steffi Graf. He called me from a hotel room where she waiting in the lobby. I was happy to oblige.

I told Mom I had met someone and I had wanted her to meet him. He was Irish and from New York and was a writer. I was planning to go to New York City to have my surgery to hopefully clear up the dysplasia and rid me of probable cervical precancer.

Mom was supposed to take me to the

hospital the morning of, but I could tell she was not going to be able to make it. She was still drinking, and even though she probably could have rallied, I didn't want to be around her. I couldn't deal with her drinking and with going under the knife at the same time. This seemed to be a pattern. But she was always around to attend to me when I was sick. Maybe surgery and death terrified her. Justifying again, am I?

I suddenly broke up with Chris a week before the operation out of fear that I had not given myself a real chance to be free. I thought that the feelings I had for him had to be false rebound emotions. But I called him every day during this breakup.

He finally said, "You know you broke up with me, right? Technically you can't call me every day if we are broken up."

"Oh, yeah, right. . . . Well, bye, then, I guess."

I admit I made one last call before the impending surgery. I was actually scared and just wanted to hear his voice.

I called his cell and he sounded different so I asked where he was. He was in Vermont visiting his writing partner for a few days. I told him I just wanted to call him before my surgery and he asked if anybody was going to take me to the hospital. I said no, which was true, but my mom was going to pick me up. He volunteered to drive in to take me and meet my mom. It seemed like a lot, but I said yes before I could change my mind.

He came in to take me to the hospital and he met my mom for the first time. I went under and the two of them went for a walk and a bite to eat at some diner. While on the walk, Mom handed Chris an envelope and asked him to keep it safe for her. She needed to mail it and would do so after the meal. It was a hot summer day and Chris kept the envelope in his breast pocket for hours. After the meal, she took it back from him. He asked her what it was and she replied that it was her dog's stool sample — her Maltese had had diarrhea. She thought it was hysterical. He knew instantly what he was getting himself into.

The operation ended up being much more invasive than they had anticipated. They practically had to remove my entire cervix. I recovered in Vermont with Chris and his friends, and I finally admitted once and for all that he was my boyfriend.

Mom seemed to like Chris. His parents were from New York and were from the same era and background. Chris's family consisted mainly of firemen, cops, and nurses. They were the kind of people Mom had known growing up and always felt akin to.

On a trip to Ireland over the millennium a year after we started dating Chris gave me a promise ring. I nearly passed out when he showed me the box while we were overlooking Dingle Bay on the last sunset of 1999. He saw the look of terror and pressure on my face and quickly said it was only a promise ring. I had no desire to even think about getting married again.

A year later, when he was finally prepared to propose, ring in hand, he got the shock of his life. The man who sold him the ring had his sister secretly photograph Chris leaving the store after the purchase. I had no idea he had bought the ring, and when he opened the paper that morning he turned sickly pale.

I saw the photo, slammed the paper shut, and said, "Oh God, I am so sorry, Chris. . . . Whatever you were going to do, don't."

"What?!"

"I mean do it, but reclaim the time and do it at another time."

"Oh, OK, wow. . . . How could he . . . How could they . . . ?"

I felt terrible that because I was famous, his first time proposing was ruined. I felt terrible because unfeeling people and the press once again chose to rob me of the beauty of my personal experiences for their own profit.

I told Mom about the whole thing and she said, "That's a shame, honey, but you can make it your own again."

I wonder if she was secretly a tad bit relieved that the press still paid attention.

I put it out of "our" minds, but when Chris finally did surprise me a few months later by proposing to me in Mexico, I said "Yes!" and then had the jeweler's name buffed out of the ring.

And a year after he gave me the promise ring, I was saying, "I do."

Before we got married, the in-laws were all sitting at a diner in LA and the mothers began talking about what they wanted to be called by their grandchildren. My mother-in-law claimed "Cha Cha" and my mother coined herself "Toots." God forbid they be called Nana or Grandma or Granny. . . .

I loved the idea of having children with Chris. Despite my fears about my cervix, I was encouraged by my doctor and told it should all be fine. Chris and I wanted to start as soon as we could.

My father was going through chemo at

the time, so we decided that instead of New York City we would get married where he lived, in Palm Beach, Florida. Dad's close friend Terry Kramer had a stunningly beautiful home on the water and graciously offered to have us hold the wedding there. I humbly accepted but on one condition: that we hold the reception in a tent outside. As much as I really wanted to be seated inside, surrounded by the priceless paintings and incredibly precious art and furniture, I didn't trust any of our relatives not to do something somehow damaging. This home housed original Picassos both from his Blue Period and his later works. Many masters were on the walls, and real Fabergé eggs were scattered like confetti. I pictured my mother feeling up a server or kissing a portrait with fire engine–red lipstick, or one of Chris's old friends stealing the Cuban cigars or somehow pocketing an egg or silver monogrammed matchbox.

My mother had gotten another DUI a few months before the wedding and was placed in mandatory rehab. Her license was suspended and she went under psychiatric treatment. I was called when she was first arrested and put in the hospital for observation. They said she was confused and they would keep her overnight. I tried to have them keep her in for a few days but she insisted on leaving. She could not drive and had to take a taxi home.

The courts decided that she should go to a mandatory alcohol treatment facility. I was relieved and thrilled and thought the timing was perfect. She would be out just in time to get her life together and be at the wedding sober. She would even make the shower.

My girlfriend Sherie from Broadway threw me a shower. I did not want to have a typical shower because we needed nothing, but I did want to celebrate and also give Chris's friends and family a chance to do so as well. We had a crafty type of shower, where we all put together mosaic tiles to be put some place in our home. Mom and my mother-in-law and sister-in-law all seemed to be getting along beautifully. Mom did not drink the mimosas and acted fine, but I could tell she was a bit vulnerable. She was just not able to relax. She was awkward and restrained and I felt bad because I could tell she was struggling. I must admit, though, I was much less on my guard believing she would not drink that day and was subsequently seemingly able to relax a bit and basically enjoy the festivities.

I had a romantic idea — maybe I could

invite Mom's old love, Antonio Rius from Rio, to be her date to the wedding. I'd found his number and called him years before, only to find out he'd had a stroke and didn't want her to see him in such poor (and disfigured) health. I encouraged her to try him again, though. But it still wasn't meant to be, sadly — when she finally called, he was thrilled to hear her voice. He was doing better, but had married his nurse only two months earlier. Another chance at happiness lost.

"But I waited. . . ."

The wedding date arrived. The hostess was incredibly generous and housed the whole family. My mom and Lila were in one room and Chris and I in another.

Dad and Didi threw the rehearsal dinner, and Cristiana organized the after-party. It went off without drama — it was actually rather peaceful in Dad's home. Mom did not drink that night and it was looking like it was all calm on the Teri front.

We had not hired a wedding planner, which in hindsight was a huge mistake. To save on costs and keep it simple we had decided to do it all ourselves. With the money saved we splurged on hiring Tuck and Patti to perform. The planning was relatively easy and I had assistants to help, but once in Florida I realized I really needed extra support. I had to organize the entire event myself. I could not rely on my mother for a myriad of reasons and the pressure was too much for any of my in-laws. We needed a person other than the bride or groom to take charge. I had two assistants helping, and Gavin's guys were taking care of security, but nobody had been designated as the captain of the ship. The problem was that without a point person, the mothers began to get involved. The day before the wedding, during the rehearsal portion of the day, I was being pulled in all directions. There was no one to tell me where to go and yet people also needed instruction. I instantly wished I had had a logistics director. It became obvious that I was getting a bit harried.

At one point my mother-in-law and Mom were wandering around aimlessly, trying to be helpful. My mother-in-law evidently said to my mother, "Can I help you, Teri?"

Mom responded with "No, thank you. . . ." And as she turned away, Mom added, "You fucking cunt."

Oh, dear God. Chris heard it but I did not. My assistant told me what had transpired and I knew alcohol had finally reared its ugly head. Chris and I both prayed his mother had not heard. She was gracious and never mentioned a thing, but it was a horror show. Then, not too long after that, Cha Cha took it upon herself to order my assistant Patty to come to my rescue. Everybody was on high stress alert and acting out. Patty had been my assistant for eleven years and always knew when I did and when I did not need anything. She was insulted. She did have it all under control but admittedly was getting a bit flustered by the tension and mounting confusion. I make it a rule never to order my assistants to do anything. I apologized to my longtime and excruciatingly (for her, I'm sure) loyal employee, explaining that tensions were high and these strong mothers were simply needing to be needed.

On the day of the wedding our hostess held a lovely lunch for the houseguests. Didi stayed at their house to deal with the rehearsal-dinner aftermath, and I went to get a massage with my sisters. Mom stayed at the house for lunch and was evidently charming and on point. She and my dad laughed together and were very sweet with each other. Mom was gracious and not inappropriate and seemingly very in her own skin. She did not drink any of the delicious wine that flows like water at this stunning home. I will always regret not witnessing my mother and this meal.

On the wedding day, I was getting ready and putting on my big princess wedding dress. I was getting the veil adjusted and my father awkwardly came up to the room and said he had to ask me a quick question. He pulled out a letter from a buddy of his who freelanced for *People* magazine. The guy was begging my father to just be able to be invited to the BBQ the following day so he could cover it for the magazine.

I looked at my father and, pointing to myself, said, "Dad . . . *wedding dress* . . . *bride*! Can we not discuss this right now, please?"

"I'm just saying, he's a nice guy and he's a buddy of mine from —"

"I am sure he is, Dad, but I am not going to discuss this with you right now, seconds before I am going to actually walk down the aisle."

"OK."

"Don't worry, Dad, I get it. We will figure something out. But please let's just focus on this first."

I was standing in the doorway, surrounded by beautiful marble pillars and shiny steps, and I was about to walk out and down the path to my waiting groom. Mom would be walked down the aisle by my brother-in-law, and my stepsister, Diana, was my maid of honor. Her girls were flower girls and my other sister Marina was going to do a reading. Our youngest sister, Olympia, was serving as the oldest ring bearer ever and helped the flower girls down the aisle.

I was helping my dad navigate his Rollei camera, which did not fit in his pocket, and I could tell he was nervous. It was the second time he'd walk me down an aisle, but we all knew this was different. Chris had actually flown to Florida to ask him for my hand and that impressed my father more than ever.

It was about time for me to start walking. I looked at my mom and said, "Well, Mom, this is it. I am about to go get married. Tell me something."

She motioned for me to come closer, and I did. I leaned in and she sloppily whispered into my ear, "No *People* magazine cover."

I reacted so suddenly and actually shoved her away. I pulled back in a daze and stared at her. I saw the look. The lips were dry and the liner had begun to bleed slightly into her wrinkles. She had obviously been drinking from some stash or had made some arrangement with the staff. She was on her way.

She cocked an eyebrow and pursed her lips into a smirk and said, "What?! I'm just saying. No *People* magazine cover."

She wanted to be the one who perpetually controlled my image. It was all she knew. She could not give me advice, support, or words of wisdom. She did not have any. She knew nothing but how to try to dictate my public persona. The shove was on the wedding video but I had it erased.

I felt so terribly sad for her at that moment. I got it. She had no idea how to just be my mom and was lonelier than hell. She felt she was losing me all over again.

I grabbed Dad's camera as he fumbled to try to fit it in his pocket and I hurriedly put it on a table. I wanted him to watch, not to take photos during the ceremony. I wanted him to be present. I looked at him and at my mother and I thought it was all crazy. I panned past my father, who was adjusting his jacket, and then to my mom, who looked like a little orphaned kid, and then I looked out to the lawn by the water to where Chris stood in his white suit, his hands clasped in front and his neck craned to see me. I thought, *Crazy to my right. Crazy to my left. Not crazy ahead. Finally, not crazy. Just walk toward your future, Brooke. You get to leave the crazy and go to this man you love.*

During the reception, people started making toasts. There were a few comedians in attendance and I swear I saw them working on their speeches *during* the actual ceremony. Comedians are like that. Each one wanted to be the funniest.

They were all great. Once I got over the fact that I did not think any of them had paid attention to their best friend's vows, I laughed harder than anybody. Dad got up to make a toast. He was always tremendous at making toasts and was warm and funny and even got a bit teary. He held out his glass and you could hear a pin drop. I knew he would not drink its contents because he had given up drinking a while earlier.

My eye was immediately drawn to his beautiful hand with his gold bracelet and crest ring, and I suddenly saw my father through a child's eyes. He held his pinky slightly extended, not from affectation but from necessity. His hands were just too big to fit the stem. He explained how impressed he had been that Chris had asked for his permission and he was comforted that I had found a man who made me so relaxed and happy. It was a beautiful moment.

But the next thing I knew, the owner of this stunning estate, who was also named Terry (only spelled differently) and was also quite a larger-than-life character, was suddenly guiding my now drunk mother up toward the mike. They were both Leos and loved to be in control. They were quite a team. She must have thought it safer to accompany my mom in case something went awry. My heart sank. *Oh, Mama, please don't do this. You are better than this.* She could never speak in public unless drinking. She actually could do very little without the numbness of liquor. She was so insecure about how she spoke and sounded that she lost her train of thought and would go vulgar so the shock value distracted everybody and counteracted everything. If she was sober when toasting, she would just say, "I love you with all my heart." And then be done.

Hostess Terry explained she thought it

would be funny for the two powerful Terrys to make a toast together. She said something first and then it was Mom's turn. I started to feel like I was in the middle of a car accident right before impact. I heard nothing and my vision narrowed to a pinpoint. All I saw were my mother's red lips moving. She bizarrely made the toast about her and I began to clap the second I regained my hearing and felt the first pause between her (slurred) words. Mom brought attention to this vaudeville hook, this gong-show gong she said I was wielding, and blurted out some remark regarding my being rude as usual.

"Sure, look at her trying to get rid of the old lady. It's OK, I'm almost done."

I just wanted it over so she would not

embarrass herself. I was not angry, but I was humiliated for her. I was so pained to see Mom doing this in front of my father and Didi. She did end with something sweet but I knew she had just perpetuated her already less-than-stellar reputation. For the first time in my life I suddenly felt strangely jealous of my stepmother, because unlike my mother, she easily commanded more respect. Why hadn't Mom allowed her last impression from lunch to be her new image? Thank God Mom did not mention my father's wife, who remained reticent and graceful as usual.

Chris was ultimately OK with it all because his friends were funny and my dad laughed his booming laugh, which resonated throughout the tent. The comedians all mentioned that they were in a gazillion-dollar estate and they had all been led to a tent in order to bypass the house entirely. That was my plan, and even though I missed being surrounded by the fantasy of luxury, I would breathe easier because of my decision.

In the end, however, Chris's friend did steal the Cuban cigars and I would get a call late that night from the police regarding my infamous drunk mother.

Chris and I had met up with some friends

after all the festivities and were enjoying the warm weather and the water when I got a call that the police had been called to the house because my mom was being disorderly. I don't know who called them, but clearly she needed some kind of help. The medics asked her a series of questions. Of course she knew the answer to each one. She could access names, dates, numbers, and so on. So fuck all of you, she was fine!

Terry Kramer had seemingly no intention of pressing charges. Because Mom had been on private property, there was nothing anyone could do. Chris and I were told that Mom had gone to her room and things had calmed down. I was absolutely mortified and grossed out and had lost all respect in a way I had never experienced before. I did not care how sad or sick she was. It was outrageous and selfish and unfair for her to do this to our generous hostess, and on her only daughter's wedding day. Mom was burying herself, and all hopes I held of the Teri Terrific from brunch the day before becoming her new and improved image were dashed.

Chris and I left for Bali on our honeymoon. I did not look back until I had to. I have no memory of how she got home but knew she would figure it out. I remembered

Paris and Big Sur and her disappearing into the dark and wandering on a highway in the middle of nowhere while on a book tour in some city. And I remembered her inevitable reappearances when you thought it impossible. She would do what she wanted and get back to where she was headed when she was good and ready. Her wake or those caught up in it never concerned her. She was her own riptide.

Mom made alienating herself from people her personal art form. She did it so consistently and so often with those she loved that she found herself decidedly alone and isolated with the booze. She could hurt people like no other. I believe it was because her capacity to love was immeasurable. She knew how to hook into people and register with them deeply, but if it got too close or she felt an ounce of vulnerability, she would lash out. I was the only one who kept returning for both the love and the lashes. She was, as always, my mom.

Chris and I wanted to start a family as soon as possible, but it would not be as easy as we had hoped. We had *not* been actively trying to get pregnant, but for the past two years we had discussed being fine even if I were to become a pregnant bride (and thus need to alter my wedding dress). It had not happened as of yet and we assumed it was because of our busy schedules and stress. We had not really factored in my cervix because surgery had been successful, and the threat of cancer had been our main focus.

Upon consulting with a doctor, we learned that because so much of my cervix had been removed, it was proving almost impossible for me to become pregnant naturally. We immediately started the process of IVF. It was a crazy experience with hormones and drugs and shots. But after the first successful transfer of my fertilized eggs, I became pregnant. We were so thrilled, we told all our friends and relatives. Mom sounded teary on the phone and offered up a name for the baby. She assumed it would be a girl and we should name her Willow. We thought it was too soon to pick names. Not because of losing the baby, but because we needed to do my favorite thing and make lists!

Within three months, I was writhing in our bedroom, enduring an insanely surreal and painful miscarriage. By the time the night was over I had banned Chris from coming near me, only allowing our new dog, Darla, to sleep at my feet. I was exhausted and angry.

I was again different after that night. I lost innocence and a belief that everything would turn out OK. Like most children, when I was a little kid I had an incredibly naïve belief that all things would be positive and work out the way I wanted. I believed perpetually that my mother would one day stop drinking and be healthy and happy because she was sober. I held on tightly to that hope. I even believed that if I had babies Mom would become a sweet, happy, fun-loving little old grandmother.

I always knew I wanted to be a mother, but I also believed that being a mother would give me freedom — freedom from my mother's drinking and the hurt she caused me. I believed I would need less from her and be freer to have compassion for her while personally remaining safe. My energy could be redirected.

For some reason, after all the disappointments regarding her drinking and my being let down, I held on to the belief that if I had a baby, it would heal and right everything. There was no connection except in the expectation I placed on these possibilities with all my heart. When I lost this baby, I was heartbroken. I felt as if I had finally been defeated and I was not slated for conventional happiness.

I became convinced that I was not allowed to be normal and that I would not be allowed to have babies. I got very dark.

My first call the next day was to my mother. She was very sad but quickly added that as long as I was OK, that was what mattered. We would have another. And that was it. She had no other words of empathy.

I could not believe the pauses on the other end of the phone.

"Mom, are you sure there is not anything you want to tell me?"

"Nope."

"Well, OK. I love you, Mama."

"I love you, too, sweetheart."

I hung up and finally got really angry.

Wasn't this the moment when the mother was supposed to say to her grieving child some words of empathy or compassion from her own experience? We'd hardly talked about the mysterious Baby John since my outburst all those years ago, but I knew Mom, too, had experienced some kind of a loss and she might be able to identify with me or offer support.

And even if Mom had no connection to such a personal loss, wasn't she supposed to come up with something like "Oh, honey, it is much more common than you think. It's your body's way of telling you the baby was not strong enough." Or even, "There is another angel in heaven, my darling."

I just couldn't believe that she could not finally come clean about the baby boy she had supposedly lost after delivery. I was in pain and sad and I had nowhere to turn.

I dialed her house once again. "Mom, are you sure there is *nothing* you want to share with me at this moment in my life?"

"Nope, not that I can think of."

"OK, well, can I ask you a question?"

"Sure."

"Was there ever a baby . . ."

Pause.

"Was there . . . like, a boy . . ."

"Ah, why would you want to talk about such things?"

"Well is there a . . . grave?"

"Maybe."

OK, then, if this is so painful for her that she can't even help her only daughter not feel so alone, at a devastating time like this, then . . . I got nothin'.

I let her off the hook and never brought it up to her again. I would never know any more while my mother was still alive and physically able to communicate.

We would go through six IVF attempts after the first successful transfer. The difference was that because of the violence of the miscarriage, the scar tissue on my cervix had been stretched enough for me to get pregnant vaginally. The first successful attempt at implantation had been completed via my belly button. This would be the possible spiritual "reason" for the loss. By the time we got to the sixth try, we were exasperated. I had had some frozen embryos and some were fresh (six in all), and I could barely take it anymore.

I told the doctor I did not care if I had triplets; I wanted all six to be implanted in me and we would see. Lucky seven it was, and we finally returned home from a routine visit with a positive pregnancy test. And miraculously only one took. And unbelievably, the one embryo strong enough to make it had been a member of the original bunch. She had been frozen for two whole years.

This time we kept it a secret until we heard the heartbeat.

We called our parents during the sonogram and put the phone up to the machine to hear the heart. My mom recognized the sound immediately and began to cry. "Oh, my darling, I'm so happy for you." (Probably just for me — she didn't mention "that man" [Mom's favorite moniker for Chris] to whom I was married.) My dad thought it was a dog panting. We shared the good news with a slightly tempered excitement simply because of the long journey we had been on to get here. We did all the tests, including the amniocentesis, and we were relieved every time we got good news. When I got the formal call that the amnio had been normal, I burst into tears. Chris's parents were in town and we were having pizza at John's, uptown. I nervously picked up the call, and when I hung up, I was going to be a mother.

I don't remember telling my mom about the amnio. I also don't remember ever letting my mother feel my belly when the baby was moving. It seemed too physically intimate.

Chris and I bought a loft in SoHo with great light. The plan had been to stay in LA as long as possible because Chris had a job there and then come to New York City later in my third trimester. I wanted our baby to be born in New York City and Chris was on board. Plus, I was considered a high-risk pregnancy because of my compromised cervix, and the doctor did not want me doing too much traveling. I always loved that term: *compromised cervix*. As if my cervix had been involved in a lengthy legal negotiation and had been forced to reach some settlement. Well. It was better than the word *incompetent,* so I took it.

This high-risk state also meant that I could not visit my sick father. I needed a specialist in these types of deliveries and nobody wanted to put me or the baby in jeopardy.

Three weeks before leaving for New York City to deliver my baby, I was at the LA dog park saying bye to some friends when my cell phone rang. It was my stepsister.

"Say what you want to your dad, and say it now."

She put the phone up to his ear and I said: "I love you, Dad. And I've always been proud you were my father. Please don't be scared."

According to Cristiana, Dad moved his toes.

That was the last time I would ever talk to him. He passed away that afternoon shortly after we were on the phone. We had already chosen a first name for the baby, Rowan, and I decided Dad's first name would be her middle name. She was to be Rowan Francis Henchy.

I phoned my mother to tell her that Dad had died, and she began to cry, repeating, "Oh, Brookie, oh, Brookie."

We had not really discussed my dad's illness. Through her lonely tears she asked me if he had said anything about her to me.

"What?!"

"Did he mention me?"

"No, Mom, he did not mention you. How could you ask me that right at this moment? No, he did not talk about *you!"*

I knew that was being cruel but I said it anyway.

I sobbed the entire plane ride to New York City.

I went to term.

CHAPTER SIXTEEN: I KNOW YOUR KIND

I was eight months pregnant and a good friend of ours from California was throwing me a coed baby shower in our newly acquired SoHo loft. All my life I'd lived on the Upper East Side, but moving downtown was the best decision we ever made. It felt like a fresh start. It was a bit grittier than the Upper East Side but more forgiving and varied. We decided not to cancel the shower because of my father's death but to instead try to celebrate his life as well as the one growing inside of me. I was incredibly sad that my dad would never meet my children, but I tried to forget the reality of the loss.

I had not seen my mom in a while and I was very nervous because I was pretty emotional and didn't want her to cause any trouble. But when she arrived she was surprisingly happy and not even sneaking alcohol. It was a beautiful and intimate shower, even if it was slightly bittersweet. I was shocked, amazed, and unbelievably relieved that Mom did not drink, and probably would have lost my mind if she had. Maybe somewhere in her subconscious she sensed that, but I doubt it. I just got lucky.

Three weeks later, in mid-May, my water broke. It was 5:00 A.M., at the crack of dawn, and I had gotten up to use the bathroom. It was a few days before her due date and two days before my father's birthday. I had hoped she would be born on my dad's birthday. But Rowan was breech and chose to turn the night before my water broke. I'm sure she did it on purpose just to make sure I knew she was her own person.

When my water broke I did not go right to the hospital or call anybody. I called out to Chris, who had been up all night celebrating at the upfronts, which is when networks present their new shows to advertisers and affiliates. I yelled to him from the bathroom and asked him to check the *What to Expect When You're Expecting* book to see what to do when your water breaks. He waited a few moments and then said that the book said to go back to bed. I brought a towel to bed, went back to sleep, and had an amazing two-hour nap. I had a blowout scheduled for 9:00 A.M. so I figured I could go to the hospital with smooth hair. I hoped I would not go into labor until after the blowout was done.

I awoke and called my stepsister, Diana. I casually mentioned that my water had broken and she screamed at me, "Why are you not at the hospital?"

"Because I'm not having contractions and they'd probably just send me home."

"Oh my God, no, that is not right. Go to the hospital now. You can get an infection if your water breaks and you don't tend to it."

I lunged at Chris and asked him to tell me, again, what the book had said.

"What book?"

"Oh my God, you didn't even look at the book when I asked you! The baby may get an infection or I might because my water broke and I did nothing. Get me to the hospital *now*!"

Once safely at the hospital, we began phoning relatives and some close friends. I did not get an infection and I ended up needing to be induced. However, after being on Pitocin for twenty-four hours with practically no dilation, I needed an emergency C-section.

Mom and Chris's parents had all arrived at the hospital. As I was being wheeled into the OR, I saw Mom from my lying-down position on the gurney and I had such a strange feeling inside. I knew she was going to kiss me either on the lips or the forehead and I was instantly sick to my stomach at the thought that she might have cold, slightly clammy lips. I was sure she was nervous because only Chris was allowed to be in the OR with me.

I also resisted yelling out to her to tell me I was going to be OK. I suddenly felt like I could never ask her that question ever again. I knew for the first real time that she could not possibly know the answer to this question that I had been asking her since she was able to make it rain. I sometimes weaken and ask Chris this question. Sometimes you just want to hear someone say, "Yes, it's all going to be fine," even if you know that they couldn't possibly know the truth.

The delivery was horrendous. I was conscious and had had an epidural but I was very aware that things were not going smoothly. First of all, I heard the doctor yell, "Cord wrapped, cord wrapped!"

Evidently, when Rowan turned the night before, she had wrapped the umbilical cord around her body and neck in three places. Thank God I did not push.

My uterus had herniated and I had lost a tremendous amount of blood. Another doctor was called in to assist. The baby was fine, fortunately, but the doctor had to concentrate on trying to keep me alive. The nurses took her away and I told Chris to go with them.

"Go with the baby, go with her."

I had heard that babies got switched sometimes and I was paranoid.

Once I was alone with the team of doctors and nurses, the terror set in. I was terrified of dying. I suddenly did want my mommy to tell me I was going to be OK after all. I had just had a baby, but I felt more like a baby than I have ever felt in my life. "Mommy, where are you?" was ringing in my ears. The doctor was able to assure me that the worst that would happen was a blood transfusion and a hysterectomy. I couldn't have cared less about losing my uterus. I wanted to live.

I also instantly got jealous of Chris for being alive and with our baby and hated my mother for being so careless with her own life by abusing her health with alcohol. And here I was split down the middle and fanned out like an opened minibox of cereal! It all came out as feelings of abandonment. I was sad and miserable — I couldn't believe how cold the OR suddenly felt. I got stitched back together and was allowed to own my uterus for another twenty-four hours. Ooh, goody! They were going to watch me, and if the bleeding stopped, I would not need the hysterectomy. I had always been fascinated by the fact that the word *hysterectomy* was born out of the word *hysteria* and was designed to fix women who were acting crazy during menstruation. It made sense to me now.

Once I was back in my room, they brought Rowan to me to breast-feed. My mother had never breast-fed me and, while watching the nurse hold my newborn baby up to my chest, had the strangest look on her face. Mom kept herself tucked in between the side table and the side of my bed and draped her left arm over the back headboard of the hospital bed. I felt crowded but also strangely glad she was quiet, while making her best attempt to be near me without trying to control something she knew nothing about. She was shockingly still sober. Maybe she was deeply afraid something was going to happen to me.

I was exhausted and beginning to really struggle. I was beginning to feel stranger and sadder than I had ever felt in my life. I felt like I didn't recognize anyone around me. I knew who they were, but I felt they were all on a shore celebrating while I was underwater trying not to drown. I have pictures of the nurse holding Rowan up to my breast and I have fear all over my face. My mother was quiet and non-communicative. She looked like she was in shock.

Chris's family and some friends were milling around and all focusing on the baby. Chris held her practically the entire time. I don't remember ever asking to hold Rowan myself. I had seen so many photos of friends and relatives from their hospital beds holding their newborns and looking at them with utter devotion and loving awe. I am sitting bare breasted and hooked up to machines, looking at almost everybody else except Rowan. I had this overriding feeling that she already did not like me.

This was obviously the beginning of severe postpartum depression. None of us knew what it was yet, but it would last much longer and cause damage to all of us in different ways. Thank God Rowan would remain unscathed. I eventually wrote a book about this experience, *Down Came the Rain,* but at the moment I had to concentrate on avoiding both a blood transfusion and a hysterectomy. My twenty-four hours of being watched were not yet over. I was not out of the woods yet and I could not seem to focus on anything other than my health and my own life.

People who wanted to see the happy mother and child came and went, and I kept a close eye on my mom. She seemed so out of sorts and slightly sad. I kind of felt like shaking her, but I didn't know what I would say. She seemed to want to be needed but she was so uncomfortable. It was as if she felt like she did not belong. She was as much related to this baby as Chris's parents, and yet she seemed to be receding into the background. In a surreal way, we both were but for different reasons. We were both out of sorts, equally at risk of not surviving. Mom dealt by being eerily quiet and I, too, chose reticence as a way to stay afloat.

It was time for Rowan and me to rest. Mom and Lila went to P. J. Clarke's to eat and I slept. Rowan was in a crib next to my bed and was attached to a light to help build up her bilirubin. She was a bit jaundiced and needed the vitamin D. She looked like a little alien on a mini wooden stretcher. I can't remember when Mom and Lila returned but I recall them coming back separately. Lila came in first and was mumbling something about how Mom had not wanted to leave the restaurant.

Chris had set up chairs in a kind of circle in the middle of my room and inclined toward my bed. He knew many people would be coming and going and want to hold the baby. Mom arrived after Lila and she walked into the room totally hammered and ready to fight. A male nurse, with whom she was overtly flirting, was guiding her into the room. We got the feeling that Mom had been in the building for a little while and had inappropriately made her presence known. She may or may not have pinched or slapped him on the butt but he ushered her into the room and then made a quick exit. I had an inkling that because she was my mom they were stretching their tolerance.

Mom came in the room as the family

members were passing Rowan around to be held. They all took turns, and when it was Mom's turn, she reached out to hold the swaddled newborn, only to almost drop her in the process. Rowan only weighed seven and a half pounds, but Mom fumbled her and the baby almost fell to the floor. I could tell she was drunk, but I could not even speak. I was mute and exhausted and felt like I was out of my body and hovering unnoticed. I watched in stilled horror and felt as if I had just been forced to ride a terrifying Ferris wheel for a second time. As if the operator would not let me get off.

Chris leapt up, grabbed the baby from her hands, and got right up in my mother's face. He told her that she was not allowed to hold Rowan in her condition. He took a strong stance and told her she was drunk and could do whatever the hell she wanted to herself, but was not allowed to jeopardize our baby. His face was red with anger, and he said, in fact, he would like her to leave this room right now.

Nobody else said a word. I don't even remember Rowan uttering a peep. Chris followed my mother to the doorway to make sure she didn't do anything sudden. She turned face-to-face with him in the doorway, pointing at him and tapping her forefinger on his chest in a threatening way.

"Oh, I know your kind," she said.

She pushed back and staggered off and out into the night.

Chris came over to me immediately and apologized and said he was so sorry, but he had to draw the line at our baby. I was relieved she was gone but profoundly sad that it had to be that way. I thanked Chris for defending us, even though I knew he was just defending his daughter. That was the man I knew he was and the father I wanted for my children. But overall, I was just fatigued by everything.

My in-laws were trying to act normal and were successfully avoiding discussing anything but this perfect baby. I could tell Lila was angry and sad and hurt and frustrated by having to deal with Mom again and again. Nobody had any authority over my mother. Even in this supposedly blessed and happy moment, she could not be happy or healthy.

My heart was breaking for a few reasons and it would soon become evident that I had reached an emotional limit. The cumulative and recent pain and sorrow had caught up to me and I was breaking apart. My heart ached for everybody I loved and was now breaking for myself. I fell asleep that night looking at this little stranger under her orange light and I envied her. This baby was allowed to be helpless. I had never been permitted to be so.

The next day the doctor came and told us Rowan's hips had not fully formed and she would need to wear a strong Velcro brace for a few months. I sat there on my hospital bed and could not grasp anything. I hated breast-feeding, I had lost a lot of blood and was weak, my baby was yellow and needed a paddle attached to her with intense light, and now her hip sockets had not formed and she needed to wear a brace that made her look like a marionette whose knees were stuck bent up. I did not have the strength to feel happy or available to the present potential of joy. Rowan was in a brace, but I felt like I was in a straightjacket.

I was able to keep my uterus and my life and I was soon released.

At home, it seemed that nobody could help me. I continued to struggle with breast-feeding, I could not stop crying, and I had horrible visions of Rowan getting hurt. I would get dizzy at the powder smell of the diapers. I'd huddle in the shower with hot water pounding down on me and not move for extended periods of time. Food had no taste or appeal. I actually still haven't eaten lasagna since my mother-in-law made a pan of it that first week. I had taken one bite and could not even swallow. I had such trouble producing milk for my baby because I was not nourishing my own body.

On one incredibly low day, Chris went out to get a changing table because we were totally unprepared for the arrival. For some reason I had not been proactive about setting up a nursery. I knew the due date but had not bought the necessary furniture and had only set up the nursery by getting a rocker that had actually been a gift.

Chris came back from a store (ironically called buybuy Baby), empty-handed. He sat down on the edge of the bed and began to cry. He said he had seen happy mothers holding their newborns, and pregnant mothers smiling and shopping.

"What is wrong with you? You don't sing to her or kiss her."

I felt my world end. I could only answer that I did not know and that I was so sorry. I left him in our room and hobbled out to see my mom, who was sitting on our leather tufted coffee table in the living room. I slumped in the chair in front of her and began to cry. She asked me what was the matter, and I looked at her and with dismay said, "I made Chris cry."

"I made him cry?" she asked.

"What?! Oh my God, Mom, *no,* not *you. I made Chris cry! You* are not the important one here. Get out of this house right now or I am going to jump out of the fucking window. Get out — I mean it!"

She just sat there motionless and trying to be invisible. I cried and escaped back to the bedroom, disgusted. I knew her hearing was deteriorating but I could not believe that she heard something about her — and not about Chris or me — in what I was crying about. Just like when Dad died and she asked me if he had asked about her, my husband was crying and she thought she had caused his tears. It was all about her in her mind, not out of narcissism but out of fear and insecurity. Mom had just stared at me and had become helplessly still. Her eyes looked like those of a scared little kid witnessing something horrible.

I realized the problem did not actually concern her. There was something terrible wrong in my life and it affected all those around me. I did not know where to turn.

I would soon get a baby nurse to help out for a week, which turned into a year. I got help from a doctor who referred me to a pharma-psychologist who prescribed me the proper combination of medication. I also began to eat better and began to exercise again by taking Rowan on long hikes around the neighborhood in New York and LA.

Things settled down and I stopped hating my mother for not knowing what I needed. How could I expect her to talk about her experiences from a place of wisdom and understanding when she had never spent any time on self-reflection? I realize today that she was scared most of the time and lonely all of the time. I was eventually even able not to punish my mother for continuing to call Rowan "Brookie." We invited her out to California because, no matter what, I wanted her to know my baby and I wanted Rowan to know this grandmother as well.

I didn't realize, though, that this was the beginning of a new phase in our relationship and my mother's health. Mom started being more and more helpless. The next few years would be a challenge in an all new way.

In the months after Rowan was born, there were a few times that Mom visited us in LA and seemed to be in a quieter place. I was going back and forth between New York and New Jersey and LA, but for the beginning of Rowan's life we were primarily living in Santa Monica. Chris was working on a new TV show and we were living in a house on the west side of town. Rowan was only a few months old but was getting so big so fast, and I really wanted Mom to see that I was doing a good job taking care of my baby. She enjoyed playing with Rowan and putting pink sponge rollers on her few bits of baby hair. Mom would spend the first few days seemingly not drinking, but by day three it was always clear she did not want to be under my watchful eye.

Not watching my mother was never something I could do. I always fell right into a codependent routine of scrutinizing her every move and trying to anticipate those I had yet to see. I wanted my mother around because that way I knew she was alive. But she made me crazy in ways I could not believe. She would say things under her breath or I'd see an expression of judgment in her eyes and I would have to address or fight it. Even if I left the room and counted to ten or practiced deep breathing, I would have the urge to wrap my hands around her throat and squeeze. Even when I'd try to be sweet, it felt forced because she made me nervous. Oh, how my mom could unsettle me and undo all the work I had done on myself to live a healthy and self-actualized life. And why did I still seek her approval?

I still would rather have her be around than alone and in an echoing house in New Jersey. It was a relief to have her arrive safely off the plane and a relief to see her leave. She was OK with Rowan but was never left alone with her in those early days.

I wanted to have her go on these walks with me while I pushed Rowan in a stroller around the neighborhood. I had had such good deep conversations with Gemma, our baby nurse, on these walks, and I would have loved the Hallmark moment with my mom as well. Sadly, Mom's knees were bad and her arthritis was making it very hard for her to do any walking. She was perfectly comfortable to sit and watch movies for hours. It seemed it was the only activity we occasionally still enjoyed together. For some reason it bothered me when she sat doing nothing all day, just watching movies. And for some reason I didn't trust that she was not also trying to snoop around my office or even pocket little things just because she felt entitled to do so. It was very strange but Mom wanted any form of control she could find, even if it meant stealing back a little ashtray or coaster we had gotten in Europe on one of our earlier trips.

Her health did seem to be declining and it was beginning to be apparent that alcohol consumption was not her only issue. It would be years before the problem would be diagnosed, but she was somehow increasingly different and booze was surprisingly no longer the only problem.

When I once went back to Haworth when Rowan was about six months old, it became even clearer to me that drinking or not, Mom was not completely coherent. She would get confused or not be able to follow a story. This particular night in Haworth, Rowan was sick and I really did not feel secure with my mom helping. She began drinking, only in the evening, but I realized that I was totally alone in caring for my sick infant. I had no car because I had been dropped off at my mother's for the night and her car was in the shop. She had had her license taken away from her anyway, so she wouldn't be needing a car. I was going to help her sort through some closets that needed cleaning out that evening, but Rowan had gotten a fever and instead I had to keep a close eye on her.

Chris told me to call a car and leave immediately. Leaving abruptly was proving problematic, but I figured since I was near a police station and hospital I had a potential escape plan. I called the doctor and he said just to keep an eye on her fever. If it got past 103, then I should worry. I tried to cool her face off with cool compresses.

It was a real traumatic night for me because I felt so alone and so afraid for my daughter. I had my own child to care for and it really hit home for me that I could not rely on my mother to help. All my life I felt secure knowing I could handle my mom and take care of myself. I also always believed she actually did take care of me growing up. I had survived, hadn't I? This feeling with my own baby girl felt very different and deeply unsettling. Suddenly all bets were off and I hated my mother and her incompetence.

I consciously separated myself from my

mom and her issues, and survival kicked in. But this time it was not for myself but for my infant. Something deep within me shifted and I made Rowan my only emotional and physical focus. My daughter became my only priority. I realized, completely, that I could not count on my mother to help my daughter or me. And most likely not even herself.

All throughout my life I had held out hope that my mother would one day ultimately show up for me and give me the freedom not to worry about her or put her needs ahead of mine. In these moments of fear for my daughter's health, I realized that it was up to me to reclaim that freedom on my own. She would never be able to bestow on me such peace and autonomy. Rowan slept and I stayed awake to watch her breathing. As I lay awake listening to Rowan's labored breathing and praying for her fever to break, I hated my mom and I redefined my loyalty. By dawn Rowan's fever had broken. I was exhausted but buoyed by the fact that the worst was over. I returned to New York City and never discussed any of it with my mom. There was no point.

Two years later, living in New York again, I was planning to appear in the musical *Chi-*

cago for the second time as Roxie Hart, this time trading London's West End for Broadway. I had called my IVF doctor to say that I wanted to start the process of getting pregnant during my run in the show. I would need a few months of medication, and being in a show was the best time to do it, because I am always my healthiest when performing. After some routine blood tests the doctor called back to tell me that the process would not be necessary because I was already pregnant. I was stunned and elated but now suddenly afraid of doing eight shows a week while pregnant. The doctor said not to do any extra exercise and I would be fine.

Mom came to my opening night on Broadway and seemed happy to be included, but very distant. She seemed uncomfortable and unable to articulate herself. I had been getting more short and curt with her recently because she couldn't even seem to order the food she wanted at a restaurant. She whispered instead of speaking loud enough to be heard, and I would often impatiently hurry her on and speak to her in a condescending tone. I could not seem to stop myself from lashing out. I would get frustrated and oddly embarrassed.

I would get impatient and raise my voice,

saying, "Mom, *what* do you want to *eat*?"

I would then just pick for her and apologize to the server out of embarrassment for my mother's lack of focus. I felt mortified that she was acting like a little kid and I was ashamed of my own impatience. Later, Rowan would stick up for Toots and tell me not to be mean to her, scolding me.

Other strange things happened as well. Chris came into the kitchen one afternoon and saw my mother place a ceramic bowl of soup onto an open flame on the stove. He stopped her and said, "Teri, that should be in a metal pot."

"I know but it's faster this way. Take out the middleman."

Luckily, he managed to avert disaster by offering to help and, in fact, serve her. This soup incident sent up our first warning sign. This was beyond my mother's normal eccentric nature.

Soon after that, I decided to get rid of my entire set of Fiestaware dishes and cups that Mom and I had collected over the years at various flea markets. I now wanted clean, uniform-looking china. I went to Sur La Table and bought simple white bowls and plates and mugs. As I was taking the stickers off the bottoms of the mugs it occurred to me that this task might be something my mother could help me with. She was thrilled that I asked for her help. She stood at the kitchen island and began peeling off the tiny SKU labels from the bottom of the pieces.

I watched her out of the corner of my eye and was sadly fascinated by the precision with which she picked away at the edges with the tip of the painted red nail of her index finger. She moved slowly and with focused concentration, and added each little sticker to a mounting pile stuck to the marble top of the counter. She reminded me of the autistic children I had studied temporarily after I graduated from college as research for a part in a shitty movie I did. She was at first quiet and seemingly content, but she could not seem to finish the job. I kept watching her while pretending to do other things. She skipped some stickers and labored over others, and then would get distracted and forget she was working on a task at all. A task that should have taken fifteen minutes took over two hours and was completely disorganized.

Watching her inability to complete any seemingly simple task spurred deep curiosity in me. Was she brain damaged from a ministroke she had suffered a few years back? Was the hematoma that I had seen and touched at St. Vincent's when I received the dead turtle more damaging than I thought, or was excessive alcohol all to blame?

I tried another kitchen task. I asked Mom to set the dining room table with the new flatware I had also just ordered. I gave her enough for twelve settings. Now, it had been my mother who had taught me the proper way to set a formal dinner table. She was from Newark but she made sure she was skilled in proper etiquette. I learned from a young age which utensil went where and why. Mom disappeared into the dining area to set the table. We were not having a dinner, but I did not tell her that. She was gone for about two hours. When I checked in on her, nothing she'd done made sense. She could not seem to finish the job. I can't say I handled it well. I would like to be able to write that I calmly helped her and encouraged her like I would a child. I did not. I got disgusted and impatient and used the moment to chastise her and shame her. I was striking back and felt ugly and ashamed but I could not stop this lashing out.

"Seriously, Mom, you can't even set a table. Really?"

She got that terrible wide-eyed — scared, cornered, and broken — look in her expression and she went still again. Instead of lashing back or cursing at me as I had seen so many times, she looked like a little kid being shamed by her mommy. I was not proud of my behavior but felt so pouty and bratty. I wanted to stamp my feet and cry, "It's not fair!"

It was as if I had reverted to that little brat from Mom's return from St. Mary's.

It is a very unsettling feeling to see your parents really helpless and vulnerable. I was so frustrated that I had taken care of her my whole life, and that now, when the big dramas seemed to have subsided, it felt even worse. I was getting angry that when I had thought she might have finally settled down a bit and had finally become a sweet or calmer grandma, she now seemed impaired and even more helpless. The promised land I believed in had never materialized and now we were in a different kind of hell. What had it all been for?

Something was not right in her head. Was her brain pickled by booze? Or was it something else?

■ ■ ■ ■

Part Five

■ ■ ■ ■

I will always be your daughter and you my mother even if the manifestation of that is not what either of us dream of.
— *Card to Teri from Brooke*

CHAPTER SEVENTEEN:
TAG SALE

Life around my mother began to be even more unsettled and intense, but for entirely new reasons. I was beginning to get worried and sad because alcohol was seriously beginning to be the least of my worries. For forty years my focus had been on her drinking. Now I almost wished that the booze was the problem. My chest would tighten every time I saw the look of fear on her face when she was asked a question. She looked like a little kid in a foreign land having been separated from her mommy.

Chicago went well and I finished my run just as my belly was beginning to look like I was hiding half a soccer ball in it. I told my mother I was pregnant and called her again when I heard my daughter's heartbeat. Mom cried this time, too.

It was about this time that I really began to feel distant from my mom. When I had Rowan I was still so enmeshed with my mother, but with this baby I felt a new level of freedom. I am not sure what to attribute this liberation to, but I really just started to feel like I was finally growing up. Time had passed since my dad's death. I didn't care, honestly, if my mom drank or not. And I was about to have two children under the age of three. Life was shifting.

Sadly, the realization dawned on me that I was becoming a mother at the same time I was beginning to lose my own. I am reminded of the fact that in every Disney movie from *Bambi* to *Frozen* the mothers all are dead or die within the first few minutes. Is that what it takes to start your own story? One's narrative morphs with one's current perspective of the truth. But must one's mother die for a person to fully individuate?

I started getting the heavy feeling that it was too late for my mom to ever really be happy and for me to make up for the time I had lost whenever she was drunk.

Maybe when I blurted out "If you die, I'll die" all those years ago I was onto something. Maybe a part of me would have to die to continue. I used to honestly feel that if Mom died I would actually stop living. Now I had my own children to live for and I had my own life to fully live.

It started getting very sad to me when I realized I was actually, slowly, losing my mother and there was little to be done about it. I felt like I had lost her my entire life. I had fought for her and had fought against her for so many years and was not sure what I had to show for it. She was fading just as I was beginning to come into focus.

Mom was mostly living in her new condominium in New Jersey. It was becoming evident that this would probably not last long. It was getting harder and harder for her to take care of herself. She was starting to show real signs of forgetfulness and she began speaking less and even more quietly. She was hardly drinking and when she did it wasn't to excess. I had actually given up trying to get her to quit drinking. In fact, I began to pour her wine like I would for anybody else at the table. Why not? I had contacted lawyers and begun the legal process of being designated her health and legal proxy. It was evident Mom was on a path toward being declared incompetent with regard to her personal care. She had a couple of friends who'd drive her places and I'd arrange any other necessary travel. I was no longer worried she could drive, and I just had to make sure she didn't hurt herself by accident in some way while unattended.

I visited her when I could. In my spare time I continued to go through her storage units to take inventory and sell some more items to help her pay her bills. Over the course of our lifetime together Mom and I had owned six homes. There was a period where we owned them all at the same time! Once I convinced my mother to start unloading some real estate so as to maintain some financial liquidity, we suddenly had more furniture than we could ever use. That did not stop her from buying more. Mom often bought furnished houses, but every time she sold a house, she kept its contents. My mom could never part with a thing. After the collection expanded out of several storage units, my mother ended up renting a warehouse in Paterson, New Jersey, that was literally the size of an airplane hangar. She filled it top to bottom and had been paying rent on it for years.

The big problem, however, was the actual manner in which Mom stored her treasures. There was no rhyme or reason to any of it and hardly anything was marked. The boxes were stacked on top of each other, reaching up as high as the ceiling. She had clothes, linens, silverware, fabric, jewelry, more clothes, books, art, film reels, bikes, toys, tools, stereo equipment, countless rugs, built-in cabinets she had ripped out from places, machinery of sorts, Hollywood memorabilia, and furniture galore. Most of it was real quality. But who needed four roll-top desks or the built-in cabinetry from our town house on Sixty-Second and Lexington Avenue? My assistant Dan started helping me sort through everything. We never knew what we would find, but you knew there would be a story attached.

For example, she had two wardrobe-size cardboard boxes chock-full of Beanie Babies. She had become one of those people who collected them with the plan of cashing in one day. She never traded or sold them, though, but simply kept buying hoards of the little ridiculous stuffed animals. The whole thing creeped me out. But I had learned to pick my battles. Either they would sell or I would find a place to donate them.

I thought I would donate the boxes to a children's hospital but was told they could not take stuffed animals because of the germs. I then found out that my aunt Lila knew somebody who would fill a suitcase and bring it to children in developing countries. She could only take one suitcase, however, and would not be making another

511

trip for months. I decided to rummage through the boxes before separating them to be sold. My assistant thought it was a waste of my time. They were obviously just boxes full solely of Beanie Babies.

I explained to him that he did not really know my mother. Something told me I needed to go through all of them. Well, at the bottom of one of the wardrobe boxes was a little piece of crumpled-up tissue. Inside said tissue was a 14-karat gold, diamond-encrusted Harry Winston watch. Mom had always hidden things places and then forgot where they were. I found lose semiprecious stones in dental-floss containers and a 24-karat gold purse inside another flea market clutch. There were real Louis Vuitton and Chanel bags mixed in with knockoffs, and I had to beg Dan to go into their stores and ask for help telling the difference between them. I don't think it was about fear of theft as much as she was just eccentric and loved being in control. Mom would go to all lengths for a laugh or just to have something over on somebody.

In April 2006 our second daughter, Grier Hammond Henchy, was born. Now I had two daughters under the age of three. Even though Grier was born in LA, we had decided that when she started school we would move the girls back to New York and get their education in Manhattan. I had always wanted to have my girls have a New York City upbringing. Mom had been making reckless decisions — like letting a guy who worked at the gas station move into her living room. She was found wandering barefoot and confused around a school parking lot.

We decided it was time to move her to an assisted-living facility.

Mom went willingly, but when she arrived she hated it because she was not like "these people." It was just like it was back in rehab all those years ago. The way she saw it, she was never as bad as the other people in these places. The tough part for me was that Mom really didn't look as old as the other residents. They all actually did seem older and more out of it than she did. She didn't mumble as much as they did and had not begun to shuffle with her socked feet wedged into bedroom slippers.

As soon as she was checked in she started asking me when she could leave. I have to admit that although it was a relief to have her accounted for, I felt terrible that she needed such a place. I felt guilty for "putting her away." She used to love to paint the picture to people of her being eventually locked up and me sliding a tray of food to her under the door. "Peter and the tray," she called it, reminding me of the Peter-like betrayal she'd always expected.

I justified it all by saying to myself that it was temporary. I secretly felt she was somehow superior to the others. I thought she would snap out of it. She had to. It couldn't end like this.

Having her in a facility gave me the freedom to handle the sale of her homes and have tag sales for the excess crap. I discovered that she had been shopping on QVC and HSN for copious amounts of jewelry. She had burned through money I had allotted her over the years and had even siphoned from a retirement fund. There were hundreds and hundreds of little boxes and bags filled with birthstone rings and earrings. I had never seen so many cubic-zirconia items in one area. She bought in bulk and had intended to give it all away to friends and employees and one of each to her granddaughters. It was insane. In addition she had various collections of everything from taxidermy, vintage record players, quilts, tiles, antique doors, or orange crates filled with door fittings. She had milk-glass table settings, Depression-glass collections, rugs, sterling-silver settings for twelve, over a thousand vintage tablecloths, assortments of paint-by-number art mixed in with period oil portraits, bolts of fabric, multiple pieces of antique furniture, and unfinished crafts from the seventies.

I had to sort through it all and decide what to do with it. I basically kept the good stuff and put the rest up for sale. We had three more massive two-day tag sales to rid ourselves of the clutter. We made a good chunk of money on these sales and the money went directly to her living costs.

One day I called to speak to my mother and they said she had gone out with a male friend. My mother had two friends at this point and I was one of them. The other was an accountant's assistant who had been helping Mom pay bills. She was a woman.

I asked with whom she had gone out and to where, and why had they not called me?

They said that a man came to visit her and that Mom seemed to know him, so she left with him. The jailbreak had been a success. He was not on the accepted list of visitors and these idiots had no idea that they were allowing my mother to be checked out by a *National Enquirer* reporter. My head exploded with rage.

This bozo snuck Mom directly to the

bank, at her request, and she had tried to take out money. I actually guessed she would go back to Haworth, because she maintained her account there and was always talking about money and being stolen from. She wanted to flee and this was her ticket to escape. I hung up on the numbnut attendant at the facility and immediately called the bank and asked if my mom was there. They informed me that yes, she was. A man in fact had accompanied her. She was trying to withdraw money from her account at that moment.

I explained in an agitated tone that this man was not a friend and had basically kidnapped her. I begged them to please not release any funds, saying that she had been under psychiatric observation and was currently living in an assisted-living facility. I had no legal right, technically, to stop anything, because the account was in her name. I made a dramatic, agitated, yet crystal-clear case and explained that my mom was not of sound mind and would do something damaging with any money. They agreed to deny her access this time but would need more documentation on the legal restrictions, which were always being prepared.

I thanked them profusely and said I would

get the paperwork ASAP. I had by then known these bank clerks, policemen, and mailmen for over twenty-five years.

Mom got very angry that she was denied access to her account and stormed off. The bank had said it was some paperwork mix-up and told her to ask her daughter to help. The slimeball reporter next took Mom to a diner, where she proceeded to blab all about her horrible daughter over a cheeseburger. She told the dramatic details of how I "divorced" my own mother and stole everything from her. She went on a tirade about evil Perry and how he had brainwashed me. She loved saying I had basically joined the Agassi cult. Mom painted herself as a true victim and me as the ultimate betrayer. "Hiya, Peter!"

He took copious notes and had the story of a lifetime. America's Sweetheart was actually a Daughter Dearest! He had gotten everything he wanted, and Mom loved being able to vent and be heard. She felt wronged in every way and was letting the world know the "truth." He dropped her back at the facility with the same ease with which he had had her removed.

I moved her out of the facility the next day and sued the *Enquirer*. I won the case and gave the money to Alzheimer's research.

The story was blocked and I was ultimately protected.

Because of the wandering situation and the trust in strangers, as well as her mounting paranoia, I had Mom analyzed and consequently declared incompetent. My request to become legally affirmed her health proxy and guardian was thus immediately facilitated. Once again I was taking care of her, but this time it was out of necessity, not obsession. I tried to be upfront about it with her but was worried she would feel like I was trying to find more ways to betray her and steal from her. She seemed not to grasp anything that I tried to explain. Having more control made it much easier with regards to real estate sales and other legal decisions. I found another facility in New York City that specialized in patients with Alzheimer's and the many other forms of dementia. It was located on the Upper East Side at Eightieth and York. It only took two trains to get to and was close to Mom's and my old neighborhood.

Plus, I could sleep at night knowing she was closer to me in New York City, and with any luck I would not be getting any more phone calls from the police. In addition I could have my children still spend visits with her, which made her smile.

As a part of the entrance protocol, Mom had to be taken to a psychiatrist to be analyzed. I took her to a small office on the ground level of a big brick building. The doctor asked Mom simple questions about the weather, the day, and who our president was. It happened to be Presidents' Day so the question regarding our president was clearly appropriate.

But when asked the question, Mom couldn't remember the president's name. It was a cloudy day, and when asked about the weather, Mom smiled and said it was a great day outside because her daughter was with her. She recalled her birthday and other details about herself with no problem, but it was clear there was some sort of impairment.

The next part of the test involved her answering some comparison questions. There was clearly one best answer to each comparison. This showed me something so extraordinary and sweet and heartbreaking.

"How are a boat and a vehicle the same?"

"They both have motors."

"How are a baby and a bud the same?"

"They both smell really good."

She failed.

This last question killed me, because it was so clear as to the way she thought. She thought with an innocence of a child. Some boats did have motors, and buds and babies did smell pretty delicious. She would not get cognitive credit for being anything but literal. Varied interpretation was not the desired goal. I tried to argue that they were not entirely wrong answers. Yet again I felt the need to stick up for my mother in front of a total stranger. The doctor later explained to me that based on all the tests and the brain scan, Mom was showing signs of developing dementia. All my frustrations, fear, and worry and what little anger I really and rarely possessed melted in abject, gut-wrenching, and profound sadness.

Of all the things I thought my mother would be dying of, dementia was not one of them. Her brain had so long remained seemingly sharp. Because of her wit and ability to notice details in human behavior, I thought her mind would be the last to go. I was sure it would be her liver that went. She was also from hearty German and Irish stock, and because her mother had lived past ninety, I was sure my mom would outlast all of us, or at least her wretched mother.

I took her back to the new facility. It still didn't feel as if Mom really belonged in a place like this. She didn't seem like the other people, at least from my perch on self-denial hill. She still had the capacity to communicate with the staff in a way that did distinguish her from the others. She still had her wry, sarcastic approach to some things, and the staff got a kick out of her. Mom started going to Saturday Shabbat ceremony with a rabbi who loved to sing. She told him she liked the singing and the music.

As time went on, she seemed to settle in a bit more and I made my kids visit more often, even if it was only to do their homework or take her for coffee. I went as often as I could but I really hated going. The moment I would see her I would get a sick and sad feeling in the pit of my heart. She reeked of sadness. She cried every time I started to walk to the elevator to leave. I always promised to come back, but she looked like a puppy in the ASPCA commercials or a starving UNICEF orphan with tears in her eyes.

This might have been the time to talk to her and get some type of closure, but all I could ever do was tell her I loved her and run away. It was too much for me to see. But hearing "I love you" seemed to light up her eyes for a moment and I took it.

But I needed and wanted more. *Please*

come back, Mom, I thought. *Let's try this again. You can do this.*

Mom was already too far gone to have any real conversation at all and nevermind the dual apology I had imagined.

But back at home, my family was thriving. We had fully moved into the new town house downtown. Both girls asked to have their beds moved to be against the wall. I smiled inside, remembering that first night Mom and I spent in our new apartment on Seventy-Third Street. I thought about the mattress being on the floor and against the wall and wondered if genetics were playing a part. There is something very cozy and seemingly womblike about having a wall to push up against.

I resisted moving their beds for them for as long as I could because the rooms were not set up that way and moving the beds would mean blocking a window in each room. The thought of the head of a bed right under a window made me nervous, but we don't live in LA, so earthquakes are not a concern. All my fabulous decorating down the drain. My girls were not concerned with the fact that the house had been featured on the cover and inside *Architectural Digest.* They wanted beds moved and crap hung up and taped everywhere!

"OK, fine, I'll help you move your beds."

"You're the best, Mom!"

"Yeah, yeah."

I have never told my girls about the apartment on East Seventy-Third, but they both wanted to shove their beds against the wall and stack the multitude of stuffed animals all along the side. They wedge their warm little sleepy selves with their backs to the wall and now sleep through the night. My younger daughter comes in my room in the mornings and she asks to cuddle and spoon. I now pull my own little girl into my body and I am the outside spoon this time. I am constantly reminded of the glorious nights' sleep in the bare apartment and being spooned by my mommy, but my daughter and I differ when I ask her whether my arm is too heavy. She often says, "Yes, a little, Mama." I would have never told my mother her arm was heavy even if I could not breathe. God forbid she lift it off me. I guess I should feel proud my girls feel secure enough to express their feelings to me.

I look at my girls when they are asleep and I marvel at how stunning they are. Their smooth, pure faces and tiny features seem to glow. Granted, it is also because they are asleep and not fighting or talking back, but

I do understand how every mother's child is divinely perfect.

I always thought I would be a great mom. I could handle babies and take care of them and was never scared to have them entrusted to me. I could soothe them and make them smile. I could always make them fall asleep in my arms and I could get lost in their skin and delicious smell. I was never disgusted by their diapers or bored with having to attend to them constantly.

But I *never* intended for them to grow up!

I never thought past the baby stage. I assumed I'd be a good mom because I could handle infants, never once considering their being eleven.

Now, after many years, I realize that my girls could not be further apart in personality from one another. Rowan keeps her emotions deep inside whereas Grier is a walking, ticking emotional time bomb. They eat differently, dress differently, think differently, and react differently. As I write this, Rowan is eleven going on twenty-two and Grier is eight and wants to be back in my womb. In addition, they could not be more starkly different from me, and how they relate to me is nothing like how I related to my own mom.

It took me a while to realize that just giving birth to them did not mean I knew who they were. It also was a shock for me to find out they weren't me, either. I assumed that because they were babies that I understood who they were inside.

I have to ask my girls who they are. They are not me. I am not them. It is easy to want to mold them. There is a difference between teaching and crafting. It is our duty to protect and love and impart what we think are life's truths, but we really need to support our children in ways that nurture their individual selves. And I remind myself that I'm still the parent anyway.

For instance, Rowan is very clear about how her friends treat her and what her needs are. Grier once told her that her best friend was not treating her well, but she kept wanting to spend time with her. Rowan said, "Well, she is obviously not your best friend, then, because best friends don't treat each other that way!" Later I found out the reason why Rowan said what she did was that I told Rowan the same thing when her best friend was treating her a certain way. She took what I said, remembered it, and applied it to Grier's situation. But back when I was a kid and my mother's daughter,

I, like Grier, would have taken the bad treatment just to have people like me. Wow, did I actually teach her that?

I admire Rowan so much because of how sure she is of herself. When she was a baby, I would watch her at the playground trying to get kids to play with her. She would sometimes get rejected over and over and she remained unfazed. I'd hear her say, "No? . . . No? . . . No? . . . OK," and she would then simply start to dance and play on her own. She was completely content, and sure enough, in a short amount of time the same little kids would start to gravitate toward her. Before you knew it, she was like the Pied Piper.

Rowan has always been very straight-forward and black-and-white. When she was two years old, she was in her car seat in the back of my SUV and I was pulling out of our driveway in LA. I had just gotten really mad at my mother for something. I can't remember why I was crying but I was upset and quietly crying in the front seat. I was trying not to be obvious, but sure enough Rowan didn't miss a beat. She quickly asked, "Mama crying?"

I had a decision to make. Do I lie and say no, I just had something in my eye? That would send the message that it was shameful to cry in front of others and that her instincts were not correct. I had to quickly think of what my little girl needed. She needed to hear the truth but also needed to know that her world was right and her mom was OK enough to be able to keep her safe.

"Yes, bug, Mama's a bit sad, but I'm going to be fine and I love you."

"Mmn, Mama's crying."

And with that she put her thumb in her mouth and looked out the window completely satisfied. As she stared at the passing trees I thought, *What! That's all I get? I'm upset here! Come on! Nothing?*

This thought made me chuckle. How different I was from my own mother and what a different childhood Rowan was experiencing. I never was able to stop being concerned about my mother and her emotions. I could understand how she wanted my continual doting. I felt a bit lonely as I sat in the car but ultimately proud that I had not made my problems Rowan's. I don't think I ever fully believed my mom was OK or safe herself. I grew to believe it was my responsibility to keep both of us safe. Anxiety became a constant in my life beginning at a very early age, but how I handled it changed over time.

Rowan actually scared me at times growing up because she seemed so independent that I felt she didn't need me. All my mom wanted was to be needed and wanted. As Rowan grows older, she fights me on so much that our relationship often causes me confusion, frustration, fear, and pause. But every now and then she surprises me with unsolicited affection or nuanced humor. My mother and I bonded the most through our humor. It was our go-to remedy when we were having problems. I believe that comedy is one of the only ways one can truly live in the moment. I have always used humor as my biggest defense mechanism. I believe I homed in on this part of my personality early on and used it as a way to cope with life. It helped me escape Mom's alcohol. Mom and I shared a bond in comedy, and if we were laughing, we were temporarily OK. It became my vocation on and off camera.

Humor has become a point of connection between Rowan and me as well. Instead of its diffusing angst, it is just another way for us to be honest as well as vulnerable. I'll never forget the first time Rowan launched into a full-on impression of an old lady from the Bronx. She was incredible at it. For a moment I saw my younger self in her and felt emotional and strangely proud. We were with my half sisters over Thanksgiving when Rowan suddenly began asking me questions as if we were two old ladies sitting and gossiping on a stoop in the "old neighborhood." She shocked me and I jumped into the impromptu improvisation and felt so close to her. We all laughed hysterically. It was oxygen in my veins like it had been with Mom. I flashed back to skits my mom and I used to do just for one another and was very moved by all of it.

Grier and I have a very different relationship. She rarely challenges me and is incredibly affectionate with me. She had the most fun with Toots because Mom was regressing by the time she was born and could play with blocks and toys with Grier for long stretches at a time. Grier is also a mini-hoarder in training. Like my mom, who was the queen of collecting, she loved all the little dust-collecting tchotchkes my mom would give to her. Grier loves to put a coin in her "maybe need pocket" of her jeans, and it's the same kind of mini-pocket in her own jeans that Mom had pulled a nickel from when she was in the holding cell in New Orleans.

Grier is extremely emotional and once said, "You are everything that's wrong with my life!" She was mad at me for putting her sister in a time-out and crying and hated me for it. Not long after this outburst she added, "You know, Mom, the minute I say something mean to you, I wish I did not say it, but I can't stop it before it comes out of my lips." I love when my girls express such raw emotions so honestly. It hurts my feelings at times but I have to admit I am relieved that they can be so honest with their emotions and possess the freedom to express everything they feel. I think I was always way too concerned with my mom's feelings to even notice my own. The same drama that Grier embodies when she is mad is the same she shows when she is happy.

"Wow, I can't believe you love me, Mom! I don't know why I just said that!" she'd say. Or "I just love you so much it *horts*." Or "Mama, you are my heaven!"

As beautifully layered as my relationship is with my daughters, I do believe it is a much healthier one than mine was with my mom. Mine was deep and wonderful at times but extreme. It was not founded on security but on a sometimes irrational love mixed with intense codependence.

There was never any lack of love, but that's what made it hard. There was also a good deal of fear from both sides. She always feared I would leave her. I always feared something would happen to my mother or that I was not good enough for her. I never doubted her love for me but I was perpetually worried about her well-being and self-esteem — the things mothers usually worry about for their children.

My girls don't doubt my love for them, either, but they are also quite secure being away from me. They rarely feel they need to check on my state of mind or my whereabouts. I had to work on not being threatened by their autonomy because I grew up thinking that real love had to be based on codependence. Independence equaled abandonment.

In late 2011 my mother began to fade further. She was very settled into the Eightieth Street residence and I had settled into a new routine with my life and her care. I was doing *The Addams Family* on Broadway. One night after the show I was walking into one of my favorite little pubs that sold my favorite Belgian beer, Duvel. As I sat and ordered, Carmine, my bodyguard and driver on all Broadway shows, got a phone call from the facility.

Mom had complained of shortness of breath and heart palpitations. She was being taken to the emergency room. I had not yet taken off my Morticia makeup but was just going to have a quick beer before going home. I had to come straight away because she was asking for me. I chugged my beer, and Carmine and I ran out.

When I arrived at the hospital I went in to visit Mom, and an aide from the residence was feeding her bits of a ham sandwich like you would to a baby. She seemed very content being hand-fed. But Mom took one look at me, bolted up, and started to move to get dressed.

"I'm ready to go home now. I am ready to go."

She thought I had come to take her away, like Calgon, and I am sure some place deep in her consciousness, she knew if she had any emergency I would show up. I settled her a bit and told her I needed to talk to the doctor to get some information.

I stepped outside to speak to the doctor on rounds. He explained that she was checking out fine but that he was a bit concerned about her blood pressure and how disoriented and scared she seemed. He said he could not say she *had* to stay overnight, but he did suggest that it wouldn't hurt. It was late and maybe she should sleep.

That was music to my ears. I wanted her

watched and accounted for through the night. And I needed to sleep. At one point in this discussion, I glanced through the small window into Mom's room and she saw me and started to sit up again, except this time she began ripping the IV and tubes out of her veins. I burst into the room and there was blood spurting around like spin art. Here I was, with my white Morticia face and bloodstained red lips and dark kohl-lined eyes, trying to control Mom and the whipping-around tubes. It looked like a scene from *Tales from the Crypt*.

"Mom, Mom, Mom, please calm down and relax. You need those IVs to stay in for a bit."

"But I want to go home. With you."

She had not yet ripped her heart-rate monitor off and I could clearly hear the beeps of the machine. It became like a cartoon, because every time she heard something she wanted to hear, the beeps slowed and became steady, but every time I told her something she did not like or want to hear, it sped up.

"Mom, calm down, I am here." . . . Beep . . . Beep . . . Beep.

"You can't come home with me right now." . . . Beepbeepbeepbeepbeepbeepbeep.

"I will come back in the morning, which

is only in a few hours, to get you." . . . Beep . . . Beep . . . Beep.

"But, Mom, you have to stay here tonight to rest and have the doctors make sure you are OK." . . . Beepbeepbeepbeepbeepbeepbeep.

"But I'll be back." . . . Beep . . . Beep . . . Beep.

I finally settled her and they gave her something to help her relax. Carmine and I belly-laughed hysterically about the heart-monitor symphony the whole ride home. You could not make this stuff up.

CHAPTER EIGHTEEN:
THEY DIE FEETFIRST

The building that housed the facility we'd moved Mom into stood alone and was dedicated solely to those various forms and stages of dementia. It would prove a great fit for Mom. The staff was attentive and loving and there were many activities. There was a salon and outings and crafts and musical events. A rabbi came to offer services and a priest came every Sunday.

Each floor had only eight residents and was well staffed. The higher floors were designated for those patients further along in their decline. Mom began on a lower floor and could often be found sitting at the small reception area fully dressed and perpetually ready to leave, lipstick and all. As the first year progressed she stayed on a lower floor, but as she entered her second year the director suggested that Mom be moved to a higher floor. She was beginning to show signs of incontinence and was taking her Depends off and hiding them behind her armoire in her room. She then would have accidents and . . . evidently it was not pretty. I did not want to hear the details, but to them it was just another day at the office. The first time the situation was described to me, I got instantly sick. I had just gotten past the diaper stage with my daughters a few years prior. This was an utterly different thing. My God. I was not prepared to deal with adult diapers.

In the summer of 2012, Mom was moved to a higher floor and I visited as often as I could. I remember a woman I had seen often at the facility around that time, whose husband had also been suffering from dementia, asking to come in to say a word. I always thought this lady was incredibly put together. She was beautiful and effortlessly chic. I would be in my sweatpants and sweater, feeling like I was somehow being disrespectful by not dressing up more. I would see her thin frame in a woolen herringbone suit with an A-line skirt, telling her husband she loved him over and over in a cheery tone or feeding him pastina. It made me well up with tears. She came in and said she wanted to thank my mom. She wanted me to know that my mom had made the place "real" for her.

She explained that in her early months at the residence she would see my mom dressed up and with her lipstick on downstairs sitting with the receptionist for hours at a time. Mom wanted the company and to be the welcoming committee. This woman said that Mom had always been so nice and thoughtful to her, complimenting her on her outfit or jewelry whenever she'd arrive to visit her husband.

The truth was I'd been watching the woman for months. I'd see her dancing with him during holiday get-togethers when there was live music. I'd think about them dancing at their wedding, and then consider how tragic it must be to have your husband not recognize you. I guess I was projecting to avoid the sadness that engulfed me the day my mom could not recall my name. In the summer of 2012, I asked her what my name was and she just stared and appeared to be searching for some clue. She lit up every time she saw me and could point to my pictures in magazines but could not access my name. I was familiar to her but she could never retrieve my name again. I even joked to her once that I was an "icon," and surely she was able to recall the eighties? Nothing.

Even though I retained my humor, it all

kept chipping away at my soul.

I began spending even more time with Mom and would sometimes just go sit with her and read a book. But one night, when I was away, I got an alarming call. She must have fallen in the bathroom, and was complaining about pain and acting agitated. The facility decided to send her to the ER. I was called and went to go see what was happening. There were so many doctors coming and going and asking me questions that I couldn't answer. I was supposed to be the closest person in her life, but I could hardly answer one question regarding her wishes or her medical history. In the end, they discovered that she'd broken her arm, but things quickly got worse.

I called Lila in Arizona and told her Mom was in the hospital and also hadn't been eating. She had gotten a feeding tube and evidently had gotten pneumonia because she was not swallowing and her lungs had had some fluid in them. The main doctor handed me a form and asked what my mother's wishes were regarding DNR. I had actually never heard of a DNR (which means a "do not resuscitate" order, but to me at that moment I could only think "do not run").

I stood out in the hospital corridor on an iPhone whose reception went in and out because of all the machines and signals, and I told Lila my mother might need surgery and asked her if my mother had ever given her any inkling as to her wishes should she die on the table during an operation. Her reply was the last thing I expected.

"All I can think about is that little boy."

"Excuse me?"

"All I can think of is that little boy."

"What does any of this have to do with what I just asked you? Does she want to be resuscitated or not?"

"Oh, your mother never planned on dying."

Holy fuck! I thought. I was going insane. The doctors were all waiting inside the tiny room for me to check a box and they gave me the impression that time was of the essence, and I was just now actually learning a hugely powerful piece of information. I settled my reeling mind and regained my composure.

"Are you intimating that there is a grave some place and I need to start to find it so Mom can be buried next to a brother I never met? And does that mean she wants DNR or not?"

"Well, I remember a medallion that the

priest gave your mother and me. I had it for years but it fell down the drain and when I found it, it was all black. He gave them to us after doing a small Mass for the baby. I think he was buried but can't remember where."

"You know what, I'll call you back! Thank you, and I'll keep you posted as soon as I get more info."

I checked the box for "Do Not Resuscitate." I reasoned that if she went, she would not be able to withstand the defibrillator paddles anyway. She was Catholic so I assumed she would let God make up his own mind. And even if Mom had wanted to be kept alive at all costs forever, I didn't want that. I was sure I couldn't handle it.

I signed the sheet, and as I was bent over the clipboard atop the tray table, my mom's favorite necklace, which I'd recently begun wearing, swung out over the page. It was a big gold medal of the Virgin Mary that some guy had given her along with a little aluminum disk, exactly like the one that Lila had just described to me. I had seen this medal my entire life and never knew why she wore it. I went home in slight shock at the day's events.

I was informed that the doctor had chosen not to operate on her arm for fear that the surgery might be too stressful. Mom was actually recovering and would probably be able to leave the hospital in a day or two, once the pneumonia cleared. DNR was no longer on the table, but the medal still was.

It was time to deal with the other matter. I got a glass of wine and called Lila back.

Now, finally, I heard the true story about Baby John, a secret Mom had kept almost her whole life. Mom had gotten pregnant with a man named Philip Brady. She gave birth to a boy and named him John after her dad and brother.

She had met the father at the Peppermint Lounge in Manhattan. He was married. He knew she was pregnant. Mom promised not to get him in trouble for having an affair. She must have said she wouldn't say a thing to anybody or ask for money, but wanted to have the baby. This was obviously Mom's modus operandi, a modern and sadly sweet one at that.

As far as I can tell, Mom had also been with Murray (the same boyfriend she'd surprised by removing her fur coat), who was eighteen years her senior. Somehow they were dating when Mom went into labor and he was at the hospital for the delivery. He was convinced the kid was his, and his name was put on the birth certificate. She had the baby, but Lila told me that he died in the hospital within twenty-four hours. The baby maintains Murray's last name and supposedly is buried somewhere in New York. At the burial, a priest evidently performed a service and then returned to give that saint's charm to both my mom and Lila, her best friend and my future godmother. I assume Lila had been meant to be named godmother to Baby John as well.

It all made more sense now. Her terror when she had me so early. The fear, the squeaky door, the poop, the worry about the crib turned to the wall indicating a kid would be adopted. The strap attached around the chest. She panicked because she'd had a loss before. She was gripping on to a life — hers, mine, and Baby John's.

The memory must have been too devastating for her to drudge up, and my own miscarriage must have derailed her and thrust her back to that horrible memory of her own loss. No wonder she couldn't help me.

I remember sitting on the floor with my friend Stephanie years earlier, after my failed attempts at conception and my eventual miscarriage, thinking, *Why am I not allowed to be normal and have a baby like anybody else? I don't work properly. I am a failure.* Mom always wanted me to be special, and I worried that this failure to become a mother was a by-product of being so "unique." Of course I wasn't normal. I was Brooke Shields. I wasn't perfect, though, obviously, was I?

No matter what it all meant, I had finally learned the whole story, or as much as was available.

Once Mom was back at the residence, it seemed that she was exhausted and began spending most of her time in her own room instead of in the floor's common area with the TV. She had totally stopped her reception-area visits. Her sister-in-law and nephew and nieces came to visit, as did Lisa, Bob, Lila, Stephanie, and Lyda and a couple other close friends of mine who knew my mom in her later years. Her full-blood sister never bothered. It was tough on Diana and she explained she did not want to see Mom the way she was. She was satisfied remembering the laughter and the fun all of us had had together.

I was with Mom the whole time at the end. It was so hard to watch her all bent and rigid as if rigor mortis had already begun to take hold. Except for the liquids that gave her pneumonia in the hospital, Mom had not eaten in almost a month. We called in hospice to start to visit once or twice a week. When I told them how long she had gone without food, they said they had never seen anything like it before. Of course not. This was Teri Terrific. She defied the odds. This was about a few weeks until the end.

Her face was becoming pale and twisted and she'd bite anything that got near her mouth, including Lisa's neck once as she was trying to tuck in a sheet. Either her lips were tightly pursed or her mouth gaped open. Her skin was remarkably smooth, soft, and unwrinkled.

The only sounds she emitted were dry mumbles, where her chin would flap like a ventriloquist dummy and her lips would dryly flutter. Cries of resistance could be heard every time someone tried to move her at all. Her fractured arm must have been excruciatingly painful. Her hospice aides flipped her over like a dead body in order to wash her and change her diaper and powder her. The bizarrely green-brown contents of her body were just the same color as an infant's.

Her fists were clenched, and whenever I tried to open her fingers to clean her palms, she would try to bite my hands and scream through clenched teeth. She once bit the lose skin that covered my knuckle. She clenched down and simply would not let go and just bit and bit. As at the elbow, there are no nerve endings, so I just let her bite as much as she wanted. She wasn't strong enough to break the skin. She was never able to relax, not once during that time. To get disengaged from her clenches, I pried her jaw open like I do with my dogs when they pick up something from the ground and won't give it back to me. Biting never seemed to give her any relief, either. I guess she simply did not want to go. The feeling of fear radiated from her and all throughout the room.

At times Mom had fits of emotion, widening her eyes and looking terrified. At others, she would gaze up with a deeply worried expression and stare at a spot on the ceiling, scared and with seeming anticipation toward something. Lila told me she was looking at the angels, but she looked too frightened to me. She looked like she was seeing the Grim Reaper. I thought anything divine was supposed to elicit beautiful and relaxed emotions. Mom's eyes pooled with fear and panic.

■ ■ ■ ■

The end finally arrived in late October 2012. As the fates would dictate, it happened that this period of time was devastating not just for me but for the entire East Coast as well. Hurricane Sandy had ravaged New York City as well as the entire coastline.

It was the deadliest and most destructive of the year and the second costliest in US history. Unofficially known as Superstorm Sandy, it hit New York and New Jersey on October 29 and created havoc. In the city alone we were experiencing a widespread power outage and a halt to life as we knew it. I was getting the feeling that Mom was getting close to dying because she was so unresponsive.

I did not have the awareness or the perspective to see the personal symbolism in all of it. New York City had no electricity, no water, no public transportation, and the National Guard was patrolling the streets. And those of us in Manhattan were considered the lucky ones. Other parts of the city looked like war-torn areas in need of real relief.

There was no gas to be bought, so when

our car made its last trip uptown for me to get to Mom I had no way of getting back. So I stayed there. There was a declaration of a statewide state of emergency and Governor Cuomo had requested a pre-disaster declaration on October 26. I joked to my mom that if only I had gone to her years ago and requested a pre-disaster declaration, maybe things would have turned out differently.

I came to refer to all of it as Hurricane Teri. Close friends would nod in agreement when I said it was all by design. My mom would never allow herself to be overshadowed by anything, especially not a hurricane with a name like Sandy. It was as if Mom were spiritually declaring, "Fuck you, Sandy! I'm Teri and ya ain't seen nothin' yet!"

I'd joke that she had orchestrated the whole thing so I would have to stay by her side. I was by no means minimizing the pain and loss and devastation that Sandy created and that countless were still enduring — I was trying to stay present and intact, and humor was once again my only resource.

On October 30, the night before she died, I was sitting in a chair next to her bed and three women from the staff, who had ended their workday, popped their heads in and asked if they could say good-bye. I was surprised. I'd been coming there for weeks — how did they know now was the time to say good-bye?

They handed me a three-quarters-full bottle of Poland Spring water. Since we were smack in the middle of Sandy's wrath and were rationing everything, I made no mention of the cracked seal on the cap. (It didn't cross my mind that this residence had generators and hoards of supplies should disaster strike. Everything was available that people needed.)

I took the plastic bottle and held it in my hand and thanked them. The more maternal one of the three kept saying, "We are worried about you. You have not eaten or had anything to drink in a while and we are worried you are not staying hydrated."

I said I was fine. A friend of mine had brought me soup earlier, and to be honest, I was (shh . . .) planning on having a snuck-in Duvel in a bit. They stood for a while and then suddenly, strangely, all plopped down on the floor in Mom's tiny room. Well, I figured they were planning on staying for a while so I joined them. Mom was propped up as usual on multiple pillows and showed no signs of awareness that anybody was in the room.

The same staff member reiterated that they were concerned that I was not staying hydrated. I needed to drink! *OK,* I thought. *Wow, stop bugging me. . . . I will show you that I will drink.*

I took a huge swig of what I thought would be water from my little plastic bottle, only to discover that my throat was on fire with pure, marshmallow-flavored vodka! Not wanting to seem unappreciative or square at all, I sputtered, "Wow . . . thanks. . . . I needed that!"

Smiling and nodding, one of the ladies proudly announced it was very new and was called Fluffed vodka. Wasn't it delicious? Huh? I felt like gagging. I hate any flavored anything. I drink my vodka straight and with a twist. No chocolate, cake, eggnog, or cotton-candy-flavored vodka for me, ever. But, I guess, it was time to make an exception. Down the hatch with another smaller gulp.

Then one by one each of these beautiful, hardworking, warm relative strangers began pouring shots from their own vodka in plastic bottles, into tiny pill cups, like I'd seen in the movie *One Flew Over the Cuckoo's Nest,* and raising them to my mom. The toasts began. We raised our mini "glasses" as each person told her version of how my mom had affected her life.

One woman still in her hairnet began by saying, "I call her 'My T.' " Another said she liked to call her "Teri Town." Others preferred "Mamma T" or "T" or simply "T-town."

Mom lay catatonic in her bed, mouth open, seemingly oblivious to what was happening. The bottom half of her body looked like it had melded into the mattress. Only her head and shoulders, propped up on the pillows, seemed to be in the room.

One story involved Mom going up to a woman and saying what a beautiful smile she had — the first time she had ever received such a compliment in her life. Another told a story about a daytime attendant who always asked incredibly obvious questions. Mom's new friend was wheeling in the lunch tray, like she did every day at the same time, and this person asked if it was lunchtime. The attendant rolled her eyes, and Mom, seeing the exchange, made a face accompanied by a rude gesture, signifying that she, too, thought the question was dumb. Mom made people feel noticed.

Another toast included how Mom knew when one of the ladies was having a bad day and was trying not to show it to the residents. Mom went over to her and said that no matter what was going on in her life, it would all end up OK in the long run.

She touched these women in varying ways and they kept repeating how much the staff as a whole had adored her. One of the women said that she always knew that Mom "had a little Dominican in her." As did I, evidently, from the way I "gulped down that vodka!" This comment incited a mini-debate over whether Mom was more Dominican, Puerto Rican, or Cuban and what the merits of all were.

This woman had once been asked by her supervisor to get a bottle of wine that was hidden under my mom's bed. She was to tell Mom that she could have the bottle but just not keep it under her bed. The bottle would be safe in the main office downstairs and Mom could have it whenever she wished (I had no idea Mom was getting access to wine from the inside, but it didn't surprise me). She entered her room and asked Mom for the bottle, and Mom complied readily by proceeding to pull out from under her bed an entire *case* of red wine as if it was the most normal thing in the world. Why have just one bottle at hand when you can get a whole case? Makes sense. Take out the middleman.

I shared a story about how Mom once used a turkey baster to infuse the breakfast melons with vodka while we were on a river-rafting trip down the Salmon River. The ladies loved that one.

These stories continued until the staff had felt like they had gotten a chance to tell me what Mom had meant to them and how funny and sensitive she had been. I was not at all surprised by any of this, because it had always been my mother's way. She always immediately connected with the staff at places to make sure that they never felt like she was better than they were. She always said that the working people were her people. Mom had a talent of making strangers feel special. She put me on a pedestal while placing herself, pinned, under it.

To end the good-bye, the first staff member held up a plastic pill cup filled with Fluff vodka and motioned to me that she wanted to put a bit on Mom's lips as a toast.

I said, "Sure, it's not like it's gonna kill her. Go on, give it to her." Now, Mom's mouth had been open for days by this point. The cup was pressed to her lips, and in the same reaction that caused Mom to bite my finger and Lisa's neck, Mom's teeth clamped onto that cup like the Jaws of Life. Even though she basically did that to anything that got near her mouth, it was pretty funny. I didn't ruin the "funny" part with an explanation. The women all squealed with laughter and a declaration of Mom's love of booze. All at once there was a ceremonious raising of the last cup to God, and Mom, and life, and those we love. It was one of the most surreal moments I have ever experienced. It was tragic and sweet and real and odd and funny and profoundly heartbreaking.

Finally, it was time for them to leave. I thanked them for what was now my empty bottle and I was then alone again with my near-death mother.

The Fluff vodka had made me tired, thankfully. I had no way to get home because of the continued mass-transit strike and lack of gas. I had no place to be. My kids were fine, bunking with evacuated friends at my home, where we had a wood-burning fireplace and candles. The city was shut down entirely and I had had Fluff vodka for dinner. I decided I would get into the bed with Mom and get some rest.

I slept in the bed with Mom the whole night, not waking up once. I raised the side rails so I would not tumble off during the wee hours and set off some alarms or sensors. I slept hard. I have no memory of my dreams.

That next day the daytime hospice nurse arrived at 9:00 A.M. and changed Mom's diaper and bedding and washed her hair. Mom loved animal prints. In her tiny freestanding blond-wood closet she had two leopard-print blouses. One was made of slightly stiff cotton with neon accents. The other was silk with a smaller print and no accompanying obnoxious color. I started to give the aide the silk one and then selfishly and morbidly changed my mind. I wanted the silk one for myself, and with dark humor joked to myself that it would be a shame to burn the more expensive silk one. I knew that if it had been anybody else in that bed and Mom and I had been making the same decision, we would have made the same joke.

Mom was now dressed from the waist up with her hair combed. I tried to pry her fingers open to put in some talc. Her fingers were so clenched, and as had become the ritual, she screamed through a once again clenched jaw and tried to pull herself up to bite me with the front of her teeth. I gave up and just calmly said, "OK, Mama, it's

OK, no powder."

The attendant tucked in the sheets and was changing Mom's socks. I rolled my eyes and shook my head when I saw that both pairs of socks were actually the gray unisex kind with no elastic that the airlines sometimes give away. The no-elastic part was fine, but it still struck me as funny, typical, and gut-stabbingly tragic that they were the same socks the airlines provided. They are usually offered only in business class, though, so maybe Mom thought them special and herself fancy. Mom just loved anything free, including the menus on airplanes or the tiny dishes for butter. Back in the day, Mom would take everything from everywhere. She wiped clean anything travel-size she could get her hands on at hotels and on planes and from cleaning carts. She even pilfered the linens from Japan Airlines' table setting from first class.

The worst was one year on Halloween when she decided that instead of candy, she would make little care bags of mini toiletries to hand out. I begged her not to and suggested we instead donate the stash to a women's shelter. Disaster and humiliation diverted as mini Butterfingers and Hershey's Kisses replaced the shampoos and conditioners.

Well, this day was Halloween and the recollection gave me pause. This pause would turn out to include the last smile I would feel on my face while she was alive.

I was shocked out of the moment by the insensitive aide, who grabbed Mom's airline-sock-covered feet and announced, "Oh, so cold. Yup, in my country we say they die feetfirst. Yup, that's what they say. . . . Feetfirst!"

I did not know or care to which country this woman was referring. I did, however, wish she was currently in it. I could not believe the lack of compassion she was exhibiting. However, I did go feel my mom's feet, and they were indeed colder than the rest of her and colder than usual. But it was almost November so I overlooked the callous comment. I could never really bring myself to say she was dying.

I put the blanket over Mom's gray socks and pulled my chair around to the side of the bed. I sat in it facing her. I put a classical music station on my iPhone and held it up to her left ear. I saw no flicker of acknowledgment of the music but tried to believe the people who told me that the hearing was the last thing to go.

I sat trying to read a book and kept glancing up at her eyes to see if there was any movement under the lids. I periodically held the back of my hand to her open mouth to feel air, just like the mirror Mom held to my mouth to check for steam. I'd also stare at the sheet over her chest to make sure it was still rising and falling with her breath. All of a sudden my iPhone chirped and it was Lisa calling. The phone call interrupted the music. There was still almost no movement from Mom. But every so often a slight, almost imperceptibly faint rise in the white cotton sheet would occur. I breathed then, too. Mom's body seemed so heavy and flat, as if it had melted into the bed like Silly Putty in the sun.

I picked up the phone and with the other hand touched Mom's left arm. I had long since stopped trying to hold her hand because she would clench her fist tighter if I even tried to shove my fingers in between hers. I was giving Lisa the update when Mom suddenly and violently clamped closed her mouth with a smacking sound, teeth crashing, and then equally as quickly and forcefully sucked in a widemouthed breath. She then brought her lips back together. I blurted out to Lisa that something was happening and I had to hang up. I dropped the phone and stared at Mom's chest. It was still slightly rising up and down like the pulse of the light on an at-sleep computer.

I worriedly shot a glance over at the aide, who was sitting in the comfy chair at the window, oblivious and fully engaged in her Sudoku puzzle. As much as I hated this woman and her cold-footed country, I still thought it better to have her around in case I was missing some kind of sign. This was a ridiculous idea, because she was not paying attention and, in the end, I had resented her being in the room.

Then it happened again. Another gasp of breath followed by a tight clap together of her lips. My adrenaline started pumping and I began to panic. I counted beats in between these gasps: one, two, three, four, gasp, shut . . . one, two, three, four, gasp, shut.

I just stared and was startled off my seat with each lurch of her breathing and accompanying gaped mouth. The time in between them varied as did the seconds in the open position. There would be nothing and I'd think maybe she died and then, bam, another gasp. There was no rattle like I had anticipated. Finally I said, "Ah, Mom? What are you doin' to me!?"

I was on the edge of my chair in a surreal and seemingly suspended state, focused and watching and waiting, but unclear as to what for! I was holding my breath in sync with hers, and it was like she died a hundred times! I took another quick peek to see if the aide was watching, which she was not, and returned to Mom. When her mouth was clamped shut I kept uttering "Ahhh?" in an attempt to ask the oblivious aide if *this* was *it*? But then Mom would pop her mouth open again and grab a mouth of air.

Mom continued to do this for what felt like an hour but what was, in actuality, only about thirty seconds. I stared, waiting for each gasp. And then, as suddenly and as without warning as it had all began, it just stopped. I waited for it to occur again. Nothing. It was the opposite of what I thought would happen. I always thought it would be an exhale — a slightly pushed-out pop of air coming from the back of someone's throat — that signaled the end. That was what the movies showed, often. Instead, my mother's mouth simply stopped opening. Nothing else happened.

It all just stopped happening. *She* stopped happening.

I exclaimed, "Ah, is that it? Is this It? Did it just happen? Ah, excuse me, whatever your name is, is she . . . ah . . . done?" I checked my phone for the time. It was

11:37. I couldn't help but release a quiet crying chuckle and say, "Oh, Mom, of course it's a thirty-seven."

Thirty-seven had always been my mom's favorite number. I never remembered why and always forgot to ask her, but I did remember that we always bet on horses or picked numbers that had a thirty-seven in them. I had been desperate for signs of any kind during the entire dying ordeal and instantly prayed that this thirty-seven was one of them. Of what, though, I could not tell you.

The aide got up in slow fucking motion and came over to feel for a pulse. Now it was my mouth that was open. She just nodded at me and muttered that she had called it. . . . "Yup, they always go feetfirst." Oh, I wanted to punch her and stick a plane ticket in her mouth. This woman then suddenly acted sweet. She gently placed my mom's hands back on her stomach, slightly overlapping each other like you see on dead people in open coffins. She then whispered some quick words that felt like a "Go with God or peace" or some sort of a sentiment, but I did not comprehend any of it. I could no longer decipher sounds. I felt like I was in a sound booth with the volume for the outer room turned off. Only the sound of my own heart pounding in my head kept me from passing out.

Oh my God. . . . Wait, no, wait a minute, can we go back?! Just for a minute. I have to grab something. I just need to get it.

I had this overriding urge to believe that I just needed to go retrieve something and therefore Mom could not die just yet because I needed to get my stuff. She had to wait to leave. She had to say something to me. Please, God, bring her back just so we can say good-bye with words and sounds and with closure. She needed to tell me something, anything and that she knew that I had always loved her deeply and that I was sorry if she ever felt hurt.

Wait — if I stare long enough at her, she will wake up for sure.

I took a deep inhale to calm down, cleared my eyes, and stood up over Mom to look at her face. I hoped she could somehow pop up and comfort me. I still wanted my mommy to tell me she loved me and it would be OK.

It was not that her face looked "peaceful," but it was true that she was no longer grimacing. What struck me, however, was that she no longer looked like my mother. She was not in there. Her skin was still so beautiful and almost iridescent. It was like silk velvet and her forehead was still warm. I desperately wanted to kiss it before she got cold so I could still feel the warmth of the living. I kissed her and told her I loved her and then added that she could come back . . . *now.*

But I was talking to a stranger and an it. I wanted to shake this being and tell it to give me back my mother. Then I realized I was not talking to a dead person but was addressing something else entirely. Something that looked nothing like Teri, or even human really. The woman I had shared life with was no longer in there. This thing lying in the bed was an inanimate object — an emptied package. I had heard all sorts of versions of the body being only a vessel, but they had never really struck me until this moment.

Maybe it is the soul or the spirit — or a myriad of different labels — but all I can say is my mom was no longer in the room. Her essence seemed to have instantly disappeared. I said out loud but to myself, "She's not in there anymore. Who is this body?" The room got very foggy and it felt alien.

I felt the panic starting to mount yet again and my eyes darted all around trying to find something I could recognize. Where had my mom gone? Where was I? Flashbacks of when I was a little kid and did not know my mother's whereabouts coursed through my body. On a floral chintz-covered armchair (oh, how my mom loved her floral and especially her chintz fabrics) sat a huge stuffed doll I had made when I was nine. It had a completely disproportionate body made out of heavy white linen. The chest and lower half formed a square and the arms and legs were tiny and stuck out like a brontosaurus. She had glued rows of thick yellow yarn on top of and around her head. I had given her a blue-jean-overall skirt. That was the best I could do and had to rely on my mom to sew in the blue eyes, small nose, and little lips that looked like a perfect bow. It had been one of the first things I had ever really sewn and Mom made me feel like it had been worthy of awards. I recognized this doll as the only real thing left in the room.

My mom was no longer occupying the space, and I did not know where she had gone. All I knew was that I had to *leave.* I had to get out of that room.

I grabbed the doll, a tiny stamp-size photo of me as a baby in a sterling-silver heart frame that was by the bed, and my purse and opened the emergency door. The buzzer always buzzed while the door was open and I had gotten used to it. Today, however, it seemed suddenly extra loud and long. I ran into one of the downstairs offices, half-thinking she'd be right behind me and I was busting her free from a cell. I brought with me a charger I had borrowed. If only I had thought to bring the charger down a little earlier, Mom would have waited longer to die. I was sure of it. That was the thing I needed to do to keep Mom alive. I tried to explain to the staff that I just had to return their charger. I just had to. I was never coming back there again to do it. "Here is your charger. Thank you." I knew when I turned to leave that I would not be back. I ran out to Eightieth Street and turned west toward First Avenue.

I got to the corner and stopped, not sure what to do next. I needed to get back to some place. I remember feeling like this on 9/11. I ran out of my apartment on Fiftieth Street and just started speed-walking up First Avenue. That day, like today, I had no idea where I was headed. Some taxis had begun to run again but I was suddenly afraid to get into one. Chris was in LA and not picking up his phone. I left him a message about my mom and just began pacing in a small radius on the southeast corner of

Eighteenth Street and First Avenue.

As I was looking up and down the avenue, a beautiful foreign girl was crossing the street in front of me. She may have been from Brazil or Spain — I couldn't tell — but she was very pretty, except for the cigarette that was hanging from her red-lipped mouth. As she passed, she recognized me and started excitedly to try to talk to me about *"Laguna Blu."* I began to feel like I'd black out right there. I think I said thank you and that she had pretty hair and then I tried to look away.

She was staring at me with a kind, questioning look. She asked if I was OK. I blurted out to her that I was not OK and that my mom had just died. Could I have one of her cigarettes? I do not smoke. I have never been a smoker. The times I have been drinking and have tried to join in, I felt incredibly and uselessly sick. But in this moment I wanted to feel that sick sensation even just to know that I was in fact still alive. I wanted to fill my body with disgusting smoke and nicotine and get that head rush and feel the sweating that precedes vomiting. She gave me one and went on her way after trying to say something sweet in broken English. I took two drags on the cancer stick and threw it out. I was alone

565

on the street again and had no idea where to turn.

I did not look for a cab but instead went inside a kosher meat market on that block. Standing by the refrigerated items, I called my friend Stephanie and asked if she'd come meet me here because I needed to go home and cook steaks. I was crying and saying how horrible it was to see what I had just seen and that I was afraid to be alone.

She said she'd meet me ASAP and told me to hold it together. An old couple was buying some meat nearby and had obviously heard me on the phone. I had not tried to be discreet. In fact, I believe I had purposely talked loud enough to not be alone. I knew they, too, had recognized me, and I secretly hoped that if they knew I was sad, they would say something wise to offer me comfort. It is amazing to me the comfort of strangers in moments of dire straits.

I was beginning to have the feeling I used to get as a teenager when I felt like I was disappearing. It usually happened in large crowds and I believed that if I screamed, nobody would hear me. I caught their eyes and tried to smile. Maybe they would understand my fear and pain. The old man nodded and said, "We know who you are." The woman then chimed in with some type of "circle of life" comment and I instantly hated them. I was so jealous of their old age and their seeming happiness and of the fact that they had one another. How could they know what my mom felt or how I was doing? How dare they try to help me? Who did they think they were? Fuck them!

I nodded, bought my meat, and went to wait on the street. I started to beat myself up for talking loudly on the phone and for looking to strangers for recognition of my pain. It was an affliction of mine of which I thought I had been cured and felt angry to have seen it rear its ugly head once again. Thankfully, Steph got to me and we drove downtown together. By the time we arrived at the house, Lisa was already there. She knew something was going to happen and cleared her day. I must have called her to tell her but did not remember much from the previous hour. Chris got me on my cell and I told him I couldn't talk because the girls were with me and if I stayed on the phone all I would be able to do was cry, hearing his voice. My mom loved Lisa and Stephanie like her own daughters and they knew her better than any of my friends. It made perfect sense to have us all together.

Another friend from our school arrived as well. I must have called her, too. I don't remember calling anybody but Stephanie. All I remember from the rest of the day and night was a big fire in the living room, steaks on the grill, and lots of wine. We managed some morbid humor so as to keep me from careening off a cliff.

Overall, I was numb. I was not tired but I knew I could not handle being awake much longer. Being awake was simply too dangerous. I was offered a sleeping pill but was terrified that I would have some kind of hallucination and not make it through the night. Some more wine seemed to do the trick, and I promised my friends it was safe for them to leave. My girls came home from a friend's house and let me sleep. Chris must have told the girls about their Toots. In the morning I opened my door to find a note from Grier that read, "Dear Mom I am sorry about your mom but she will be OK. It's OK to be sad. . . . I love you. . . ." She had erased something under the "I love you." "You will see her soon. . . ." I cried at how sweet the note was and then burst into hysterics at the part she erased.

It was October 31. The day that Hurricane Sandy dissipated, Mom dissipated, too.

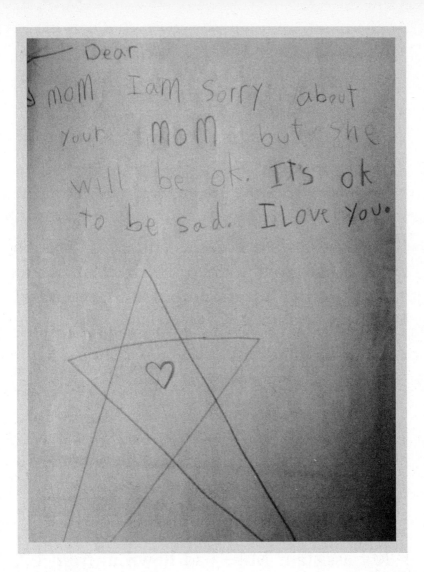

CHAPTER NINETEEN: CREMATION/LOOK, MA, NO PANTS!

The funeral home came and took Mom's body. I had gone there a few weeks prior to make all the arrangements. The funeral director had told me to also contact the church ahead of time, which I did. Afterward I even stopped at Finnegans Wake for a cold beer after speaking to the priest. It was a mini-tribute. One of Mom's old haunts when we lived on Seventy-Third Street. It was easiest to find her there because it was often the first stop and was just at the end of our block. I didn't even have to cross the street.

My assistant Mike had flown in from LA to help me prepare for the memorial. In the two days that he had been in New York City I suddenly decided to have him go through all my closets with me. We did a massive frenzy of a purge. I needed to stay busy because I was afraid to feel. I could not stop myself from whipping around my house and cleaning it all out. I combined my stuff with my mother's from the residence and we lugged four grossly heavy black garbage bags into our car. Mike had finally found gas, from a Hasidic Jewish man who had a minipump under a bridge in Brooklyn. It was surreal but Mike followed up on a tip from a buddy and we had wheels to get to the Upper East Side funeral home. Mom had a favorite thrift store that had been around for decades. It was the same one in which she bought her Puccis and my infamous gauchos.

Parking was hard and we could only find a spot five blocks away. Sweating and running, we lugged the bags across middles of streets and finally reached the store. I deposited the mother lode, and the little ladies behind the counter were thrilled. They recognized me but, when they heard my mother had died, did not ask for a picture. I explained it was my mother's stuff as well as mine and she had died two days prior. I needed to keep saying it to believe it was actually real. I joked to Mike that I should have said "the mother loaded," because Mom would have thought it funny and a bit outrageous. We rushed home because we still had no power and the house was empty and without an alarm.

The funeral director called and explained to me that they were going to use a different facility for cremation because their regular one had lost power due to the storm. I told him Mom would prefer the one without the power! I think he got the joke but was afraid to laugh. Funeral homes make me laugh nervously. Otherwise it is all just too horrible.

They had taken Mom's body to be embalmed so I could view her and say goodbye. Two days later I was called and told she was ready for me to see. I was first shown the vessels to choose from for after cremation but was unhappy with the choices so I said I would buy my own.

I was then sent up to the ice-cold viewing room. It was huge and empty except for Mom's basic wooden coffin at the far end. They said they have to keep the room cold because if not the bodies thaw. A detail I did not need to know. He closed the door and I stood for a moment before moving. I then walked across the huge empty room and it felt like an hour-long trip. There she was in her shitty stiff cotton leopard-and-neon-printed shirt and nothing on the bottom. I looked. Under the cover was just a plastic tarp and I did not see her big grandma panties, either. I did not inspect too closely for obvious reasons but I had to know about the stuff they don't show you. It did strike me as morbidly funny and knew that Mom would get a chuckle out of it all as well.

"Look, Ma, no pants!" I said. "Oh, Mom . . . here we go. Haven't you taken this far enough? You are not getting up, are you? I love you, you know that, right? God damn it, Mom. Really? We could have had more laughs. My babies are really funny, too. I am sorry."

And with that, I put the weird square-bodied doll in the box with her and placed my picture in the little heart frame, which by the way was one of the party favors from my sweet-sixteen birthday. Mom had over two hundred made with a picture of me as a baby inside. We would always find the extras hidden in surprising places. I tried to put the small frame in her now freezing hands but once again could not open her fingers because this time she was actually dead and stiff. I attempted to wedge it under the clasped part but it felt too Sopranos-like. I settled on placing it on her sunken chest and pictured it rolling off during her transfer to the crematorium facility in Long Island City.

I had to kiss her forehead, which was

indeed freezing and such a contrast to the moments right after her death. I am glad I did it, but wish I had not. My lips will forever remember the cold, smooth skin. She still didn't jump up or tell me it was all OK. And it wasn't OK. None of it had been but here we were. This was indeed it. The moment I had been afraid of my whole life.

"I love you, Mama. Bye."

I walked out, looking back once more and wanting to rush in and shake her. I was so truly alone. And she was so not ready to go.

I was quiet in the car as we drove away.

Three days later I got another call from the funeral director. He was hemming and hawing and I could tell something was wrong.

"Yeah . . . hi. . . . Well, you know how I said that we were using a different facility to do your mother's cremation?"

"Yes?"

"Well . . . yeah. . . . OK, well . . . we um, we started the process. . . ."

"Yeah?"

"And then, um, well, that facility lost power as well. So we had to then have your mom sent to a different one."

"OK . . . So was she . . . ah, lumpy . . . or just done from the waist down, or . . . You know what, *don't* tell me. I don't need to

574

know I am good. . . . Thank you."

I went shopping at antique stores for a sterling-silver container of some kind. I even toyed with the idea of its being a martini shaker as an inside joke. I could not find one big enough. Neither did my mother, obviously!

Anyway, I ended up buying a sterling-silver round jar with a lid that probably had been used for biscuits or cookies. It must have been some kind of retirement gift because it had engraving in a foreign language and a date around the lip of the lid and was very heavy. My plan was to put her on my bar and nestle her among the array of glass bottles and sterling knickknacks and stirrers. I figured this way she could remain forever close to the two most important things in her life: me and booze.

I know the joke would not be lost on her and that she would actually appreciate it. It is not against Catholicism to cremate, but a burial and a headstone is more often the norm. But "dust to dust" sounds more like cremation than decomposition if you ask me. There is not even a skeleton left after the oven. Catholics love funerals and a place to visit their dead, so I will eventually find her a spot in a mausoleum in the city if I can. But cremating her was what I wanted, and I did what I wanted to do. I did not like the idea of her in a box under the ground because it did not feel finished to me. She was never a woman to be contained. She was the kind who would rather go down in a blaze of glory than be in a box. It seemed fitting. I wanted her with me as well as near or in her favorite places.

This would end up being easier to do than expected because she, of course, did not entirely fit in the cookie jar. When the funeral director handed me the jar, he also handed me a canvas bag with the name of the funeral home printed on the side. It was shockingly heavy. I felt like I had just visited a gift shop in a theme park that had happened to be death themed. The director sheepishly said that she didn't fit in the jar, "So the rest of her is in this plastic sealed bag and blond wooden box. Sorry about that." At this point that was the least of my worries. I was just glad they finished all of her.

The wooden box sits next to our beloved dog Darla in a cabinet. I have yet to decide what to do with either of them. The sterling biscuit container indeed sits on my antique marble bar table amid the beautiful bottles and antique decanters and items we collected from all over the world. I can't wait to feel her watching me.

While Mom was dying I tried to keep giving myself the benefit of every doubt. I was there and loving. Toward the end, I consciously made myself breathe and stay present in every moment. If I drifted in attempt to escape the situation, I would snap back and touch her arm and tell her I loved her. I said what I thought I wanted to say. I said what I thought she would want to hear. I said words but it never felt cathartic or sufficient. And I will never know if she heard me or not.

I would have to remind myself that every time I visited her I did hug her and tell her I loved her. It had to have an impact. But it never seemed enough for either one of us.

It never felt satisfying and I never exhaled. I didn't think I started early enough, while she was able to respond. I kept beating myself up for not doing something differently. I kept having that gnawing feeling that I waited too long to start really spending time with her. But then I remember how impossibly hard it had been to be around her. I had created a distance so as to form my own life. I had to leave so I could return.

And yet I look back, and I realize I really tried. I did my honest best. I never fully abandoned her all those years. While in the facility I always went back in for another hug or to say I love you again. She would sometimes smile and mumble it back or she'd start to cry as I was walking away. Had my lifetime of devotion registered with her at all? It really was not supposed to end this way. Or maybe it simply was?

In the end I wanted her to forgive me for the "divorce" and for stripping the entire office and for putting her in a facility. I admit I do carry some residual guilt. But I did get a bit of a reprieve when Lisa told me that Mom said to her, "I can't believe Brookie did that to me with the office," then with a pursed-lip smirk added, "That took *balls*." Lisa said it was as if she was proud and had taught me well.

I got nothing like that from her during her dying days. Before she left this earth I never had that moment with her alone where she gave me peace of mind and heart. I never did with Dad, either. But the problem is they are the ones doing the dying. They can't make it about us, the living. But if she had been peaceful I might have been able to exhale. I don't know if my mother had ever been at peace.

Now that she's gone, I'm not sure what I miss. I miss the earlier years and who I believed she was. I missed our unabashed laughter. But most of all what I think I miss is potential. I was always waiting for the drama to be over. I believed one day it would all be fine. She would be normal and sober and happy and we could relax and enjoy all we had experienced in life. Her alcoholism permeated our lives and it was on a rampage to steamroll our dreams. Mom was not strong enough to fight it. But honestly the alcoholism didn't kill me. What did me in was the *hope*. I was never ever released from the hope. There was never any freedom from it.

I miss my mommy, but do I miss the idea of her more? I wanted to feel more relieved for her when she passed, but I don't feel that way. Mostly I just feel sad. It seems like such a shame and such a waste actually. And yet maybe if she had been healthier, my life would not have turned out as extraordinary. I can't regret any of my life but I do regret for her. I am OK. I was always going to be OK. She was not and that is simply sad to me. All I ever really wanted was for Mom to be happy and healthy minded. I wanted this mostly for her but it would have been an amazing gift for so many.

I also wanted my mom to accept me entirely and support my decisions. But like

I have said about my own children, we are not the same people. I wanted her to agree with me and it could not happen. I often had to force myself to go against her. I wanted her to be independent, and at the same time I wanted her to help me be independent. Two things that threatened her to the core. Independence equaled loneliness for her. She claimed she was independent, but it scared her to death.

There's an Erich Fromm quote I love: "The mother-child relationship is paradoxical and, in a sense, tragic. It requires the most intense love on the mother's side, yet this very love must help the child grow away from the mother, and to become fully independent." I did become my own person, but am not sure I was or will ever be completely independent of her. I was born from her.

Once we stopped living together full-time I didn't want Mom to be alone. I wanted her to maximize her many creative talents. She used to help cast male cowboys for Bruce Weber. Why not go into casting? She collected linens. Maybe open a linen shop? I wanted her to streamline her life and not become a slave to her possessions like she warned me against becoming. I wanted her to not be lonely. Admittedly, I would have been jealous — and even squeamish — if she had a relationship. But I'd get over it, because I'm a big girl. Plus, if she'd had one, it could have freed me considerably. At times I wished I had a sibling from her to carry the burden. I envisioned her traveling or having a fabulous shop in New York and fun colorful friends. I wanted us to have great holidays and family gatherings. Nothing is ever like it is in the movies.

I guess I harbored such romantic visions about who she could have been because I really believed they were options. I saw it all. Why couldn't she? I wanted her to never drink a drop of alcohol ever again and be released from her crippling addiction. I wanted her to know how fabulous I thought she was and how much more I thought she could enjoy. I wanted her to feel loved and to have truly loved herself. But that last key desire of mine never happened. Instead, she was sad inside and alienated everybody around her. Her loneliness was epic and I felt like I was watching a life squandered.

And, because she was not communicating at all at the end, her dying was even more frustrating and I felt increasingly helpless. I could not snap my fingers and change any of it. It is a crazy, gut-churning feeling to be alive while somebody is actually dying. We should not have been done yet but maybe you never are. Maybe it never is enough. Maybe that's the point. Maybe life just needs to be lived, period. Mom was leaving this world and I could not stop it from happening. My mother did not want to die but she spent a lifetime killing herself.

I will never feel like I said good-bye to either of my parents. But honestly, nothing would have been enough. I prayed she would hold my hand once more, make eye contact, or say I love you. They say that the hearing is one of the last senses to go and that she could hear me telling her I loved her, but I will never know. I will never know what she was or was not feeling. She seemed horribly scared to me and not at all peaceful. Maybe people just make that stuff up to help the living, grieving people? I have played and replayed those last few days and her last moments. I've done it drunk; I've done it sober. I've done it in therapy and out loud to myself when I'm alone. And I still can't fucking grasp it. I wanted to be there, and I was, but the horrific image will be etched on my retinas for the rest of my life. I would have beaten myself up if I weren't there, but I will forever regret seeing what I saw. I cannot believe my mother no longer exists. She is no longer present in this world. I simply can't believe it.

I understand nothing more about death than I ever have before. In fact, because I can no longer just imagine what it would look like, I no longer have the luxury of painting it the way I want to see it. I did *see* it and I did not like one bit of it. I saw it and I still don't get it. I have no clue as to what really happened or happens.

For me it helps to believe that there is a God of some kind because it means that maybe Mom is not alone.

I hope and pray that our loved ones find peace and are only dead to the material world. I wanted nothing more than to know Mom ended happy in her heart. Maybe that's why she looked so unfamiliar the second she died. Maybe the body is just a temporary house. There has to be more than this. There has to be something else. I know this world can't possibly be all there is. I have to believe she went somewhere, because otherwise it's just that she no longer is. I simply hate to bear that thought. I wanted some sort of proof she still occupied somewhere. I wanted a sign or to feel a "presence." But that is not the way it worked for me, evidently. I now know why people seek mediums or psychics. They want to believe and will take any proof.

Now Mom is just ashes. If I think about it too much, I can work myself up into frenzy. I can get claustrophobic and sweaty at the thought that I can't touch her or go back to the way it was earlier and in good times. Now she is not anywhere I can get to or even get away from. She has been reduced to dust divided into two containers. Not sure what to do with that reality. My religion only tempers me to a certain extent. I love it in theory but when somebody you love goes away forever, it just feels so final. I know love never dies, but if given a choice I really would prefer David and my dad and my dog and my mother to all be alive. I would only want my mother to be alive if she was sober and happy, though! Otherwise, keep her until she's prepared to be so.

My kids dealt differently with Mom's death. Grier cried when she was sleepy and brought up angels and heaven a lot. Rowan was stoic and only worried that it meant I would die soon, too. I always hated when people said how we are all constantly dying so I did not respond to Rowan with that. I reassured my daughters that I was fine and would be around a lot longer. I believe all kids deeply want to hear that.

Just because I no longer had a mother it did not mean I was no longer a mother. It actually hit me as very strange not to gauge any of my actions toward my children based on my mother's reactions or opinions. Even though Mom did not spend a great deal of time around my girls and me together, I always had her in the back of my mind. And she only had me in the front of hers. It was as if I alone existed in and for her life. I can still hear her opinions in my head today, but because she is now not actually alive, I don't feel the need to defend myself or yield to her way of doing things. The noise of her is turning down its volume in my thoughts. This is a bit of a relief because I no longer have to feel not good enough for her. She is dead and can't affect the course of my days anymore. That I welcome.

One night in bed Grier made two half ovals with both her hands as if she were about to bite into a burger. She said that this was us. We were together. I saw it as we were separate but also whole because of the other half. We started pretending we were eating big burgers and saying *"Yum."*

She then made one half oval move a bit up and the other slightly down so they were no longer parallel. "This is Rowan and me," she said. My heart cracked. I prayed her relationship with her sister would improve but right then it was all about fighting.

I explained that it would not always feel like that between her and her sister. I promised that Rowan loved her younger sister and said I believed that they would one day be closer.

She then made half a heart with her left hand and fingers and then did the same with her right hand. She first held them apart and then slowly closed the two sides to form the heart. She then said, "Mom, it's like this *heart* is our home."

Often it's at bedtime that I am moved to tears.

The other night I was lying down with Grier as I always try to do before she goes to sleep. Rowan stopped asking me to stay with her a while ago so I am savoring the one who still wants me. Grier asks to cuddle and I have to fight not falling asleep and waking up at 4:00. Sometimes I ask what she is thinking. Lately she has been saying she often thinks about Toots and Pop-Pop. I can tell she knows this will touch me and she wants to let me know she cares. I asked her what she was thinking about them. She never met my dad but hears stories all the time about him. She said she was thinking of what she would be doing with them if they were here now. I asked her what that would be. "Well, I think I would be reading my journal to Pop-Pop and I'd for sure be showing Toots my gymnastics."

I asked her if she was sad or missed Toots. Mom scared Rowan as time went on, but she played with Grier like a kid and had deteriorated mentally by the time Grier was old enough to know her. They played like buddies together and adored little trinkets. Of course Mom had bought the expired Happy Meal toys from a tag sale and kept giving them to Grier. I kept throwing them out because I hate the clutter my mother always represented.

Grier said she did miss my mother but was not sad because every time she felt like she missed her she would just realize that she could talk to her and that she would always be in her heart. Grier tapped both her hands on her chest and mentioned that even in school if she thought of Toots she could think of her as being inside her own heart. "Right here. And I don't feel sad. I can talk to her from here." This blew my mind and I promised to try to do the same thing. Mom once told me that she was trying a new therapy that when she wanted a drink she would tap on her chest bone with her fingers to remind her not to take the drink. She said it was supposed to trigger some kind of sense memory and help with addiction. Of course, she probably was just doing it at a bar and the bartender thought she was signaling that he serve her another drink. Anyway, I told Grier that that was beautiful and I would do the same from then on.

I know I have said that we keep those we love forever in our hearts, but hearing her repeat it with her little hands over her heart and in her tiny voice made me weep. I hope I can find that same comfort in my own heart that I seem to have taught her to have. Or maybe I didn't teach that? Maybe she taught it to me?

Grier provided one sort of comfort to me. Rowan did, too, but in a very different way. Rowan convinced me to let her get her ears pierced at the age of ten. It was six months after Mom died. I recalled that I was twelve when my mom took me to get both our ears pierced. She had never had hers done and wanted to do it with me. I went first!

I actually had always intended to only let Rowan get her ears done when she was twelve, but walked into my own trap. She had asked me at age nine and I said no, not until you are double digits! Forgetting completely that ten and eleven were indeed double digits prior to twelve, I had to follow through. I did go to college, I swear.

She and her cousin wanted to get them done together and it was to be a special birthday event for Rowan. Her cousin graciously waited until Rowan's actual birthday to get hers done at the same time.

My oldest half sister, Marina, lives uptown and suggested we go to her dermatologist. I had thought Claire's would have been the better bet and cheaper, too. Not that I try to ever skimp on my daughters where their physical well-being is concerned, but I had gotten my ears pierced at a mall in New Jersey when I was twelve and my ears didn't get infected and fall off. The mall kiosks did countless lobes a day and had it down from my point of view. I did not yet realize that the venue would turn out to be the least of my worries. But Rowan wanted to go up-town to be with her cousin, and my sister made an appointment.

Rowan and I were rushing late as usual and her cousin had already gone in. By the time we arrived, the cousin was smiling with two wonderfully pierced ears. Rowan sat down next and the doctor came in. She drew the dots on the lobes and asked me what I thought.

Remember, when I was young my mother was never, ever wrong in my eyes. She always had a question or a suggestion when we were at the doctor's as well as every other area in which she was completely untrained. She possessed impressive instincts in a variety of situations and I always trusted her above all. She often questioned the professionals and they often complimented her on her observations. She was also always bluffing her way through. I, however, thought she was God. Mom, therefore, could have had the lower right side of my chin and the outer left side of my eyebrow each pierced and tell me they were even and I would have looked in the mirror and seen perfect symmetry.

Unlike my mother, I usually ask Rowan her opinions before voicing my own. But in this case I spoke up first. I looked at each lobe and said that I had to be honest — I wasn't sure the dots looked centered. I wanted them each centered in the middle of the lobe. The doctor exclaimed that that was exactly why she asked the mothers. She wanted moms to give the stamp of approval. She did not say if she agreed or not. I felt so good at the moment — Rowan must have thought that her mother was even smarter than the doctor.

What I had not taken into consideration was that first of all, I was *not* a doctor, and second, my daughter's lobes (like the rest of the population's) were different in size from one another. The board-certified surgeon was, in fact, taking this into consideration. The dots were redrawn and the deed was done. I took one look at the final product and, getting instantly sick to my stomach, realized that I had inadvertently caused the holes to actually be uneven. Yes, thanks to my expertise, each lobe was pierced in its center, but when looked at head-on, one gold ball was, in fact, a bit higher than the other. I did not say a word, partially because I could not breathe, but mostly because I was terrified of my daughter's reaction.

I paid the ridiculously large bill, we all made a big fuss at how big our girls were, and we separated. I took Rowan back downtown and envisioned my sister and the family all celebrating my niece's perfect lobes. I was resigned to try to suppress all the feelings that were creeping into my consciousness. "This too shall pass" had become a useful mantra for me over the years, and I was reminding myself of it once again for comfort.

I continually tried to forget about it but with little success. However, Rowan didn't seem to comment so I thought maybe the bullet had been dodged. It gnawed at me, as things tend to do, and try as I might I could not suppress my self-hatred for having marred our firstborn.

A few months passed and Fourth of July weekend was upon us. After being asked the same question every week leading up to this holiday, I finally told Rowan she could indeed put on new earrings for the first time. I took her to get some fun earrings and the choice was a monumental one. After about an hour, I was numb. She chose a small cardboard square full of multicolored little Gummy Bears. We went home and the ceremonious changing of the earrings began.

Because I could not find music associated with the changing of the guard at Buckingham Palace, I found Bob Dylan's '78 single with that exact same title and gave it a shot. As we were swabbing each lobe with alcohol and talking about how exciting it would be for her to show off her ears to the families who were soon coming over for the Fourth of July BBQ, Rowan breezily said, "Mom, I think when you switched the dots on my ears, you actually made them uneven."

I almost instantaneously threw up. I no longer heard any music and had the feeling that I was falling into an abyss. My world suddenly narrowed. Mustering a voice that wouldn't betray my true emotions, I calmly retorted, "Really? I don't know, I think they look great."

We completed the switch and I sent her to put on her bathing suit. I quietly snuck into the next room and asked Chris if I could have a word. He'd definitely have a solution. I began deep breathing and when he arrived, I said I had something I needed to tell him and that I really needed his support and his help. I begged him first to tell me that we could fix it and it would all be OK. He had such compassion in his eyes and in the past has repeatedly met such frightening moments like these (for me) with true calm and honest but practical advice.

But his faced changed with the news and he just turned and left the room to look at our daughter. Suddenly he burst back into the room and blurted out, "One Gummy Bear's feet are sitting fine and the other Gummy Bear's feet are dangling off her lobe. She looks ridiculous. You are not a doctor. Why did you interfere? I can't believe you."

I was stunned and in shock. He had never reacted to me like this. He was defending her and was so angry and disappointed in me. I myself could not believe it. I was also instantly jealous of Rowan. And after I emotionally prefaced the entire situation by saying I felt terrible and needed help to fix it. This was fixing nothing.

Seething, I silently put on a bathing suit and a long caftan cover-up. I got a fresh bottle of sauvignon blanc from a local vineyard from the fridge and brought the whole thing out to the pool, just as I had seen my mom do countless times, except with red. I had every intention of finishing the bottle by myself, but to maintain a modicum of dignity and a semblance of being a lady, I was sure to bring a glass. Never let it be said I'm not a lady! I calmly went out to a chaise lounge by the pool and settled in for the long haul through my rambling and conflicting thoughts. Looking like the mother in *August: Osage County* before needing a binge, I hunkered down.

I stayed on that lounge chair growling inside and steadily drinking that entire bottle of wine. Maybe I was more similar to my mother than I thought. Friends began showing up for the BBQ but I did not move one limb, nor did I speak. I just lay their stewing, bottle in hand, and nodding like an old silent-film star to friends as they arrived. Everybody made himself or herself at home.

They knew me enough to just let me go through whatever it was that I was going through.

I let Chris be host and invisibly watched the scene unfold. I was so hurt and mad at my husband and so enraged with myself for interfering. I was angry with my mother for always seeming to be right, in my eyes. I was mad that I could not become the same sort of maternal superhero I thought she was. I was mad at Rowan for questioning me. As the backyard began to fill with noises of screaming kids and mingling adults, my wine-calmed mind drifted to an old video. In it I was about nine years old and Mom and I were on vacation visiting with Lila in Tucson, Arizona. She was working at the Biltmore Hotel and they had a huge pool and great pizza and frozen yogurt. Lila must have been videotaping me in the pool.

In the video, Mom is teaching me to dive from a diving board and swim the length of a pool. It was in the early afternoon and already blistering hot, but there she was, sitting on the edge of a metal and plastic slatted lounge chair in blue jeans and a button-down blouse. Just like a coach training his Olympian hopeful, Mom was calling out instructions to me with the utmost confidence.

Mom kept declaring, "Brookie, think out, not down, when you dive. Think out, always think out and to the other end of the pool." I can see her left arm swinging up and out, indicating a forward fluid motion all the way to the far end of the huge pool. I repeatedly dived off the board and resurfaced with the same gasp, spitting out the important question "How'd I do, Mom? How was that?"

It was seemingly very sound advice and made a great deal of sense. I guess it is important to always aim in the direction of where you want to end up while diving or doing anything else in life. However, I am not quite positive that her directions were founded on any true knowledge of how to dive. And she was so sure of her own advice, I took it as absolute truth. I just breathlessly continued on in my pursuit of the out-and-far dive, trying not to throw up from the inevitable belly flop.

It wasn't until years later, while watching this video, I remembered that my mother never learned how to swim! Mom avoided water — her uncle had drowned and I'm sure her mother never taught her — but I never knew any of that until I was an adult. I always just thought Mom didn't like being in water. She would wade in the shallow end at times or I would hang off her legs as she sat on the edge. On a cruise ship once, when I was about five, I went swimming and the water started sloshing around. I began to flounder. Mom didn't jump in but grabbed a server and he pulled me out to safety. Looking back, I never had any real evidence that she could swim. I had pictured her frolicking in the ocean, but I don't remember her ever actually swimming, let alone doing a dive.

What struck me was how convinced I was that my mom knew of what she was instructing. I never doubted my mother's ability in anything she did. Why would it ever cross my mind that she could not have been able to save me were I to have begun drowning?

Back on my chaise I was wakened from my daydream by a loud cannonball in the actual pool in front of me.

I looked at Rowan frolicking around and thought, *How come you question me so much? Why am I not your queen?* Suddenly, after years of professing that I wanted and planned on nurturing my daughter's independence and raising her as a healthy, secure, and unique young girl, I now wanted to take it all back and instill in her the same blind faith I held for Mom. I had always professed that I wanted to nurture my girls' independence and help thwart inevitable insecurities. Yet as soon as I became threatened, I changed my tune and wanted her to be as dependent on me and reverential toward me as I had been on and toward my mom. I wanted my daughter to look up to me with that vintage, unconditional love I had always had in my heart and mind for my mama. The moment I felt threatened, I changed my tune. I did want her to believe I was always right. Of course I hoped she was self-confident, but I sure as hell didn't want her to challenge me or think me fallible.

I realized I envied her independence. I was threatened by the fact that even at such an early age, she had begun to individuate. I ached from loving her and all the feelings that brought up.

In that doctor's office I had just wanted to be right. I wanted Rowan to think me smarter than everybody, including the trained professional. In recounting the earring story to her friends, I wanted her to say, "My mommy is the best; she knows even more than the doctors do."

After yet another cannonball the dog started barking. It was a signal to shift my focus back to the present. No more time to wallow in my self-pity and anger. I was beginning to get self-conscious alone on the lounge chair, and I shifted my thoughts. I had the reality of the uneven holes with which to contend but could not immediately do anything about them. In my defense, the corrected dots were clearly centered in the middle of each of her lobes. However, one had to look at only one lobe at a time to see that. Look at my daughter head-on and it was another story.

Fortified by the haze of the sauvignon blanc and renewed by the desire to fix what I had broken by myself, I settled the dog and resolved to contact the doctor the next day to review the options. Just as I experienced a hint of relief and renewed focus, a game of chicken was loudly being assembled in the pool.

It was Rowan on her dad's shoulders against another schoolmate on her dad's. Right before the match began, Rowan called out to the crowd. "People, I have an announcement to make. People . . . I . . . have . . . pierced . . ."

Oh my God, I thought, *here it comes — she's going to throw me under the bus!* I braced myself.

"Ears! Yes, that's right people, I, Rowan Francis Henchy, have . . . perfectly symmetrically pierced ears! *Bam!*"

She did some hip-hop gesture with both

her hands to punctuate this declaration.

Stunned, I just stared at her. Emotionally inverted by a joy I had not expected, my eyes welled once again. Rowan had obviously intuited the whole picture so clearly and wanted to take care of me. I slammed up against feelings of relief and joy as well as guilt and embarrassment at how much I, too, needed her approval. This dynamic was so complex and layered.

I felt so proud of my little girl's heart and her innate spirit, yet shrunk with shame that I had created a situation in which she felt the need to care for me. I silently vowed not to make my shortcoming her responsibility ever again. I should have remembered how I acted when she asked about my crying in the car all those years back. Rowan was being her grounded self, wanting everything to be OK. Standing chest-deep in the water with Rowan on his shoulders, Chris just shook his head and half smiled. His expression suggested pique, defeat, and pride.

We all celebrated the day of independence, and the irony was not overlooked on my part. I, too, shook my head.

That night Chris and I did not discuss the events of the day but instead quietly readied ourselves for bed. He broke the silence with the acknowledgment that a bigger conversation was necessary but sleep was calling.

The next day, after reaching the doctor and explaining my dilemma, I had a plan to offer. Taking Rowan aside, I admitted to having made a mistake and explained that we could take one earring out, let the hole close, and get it repierced. I emotionally added that I loved her so much and I had just wanted it to be perfect and for her to think her Mom was cool. I thanked her for what she did in the pool and said I really appreciated it. She asked me if I thought her ears looked OK. I said I honestly did. Rowan looked at herself in the mirror and then turned back me and said, "Mom, you didn't do it on purpose and besides nobody is going to ever notice. Can I go play now?"

I exhaled and was awed by how self-confident and forthright my ten-year-old was. Had I had anything to do with that?

I realized once again I still had a lot to learn. I forgave my husband completely. I would have been mad at me, too. I admitted to my own mistakes and where my own insecurities reared their ugly heads. I brought up the necessity of our being a united front at all times in front of the girls and we could always hash out our own differences in private.

It is not about not becoming my mother

as a mom. Nor is it about being her. It is about being as much of myself as possible and defining my individual relationship with my girls with respect for how they feel as well as how I feel. Using those lessons I have learned that I value and leaving the ones I don't behind. Rowan and I were both free enough to be ourselves and together managed to find an honest and healthy way out of a decent-size problem. I don't know all the answers but together we can learn.

I have to come clean and say that this was not the end of the Gummy Bear saga. A year later Rowan out of the blue asked if she could repierce her one ear. I said sure and we went to Claire's that afternoon. A new hole was pierced and it was not dangerously close to the old one. She even convinced me to get a third in my left ear. How could I say no? It was a little bonding moment and funny that this time, too, she went first, just as I had when my mom and I got our ears pierced together when I was young.

Who knew that little, uneven, plastic Gummy Bears could penetrate so many layers. Literally!

CHAPTER TWENTY: RETURNING HOME

In January 2013, Chris and I began looking for a house out at the beach. I hadn't spent time in the Hamptons in years. My dad's family had moved to Palm Beach and soon those beaches replaced the sand of my youth. However, Chris and I and the girls soon began getting invited to visit with various families from school who had Hamptons houses. Driving back into the city on Sunday night we'd talk about how much fun we all had and how relaxing it had all been. I began to reestablish a bond with the area, visiting the playground on which I had skinned my knee and crawling under the trellis under which I used to find tiny frogs. I'd run into people of all ages that I knew from my childhood. Invariably after I'd introduce them to my husband and daughters, these old friends would begin to reminisce about my father and tell me how missed he was. I even got to show Chris and the girls pictures of my grandfather that hung on the walls at the Meadow Club.

It was all very familiar and somehow comforting. It felt different, though, and as if this time my entry into this community had been generated by me. It was via my husband and girls that I had come to want to celebrate my roots. After a while, it became clear that Chris and I wanted our own place somewhere at the beach.

One random day, after years of wishing for and working toward the possible purchase of a second home, Chris just said, "What are we waiting for? We work to live, so why don't we invest in a house and enjoy it? It doesn't have to be in Southampton, either." We began the hunt and after a fun and exhausting search during the dead of winter, just three months after Mom's death, we found the perfect place — a modest, yet roomy house in the town of Southampton, about a mile from the water. It was fully renovated, would fit many guests comfortably, and had a big backyard and a freshwater pool. Our dream house was finally a reality.

We had cast a wide net and had looked everywhere from Southampton to Montauk. How funny it was that we should end up right back where it had all begun! Suddenly,

I was with a Realtor, driving past the place in which I learned how to swim and do the box step.

How serendipitous it had been to have been accepted at the perfect school and then become friends with people who all lived near one another in the town I actually loved. And how strange and amazing that it was my daughters who had brought me back to the place my mother had loved and to a life she had coveted. And how strangely sad it was that Mom would never see it.

The sale went through and I set out immediately to decorate. Given my mother's inability to ever finish decorating any of her homes, I was even more intent on quickly assembling furniture in every room. My goal was for each room to be livable and uncluttered. I promised Chris that I would not spend any money, but could easily furnish the place with what I currently had in storage. Dan and I had spent almost five years going through my mother's storage spaces — Beanie Babies, Louis Vuitton purses, and all the rest — and it happened that we were just about to finish and leave the space for good.

The day we emptied the unit completely and had trekked to Paterson for the last time it seemed almost too good to be true.

Mom had been moved to the new facility in Manhattan and had declined in mental health so that she had given up trying to fight me on the warehouse. She just knew I had sold some stuff and had money for her. I assured her I kept the jewelry and most of the art and special furniture, but maybe we did not need twelve Erté sculptures. Two would suffice. She seemed to be mollified by the amounts of cash we made at the three huge tag sales and the tax deductions from donations. As we drove away from the now cavernous unit, I looked out the window and saw the bronze monument of Lou Costello and a little park dedicated to him. He had been from Paterson. Abbot and Costello had always been a favorite for both my mom and me. We'd rush back from church Sunday afternoons to watch it together on Seventy-Third Street. Amid the seediness of this area stood this plump little man with a smile on his face. It looked as if he were waving me good-bye.

Now it was time to start decorating the beach house. Chris was away the weekend the movers came to Southampton for the big move, so I had free reign. I called in my personal troops and was determined to use as much preexisting stuff as I could.

For three full days, three of us worked nonstop, getting all of my mother's furniture and art scattered and perfectly placed. We staged it as if it were a movie set. We put down rugs and hung art. We made up the beds with various antique linens. In every room we found mismatched but functioning end tables, lamps, chests, and more. We moved a huge oak table by ourselves down a flight of stairs and into a basement to be used as a wrapping, craft, and work table. I wanted it to look cozy and eclectic and like we had lived there for years. We were able to fill the small pool house with towels and couches and a few coffee tables. An enormous collection of earthenware green vases that Mom and I had collected from various antique markets lined an old oak baker's rack. The Van Briggles, Roseville, and USA pieces added color to the room. We'd only take one break a day to eat dinner.

By the time Chris arrived I was shattered physically and mentally. I was an emotional wreck, having engaged with my mom's belongings so intensely over the past few days. Many memories were attached to all the pieces, and it felt like each one was imbued with her spirit. My mother's stuff was finally being put to use after decades of being paid for and transported all over the

United States. This was the first time some of the pieces had ever even been put to use. She would collect just to collect. She amassed for future homes she wouldn't even buy. Seeing it all finally staged perfectly in a home Mom would never see gave me pause. Mom never arrived at a place to actually use and enjoy her things.

Chris gave me a huge hug and was obviously blown away by how much work we had done. He marveled that it looked like a "completely decorated home." But I couldn't help but think his comment was like what you say when you see an ugly baby for the first time and don't want to insult the parents. He must have caught a glimpse of an expression on my assistant's face as he hugged me that suggested he tread lightly. He smiled and said, "It's great, babe. I'm starving; let me shower and take you all to a great meal."

At dinner Chris, sensing my fragile and fatigued state, lifted a glass and made a toast to us and to all the hard work we had accomplished. Cheers to our new amazing home! He then added a special toast to me, calling me "Mom" and saying he knew how much I was doing and that it was all truly appreciated. I felt so relieved he was there and let out a sigh that represented a mixture of weariness and relief. I drank my martini straight up with a twist and didn't realize the poignancy of the order until later. That had ultimately been my mom's drink of choice. We all counted our blessings and talked about all the things we wanted to do in our new home.

Later that night, I lay in bed, wide-eyed and staring up at the ceiling. Chris asked, "Babe, what is it? Are you OK?" In a trance-like voice I responded, "I hate everything, I'm getting rid of it *all.*"

Suddenly, I hated everything. It was eclectic all right, but seemingly done by a color-blind crazy hoarder person. I hated the old-fashioned style, I hated the smell, I hated the fact that Mom saved it all and that we had paid for the storage all these years. I hated her hoarding it, and us waiting and waiting for a dream house and a place in which we would be happy and at peace with one another. I hated that I gave so much of my own time to the navigation of it all.

What was meant to have been a fresh start for us all had developed into an experiment in clutter, in being stuck in the past, and in how *not* to decorate a beach house. I had hoped and believed the pieces would work and that this eclectic amassing of furniture and things would make for a charming beach home. But the truth was, I had outgrown the stuff. Assembled all together, after all this time, it just seemed dated. None of it felt like my taste anymore. I was no longer that person. I had changed and was no longer "shabby chic meets uptown Manhattan meets tramp art meets Connecticut housewife."

I felt sad, stupid, and slightly frustrated by the years that had gone into these past three days. I lay still and felt an unsettling sense of rage and sadness inside. I was surrounded by the things my mom savored, in a house she would have loved, yet she was not there to see any of it. And I didn't even like it in the end. It felt it had all been for nothing.

I knew not whether to scream or cry, but I was clear about one thing: I had to rid myself of almost everything. I realized it could possibly be considered excessive, but I knew it was necessary. Suddenly, I didn't care about spending money on new pieces. I had some cash left from the tag sales and I wasn't going to go on a crazy buying spree. I just needed this home to reflect the *me* I was today and the family I had created. Some might say I was ascribing way too much to inanimate objects, but this was my entire past and my upbringing and the life I had only shared with my mother. These things represented our unfulfilled dreams. Now I saw it all as only holding an obsolete promise. I had attached so much to these *things*. I saw in them a feeble chance to go back and make right the "almosts" in our life. I saw it all laid out and knew I could never go back. Mom and I never finished a home and enjoyed it together. We just kept chasing the stuff and the destinations and never inhabited them. It felt like a real end to a huge period of longing.

The next day I started peeling away the things that gave me the most anxiety. I found an antiques dealer in the next town over and engaged him to help me sell most of it. He was hesitant at first because he said people often came to him with pieces left to them by family. They usually held only emotional value to the individual but usually little else.

Undeterred, I sent him photos and measurements and we were in business. I have to say that the pieces were all exquisite. They had real value and were in pristine shape. This guy said that in all his years of being in this business, he had never seen such a cohesive, quality, beautiful collection. He could easily move this stuff and give me half the proceeds. I then could buy items we all really loved and wanted to live among. It made sense, and I did just that.

I soon realized that this had actually been an important part of my particular mourning process. I had needed to go through the entire process — cleaning out the storage space, seeing everything that was there, placing it all in our new home, paying tribute to what my mom and I had collected and the path it had taken, and then being *done* with it.

I kept a few special items with which I could not part and decided to work just enough of them in to feel good and connected to my mom. With the money I received I bought and decorated the place to reflect my husband and me and us as a family. It was a liberating process and a telling one.

Six months later it was our first Christmas in this house, and to quote my girls, it promised to be "the best one ever!"

For the first time since I can remember, I was also not alone in the holiday decorating. As a kid I decorated our tree every year all by myself. I'd take a minimum of four hours to place the multicolored mini-lights on practically every needle. I would then deck out the tree with so many ornaments you could barely see the branches. I loved the ritual of it all. I would stay up all night if I had to use everything. I was methodical and maniacal and felt such commitment and peace doing it all by myself. Mom never liked doing the tree.

I would start after dinner and then we would go to midnight Mass. I always resumed after Mass and would sometimes stay up to 4:00 A.M. I never turned on the lights until the whole tree was done. My favorite part was when I'd finally take the ridiculously long assembly of plugs that had been stacked and attached and put the last one in the socket. The tree would glow and it was so bright you could read a book under it.

I'd switch it on and enjoy the light and the intense quiet. Mom would be getting ready for bed and I'd do the reveal for her — "Ta-da, Mama!" — and then go into my room and go to bed, incredibly excited for Santa to come. I'd leave the tree without presents and in the morning there would be so many wrapped packages surrounding the base that one would not believe we were a household of two. Most of the gifts would be spilling out of a Christmas stocking the size of a young child. Mom had found the enormous stocking at some store and thought I deserved it.

Christmas morning was always amazing and we would usually go to Bob's family's house for an Armenian-style family Christmas. The day after Christmas I'd go to my dad's house and have the holiday with my family there. Mom's relatives were never a part of our lives in these later years.

Now it was my turn to create traditions in my own home. And I was taking it incredibly seriously. I roll-called my platoon and we put together a plan. Everyone happily got to work. I dreaded the day my girls stopped believing in Santa (and vowed to never pass out like my mom had done so many years ago and reveal the truth). Santa would come during the night when they were all asleep for as long as possible.

This year one daughter did the outside lights with Chris's mom, another child did the fireplaces and powder room, I completed the dining room table, and we all did the tree together. For the record, I did not redo the placement of any of the lights or the ornaments when my girls were not looking! The house was stunning. Because it was to be the first family dinner at my new special table, I wanted it to be just right. I had recently convinced my husband to let me get a large oval zinc-top table that had two massive debarked tree trunks as its base. Even though Chris started out being unsure, thankfully, its dominating presence grew on him and we kept the table. Since the table was my domain, I went about the decorating in a way that would make Colin Cowie proud.

First, I placed two fresh garlands from a local farm along the length of the table crossing in and out of the other through the center. I next wrapped tiny battery-operated mini-lights on thin wire, which I had splurged on from Restoration Hardware, around white balls made of seashells. I made two pyramids of three balls each and encased them under glass domes and located them toward the center of the table amid the green garland. Two sterling candelabras that my mom bought at an antique place ages ago bracketed my center masterpiece. To finish it off, I scattered a few huge pinecones and nestled a few silver birds and mini-conches into the green. I thought I'd add a bit of beach into Christmas. I lit the candles, stood back, and as the holiday music wafted through the otherwise quiet house, I thought it was the best-smelling room and most beautiful table I had ever set.

Chris made a feast and we all sat down and toasted to it all. As I sipped my glass I slowly looked around the table at the smiling faces. Everyone was eating, talking, and enjoying the meal and the setting. I suddenly thought, *Who are these people and why are they in my house?* I started to feel like I was receding into the atmosphere. What were they all doing in my home and at my table? Where was my mom? I looked at all their faces and finally settled on my girls' backlit silhouettes. They seemed to have left me. They looked so happy and in their own skin. They were playing some joke on their "Opah," which is what they call Chris's dad, and it occurred to me that they, my daughters, were actually related to these people. They were blood, and I, somehow, was the outsider.

This thought seemed to suggest to me that all the people at this table were related to each other except me. I saw Chris and his sister, Michele (who the girls call Aunt Mimi), both their parents, and the sole Henchy grandchildren. All of them, including Mimi's husband for some reason, were all one big happy family rejoicing in Christmas. Where had my family and my life gone?

Sitting there, as the noises became more indiscernible, it slowly dawned on me that I no longer had any parent with whom to share this day. I felt orphaned.

I started to feel as if I could sneak away from the table while they all laughed and celebrated and walk out of the house and just keep going. My kids would be fine. Look at the great family they had! They might miss me, but not for long, and they would grow up just fine. Look at all those Disney princesses — their moms had been vanished from their lives way earlier than this and their futures turned out to be more glorious than they could have imagined. Maybe it was even better for my kids if I, too, vanished.

Chris startled me by repeating some question even louder and I regained consciousness and tried to shake off my mood. I got a huge lump in my throat and tried to smile it down. I lingered with the feeling for another second, though, and recognized it as similar to a sensation I encountered years back and at the beginning of my bout with PPD. I resisted the urge to panic.

I finished my glass and slowly refilled it with champagne, watching every bubble trying to stay afloat and feeling slightly like one of those helpless bubbles. Nobody seemed to have noticed my "absence" and I attempted successfully to reengage in the table chatter.

After dinner, as I was clearing the table, my husband said, "I see that look in your eyes. You are leaving again, aren't you? You are retreating and I want to go on record and say that I am a witness to your starting to disappear." I looked at him with tears starting to well up my eyes and said, "I have no parents." He held me tight and said he understood.

Do you? I thought. *Does anybody really know what it feels like to lose a mom, until it happens?* No matter what the quality or situation of one's life, the end of a living mother is profound.

I was happy for Chris's sake that he didn't know from experience what I was feeling, of course. And I also knew that he was really just saying that I had him and the girls, and that he was aware I was struggling. I didn't feel like Christmas-crying anymore. So I took a deep breath and told him I loved him and the girls, so much it "horts."

Later that night I went over it in my head. How could it be that I had everything in place, but there remained a huge void?

I found the wonderful husband and grounded relationship, my kids were healthy, we had the full and vibrant home with the tree and the decorations and the music, and even the *snow,* for Christ's sake. I had everything I had always wanted, but now I had no mom. She used to be my barometer for joy. If she was happy, I was happy. I wanted to show her how well it had all turned out. Sure, life had kicked us in the ass for various reasons but no one's exempt from that and there had been and currently was a tremendous amount of good. The blessings were continuing. I wanted to show off my beautiful table and how I had utilized the special possessions she herself had taught me about and collected. I knew she'd love it when she saw it.

Denial can be so very shrewd. The first year after Mom died didn't seem to be so bad. Because Mom had been failing for a while, there had been a few recent celebrations during which we were not together. That first year I just tricked myself into thinking Mom was not with me because she was still at the assisted-living facility. But this Christmas was a shock. It had been about a year and two months and I still had not had any dreams about Mom or any emotional outbursts. I suppose it was crafty denial, but I was beginning to realize that my mourning had only just begun.

I now needed to do what Mom was never capable of doing — let go, even just a little bit. Because I wish she knew she didn't ever have to let me go. All she needed to do was stretch her arms out farther and relax her fingers.

EPILOGUE

Dear Mom,

My first feeling is that I miss you very much. It is hardest on your birthday and on my birthday, because those were the days that we celebrated each other. I never thought I could live without you. To see you dying in that bed with its rails and thin sheets, in a curled-up and scared position, devastated me. Watching you actually die was one of the hardest, more unreal things I have ever experienced, and it was the day I had dreaded most my whole life.

I never felt as though I told you enough how much I loved and appreciated you. I wish we had had a heart-to-heart while you were still of sound mind. You always said, "Let's talk," but it never happened. I think we wanted to avoid disrupting the good times. Or, when we did try, we'd just fight or not know what to say.

It was as if the intimacy was too scary and embarrassing.

I still feel as though I knew and understood you better than anyone else in your life, and that was hard to do because you so rarely told anybody how you were feeling. And yet I feel as though I never got the full story. I think I hated your drinking so much because the you I knew existed and loved was stolen away from me.

I was always free enough to sob to you, but it did not bring us closer. I think that was because I was your baby in those moments and you felt needed. But as I grew up and tried to make changes, these moments were fewer and farther between. It was as if we no longer knew who we were together.

I also have to believe that because you never really lived in sobriety, even your dry days were colored by your addiction. You were ambitious and street smart, and although also intensely loving, and often well intended, you were also an addict. It was as if you were not only addicted to alcohol but also addicted to me. You never did the work to fully embrace sobriety, and you robbed yourself. I became the meaning in your life when it would have served you to find the meaning from within.

I see now how much pain and sadness you carried. I believe your heart was such a fully feeling heart that you were not strong enough to heal each time it was broken. I have read some of your old journals and was deeply affected by how you regarded yourself. You always proclaimed how tough you were and how strong you were, but you never seemed to feel good enough. It is hard to love ourselves, but I have learned to love who I am inside. I can always strive to be better, but I am enough. I don't know if you ever really did love who you were. I don't believe your mom ever helped you to believe in your own self-worth as you did for me.

I know I fought you, but it never meant I did not love you or did not need you. Your approval meant the world to me, as did your happiness. That was the hard part, because I wanted your approval for my growing up independently of you, yet I feared my independence was the root of your unhappiness. But if I had not fought to differentiate myself from you and from our tight bond, I would not have been able to survive. I'm sorry for the way I handled our "divorce," but I did not have the strength to break away from the life we were living without taking drastic measures.

I loved you so much, Mama, that for so long I put you before me. I blindly defended you because you were my mom. It was often just that simple. As a mom, I admit I sometimes wish my daughters looked up to me with the same undaunted devotion as I did you because I imagine it felt good. But I also don't want them to have to carry that burden. I carried you because I loved you and needed you, but I needed to learn to care for myself, too. I remained conflicted because I felt like you never really let me in, yet you absorbed me so far in that I could hardly find my way out.

I appreciated you and all you gave me in my life. It was very hard to get past the alcohol and yet, when you were not drinking, we were so unique and glorious together. The laughter healed everything.

I am just so sad that you were so sad and that you could not get your life straightened out or fully actualized. And yet, it was your life, and you chose to do with it what you wanted.

I remember when we were being interviewed by Barbara Walters when I was sixteen. When Barbara asked you what message you wanted to leave with the public, you simply and resolutely said, "I'm not going to change." And you didn't. But in life I believe change is healthy and necessary for growth. You saw it as defeat, and I believe that was unfortunate. I knew you meant that you were never going to take criticism lying down or cave to others' wills, but it also carried into your life.

I realized that up until the end I was fighting the same fight. I was navigating your demons. I was trying to do for you what only you could do for yourself. I was never going to "fix" you. I see, too, that much of your unhappiness was independent of anything I did or was, but as a child, one carries that responsibility. I did not have faith that you would be OK, so I kept trying to be the source of your happiness and self-worth.

I wrote this book as a way to shed light on your complicated yet vibrant and, at times, tragic personality. I wanted you to live longer. I wanted you to be a more integral part of our lives, but the booze

625

killed everything. You died too early. You had more to enjoy and do. We had more to laugh about.

But we did share an extraordinary life together, and you taught me so many wonderful things. I learned about humor, survival, and perseverance. I learned the power of observation and the necessity of generosity and good manners. I learned how to always work hard and try my best. I even learned how to have better posture. "Stand up straight, Brookie. . . . And keep your head held up high."

I learned how to "never take no for an answer" and how to fight for what I want. I learned how to pick myself up when I fall and never allow defeat to define me. You taught me to cast off any negative comments often hurled at me and not to "sweat the small stuff."

You taught me to look for the good in people and to admit that life could always be worse. You taught me how to adapt to my surroundings and to jump into life with both feet. You taught me how to find treasures at flea markets, to love both NECCO and Choward's Violet candies, sneak into a second movie, and be silly for a laugh. I learned to dab perfume in various, and even precarious, places because "ya never know where you might be kissed." And most important, you taught me to "never say fuck in front of the B-A-B-Y!"

Throughout the good and the bad, I would not have traded you for any other mother. I would have exchanged some of your behaviors, sure, but I can say that about practically everyone I know, including myself. You did the best you could, and so did I.

It is sad, though, and that was the overriding emotion that permeated my life throughout writing this book. Sadness. I wish I had written this letter while you were still aware.

Neither writing the book nor this letter felt at all cathartic. People speculated it would, but in actuality it all just gave me a heavy heart. But soon I will only remember the good.

I am choosing now to concentrate on and revel in only the wonderful memories. They are as much a part of me and us as are the bad ones. I have always loved you, and I am thankful for all you were. That will be your legacy.

From now on, when it rains, I will know it's just you up there being bossy.

And from now on when I throw my kisses at the moon, I will hurl some your way.

I love you, Mama,
XX, Your baby girl

ACKNOWLEDGMENTS

I wish to say thank you to my literary agent, Stephen Barr, for his layered insight and basically just for the way his brain works; to my focused and incredibly organized and attentive editor, Jill Schwartzman, for filing every tiny random memory I sent to her at all hours of the night; to her assistant, Stephanie, who didn't let a little thing like pregnancy derail her when it came to getting my changes transcribed and in on a deadline; to my godmother, Lila, for her years of support and for helping me reconstruct history; to my great friend Lyda for being attached to the past in the same way I am and for helping me remember all the details; to my friend and archivist Mike for knowing more about my life than I do and for caring and for tirelessly keeping track of every bit of the past forty-nine years; to my babysitters Kelly and Lauren for keeping my kids busy and alive while I slogged away

629

at writing this book and for listening to me read out loud and for typing faster than I will ever be able to. To my assistant Dan, for caring for me and for becoming a part of our family. To Lisa, for remaining my "sassy." To my husband, Chris, just because he asked me to marry him; and to my smart and stunning daughters, who inspire me to be a better person and who take my breath away because I love them so deeply. And finally to my mom, for loving me.

ABOUT THE AUTHOR

Brooke Shields is an award-winning actress and a Princeton graduate with honors in French Literature. She starred in iconic films such as *Pretty Baby, The Blue Lagoon,* and *Endless Love.* She is a renowned model and starred in the long-running TV show *Suddenly Susan* and the critically acclaimed *Lipstick Jungle.* She has appeared on Broadway multiple times and wrote and performed in her own one-woman show, *In My Life.* She wrote the *New York Times* bestseller *Down Came the Rain* and also penned two children's books. She lives in New York City with her husband, writer and producer Chris Henchy, and their two daughters.

The employees of Thorndike Press hope you have enjoyed this Large Print book. All our Thorndike, Wheeler, and Kennebec Large Print titles are designed for easy reading, and all our books are made to last. Other Thorndike Press Large Print books are available at your library, through selected bookstores, or directly from us.

For information about titles, please call:
  (800) 223-1244

or visit our Web site at:
  http://gale.cengage.com/thorndike

To share your comments, please write:
  Publisher
  Thorndike Press
  10 Water St., Suite 310
  Waterville, ME 04901

relationships was already convincing, and the DNA-based conclusions confirmed what the anatomists had already concluded. But DNA was also able to resolve the problem at which anatomy had failed—the relationships between humans, gorillas, and chimpanzees. As Figure 1 shows, humans differ from either common chimps or pygmy chimps in about 1.6 percent of their (our) DNA, and share 98.4 percent. Gorillas differ somewhat more, by about 2.3 percent, from us or from either of the chimps.

Let's pause to let some of the implications of these momentous numbers sink in:

The gorilla must have branched off from our family tree slightly before we separated from the common and pygmy chimpanzees. The chimpanzees, not the gorilla, are our closest relatives. Put another way, the chimpanzees' closest relative is not the gorilla but humans. Traditional taxonomy has reinforced our anthropocentric tendencies by claiming to see a fundamental dichotomy between mighty man, standing alone on high, and the lowly apes all together in the abyss of bestiality. Now, future taxonomists may see things from the chimpanzees' perspective: a weak dichotomy between slightly higher apes (the *three* chimpanzees, including the "human chimpanzee") and slightly lower apes (gorillas, orangutans, gibbons). The traditional distinction between "apes" (defined as chimps, gorillas, etc.) and humans misrepresents the facts.

The genetic distance (1.6 percent) separating us from pygmy or common chimps is barely double that separating pygmy from common chimps (0.7 percent). It's less than that between two species of gibbons (2.2 percent), or between such closely related North American bird species as red-eyed vireos and white-eyed vireos (2.9 percent). The remaining 98.4 percent of our DNA is just normal chimp DNA. For example, our principal hemoglobin, the oxygen-carrying protein that gives blood its red color, is identical in all of its 287 units with chimp hemoglobin. In this respect as in most others, we are just a third species of chimpanzee, and what's good enough for common and pygmy chimps is good enough for us. Our important visible distinctions from the other chimps—our upright posture, large brains, ability to speak, sparse body hair, and peculiar sexual lives—must be concentrated in a mere 1.6 percent of our genetic program.

If genetic distances between species accumulated at a uniform rate with time, they would function as a smoothly ticking clock. All that would be required to convert genetic distance into absolute time since the last common ancestor would be a calibration, furnished by a pair of species for which we know *both* the genetic distance *and* the time of divergence as dated independently by fossils. In fact, two independent calibrations are available for higher primates. On the one hand, monkeys diverged from apes between twenty-five and thirty million years ago according to fossil evidence, and now differ in about 7.3 percent of their DNA. On the other hand, orangutans diverged from chimps and gorillas between twelve and sixteen million years ago and now differ in about 3.6 percent of their DNA. Comparing these two examples, a doubling of evolutionary time, as one goes from twelve-to-sixteen to twenty-five-to-thirty million years, leads to a doubling of genetic distance (3.6 to 7.3 percent of DNA). Thus, the DNA clock has ticked relatively steadily among higher primates.

With those calibrations, Sibley and Ahlquist estimated the following time scale for our evolution. Since our own genetic distance from chimps (1.6 percent) is about half the distance of orangutans from chimps (3.6 percent), we must have been going our separate way for about half of the twelve to sixteen million years that orangutans had to accumulate their genetic distinction from chimps. That is, the human and "other chimp" evolutionary lines diverged around six to eight million years ago. By the same reasoning, gorillas parted from the common ancestor of us three chimpanzees around nine million years ago, and the pygmy and common chimps diverged around three million years ago. In contrast, when I took physical anthropology as a college freshman in 1954, the assigned textbooks said that humans diverged from apes fifteen to thirty million years ago. Thus, the DNA clock strongly supports a controversial conclusion also drawn from several other molecular clocks based on amino-acid sequences of proteins, mitochondrial DNA, and globin pseudogene DNA. Each clock indicates that humans have had only a short history as a species distinct from other apes, much shorter than paleontologists used to assume.

WHAT DO THESE RESULTS imply about our position in the animal kingdom? Biologists classify living things in hierarchical categories, each less distinct than the next: subspecies, species, genus, family, superfamily, order, class, and phylum. The *Encyclopedia Britannica* and all the biology texts on my shelf say that humans and apes belong to the same order, called Primates, and the same superfamily, called Hominoidea, but to separate families, called Hominidae and Pongidae. Whether Sibley's and Ahlquist's work changes this classification depends on one's philosophy of taxonomy. Traditional taxonomists group species into higher categories by making somewhat subjective evaluations of how important the differences between species are. Such taxonomists place humans in a separate family because of distinctive functional traits like large brain and bipedal posture, and this classification would remain unaffected by measures of genetic distance.

However, another school of taxonomy, called cladistics, argues that classification should be objective and uniform, based on genetic distance or times of divergence. All taxonomists agree now that red-eyed and white-eyed vireos belong together in the genus *Vireo,* the various species of gibbons in the genus *Hylobates.* Yet the members of these pairs of species are genetically more distant from each other than are humans from the other two chimpanzees, and diverged longer ago. On this basis, then, humans don't constitute a distinct family, or even a distinct genus, but belong in the same genus as common and pygmy chimps. Since our genus name *Homo* was proposed first, it takes priority, by the rules of zoological nomenclature, over the genus name *Pan* coined for the "other" chimps. So there are not one but three species of genus *Homo* on earth today: the common chimpanzee, *Homo troglodytes;* the pygmy chimpanzee, *Homo paniscus;* and the third chimpanzee or human chimpanzee, *Homo sapiens.* Since the gorilla is only slightly more distinct, it has almost equal right to be considered a fourth species of *Homo.*

Even taxonomists espousing cladistics are anthropocentric, and the lumping of humans and chimps into the same genus will undoubtedly be a bitter pill for them to swallow. There is no doubt, however, that whenever chimpanzees learn cladistics, or whenever taxonomists from Outer Space visit Earth to inventory its inhabitants, they will unhesitatingly adopt the new classification.

WHICH PARTICULAR GENES are the ones that differ between humans and chimps? Before we can consider this question, we need first to understand what it is that DNA, our genetic material, does.

Much or most of our DNA has no known function and may just constitute "molecular junk": i.e., DNA molecules that have become duplicated or have lost former functions, and that natural selection hasn't eliminated from us because they do us no harm. Of our DNA that does have known functions, the main functions have to do with the long chains of amino acids called proteins. Certain proteins make up much of our body's structure (such as the proteins keratin of hair or collagen of connective tissue), while other proteins termed enzymes synthesize and break down most of our body's remaining molecules. The sequences of the component small molecules (nucleotide bases) in DNA specify the sequence of amino acids in our proteins. Other parts of our functional DNA regulate protein synthesis.

Those of our observable features that are easiest to understand genetically are ones arising from single proteins and single genes. For instance, our blood's oxygen-carrying protein, which I have already mentioned, hemoglobin, consists of two amino-acid chains, each specified by a single chunk of DNA (a single "gene"). Those two genes have no observable effects except through specifying the structure of hemoglobin, which is confined to our red blood cells. Conversely, hemoglobin's structure is totally specified by those genes. What you eat or how much you exercise may affect how much hemoglobin you make, but not the details of its structure.

That's the simplest situation, but there are also genes influencing many observable traits. For example, the fatal genetic disorder known as Tay-Sachs disease involves many behavioral as well as anatomical anomalies: excessive drooling, rigid posture, yellowish skin, abnormal head growth, and other changes. We know in this case that all these observable effects result somehow from changes in a single enzyme specified by the Tay-Sachs gene, but we don't know exactly how. Since that enzyme occurs in many tissues of our bodies and breaks down a widespread cellular constituent, changes in that one enzyme have wide-ranging and ultimately fatal consequences. Conversely, some traits, such as your height as an adult, are influenced simultaneously by many genes and also by environmental factors (e.g., your nutrition as a child).

While scientists understand well the function of numerous genes that specify known individual proteins, we know much less about the function of genes involved in complexly determined traits, like most behaviors. It would be absurd to think that a human hallmark such as art, language, or aggression depends on a single gene. Behavioral differences among individual humans are obviously subject to enormous environmental influences, and it's very controversial what role genes play in such individual differences. However, for those behaviors that differ consistently between chimps and humans, genetic differences are likely to be involved, even though we can't yet specify the genes responsible. For instance, the ability of humans but not chimps to speak surely depends on differences in genes specifying the anatomy of the voice box and the wiring of the brain. A young chimpanzee brought up in a psychologist's home along with the psychologist's human baby of the same age still continued to look like a chimp and didn't learn to talk or walk erect. But whether an individual human grows up to be fluent in English or Korean is independent of genes and dependent solely on childhood linguistic environment, as proved by the linguistic attainments of Korean infants adopted by English-speaking parents.

With this as background, what can we say about the 1.6 percent of our DNA that differs from chimp DNA? We know that the genes for our principal hemoglobin don't differ, and that certain other genes do exhibit minor differences. In the nine protein chains studied to date in both humans and common chimps, only five out of a total of 1,271 amino acids differ: one amino acid in a muscle protein called myoglobin, one in a minor hemoglobin chain called the delta chain, and three in an enzyme called carbonic anhydrase. But we don't yet know which chunks of our DNA are responsible for the functionally significant differences between humans and chimps to be discussed in Chapters 2 to 7: the differences in brain size, anatomy of the pelvis and voice box and genitalia, amount of body hair, female menstrual cycle, menopause, and other traits. Those important differences certainly don't arise from the five amino-acid differences detected to date. At present, all we can say with confidence is this: much of our DNA is junk; at least some of the 1.6 percent that differs between us and chimps is already known to be junk; and the functionally significant differences must be confined to some as-yet-unidentified small fraction of 1.6 percent.

Within that small differing fraction of our DNA, some differences have bigger consequences for our bodies than do others. To begin with, most amino acids of proteins can be specified by at least two alternative sequences of nucleotide bases in DNA. Changes in nucleotide bases from one such sequence to an alternative one are "silent" mutations: they produce no change in the amino-acid sequences of proteins. Even when a change in one base does cause one amino acid to be replaced by another, some amino acids are very similar to certain others in their chemical properties, or are located in relatively insensitive parts of a protein.

But other parts of a protein are crucial to the protein's function. Replacing an amino acid in such a part with a chemically dissimilar amino acid is likely to produce some detectable effect. For instance, the disease sickle-cell anemia is an often-fatal condition, resulting from a change in our hemoglobin's solubility, resulting in turn from a change in just one of hemoglobin's 287 amino acids, resulting in turn from a change in just one of the three nucleotides specifying that amino acid. That change, however, replaces a negatively charged amino acid with one lacking net charge, thereby changing the electrical charge on the whole hemoglobin molecule.

While we don't know which particular genes or nucleotide bases are the crucial ones accounting for our observed differences from chimps, there are numerous precedents for one or a few genes having big impacts. I just mentioned the many big and visible differences between Tay-Sachs patients and normal people, all somehow arising from a single change in one enzyme. That's an example of differences among individuals of the same species. As for differences between related species, a good example is provided by the cichlid fishes of Africa's Lake Victoria. Cichlids are popular aquarium species, of which about two hundred are confined to that one lake, where they evolved from a single ancestor within perhaps the last 200,000 years. Those two hundred species differ among themselves in their food habits as much as do tigers and cows. Some graze on algae, others catch other fish, and still others variously crush snails, feed on plankton, catch insects, nibble the scales off other fish, or specialize in grabbing fish embryos from brooding mother fish. Yet all those Lake Victoria cichlids differ from each other on the average by only about 0.4 percent of their DNA studied. Thus, it took even fewer genetic mutations to change a snail crusher into a specialized baby killer than it took to produce us from an ape.

*   *   *

Do THE NEW FINDINGS about our genetic distance from chimps have any broader implications, besides technical questions of taxonomic names? Probably the most important implications concern how we think about the place of humans and apes in the universe. Names are not just technical details but express and create attitudes. (To convince yourself, try greeting your spouse this evening either as "my darling" or as "you swine," using the same expression and tone of voice). The new findings do not specify how we *should* think about humans and apes. But, just as did Darwin's *Origin of Species,* they will probably influence how we *do* think, and it will probably take us many years to readjust our attitudes. I'll mention just one example of a controversial area that might be affected: our use of apes.

At present we make a fundamental distinction between animals (including apes) and humans, and this distinction guides our ethical code and actions. For instance, as I noted at the start of this chapter, it's considered acceptable to exhibit caged apes in zoos, but it's not acceptable to do the same with humans. I wonder how the public will feel when the identifying label on the chimp cage in the zoo reads "*Homo troglodytes.*" Yet, if it were not for the sympathetic interest in apes that many people gain at zoos, there might be much less public financial support for conservationists' efforts to protect apes in the wild.

I also noted earlier that it's considered acceptable to subject apes, but not humans, without their consent to lethal experiments for purposes of medical research. The motive for doing so is precisely that apes are so similar to us genetically. They can be infected with many of the same diseases as we can, and their bodies respond similarly to the disease organisms. Thus, experiments on apes offer a far better way to devise improved medical treatments for humans than would experiments on any other animals.

This ethical choice poses an even more difficult problem than does caging apes in zoos. After all, we regularly cage millions of human criminals under worse conditions than zoo apes, but there is no socially accepted human analogue of medical research on animals, even though lethal experiments on humans would provide medical scientists with far more valuable information than do lethal experiments on chimps. Yet the human experiments performed by Nazi concentration-camp physicians are widely viewed as one of the most abominable of all the Nazis' abominations. Why is it okay to perform such experimentation on chimps?

Somewhere along the scale from bacteria to humans, we have to decide where killing becomes murder, and where eating becomes cannibalism. Most people draw those lines between humans and all other species. However, quite a few people are vegetarians, unwilling to eat any animal (yet willing to eat plants). And an increasingly vocal minority, belonging to the animal-rights movement, object to medical experiments on animals—or at least on certain animals. That movement is especially exercised about research on cats and dogs and primates, less concerned about mice, and generally silent about insects and bacteria.

If our ethical code makes a purely arbitrary distinction between humans and all other species, then we have a code based on naked selfishness devoid of any higher principle. If our code instead makes distinctions based on our superior intelligence, social relationships, and capacity for feeling pain, then it becomes difficult to defend an all-or-nothing code that draws a line between all humans and all animals. Instead, different ethical constraints should apply to research on different species. Perhaps it's just our naked selfishness, reemerging in a new disguise, that would advocate granting special rights to those animal species genetically closest to us. But an objective case, based on the considerations I just mentioned (intelligence, social relationships, etc.), can be made that chimps and gorillas qualify for preferred ethical consideration over insects and bacteria. If there's any animal species currently used in medical research for which a total ban on medical experimentation can be justified, that species is surely the chimpanzee.

The ethical dilemma posed by animal experiments is compounded for chimps by the fact that they are endangered as a species. In this case, medical research not only kills individuals but threatens to kill the species itself. That's not to say that demands for research have been the sole threat to wild chimp populations; habitat destruction and capture for zoos have also been major threats. But it's enough that research demands have been a significant threat. The ethical dilemma is further compounded by other considerations: that on the average several wild chimps are killed in the process of capturing one alive (often a young animal that was being carried by its mother) and delivering it to a medical research lab; that medical scientists have played little role in the struggle to protect wild chimp populations, despite their obvious self-interest in doing so; and that chimps used for research are often caged under cruel conditions. The first chimp that I saw being used for medical research had been injected with a slow-acting lethal virus and was being kept alone for the several years until it died, in a small indoor cage devoid of play objects, at the U.S. National Institutes of Health.

Breeding chimps in captivity for research use avoids objections based on depleting wild chimp populations. But that still doesn't get around the basic dilemma, any more than enslaving children of U.S.-born blacks after abolition of the African slave trade made black slavery in the nineteenth-century U.S. acceptable. Why is it okay to experiment on *Homo troglodytes,* but not on *Homo sapiens?* Conversely, how should we explain to parents whose children are at risk of dying from diseases now being studied in captive chimps that their children are less important than chimps? Ultimately, we the public, not just scientists, will have to make these terrible choices. All that is certain is that our view of man and apes will determine our decision.

Finally, changes in our attitudes about apes may be crucial in determining whether apes will survive at all in the wild. At present, their populations are threatened especially by destruction of their rainforest habitats in Africa and Asia, and by legal and illegal capture and killing. If present trends continue, the mountain gorilla, orangutan, pileated gibbon, Kloss's gibbon, and possibly some other apes as well will exist only in zoos by the time this year's crop of human babies enters college. It's not enough for us to preach to the governments of Uganda, Zaire, and Indonesia about their moral obligation to protect their wild apes. These are impoverished countries, and national parks are expensive to create and maintain. If we as the third chimpanzee decide that the other two chimpanzees are worth saving, those of us in the richer countries will have to bear most of the expense. From the point of view of the apes themselves, the most important effect of what we've recently learned about the tale of three chimpanzees will be on how we feel about footing that bill.

CHAPTER 2

The Great Leap
Forward

F OR MOST OF THE MANY MILLIONS OF YEARS SINCE OUR LINEAGE diverged from that of apes, we remained little more than glorified chimpanzees in how we made our living. As recently as forty thousand years ago, western Europe was still occupied by Neanderthals, primitive beings for whom art and progress scarcely existed. Then there came an abrupt change, as anatomically modern people appeared in Europe, bringing with them art, musical instruments, lamps, trade, and progress. Within a short time, the Neanderthals were gone.

That Great Leap Forward in Europe was probably the result of a similar leap that had occurred over the course of the preceding few tens of thousands of years in the Near East and Africa. Even a few dozen millennia, though, is a trivial fraction (less than 1 percent) of our long history separate from ape history. Insofar as there was any single point in time when we could be said to have become human, it was at the time of that leap. Only a few more dozen millennia were needed for us to domesticate animals, develop agriculture and metallurgy, and invent writing. It was then but a short further step to those monuments of civilization that distinguish humans from animals across what used to seem an unbridgeable gulf—monuments such as the "Mona Lisa" and *Eroica Symphony,* the Eiffel Tower and Sputnik, Dachau's ovens and the bombing of Dresden.

This chapter will confront the questions posed by our abrupt rise to humanity. What made it possible, and why was it so sudden? What held back the Neanderthals, and what was their fate? Did Neanderthals and modern peoples ever meet? If so, how did they behave toward each other?

Understanding the Great Leap Forward isn't easy, and writing about it isn't easy either. The immediate evidence comes from technical details of preserved bones and stone tools. Archaeologists' reports are full of terms obscure to the rest of us, such as "transverse occipital torus," "receding zygomatic arches," and "Châtelperronian backed knives." What we really want to understand—the way of life and the humanity of our various ancestors—isn't directly preserved but only inferred from those technical details of bones and tools. Much of the evidence is missing, and archaeologists often disagree over the meaning of such evidence as has survived. Since the books and articles listed in Further Readings, pages 373–74, will slake the interest of readers curious to learn more about receding zygomatic arches, I'll emphasize instead the inferences from bones and tools.

To place human evolution in a time perspective, recall that life originated on Earth several billion years ago, and that the dinosaurs became extinct around sixty-five million years ago. It was only between six and ten million years ago that our ancestors finally became distinct from the ancestors of chimps and gorillas. Hence human history constitutes only an insignificant portion of the history of life. Science-fiction films that depict cavemen fleeing from dinosaurs are just that, science fiction.

The shared ancestor of humans, chimps, and gorillas lived in Africa, to which chimps and gorillas are still confined, and to which we remained confined for millions of years. Initially, our own ancestors would have been classified as merely another species of ape, but a sequence of three changes launched us in the direction of modern humans. The first of these changes had occurred by around four

million years ago, when the structure of fossilized limb bones shows
that our ancestors were habitually walking upright on the two hind
limbs. In contrast, gorillas and chimps walk upright only occasionally, and usually proceed on all fours. The upright posture freed our
ancestors' forelimbs to do other things, among which toolmaking
proved the most important.

The second change occurred around three million years ago, when
our lineage split into at least two distinct species. As background,
reflect that members of two animal species living in the same area
must fill different ecological roles and do not normally interbreed
with each other. For example, coyotes and wolves are obviously
closely related and (until wolves were exterminated in most of the
United States) lived in many of the same areas of North America.
However, wolves are larger, mainly hunt big mammals like deer and
moose, and often live in large packs, whereas coyotes are smaller,
mainly hunt small mammals like rabbits and mice, and usually live
in pairs or small groups. Coyotes usually mate with coyotes, wolves
with wolves. In contrast, every human population living today has
interbred with every other human population with which it has had
extensive contact. Ecological differences among existing humans are
entirely a product of childhood education: it's not the case that some
of us are born with sharp teeth and equipped to hunt deer, while
others are born with grinding teeth, gather berries, and don't marry
the deer hunters. Hence all modern humans belong to the same
species.

On perhaps two occasions in the past, though, the human lineage
split into separate species, as distinct as wolves and coyotes. The most
recent such occasion, which I'll describe later, may have been at the
time of the Great Leap Forward. The earlier such occasion was
around three million years ago, when our lineage split into two: a
man-ape with a robust skull and very big cheek teeth, assumed to
eat coarse plant food, and often referred to as *Australopithecus robustus* (meaning "the robust southern ape"); and a man-ape with a
more lightly built skull and smaller teeth, assumed to have an om-
nivorous diet, and known as *Australopithecus africanus* ("the southern ape of Africa"). The latter man-ape evolved into a larger-
brained form termed *Homo habilis* ("man the handyman").
However, fossil bones that some paleontologists consider to represent male and female *Homo habilis* differ so much from each other

THE HUMAN FAMILY TREE

Cro-Magnon

Asians

Anatomically
modern
Africans

Neanderthal   100,000

H. sapiens   500,000

H. erectus

Third Man   1.7 million

H. habilis

A. robustus

A. africanus

3 million

Apes

Upright hominid   6 million years ago

Figure 2. Several branches of our family tree have become extinct, including those belonging to the robust australopithecines, Neanderthals, and possibly a poorly understood "Third Man" and an Asian population contemporary with Neanderthals. Some descendants of *Homo habilis* survived to evolve into modern humans. To recognize by different names the changes in fossils representing this line, they are somewhat arbitrarily divided into *Homo habilis,* then *Homo erectus* beginning around 1.7 million years ago, then *Homo sapiens* beginning around 500,000 years ago. *A.* stands for the genus name of *Australopithecus, H.* for *Homo.*

in skull size and tooth size that they may actually imply another fork in our lineage yielding two distinct *habilis*-like species: *Homo habilis* himself, and a mysterious "Third Man." Thus, by two million years ago there were at least two and possibly three protohuman species.

The third and last of the big changes that began to make our ancestors more human and less apelike was the regular use of stone tools. This is a human hallmark with clear animal precedents: woodpecker finches, Egyptian vultures, and sea otters are among the other animal species that evolved independently to employ tools in capturing or processing food, though none of these species is as heavily dependent on implements as we now are. Common chimpanzees also use tools, occasionally of stone, but not in numbers sufficient to litter the landscape. But by around 2½ million years ago very crude stone tools appear in numbers in areas of East Africa occupied by the protohumans. Since there were two or three protohuman species, who made the tools? Probably the light-skulled species, since both it and the tools persisted and evolved.

With only one human species surviving today but two or three a few million years ago, it's clear that one or two species must have become extinct. Who was our ancestor, which species ended up instead as a discard in the trash heap of evolution, and when did this shakedown occur? The winner was the light-skulled *Homo habilis,* who went on to increase in brain size and body size. By around 1,700,000 years ago the differences were sufficient for anthropologists to give our lineage a new name, *Homo erectus,* meaning "the man that walks upright." (*Homo erectus* fossils were discovered before all the earlier fossils I've been discussing, so anthropologists didn't realize that *Homo erectus* wasn't the first protohuman to walk upright). The robust man-ape disappeared somewhat after 1,200,000 years ago, and the "Third Man" (if he ever existed) must have disappeared by then also. As for why *Homo erectus* survived and the robust man-ape didn't, we can only speculate. A plausible guess is that the robust man-ape could no longer compete, since *Homo erectus* ate both meat and plant food, and since tools and a larger brain made *Homo erectus* more efficient at getting even the plant food on which his robust sibling depended. It's also possible that *Homo erectus* gave his sibling a direct push into oblivion, by killing him for meat.

All the developments that I've been discussing so far were played out within the continent of Africa. The shakedown there left *Homo erectus* as the sole protohuman on the African stage. It was only around one million years ago that *Homo erectus* finally expanded his horizons. His stone tools and bones show that he reached the Near East, then the Far East (where he is represented by the famous fossils known as Peking Man and Java Man) and Europe. He continued to evolve in our direction by an increase in brain size and in skull roundness. By around 500,000 years ago, some of our ancestors looked sufficiently like us, and different from earlier *Homo erectus,* that they are classified as our own species (*Homo sapiens,* meaning "the wise man"), though they still had thicker skulls and brow ridges than we do today.

Readers unfamiliar with details of our evolution might be forgiven for assuming that the appearance of *Homo sapiens* constituted the Great Leap Forward. Was our meteoric ascent to *sapiens* status half-a-million years ago the brilliant climax of Earth history, when art and sophisticated technology finally burst upon our previously dull planet? Not at all: the appearance of *Homo sapiens* was a nonevent. Cave paintings, houses, and bows and arrows still lay hundreds of thousands of years off in the future. Stone tools continued to be the crude ones that *Homo erectus* had been making for nearly a million years. The extra brain size of those early *Homo sapiens* had no dramatic effect on our way of life. That whole long tenure of *Homo erectus* and early *Homo sapiens* outside Africa was a period of infinitesimally slow cultural change. In fact, the sole candidate for a major advance was possibly the control of fire, for which caves occupied by Peking Man provide one of the earliest indications in the form of ash, charcoal, and burnt bones. Even that advance—if those cave fires really were man-lit rather than caused by lightning—would belong to *Homo erectus,* not *Homo sapiens.*

The emergence of *Homo sapiens* illustrates the paradox discussed in the previous chapter: that our rise to humanity was not directly proportional to the changes in our genes. Early *Homo sapiens* had progressed much further in anatomy than in cultural attainments along the road up from chimpanzeehood. Some crucial ingredients still had to be added before the Third Chimpanzee could conceive of painting the Sistine Chapel.

*   *   *

How did our ancestors make their living during the 1½ million years that spanned the emergence of *Homo erectus* and *Homo sapiens*?

The only surviving tools from this period are stone tools that can charitably be described as very crude, in comparison with the beautiful polished stone tools made until recently by Polynesians, American Indians, and other modern Stone Age peoples. Early stone tools vary in size and shape, and archaeologists have used those differences to give the tools different names, such as "hand axe," "chopper," and "cleaver." These names conceal the fact that none of those early tools had a sufficiently consistent or distinctive shape to suggest any specific function, as do the obvious needles and spear points left by the much later Cro-Magnons. Wear marks on the tools show that they were variously used to cut meat, bone, hides, wood, and nonwoody parts of plants. But any size or shape of tool seems to have been used to cut any of those things, and the tool names applied by archaeologists may be little more than arbitrary divisions of a continuum of stone forms.

Negative evidence is also significant here. Many advances in tools that appear after the Great Leap Forward were unknown to *Homo erectus* and early *Homo sapiens*. There were no bone tools, no ropes to make nets, and no fishhooks. All the early stone tools may have been held directly in the hand; they show no signs of having been mounted on other materials for increased leverage, as we mount steel axe blades on wooden handles.

What food did our early ancestors get with those crude tools, and how did they get it? At this point, anthropology books usually insert a long chapter entitled something like "Man the Hunter." The point here is that baboons, chimps, and some other primates occasionally prey on small vertebrates, but recently surviving Stone Age people (like Bushmen) did a lot of big-game hunting. So did Cro-Magnons, according to abundant archaeological evidence. There's no doubt that our early ancestors also ate some meat, as shown by marks of their stone tools on animal bones and by wear marks on their stone tools caused by cutting meat. The real question is: how *much* big-game hunting did our early ancestors do? Did big-game hunting skills improve gradually over the past 1½ million years, or was it only after the Great Leap Forward that they made a large contribution to our diet?

Anthropologists routinely reply that we have been successful big-game hunters for a long time. The supposed evidence comes mainly from three archaeological sites occupied around 500,000 years ago: a cave at Zhoukoudian near Beijing, containing bones and tools of *Homo erectus* ("Peking Man") and bones of many animals; and two noncave (open-air) sites at Torralba and Ambrona in Spain, with stone tools plus bones of elephants and other large animals. It's usually assumed that the people who left the tools killed the animals, brought their carcasses to the site, and ate them there. But all three sites also have bones and fecal remains of hyenas, which could equally well have been the hunters. The bones of the Spanish sites in particular look as if they came from a collection of scavenged, water-washed, trampled carcasses such as one can find around African waterholes today, rather than from human hunters' camps.

Thus, while early humans ate some meat, we don't know how much meat they ate, or whether they got the meat by hunting or scavenging. It's not until much later, around 100,000 years ago, that we have good evidence about human hunting skills, and it's clear that humans then were still very *ineffective* big-game hunters. Hence human hunters of 500,000 years ago and earlier must have been even more ineffective.

The mystique of Man the Hunter is now so rooted in us that it's hard to abandon our belief in its long-standing importance. Today, shooting a big animal is regarded as an ultimate expression of macho masculinity. Trapped in this mystique, male anthropologists like to stress the key role of big-game hunting in human evolution. Supposedly, big-game hunting was what induced protohuman males to cooperate with each other, develop language and big brains, join into bands, and share food. Even women were supposedly molded by men's big-game hunting: women suppressed the external signs of monthly ovulation that are so conspicuous in chimps, so as not to drive men into a frenzy of sexual competition and thereby spoil men's cooperation at hunting.

As an example of the purple prose spawned by this men's locker-room mentality, consider the following account of human evolution by Robert Ardrey in his book *African Genesis:* "In some scrawny troop of beleaguered not-yet-men on some scrawny forgotten plain a radian particle from an unknown source fractured a never-to-be-forgotten gene, and a primate carnivore was born. For better or for worse, for tragedy or for triumph, for ultimate glory or ultimate damnation, intelligence made alliance with the way of the killer, and

Cain with his sticks and his stones and his quickly running feet
emerged on the high savannah." What pure fantasy!

Western male writers and anthropologists aren't the only men
with an exaggerated view of hunting. In New Guinea I've lived with
real hunters, men who recently emerged from the Stone Age. Conversations at campfires go on for hours over each species of game
animal, its habits, and how best to hunt it. To listen to my New
Guinea friends, you would think that they eat fresh kangaroo for
dinner every night and do little each day except hunt. In fact, when
pressed for details, most New Guinea hunters admit that they have
bagged only a few kangaroos in their whole lives.

I still recall my first morning in the New Guinea highlands, when
I set out with a group of a dozen men armed with bows and arrows.
As we passed a fallen tree, there was suddenly much excited shout-
ing, men surrounded the tree, some spanned their bows, and others
pressed forward into the brush pile. Convinced that an enraged boar
or kangaroo was about to come out fighting, I looked for a tree that
I could climb to a perch of safety. Then I heard triumphant shrieks,
and out of the brush pile came two mighty hunters holding aloft their
prey: two baby wrens, not quite able to fly, weighing about one-third
of an ounce each, and promptly plucked, roasted, and eaten. The rest
of that day's catch consisted of a few frogs and many mushrooms.

Studies of most modern hunter-gatherers with far more effective
weapons than early *Homo sapiens* show that most of a family's calories
comes from plant food gathered by women. Men catch rabbits and
other small game never mentioned in the heroic campfire stories.
Occasionally the men do bag a large animal, which does indeed
contribute significantly to protein intake. But it's only in the Arctic,
where little plant food is available, that big-game hunting becomes
the dominant food source. And humans didn't reach the Arctic until
within the last few dozen millennia.

I would guess that big-game hunting contributed only modestly to
our food intake until *after* we had evolved fully modern anatomy and
behavior. I doubt the usual view that hunting was the driving force
behind our uniquely human brain and societies. For most of our
history we were not mighty hunters but skilled chimps, using stone
tools to acquire and prepare plant food and small animals. Occasionally, men did bag a large animal, and then retold the story of that rare
event incessantly.

* * *

IN THE PERIOD just before the Great Leap Forward, at least three distinct human populations occupied different parts of the Old World. These were the last truly primitive humans, supplanted by fully modern people at the time of the Great Leap. Let's consider those among the last primitives whose anatomy is best known and who have become a metaphor for brutish subhumans: the Neanderthals.

Where and when did they live? Their geographic range extended from western Europe, through southern European Russia and the Near East, to Uzbekistan in Central Asia near the border of Afghanistan. (The name "Neanderthal" comes from Germany's Neander Valley [valley = *Thal*, or *Tal*, in German], where one of the first skeletons was discovered). As to the time of their origin, that's a matter of definition, since some old skulls have characteristics anticipating later full-blown Neanderthals. The earliest "full-blown" examples date to around 130,000 years ago, and most specimens postdate 74,000 years ago. While their start is thus arbitrary, their end is abrupt: the last Neanderthals died somewhat after 40,000 years ago.

During the time that Neanderthals flourished, Europe and Asia were in the grip of the last Ice Age. Neanderthals must have been a cold-adapted people—but only within limits. They got no further north than southern Britain, northern Germany, Kiev, and the Caspian Sea. The first penetration of Siberia and the Arctic was left to later, fully modern humans.

Neanderthals' head anatomy was so distinctive that, even if a Neanderthal dressed in a business suit or designer dress were to walk down the streets of New York or London today, everybody else (all the homines sapientes) on the street would be staring in shock. Imagine converting a modern face to soft clay, gripping the middle of the face from the bridge of the nose to the jaws in a vise, pulling the whole midface forward, and letting it harden again. You'll then have some idea of a Neanderthal's appearance. Their eyebrows rested on prominently bulging bony ridges, and their noses and jaws and teeth protruded far forward. Their eyes lay in deep sockets, sunk behind the protruding nose and brow ridges. Their foreheads were low and sloping, unlike our high vertical modern foreheads, and their lower jaws sloped back without chins. Despite these startlingly primitive features, Neanderthals' brain size was nearly 10 percent *greater* than ours!

A dentist who examined a Neanderthal's teeth would have been in for a further shock. In adult Neanderthals the incisors (front teeth) were worn down on the outer-facing surface, in a way found in no modern people. Evidently, this peculiar wear pattern somehow resulted from a use of their teeth as tools, but what exactly was that function? As one possibility, they may have routinely used their teeth as vises to grip objects, like my baby sons, who gripped their milk bottles in their teeth and ran around with their hands free. Alternatively, Neanderthals may have bitten hides with their teeth to make leather, or bitten wood to make wooden tools.

While a Neanderthal in a business suit or dress would attract attention today, one in shorts or a bikini would draw gasps. Neanderthals were more heavily muscled, especially in their shoulders and neck, than all but the most avid modern bodybuilders. Their limb bones, which took the force of those big muscles' contracting, had to be considerably thicker than ours to withstand the stress. Their arms and legs would have looked stubby to us, because the lower leg and forearm were relatively shorter than ours. Even their hands were much more powerful than ours; a Neanderthal's handshake would have been literally bone-crushing. While their average height was only around five feet four inches, their weight would have been at least twenty pounds more than that of a modern person of that height, and this excess was mostly in the form of lean muscle.

One other possible anatomical difference is intriguing, though its reality as well as its interpretation are quite uncertain. A Neanderthal woman's birth canal may have been wider than a modern woman's, permitting her baby to grow inside her to a bigger size before birth. If so, a Neanderthal pregnancy might have lasted one year, instead of our nine months.

Besides their bones, our other main source of information about Neanderthals is their stone tools. As I described for earlier human tools, Neanderthal tools may have been simple hand-held stones not mounted on separate parts such as handles. The tools don't fall into distinct types with unique functions. There were no standardized bone tools, no bows and arrows. Some of the stone tools were undoubtedly used to make wooden tools, which rarely survive. One notable exception is a wooden thrusting spear eight feet long, found in the ribs of a long-extinct species of elephant at an archaeological site in Germany. Despite that (lucky?) success, Neanderthals were probably not very good at big-game hunting, because Neanderthal population densities (to judge from the number of their sites) were much lower than those of later Cro-Magnons, and because even anatomically more modern people living in Africa at the same time as the Neanderthals were undistinguished as hunters.

If you say "Neanderthal" to friends and ask for their first association, you'll probably get back the answer "caveman." While most excavated Neanderthal remains do come from caves, that's surely an artifact of preservation, since open-air sites would be eroded much more quickly. Among my hundreds of campsites in New Guinea, one was in a cave, and that's the only site where future archaeologists are likely to find my pile of discarded tin cans intact. The archaeologists will also be deceived into considering me a caveman. Neanderthals must have constructed some type of shelter against the cold climate in which they lived, but those shelters must have been crude. All that remains is a few piles of stones and some postholes, compared to the elaborate remains of houses built by the later Cro-Magnons.

The list of other quintessentially modern human things that Neanderthals lacked is a long one. They left no unequivocal art objects. They must have worn some clothing in their cold environment, but it had to be crude, as they lacked needles and other evidence of sewing. They evidently lacked boats, as no Neanderthal remains are known from Mediterranean islands or even from North Africa, just eight miles across the Straits of Gibraltar from Neanderthal-populated Spain. There was no long-distance overland trade: Neanderthal tools are made of stones available within a few miles of the site.

Today we take cultural differences among people inhabiting different areas for granted. Every human population alive today has its characteristic house style, implements, and art. If you were shown chopsticks, a Guinness beer bottle, and a blowgun and asked to associate one object each with China, Ireland, and Borneo, you'd have no trouble giving the right answers. No such cultural variation is apparent for Neanderthals, whose tools look much the same whether they come from France or Russia.

We also take cultural progress with time for granted. The wares from a Roman villa, medieval castle, and 1990 New York apartment differ obviously. In the year 2000 my sons will look with astonishment at the slide rule I used for calculations throughout the 1950s: "Daddy, are you *really* that old?" But Neanderthal tools from 100,000 and 40,000 years ago look essentially the same. In short, Neanderthal tools had no variation in either time or space to suggest that most human of characteristics, *innovation*. As one archaeologist put it, Neanderthals had "beautiful tools stupidly made." Despite Neanderthals' big brains, something was still missing.

Grandparenting, and what we consider old age, must also have been rare among Neanderthals. Their skeletons make clear that adults might live to their thirties or early forties, but not beyond forty-five. If we lacked writing *and* if none of us lived past forty-five, just think how the ability of our society to accumulate and transmit information would suffer.

I've had to mention all these subhuman qualities of Neanderthals, but there are three respects in which we can relate to their humanity. First, virtually all well-preserved Neanderthal caves have small areas of ash and charcoal indicating simple fireplaces. Hence, although Peking Man may have already used fire hundreds of thousands of years earlier, Neanderthals were the first people to leave undisputed evidence of fire's regular use. Neanderthals may also have been the first people who regularly buried their dead, but that's disputed, and whether it would imply religion is a matter of pure speculation. Finally, they regularly took care of their sick and aged. Most skeletons of older Neanderthals show signs of severe impairment, such as withered arms, healed but incapacitating broken bones, tooth loss, and severe osteoarthritis. Only care by young Neanderthals could have enabled such older Neanderthals to stay alive to the point of such incapacitation. After my long litany of what Neanderthals lacked, we've finally found something that lets us feel a spark of kindred spirit in these strange creatures of the last Ice Age—nearly human in form, and yet not really human in spirit.

Did Neanderthals belong to the same species as we do? That depends on whether we could and would have mated and reared a child with a Neanderthal man or woman, given the opportunity. Science-fiction novels love to imagine the scenario. You remember the blurb on many a back cover: "A team of explorers stumbles on a steep-walled valley in the center of deepest Africa, a valley that time forgot. In this valley they find a tribe of incredibly primitive people, living in ways that our Stone Age ancestors discarded thousands of years ago. Do they belong to the same species as we do? There's only one way to find out, but who among the intrepid explorers can bring himself [male explorers, of course] to make the test?" At this point one of the bone-chewing cavewomen suddenly is described as beautiful and sexy in a primitively erotic way, so that modern novel readers will find the brave explorer's dilemma believable: does he or doesn't he have sex with her?

Believe it or not, something like that experiment actually took place. It happened repeatedly around forty thousand years ago, at the time of the Great Leap Forward.

I MENTIONED that the Neanderthals of Europe and western Asia were just one of at least three human populations occupying different parts of the Old World around 100,000 years ago. A few fossils from eastern Asia suffice to show that people there differed from Neanderthals as well as from us moderns, but too few bones have been found to describe these Asians in more detail. The best-characterized contemporaries of the Neanderthals are those from Africa, some of whom were virtually modern in their skull anatomy. Does this mean that, 100,000 years ago in Africa, we have at last arrived at the watershed of human cultural development?

Surprisingly, the answer is still "no." The stone tools of these modern-looking Africans were very similar to those of the decidedly unmodern-looking Neanderthals, hence we refer to them as "Middle Stone Age Africans." They still lacked standardized bone tools, bows and arrows, nets, fishhooks, art, and cultural variation in tools from place to place. Despite their mostly modern bodies, these Africans were still missing something needed to endow them with full humanity. Once again, we face the paradox that mostly modern bones, and presumably mostly modern genes, aren't enough by themselves to produce modern behavior.

Some South African caves occupied around 100,000 years ago provide us with the first time point in human evolution when we have detailed information about what people actually were eating. Our confidence stems from the fact that the African caves are full of stone tools, animal bones with cut marks from stone tools, and human bones, but few or no bones of carnivores like hyenas. Thus, it's clear that people, not hyenas, brought the bones to the caves. Among the bones are many of seals and penguins, as well as shellfish such as limpets. That makes Middle Stone Age Africans the first people for whom there is even a hint that they exploited the seashore. However, the caves contain very few remains of fish or flying seabirds, undoubtedly because people still lacked the fishhooks and nets needed to catch fish and birds.

The mammal bones from the caves include those of quite a few medium-sized species, among which those of an antelope called eland predominate by far. Eland bones in the caves represent eland of all ages, as if people had somehow managed to capture a whole herd and kill every individual. At first, the relative abundance of eland among hunters' prey is surprising, since the caves' environment 100,000 years ago was much as it is today and since eland is now one of the least common large animals in the area. The secret to the hunters' success with eland probably lay in the fact that eland are rather tame, not dangerous, and easy to drive in herds. This suggests that hunters occasionally managed to drive a whole herd over a cliff, explaining why the distribution of eland ages among the cave kills is like that in a living herd. In contrast, more dangerous prey, such as Cape buffalo, pigs, elephants, and rhinos, yield a very different picture. Buffalo bones in the caves are mainly of very young or very old individuals, while pigs, elephants, and rhinos are virtually unrepresented.

Hence Middle Stone Age Africans can be considered big-game hunters, but only barely. They either avoided dangerous species entirely or confined themselves to weak old animals or babies. Those choices reflect sound prudence on the hunters' part, since their weapons were still spears for thrusting rather than bows and arrows. Along with drinking a strychnine cocktail, poking an adult rhino or Cape buffalo with a spear ranks as one of the most effective means of suicide that I know. Nor could the hunters have succeeded often at driving eland herds over cliffs, since elands weren't exterminated but continued to coexist with hunters. As with earlier peoples and modern Stone Age hunters, I suspect that plants and small game made up most of the diets of these not-so-great Middle Stone Age hunters. They were definitely more effective than chimpanzees, but not up to the skill of modern Bushmen and Pygmies.

The scene that the human world presented from around 100,000 to somewhat before fifty thousand years ago was this. Northern Europe, Siberia, Australia, oceanic islands, and the whole New World were still empty of people. In Europe and western Asia lived the Neanderthals; in Africa, people increasingly like us moderns in their anatomy; and in eastern Asia, people unlike either the Neanderthals or Africans but known from only a few bones. All three of these populations were, at least initially, still primitive in their tools, behavior, and limited innovativeness. The stage was set for the Great Leap Forward. Which among these three contemporary populations would take that leap?

THE EVIDENCE for an abrupt rise is clearest in France and Spain, in the Late Ice Age around forty thousand years ago. Where there had previously been Neanderthals, anatomically fully modern people (often known as Cro-Magnons, from the French site where their bones were first identified) now appear. Had one of those gentlemen or ladies strolled down the Champs Élysées in modern attire, he or she would not have stood out from the Parisian crowds in any way. As significant to archaeologists as the Cro-Magnons' skeletons are their tools, which are far more diverse in form and obvious in function than any in the earlier archaeological record. The tools suggest that modern anatomy had at last been joined by modern innovative behavior.

Many of the tools continued to be of stone, but they were now made from thin blades struck off larger stones, thereby yielding ten times more cutting edge from a given quantity of raw stone than obtainable previously. Standardized bone and antler tools appeared for the first time. So did unequivocal compound tools of several parts tied or glued together, such as spear points set in shafts or axe heads fitted onto wooden handles. Tools fall into many distinct categories whose function is often obvious, such as needles, awls, mortars and pestles, fishhooks, net sinkers, and rope. The rope (used in nets or snares) accounts for the frequent bones of foxes, weasels, and rabbits at Cro-Magnon sites, while the rope, fishhooks, and net sinkers explain the bones of fish and flying birds at contemporary South African sites.

Sophisticated weapons for safely killing dangerous large animals at a distance now appear—weapons such as barbed harpoons, darts, spear throwers, and bows and arrows. South African caves occupied by people now yield bones of such vicious prey as adult Cape buffalo and pigs, while European caves are full of bones of bison, elk, reindeer, horse, and ibex. Even today, hunters armed with high-powered telescopic rifles find it hard to bag some of these species, which must have required highly skilled communal hunting methods based on detailed knowledge of each species' behavior.

Several types of evidence testify to the effectiveness of Late Ice Age people as big-game hunters. Their sites are much more numerous than those of earlier Neanderthals or Middle Stone Age Africans, implying more success at obtaining food. Numerous species of big animals that had survived many previous ice ages became extinct toward the end of the last Ice Age, suggesting that they were exterminated by human hunters' new skills. These likely victims, to be discussed in later chapters, include the mammoths of North America, Europe's woolly rhino and giant deer, southern Africa's giant buffalo and giant Cape horse, and Australia's giant kangaroos. Evidently, the most brilliant moment of our rise already contained the seeds of what may yet prove a cause of our fall.

Improved technology now allowed humans to occupy new environments, as well as to multiply in previously occupied areas of Eurasia and Africa. Australia was first reached by humans around fifty thousand years ago, implying watercraft capable of crossing water gaps as wide as sixty miles between eastern Indonesia and Australia. The occupation of northern Russia and Siberia by at least twenty thousand years ago depended on many advances: sewn clothing, whose existence is reflected in eyed needles, cave paintings of parkas, and grave ornaments marking outlines of shirts and trousers; warm furs, indicated by fox and wolf skeletons minus the paws (removed in skinning and found in a separate pile); elaborate houses (marked by postholes, pavements, and walls of mammoth bones), with elaborate fireplaces; and stone lamps to hold animal fat and light the long Arctic nights. The occupation of Siberia and Alaska in turn led to the occupation of North America and South America around eleven thousand years ago.

Whereas Neanderthals obtained their raw materials within a few miles of home, Cro-Magnons and their contemporaries throughout Europe practiced long-distance trade, not only for raw materials of tools but also for "useless" ornaments. Tools of high-quality stone

WORLD CONQUEST

Figure 3. This map illustrates stages in the spread of our ancestors from their African origins to populate the world. Numbers stand for estimated number of years before the present. Further discoveries of older archaeological sites may well show that some regions, such as Siberia or the Solomons, were colonized earlier than the estimated dates shown here.

such as obsidian, jasper, and flint are found hundreds of miles from where those stones were quarried. Baltic amber reached southeast Europe, while Mediterranean shells were carried to inland parts of France, Spain, and the Ukraine. I saw very similar patterns in modern Stone Age New Guinea, where cowry shells prized as decorations were traded up to the highlands from the coast, bird-of-paradise plumes were traded back down to the coast, and obsidian for stone axes was traded out from a few highly valued quarries.

The evident aesthetic sense reflected in Late Ice Age trade in ornaments relates to the achievements for which we most admire the Cro-Magnons: their art. Best known, of course, are the rock paintings from caves like Lascaux, with stunning polychrome depictions of now-extinct animals. But equally impressive are the bas reliefs, necklaces and pendants, fired-clay ceramic sculptures, Venus figurines of women with enormous breasts and buttocks, and musical instruments ranging from flutes to rattles.

Unlike Neanderthals, few of whom lived past the age of forty, some Cro-Magnon skeletons indicate survival to sixty. Many Cro-Magnons, but few Neanderthals, lived to enjoy their grandchildren. Those of us accustomed to getting our information from the printed page or television will find it hard to appreciate how important even just one or two old people are in preliterate society. In New Guinea villages it often happens that younger men lead me to the oldest person in the village when I stump them with a question about some uncommon bird or fruit. For example, when I visited Rennell Island in the Solomons in 1976, many islanders told me what wild fruits were good to eat, but only one old man could tell me what other wild fruits could be eaten in an emergency to avoid starvation. He remembered that information from a cyclone that had hit Rennell in his childhood (around 1905), destroying gardens and reducing his people to a state of desperation. One such person in a preliterate society can thus spell the difference between death and survival for the whole society. Hence the fact that some Cro-Magnons survived twenty years longer than any Neanderthal probably played a big role in Cro-Magnon success. Living to an older age required not just improved survival skills but also some biological changes, possibly including the evolution of human female menopause.

I've described the Great Leap Forward as if all those advances in tools and art appeared simultaneously forty thousand years ago. In fact, different innovations appeared at different times. Spear throwers appeared before harpoons or bows and arrows, while beads and pendants appeared before cave paintings. I've also described the changes as if they were the same everywhere, but they weren't. Among Late Ice Age Africans, Ukrainians, and French, only the Africans made beads out of ostrich eggs, only the Ukrainians built houses out of mammoth bones, and only the French painted woolly rhinos on cave walls.

These variations of culture in time and space are totally unlike the unchanging monolithic Neanderthal culture. They constitute the most important innovation that came with our rise to humanity: namely, the capacity for innovation itself. To us today, who can't picture a world in which Nigerians and Latvians in 1991 have virtually the same possessions as each other and as Romans in 50 B.C., innovation is utterly natural. To Neanderthals, it was evidently unthinkable.

Despite our instant sympathy with Cro-Magnon art, their stone tools and hunter-gatherer life-style make it hard for us to view them as other than primitive. Stone tools evoke cartoons of club-waving cavemen uttering grunts as they drag a woman off to their cave. But we can form a more accurate impression of Cro-Magnons if we imagine what future archaeologists will conclude after excavating a New Guinea village site from as recently as the 1950s. The archaeologists will find a few simple types of stone axes. Virtually all other material possessions were made of wood and will have perished. Nothing will remain of the multistory houses, beautifully woven baskets, drums and flutes, outrigger canoes, and world-quality painted sculpture. There will be no trace of the village's complex language, songs, social relationships, and knowledge of the natural world.

New Guinea material culture was until recently "primitive" (i.e., Stone Age) for historical reasons, but New Guineans are fully modern humans. New Guineans whose fathers lived in the Stone Age now pilot airplanes, operate computers, and govern a modern state. If we could carry ourselves back forty thousand years in a time machine, I suspect that we would find Cro-Magnons to be equally modern people, capable of learning to fly a jet plane. They made stone and bone tools only because no other tools had yet been invented; that's all they had the opportunity to learn.

It used to be argued that Neanderthals evolved into Cro-Magnons within Europe. That possibility now seems increasingly unlikely. The last Neanderthal skeletons from somewhat after forty thousand years ago were still "full-blown" Neanderthals, while the first Cro-Magnons appearing in Europe at the same time were already anatomically fully modern. Since anatomically modern people were already present in Africa and the Near East tens of thousands of years earlier, it seems much more likely that anatomically modern people invaded Europe from that direction than that they evolved within Europe.

What happened when invading Cro-Magnons met the resident Neanderthals? We can be certain only of the end result: within a short time, no more Neanderthals. The conclusion seems to me inescapable that Cro-Magnon arrival somehow caused Neanderthal extinction. Yet many archaeologists recoil at this conclusion and invoke environmental changes instead. For example, the *Encyclopedia Britannica*'s fifteenth edition concludes its entry for Neanderthals with the sentence "The disappearance of the Neanderthals, although it cannot yet be fixed in time, was probably the result of being creatures of an interglacial period unable to avoid the ravages of another Ice Age." In fact, Neanderthals thrived during the last Ice Age, and suddenly disappeared over thirty thousand years after its start and an equal time before its end.

My guess is that events in Europe at the time of the Great Leap Forward were similar to events that have occurred repeatedly in the modern world, whenever a numerous people with more advanced technology invades the lands of a much less-numerous people with less-advanced technology. For instance, when European colonists invaded North America, most North American Indians proceeded to die of introduced epidemics; most of the survivors were killed outright or driven off their land; some of the survivors adopted European technology (horses and guns) and resisted for some time; and many of the remaining survivors were pushed onto lands that Europeans did not want, or else intermarried with Europeans. The displacement of Aboriginal Australians by European colonists, and of southern African San populations (Bushmen) by invading iron-age Bantu speakers, followed a similar course.

By analogy, I guess that Cro-Magnon diseases, murders, and displacements did in the Neanderthals. If so, then the Cro-Magnon-Neanderthal transition was a harbinger of what was to come, when the victors' descendants began squabbling among themselves. It may at first seem paradoxical that Cro-Magnons prevailed over the far more muscular Neanderthals, but weaponry rather than strength would have been decisive. Similarly, it's not gorillas that are now threatening to exterminate humans in central Africa, but vice versa. People with huge muscles require lots of food, and they thereby gain no advantage if slimmer, smarter people can use tools to do the same work.

Like the Great Plains Indians, some Neanderthals may have learned some Cro-Magnon ways and resisted for a while. This is the only sense I can make of a puzzling culture called the Châtelperronian, which coexisted in western Europe along with a typical Cro-

Magnon culture (the so-called Aurignacian culture) for a short time after Cro-Magnons arrived. Châtelperronian stone tools are a mixture of typical Neanderthal and Cro-Magnon tools, but the bone tools and art typical of Cro-Magnons are usually lacking. The identity of the people who produced Châtelperronian culture was debated by archaeologists until a skeleton unearthed with Châtelperronian artifacts at Saint-Césaire in France proved to be Neanderthal. Perhaps, then, some Neanderthals managed to master some Cro-Magnon tools and hold out longer than their fellows.

What remains unclear is the outcome of the interbreeding experiment posed in science-fiction novels. Did some invading Cro-Magnon men mate with some Neanderthal women? No skeletons that could reasonably be considered Neanderthal-Cro-Magnon hybrids are known. If Neanderthal behavior was as relatively rudimentary, and Neanderthal anatomy as distinctive as I suspect, few Cro-Magnons may have wanted to mate with Neanderthals. Similarly, although humans and chimps continue to coexist today, I'm not aware of any matings. While Cro-Magnons and Neanderthals weren't nearly as different, the differences may still have been a mutual turnoff. And if Neanderthal women were geared for a twelve-month pregnancy, a hybrid fetus might not have survived. My inclination is to take the negative evidence at face value, to accept that hybridization occurred rarely if ever, and to doubt that living people of European descent carry any Neanderthal genes.

So much for the Great Leap Forward in western Europe. The replacement of Neanderthals by modern people occurred somewhat earlier in eastern Europe, and still earlier in the Near East, where possession of the same area apparently shifted back and forth between Neanderthals and modern people from ninety thousand to sixty thousand years ago. The slowness of the transition in the Near East, compared to its speed in western Europe, suggests that the anatomically modern people living around the Near East before sixty thousand years ago had not yet developed the modern behavior that ultimately let them drive out the Neanderthals.

Thus, we have a tentative picture of anatomically modern people arising in Africa over a hundred thousand years ago, but initially making the same tools as Neanderthals and having no advantage over them. By perhaps sixty thousand years ago, some magic twist of behavior had been added to the modern anatomy. That twist (of which more in a moment) produced innovative, fully modern people who proceeded to spread westward from the Near East into Europe, quickly supplanting Europe's Neanderthals. Presumably, those modern people also spread east into Asia and Indonesia, supplanting the earlier people there, of whom we know little. Some anthropologists think that skull remains of those earlier Asians and Indonesians show traits recognizable in modern Asians and Aboriginal Australians. If so, the invading moderns may not have exterminated the original Asians without issue, as they did the Neanderthals, but instead interbred with them.

Two million years ago, several protohuman lineages had coexisted side by side until a shakedown left only one. It now appears that a similar shakedown occurred within the last sixty thousand years, and that all of us alive in the world today are descended from the winner of that shakedown. What was the last missing ingredient whose acquisition helped our ancestor to win?

THE IDENTITY of the ingredient that produced the Great Leap Forward poses an archaeological puzzle without an accepted answer. It doesn't show up in fossil skeletons. It may have been a change in only 0.1 percent of our DNA. What tiny change in genes could have had such enormous consequences?

Like some other scientists who have speculated about this question, I can think of only one plausible answer: the anatomical basis for spoken complex language. Chimpanzees, gorillas, and even monkeys are capable of symbolic communication not dependent on spoken words. Both chimpanzees and gorillas have been taught to communicate by means of sign language, and chimpanzees have learned to communicate via the keys of a large computer-controlled console. Individual apes have thus mastered "vocabularies" of hundreds of symbols. While scientists argue over the extent to which such communication resembles human language, there is little doubt that it constitutes a form of symbolic communication. That is, a particular sign or computer key symbolizes a particular something else.

Primates can use not just signs and computer keys, but also sounds, as symbols. For instance, wild vervet monkeys have a natural form of symbolic communication based on grunts, with slightly different grunts to mean "leopard," "eagle," and "snake." A month-old chimpanzee named Viki, adopted by a psychologist and his wife and reared virtually as their daughter, learned to "say" approximations of four words: "papa," "mama," "cup," and "up." (The chimp breathed rather than spoke those words.) Given this capability for symbolic communication using sounds, why have apes not gone on to develop much more complex natural languages of their own?

The answer seems to involve the structure of the larynx, tongue, and associated muscles that give us fine control over spoken sounds. Like a Swiss watch, all of whose many parts have to be well designed for the watch to keep time at all, our vocal tract depends on the precise functioning of many structures and muscles. Chimps are thought to be physically incapable of producing several of the commonest human vowels. If we too were limited to just a few vowels and consonants, our own vocabulary would be greatly reduced. For example, take this paragraph, convert all vowels other than "a" or "i" to either of those two, convert all consonants other than "d" or "m" or "s" to one of those three, and then see how much of the paragraph you can still understand.

That's why it's plausible that the missing ingredient may have been some modifications of the protohuman vocal tract to give us finer control and permit formation of a much greater variety of sounds. Such fine modifications of muscles need not be detectable in fossil skulls.

It's easy to appreciate how a tiny change in anatomy resulting in capacity for speech would produce a huge change in behavior. With language, it takes only a few seconds to communicate the message, "Turn sharp right at the fourth tree and drive the male antelope toward the reddish boulder, where I'll hide to spear it." Without language, that message could not be communicated at all. Without language, two protohumans could not brainstorm together about how to devise a better tool, or about what a cave painting might mean. Without language, even one protohuman would have had difficulty thinking out for himself or herself how to devise a better tool.

I don't suggest that the Great Leap Forward began as soon as the mutations for altered tongue and larynx anatomy arose. Given the right anatomy, it must have taken humans thousands of years to perfect the structure of language as we know it—to arrive at the concepts of word order and case endings and tenses, and to develop vocabulary. In Chapter 8 I'll consider some possible stages by which our language might have become perfected. But if the missing ingredient did consist of changes in our vocal tract that permitted fine control of sounds, then the capacity for innovation would follow eventually. It was the spoken word that made us free.

This interpretation seems to me to account for the lack of evidence for Neanderthal-Cro-Magnon hybrids. Speech is of overwhelming importance in the relations between men and women and their children. That's not to deny that mute or deaf people learn to function well in our culture, but they do so by learning to find alternatives for a spoken language that already exists. If Neanderthal language was much simpler than ours or nonexistent, it's not surprising that Cro-Magnons didn't choose to marry Neanderthals.

I'VE ARGUED that we were fully modern in anatomy and behavior and language by forty thousand years ago, and that a Cro-Magnon could have been taught to fly a jet airplane. If so, why did it take so long after the Great Leap Forward for us to invent writing and build the Parthenon? The answer may be similar to the explanation why the Romans, great engineers that they were, didn't build atomic bombs. To reach the point of building an A-bomb required two thousand years of technological advances beyond Roman levels, such as the invention of gunpowder and calculus, the development of atomic theory, and the isolation of uranium. Similarly, writing and the Parthenon depended on tens of thousands of years of cumulative developments after the arrival of Cro-Magnons—developments that included the bow and arrow, pottery, domestication of plants and animals, and many others.

Until the Great Leap Forward, human culture had developed at a snail's pace for millions of years. That pace was dictated by the slow pace of genetic change. After the leap, cultural development no longer depended on genetic change. Despite negligible changes in our anatomy, there has been far more cultural evolution in the past forty thousand years than in the millions of years before. Had a visitor from Outer Space come to the Earth in Neanderthal times, humans would not have stood out as unique among the world's species. At most, the visitor might have mentioned humans along with beavers, bowerbirds, and army ants as examples of species with curious behavior. Would the visitor have foreseen the change that would soon make us the first species, in the history of life on Earth, capable of destroying all life?

PART TWO

AN ANIMAL
WITH A STRANGE
LIFE CYCLE

We've just traced our evolutionary history through the appearance of humans with fully modern anatomy and behavioral capabilities. But that background doesn't prepare us to go straight on to consider the development of human cultural hallmarks, such as language and art. That's because we took up only the evidence of bones and tools. Yes, our evolution of large brains and upright posture was prerequisite to language and art, but wasn't enough by itself. Human bones alone don't guarantee humanity. Instead, our rise to humanity also required drastic changes in our life cycle, which will be the subject of Part Two.

For any species one can describe what biologists term its "life cycle." That means traits such as the number of offspring produced per litter or birth, the parental care (if any) that offspring receive from the mother or father, social relations between adult individuals, how a male and female select each other to mate with, frequency of sexual relations, menopause (if any), and life expectancy.

We take the forms of these traits as they exist in humans for granted, as the norm. But our life cycle is actually bizarre by animal standards. All the traits that I've just mentioned vary greatly between species, and we are extreme in most respects. To mention only some obvious examples, most animals produce litters much larger than one baby at a time, most animal fathers provide no parental care, and few other animal species live even a small fraction of three score years and ten.

Of these exceptional features of ours, some are shared by apes, suggesting that we merely retained traits already acquired by our apelike ancestors. For instance, apes too usually give birth to one baby at a time and live for several decades. Neither of these things is true of the other animals most familiar (but less closely related) to us, such as cats, dogs, songbirds, and goldfish.

In others of these respects, we're greatly different even from apes. Here are some obvious differences whose functions are well understood. Human babies continue to have all food brought to them by their parents even after weaning, whereas weaned apes gather their own food. Most human fathers as well as mothers, but only chimpanzee mothers, are closely involved in caring for their young. Like seagulls but unlike apes or most other mammals, we live in dense breeding colonies of nominally monogamous couples, some of whom also pursue extramarital sex. All these traits are as essential as large brain cases for the survival and education of human offspring. That's because our elaborate, tool-dependent methods of obtaining food make weaned human infants incompetent to feed themselves. Our infants first require a long period of food provisioning, training, and protection—an investment much more taxing than that facing the ape mother. Hence human fathers who want their offspring to survive to maturity have generally assisted their mates with more than just sperm, the sole parental input of an orangutan father.

Our life cycle also differs from that of wild apes in more subtle respects, whose functions are nevertheless still discernible. Many of us live longer than most wild apes: even hunter-gatherer tribes include some old individuals who are enormously important as repositories of experience. Men's testes are much larger than those of gorillas but smaller than those of chimps, for reasons that this book will explain. We regard human female menopause as inevitable, and I'll show why it makes good sense for humans, but it's almost unprecedented among other mammals. The closest mammalian parallel is among some tiny mouselike marsupials in Australia, and it's their males, not their females, that undergo menopause. Our longevity, testis size, and menopause were also prerequisites to our humanity.

Still other features of our life cycle differ far more drastically from those of apes than do our testes, yet the functions of those remaining novel features of ours remain hotly debated. We are unusual in having sex mainly in private and for fun, rather than mainly in public and only when the female is able to conceive. Ape females advertise the time when they are ovulating; human females conceal it even from themselves. While anatomists understand the value of men's moderate testis size, an explanation for men's relatively enormous penis still escapes us. Whatever their explanation, all these features, too, are part of what defines humanity. Certainly, it is hard to picture how fathers and mothers could cooperate harmoniously at rearing their children if human females resembled some primate females in having their genitalia turn bright red at the time of ovulation, becoming sexually receptive only at that time, flaunting their red badge of receptivity, and proceeding to have sex in public with any passing male.

Thus, human society and child rearing rest not only on the skeletal changes mentioned in Part One, but also on these remarkable new features of our life cycle. Unlike the case with our skeletal changes, however, we can't follow through our evolutionary history the timing of each of these life-cycle changes, because they leave no direct fossil imprint. As a result, they receive only brief attention in paleontology texts despite their importance. Archaeologists have recently discovered a Neanderthal hyoid bone, one of the key pieces of our speech-producing equipment, but as yet no trace of a Neanderthal penis. We don't know whether *Homo erectus* was already on the road to evolving a preference for having sex in private, in addition to having evolved his and her well-documented large brain. We can't even prove through fossils, as we can for our large brain size, that we rather than living apes are the ones whose life cycles diverged most from the ancestral condition. Instead, we have to be content with merely inferring that conclusion from the fact that our life cycles are exceptional compared not just to living apes but also to other primates, suggesting that we were the ones who did more changing.

Darwin established in the mid-nineteenth century that animals' anatomy has evolved through natural selection. Within this century, biochemists have similarly traced how animals' chemical makeup has evolved through natural selection. But so has animals' behavior, including reproductive biology and sexual habits in particular. Life-cycle traits have some genetic basis and vary quantitatively among individuals of the same species. For instance, some women are genetically predisposed to give birth to twins, while we're all aware that genes for long life span run in some families more than in others. Life-cycle traits affect our success in passing on our genes, through affecting our success in wooing mates, conceiving, rearing babies, and surviving as adults. Just as natural selection tends to adapt an animal's anatomy to its ecological niche and vice versa, so natural selection also tends to mold animals' life cycles. Those individuals leaving the most numerous surviving offspring promote their genes for life-cycle traits as well as for bones and chemical makeup.

A difficulty with this reasoning is that it seems as if some of our traits, such as menopause and aging, would reduce (rather than enhance) our output of offspring and shouldn't have resulted from natural selection. It often proves profitable to try to understand these paradoxes through the concept of "trade-offs." In the animal world there's nothing that's free or pure good. Everything involves costs as well as benefits, by using space, time, or energy that could have been devoted to something else. You might otherwise have thought that women who never underwent menopause would leave more descendants than women designed as they actually are. But we'll see that consideration of the hidden costs of forgoing menopause suggests why evolution didn't design these strategies into us. The same considerations illuminate such painful questions as why we grow old and die, and whether we're better off (even in a narrow evolutionary sense) in being faithful to our spouses or in pursuing extramarital affairs.

I've been assuming in this discussion that our distinctively human life-cycle traits have some genetic basis. The comments that I made in Chapter 1 about the function of genes in general apply here as well. Just as our height and most of our other observable traits aren't influenced by just a single gene, there surely isn't a single gene specifying menopause or monogamy. In fact, we know little about the genetic bases of human life-cycle traits, though selective breeding experiments in mice and sheep have illuminated the genetic control of their testis size. Enormous cultural influences obviously operate on our motivation for providing child care or seeking extramarital sex, and there is no reason to believe that genes contribute significantly to differences among individual people in these traits. However, genetic differences between humans and the other two chimpanzee species probably do contribute to the consistent differences in many life-cycle traits between all human populations and all chimpanzee populations. There is no human society, regardless of its cultural practices, whose men have chimpanzee-sized testes and whose women forgo menopause. Among those 1.6 percent of our genes that differ between us and chimps and that have any function, a significant fraction is likely to be involved in specifying traits of our life cycle.

In our discussion of our uniquely human life cycle, we'll begin by taking up the distinctive features of human social organization and of sexual anatomy, physiology, and behavior. As already mentioned, features that make us strange among animals include our societies of nominally monogamous couples, our genital anatomy, and our constant and generally private pursuit of sex. Our sex lives are reflected not only in our genitalia but also in the relative sizes of men's and women's bodies (much more equal than are the bodies of male and female gorillas or orangutans). We'll see how some of these familiar distinctive features have known functions, while others continue to defy understanding.

No honest discussion of the human life cycle could get away with noting that we're nominally monogamous and just leaving it at that. Pursuit of extramarital sex is obviously greatly influenced by each individual's particular upbringing and by the norms of the society in which the individual lives. Despite all that cultural influence, we're left with having to explain the facts that *both* the institution of marriage *and* the occurrence of extramarital sex have been reported from all human societies; but that extramarital sex is unknown in gibbons, although they do practice "marriage" (i.e., lasting male-female pairing to rear offspring); and that the question of extramarital sex is meaningless for chimpanzees because they don't practice "marriage." Thus, an adequate discussion of our uniquely human life cycle must account for our combination of marriage with extramarital sex. As I'll show, animal precedents exist to help us make evolutionary sense of our combination: men and women tend to differ in their attitudes toward extramarital sex much as geese and ganders do.

We'll then turn to another distinctive human life-cycle trait: how we select our sex partners, marital or otherwise. That problem scarcely arises for baboon troops, in which there is little selection: any male tries to mate with each female as she comes into heat. While common chimpanzees do some picking of their sex partners, they're still much less selective and much more promiscuously baboonlike than are humans. Mate selection is a decision of major consequence in the human life cycle, because married couples share parental responsibilities as well as sexual involvement. Precisely because care of human children demands such heavy and prolonged parental investment, we have to select our coinvestor much more carefully than does a baboon. Nevertheless, it turns out that we can find animal precedents for our procedure in choosing sex partners, by going beyond primates to rats and birds.

Those mate-selection criteria of ours prove relevant to the vexed question of human racial variation. Humans native to different parts of the globe vary conspicuously in external appearance, as do gorillas, orangutans, and most other animal species occupying a sufficiently extensive geographic range. Some of the geographic variation in our appearance surely reflects natural selection molding us to local climate, just as weasels in areas with winter snow develop white fur in winter for better camouflage and survival. But I'll argue that our visible geographic variability arose mainly through sexual selection, as a result of our mate-choice procedures.

To bring the discussion of our life cycle to an end, I'll ask why our lives themselves have to come to an end. Aging is another feature of our life cycle so familiar that we take it for granted: of course we'll all grow old and eventually die. So will all individuals of all animal species, but different species age at very different rates. Among animals we are relatively long-lived and became even more so around the time that Cro-Magnons replaced Neanderthals. Our longevity has been important for our humanity, by permitting effective transmission of learned skills between generations. But even humans grow old. Why is aging inevitable, given our extensive capacity for biological self-repair?

Here, more than anywhere else in this book, the importance of thinking in terms of evolutionary trade-offs becomes clear. As measured by leaving increased numbers of offspring, it paradoxically just wouldn't pay us to make the increased investment in self-repair mechanisms required to live longer. We'll see that the trade-off concept also illuminates the puzzle of menopause: a shutdown of childbearing, paradoxically programmed by natural selection so that women can leave more surviving children.

CHAPTER 3

The Evolution
of Human Sexuality

NO WEEK PASSES WITHOUT PUBLICATION OF YET ANOTHER BOOK about sex. Our desire to read about sex is surpassed only by our desire to practice it. Hence, you might suppose, the basic facts of human sexuality must be familiar to lay people and understood by scientists. Just test your own grasp of sex by trying to answer these five easy questions:

Among the various ape species and man, which has by far the biggest penis, and what for?

Why should men be bigger than women?

How can men get away with having much smaller testes than do chimpanzees?

Why do humans copulate in private, while all other social animals do it in public?

Why don't women resemble almost all other female mammals in having easily recognized days of fertility, with sexual receptivity confined to those days?

If you jumped at "the gorilla" as your answer to the first question, put on a dunce cap; the correct answer is man. If you gave any intelligent answers to the next four questions, publish them; scientists are still debating rival theories.

These five questions illustrate how hard it is to explain the most obvious facts of our sexual anatomy and physiology. Part of the problem is our hang-ups about sex: scientists did not begin to study it seriously until recently, and they still have trouble being objective. Another difficulty is that scientists can't do controlled experiments on sexual practices of us humans, as they can on our cholesterol intake or toothbrushing habits. Finally, sex organs don't exist in isolation: they are adapted to their owners' social habits and life cycle, which are in turn adapted to food-gathering habits. In our own case that means, among other things, that evolution of human sex organs has been intertwined with that of human tool use, large brains, and child-rearing practices. Our progress from being just another species of big mammal to being uniquely human therefore depended on the remodeling not just of our pelvises and skulls, but also of our sexuality.

GIVEN KNOWLEDGE of how an animal feeds, a biologist can often predict the animal's mating system and genital anatomy. In particular, if we want to understand how human sexuality got to be the way it is, we have to begin by understanding the evolution of our own diet and our society. From the vegetarian diet of our ape ancestors, we diverged within the last several million years to become social carnivores as well as vegetarians. Yet our teeth and claws remained those of apes, not of tigers. Our hunting prowess depended instead on large brains: by using tools and operating in coordinated groups, our ancestors were able to hunt successfully despite their deficient anatomical equipment, and they regularly shared food with each other. Our ability to gather roots and berries as well came to depend on tools and thus also to require large brains.

As a result, human children took years to acquire the information and the practice needed to be efficient hunter-gatherers, just as they still take years to learn how to be farmers or computer programmers today. During those many years after weaning, our children are still too ignorant and helpless to acquire their own food; they depend entirely on us parents to bring food to them. These habits are so natural to us that we forget that baby apes gather food as soon as they are weaned.

The reasons that human infants are totally incompetent at food gathering are actually twofold: mechanical and mental. First, making and wielding the tools used to obtain food requires fine finger coordination that children take years to develop. Just as my four-year-old sons still can't tie their own shoelaces, four-year-old hunter-gatherer children can't sharpen a stone axe or build a dugout canoe. Second, we depend on much more brainpower than do other animals in acquiring food, because we have a much more varied diet and more varied and complicated food-gathering techniques. For instance, New Guineans with whom I work typically have separate names for about a thousand different species of plants and animals living in the vicinity. For each of those species they know something about its distribution and life history, how to recognize it, whether it is edible or otherwise useful, and how best to capture or harvest it. All this information takes years to acquire.

Weaned human infants can't support themselves because they lack these mechanical and mental skills. They need adults to teach them, and they also need adults to feed them for the decade or two that they are being taught. As is true of so many other human hallmarks, these problems of ours too have animal precedents. In lions and many other species, the young must be trained to hunt by their parents. Chimpanzees too have a varied diet, employ varied foraging techniques, and assist their young in obtaining food, while common (but not pygmy) chimps make some use of tools. Our distinction isn't absolute but one of degree: for us the necessary skills and hence the parental burden are far greater than for lions or chimpanzees.

The resulting parental burden makes parental care by the father as well as the mother important for a child to survive. Orangutan fathers provide their offspring with nothing beyond their initial donation of semen; gorilla, chimpanzee, and gibbon fathers go beyond that to offer protection; but hunter-gatherer human fathers provide some food and much teaching as well. Human food-gathering habits require a social system in which a male retains his relationship with a female after fertilizing her, in order to assist in rearing the resulting child. Otherwise, the child would be less likely to survive, and the father less likely to pass on his genes. The orangutan system, in which the father departs after copulation, wouldn't work for us.

But the chimpanzee system, in which several adult males are likely to copulate with the same estrous female, also wouldn't work for us. The result of that system is that a chimpanzee father has no idea which infants in the troop he has sired. For the chimp father that's no loss, as his exertions on behalf of troop infants are modest. For the human father, however, who will contribute significantly to the care of what he thinks is his child, he had better have some confidence in his paternity—e.g., through having been the exclusive sexual partner of the child's mother. Otherwise, his child-care contribution may help pass on some other man's genes.

Confidence in paternity would be no problem if humans, like gibbons, were scattered over the landscape as separate couples, so that each female would only rarely encounter a male other than her consort. But there are compelling reasons why almost all human populations have consisted of groups of adults, despite the paranoia about paternity that this causes. Among the reasons: much human hunting and gathering involves cooperative group efforts among men, women, or both; much of our wild food occurs in scattered but concentrated patches, able to sustain many people; and groups offer better protection against predators and aggressors, especially against other humans.

In short, the social system we evolved to accommodate our un-apelike food habits seems utterly normal to us, but is bizarre by ape standards and is virtually unique among mammals. Adult orangutans are solitary; adult gibbons live as separate monogamous, male-female pairs; gorillas live in polygamous harems, each consisting of several adult females and usually one dominant adult male; common chimpanzees live in fairly promiscuous communities consisting of scattered females plus a group of males; and pygmy chimpanzees form even more promiscuous communities of both sexes. But our societies, like our food habits, resemble those of lions and wolves: we live in bands containing many adult males *and* many adult females. Furthermore, we diverge from even lions and wolves in how those societies are organized: our males and females are paired off with each other. In contrast, any male lion within a lion pride can and regularly does mate with any of the pride's lionesses, making paternity unidentifiable. Our peculiar societies instead have their closest parallels in colonies of seabirds, like gulls and penguins, which also consist of male-female pairs.

At least officially, human pairing is more or less monogamous in most modern political states, but is "mildly polygynous" among most surviving hunter-gatherer bands, which are better models for how mankind lived over the last million years. (This description omits consideration of extramarital sex, through which we become effectively more polygamous and whose scientifically fascinating aspects I'll discuss in the next chapter.) By "mildly polygynous," I mean that most hunter-gatherer men can support only a single family, but a few powerful men have several wives. Polygyny on the scale of elephant seals, among which powerful males have dozens of wives, is impossible for hunter-gatherer men, because they differ from elephant seals in having to provide child care. The big harems for which some human potentates are famous didn't become possible until the rise of agriculture and centralized government let a few princes tax everyone else in order to feed the royal harem's babies.

Now LET'S SEE how this social organization shapes the bodies of men and women. Take first the fact that adult men are slightly bigger than similar-aged women (about 8 percent taller and 20 percent heavier, on the average). A zoologist from Outer Space would take one look at my five-foot-eight wife next to me (five-feet-ten), and would instantly guess that we belonged to a mildly polygynous species. How, you may ask, can one possibly guess mating practices from relative body size?

It turns out that, among polygynous mammals, average harem size increases with the ratio of the male's body size to the female's body size. That is, the biggest harems are typical of species in which males are much larger than females. For example, males and females are the same size among gibbons, which are monogamous; male gorillas, with a typical harem of three to six females, weigh nearly double each female; but the average harem is forty-eight wives for the southern elephant seal, whose three-ton male dwarfs his seven hundred-pound wives. The explanation is that, in a monogamous species, every male can win a female, but in a very polygynous species most males languish without any mates, because a few dominant males have succeeded in rounding up all the females into their harems. Hence, the bigger the harem, the fiercer is the competition among males and the more important it is for a male to be big, since the bigger male usually wins the fights. We humans, with our slightly bigger males and slight polygyny, fit this pattern. (However, at some point in human evolution, male intelligence and personality came to count for more than size: male basketball players and sumo wrestlers don't tend to have more wives than male jockeys or coxswains.)

Because competition for mates is fiercer in polygynous than monogamous species, the polygynous species also tend to have more marked differences between males and females in other respects besides body size. These differences are the secondary sexual characteristics that play a role in attracting mates. For instance, males and females of the monogamous gibbons look identical at a distance, while male gorillas (befitting their polygyny) are easily recognized by their crested heads and silver-haired backs. Here too, our anatomy reflects our mild polygyny. The external differences between men and women aren't nearly as marked as sex-related differences in gorillas or orangutans, but the zoologist from Outer Space could probably still distinguish men and women by the body and facial hair of men, men's unusually large penises, and the large breasts of women even before first pregnancy (in this we are unique among primates).

PROCEEDING NOW to the genitalia themselves, the combined weight of the testes in the average man is about 1½ ounces. This may boost the macho man's ego when he reflects on the slightly lower testis weight in a 450-pound male gorilla. But wait: our testes are dwarfed by the 4-ounce testes of a 100-pound male chimpanzee. Why is the gorilla so economical, and the chimp so well-endowed, compared to us?

The Theory of Testis Size is one of the triumphs of modern physical anthropology. By weighing the testes of thirty-three primate species, British scientists identified two trends: species that copulate more often need bigger testes; and promiscuous species in which several males routinely copulate in quick sequence with one female need especially big testes (because the male that injects the most semen has the best chance of being the one to fertilize the egg). When fertilization is a competitive lottery, large testes enable a male to enter more sperm in the lottery.

MALES, AS FEMALES SEE THEM

female

chimp

man

orangutan

gorilla

Figure 4. Humans and great apes differ with respect to the relative body size of males and females, penis length, and testis size. The main circles represent the body size of the male of each species relative to that of the female of the same species. Female body size is arbitrarily shown as the same for all species at upper right. Thus, chimps of both sexes weigh about the same; men are slightly larger than women; but male orangutans and gorillas are much bigger than females. The arrows on the male symbols are proportional to the length of the erect penis, while the twin circles represent testis weight relative to that of the body. Men have the longest penises, chimps the largest testes, and orangutans and gorillas the shortest penises and smallest testes.

Here's how these considerations account for the differences in testis size among the great apes and humans. A female gorilla does not resume sexual activity until three or four years after giving birth, and she is receptive for only a couple of days a month until she becomes pregnant again. Even the successful male gorilla with a harem of several females experiences sex as a rare treat: if he is lucky, a few times a year. His relatively tiny testes are quite adequate for

FEMALES, AS MALES SEE THEM

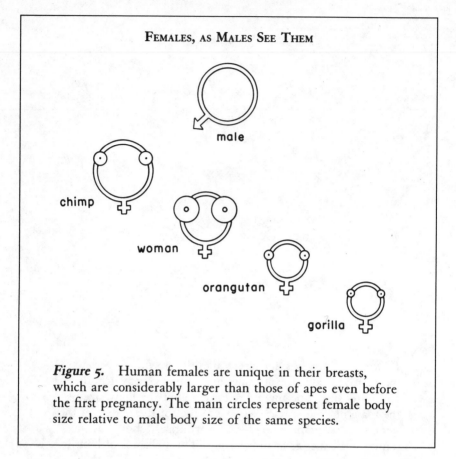

Figure 5. Human females are unique in their breasts, which are considerably larger than those of apes even before the first pregnancy. The main circles represent female body size relative to male body size of the same species.

those modest demands. The sex life of a male orangutan may be somewhat more demanding, but not much. However, each male chimp in a promiscuous troop of many females lives in sexual nirvana, with nearly daily opportunities to copulate for a common chimp and several daily copulations for the average pygmy chimp. That, plus his need to outdo other male chimps in semen output if he is to fertilize the promiscuous females, explains his need for gigantic testes. We humans make do with medium-sized testes, because the average man copulates more often than gorillas or orangutans but less often than chimps. In addition, the typical woman in a typical menstrual cycle does not force several men into sperm competition to fertilize her.

Thus, primate testis design well illustrates the principles of trade-offs and evolutionary cost/benefit analyses explained on pages 62–65.

Each species has testes big enough to do their job, but not unnecessarily larger ones. Bigger testes would just entail more costs without proportional benefits, by diverting space and energy from other tissues and increasing the risk of testicular cancer.

From this triumph of scientific explanation we descend to a glaring failure: the inability of twentieth-century science to formulate an adequate Theory of Penis Length. The length of the erect penis averages 1¼ inches in a gorilla, 1½ inches in an orangutan, 3 inches in a chimp, and 5 inches in a man. Visual conspicuousness varies in the same sequence: a gorilla's penis is inconspicuous even when erect because of its black color, while the chimp's pink erect penis stands out against the bare white skin behind it. The flaccid penis is not even visible in apes. Why does the human male need his relatively enormous, attention-getting penis, which is larger than that of any other primate? Since the male ape successfully propagates his kind with much less, does not the human penis represent largely wasted protoplasm that would be more valuable if devoted, say, to the cerebral cortex or improved fingers?

Biologist friends to whom I pose this conundrum usually think of distinctive features of human coitus in which they suppose a long penis might somehow be useful: our frequent use of the face-to-face position, our acrobatic variety of coital positions, and the leisurely duration of our coital bouts. None of these explanations survives close scrutiny. The face-to-face position is also a preferred one for orangutans and pygmy chimps, and is used occasionally by gorillas. Orangs vary face-to-face copulation with dorsoventral and sideways positions, and do it while hanging from branches of trees: surely that demands more penile acrobatics than our comfortable boudoir exercises. Our mean duration of coitus (about four minutes for Americans) is much longer than for gorillas (one minute), pygmy chimps (fifteen seconds), or common chimps (seven seconds), but shorter than for orangutans (fifteen minutes) and lightning-fast compared to the twelve-hour-long copulations of marsupial mice.

Since these facts make it unlikely that special features of human coitus demand a large penis, a popular alternative theory is that the human penis has also become an organ of display, like a peacock's tail or a lion's mane. This theory is reasonable but begs the question: what type of display, and to whom?

Proud male anthropologists unhesitatingly answer: an attractive display, to women. But the anthropologists' answer represents mere wishful thinking. Many women say that they are turned on by a man's voice, legs, and shoulders more than by the sight of his penis. A telling point is that the women's magazine *Viva* initially published photos of nude men but dropped them after surveys showed lack of female interest. When *Viva*'s nude men disappeared, the number of female readers increased, and the number of male readers decreased. Evidently the male readers were the ones buying *Viva* for its nude photos. While we can agree that the human penis is an organ of display, the display is intended not for women but for fellow men.

Other facts confirm the role of a large penis as a threat or status display toward other men. Recall all the phallic art created by men for men, and the widespread obsession of men with their penis size. Evolution of the human penis was effectively limited by the length of the female vagina: a man's penis would damage a woman if it were significantly larger. However, I can guess what the penis would look like if this practical constraint were removed and if men could design themselves. It would resemble the penis sheaths (phallocarps) used as male attire in some areas of New Guinea where I do fieldwork. Phallocarps vary in length (up to two feet), diameter (up to 4 inches), shape (curved or straight), angle made with the wearer's body, color (yellow or red), and decoration (e.g., a tuft of fur at the end). Each man has a wardrobe of several sizes and shapes from which to choose each day, depending on his mood that morning. Embarrassed male anthropologists interpret the phallocarp as something used for modesty or concealment, to which my wife had a succinct answer on seeing a phallocarp: "The most immodest display of modesty I've ever seen!"

Thus, astonishing as it seems, important functions of the human penis remain obscure. Here is a rich field for research.

PASSING NOW from anatomy to physiology, we are immediately confronted by our sexual-activity pattern, which must be considered freakish by the standards of other mammal species. Most mammals are sexually inactive most of the time. They copulate only when the female is in estrus—i.e., when she is ovulating and capable of being fertilized. Female mammals apparently "know" when they are ovulating, for they solicit copulation then by presenting their genitals toward males. Lest a male miss the point, many female primates go further: the area around the vagina, plus in some species the buttocks and breast, swells up and turns red, pink, or blue. This visual advertisement of female availability affects male monkeys in the same way that the sight of a seductively dressed woman affects male humans. In the presence of females with brightly swollen genitals, male monkeys stare much more often at the female's genitals, develop higher testosterone levels, attempt to copulate more often, and penetrate more quickly and after fewer pelvic thrusts than in the presence of females not displaying their wares.

Human sexual cycles are quite different. The human female maintains her sexual receptivity more or less constantly, instead of having it sharply confined to a short estrus phase. Indeed, despite numerous studies aimed at settling whether a woman's receptivity varies at all through her cycle, there is still no agreement about the answer—nor about the cycle phase when receptivity is maximal if it does vary.

So well concealed is human ovulation that we did not have accurate scientific information on its timing until around 1930. Before that, many physicians thought that women could conceive at any point in their cycle, or even that conception was most likely at the time of menstruation. In contrast to the male monkey, who has only to scan his surroundings for brightly swollen lady monkeys, the unfortunate human male has not the faintest idea which ladies around him are ovulating and capable of being fertilized. A woman herself may learn to recognize sensations associated with ovulation, but it is often tricky, even with the help of thermometers and ratings of vaginal mucus quality. Furthermore, today's would-be mother, who tries in such ways to sense ovulation in order to achieve (or avoid) fertilization, is responding by cold-blooded calculation to hard-won, modern book knowledge. She has no other choice; she lacks the innate, hot-blooded sense of sexual receptivity that drives other female mammals.

Our concealed ovulation, constant receptivity, and brief fertile period in each menstrual cycle ensure that most copulations by humans are at the wrong time for conception. To make things worse, menstrual-cycle length varies more between women, or from cycle to cycle in a given woman, than for other female mammals. As a result, even young newlyweds who omit contraception and make love at maximum frequency have only a 28 percent probability of conception per menstrual cycle. Animal breeders would be in despair if a prize cow had such low fertility, but in fact they can schedule a *single* artificial insemination so that the cow has a 75 percent chance of being fertilized!

Whatever the main biological function of human copulation, it isn't conception, which is just an occasional by-product. In these days of growing human overpopulation, one of the most ironic tragedies is the Catholic Church's claim that human copulation has conception as its natural purpose, and that the rhythm method is the only proper means of birth control. The rhythm method would be terrific for gorillas and most other mammal species, but not for us. In no species besides humans has the purpose of copulation become so unrelated to conception, or the rhythm method so unsuited for contraception.

For animals, copulation is a dangerous luxury. While occupied *in acto flagrante,* an animal is burning up valuable calories, neglecting opportunities to gather food, vulnerable to predators eager to eat it, and vulnerable to rivals eager to usurp its territory. Hence copulation is something to be accomplished in the minimum time required to do the job of fertilization. In contrast, human sex, as a device to achieve fertilization, would have to be rated a huge waste of time and energy, an evolutionary failure. Had we retained a proper estrus cycle like other mammals, the wasted time could have been diverted by our hunter-gatherer ancestors to butchering more mastodons. By this results-oriented view of sex, any hunter-gatherer band whose females advertised their estrus period could thereby have fed more babies and outcompeted neighboring bands.

Thus, the most hotly debated problem in the evolution of human reproduction is to explain why we ended up with concealed ovulation, and what good all our mistimed copulations do for us. For scientists, it's no answer just to say that sex is fun. Sure, it's fun, but evolution made it that way. If we weren't getting big benefits from our mistimed copulations, mutant humans who had evolved not to enjoy sex would have taken over the world.

Related to this paradox of concealed ovulation is the paradox of concealed copulation. All other group-living animals have sex in public, whether they are promiscuous or monogamous. Paired seagulls mate in the middle of the colony; an ovulating female chimpanzee may mate consecutively with five males in each other's presence. Why are we unique in our strong preference for copulating in private?

Biologists are currently arguing over at least six different theories to explain the origin of concealed ovulation and concealed copulation in humans. Interestingly, the debate proves to be a Rorschach test for the gender and outlook of the scientists involved. Here are the theories and their proponents:

1. *Theory preferred by many traditional male anthropologists.* According to this view, concealed ovulation and copulation evolved in order to enhance cooperation and reduce aggression among male hunters. How could cavemen bring off the precise teamwork needed to spear a mammoth if they had been fighting that morning for the public favors of a cavewoman in estrus? The implicit message of this theory: women's physiology is important chiefly for its effect on bonds between men, the real movers of society. However, one can broaden this theory to make it less blatantly sexist: visible estrus and sex would disrupt human society by affecting female/female and male/female as well as male/male bonds.

To illustrate this broadened version of the prevalent theory, consider the following scene from an imaginary soap opera, showing what life would be like for us modern hunter-gatherers if we did not have concealed ovulation and private copulation. Our soap opera stars Bob and Carol and Ted and Alice and Ralph and Jane. Bob, Alice, Ralph, and Jane work together in an office where the men hunt contracts and the women gather accounts payable. Ralph is married to Jane. Bob's wife is Carol, and Alice's husband is Ted. Carol and Ted work elsewhere.

One morning, Alice and Jane both discover on awakening that they have turned bright red in order to advertise impending ovulation and sexual receptivity. Alice and Ted make love at home before they go off in their separate directions to work. Jane and Ralph go together to work, where they copulate occasionally on the office sofa in the presence of their coworkers.

Bob cannot help lusting for Alice and Jane when he sees them bright red and sees Jane and Ralph copulating. He is unable to concentrate on his work. He repeatedly propositions Jane and Alice.

Ralph drives Bob away from Jane.

Alice is faithful to Ted and rejects Bob, but the hassle also interferes with her work.

All day, Carol in her office elsewhere is seething with jealousy at the thought of Alice and Jane, because Carol knows that Alice and Jane are bright red and attractive to Bob, while she (Carol) is not.

As a result, the office succeeds in bagging few contracts and accounts. In the meantime, other offices, where ovulation is concealed and where copulation is private, prosper. Eventually, Bob, Alice, Ralph, and Jane's office goes extinct. The only offices that survive are those with concealed ovulation and copulation.

This parable suggests that the traditional theory, by which concealed ovulation and copulation evolved to promote cooperation within human societies, is plausible. Unfortunately, there are other, equally plausible theories that I'll now explain more briefly.

2.   *Theory preferred by many other traditional male anthropologists.* Concealed ovulation and copulation cement the bonds between a particular man and woman, thereby laying the foundations of the human family. A woman remains sexually attractive and receptive so that she can satisfy a man sexually all the time, bind him to her, and reward him for his help in rearing her baby. The sexist message: women evolved to make men happy. Left unexplained by this theory is the question why pairs of gibbons, whose unflinching devotion to monogamy should make them role models for the Moral Majority, remain constantly together despite having sex only every few years.

3.   *Theory of a more modern male anthropologist.* (Donald Symons). Symons noted that a male chimpanzee who kills a small animal is more likely to share the meat with an estrous female than with a nonestrous female. This suggested to Symons that human females might have evolved a constant state of estrus in order to ensure a frequent meat supply from male hunters by rewarding them with sex. As an alternative theory, Symons noted that women in most hunter-gatherer societies have little say in selection of a husband. The societies are male-dominated, and male clans just suit themselves by exchanging daughters in marriage. However, by being constantly attractive, even a woman wed to an inferior male could privately seduce a superior male and secure his genes for her children. Symons's theories, while still male-oriented, at least represent

a step forward in that he views women as cleverly pursuing their own goals.

4. *Theory produced jointly by a male biologist and a female biologist* (Richard Alexander and Katherine Noonan). If a man could recognize signs of ovulation, he could use that knowledge to fertilize his wife by copulating with her only while she's ovulating. He could then safely neglect her the rest of the time and go off and philander, secure in the knowledge that the wife he left behind was unreceptive, if not already fertilized. Hence women evolved concealed ovulation to force men into a permanent marriage bond, by exploiting male paranoia about fatherhood. Not knowing the time of ovulation, a man must copulate often with his wife to have a chance of fertilizing her, and that leaves him less time to develop dalliances with other women. The wife benefits, but so does the husband. He gains confidence in his paternity of his children, and he need not worry that his wife will suddenly attract many competing men by turning bright red on a particular day. At last, we have a theory seemingly grounded in sexual equality.

5. *Theory of a female sociobiologist* (Sarah Hrdy). Hrdy was impressed by the frequency with which many primates—including not only monkeys but also baboons, gorillas, and common chimps—kill infants not their own. The bereaved mother is thereby induced to come into estrus again and often mates with the murderer, thus increasing his output of progeny. (Such violence has been common in human history: male conquerors kill the vanquished men and children but spare the women.) As a countermeasure, Hrdy reasoned, women evolved concealed ovulation in order to manipulate men by confusing the issue of paternity. A woman who distributed her favors widely would thereby enlist many men to help feed (or at least not to kill) her infant, since many men could suppose themselves to be the infant's father. Whether this theory is right or wrong, we must applaud Hrdy's overturning of conventional masculine sexism and her transferring of sexual power to women.

6. *Theory of another female sociobiologist* (Nancy Burley). The average seven-pound human newborn weighs double a newborn gorilla, but the two-hundred-pound gorilla mother dwarfs the average

human mother. Because the human newborn is so much larger in relation to its mother than are newborn apes, birth is exceptionally painful and dangerous in humans. Until the advent of modern medicine, women often died in childbirth, whereas I have never heard of such a fate's befalling a female gorilla or chimpanzee. Once humans had evolved enough intelligence to associate conception with copulation, estrous women could have chosen to avoid copulating at the time of ovulation, and could have thereby spared themselves the pain and peril of childbirth. But such women would have left fewer descendants than did women who could not detect their ovulation. Thus, where male anthropologists saw concealed ovulation as something evolved by women for men (Theories 1 and 2), Nancy Burley sees it as a trick that women evolved to deceive themselves.

WHICH OF THESE SIX THEORIES for the evolution of concealed ovulation is correct? Not only are biologists uncertain; it is only in recent years that the question has begun to receive serious attention. This dilemma exemplifies a pervasive problem in establishing causation in evolutionary biology, as well as in history, psychology, and many other fields where one can't manipulate variables to perform controlled experiments. Such experiments would afford the most convincing way to demonstrate cause or function. If we could remodel one tribe of people so that all women advertised their day of ovulation, we could then see whether cooperation within or between couples broke down, or whether the women used their new knowledge to avoid becoming pregnant. In the absence of such experiments, we can never be certain what human society would really be like today without concealed ovulation.

If it's hard to determine the function of things happening today under our eyes, how much harder must it be to determine functions in the vanished past! We know that human bones and tools were different hundreds of thousands of years ago, when concealed ovulation may have been evolving. Probably human sexuality, including the function of concealed ovulation, may also have been different then, in ways now hard for us to picture. Interpretation of our past runs the constant risk of degenerating into mere "paleopoetry": stories that we spin today, stimulated by a few bits of fossil bone, and expressing like Rorschach tests our own personal prejudices, but devoid of any claim to validity about the past.

Nevertheless, having mentioned six plausible theories, I can't just walk away from the problem without attempting some synthesis. Here again, we come up against another pervasive problem in establishing causation. It's rare for complex phenomena like concealed ovulation to be influenced by only a single factor. It would be as silly to seek a single cause of concealed ovulation as to claim that there was a single root cause of World War I. Instead, there were many somewhat independent factors in the period 1900–14 pushing toward war, others pushing toward peace. War finally broke out when the net weight of factors tipped toward war. But that doesn't excuse going to the opposite extreme, and "explaining" complex phenomena by an unweighted laundry list encompassing every conceivable factor.

As a first step toward pruning down our laundry list of six theories, let's realize that, whatever factors caused our distinctive sexual habits to evolve in the distant past, they wouldn't be persisting today if there weren't some factors still sustaining them. But the factors responsible for their initial appearance needn't have been the same as the ones now operative. In particular, although the factors behind Theories 3, 5, and 6 may have been major ones long ago, they don't seem to be so now. Only a minority of modern women use sex to obtain food or other resources from many men, or to confound paternity and induce many men simultaneously to support the woman's child. Postulates of their former role are paleopoetry, albeit plausible paleopoetry. Let's just content ourselves with trying to understand why concealed ovulation and frequent private copulation might make sense now. At least our guesses can be guided by introspection about ourselves plus observations of others.

The factors behind Theories 1, 2, and 4 seem to me still operative today, and to be facets of the same paradoxical feature of human social organization. That paradox is that a man and woman desirous for their child (and genes) to survive must cooperate with each other for a long time to rear their child, *but* must also cooperate economically with other couples living close by. It's obvious that regular sexual relations between a man and woman intensifies their connection, compared to their connections with other women and men whom they see daily but with whom they are not involved sexually. Concealed ovulation and constant receptivity advance this "new" function of sex (new by the standards of most mammals) as a social cement, not just a device for fertilization. This function is not, as in the traditional male-chauvinist version of Theories 1 and 2, a sop thrown by a cold, calculating woman to a sex-starved man, but instead an inducement for both sexes. Not only have all signs of female ovulation vanished, but the act of sex itself takes place privately, to emphasize the distinction between sexual and nonsexual partners within the same close group. As for the objection that gibbons remain monogamously involved without the reward of constant sex, that's easy to explain: each gibbon couple has minimal social and no economic involvement with other gibbon couples.

Human testis size also seems to me an outcome of that same basic paradox of human social organization. While our testes are larger than a gorilla's, because we have frequent sex for fun, they're still smaller than a chimpanzee's, because we're more monogamous. The oversized human penis may have evolved as an arbitrary sexual display symbol, as arbitrary as a lion's mane or a woman's enlarged breasts. Why weren't lionesses the ones to develop enlarged breasts, lions an oversized penis, and men a mane? If they had, those permuted signals could have functioned equally well. That it didn't come out that way may be just an accident of evolution, a result of each species' and sex's relative ease of evolving those various structures.

But there's still something basic missing from our discussion so far. I've talked about an idealized form of human sexuality: monogamous couples (plus a few polygynous households), husbands confident in their paternity of their wives' children, and husbands helping their wives with child rearing rather than neglecting the kids in order to philander. As justification for discussing this fictitious ideal, I maintain that actual human practice is much closer to this ideal than to baboon or chimpanzee practice. But the ideal is still fictitious. Any social system with rules of conduct is open to the risk of individuals' cheating when they find the advantages of cheating to outweigh the burden of sanctions. The question is thus a quantitative one: does cheating become so regular that the whole system collapses, or does cheating occur but not so often as to destroy the system, or is cheating vanishingly rare? As translated for human sexuality, that question becomes: are 90 percent, 30 percent, or 1 percent of human babies fathered extramaritally? Let's now confront that question and its consequences.

CHAPTER 4

The Science
of Adultery

P EOPLE HAVE MANY REASONS TO LIE WHEN ASKED WHETHER THEY HAVE committed adultery. That's why it's notoriously difficult to get accurate scientific information about this important subject. One of the few existing sets of hard facts emerged as a totally unexpected by-product of a medical study, performed nearly half a century ago for a different reason. That study's findings have never been revealed until now.

I recently learned those facts from the distinguished medical scientist who ran the study. (Since he does not wish to be identified in this connection, I shall refer to him as Dr. X.) In the 1940s Dr. X was studying the genetics of human blood groups, which are molecules that we acquire only by inheritance. Each of us has dozens of blood-group substances on our red blood cells, and we inherit each substance either from our mother or from our father. The study's research plan was straightforward: go to the obstetrics ward of a highly respectable U.S. hospital; collect blood samples from one thousand newborn babies and their mothers and fathers;

identify the blood groups in all the samples; and then use standard genetic reasoning to deduce the inheritance patterns.

To Dr. X's shock, the blood groups revealed nearly 10 percent of those babies to be the fruits of adultery! Proof of the babies' illegitimate origin was that they had one or more blood groups lacking in both alleged parents. There could be no question of mistaken maternity: the blood samples were drawn from an infant and its mother soon after the infant emerged from the mother. A blood group present in a baby but absent in its undoubted mother could only have come from its father. Absence of the blood group from the mother's husband as well showed conclusively that the baby had been sired by some other man, extramaritally. The true incidence of extramarital sex must have been considerably higher than 10 percent, since many other blood-group substances now used in paternity tests were not yet known in the 1940s, and since most bouts of intercourse do not result in conception.

At the time that Dr. X made his discovery, research on American sexual habits was virtually taboo. He decided to maintain a prudent silence, never published his findings, and it was only with difficulty that I got his permission to mention his results without betraying his name. However, his results were later confirmed by several similar genetic studies whose results did get published. Those studies variously showed between about 5 and 30 percent of American and British babies to have been adulterously conceived. Again, the proportion of the tested couples of whom at least the wife had practiced adultery must have been higher, for the same two reasons as in Dr. X's study.

We can now answer the question whether extramarital sex is for humans a rare aberration, a frequent exception to a "normal" pattern of marital sex, or so frequent as to make a sham of marriage. The middle alternative proves to be the correct one. Most fathers really are raising their own children, and human marriage is not a sham. We're not just promiscuous chimpanzees pretending to be otherwise. Yet it's also clear that extramarital sex is an integral, albeit unofficial, part of the human mating system. Adultery has also been observed in many other animal species whose societies resemble ours in being based on male and female coparents with a lasting bond. Since such lasting bonds don't characterize common chimpanzee or pygmy chimpanzee society, it's meaningless to talk of adultery in chimps. We must have reinvented it after our chimp-like ancestors had rendered it obsolete. Thus, we can't discuss human sexuality, and its role in our rise to humanity, without carefully considering the science of adultery.

Most of our information about adultery's incidence has come from researchers asking people about their sex lives, rather than from blood-grouping their babies. Since the 1940s, the myth that marital infidelity is rare in the U.S. has been publicly exploded by a long succession of surveys, beginning with the Kinsey report. Nevertheless, even though this is the supposedly liberated 1990s, we are still profoundly ambivalent about adultery. It is thought of as exciting: no television soap opera could attract many viewers without it. It has few rivals as a basis of jokes. Yet, as Freud pointed out, we often use humor to deal with things intensely painful. Throughout history, adultery has had few rivals as a cause of murder and human misery. In writing about this subject, it's impossible to remain completely serious, but it's also impossible not to be revolted at the sadistic institutions by which societies have attempted to deal with extramarital sex.

WHAT MAKES A MARRIED PERSON decide to seek or avoid adultery? Scientists have theories to explain many other things, so it should not be surprising that there is also a theory of extramarital sex (abbreviated EMS, and not to be confused with premarital sex = PMS, in turn not to be confused with premenstrual syndrome = PMS). With many species of animals the problem of EMS never arises, because they don't opt for marriage in the first place. For instance, a female Barbary macaque in heat copulates promiscuously with every adult male in her troop and averages one copulation per seventeen minutes. However, some mammals and most bird species do opt for "marriage." That is, a male and a female form a lasting pair bond to devote care or protection to their joint offspring. Once there is marriage, there is also the possibility of what sociobiologists euphemistically term "the pursuit of a mixed reproductive strategy" (abbreviated MRS). In plain English, that means being married while simultaneously seeking extramarital sex.

Married animals vary enormously in the degree to which they mix their reproductive strategies. There appears to be no recorded instance of EMS in the little apes called gibbons, while snow geese indulge regularly. Human societies similarly vary, but I suspect that none comes close to the faithful gibbons. To explain all this variation, sociobiologists have found it useful to apply the reasoning of game theory. That is, life is considered an evolutionary contest whose winners are those individuals leaving the largest number of surviving offspring.

Contest rules are set by the ecology and reproductive biology of the particular species. The problem is then to figure out which strategy is most likely to win the contest: rigid fidelity, pure promiscuity, or a mixed strategy. But I must make one thing clear right at the outset. While this sociobiological approach certainly proves useful for understanding adultery in animals, its relevance for human adultery is an explosive issue to which I shall return.

The first thing one realizes when one starts to think about the contest is that the best game strategy differs between males and females of the same species. This is because of two profound differences between the reproductive biology of males and females: in the minimum necessary reproductive effort, and in the risk of being cuckolded. Let's consider these differences, which are painfully familiar to humans.

For men, the minimum effort needed to sire an offspring is the act of copulation, a brief expenditure of time and energy. The man who sires a baby by one woman one day is biologically capable of siring a baby by another woman the next day. For women, however, the minimum effort consists of copulation plus pregnancy plus (throughout most of human history) several years spent nursing—a huge commitment of time and energy. Thus, a man potentially can sire far more offspring than can a woman. A nineteenth-century visitor who spent a week at the court of the Nizam of Hyderabad, a polygamous Indian potentate, reported that four of the Nizam's wives gave birth within eight days, and that nine more births were anticipated for the following week. The record lifetime number of offspring for a man is 888, sired by Emperor Moulay Ismail the Bloodthirsty of Morocco, while the corresponding record for a woman is only sixty-nine (a nineteenth-century Moscow woman specializing in triplets). Few women have topped twenty children, whereas some men easily do so in polygynous societies.

As a result of this biological difference, a man stands to gain much more from EMS or polygamy than does a woman—if one's sole criterion is number of offspring born. (To female readers about to stop reading in outrage, or to male readers about to cheer, I warn you now: keep reading, there is much more to the question of EMS.) For human EMS the statistical evidence is naturally hard to come by, but for human polygamy it is readily available. In the sole polyandrous society for which I could find data, the Tre-ba of Tibet, women with two husbands average *fewer* children, not more children, than women with one husband. In contrast, nineteenth-century American Mormon men realized big benefits from polygyny: men with one wife averaged only 7 children, but men with two wives averaged 16 children, and those with three wives averaged 20. Polygynous Mormon men as a group averaged 2.4 wives and 15 children, while polygynous Mormon church leaders in particular averaged 5 wives and 25 children. Similarly, among the polygynous Temne people of Sierra Leone, a man's average number of children increases from 1.7 to 7 as his number of wives increases from 1 to 5.

The other sexual asymmetry relevant to mating strategy involves confidence that one really is the biological parent of one's putative offspring. A cuckolded animal, deceived into rearing offspring not its own, has thereby lost the evolutionary game while advancing the victory of another player, the real parent. Barring a switch of babies in the hospital nursery, women cannot be "cuckolded": they see their baby emerge from them. Nor can there be cuckoldry of males in animal species practicing external fertilization (i.e., fertilization of eggs outside the female's body). For instance, some male fish watch a female shed eggs, then immediately deposit sperm on the eggs and scoop them up to care for them, secure in their paternity. However, men and other male animals practicing internal fertilization— fertilization of eggs inside the female's body—can readily be cuckolded. All that the putative father knows for sure is that his sperm went into the mother, and eventually an offspring came out. Only observation of the female throughout her whole fertile period can absolutely exclude the possibility that some other male's sperm also entered and did the actual fertilizing.

An extreme solution to this simple asymmetry is the one formerly adopted by southern India's Nayar society. Among the Nayar, women freely took many lovers simultaneously or in sequence, and husbands accordingly had no confidence in paternity. To make the best of a bad situation, a Nayar man did not live with his wife or care for his supposed children, but he instead lived with his sisters and cared for his sisters' children. At least, those nieces and nephews were sure to share one-quarter of his genes.

Bearing in mind these two basic facts of sexual asymmetry, we can now examine what is the best game strategy, and when EMS pays. Let's examine three game plans of increasing complexity.

Game Plan 1. A man should always seek EMS, because he has so little to lose and so much to gain. Consider the hunter-gatherer conditions prevailing throughout most of human evolution, under which a woman could at best rear about four children in the course of her life. Through one dalliance, her otherwise faithful husband could increase his lifetime reproductive output from four to five: an enormous increase of 25 percent, for only a few minutes' work. What's wrong with this dazzlingly naïve reasoning?

Game Plan 2. A moment's reflection should expose a basic flaw of Game Plan 1: it considers only the potential benefits of EMS to a man and ignores his potential costs. Obvious costs would include: the risk of detection and injury or murder by the husband of the woman sought as EMS partner; the risk that one's own wife will desert; the risk of being cuckolded by one's wife while one is off seeking EMS; and the risk that one's legitimate children will suffer through one's neglect of them. Thus, according to Game Plan 2, the would-be Casanova, like a sophisticated investor, should seek to maximize his gains while minimizing his losses. What reasoning could be more impeccably judicious?

Game Plan 3. The man silly enough to be satisfied with Game Plan 2 has obviously never approached a woman with an offer of EMS or PMS. Worse yet, the silly man has never even thought about the statistics of human heterosexual intercourse, which dictate that, for every bout of EMS by a man, there must be one bout of EMS (or at least PMS) by a woman. Game Plans 1 and 2 share the flaw that they ignore considerations of the woman's strategy, without which any male strategy is doomed to failure. So an improved Game Plan 3 must combine a male strategy and a female strategy. But, since one husband suffices to realize a woman's maximum reproductive potential, what could possibly attract a woman to EMS or PMS? This question puzzles the current generation of theoretical sociobiologists with a purely intellectual interest in EMS, just as it has taxed the ingenuity of would-be male adulterers throughout human history.

To PROCEED FURTHER with our theoretical exploration of Game Plan 3, we need rigorous empirical data on EMS. Because surveys of people's sexual habits are notoriously unreliable, let's first turn to some recently published studies of birds that nest as mated pairs in large colonies. These, rather than our closest relatives the apes, are the animals whose mating system most closely resembles our own. Compared to us, birds have the disadvantage that one can't ask them about their motives for EMS, but this is no great loss, as our answers are often lies anyway. The great virtue of colonial birds for EMS research is that one can band the birds in a colony, then sit nearby for hundreds of hours and determine exactly who does what with whom. I am unaware of equivalent information for a large human population.

Important recent observations of adultery among birds were made on five species of herons, gulls, and geese. All five nest in dense colonies composed of nominally monogamous male-female pairs. One parent alone is incapable of rearing a chick, as an unguarded nest is likely to be destroyed while the parent is off food-gathering. Nor is a male capable of feeding or guarding two families simultaneously. Thus, among the ground rules of mating strategy for these colonial birds are the following: polygamy is forbidden; copulation with or by an unmated female is pointless, unless she soon acquires a mate to care for the resulting offspring: but surreptitious fertilization by one male of another male's mate is a viable strategy.

The first study involved great blue herons and great egrets at Hog Island, Texas. In these species the male builds a nest and stays there to court visiting females. Eventually a male and female accept each other and copulate about twenty times. The female then lays eggs and goes off to spend most daylight hours feeding, while the male remains to guard the nest and eggs. During the first day or two after pairing, the male often resumes courting any passing female as soon as his mate leaves to feed, but EMS does not result. Instead, the male's halfway-unfaithful behavior seems to constitute "divorce insurance" that lines up a backup mate for him in case his own mate deserts (she does desert him in up to 20 percent of the pairings reported). The passing "backup" female pursues the courtship out of ignorance: she is seeking a mate and has no way of knowing that the male is already mated, until his spouse returns (which she does at frequent intervals) and drives them off. Eventually, the male gains complete confidence that he will not be deserted, and he ceases to court any passing females.

In the second study, of little blue herons in Mississippi, behavior that might have originated as divorce insurance took a more serious turn. Sixty-two cases of EMS were documented, mostly between a female on her nest and a male from the neighboring nest while the female's mate was busy finding food. Most females initially resisted but then ceased resisting, and some females engaged in more EMS than marital sex. To reduce his own risk of being cuckolded, the adulterous male did his feeding as quickly as possible, returned often to his own nest to guard his mate, and traveled no further than neighboring nests to seek EMS. EMS was usually timed to occur when the female chosen had not yet completed egg laying and could still be fertilized. However, adulterous copulations were quicker than marital copulations (eight versus twelve seconds), hence possibly less effective at fertilizing, and nearly half of all nests involved in EMS were subsequently abandoned.

Among herring gulls in Lake Michigan, 35 percent of mated males were observed to engage in EMS. This percentage is nearly the same as the value of 32 percent reported for young American husbands in a study published by Playboy Press in 1974. But there is a big difference between gulls and humans in female behavior. Whereas Playboy Press reported EMS for 24 percent of young American wives, every mated female gull virtuously rejected adulterous male advances and never solicited the neighboring male in her own mate's absence. Instead, all cases of male EMS involved unmated female gulls practicing PMS. To decrease his own risk of being cuckolded, the male spent more time chasing intruders away from his nest when his mate was fertile than when she was not fertile. As for how the male induced his mate to remain faithful during the time that he was off seeking EMS, his secret—like that of some married men similarly pursuing a mixed reproductive strategy—consisted of feeding her diligently and copulating often whenever she was receptive.

Our final set of rigorous data involves snow geese breeding in Manitoba. Just as I already explained for little blue herons, EMS in snow geese mainly involves a male approaching an initially resisting female on a neighboring nest in the absence of her mate. The mate's absence is usually because he himself is off seeking EMS. It may seem as if the male thereby loses as much as he gains, but a male goose is not so dumb. As long as the female is still laying eggs, her mate remains to guard her. (A nesting female is propositioned fifty times less often in her mate's presence than in his absence.) Only after the female has finished laying does her mate go off on EMS quests, with his paternity assured at home.

Such bird studies illustrate the value of a scientific approach to adultery. They have revealed a series of sophisticated strategies by which adulterous male birds try to have it both ways, so as to obtain confidence of paternity at home while sowing their seed abroad. The strategies include wooing unmated females for "divorce insurance," as long as one feels unsure of one's wife's fidelity; guarding one's fertile spouse; feeding her copiously and copulating with her often, to induce her to remain faithful in one's absence; and coveting one's neighbor's spouse at a time when she is fertile and one's own spouse is no longer fertile. However, not even these applications of the scientific method in all its power sufficed to clarify what, if anything, female birds gain from EMS. One possible answer is that female herons weighing desertion of their mates may use EMS to shop around for a new mate. Another is that some unmated female gulls in colonies with a deficit of males may get fertilized by PMS, and then try to rear the chicks with the help of another, similar female.

The chief limitation of these colonial bird studies is that the females often seem to be unwilling participants in EMS. For understanding of a more active female role, we have no choice but to turn to human studies, riddled as they are with problems of cultural variation, observer bias, and dubiously reliable survey responses.

SURVEYS COMPARING MEN WITH WOMEN in various cultures scattered around the world typically purport to find the following differences: men are more interested in EMS than are women; men are more interested than women in seeking a variety of sexual partners for the sake of variety itself; women's motives for EMS are more likely to be marital dissatisfaction and/or a desire for a lasting new relationship; and men are less selective in taking on casual female sexual partners than women are in taking on casual male partners. For example, among the New Guinea highlanders with whom I work, a man will say he seeks EMS because sex with his own wife (or even wives, in the case of polygynous men) inevitably becomes boring, while a woman who seeks EMS does so mainly because her husband cannot satisfy her sexually (e.g., because of old age). In the questionnaires that several hundred young Americans filled out for a computer dating service, women expressed stronger partner preferences than men did in almost every respect: intelligence, status, dancing ability, religion, race, etc. The only category in which men were more selective than women was physical attractiveness. After dates the men and women filled out "debriefing" questionnaires, with the result that two and a half times as many men as women expressed strong romantic attraction to their computer-selected partner. Thus, the women were choosier, the men more undiscriminating, in their reactions to partners.

Obviously, we are on shaky ground if we expect an honest answer when we ask people their attitudes about EMS. However, people also express their attitudes in laws and behaviors. In particular, some widespread hypocritical and sadistic features of human societies stem from two fundamental difficulties that men face in seeking EMS. First, a man who pursues an MRS is trying to have it both ways: he wishes to obtain sex with other men's wives, while denying sex with his own wife (or wives) to other men. Thus, some men inevitably gain at the expense of other men. Second, as we have discussed, there is a realistic biological basis for men's widespread paranoia about being cuckolded.

Adultery laws provide a clear example of how men have dealt with these dilemmas. Until recently, essentially all such laws—Hebraic, Egyptian, Roman, Aztec, Moslem, African, Chinese, Japanese, and others—were asymmetrical. They existed to secure a married man's confidence in his paternity of his children, and for no other purpose. Hence these laws define adultery by the marital status of the participating woman; that of the participating man is irrelevant. EMS by a married woman is considered an offense against her husband, who is commonly entitled to damages, often including violent revenge or else divorce with refund of the bride price. EMS by a married man is not considered an offense against his wife. Instead, if his partner in adultery is married, the offense is against her husband; if she is unmarried, the offense is against her father or brothers (because her value as prospective bride is reduced).

No criminal law against male infidelity even existed until a French law of 1810, and that law only forbade a married man to keep a concubine in his conjugal house against his wife's wishes. Viewed from the perspective of human history, the absence or near-symmetry of modern western adultery laws is a novelty that only appeared in the last 150 years. Even today, prosecutors, judges, and juries in the United States and England often reduce a homicide charge to manslaughter of the lowest degree, or else acquit altogether, when a husband kills an adulterous wife or her lover caught in the act.

Perhaps the most elaborate system to uphold confidence of paternity was that maintained by Chinese emperors of the T'ang Dynasty. For each of the emperor's hundreds of wives and concubines, a team of court ladies kept records on dates of menstruation, so that the emperor could copulate with that wife on a date likely to result in fertilization. Dates of copulation were also recorded, and as an auxiliary form of record keeping, were commemorated by an indelible tattoo on the woman's arm and by a silver ring on her left leg. It goes without saying that equal thoroughness was applied to excluding men other than the emperor from the harem.

Men of other cultures have resorted to less complicated but even more repulsive means of ensuring paternity. These measures limit sexual access to wives, or else to daughters or sisters who would command a high bride price if delivered as proven virgin goods. Relatively mild measures include close chaperoning or virtual imprisonment of women. Similar purposes are served by the code of "honor and shame" widespread in Mediterranean countries. (Translation: EMS for me but not for you; only the latter is a shame to *my* honor.) Stronger measures include the barbaric mutilations euphemistically and misleadingly termed "female circumcision." These consist of removal of the clitoris or most of the external female genitalia to reduce female interest in sex, marital or extramarital. Men bent on total certainty invented infibulation: suturing a woman's labia majora nearly shut, so as to make intercourse impossible. An infibulated wife can be deinfibulated for childbirth or for reinsemination after each child is weaned, and can be reinfibulated when the husband takes a long trip. Female circumcision and infibulation are still practiced in twenty-three countries today, from Africa through Saudi Arabia to Indonesia.

When adultery laws, imperial records, and coercive restraint still fail to ensure paternity, murder is available as a last resort. The role of sexual jealousy as one of the commonest causes of homicide emerges from studies in many American cities and in many other countries. Usually, the murderer is a husband while the victim is his adulterous wife or her lover; or else the lover kills the husband. The table on the facing page gives some actual numbers for murders committed in Detroit in 1972. Until the formation of centralized political states provided soldiers with loftier motives, sexual jealousy also loomed large in human history as a cause of war. It was Paris's seduction (abduction, rape) of Menelaus's wife Helen that provoked the Trojan War. In the modern New Guinea highlands, only disputes over ownership of pigs rival disputes over sex at triggering war.

Asymmetric adultery laws, tattooing of wives after insemination, virtual imprisonment of women, genital mutilation of women: these behaviors are unique to the human species, defining humanity as much as does invention of the alphabet. More exactly, they are new means to the old evolutionary goal of males' promoting their genes. Some of our other means to this goal are ancient ones shared with many animals, including jealous murder, infanticide, rape, intergroup warfare, and adultery itself. Human male infibulators stitch the vagina closed; some male animals achieve the same result by cementing a female's vagina after copulating with her.

Sociobiologists have had considerable success at understanding the marked differences among animal species in details of these practices. As a result of recent research, it is no longer controversial to conclude that natural selection caused animals to evolve behaviors, as well as anatomical structures, that tend to maximize the number of their descendants. Few scientists doubt that natural selection molded human anatomy. However, no theory has caused such bitter divisions among my fellow biologists today as the claim that natural selection likewise molded our social behavior. Most of the human behaviors discussed in this chapter are considered barbaric by modern western society. Some biologists are outraged not only by the behaviors themselves but also by sociobiological explanations for the evolution of the

Breakdown of murders caused by sexual jealousy
in the U.S. city of Detroit in 1972

Total: 58 murders

47 murders precipitated by jealous man:
   16 cases: jealous man killed the unfaithful woman
   17 cases: jealous man killed the rival man
   9 cases: jealous man was killed by the accused woman
   2 cases: jealous man was killed by the accused woman's
       relatives
   2 cases: jealous man killed unfaithful homosexual male
       lover
   1 case: jealous man killed innocent bystander
       accidentally

11 murders precipitated by jealous woman:
   6 cases: jealous woman killed the unfaithful man
   3 cases: jealous woman killed the rival woman
   2 cases: jealous woman was killed by the accused man

behaviors. To "explain" a behavior seems uncomfortably close to defending it.

Like nuclear physics and all other knowledge, sociobiology is available for abuse. People have never lacked pretexts to justify the abuse or killing of other people, but ever since Darwin formulated his theory of evolution, evolutionary reasoning has also been abused as such a pretext. Sociobiological discussions of human sexuality can be seen as seeking to justify men's abuse of women, analogous to the biological justifications advanced for whites' treatment of blacks or Nazis' treatment of Jews. In the critiques that some biologists have directed at sociobiology, two fears recur: that a demonstrated evolutionary basis for a barbaric behavior would seem to justify it; and that a demonstrated genetic basis for the behavior would imply the futility of attempts at change.

In my view, neither fear is warranted. As for the first fear, one can seek to understand how something arose, regardless of whether one considers that something admirable or abominable. Most books analyzing the motives of murderers are not written in an effort to justify murder, but instead to understand its causes as a way of preventing it. As for the second fear, we are not mere slaves to our evolved characteristics, not even to our genetically acquired ones. Modern civilization is fairly successful at thwarting ancient behaviors like infanticide. One of the main objectives of modern medicine is to thwart the effects of our harmful genes and microbes, despite our having come to understand why it's natural for those genes and microbes to tend to kill us. Thus, the case against infibulation does not collapse even if the practice can be shown to be genetically advantageous to male infibulators. Instead, we condemn it because we hold the mutilation of one person by another to be ethically loathsome.

While sociobiology is thus useful for understanding the evolutionary context of human social behavior, this approach still shouldn't be pushed too far. The goal of all human activity can't be reduced to the leaving of descendants. Once human culture was firmly in place, it acquired new goals. Many people debate today whether to have children, and many decide that they prefer to devote their time and energy to other activities. I claim only that evolutionary reasoning is valuable for understanding the origin of human social practices; I don't claim that it's the only way to understand their current forms.

In short, we evolved, like other animals, to win at the contest of leaving as many descendants as possible. Much of the legacy of that game strategy is still with us. But we have also chosen to pursue ethical goals, which can conflict with the goals and methods of our reproductive contest. Having that choice among goals represents one of our most radical departures from other animals.

CHAPTER 5

How We Pick Our Mates
and Sex Partners

ARE THERE ANY UNIVERSAL STANDARDS OF HUMAN BEAUTY AND SEX appeal accepted by peoples as different in appearance as Chinese, Swedes, and Fijians? If not, do we inherit our particular taste in marriage partner through our genes, or do we learn it by looking at other members of our society? How, really, do we pick our sex partners and spouses?

It may be surprising to realize that this problem is one that arose anew during the evolution of the human species—or at least became much more important for us than for the other two chimpanzees. As we've already discussed, our familiar human mating system, based ideally on couples' maintaining ongoing involvement, is a human innovation. Pygmy chimps are the opposite of sexually selective: females mate in sequence with many males, and there is much sexual activity between females and between males as well. Common chimps are not so completely promiscuous—a male and female may sometimes go off and "consort" with each other for a few days—but they still rank as promiscuous by human standards. However, humans are much more selective sexually, since rearing a human child is difficult (at least for hunter-gatherers) without a father's help, and since sex becomes part of the cement that differentiates coparents from other men and women frequently encountered. Choosing a mate or sex partner is not so much a human invention as a reinvention of something practiced by many other (nominally) monogamous animals with lasting pair bonds, and lost by our chimpanzeelike ancestors. Those choosy animals include many bird species, plus our distant ape relatives the gibbons.

We just saw in the last chapter that this ideal depiction of a human society based on monogamous couples coexists with a good deal of extramarital sex. Sex appeal plays an even greater role in our choices of extramarital partners than of spouses, with adulterous women tending to be more finicky than adulterous men. Thus, selection of sex partners, married or otherwise, is another important piece of what defines humanity. It's as basic to our rise from chimpanzee status as is our remodeled pelvis. We'll see that much of what we think of as human racial variation may have arisen as a by-product of the beauty standards by which we pick our bedmates.

IN ADDITION to this theoretical interest, the question how we make these choices is of much personal interest. It preoccupies most of us for much of our lives. Those of us who are still unattached spend daily hours dreaming about whom we will consort with or marry. The question becomes more intriguing when we compare what turns on different people within the same culture. Think of the men or women that you find sexually attractive. If you're a man, for instance, do you prefer women who are blond or brunette, flat-chested or buxom, and with big or small eyes? If you're a woman, do you like men who are bearded or smooth-shaven, tall or short, and smiling or scowling? Probably you don't just go for anyone, but only certain types attract you. Everyone can name friends who got divorced, then chose a second spouse who was the exact image of the first one. A colleague of mine went through a long series of plain, slim, brown-haired, round-faced girlfriends, until he finally found one he got along with and married her. Whatever your own preference, you'll have noticed that some of your friends have completely different tastes.

The particular ideal that each of us pursues is an example of what are called "search images." (A search image is a mental picture against which we compare objects and people around us in order to be able to recognize something quickly, like a Perrier bottle amidst all the other bottled waters on the supermarket shelf, or one's child at a playground with other kids.) How do we develop our private search image for a mate? Do we seek someone familiar and similar to us, or are we more turned on by someone exotic? Would most European men really marry a Polynesian woman if given the chance? Do we seek someone complementary to us so as to fulfill our needs? For instance, there undoubtedly are some dependent men who marry a mothering woman, but how typical are such pairings?

Psychologists have tackled this question by examining many married couples, measuring everything conceivable about their physical appearance and other characteristics, and then trying to make sense out of who married whom. A simple numerical way of describing the result is by means of a statistical index called the correlation coefficient. If you line up one hundred husbands in order of their ranking for some characteristic (say, their height), and if you also line up their one hundred wives with respect to the same characteristic, the correlation coefficient describes whether a man tends to be at the same position in the husbands' line-up as his wife is in the wives' line-up. A correlation coefficient of plus 1 would mean perfect correspondence: the tallest man marries the tallest woman, the thirty-seventh-tallest man marries the thirty-seventh-tallest woman, and so on. A correlation coefficient of minus 1 would mean perfect matching by opposites: the tallest man marries the shortest woman, the thirty-seventh-tallest man marries the thirty-seventh-shortest woman, and so on. Finally, a correlation coefficient of zero would mean that husbands and wives assort completely randomly by height: a tall man is as likely to marry a short woman as a tall woman. These examples are for height, but correlation coefficients can also be calculated for anything else, such as income and IQ.

If you measure enough things about enough couples, here is what you'll find. Not surprisingly, the highest correlation coefficients— typically around +0.9—are for religion, ethnic background, race, socioeconomic status, age, and political views. In other words, most husbands and wives prove to be of the same religion, ethnic background, and so on. Perhaps you also won't be surprised that the next-highest correlation coefficients, usually around +0.4, are for measures of personality and intelligence, such as extroversion, neatness, and IQ. Slobs tend to marry slobs, though the chances of a slob marrying a compulsively neat person aren't as low as the chances of a political reactionary marrying a left-winger.

What about matching of husbands and wives for physical characteristics? The answer isn't one that would leap out at you immediately if you just looked at a few married couples. That's because we don't select our own mates for their bodies as carefully as we select the mates of our show dogs, race horses, and beef cattle. But we select nevertheless. If you measure enough couples, the answer that finally emerges is unexpectedly simple: *on the average,* spouses resemble each other slightly but significantly in almost every physical feature examined.

That's true of all obvious traits you'd first think of when asked to design your ideal beloved—his or her height, weight, hair color, eye color, and skin color. But it's also true of an astonishing variety of other traits that you probably wouldn't have mentioned in your description of the perfect sex partner. Those other traits include ones as diverse as breadth of nose, length of earlobe or middle finger, circumference of wrist, distance between eyes, and lung volume! Experimenters have made this finding for people as diverse as Poles in Poland, Americans in Michigan, and Africans in Chad. If you don't believe it, try noting eye colors (or measuring ear lobes) the next time you are at a dinner party with many couples, and then get your pocket calculator to give you the correlation coefficient.

Coefficients for physical traits are on the average +0.2—not so high as for personality traits (+0.4) or religion (+0.9), but still significantly higher than zero. For a few physical traits the correlation is even higher than 0.2—e.g., an astonishing 0.61 for length of middle finger. At least unconsciously, people care more about their spouse's middle-finger length than about his or her hair color and intelligence!

IN SHORT, like tends to marry like. Among the obvious explanations that contribute to these results, one is propinquity: we tend to live in neighborhoods defined by socioeconomic status, religion, and ethnic background. For instance, in large American cities one can point to the rich neighborhoods and the poor neighborhoods, and also to the

Jewish section, Chinese section, Italian section, black section, and so on. We meet people of the same religion when we go to church, and we tend to meet people of similar socioeconomic status or political views in many of our daily activities. Since those contacts give us far more opportunities to meet people like us than unlike us in these respects, of course we're more likely to marry someone of our religion, socioeconomic status, and so on. But we don't live in neighborhoods grouped by length of earlobe, so there must be some other reason why spouses tend to be matched in that respect as well.

Another obvious reason why likes tend to marry likes is that marriage isn't just a choice; it's a negotiation. We don't go out searching until we find a person with the right eye color and length of middle finger, then announce to that person, "You are marrying me." For most of us, marriage results from a proposal rather than a unilateral announcement, and the proposal is the culmination of some sort of negotiation. The more similar a man and woman are in political views, religion, and personality, the smoother will be the negotiation. The match in personality traits is on the average closer for married couples than for dating couples, closer for happily than unhappily married couples, and closer for couples who stay married than for those who get divorced. But this still doesn't explain spousal resemblance in earlobe length, which is only rarely cited as a factor in divorce.

The remaining factor deciding whom you'll marry, besides propinquity and smoothness of negotiation, is surely sexual attraction based on physical appearance. That in itself is no surprise. Most of us are aware of our preferences in obvious visible features like height, build, and hair color. What's initially surprising is the importance of so many other physical traits that we usually don't consciously notice, such as earlobes, middle fingers, and interocular distances. Nevertheless, all those other traits contribute unconsciously to the snap decisions we make when we're introduced to someone and a voice inside tells us, "She's my type!"

Here's an example. When my wife and I were introduced to each other, I instantly found Marie attractive and vice versa. In retrospect, I can understand why: we're both brown-eyed, similar in height and build and hair color, and so on. But, on the other hand, I also had a sense that there was something about Marie that didn't quite match my ideal, even though I couldn't figure out what exactly it was. Not until Marie and I first went to a ballet together did I solve the puzzle. I lent Marie my opera glasses, and when she passed them back to me, I found that she had pushed the eyepieces so close together that I couldn't see through them until I had spread them apart again. I then realized that Marie has more close-set eyes than I do, and that most women whom I had pursued before had wide-set eyes like my own. Thanks to Marie's earlobes and other merits, I've been able to make peace with my and her mismatched interocular distances. Nevertheless, the episode with the opera glasses made me appreciate for the first time that I have always found wide-set eyes a turn-on, even though I hadn't been explicitly aware of it.

So we tend to marry someone who looks like us. But—wait a minute. The men who look most similar to a woman are the men who share half of her genes: her father or brother! Similarly, the best-matched mate for a man would be his mother or sister! Yet most of us obey the incest taboo and certainly do not marry our parent or sibling of the opposite sex.

Instead, I'm saying that people tend to marry a person who *looks like* the parent or sibling of the opposite sex. That's because we begin already as children to develop our search image of a future sex partner, and that image is heavily influenced by the people of opposite sex whom we see most often. For most of us that's our mother (or father) and sister (or brother), plus close childhood friends. Our behavior is summed up by a popular song of the 1920s,

> *I want a girl*
> *Just like the girl*
> *That married dear old Dad . . .*

At this point, you are probably turning to your spouse or significant other, pulling out your tape measure, and discovering gross mismatch between your and his (or her) earlobes. Or perhaps you've pulled out a photo of your mother or sister, and you detect not the faintest resemblance when you hold it beside your spouse. If your wife isn't a dead ringer for your mother, don't stop reading, and conversely don't get worried that you should see a psychiatrist about your pathological search image. After all, remember:

1. Studies consistently show that factors like religion and personality influence our choice of spouse much more strongly than does physical appearance. I'm merely saying that physical traits have *some* influence. In fact, I'd predict much higher correlation coefficients for physical traits between casual sex partners than between spouses. That's because we can select casual sex partners solely on the basis of physical attraction, without regard to religion or political views. This prediction awaits testing.

2. Remember also that your search image could have been influenced by any of the people of opposite sex that you regularly saw around you as you were growing up. That includes playmates and siblings as well as parents. Perhaps your spouse resembles the little girl next door, rather than Mother.

3. Finally, remember that lots of independent physical traits enter into our search images, so most of us end up with a mild average resemblance to our spouses in many traits, rather than with a very close resemblance in a few traits. This idea is known as the "buxom redhead theory." If a man's mother and sister were both buxom redheads, he might grow up to consider buxom redheads very exciting. But redheads are relatively rare, and buxom redheads still rarer. Furthermore, the man's preference even in a casual sex partner is likely to depend on some other physical traits as well, and his preference in a wife will certainly depend on her views about children, politics, and money. As a result, among a group of sons of buxom redheads, a few lucky ones will find a girl like Mother in those two respects, some will have to settle for buxom nonredheads, others for nonbuxom redheads, and most for run-of-the-mill nonbuxom brunettes.

You may also be objecting at this point that my argument applies only to societies where spouses pick each other. As friends from India and China are quick to remind me, that's a peculiar custom of the twentieth-century U.S. and Europe. It wasn't true of the U.S. and Europe in the past, and it's still not true of most of the world today, where marriages are instead arranged by the families involved. The bride and groom often aren't even introduced until the wedding day. How could my argument possibly apply to such marriages?

Of course it couldn't, if one is talking just about legal marriages. But my argument would still apply to choice of extramarital sex partners, who may father a nontrivial fraction of children, just as blood-group studies proved for American and British children. In fact, I'd expect that if extramarital fathering is frequent even in societies where a woman already exercises her sexual preferences in choosing a husband, it may be even more frequent in societies with arranged marriages, where a woman's choice can only be expressed extramaritally.

IT'S NOT JUST THE CASE, then, that Fijian men prefer Fijian women over Swedish women, and vice versa: our search images are much more specific. However, these insights still leave questions unanswered. Did I inherit or learn my search image for someone like Mother? If I were offered the choice of sex with my sister or a strange woman, I would certainly reject the offer of my sister and probably my first cousin, but would I prefer my second cousin over a strange woman (because the cousin probably resembles me more)? There are some crucial experiments that would settle these questions—e.g., keeping a man in a large cage with his female first, second, third, fourth, and fifth cousins, counting how many times he had sex with each, and repeating the experiment with many men (or women) and their cousins. Alas, such experiments are hard to do in humans, but they've been done for several animal species, with instructive results. I'll give just three examples: the cousin-loving quail, and the perfumed mice and rats. (We can't use our closest relatives the chimpanzees for these examples, since they're so unselective.)

Consider first the case of Japanese quail, which normally grow up with their biological parents and siblings. However, it's also possible to "cross-foster" quail by switching eggs between quail mothers and their nests before the eggs hatch. In that way, a baby quail may be reared by foster parents and grow up with "pseudo-siblings"—i.e., litter mates among whom the baby hatched but to whom the baby isn't genetically related.

The preferences of male quail have been tested by putting a male in a cage with two females and observing with which female the male spent more time or copulated. When a male was given a choice between females that he had never seen before (although some were his relatives that had been separated from him before hatching), he preferred his first cousin to his third cousin or an unrelated female, but he also preferred his first cousin to his sister. Evidently, male quail as they grow up learn the appearance of their sisters (or mother) with whom they are reared, then seek a mate that is very similar but not *too* similar. In fancy technical language, biologists term this the Principle of Optimal Intermediate Similarity. Like other things in life, inbreeding seems to be good in moderation—a little inbreeding, but not too much. For instance, among unrelated females a male prefers an unfamiliar one over a familiar one with whom he grew up (a "pseudo-sister," who pushes the male's not-too-much-incest button).

Mice and rats similarly learn in childhood what to look for in mates, but they choose by smell more than by appearance. When infant female mice were reared by parents sprayed repeatedly with Parma Violet perfume, the females on reaching adulthood sought out Parma Violet–scented males in preference to unscented males. In another experiment, infant male rats were reared by mother rats whose nipples and vagina were sprayed with lemon odor, then the male on reaching adulthood was put in a cage with a lemon-smelling or unscented female rat. Each such encounter was videotaped and played back to note the times of key events. It turned out that males with scented mothers mounted and ejaculated more quickly when placed with a scented female than an unscented one, while the reverse was true for males with unscented mothers. For example, sons of scented mother rats were so excited by a scented sex partner that they ejaculated in only 11½ minutes, while they took over 17 minutes to ejaculate with an unscented female. But sons of unscented mother rats took over 17 minutes with the *scented* partner and only 12 minutes with the *unscented* partner. Obviously, the males had learned to be sexually excited by their mother's smell (or lack of smell); they did not inherit the knowledge.

WHAT DO THESE EXPERIMENTS on quail, mice, and rats show? The message is clear: animals of those species learn to recognize their parents and siblings as they grow up, then are programmed to seek out an individual fairly similar to the parent or sibling of opposite sex—but not Mother or Sister herself. They may *inherit* some search image of what constitutes a rat, but they evidently *learn* their search image of who in particular is a beautiful, eligible rat.

We can immediately appreciate what experiments are needed to get unequivocal proof of this theory for humans. We should take an average happy family, spray Father every day with Parma Violet, spray Mother's nipples daily with lemon oil while she is nursing, and then wait twenty years to see whom the sons and daughters marry. Alas, we would be frustrated by the many obstacles to establishing Scientific Truth for humans. But some observations and accidental experiments still let us tiptoe toward the truth.

Take the incest taboo. Scientists debate whether the taboo itself in humans is instinctive or learned. Given that we somehow acquire an incest taboo, do we learn to whom to apply it, or do we inherit that information in our genes? Normally we grow up with our closest relatives (parents and siblings), so our subsequent avoidance of them as sex partners could equally well be genetic or learned. But adoptive brothers and sisters also tend to avoid incest, suggesting learned avoidance.

This conclusion is strengthened by an interesting set of observations made in Israeli kibbutzim—the collective settlements whose members house, school, and care for all their children together as a large group. Kibbutz children live from birth until young adulthood in intimate association with each other, like a gigantic family of brothers and sisters. If propinquity were the main factor influencing whom we marry, most kibbutz children should marry within the kibbutz. In fact, a study of 2,769 marriages contracted by kibbutz-reared children turned up only thirteen between children from the same kibbutz; all the other children married outside the kibbutz on reaching maturity.

Even those thirteen cases turned out to be the exceptions that proved the rule: all involved couples one of whom had moved into that kibbutz only after the age of six! Among children reared in the same peer group since birth, there were not only no marriages, but also no cases of adolescent or adult heterosexual activity at all. This is astonishing restraint on the part of nearly three thousand young men and women who enjoyed daily opportunities for sexual involvement with each other, and who had far fewer opportunities for involvement with outsiders. It illustrates dramatically that the period between birth and age six is a critical time for formation of our sexual preferences. We *learn,* however unconsciously, that our intimate associates from that period are ineligible as sex partners when we become mature.

We also appear to learn the part of our search image that tells us whom to seek, not just the part that tells us whom to avoid. For instance, a friend of mine who is 100 percent Chinese herself happened to grow up in a community in which every other family was white. Eventually she moved as an adult to an area with many Chinese men, and for some time she dated both Chinese and white men, but came to realize that it was the whites who attracted her. She has been married twice, both times to white men. Her own experiences led her to ask her Chinese women friends about their backgrounds. It turned out that most of her friends reared in white enclaves also ended up marrying white men, while those reared in Chinese neighborhoods married Chinese men—although all had plenty of men of both types from whom to choose during their young adult years. Hence those who surround us as we grow up, though ineligible themselves as eventual mates, nevertheless shape our beauty standards and search images.

Think to yourself: what sort of men or women do you find physically attractive, and where did you develop that taste? I'd guess that most people, like me, can trace their preferences to the appearance of parents or siblings or childhood friends. So don't be discouraged by all those old generalizations about sex appeal—"Gentlemen prefer blondes," "Men seldom make passes at girls who wear glasses," etc. Each such "rule" applies only to some of us, and there are plenty of men out there whose mothers were myopic brunettes. Fortunately for my wife and me—both of us brunettes requiring glasses, born of brunette glasses-wearing parents—beauty is in the eye of the beholder.

CHAPTER 6

Sexual Selection,
and the
Origin of Human Races

WHITE MAN! LOOKIM THIS-FELLER LINE THREE-FELLER MAN.
This-feller number-one he belong Buka Island, na nother-feller
number-two he belong Makira Island, na this-feller number-three he
belong Sikaiana Island. Yu no savvy? Yu no enough lookim straight?
I think, eye-belong-yu he bugger-up finish?"

No, damn it, my eyes-belong-me were not ruined beyond repair. It
was my first visit to the Solomon Islands in the Southwest Pacific,
and I told my scornful guide through the medium of pidgin English
that I saw perfectly well the differences between those three men in
a row over there. The first one had jet-black skin and frizzy hair, the
second had much lighter skin and frizzy hair, and the third had
straighter hair and more slanted eyes. The only thing the matter with
me was that I had no experience of what people from each particular
Solomon island looked like. By the end of my first trip through the
Solomons, I too could identify people to islands by their skin and hair
and eyes.

In those variable features, the Solomons are a microcosm of humanity. Simply by looking at a person, even laymen can often tell

what part of the world that person comes from, and trained anthropologists may be able to "place" him or her to the right part of the
right country. For example, given one person each from Sweden,
Nigeria, and Japan, none of us would have any trouble deciding at a
glance which person was from which country. The most visibly
variable features in clothed people are of course skin color, the color
and form of the eyes and hair, body shape, and (in men) the amount
of facial hair. If the people to be identified were undressed, we might
also notice differences in amount of body hair, the size and shape and
color of a woman's breasts and nipples, the form of her labia and
buttocks, and the size and angle of a man's penis. All those variable
features contribute to what we know as human racial variation.

Those geographic differences among humans have long fascinated
travelers, anthropologists, bigots, and politicians, as well as the rest of
us. Since scientists have solved so many arcane questions about obscure unimportant species, surely you might expect them to have
answered one of the most obvious questions about ourselves: "Why
do people from different areas look different?" Our understanding of
how humans came to differ from other animals would remain in-
complete if we didn't also consider how, in the process, human
populations acquired their most visible differences from each other.
Nevertheless, the subject of human races is so explosive that Darwin
excised all discussion of it from his famous 1859 book *On the Origin
of Species.* Even today, few scientists dare to study racial origins, lest
they be branded racists just for being interested in the subject.

But there's another reason why we don't understand the significance of human racial variation: it proves to be an unexpectedly
difficult problem. Twelve years after Darwin wrote his book attributing the origin of species to natural selection, he wrote another book
898 pages long, attributing the origin of human races to our sexual
preferences, which I described in the last chapter, and entirely re-
jecting a role of natural selection. Despite that verbal overkill, many
readers were unconvinced. To this day, Darwin's theory of sexual
selection (as he called it) remains controversial. Instead, modern biologists generally invoke natural selection to explain the visible differences among human races—especially the differences in skin color,
whose relation to sun exposure seems obvious. However, biologists
can't even agree on why natural selection led to dark skin in the
tropics. I shall explain why I believe natural selection to have played

only a secondary role in our racial origins, and why Darwin's preference for sexual selection seems to me correct. I thus consider visible human racial variation to be largely a by-product of the remodeled human life cycle.

First, to place matters in perspective, let's realize that racial variation is not at all confined to humans. Most animal and plant species with sufficiently wide distributions, including all higher ape species except the geographically localized pygmy chimp, also vary geographically. So marked is variation in some bird species, such as North America's white-crowned sparrow and Eurasia's yellow wagtail, that experienced bird-watchers can identify an individual bird's approximate birthplace by its plumage pattern.

Variation in apes encompasses many of the same characteristics that vary geographically in humans. For example, among the three recognized races of gorillas, western lowland gorillas have the smallest bodies and rather gray or brown hair, while mountain gorillas have the longest hair, and eastern lowland gorillas share black hair with mountain gorillas. Races of white-handed gibbons similarly vary in hair color (variously black, brown, reddish, or gray), hair length, tooth size, protrusion of the jaws, and protrusion of the bony ridges over the eyes. All these traits that I have just mentioned as varying among gorilla or gibbon populations also differ among human populations.

How does one decide whether recognizably distinct animal populations from different localities constitute different species, or belong instead to the same species and just constitute different races (also known as subspecies)? As I have explained, the distinction is based on interbreeding under normal circumstances: members of the same species may interbreed normally if given the opportunity, while members of different species don't. (But closely related species that wouldn't normally interbreed in the wild, like lions and tigers, may do so if a male of one is caged with a female of the other and given no other choice.) By this criterion, all living human populations belong to the same species, since some interbreeding has occurred whenever humans from different regions have come into contact— even people as dissimilar in appearance as African Bantus and Pygmies. With humans as with other species, populations may intergrade into each other, and it becomes arbitrary which populations to group as races. By the same criterion of interbreeding, the large gibbons known as siamangs are a species distinct from the smaller gibbons, since both occur together in the wild without hybridizing. This is also the criterion for considering Neanderthals possibly as a distinct species from *Homo sapiens,* since hybrid skeletons have not been identified despite apparent Cro-Magnon-Neanderthal contact.

Racial variation has characterized humans for at least the past several thousand years, and possibly much longer. Already around 450 B.C., the Greek historian Herodotus described the Pygmies of West Africa, the black-skinned Ethiopians, and a blue-eyed, red-haired tribe in Russia. Ancient paintings, mummies from Egypt and Peru, and bodies of people preserved in European peat bogs confirm that people several thousand years ago differed in their hair and faces much as they do today. Origins of modern races can be pushed back still further, to at least ten thousand years ago, since fossil skulls of that age from various parts of the world differ in many of the same respects that modern skulls from the same regions differ. More controversial are the studies of some anthropologists, contested by others, reporting continuity of racial skull characteristics for hundreds of thousands of years. If those studies are correct, then some of the human racial variation that we see today may predate the Great Leap Forward, and may have gone back to *Homo erectus* times.

Now LET'S TURN to the question whether natural selection or sexual selection has made the larger contribution to those visible geographic differences of ours. Take first the arguments about natural selection, the selection of traits that enhance survival. No scientist denies today that natural selection does account for many of the differences between species, like the fact that lions have paws with claws while we have grasping fingers. No one denies either that natural selection explains some geographic variation ("racial variation") within some animal species. For instance, Arctic weasels that live in areas covered by winter snow change color from brown in summer to white in winter, while more southerly weasels stay brown all year. That racial difference enhances survival, because white weasels against a brown background would be glaringly conspicuous to their prey but are camouflaged against snow.

By the same token, natural selection surely explains *some* geographic variation in humans. Many African blacks but no Swedes have the sickle-cell hemoglobin gene, because the gene protects against malaria, a tropical disease that would otherwise kill many Africans. Other localized human traits that surely evolved through natural selection include the big chests of Andean Indians (good for extracting oxygen from thin air at high altitudes), the compact shapes of Eskimos (good for conserving heat), the slender shapes of southern Sudanese (good for losing heat), and the slitlike eyes of north Asians (good for protecting eyes against cold and against sun glare off the snow). All these examples are easy to understand.

Can natural selection similarly explain the racial differences that we think of first, those in skin color and eye color and hair? If so, one might expect that the same trait (e.g., blue eyes) would reappear in different parts of the world with similar climates, and that scientists would agree on what the trait is good for.

Seemingly the simplest trait to understand is skin color. Our skins run the spectrum from various shades of black, brown, copper, and yellowish to pink with or without freckles. The usual story to explain this variation by natural selection goes as follows. People from sunny Africa have blackish skins. So too (supposedly) do people from other sunny places, like southern India and New Guinea. Skins are said to get paler as one moves north or south from the equator, until one reaches northern Europe, with the palest skins of all. Obviously, dark skins evolved in those people who were exposed to much sunlight. That's just like the skins of whites tanning under the summer sun (or in tanning parlors!), except that tanning is a reversible response to sun rather than a permanent genetic one. It's equally obvious what good a dark skin does in sunny areas: it protects against sunburn and skin cancer. Whites who spend lots of time outdoors in the sun tend to get skin cancer, and they get it on exposed parts of their body like their head and hands. Doesn't that all make sense?

Unfortunately, it's really not so simple at all. To begin with, skin cancer and sunburn cause little debilitation and few deaths. As agents of natural selection, they have an utterly trivial impact compared to infectious diseases of childhood. Many other theories have instead been proposed to explain the supposed pole-to-equator gradient in skin color.

One favorite competing theory notes that the sun's ultraviolet rays promote vitamin D formation in a layer of our skin beneath the main pigmented layer. Thus, people in sunny tropical areas might have evolved dark skin to protect them against the risk of kidney disease caused by too much vitamin D, while people in Scandinavia with its long, dark winters evolved pale skins to protect them against the risk of rickets caused by too little vitamin D. Two other popular theories: dark skins are to protect our internal organs against overheating by the tropical sun's infrared rays; or—just the opposite—dark skins help keep tropical people warm when the temperature drops. And if those four theories aren't enough for you, consider four more: that dark skins provide camouflage in the jungle, or that pale skins are less sensitive to frostbite, or that dark skins protect against beryllium poisoning in the tropics, or that pale skins cause deficiency of another vitamin (folic acid) in the tropics.

With at least eight theories in the running, we can hardly claim to understand why people from sunny climates have dark skins. That in itself doesn't refute the idea that, somehow, natural selection caused the evolution of dark skins in sunny climates. After all, dark skins could have multiple advantages, which scientists may sort out some- day. Instead, the heaviest objection to any theory based on natural selection is that the association between dark skins and sunny cli- mates is a very imperfect one. Native peoples had very dark skins in some areas receiving relatively little sunlight, like Tasmania, while skin color is only medium in sunny areas of tropical Southeast Asia. No American Indians have black skins, not even in the sunniest parts of the New World. When one takes cloud cover into account, the world's most dimly lit areas, receiving a daily average of under 3½ hours of sunlight, include parts of equatorial West Africa, South China, and Scandinavia, inhabited respectively by some of the world's blackest, yellowest, and palest peoples! Among the Solomon Islands, all of which share a similar climate, jet-black people and lighter people replace each other over short distances. Evidently, sunlight has not been the sole selective factor that influenced skin color.

The first response of anthropologists to these objections is to raise a counterobjection: the time factor. This argument tries to explain away the cases of pale-skinned people in the tropics by claiming that those particular peoples migrated to the tropics too recently to have evolved black skins. For example, the ancestors of American Indians may have reached the New World only eleven thousand years ago:

perhaps that hasn't been long enough to evolve black skins in the tropical Americas. But if you're going to evoke the time factor to explain away objections to the climate theory of skin color, then you also have to consider the time factor for peoples who supposedly support that theory.

One of the prime supports of the climate theory is the pale skins of Scandinavians, living in the cold, dark, foggy North. Unfortunately, Scandinavians have been in Scandinavia for an even shorter time than American Indians have been in the Amazon. Until about nine thousand years ago, Scandinavia was covered by an ice sheet and could hardly have supported any people, pale-skinned or dark-skinned. Modern Scandinavians reached Scandinavia only around four or five thousand years ago, as a result of the expansion of farmers from the Near East and of Indo-European speakers from southern Russia. Either Scandinavians acquired their pale skins long ago in some other area with a different climate, or else they acquired them in Scandinavia within half the time that Indians have spent in the Amazon without becoming dark-skinned.

The sole people in the world about whom we can be certain that they spent the last ten thousand years in the same location were the natives of Tasmania. Lying south of Australia, at the temperate latitude of Chicago or Vladivostok, Tasmania used to be connected to Australia until it was cut off by rising sea level ten thousand years ago and became an island. Since modern Tasmanian natives didn't have boats capable of going more than a few miles, we know that they were derived from colonists who walked out to Tasmania at the time of its connection to Australia, and who remained there continuously until they were exterminated by British colonists in the nineteenth century. If any people had enough time for natural selection to match their skin color to their local temperate-zone climate, it was the Tasmanians. Yet they had blackish skins, supposedly adapted to the equator.

If the case for natural selection of skin color seems weak, that for hair color and eye color is virtually nonexistent. There are no consistent correlations with climate, and not even any halfway-plausible theories for the supposed advantage lent by each color type. Blond hair is common in cold, wet, dimly lit Scandinavia and also among Aborigines of the hot, dry, sunny desert of central Australia. What do those two areas have in common, and how does being blond help both Swedes and Aborigines to survive? Blue eyes are common in Scandinavia and supposedly help their owners see farther in dim, misty light. But that speculation is unproven, and all my friends in the even dimmer, mistier mountains of New Guinea see just fine with their dark eyes.

The racial traits for which it seems most absurd to seek an explanation based on natural selection are our variable genitalia and secondary sex characteristics. Are hemispherical breasts an adaptation to summer rainfall and conical breasts an adaptation to winter fog, or vice versa? Do the protruding labia minora of Bushman women protect them against pursuing lions, or reduce their water losses in the Kalahari Desert? You surely don't think that men with hairy chests can thereby keep warm while going shirtless in the Arctic, do you? If you do think so, then please explain why women don't share hairy chests with men, since women also have to keep warm.

FACTS SUCH AS THESE were what made Darwin despair of imputing human racial variation to his own concept of natural selection. He finally dismissed the attempt with a succinct statement: "Not one of the external differences between the races of man are of any direct or special service to him." When Darwin came up with a theory that he preferred, he termed it "sexual selection" to contrast with natural selection, and he devoted an entire book to explaining it.

The basic notion behind this theory is easily grasped. Darwin noted many animal features that had no obvious survival value but that did play an obvious role in securing mates, either by attracting an individual of the opposite sex or by intimidating a rival of the same sex. Familiar examples are the tails of male peacocks, the manes of male lions, and the bright red buttocks of female baboons in estrus. If an individual male is especially successful at attracting females or intimidating rival males, that male will leave more descendants and will tend to pass on his genes and traits—as a result of sexual selection, not natural selection. The same argument applies to female traits as well.

For sexual selection to work, evolution must produce two changes simultaneously: one sex must evolve some trait, and the other sex must evolve in lockstep a liking for that trait. Female baboons could hardly afford to flash red buttocks if the sight revolted male baboons to the point of their becoming impotent. As long as the female has it and the male likes it, sexual selection could lead to any arbitrary trait, just as long as it doesn't impair survival too much. In fact, many traits produced by sexual selection do seem quite arbitrary. A visitor from Outer Space who had yet to see humans could have no way of predicting that men rather than women would have beards, that the beards would be on the face rather than above the navel, and that women would not have red and blue buttocks.

That sexual selection really can work was proved by an elegant experiment carried out by the Swedish biologist Malte Andersson on the long-tailed widowbird of Africa. In this species the male's tail in the breeding season grows to twenty inches long, while the female's tail is only three inches. Some males are polygamous and acquire up to six mates, at the expense of other males who get none. Biologists had guessed that a long tail served as an arbitrary signal by which males attracted females to join their harem. Hence Andersson's test was to cut off parts of the tails from nine males so that their tails were only six inches long. He then glued those cut segments to the tails of nine other males to give them thirty-inch tails, and he waited to see where the females built their nests. It turned out that the males with the artificially lengthened tails attracted on the average over four times as many mates as the males with artificially shortened tails.

Perhaps our first reaction to Andersson's experiment is: Those dumb birds! Imagine a female selecting a particular male to father her offspring merely because his tail is longer than other males' tails! But before we get too smug, let's consider again what we learned in the last chapter about how we humans select our own mates. Are our criteria such good indicators of genetic worth? Don't some men and women set disproportionate value on the size or form of certain body parts, which are really nothing more than arbitrary signals for sexual selection? Why did we evolve to pay any attention at all to a beautiful face, which is useless to its owner in the struggle for survival?

In animals some of the traits that vary racially are ones produced by sexual selection. For instance, lions' manes vary in length and in color. Similarly, snow geese occur in two color phases, a blue phase commoner in the western Arctic and a white phase commoner in the eastern Arctic. Birds of each phase prefer a mate of the same phase. Could human breast shape and skin color similarly be the outcome of sexual preferences that vary arbitrarily from area to area?

After 898 pages of his book Darwin convinced himself that the answer to this question was a resounding "yes." He noted that we pay inordinate attention to breasts, hair, eyes, and skin color in selecting our mates and sex partners. He noted also that people in different parts of the world define beautiful breasts, hair, eyes, and skin by what is familiar to them. Thus, Fijians, Hottentots, and Swedes each grow up with their own learned, arbitrary beauty standards, which tend to maintain each population in conformity with those standards, since individuals deviating too far from the standards would find it harder to obtain a mate.

Darwin died before his theory could be tested against rigorous studies of how people actually do select their mates. Such studies have proliferated in recent decades, and I summarized the results in the preceding chapter. There I showed that people tend to marry individuals who resemble themselves in every conceivable character, including hair and eye and skin color. To explain that seeming narcissism of ours, I reasoned that we develop our beauty standards by imprinting on the people we see around us in childhood—especially on our parents and siblings, the people we see the most. But our parents and siblings are also the people to whom we bear the strongest physical resemblance, since we share their genes. Thus, if you're a fair-skinned, blue-eyed blond who grew up in a family of fair-skinned blue-eyed blonds, that's the sort of person whom you'll consider most beautiful and will seek as a mate.

To test that imprinting theory of human mate choice rigorously, one would have to do experiments like shipping some Swedish babies to adoptive parents in New Guinea, or painting some Swedish parents permanently black. Then, after waiting twenty years for the babies to grow up, one could study whether they preferred Swedes or New Guineans as sex partners. Alas, once again, the Search for Truth about humans founders on practical problems. But such tests can be performed with full experimental rigor on animals.

Take snow geese, for example, with their blue and white color phases. Do white geese learn or inherit their preference in the wild for white geese over blue ones? Canadian biologists hatched gosling eggs in an incubator, then put the goslings into a nest of goose "foster parents." When those goslings grew up, they chose mates with the color of the foster parents. When goslings were reared in a large mixed flock of both blue and white birds, they showed no preference between blue and white prospective mates on reaching adulthood. Finally, when the biologists dyed some white parents pink, their offspring came to prefer pink-dyed geese. Thus, geese do not inherit but learn a color preference, by imprinting on their parents (and on their siblings and playmates).

How, THEN, do I think that people in different parts of the world evolved their differences? Our insides remained invisible to us and were molded only by natural selection, with such results as that tropical Africans but not Swedes got the antimalarial defense of the sickle-cell hemoglobin gene. Many visible features of our outsides also got molded by natural selection. But, just as in animals, sexual selection had a big effect in molding the external traits by which we pick our mates.

For us humans those traits are especially the skin, eyes, hair, breasts, and genitals. In each part of the world those traits evolved in lockstep with our imprinted aesthetic preferences to reach different, somewhat arbitrary end points. Which particular human population ended up with any given eye or hair color may have been partly an accident of what biologists term the "founder effect." That is to say, if a few individuals colonize an empty land and their descendants then multiply to fill the land, the genes of those few founding individuals may still dominate the resulting population many generations later. Just as some birds of paradise ended up with yellow plumes and others with black plumes, so some human populations ended up with yellow hair and others with black hair, some with blue eyes and others with green eyes, some with orange nipples and others with brown nipples.

I don't mean thereby to claim that climate has nothing whatsoever to do with skin color. I acknowledge that tropical peoples tend on the average to have darker skins than temperate-zone peoples, though there are many exceptions, and that this is probably due to natural selection, though we're unsure of the exact mechanism. Instead, I'm saying that sexual selection has been strong enough to render the correlation between skin color and sun exposure quite imperfect.

If you're still skeptical about how traits and aesthetic preferences can evolve together to different arbitrary end points, just think about our changing fashion preferences. When I was a schoolboy in the early 1950s, women rated men with crew cuts and clean-shaven faces as handsome. Since then, we've seen a parade of men's fashions, including beards, long hair, earrings, purple-dyed hair, and the Mohawk hair style. A man daring to flaunt any of those fashions in the 1950s would have revolted the girls and enjoyed zero mating success. That's not because crew cuts were better adapted to the atmospheric conditions of Stalin's last years, while a purple Mohawk has higher survival value in our post-Chernobyl era. Instead, men's appearances and women's tastes changed together, and the changes occurred far more rapidly than evolutionary changes in skin color, since no gene mutations were required. Either women came to like crew cuts because good men had them, or men adopted crew cuts because good women liked them, or something of both happened. The same goes for women's appearances and men's tastes.

To a zoologist, the visible geographic variability that sexual selection produced in humans is impressive. I've argued that much of our variability is a by-product of a distinctive feature of the human life cycle: our choosiness with respect to our spouses and sex partners. I don't know of any other wild animal species in which eye color of different populations can be green, blue, gray, brown, or black, while skin color varies geographically from pale to black and hair is either red, yellow, brown, black, gray, or white. There may be no limits, except those imposed by evolutionary time, on the colors with which sexual selection can adorn us. If humanity survives another twenty thousand years, I predict that there will be women with naturally green hair and red eyes—and men who think such women are the sexiest.

CHAPTER 7

Why
Do We Grow Old
and Die?

Death and aging constitute a mystery that we often ask about as children, deny in youth, and reluctantly come to accept as adults. I scarcely reflected on aging when I was a college student. Now that I am fifty-four years old, I find it decidedly more interesting. Life expectancy among U.S. white adults is presently about seventy-eight years for men, eighty-three for women. But few of us will survive to one hundred. Why is it so easy to live to eighty, so hard to live to one hundred, and almost impossible to live to 120? Why do humans with access to the best medical care, and animals kept in a cage with plenty of food and no predators, inevitably grow infirm and die? It's the most obvious feature of our life cycle, but there's nothing obvious about what causes it.

In the bare fact of our aging and dying we resemble all other animals. In the details, however, we've improved considerably over the course of our evolutionary history. Not a single individual of any ape species has been recorded as achieving the current life expectancy of U.S. whites, and only exceptional apes reach their fifties. Evidently, we age more slowly than do our closest relatives. Some of that slowdown may have developed recently, around the time of the Great Leap Forward, since quite a few Cro-Magnons lived into their sixties while few Neanderthals passed forty.

Slow aging is as crucial to the human life-style as are marriage, concealed ovulation, and the other life-cycle features that we've been discussing in the preceding chapters. That's because our life-style depends on transmitted information. As language evolved, far more information became available to us to pass on than previously. Until the invention of writing, old people acted as the repositories of that transmitted information and experience, just as they continue to do in tribal societies today. Under hunter-gatherer conditions, the knowledge possessed by even one person over the age of seventy could spell the difference between survival and starvation for a whole clan. Our long life span, therefore, was important for our rise from animal to human status.

Obviously, our ability to survive to a ripe old age depended ultimately upon advances in culture and technology. It's easier to defend yourself against a lion if you're carrying a spear than just a hand-held stone, and easier yet with a high-powered rifle. However, advances in culture and technology alone would not have been enough, unless our bodies had also become redesigned to last longer. No caged ape in a zoo, enjoying all the benefits of modern human technology and veterinary care, reaches eighty. We'll see in this chapter that our biology became remolded to the increased life expectancy that our cultural advances made possible. In particular, I'd guess that Cro-Magnon tools weren't the sole reason why Cro-Magnons lived on the average longer than Neanderthals. Instead, around the time of the Great Leap Forward our biology must also have changed so that we aged more slowly. That may even have been the time when menopause, the concomitant of aging that paradoxically functions to let women live longer, evolved.

THE WAY IN WHICH SCIENTISTS THINK about aging depends on whether they are interested in so-called proximate explanations or ultimate explanations. To appreciate this difference, consider the question, "Why do skunks smell bad?" A chemist or molecular biologist would answer, "It's because skunks secrete chemical compounds with certain particular molecular structures. Owing to the principles of quantum mechanics, those structures result in bad smells. Those particular chemicals would smell bad no matter what the biological function of their bad smell was."

But an evolutionary biologist would instead reason, "It's because skunks would be easy victims for predators if they didn't defend themselves with bad smells. Natural selection made skunks evolve to secrete bad-smelling chemicals; those skunks with the worst smells survived to produce the most baby skunks. The molecular structure of those chemicals is a mere incidental detail; any other bad-smelling chemicals would suit skunks equally well."

The chemist has offered a proximate explanation: i.e., the mechanism immediately responsible for the observation that was to be explained. The evolutionary biologist has instead offered an ultimate explanation: the function or chain of events that caused that mechanism to be present. The chemist and the evolutionary biologist would each dismiss the other's answer as not being "the real explanation."

Similarly, studies of aging are pursued independently by two groups of scientists who scarcely communicate with each other. One group seeks a proximate explanation, the other an ultimate explanation. Evolutionary biologists try to understand how natural selection could ever permit aging to occur, and they think that they've found an answer to this question. Physiologists inquire instead into the cellular mechanisms underlying aging, and admit that they don't yet have an answer. But I'll argue that aging can't be understood unless we seek both explanations simultaneously. In particular, I expect that the evolutionary (ultimate) explanation will help us find the physiological (proximate) explanation of aging that has so far eluded scientists.

BEFORE I CAN PURSUE THIS REASONING, I must anticipate objections of my physiologist friends. They tend to believe that something about our physiology somehow makes aging inevitable, and that evolutionary considerations are irrelevant. For instance, one such theory attributes aging to the progressive difficulties that our immune system is said to face in distinguishing our own cells from foreign cells. Physiologists subscribing to this view make an implicit assumption:

that natural selection couldn't lead to an immune system without that fatal defect. Is this belief warranted?

To evaluate this objection, let's consider biological repair mechanisms, because aging may be thought of simply as unrepaired damage or deterioration. Our first association to the word "repair" is likely to be to those repairs that cause us the most frustration—car repairs. Our cars tend to grow old and die, but we spend money to postpone their inevitable fate. Similarly, we are unconsciously but constantly repairing ourselves too, at every level from molecules to tissues or whole organs. Our own self-repair mechanisms, like those we lavish on our cars, are of two sorts: damage control and regular replacement.

An automotive example of damage control is that we replace a car's fender only if it's bashed in; we don't routinely replace the fenders at every regular oil change. The most visible example of damage control applied to our bodies is wound healing, by which we repair damage to our skin. Many animals can achieve more spectacular results: lizards regenerate severed tails, starfish and crabs their limbs, sea cucumbers their intestines, and ribbon worms their poison stylets. At the invisible molecular level our genetic material, DNA, is repaired exclusively by damage control: we have enzymes that recognize and fix damaged sites in the DNA helix while ignoring intact DNA.

The other type of repair, regular replacement, is also familiar to every car owner: we periodically change the oil, air filter, and ball bearings to eliminate slight wear, without waiting for the car to break down first. In the biological world, teeth are similarly replaced on a prescheduled basis: humans go through two sets, elephants six sets, and sharks an indefinite number, during their lifetimes. Though we humans go through life with the same skeleton with which we were born, lobsters and other arthropods regularly replace their exoskeletons by molting them and growing new ones. Still another highly visible example of scheduled repair is the continual growth of our hair: no matter how short we cut it, its growth will replace the cut portion.

Regular replacement also goes on at a microscopic or submicroscopic level. We constantly replace many of our cells: about once every few days for the cells lining our intestine, once every two months for the cells lining the urinary bladder, and once every four months for our red blood cells. At the molecular level, our protein molecules are subject to continuous turnover at a rate characteristic of each particular protein; we thereby avoid the accumulation of damaged molecules. If you compare your beloved's appearance today with a photo taken a month ago, he (or she) may look the same, but many of the individual molecules forming that beloved body are different. While all the king's horses and men couldn't put Humpty-Dumpty together again, Nature is taking us apart and putting us back together every day.

In such ways, much of an animal's body can be repaired as needed, or is regularly replaced anyhow, but the details of how much is replaceable vary greatly with the part and with the species. There is nothing physiologically inevitable about the limited repair capabilities of us humans. Since starfish can regrow amputated limbs, why can't we? What prevents us from having six sequential sets of teeth like an elephant, rather than just baby teeth and adult teeth? With four more natural sets, we wouldn't need fillings, crowns, and dentures as we got older. Why don't we protect ourselves against arthritis?—all we'd need is to replace our joints periodically, as crabs do. Why don't we guard against heart disease by periodically replacing our hearts, as ribbon worms replace their poison stylets? One might suppose that natural selection would favor the man or woman who didn't die of heart disease around age eighty but continued to live and produce babies at least until age two hundred. Why, for that matter, can't we repair or replace everything in our bodies?

The answer surely has something to do with the expense of repair. Here again, the analogy of car repair is helpful. If the boasts of the Mercedes-Benz company are to be believed, their cars are so well built that, even should you do no maintenance whatsoever—not even lubrication or oil changes—your Mercedes will still run for years. At the end of that time, of course, it will fall apart from accumulated irreversible damage. Hence Mercedes owners generally do choose to service their cars regularly. My Mercedes-owning friends tell me that Mercedes service is very expensive: hundreds of dollars every time they drive into the shop. Nevertheless, they consider the expense worth it: a serviced Mercedes lasts much longer than an unserviced Mercedes, and it's much cheaper to service your old Mercedes regularly than to discard it and buy a new one every few years.

That's how Mercedes owners reason in Germany and the United States. But suppose you were living in Port Moresby, the capital of Papua New Guinea, automobile-accident capital of the world, where any car is likely to be totaled within a year no matter how you maintain it. Many car owners in New Guinea don't go to the expense of maintaining their car: they use the saved money to help buy the inevitable next car.

By analogy, how much an animal "should" invest in biological repairs depends on the expense of the repairs, and on a comparison of the animal's expected life span with and without the repairs. But such "should" questions belong to the realm of evolutionary biology, not physiology. Natural selection tends to maximize one's rate of producing offspring that survive to leave offspring of their own. Evolution can thus be regarded as a strategy game, in which the individual whose strategy leaves the most descendants wins. The type of reasoning used in game theory is therefore helpful in understanding how we came to be the way we are.

THIS PROBLEM OF LIFE SPAN, and of investment in biological repair, is in turn one of an even broader class of evolutionary problems addressed by game theory: the mystery of what sets the maximum limit on any advantageous trait. There are lots of other biological traits, besides life span, that beg the question why natural selection hasn't made them longer or bigger or faster or made more of them. For instance, people who are big or smart or can run fast have obvious advantages over small, stupid, slow people—especially throughout most of human evolution, when we were still fending off lions and hyenas. Why didn't we evolve to become on the average even bigger, smarter, and faster than we now are?

The complication that makes these evolutionary design problems less simple than they might at first seem is this: natural selection acts on whole individuals, not on single parts of an individual. It's you, not your big brain or fast legs, that does or doesn't survive and leave offspring. Increasing one part of an animal's body may be beneficial in some obvious respect but harmful in other respects. For instance, that one larger part might not fit in well with other parts of the same animal, or it might drain off energy from other parts.

To evolutionary biologists, the magic word that expresses this complication is "optimize." Natural selection tends to mold each trait to the size, speed, or number that maximizes the survival and reproductive success of the whole animal, given the animal's basic design. Each trait in itself doesn't tend toward a maximal value. Instead, each trait converges on some optimal intermediate value, neither too big nor too small. The whole animal is thereby more successful than it would be if that trait were bigger or smaller.

Should this reasoning about animals seem abstract, think instead of our everyday machines. Essentially the same principles apply to engineering design, of machines by humans, as to evolutionary design, of animals by natural selection. For example, consider my pride and joy among my machines, my 1962 Volkswagen Beetle, the only car I've ever owned. (Car buffs will remember 1962 as the year that Volkswagen introduced the big rear window in the Beetle.) On a smooth, level highway with an assisting tailwind, my VW can go 65 mph. To BMW owners, that may sound distinctly submaximal. Why don't I junk my puny 4-cylinder 40-horsepower engine, install instead the 12-cylinder 296-horsepower engine from my neighbor's BMW 750 IL, and roar off at 180 mph down the San Diego Freeway?

Well, even I, dodo about cars that I am, know that that wouldn't work. To begin with, that huge BMW engine wouldn't fit into my VW's engine compartment, which would need enlarging. Then the BMW engine is meant to go in front, but the VW engine compartment is in back, so I'd have to change the gear box and transmission and other things. I'd also have to change the shock absorbers and brakes, designed to smooth the ride and stop a car at 65 mph but not at 180 mph. By the time I had finished modifying my VW to take the BMW engine, there wouldn't be much remaining from my original Beetle. And the modifications would have cost me a big pile of money. I'd guess that my puny 40-HP engine is optimal, in the sense that I couldn't increase my cruising speed without sacrificing other performance features of my car—as well as sacrificing other money-requiring features of my life-style.

While the marketplace *eventually* eliminates engineering monstrosities like a VW with a BMW engine, all of us can think of monstrosities that took quite a while to eliminate. To those of you who share my fascination with naval warfare, British battle cruisers are a good example. Before and during World War I, the British navy launched thirteen warships called battle cruisers, designed to be as large and with as many big guns as battleships but much faster. By maximizing speed and firepower, the battle cruisers immediately caught the public imagination and became a propaganda sensation. However, if you take a 28,000-ton battleship, keep the weight of the big guns nearly constant, and greatly increase the weight of the engines while still maintaining total weight around 28,000 tons, you have to skimp on the weight of some other parts. The battle cruisers skimped especially on weight of armor, but also on weight of small guns, internal compartments, and antiaircraft defense.

The results of this suboptimal overall design were inevitable. In 1916 H.M.S. *Indefatigable, Queen Mary,* and *Invincible* all blew up almost as soon as they were hit by German shells at the Battle of Jutland. H.M.S. *Hood* blew up in 1941, a mere eight minutes after entering battle with the German battleship *Bismarck*. H.M.S. *Repulse* was sunk by Japanese bombers a few days after the Japanese attack on Pearl Harbor, thereby acquiring the dubious distinction of being the first large warship to be destroyed from the air while in combat at sea. Faced with this stark evidence that some spectacularly maximal parts don't make an optimal whole, the British navy let its program of building battle cruisers go extinct.

In short, engineers can't tinker with single parts in isolation from the rest of a machine, because each part costs money, space, and weight that might have gone into something else. Engineers instead have to ask what *combination* of parts will optimize a machine's effectiveness. By the same reasoning, evolution can't tinker with single traits in isolation from the rest of an animal, because every structure, enzyme, or piece of DNA consumes energy and space that might have gone into something else. Instead, natural selection favors that combination of traits that maximizes the animal's reproductive output. Both engineers and evolutionary biologists have to evaluate the trade-offs involved in increasing anything: its costs as well as the benefits that it would bring.

AN OBVIOUS DIFFICULTY in applying this reasoning to our life cycles is that they have many features seeming to reduce, not to maximize, our ability to produce offspring. Growing old and dying are just one example; other examples are human female menopause, bearing one baby at a time, producing babies only once every year or so at most, and not even starting to produce babies until age twelve to sixteen.

Wouldn't natural selection favor the woman who entered puberty at age five, completed gestation in three weeks, regularly bore quintuplets, never underwent menopause, put lots of biological energy into repair of her body, lived to two hundred, and thereby left hundreds of offspring?

But posing the question in that form pretends that evolution can change our bodies one piece at a time, and ignores the hidden costs. For instance, a woman certainly couldn't reduce the length of pregnancy to three weeks without changing anything else about herself or her baby. Remember that we only have a finite amount of energy available to us. Even people doing hard exercise and eating rich food—lumberjacks or marathon runners in training—can't metabolize much more than about six thousand calories per day. How should we allocate those calories between repairing ourselves and rearing babies, if our goal is to raise as many babies as possible?

At the one extreme, if we put all our energy into babies and devoted no energy to biological repair, our bodies would age and disintegrate before we could rear our first baby. At the other extreme, if we lavished all our available energy on keeping our bodies in shape, we might live a long time but would have no energy left for the exhausting process of making and rearing babies. What natural selection must do is to adjust an animal's relative expenditures of energy on repair and on reproduction, so as to maximize its reproductive output, averaged over its lifetime. The answer to that problem varies among animal species, depending on factors such as their risk of accidental death, their reproductive biology, and the costs of various types of repairs.

This perspective can be employed to make testable predictions about how animals should differ in their repair mechanisms and rates of aging. In 1957 the evolutionary biologist George Williams cited some striking facts about aging that become comprehensible only from an evolutionary perspective. Let's consider several of Williams's examples and reexpress them in the physiological language of biological repair, by taking slow aging as an indication of good repair mechanisms.

The first example concerns the age at which an animal first breeds and produces offspring. That age varies enormously among species: few humans are so precocious as to produce babies before the age of twelve years, while any self-respecting mouse a mere two months old can already make baby mice. Animals belonging to a species whose age of first breeding is late, like us, need to devote much energy to repair, in order to ensure that they survive to that reproductive age. So we expect investment in repair to increase with age at first reproduction.

For instance, correlated with our having a much later age of first reproduction than do mice, we humans age far more slowly than mice and are presumed to repair our bodies much more effectively. Even with plenty of food and the best medical care, a mouse is lucky to reach its second birthday, while we would be unlucky not to reach our seventy-second birthday. The evolutionary reason: a human who invested no more of his/her energy in repair than does a mouse would be dead long before reaching puberty. Hence it is more worthwhile to repair a human than a mouse.

What might that postulated extra energy expenditure of ours actually consist of? At first, our human repair capabilities seem unimpressive. We can't regrow an amputated arm, and we don't regularly replace our skeleton, in the way that some short-lived invertebrates do. However, such spectacular but infrequent replacements of a whole structure probably aren't the biggest items in an animal's repair budget. Instead, the biggest expense is all that invisible replacement of so many of your cells and molecules, day after day. Even if you spend all day every day just lying in bed, you need to eat about 1,640 calories per day if you're a man (1,430 for a woman) just to maintain your body. Much of that maintenance metabolism goes to our invisible scheduled replacement. And so I'd guess that where we cost more than a mouse is in putting a bigger fraction of our energy into self-repair, and a smaller fraction into other purposes like keeping warm or caring for babies.

The second example I'll discuss involves the risk of irreparable injury. Some biological damage is potentially reparable, but there is also damage that is guaranteed to be fatal (e.g., being eaten by a lion). If you're likely to be eaten by a lion tomorrow, there's no point in paying a dentist to start expensive orthodontic work on your teeth today. You'd do better to let your teeth rot and start having babies immediately. But if an animal's risk of death from irreparable accidents is low, then there is a potential payoff, in the form of increased life span, from putting energy into expensive repair mechanisms that retard aging. This is the reasoning by which

Mercedes owners decide to pay for lubrication of their cars in Germany and the United States but not in New Guinea.

Biological analogies are that the risk of death from predators is lower for birds than for mammals (because birds can escape by flying), and lower for turtles than for most other reptiles (because turtles are protected by a shell). Thus, birds and turtles stand to gain a lot from expensive repair mechanisms, compared to flightless mammals and shell-less reptiles that will soon be eaten by predators anyway. Indeed, if one compares longevities of well-fed pets protected from predators, birds do live longer (i.e., age more slowly) than similar-sized mammals, and turtles live longer than similar-sized shell-less reptiles. The bird species best protected from predators are seabirds like petrels and albatrosses that nest on remote oceanic islands free of predators. Their leisurely life cycles rival our own. Some albatrosses don't even breed until they're ten years old, and we still don't know how long they live: the birds themselves last longer than the metal rings that biologists began putting on their legs a few decades ago in order to keep track of their ages. In the ten years that it takes an albatross to start breeding, a mouse population could have gone through sixty generations, most of which would already have succumbed to predators or old age.

As our third example, let's compare males and females of the same species. We expect more potential payoff from repair mechanisms, and lower rates of aging, in that sex with the lower accidental mortality rate. For many or most species, males suffer greater accidental mortality than females, partly because males put themselves at greater risk by fighting and bold displays. This is certainly true of human males today and has probably been so throughout our history as a species: men are the sex most likely to die in wars against men of other groups, and in individual fights within a group. Also, in many species the males are bigger than the females, but studies of red deer and of New World blackbirds show that males are thereby more likely than females to die when food becomes scarce.

Correlated with this greater accidental death rate of men, men also age faster and have a higher nonaccidental death rate than women. At present, women's life expectancy is about six years greater than that of men; some of this difference is because more men than women are smokers, but there is a sex-linked difference in life expectancy even among nonsmokers. These differences suggest that evolution has programmed us so that women put more energy into self-repair, while men put more energy into fighting. Expressed another way, it just isn't worth as much to repair a man as it is to repair a woman. But I don't mean to denigrate male fighting, which serves a useful evolutionary purpose for a man: to gain wives and to secure resources for his children and his tribe, at the expense of other men and their children and tribe.

MY REMAINING EXAMPLE of how some striking facts of aging become comprehensible only from an evolutionary perspective concerns the distinctively human phenomenon of survival past reproductive age, especially past female menopause. Since transmitting one's genes to the next generation is what drives evolution, other animal species rarely survive past reproductive age. Instead, Nature programs death to coincide with the end of fertility, because there is then no longer any evolutionary benefit to gain from keeping one's body in good repair. It's an exception in need of explanation to realize that women are programmed to live for decades after menopause, and that men are programmed to live to an age when most men are no longer busy siring babies.

But the explanation becomes apparent on reflection. The intense phase of parental care is unusually protracted in the human species and lasts nearly two decades. Even those older people whose own children have reached adulthood are tremendously important to the survival of not just their children but of their whole tribe. Especially in the days before writing, they acted as the carriers of essential knowledge. Nature has programmed us with the capacity to keep the rest of our bodies in reasonable repair even at an age when the female reproductive system itself has fallen into disrepair.

Conversely, though, we have to wonder why natural selection programmed female menopause into us in the first place. It too, like aging, can't be explained away as something physiologically inevitable. Most mammals, including human males plus chimps and gorillas of both sexes, merely experience a gradual decline and eventual cessation of fertility with age, rather than the abrupt shutdown of women's fertility. Why did that peculiar, seemingly counterproductive feature of ours evolve? Wouldn't natural selection favor the woman who remained fertile until the bitter end?

Human female menopause probably resulted from two other distinctively human characteristics: the exceptional danger that childbirth poses to the mother, and the danger that a mother's death poses to her offspring. Recall the enormous size of the human infant at birth relative to its mother: our big seven-pound babies emerging from hundred-pound mothers, compared to little four-pound gorilla babies emerging from two-hundred-pound gorilla mothers. As a result, childbirth is dangerous to women. Especially before the advent of modern obstetrics, women often died in childbirth, whereas mother gorillas and chimps virtually never do. A study of the outcome of labor in 401 pregnant rhesus monkeys recorded only a single maternal death.

Now recall the extreme dependence of human infants on their parents, especially on their mother. Because human infants develop so slowly and can't even feed themselves after weaning (unlike young apes), the death of a hunter-gatherer mother would have been likely to be fatal to her offspring up to a later age in childhood than for any other primate. A hunter-gatherer mother with several children was gambling the lives of those children at every subsequent childbirth. Since her investment in those prior children increased with their age, and since her own risk of death in childbirth also increased with her age, the odds of her gamble's paying off got worse and worse as she got older. When you already have three children alive but still dependent on you, why risk those three for a fourth?

Those worsening odds probably led through natural selection to menopausal shutdown of human female fertility, in order to protect a mother's prior investment in kids. But since childbirth carries no risk of death for fathers, men did not evolve menopause. Like aging, menopause illustrates how an evolutionary approach illuminates features of our life cycle that would otherwise make no sense. It's even possible that menopause evolved only within the past forty thousand years, when Cro-Magnons and other anatomically modern humans began frequently to survive to age sixty or more. Neanderthals and earlier humans usually died before age forty anyway, so that menopause would have brought their women no benefits if it were to occur at the same age as in modern *Femina sapiens*.

Thus, the longer life span of modern humans as compared to that of apes does not rest only on cultural adaptations, such as tools to acquire food and deter predators. It also rests on the biological adaptations of menopause and increased investment in self-repair. Whether those biological adaptations developed especially at the time of the Great Leap Forward or earlier, they rank among the life-history changes that permitted the rise of the third chimpanzee to humanity.

THE LAST CONCLUSION that I wish to draw from an evolutionary approach to aging is that it undermines the approach that has long dominated the physiological study of aging. The gerontological literature is obsessed with a search for The Cause of Aging—preferably a single cause, certainly not more than a few major causes. Within my own lifetime as a biologist, hormonal changes, deterioration in the immune system, and neural degeneration have vied in popularity for the title of The Cause, without compelling support having been adduced to date for any of the candidates. But evolutionary reasoning suggests that this search will remain futile. There *should* not be just one, or even a few, dominant physiological mechanisms of aging. Instead, natural selection should act to match rates of aging in all physiological systems, with the result that aging involves innumerable simultaneous changes.

The basis of this prediction is as follows. There's no point in doing expensive maintenance on one piece of the body if other pieces are deteriorating more rapidly. Conversely, there's no point in permitting a few systems to deteriorate long before all the others, because the cost of extra repairs on just those few systems would have bought a big increase in life expectancy. Natural selection doesn't make such pointless mistakes. By analogy, Mercedes owners shouldn't install cheap ball bearings when they are lavishing expense on all other parts of the car. Had they been so foolish, they could have doubled the lifetime of their costly car just by spending a few more dollars for better ball bearings. But it wouldn't pay either to go to the expense of installing diamond ball bearings, when all the rest of the car would have rusted away before those ball bearings wore out. Thus, the optimal strategy for Mercedes owners, and for us, is to repair all parts of our cars or bodies at rates such that everything finally collapses all at once.

It seems to me that this depressing prediction is borne out, and that this evolutionary ideal of simultaneous total collapse describes the fates of our bodies better than does the physiologists' long-sought single Cause of Aging. Signs of aging can be found wherever one looks for them. Already I am conscious in myself of tooth wear, considerable decreases in muscle performance, and significant losses in hearing, vision, smell, and taste. For all these senses, the acuity of women is greater than that of equal-aged men, whatever the age group compared. Ahead for me lies the familiar litany: weakening of the heart, hardening of the arteries, increasing brittleness of bones, decreases in kidney filtration rates, lower resistance of the immune system, and loss of memory. The list could be extended almost indefinitely. Evolution seems indeed to have arranged things so that all our systems deteriorate, and that we invest in repair only as much as we are worth.

From a practical standpoint, this conclusion is disappointing. If there had been one dominant cause of aging, curing that cause would have provided us with a fountain of youth. This thought, operating at a time when aging was thought to be largely a hormonal phenomenon, inspired some attempts at miraculous rejuvenation of old people by hormonal injections or implantation of young gonads. Such an attempt was the subject of Sir Arthur Conan Doyle's story "The Adventure of the Creeping Man," in which the aged Professor Presbury becomes infatuated with a young woman, desperately wants to rejuvenate himself, and instead is found climbing up a vine like a monkey after midnight. The great Sherlock Holmes discovers the reason: the professor has been seeking youth by injecting himself with the serum of langur monkeys.

I could have warned Professor Presbury that his myopic obsession with proximate causation would lead him astray. Had he thought of ultimate evolutionary causation, he would have realized that natural selection would never permit us to deteriorate through a single mechanism with one simple cure. Perhaps it's just as well. Sherlock Holmes worried greatly what would happen if such an elixir of life was found. "There is danger there—a very real danger to humanity. Consider, Watson, that the material, the sensual, the worldly would all prolong their worthless lives. . . . It would be the survival of the least fit. What sort of cesspool may not our poor world become?"

Holmes would be relieved to know that his worries now appear unlikely to materialize.

PART THREE

UNIQUELY
HUMAN

Parts One and Two discussed the biological foundations of our unique cultural traits. We saw that those foundations include our familiar skeletal hallmarks, such as our large braincase and our adaptations for upright gait. They also include features of our soft tissues, behavior, and endocrinology concerned with reproduction and social organization.

However, if those genetically specified features were our sole distinctions, we wouldn't stand out among animals, and we wouldn't now be threatening the survival of ourselves and other species. Other animals, such as ostriches, walk erect on two legs. Others have relatively large brains, though not as large as ours. Others live monogamously in colonies (many seabirds), or are very long-lived (albatrosses and tortoises).

Instead, our uniqueness lies in the cultural traits that rest on those genetic foundations and that in turn give us our power. Our cultural hallmarks include spoken language, art, tool-based technology, and agriculture. But if we stopped there, we'd have a one-sided and self-congratulatory view of our uniqueness. The hallmarks I just mentioned are ones that we're proud of. Yet the archaeological record shows the introduction of agriculture to have been a mixed blessing, seriously harming many people while benefiting others. Chemical abuse is a wholly ugly human hallmark. At least it doesn't threaten our survival, as do two of our other cultural practices: genocide, and mass exterminations of other species. We're uncomfortable about whether to regard these as occasional pathological aberrations, or as features no less basic to humanity than the traits we're proudest of.

All of these cultural features that define humanity are seemingly absent in animals, even in our closest relatives. They must have arisen sometime after our ancestors parted company from the other chimpanzees around seven million years ago. Furthermore, while we have no way of knowing whether Neanderthals spoke or indulged in drug abuse and genocide, they certainly didn't have agriculture, art, or the capacity to build radios. Hence these latter traits must be very recent human innovations of the last few tens of thousands of years. But they couldn't have arisen from nothing. There had to have been animal precursors, if we could only recognize them.

For each of our defining cultural traits, we need to ask: What were those precursors? When in our ancestry did the trait approach its modern form? What were the early stages of its evolution like, and can those stages be traced archaeologically? We're unique on Earth, but how unique are we in the universe?

In this part we'll consider some of the above questions for our noble, two-edged, or only mildly destructive characteristics. We'll first take up the origin of spoken language, which I suggested earlier might have triggered the Great Leap Forward, and which anyone would list among our most important distinctions from animals. On first reflection, the task of tracing the development of human language appears plainly impossible. Language before the dawn of writing left no archaeological remains, unlike our first experiments in art, agriculture, and tools. There seems to be no surviving simple human language, no animal language, that could exemplify the early stages.

In fact, there are innumerable animal precursors: the vocal communication systems evolved by many species. We're just beginning to appreciate the sophistication of some of these systems. If they exemplify a first stage, results of recent experiments at teaching language to apes represent a second stage, by revealing apes' innate capacities. The progress by which children learn to speak may trace out further stages. We'll also see that there really are some simple languages that modern humans have unconsciously invented and that prove unexpectedly instructive.

Among our unique cultural traits, art is perhaps the noblest human invention. There seems to be a gulf separating human art, supposedly created just for pleasure and doing nothing to perpetuate our genes, from any animal behavior. Yet paintings and drawings created by captive apes and elephants, whatever the motives of those animal artists, look so similar to work of human artists that they have fooled experts and have been bought by art collectors. If one nevertheless dismisses those animal artworks as unnatural productions, what is one to say about the carefully arranged colored bowers of normal male bowerbirds? Those bowers play an unquestioned crucial role in passing on genes. I'll argue that human art also had that role originally, and often still does today. Since art, unlike language, does show up in archaeological deposits, we know that human art didn't proliferate until the time of the Great Leap Forward.

Agriculture, another human hallmark, has an animal precedent but not precursor in the gardens of leafhopper ants, which lie far off of our direct lineage. The archaeological record lets us date our "reinvention" of agriculture to a time long after the Great Leap Forward, within the last ten thousand years. That transition from hunting and gathering to agriculture is generally considered a decisive step in our progress, when we at last acquired the stable food supply and leisure time prerequisite to the great accomplishments of modern civilization. In fact, careful examination of that transition suggests another conclusion: for most people the transition brought infectious diseases, malnutrition, and a shorter life span. For human society in general it worsened the relative lot of women and introduced class-based inequality. More than any other milestone along the path from chimpanzeehood to humanity, agriculture inextricably combines causes of our rise and our fall.

Abuse of toxic chemicals is a widespread human hallmark documented only within the last five thousand years, though it may well go back much earlier into preagricultural times. Unlike agriculture, it doesn't even rank as a mixed blessing but as a pure evil threatening the survival of individuals, though not of our species. Like art, drug abuse seems at first to lack animal precedents or biological functions. I'll argue, however, that it fits into a broad class of animal structures or behaviors that are dangerous to their owners or practitioners, and whose function depends paradoxically on that danger.

While animal precursors can be identified for all of our hallmarks, they still rank as human hallmarks because we're unique on Earth in the extreme degree to which we've developed them. How unique are we in the universe? Once conditions suitable for life exist on a planet, how likely are intelligent, technologically advanced life forms to evolve? Was their emergence on Earth practically inevitable, and do they now exist on innumerable planets circling other stars?

There is no direct way to prove whether creatures capable of language, art, agriculture, or drug abuse exist elsewhere in the universe, because from Earth we can't detect the existence of those traits on planets of other stars. However, we might be able to detect high technology elsewhere in the universe if it included our own capacity to send out space probes and interstellar electromagnetic signals. I'll conclude this part by examining the ongoing search for extraterrestrial intelligent life. I'll argue that evidence from a quite different field—studies of woodpecker evolution on Earth—instructs us about the inevitability of evolving intelligent life, and therefore about our uniqueness, not only on Earth but also in the accessible universe.

CHAPTER 8

Bridges to
Human Language

HUMAN LANGUAGE ORIGINS CONSTITUTE THE MOST IMPORTANT MYStery in understanding how we became uniquely human. After all, language lets us communicate with each other far more precisely than can any animals. It lets us lay joint plans, teach one another, and learn from what others experienced elsewhere or in the past. With it, we can store precise representations of the world within our minds, and encode and process information far more efficiently than can any animals. Without language we could never have conceived and built Chartres Cathedral—or V-2 rockets. These are the reasons that I speculated that the Great Leap Forward (the stage in human history when innovation and art at last emerged) was made possible by the emergence of spoken language as we know it.

Between human language and the vocalizations of any animal lies a seemingly unbridgeable gulf. As has been clear since the time of Darwin, the mystery of human language origins is an *evolutionary* problem: how was this unbridgeable gulf nevertheless bridged? If we accept that we evolved from animals lacking human speech, then our language must have evolved and become perfected with time, along with the human pelvis, skull, tools, and art. There must once have been intermediate languagelike stages linking Shakespeare's sonnets to monkey's grunts. Darwin diligently kept notebooks on his children's linguistic development, and he reflected on the languages of "primitive" peoples, in the hope of solving this evolutionary mystery.

Unfortunately, the origins of language prove harder to trace than the origins of the human pelvis, skull, tools, and art. All those latter things may survive, and can be recovered and dated, but the spoken word vanishes in an instant. In frustration, I often dream of a time machine that would let me place tape recorders in ancient hominoid camps. Perhaps I'd discover that australopithecines uttered grunts little different from those of chimpanzees; that early *Homo erectus* used recognizable single words, progressing after a million years to two-word sentences; that *Homo sapiens* before the Great Leap Forward had gotten as far as longer strings of words, but still without much grammar; and that syntax and the full range of modern speech sounds arrived only with the Great Leap.

Alas, we have no such retrospective tape recorder, and no prospects for ever getting one. How can we hope to trace speech origins without such a magic time machine? Until recently, I would have said that it was hopeless to do more than speculate. In this chapter, however, I shall try to draw on two exploding bodies of knowledge that may let us start to build bridges across the seemingly unbridgeable gulf between animal and human sounds, starting from each of its opposite shores.

Sophisticated new studies of wild-animal vocalizations, especially those of our primate relatives, constitute the bridgehead on the animal shore of the gulf. It has always been obvious that animal sounds must have been ancestral to human speech, but only now are we beginning to sense how far animals have come toward inventing their own "languages." In contrast, it has been quite unclear where to locate the bridgehead on the human shore, since all existing human languages seem infinitely advanced over animal sounds. Recently, though, it has been argued that a numerous set of human languages neglected by most linguists really does exemplify two primitive stages on the human side of the causeway.

*   *   *

MANY WILD ANIMALS communicate with each other by sounds, of which bird songs and the barking of dogs are especially familiar to us. Most of us are within earshot of some calling animal most days of our lives. Scientists have been studying animal sounds for centuries. Despite this long history of intimate association, our understanding of these ubiquitous familiar sounds has suddenly exploded because of the application of new techniques: use of modern tape recorders to record animal calls, electronic analysis of the calls to detect subtle variations imperceptible to the unaided human ear, broadcasting recorded calls back to animals to observe how they react, and observing their reactions to electronically reshuffled calls. These methods are revealing animal vocal communication to be much more language-like than anyone would have guessed thirty years ago.

The most sophisticated "animal language" studied to date is that of a common cat-sized African monkey known as the vervet. Equally at home in trees and on the ground of savanna and rain forest, vervets are among the monkey species that visitors to East African game parks are most likely to see. They must have been familiar to Africans for the hundreds of thousands of years that we have existed as the species *Homo sapiens.* They may have reached Europe as pets over three thousand years ago, and they certainly have been familiar to European biologists exploring Africa since the nineteenth century. Many lay people who have never visited Africa still know vervets from zoo captives.

Like other animals, wild vervets regularly face situations in which efficient communication and representation would help them to survive. About three-quarters of wild vervet deaths are caused by predators. If you're a vervet, it's essential to know the differences between a martial eagle, one of the leading killers of vervets, and a white-backed vulture, an equally large soaring bird that eats carrion and is no danger to live monkeys. It's essential to act appropriately when the eagle appears, and to tell your relatives. If you fail to recognize the eagle, you die; if you fail to tell your relatives, they die, carrying your genes with them; and if you think it's an eagle when it's really just a vulture, you're wasting time on defensive measures while other monkeys are safely out there gathering food.

Besides these problems posed by predators, vervets have complex social relationships with each other. They live in groups and compete for territory with other groups. Hence it's also essential to know the difference between a monkey intruding from another group, an unrelated member of your own group likely to steal food from you, and a close relative in your own group on whose support you can count. Vervets that get into trouble need ways of telling their relatives that they, and not some other monkey, are in trouble. It's also essential to know and communicate about sources of food: for instance, which of the thousand plant and animal species in the environment are good to eat, which are poisonous, and where and when the edible ones are likely to be found. For all these reasons, vervets would profit from efficient ways of communicating about and representing their world.

Despite these reasons, and despite our long and close association with vervets, we had no appreciation of their complex world knowledge and vocalizations until the mid-1960s. Since then, observations of vervet behavior have revealed that they make finely graded discriminations among types of predators, and among each other. They adopt quite different defensive measures when threatened by leopards, eagles, and snakes. They respond differently to dominant and subordinate members of their own troop, differently again to dominant and subordinate members of rival troops, differently to members of different rival troops, and differently to their mothers, maternal grandmothers, siblings, and unrelated members of their own troop. They know who is related to whom: if an infant monkey calls, its mother turns toward it, but other vervet mothers turn instead toward that infant's mother to see what she will do. It's as if vervets had names for several predator species and several dozen individual monkeys.

The first clue to how vervets communicate this information came from observations that the biologist Thomas Struhsaker made on vervets in Kenya's Amboseli National Park. He noted that three types of predators triggered different defensive measures by vervets, and also triggered alarm calls sufficiently distinct for Struhsaker to hear the differences even without making any sophisticated electronic analysis. When vervets encounter a leopard or other species of large wild cat, male monkeys give a loud series of barks, females give a high-pitched chirp, and all monkeys within earshot may run up a tree. The sight of a martial or crowned eagle soaring overhead causes vervets to give a short cough of two syllables, whereupon listening monkeys look up into the air or run into a bush. A monkey who spots a python or other dangerous snake gives a "chuttering" call, and that stimulates other vervets in the vicinity to stand erect on their hind legs and look down (to see where the snake is).

Beginning in 1977, a husband-and-wife team named Robert Seyfarth and Dorothy Cheney proved by experiments that these calls really had the different functions suggested by Struhsaker's observations. Their procedure was as follows. First, they made a tape recording of a monkey giving a call whose apparent function Struhsaker had observed (say, the "leopard call"). Then, on a later day, after locating the same troop of monkeys, Cheney or Seyfarth hid the tape and loudspeaker equipment nearby in a bush, while the other investigator (Seyfarth or Cheney) started filming the monkeys with a movie or video camera. After fifteen seconds, Scientist Number 1 broadcast the tape, and Scientist Number 2 kept filming the monkeys for one minute to see whether the monkeys behaved appropriately for the call's suspected function (e.g., whether the monkeys ran up a tree on hearing a broadcast of the supposed leopard call). It turned out that playback of the "leopard call" really did stimulate the monkeys to run up a tree, while the "eagle call" and "snake call" similarly stimulated monkeys to the behaviors that seemed to be associated with these calls under natural conditions. Thus, the apparent association between the observed behaviors and the calls had not resulted from some coincidence, and the calls did have the functions suggested by observation.

The three calls that I've mentioned by no means exhaust a vervet's vocabulary. Besides those loud and frequently given alarm calls, there appear to be at least three fainter alarms that are given less frequently. One, triggered by baboons, causes listening vervets to become more alert. A second, given in response to mammals like jackals and hyenas that prey on vervets only infrequently, makes the monkeys watch the animal and perhaps move slowly toward a tree. The remaining faint alarm call responds to unfamiliar humans and results in the vervets' quietly moving toward a bush or the top of a tree. However, the postulated functions of these three fainter alarm calls remain unproved because they have not yet been tested by playback experiments.

Vervets also utter gruntlike calls when interacting with each other. Even to scientists who have spent years listening to vervets, all these social grunts sound the same. When the grunts are recorded and displayed as a frequency spectrum on the screen of a sound-analyzing

instrument, they look the same. Only when the spectra were measured in elaborate detail could Cheney and Seyfarth detect (sometimes but not always!) average differences between the grunts given
in four social contexts: when a monkey approaches a dominant monkey, when it approaches a subordinate monkey, when it watches
another monkey, or when it sees a rival troop.

Broadcasts of grunts recorded in these four different contexts
caused monkeys to behave in subtly different ways. For example, they
looked toward the loudspeaker if the grunt had originally been recorded in the "approach dominant monkey" context, while they
looked off in the direction toward which the call was being broadcast
if it had originally been recorded in the "see rival troop" context.
Further observations of the monkeys under natural conditions
showed that the natural calls themselves had been eliciting these
subtly different behaviors.

Evidently, vervets are much more finely attuned than we are to
their calls. Merely listening to and watching vervets, without recording and playing back their calls, gave no hint that they had at least
four distinct grunts—and possibly many more. As Seyfarth writes,
"Watching vervets grunt to each other is really very much like watching humans engaged in conversation without being able to hear what
they're saying. There aren't any obvious reactions or replies to grunts,
so the whole system seems very mysterious—mysterious, that is, until
you start doing playbacks." These discoveries illustrate how easy it is
to underestimate the size of an animal's vocal repertoire.

THE VERVETS OF AMBOSELI thus have *at least* ten putative "words":
their words for "leopard," "eagle," "snake," "baboon," "other predatory mammal," "unfamiliar human," "dominant monkey," "subordinate monkey," "watch other monkey," and "see rival troop."
However, virtually every claim of any animal behavior suggestive of
elements of human language is greeted with skepticism by many
scientists, convinced of the linguistic gulf separating us from animals.
Such skeptics consider it simpler to assume that humans are unique,
and that the burden of proof should be borne by anyone who thinks
otherwise. Any claim of languagelike elements for animals is considered a more complicated hypothesis, to be dismissed as unnecessary in the absence of positive proof. Yet the alternative hypotheses by

which the skeptics instead attempt to explain animal behaviors sometimes strike me as more complicated than the simple and often plausible explanation that humans are not unique.

It seems a modest claim to propose that the different calls that vervets give in response to leopards, eagles, and snakes actually refer to these animals or are intended as communications to other monkeys. However, skeptics were disposed to believe that only humans could emit voluntary signals referring to external objects or events. The skeptics suggested that the vervet alarm calls were just involuntary expressions of the monkey's emotional state ("I'm scared out of my wits!") or of its intent ("I'm going to run up a tree"). After all, those explanations apply to some of our own "calls." If I saw a leopard coming at me, I too might scream even though there wasn't anyone around to whom to communicate. We grunt as we throw ourselves into some physical activities, like lifting a heavy object.

Suppose that zoologists from an advanced civilization in Outer Space observed me to give a trisyllabic scream "argh, leopard" and to climb a tree when I saw a leopard. The zoologists might well doubt that my lowly species could express anything beyond grunts of emotion or intent—certainly not symbolic communications. To test their hypothesis, the zoologists would resort to experiments and detailed observations. If I gave the scream regardless of whether any other human was in earshot, that would support the theory of a mere expression of emotion or intent. If I gave the scream only in the presence of another person, and only when approached by a leopard but not by a lion, that would suggest a communication with a specific external referent. And if I gave the scream to my son but remained silent when I saw the leopard stalk a man with whom I had frequently been seen to fight, the visiting zoologist would feel certain that a purposeful communication was involved.

Similar observations convinced earthling zoologists of the communicative role of vervet alarm calls. A solitary vervet chased by a leopard for nearly an hour remained silent throughout the whole ordeal. Mother vervets give more alarm calls when accompanied by their own offspring than by unrelated monkeys. Vervets occasionally give the "leopard call" when no leopard is present but when their troop is fighting with another troop and losing the fight. The fake alarm sends all combatants scrambling for the nearest tree and thereby serves as a deceptive "time-out." Hence the call is clearly a voluntary communication, not an automatic expression of fear at the sight of a leopard. Nor is the call a mere reflex grunt given in the act of climbing a tree, since a calling monkey may either climb a tree, jump out of a tree, or do nothing, depending on the circumstances.

As for the call's having a well-defined external referent, that point is especially well illustrated by the "eagle call." When they see a large, broad-winged soaring hawk, vervets usually respond with the eagle call if the hawk is a martial eagle or crowned eagle, their two most dangerous avian predators. They usually do not respond if the hawk is a tawny eagle, and almost never if it's a black-chested snake eagle or white-backed vulture, which do not prey on vervets. Seen from below, black-chested snake eagles look rather similar to martial eagles in their shared pale underparts, banded tail, and black head and throat. Vervets rate as good bird-watchers, because their lives depend on it!

These examples demonstrate that vervet alarm calls are not involuntary expressions of either fear or intent. They have an external referent that may be quite exact. They are finely targeted communications that are more likely to be given honestly if the caller cares about the listener, and that may also be given dishonestly to enemies.

Skeptics go on to dispute proposed analogies between animal sounds and human speech on the further grounds that human speech is learned, but that many animals are born with the instinctive ability to utter the sounds characteristic of their species. However, young vervets appear to learn how to utter and respond to sounds appropriately, just as do human infants. The grunts of an infant vervet sound different from those of an adult. "Pronunciation" gradually improves with age until it becomes virtually adultlike around the age of two years, somewhat less than half the age for vervet puberty. That's like human children attaining adultlike pronunciation around age five; my four-year-old sons are still sometimes hard to understand. Infant vervets don't learn reliably to give the correct response to an adult's call until the age of six or seven months. Until then, an adult's snake alarm call may send the infant jumping into a bush, the correct response to an eagle but a suicidal response to a snake. Not until the age of two years does the infant consistently emit each alarm call in the correct context. Before that age, the young vervet may call "Eagle!" not only when a martial or crowned eagle goes overhead, but also when any other bird flies over, and even when a leaf flutters down from a tree. Child psychologists refer to such behavior in our own children as "overgeneralizing"—as when a child greets not just dogs but also cats and pigeons with "bow-wow."

So FAR, I've loosely applied human concepts such as "word" and "language" to vervet vocalization. Let's now compare human vocalizations and those of subhuman primates more closely. In particular, let's ask ourselves three questions. Do vervet sounds really constitute "words"? How large are animals' "vocabularies"? Do any animal vocalizations involve "grammar" and merit the term "language"?

First, as for the question of words, it's clear at least that each vervet alarm call refers to a well-defined class of external dangers. That doesn't imply, of course, that a vervet's "leopard call" designates the same animals to a vervet as the word "leopard" does to a professional zoologist—namely, members of a single animal species, defined as a collection of potentially interbreeding individuals. Scientists already know that vervets give their leopard alarm in response not just to leopards but also to two other medium-sized cat species (caracals and servals). Hence if the "leopard call" is a word at all, it wouldn't mean "leopard" but instead "medium-sized cats that are likely to attack us, hunt in a similar way, and are best avoided by running up a tree." However, many human words are used in a similar generic sense. For example, most of us other than ichthyologists and ardent fishermen apply the generic word "fish" to any cold-blooded animal with fins and a backbone that swims in the water and might be worth eating.

Instead, the real question is whether the leopard call constitutes a word ("medium-sized cat that et cetera"), a statement ("there goes a medium-sized cat"), an exclamation ("Watch out for that medium-sized cat!!"), or a proposition ("Let's run up a tree or take other appropriate action to avoid that medium-sized cat"). At present it's not clear which of those functions the leopard call fills, or whether it fills a combination of them. Similarly, I was excited when my one-year-old son Max said "Juice," which I proudly took to be one of his first words. To Max, though, the syllable "juice" was not just his academically correct identification of an external referent with certain properties, but it also served as a proposition: "Give me some juice!" Only at a later age did Max add more syllables, like "gimme juice," to distinguish propositions from pure words. Vervets show no evidence of having reached that stage.

On the second question of size of "vocabulary," even the most advanced animals seem on the basis of present knowledge to be far behind us. The average human has a daily working vocabulary of around a thousand words; my compact desk dictionary claims to contain 142,000 words; but only ten calls have been distinguished even for vervets, the most intensively studied mammal. Animals and humans surely do indeed differ in vocabulary size, yet the difference may not be as great as these numbers suggest. Remember how slow our progress has been in distinguishing vervet calls. Not until 1967 did anyone realize that these common animals had *any* calls with distinct meanings. The most experienced observers of vervets still can't separate some of their calls without machine analysis, and even with machine analysis the distinctness of some of the suspected ten calls remains unproven. Obviously, vervets (and other animals) could have many other calls whose distinctness we haven't yet recognized.

There's nothing surprising about our difficulties in distinguishing animal sounds, when one considers our difficulties in distinguishing human sounds. Children devote much of their time for the first several years of their lives to learning how to recognize and repro- duce the distinctions in the utterances of adults around them. As adults, we continue to have difficulty distinguishing sounds in unfa- miliar human languages. After four years of high school French between ages twelve and sixteen, my problems with understanding spoken French are embarrassing compared to the abilities of any four-year-old French child. But French is easy compared to the Iyau language of New Guinea's Lakes Plains, in which a single vowel may have eight different meanings depending on its pitch. A slight change in pitch converts the meaning of the Iyau word meaning "mother- in-law" into "snake." Naturally, it would be suicidal for an Iyau man to address his mother-in-law as "beloved snake," and Iyau children learn infallibly to hear and reproduce pitch distinctions that for years confounded even a professional linguist devoting full time to the Iyau language. Given these problems of our own with unfamiliar human languages, of course we must still be overlooking distinctions within the vervet vocabulary.

However, it's unlikely that any studies on vervets will reveal to us the limits attained by animal vocal communication, because those limits are probably reached by apes rather than by monkeys. While the sounds made by chimps and gorillas seem to our ears to be unsophisticated grunts and shrieks, so did the sounds made by vervet monkeys until they were studied carefully. Even unfamiliar human languages can sound like undifferentiated gibberish to us.

Unfortunately, vocal communication by wild chimps and other apes has never been studied by the methods applied to vervets, because of logistical problems. The width of a troop's territory is typically less than two thousand feet for vervets but several miles for chimps, making it far harder to carry out playback experiments with video cameras and hidden loudspeakers. These logistical problems can't be overcome by studying groups of wild-caught captive apes in convenient-sized zoo cages, because the captives generally constitute an artificial community of individuals caught at different African locations and thrown together in a cage. As I'll discuss later in this chapter, humans caught at different African locations, originally speaking different languages, and thrown together as slaves converse in only the crudest shadow of human language, virtually without any grammar. Similarly, wild-caught captive apes must be nearly useless for studying how sophisticated the vocal communications of wild apes are. The answer will remain unknown until someone figures out how to do for wild chimps what Cheney and Seyfarth have done for wild vervets.

Several groups of scientists have nevertheless spent years training captive gorillas, common chimps, and pygmy chimps to understand and use artificial languages based on plastic chips of different sizes and colors, or on hand signs similar to those used by deaf people, or on consoles like typewriters with each key bearing a different symbol. The animals have thereby learned the meanings of up to several hundred symbols, and a pygmy chimp has recently been observed to understand (but not to utter) a good deal of spoken English. At minimum, these studies of trained apes reveal that they possess the intellectual capabilities for mastering large vocabularies, begging the obvious question whether they have evolved such vocabularies in the wild.

It's suggestive that wild gorilla troops may be seen sitting together for a long time, grunting back and forth in seemingly undifferentiated gibberish, until suddenly all the gorillas get up at the same time and head off in the same direction. One wonders whether there really was a transaction concealed within that gibberish. Because the anatomy of apes' vocal tracts restricts their ability to produce the variety of vowels and consonants that we can, the vocabulary of wild apes is unlikely to be anywhere near as large as our own. Nevertheless, I would be surprised if wild chimp and gorilla vocabularies did *not* eclipse those reported for vervets and comprise dozens of "words," possibly including names for individual animals. In this exciting field in which new knowledge is being added rapidly, we should keep an open mind on how large the vocabulary gap is between apes and humans.

The remaining unanswered question concerns whether animal vocal communication involves anything that could be considered grammar or syntax. Humans don't just have vocabularies of thousands of words with different meanings. We also combine those words and vary their forms in ways prescribed by grammatical rules (such as rules of word order) that determine the meaning of the word combinations. Grammar thereby lets us construct a potentially infinite number of sentences from a finite number of words. To appreciate this point, consider the different meaning of the following two sentences composed of the same words and endings but with different word order:

"Your hungry dog bit my old mother's leg."
or
"My hungry mother bit your old dog's leg."

If human language did not involve grammatical rules, those two sentences would have exactly the same meaning. Most linguists would not dignify an animal's system of vocal communication with the name of language, no matter how large its vocabulary, unless it also involved grammatical rules.

No hint of syntax has been discovered in the studies of vervets to date. Most of their grunts and alarm calls are single utterances. When a vervet gives a sequence of two or more utterances, all analyzed cases have proved to consist of the same utterance repeated, as has also been the case when one vervet has been recorded responding to another vervet's call. Capuchin monkeys and gibbons do have calls of several elements used only in certain combinations or sequences, but the meanings of these combinations remain to be deciphered (by us humans, that is).

I doubt that any student of primate vocalizations expects even wild chimps to have evolved a grammar remotely approaching the complexity of human grammar, complete with prepositions, verb tenses, and interrogative particles. However, it remains for the present an open guess whether any animal has evolved syntax. The necessary studies on the wild animals most likely to use grammar—pygmy or common chimps—simply have not yet been attempted.

In short, while the gulf between animal and human vocal communication is surely large, scientists are rapidly gaining understanding of how that gulf has been partly bridged from the animal side. Now let's trace the bridge from the human side. We have already discovered complex animal "languages"; do any truly primitive human languages still exist?

To HELP US RECOGNIZE what a primitive human language might sound like if there were any, let's remind ourselves of the ways in which normal human language differs from vervet vocalizations. One difference is the one of grammar that I just mentioned. Humans, but not vervets, possess grammar, meaning the variations in word order, prefixes, suffixes, and changes in word roots (like *they/them/ their*) that modulate the sense of the roots. A second difference is that vervet vocalizations, if they constitute words at all, stand only for things that one can point to or act out. One could try to argue that vervet calls do include the equivalents of nouns ("eagle") and verbs or verb phrases ("watch out for the eagle"). Our words clearly include both nouns and verbs as distinct from each other, plus adjectives. Those three parts of speech referring to specific objects, acts, or qualities are termed "lexical items." But up to half of the words in typical human speech are purely grammatical items, with no referent that one can point to.

These grammatical words include prepositions, conjunctions, articles, and auxiliary verbs (words like "can," "may," "do," and "should"). It's much harder to understand how grammatical items could evolve than it is for lexical items. Given someone who understands no English, you can point to your nose to explain what that noun means. Apes might similarly come to agree on the meanings of grunts functioning as nouns, verbs, or adjectives. How, though, do you explain the meaning of "by," "because," "the," and "did" to someone who understands no English? How could our ancestors have stumbled on such grammatical terms?

Still another difference between human and vervet vocalizations is that ours possess a hierarchical structure, such that a modest number of items at each level creates a larger number of items at the next higher level. Our language uses many different syllables, all based on the same set of only a few dozen sounds. We assemble those syllables into thousands of words. Those words aren't merely strung haphazardly together but are organized into phrases, such as prepositional phrases. Those phrases in turn interlock to form a potentially infinite number of sentences. In contrast, vervet calls cannot be resolved into modular elements and lack even a single stage of hierarchical organization.

As children, we master all this complex structure of human language without ever learning the explicit rules producing it. Not unless we study our own language in school or learn a foreign language from books are we forced to formulate the rules. So complex is human language's structure that many of the underlying rules currently postulated by professional linguists have been proposed only in recent decades. This gulf between human language and animal vocalizations explains why most linguists never discuss how human language might have evolved from animal precursors. They instead regard that question as unanswerable and unworthy even of speculation.

BECAUSE THE EARLIEST WRITTEN LANGUAGES of five thousand years ago were as complex as those of today, human language must have achieved its modern complexity long before that. Can we at least recognize linguistic missing links by searching for primitive peoples with simple languages that might represent early stages of language evolution? After all, some tribes of hunter-gatherers retain stone tools as simple as those that characterized the whole world tens of thousands of years ago. Nineteenth-century travel books abound with tales of backward tribes who supposedly used only a few hundred words or who lacked articulated sounds, were reduced to saying "ugh," and depended on gestures for their communications. That was Darwin's first impression of the speech of Tierra del Fuego Indians. But all such tales proved to be pure myth. Darwin and other western travelers merely found it as hard to distinguish the unfamiliar sounds of non-western languages as non-westerners found English sounds, or as zoologists find the sounds of vervet monkeys.

Actually, it turns out that there is no correlation between linguistic and social complexity. Technologically primitive people don't speak primitive languages, as I discovered on my first day in the New Guinea highlands among the Foré people. Foré grammar proved deliciously complex, with postpositions like those of the Finnish language, dual as well as singular and plural forms like those of Slovenian, and verb tenses and phrase construction like no language that I had encountered previously. I already mentioned the eight vowel tones of New Guinea's Iyau people, whose sound distinctions proved imperceptibly subtle to professional linguists for years.

Thus, while some peoples in the modern world retained primitive tools, none retained primitive languages. Furthermore, Cro-Magnon archaeological sites contain lots of preserved tools but no preserved words. The absence of such linguistic missing links deprives us of what might have been our best evidence about human language origins. We are forced to try more indirect approaches.

ONE SUCH APPROACH is to ask whether some people, deprived of the opportunity to hear any of our fully evolved modern languages, ever spontaneously invented a primitive language. According to the Greek historian Herodotus, the Egyptian king Psammeticus intentionally carried out such an experiment in the hope of identifying the world's oldest language. The king assigned two newborn infants to a solitary shepherd to rear in strict silence, with instructions to listen for their first words. The shepherd duly reported that both children, after mouthing nothing but meaningless babble until the age of two, ran up to him and began constantly repeating the word "becos." Since that word meant "bread" in the Phrygian language then spoken in central Turkey, Psammeticus supposedly conceded that the Phrygians were the most ancient people.

Unfortunately, Herodotus's brief account of Psammeticus's experiment fails to convince skeptics that it was carried out rigorously as described. It illustrates why some scholars prefer to honor Herodotus as the Father of Lies, rather than as the Father of History. Certainly, solitary infants reared in social isolation, like the famous wolf boy of

Aveyron, remain virtually speechless and don't invent or discover a language. However, a variant of the Psammeticus experiment has occurred dozens of times in the modern world. In this variant, whole populations of children heard adults around them speaking a grossly simplified and variable form of language, somewhat similar to what normal children themselves speak around the age of two. The children proceeded unconsciously to evolve their own language, far advanced over vervet communication but simpler than normal human languages. The results were the new languages known as creoles. Along with their precursors, which are known as pidgins, creoles may provide us with models of missing links in the evolution of normal human language.

My first experience of a creole was with the New Guinea *lingua franca* known as either Neo-Melanesian or pidgin English. (The latter name is a confusing misnomer, since Neo-Melanesian is not a pidgin but rather a creole derived from an advanced pidgin—I'll explain the difference later—and it's only one of many independently evolved languages equally misnamed as pidgin English.) Papua New Guinea boasts about seven hundred native languages within an area similar to Sweden's, but no single one of those languages is spoken by more than 3 percent of the population. Not surprisingly, a *lingua franca* was needed and arose after the arrival of English-speaking traders and sailors in the early 1800s. Today, Neo-Melanesian serves in Papua New Guinea as the language not only of much conversation, but also of many schools, newspapers, radios, and parliamentary discussions. The advertisement on page 166 will give a sense of this newly evolved language.

When I arrived in Papua New Guinea and first heard Neo-Melanesian, I was scornful of it. It sounded like long-winded, grammarless baby talk. On speaking English according to my own notion of baby talk, I was jolted to discover that New Guineans weren't understanding me. My assumption that Neo-Melanesian words meant the same as their English cognates led to spectacular disasters, notably when I tried to apologize to a woman in her husband's presence for accidentally jostling her, only to find that Neo-Melanesian "pushim" doesn't mean "push" but instead means "have sexual intercourse with."

Neo-Melanesian proved to be as strict as English in its grammatical rules. It is a supple language that lets one express anything sayable in English. It even lets one make some distinctions that cannot be expressed in English except by means of clumsy circumlocutions. For example, the English pronoun "we" actually lumps two quite different concepts: "I plus you to whom I am speaking," and "I plus one or more other people, but not including you to whom I am speaking." In Neo-Melanesian these two separate meanings are expressed by the words "yumi" and "mipela," respectively. After I have been using Neo-Melanesian for months and then meet an English speaker who starts talking about "we," I often find myself wondering, "Am I included or not in your 'we'?"

Neo-Melanesian's deceptive simplicity and actual suppleness stem partly from its vocabulary, partly from its grammar. Its vocabulary is based on a modest number of core words whose meaning varies with context and becomes extended metaphorically. For instance, while Neo-Melanesian "gras" can mean English "grass" (whence "gras bilong solwara [salt water]" means "seaweed"), it also can mean "hair," whence "man i no gat gras long head bilong em" becomes "bald man."

The derivation of Neo-Melanesian "banis bilong susu" as the word for "bra" further illustrates how supple is the core vocabulary. "Banis," meaning "fence," comes from that English word as spoken by New Guineans who have difficulty pronouncing our consonant *f* and our double consonants like *nc*. "Susu," taken over from Malay as the word for "milk," is extended to mean "breast" as well. That sense in turn provides the expressions for "nipple" ("ai [eye] bilong susu"), "prepubertal girl" ("i no gat susu bilong em"), "adolescent girl" ("susu i sanap [stand up]"), and "aging woman" ("susu i pundaun pinis [fall down finish]"). Combining these two roots, "banis bilong susu" denotes a bra as the fence to keep the breasts in, just as "banis pik" denotes pigpen as the fence to keep pigs in.

Neo-Melanesian grammar appears deceptively simple because of what it lacks or else expresses by circumlocutions. These lacks include such seemingly standard grammatical items as plural and case forms of nouns, inflectional endings of verbs, the passive voice of verbs, and most prepositions and verb tenses. Yet Neo-Melanesian has passed far beyond baby talk and vervet sounds in many other respects, including its conjunctions and auxiliary verbs and pronouns, and its ways of expressing verb moods and aspects. It is a normal complex language in its hierarchical organization of phonemes, syllables, and words. It lends itself so well to hierarchical organization of phrases and sentences that election speeches by New Guinea politicians rival the German prose of Thomas Mann in their convoluted structure.

AT FIRST, I ignorantly assumed that Neo-Melanesian was a delightful aberration among the world's languages. It had obviously arisen just in the two centuries since English ships started visiting New Guinea, but I supposed that it had somehow developed from baby talk that colonists spoke to natives they believed incapable of learning English. As it turns out, though, dozens of other languages resemble Neo-Melanesian in structure. They have arisen independently around the globe, with vocabularies variously derived largely from English, French, Dutch, Spanish, Portuguese, Malay, or Arabic. They appeared especially in plantation, fort, and trading-post situations, where populations speaking different languages came into contact and needed to communicate, but where social circumstances impeded the usual solution of each group's learning the other's language. Many cases throughout the tropical Americas and Australia, and on tropical islands of the Caribbean, Pacific, and Indian Ocean, involved European colonists importing workers who came from afar and spoke many different tongues. Other European colonists set up forts or trading posts in already densely populated areas of China, Indonesia, or Africa.

Strong social barriers between the dominant colonists and the imported workers or local populations made the former unwilling, the latter unable, to learn the other's language. Usually the colonists scorned the local people, but in China the scorn was mutual: when English traders set up a post at Canton in 1664, the Chinese would no more abase themselves by learning the foreign devils' language or teaching them Chinese than would the English learn from or teach the heathen Chinese. Even if those social barriers had not existed, the workers would have had few opportunities to learn the colonists' tongue, because workers so greatly outnumbered colonists. Conversely, the colonists would also have found it difficult to learn "the" workers' tongue, because so many different languages were often represented among the workers.

Out of the temporary linguistic chaos that followed the plantations' or forts' founding, simplified but stabilized new languages emerged. Consider the evolution of Neo-Melanesian as an example. After English ships began to visit Melanesian islands just east of New Guinea around 1820, the English also took islanders to work on the sugar plantations of Queensland and Samoa, where workers of many language groups were thrown together. From this Babel sprang somehow the Neo-Melanesian language, whose vocabulary is 80 percent English, 15 percent Tolai (the Melanesian group that furnished many of the workers), and the rest Malay and other languages.

LINGUISTS DISTINGUISH two stages in the emergence of the new languages: initially, the crude languages termed pidgins, then later the more complex ones referred to as creoles. Pidgins arise as a second language for colonists and workers who speak differing native (first) languages and need to communicate with each other. Each group (colonists or workers) retains its native language for use within its own group; each group uses the pidgin to communicate with the other group, and in addition workers on a polyglot plantation may use pidgin to communicate with other groups of workers.

Compared to normal languages, pidgins are greatly impoverished in their sounds, vocabulary, and syntax. A pidgin's sounds are generally only those common to the two or more native languages thrown together. For example, many New Guineans find it hard to pronounce our consonants *f* and *v*, but I and other native English speakers find it hard to pronounce the vowel tones and nasalized sounds rampant in many New Guinea languages. Such sounds became largely excluded from New Guinea pidgins and then from the Neo-Melanesian creole that developed from them. Words of early-stage pidgins consist largely of nouns, verbs, and adjectives, with few or no articles, auxiliary verbs, conjunctions, or prepositions. As for grammar, early-stage pidgin discourse typically consists of short strings of words with little phrase construction, no regularity in word order, no subordinate clauses, and no inflectional endings on words. Along with that impoverishment, variability of speech within and between individuals is a hallmark of early-stage pidgins, which approximate an anarchic linguistic free-for-all.

Pidgins that are used only casually by adults who otherwise retain their own separate native languages persist at this rudimentary level.

For example, a pidgin known as Russonorsk grew up to facilitate barter between Russian and Norwegian fishermen who encountered each other in the Arctic. That *lingua franca* persisted throughout the nineteenth century but never developed further, as it was used only to transact simple business during brief visits. Both those groups of fishermen spent most of their time speaking Russian or Norwegian with their compatriots. In New Guinea, on the other hand, the pidgin gradually became more regular and complex over many generations because it was used intensively on a daily basis, but most children of New Guinea workers continued to learn their parents' native languages as their first languages until after World War II.

However, pidgins evolve rapidly into creoles whenever a generation of the groups contributing to a pidgin begins to adopt the pidgin itself as its native language. (I'll discuss later what particular members of the generation do the adopting, and why they do so.) That generation then finds itself using pidgin for all social purposes, not just for discussing plantation tasks or bartering. Compared to pidgins, creoles have a larger vocabulary, much more complex grammar, and consistency within and between individuals. Creoles can express virtually any thought expressible in a normal language, whereas trying to say anything even slightly complex is a desperate struggle in pidgin. Somehow, without any equivalent of the Académie Française to lay down explicit rules, a pidgin expands and stabilizes to become a uniform and fuller language.

This process of creolization is a natural experiment in language evolution that has unfolded independently dozens of times in the modern world. The sites for the experiment have ranged from mainland South America through Africa to Pacific islands; the laborers, from Africans through Portuguese and Chinese to New Guineans; the dominant colonists, from English to Spaniards to other Africans and Portuguese; and the century, from at least the seventeenth to the twentieth. What is striking is that the linguistic outcomes of all these independent natural experiments share so many similarities, both in what they lack and in what they possess. On the negative side, creoles are simpler than normal languages in mostly lacking conjugations of verbs for tense and person, declensions of nouns for case and number, most prepositions, and agreement of words for gender. On the positive side, creoles are advanced over pidgins in many respects: consistent word order; singular and plural pronouns for the first, second, and third persons; relative clauses; indications of the anterior tense (describing actions occurring before the time under discussion, whether or not that time is the present); and particles or auxiliary verbs preceding the main verb and indicating negation, anterior tense, conditional mood, and continuing as opposed to completed actions. Furthermore, most creoles agree in placing a sentence's subject, verb, and object in that particular order, and also agree in the order of particles or auxiliaries preceding the main verb.

The factors responsible for this remarkable convergence are still controversial among linguists. It's as if you drew a dozen cards fifty times from well-shuffled decks and almost always ended up with no hearts or diamonds, but with one queen, a jack, and two aces. The interpretation I find most convincing is that of linguist Derek Bickerton, who views many of the similarities among creoles as resulting from our possessing a genetic blueprint for language.

Bickerton derived his view from his studies of creolization in Hawaii, where sugar planters imported workers from China, the Philippines, Japan, Korea, Portugal, and Puerto Rico in the late nineteenth century. Out of that linguistic chaos, and following Hawaii's annexation by the United States in 1898, a pidgin based on English developed into a full-fledged creole. The immigrant workers themselves retained their original native languages. They also learned pidgin that they heard, but they did not improve on it, despite its gross deficiencies as a medium of communication. That, however, posed a big problem for the immigrants' Hawaii-born children. Even if the kids were lucky enough to hear a normal language at home because both mother and father were from the same ethnic group, that normal language was useless for communicating with kids and adults from other ethnic groups. Many children were less fortunate and heard nothing but pidgin even at home, when mother and father came from different ethnic groups. Nor did the children have adequate opportunities to learn English because of the social barriers isolating them and their worker parents from the English-speaking plantation owners. Presented with an inconsistent and impoverished model of human language in the form of pidgin, Hawaiian laborers' children spontaneously "expanded" pidgin into a consistent and complex creole within a generation.

In the mid-1970s Bickerton was still able to trace the history of this creolization by interviewing working-class people born in Hawaii between 1900 and 1920. Like all of us, those people had soaked up language skills in their early years but then became fixed in their ways, so that their speech in their old age continued to reflect the language spoken around them in their youth. (My children too will soon be wondering why their father persists in saying "icebox" rather than "refrigerator," decades after the iceboxes of my parents' own childhood disappeared.) The old adults of various ages whom Bickerton interviewed in the 1970s gave him virtually frozen snapshots of various stages in Hawaii's pidgin-to-creole transition, depending on the subjects' birth year. In that way, Bickerton was able to conclude that creolization had begun by 1900, was complete by 1920, and was accomplished by children in the process of their acquiring the ability to speak.

In effect, the Hawaiian children lived out a modified version of the Psammeticus experiment. Unlike the Psammeticus children, the Hawaiian children did hear adults speaking and were able to learn words. Unlike normal children, however, the Hawaiian children heard little grammar, and what they did hear was inconsistent and rudimentary. Instead, they created their own grammar. That they did indeed create it, rather than somehow borrowing grammar from the language of Chinese laborers or English plantation owners, is clear from the many features of Hawaiian creole that differ from English and from the workers' languages. The same is true for Neo-Melanesian: its vocabulary is largely English, but its grammar includes many features absent from English.

I DON'T WANT to exaggerate the grammatical similarities among creoles by implying that they're all essentially the same. Creoles do vary depending on the social history surrounding creolization—especially on the initial ratio between the numbers of plantation owners (or colonists) and workers, how quickly and to what extent that ratio changed, and for how many generations the early-stage pidgin could gradually borrow more complexity from existing languages. But many similarities remain, particularly among those creoles quickly arising from early-stage pidgins. How did each creole's children come so quickly to agree on a grammar, and why did the children of different creoles tend to reinvent the same grammatical features again and again?

It wasn't because they did it in the easiest or sole way possible to devise a language. For instance, creoles use prepositions (short words preceding nouns), as do English and some other languages, but there are other languages that dispense with prepositions in favor of post-positions following nouns, or else noun case endings. Again, creoles happen to resemble English in placing subject, verb, and object in that order, but borrowing from English can't be the explanation, because creoles derived from languages with a different word order still use the subject-verb-object order.

These similarities among creoles seem likely to stem from a genetic blueprint that the human brain possesses for learning language during childhood. Such a blueprint has been widely assumed ever since the linguist Noam Chomsky argued that the structure of human language is far too complex for a child to learn within just a few years, in the absence of any hard-wired instructions. For example, at age two my twin sons were just beginning to use single words. As I write this paragraph a bare twenty months later, still several months before their fourth birthday, they have already mastered most rules of basic English grammar that people who immigrate to English-speaking countries as adults often fail to master after decades. Even before the age of two, my children had learned to make sense of the initially incomprehensible babble of adult sound coming at them, to recognize groupings of syllables into words, and to realize which groupings constituted underlying words despite variations of pronunciation within and between adult speakers.

Such difficulties convinced Chomsky that children learning their first language would face an impossible task unless much of language's structure was already preprogrammed into them. Chomsky concluded that we are born with a "universal grammar" already wired into our brains to give us a spectrum of grammatical models encompassing the range of grammars in actual languages. This prewired universal grammar would be like a set of switches, each with various alternative positions. The switch positions would then become fixed to match the grammar of the local language that the growing child hears.

However, Bickerton goes further than Chomsky and concludes that we are preprogrammed not just to a universal grammar with adjustable switches, but to a particular set of switch settings: the settings that surface again and again in creole grammars. The preprogrammed settings can be overridden if they turn out to conflict with what a child hears in the local language around it. But if a child hears no local switch settings at all because it grows up amidst the structureless anarchy of a pidgin language, the creole settings can persist.

If Bickerton is correct that we really are preprogrammed at birth with creole settings that can be overridden by later experience, then one would expect children to learn creolelike features of their local languages earlier and more easily than features conflicting with creole grammar. This reasoning might explain the notorious difficulty of English-speaking children in learning how to express negatives: they insist on creolelike double negatives such as "Nobody don't have this." The same reasoning could explain the difficulties of English-speaking children with word order in questions.

To pursue the latter example, English happens to be among the languages that uses the creole word order of subject, verb, and object for statements: for instance, "I want juice." Many languages, including creoles, preserve this word order in questions, which are merely distinguished by an altered tone of voice ("You want juice?"). However, the English language does not treat questions in this way. Instead, our questions deviate from creole word order by inverting the subject and verb ("Where are you?," not "Where you are?"), or by placing the subject between an auxiliary verb (such as "do") and the main verb ("Do you want juice?"). My wife and I have been barraging our sons from early infancy onward with grammatically correct English questions as well as statements. My sons quickly picked up the correct order for statements, but both of them are still persisting in the incorrect creolelike order for questions, despite the hundreds of correct counterexamples that my wife and I model for them every day. Today's samples from Max and Joshua include "Where it is?," "What that letter is?," "What the handle can do?," and "What you did with it?" It's as if they're not yet ready to accept the evidence of their ears, because they're still convinced that their preprogrammed creolelike rules are correct.

Now LET'S PULL TOGETHER all these animal and human studies to try to form a coherent picture of how our ancestors progressed from grunts to Shakespeare's sonnets. A well-studied early stage is represented by vervet monkeys, with at least ten different calls that are under voluntary control, are used for communication, and have external referents. The calls may function as words, explanations, propositions, or as all of those things simultaneously. Scientists' difficulties in identifying those ten calls have been such that surely more await identification, but we still don't know how large the vervet vocabulary really is. We also don't know how far other animals may have progressed beyond vervets, because the vocal communications of the species most likely to have eclipsed vervets, the common and pygmy chimp, have yet to be studied carefully in the wild. At least in the laboratory, chimps can master hundreds of symbols that we teach them, suggesting that they have the necessary intellectual equipment to master symbols of their own.

The single words of young toddlers, like "juice" as uttered by my son Max, constitute a next stage beyond animal grunts. Like vervet grunts, Max's "juice" may have functioned as some combination of a word, an explanation, and a proposition. But Max has made an enormous advance on vervets by assembling his "juice" word from the smaller units of vowels and consonants, thereby scaling the lowest level of modular linguistic organization. A few dozen such phonetic units can be reshuffled to produce a very large number of words, such as the 142,000 words in my English desk dictionary. That principle of modular organization lets us recognize far more distinctions than can vervets. For example, they name only six types of animals, whereas we name nearly two million.

A further step toward Shakespeare is exemplified by two-year-old children, who in all human societies proceed spontaneously from a one-word to a two-word stage and then to a multiword stage. But those multiword utterances are still mere word strings with little grammar, and their words are still nouns, verbs, and adjectives with concrete referents. As Bickerton points out, those word strings are rather like the pidgin languages that human adults spontaneously reinvent when necessary. They also resemble the strings of symbols produced by captive apes whom we have instructed in the use of those symbols.

From pidgins to creoles, or from the word strings of two-year-olds to the complete sentences of four-year-olds, is another giant step. In that step are added words lacking external referents and serving purely grammatical functions; elements of grammar such as word order, prefixes and suffixes, and word root variation; and more levels of hierarchical organization to produce phrases and sentences. Perhaps that step is what triggered the Great Leap Forward discussed earlier in this book. Nevertheless, creole languages reinvented in modern times still give us clues to how these advances arose, through the creoles' circumlocutions to express prepositions and other grammatical elements.

If you compare the Neo-Melanesian advertisement below with a Shakespeare sonnet, you might conclude that a huge gap still remains. In fact, I'd argue that, with an advertisement like "Kam insait long stua bilong mipela . . ." we have come 99.9 percent of the way from vervet calls to Shakespeare. Creoles already constitute expressive complex languages. For example, Indonesian, which arose as a creole to become the language of conversation and government for the world's fifth most populous country, is also a vehicle for serious literature.

Thus, animal communication and human language once seemed to be separated by an unbridgeable gulf. Now we have identified not only parts of bridges starting from both opposite shores, but also a series of islands and bridge segments spaced across the gulf. We are beginning to understand in broad outline how the most unique and important attribute that distinguishes us from animals arose from animal precursors.

NEO-MELANESIAN, IN ONE EASY LESSON

Try to understand this Neo-Melanesian advertisement for a department store:

> Kam insait long stua bilong mipela—stua bilong salim olgeta samting—mipela i-ken helpim yu long kisim wanem samting yu laikim bikpela na liklik long gutpela prais. I-gat gutpela kain kago long baiim na i-gat stap long helpim yu na lukautim yu long taim yu kam insait long dispela stua.

If some of the words look strangely familiar but don't quite make sense, read the ad aloud to yourself, concentrate on the sounds, and ignore the strange spelling. As the next step, here is the same ad rewritten with English spelling:

> Come inside long store belong me-fellow—store belong sellim altogether something—me-fellow can helpim you long catchim what-name something you likim, big-fellow na lik-lik, long good-fellow price. He-got good-fellow kind cargo long buyim, na he-got staff long helpem you na lookoutim you long time you come inside long this-fellow store.

A few explanations should help you make sense of the remaining strangenesses. Almost all the words in this sample of Neo-Melanesian are derived from English, except for the word "liklik" for "little," derived from a New Guinea language (Tolai). Neo-Melanesian has only two pure prepositions: "bilong," meaning "of" or "in order to," and "long," meaning almost any other English preposition. The English consonant *f* becomes *p* in Neo-Melanesian, as in "stap" for "staff," and "pela" for "fellow." The suffix "-pela" is added to monosyllabic adjectives (hence "gutpela" for "good," "bikpela" for "big"), and also makes the singular pronouns "me" and "you" into plural ones (for "we" and "you" plural). "Na" means "and." Hence the ad means:

> Come into our store—a store for selling everything—we can help you get whatever you want, big and small, at a good price. There are good types of goods for sale, and staff to help you and look after you when you visit the store.

CHAPTER 9

Animal Origins
of Art

Georgia O'Keeffe's drawings were slow to win recognition for her, but Siri's drawings brought her acclaim as soon as other knowledgeable artists saw them. "They had a kind of flair and decisiveness and originality"—that was the first reaction of the famous abstract expressionist painter Willem de Kooning. Jerome Witkin, an authority on abstract expressionism who teaches art at Syracuse University, was even more effusive: "These drawings are very lyrical, very, very beautiful. They are so positive and affirmative and tense, the energy is so compact and controlled, it's just incredible.... This drawing is so graceful, so delicate.... This drawing indicates a grasp of the essential mark that makes the emotion."

Witkin applauded Siri's balance of positive and negative space, and her placement and orientation of images. Having seen the drawings but knowing nothing about who made them, he guessed correctly that the artist was female and interested in Asian calligraphy. But Witkin didn't guess that Siri was eight feet tall and weighed four tons. She was an Asian elephant who drew by holding a pencil in her trunk.

De Kooning's response to being told Siri's identity was "That's a damned talented elephant." Actually, Siri was not extraordinary by elephant standards. Wild elephants often use their trunks to make drawing motions in the dust, while captive elephants often spontaneously scratch marks on the ground with a stick or stone. Hanging in many doctors' and lawyers' offices are paintings by an elephant named Carol, dozens of whose works were sold at prices of up to $500.

Supposedly, art is the noblest distinctively human attribute—one that sets us apart from animals at least as sharply as does spoken language, by differing in basic ways from anything that any animal does. Art ranks as even nobler than language, since language is really "just" a highly sophisticated advance on animal communication systems, serves an obvious biological function in helping us to survive, and obviously developed from the sounds made by other primates. In contrast, art serves no such transparent function, and its origins are considered a sublime mystery. But it's clear that elephant art could have implications for our own. At minimum, it's a similar physical activity resulting in products that even experts couldn't distinguish from human products accepted as constituting art. Of course, there are also huge differences between Siri's art and ours, not least of which is that Siri wasn't trying to communicate her message to other elephants. Nevertheless, we can't just dismiss her art as a quirk of one individual beast.

In this chapter I'll go beyond elephants to examine artlike activities of some other animals. I believe that the comparisons will help us understand the original functions of human art. Although we usually consider art to be the antithesis of science, there may really be a science of art.

To appreciate that our art must have some animal precursors, recall that it's only about seven million years since we branched off from our closest living relatives, the chimpanzees. Seven million years sounds like a lot on the scale of a human lifetime, but it is barely 1 percent of the history of complex life on Earth. We still share over 98 percent of our DNA with chimps. Hence art and those other features that we consider uniquely human must be due to just a tiny fraction of our genes. They must have arisen only a few moments ago on the evolutionary time clock.

Modern studies of animal behavior have been shrinking the list of features once considered uniquely human, such that most differences between us and so-called animals now appear to be only matters of degree. For example, I described in the preceding chapter how vervet monkeys have a rudimentary language. You may not have considered vampire bats allied with us in nobility, but they prove to practice reciprocal altruism regularly (toward other vampire bats, of course). Among our darker qualities, murder has now been documented in innumerable animal species, genocide in wolves and chimps, rape in ducks and orangutans, and organized warfare and slave raids in ants.

As absolute distinctions between us and animals, these discoveries leave us few characteristics besides art, which we managed to dispense with for the first 6,960,000 of the 7 million years since we diverged from chimps. Perhaps the earliest art forms were wood carving and body painting, but we wouldn't know it because they wouldn't have remained preserved. The first preserved hints of human art consist of some flower remains around Neanderthal skeletons, and some scratches on animal bones at Neanderthal campsites. However, the interpretation that they were arranged or scratched intentionally is in doubt. Not until the Cro-Magnons, beginning around forty thousand years ago, do we have our first unequivocal evidence for art, surviving in the form of the famous cave paintings at Lascaux, statues, necklaces, and flutes and other musical instruments.

If we're going to claim that true art is unique to humans, then in what ways do we claim that it differs from superficially similar productions of animals, like bird songs? Three supposed distinctions are often put forward: that human art is nonutilitarian, that it's just for aesthetic pleasure, and that it's transmitted by learning rather than through our genes. Let's scrutinize these claims more closely.

First, as Oscar Wilde said, "All art is quite useless." The implicit meaning a biologist sees behind this quip is that art is nonutilitarian in a narrow sense employed within the fields of animal behavior and evolutionary biology. That is, human art doesn't help us to survive or to pass on our genes, which are the readily discernible functions of most animal behaviors. Of course, most human art is utilitarian in the broader sense that the artist thereby communicates something to fellow humans, but transmitting one's thoughts to the next generation isn't the same thing as transmitting one's genes. In contrast, bird song serves the obvious functions of wooing a mate, defending a territory, and thereby transmitting genes.

Regarding the second claim, that human art is instead motivated by aesthetic pleasure, a dictionary defines art as "the making or doing of things that have form or beauty." While we can't ask mocking-birds and nightingales if they similarly enjoy the form or beauty of their songs, it's suspicious that they sing mainly during the breeding season. Hence they're probably not singing just for aesthetic pleasure.

As for human art's third claimed distinction, each human group has a distinctive art style, and the knowledge of how to make and enjoy that particular style is learned, not inherited. For example, it's easy to distinguish typical songs being sung today in Tokyo and in Paris. But those stylistic differences aren't hard-wired in our genes, as are the differences between Parisians and Japanese in their eyes. Parisians and Japanese can and often do visit each other's cities and learn each other's songs. In contrast, many species of birds (the so-called nonpasserine birds) inherit the knowledge of how to produce and respond to the particular song of their species. Each of those birds would produce the right song even if it had never heard it, and even if it had heard only the songs of other species. It's as if a French baby adopted by Japanese parents, flown in infancy to Tokyo and educated there, began spontaneously to sing the "Marseillaise."

At this point, we may seem to be light-years removed from ele-phant art. Elephants aren't even closely related to us evolutionarily. Much more relevant to us are the artworks that were produced by two captive chimpanzees named Congo and Betsy, a gorilla called Sophie, an orangutan named Alexander, and a monkey named Pablo. These primates variously mastered the media of brush or finger painting and pencil, chalk, or crayon drawing. Congo did up to thirty-three paintings in one day, apparently for his own satisfaction, as he didn't show his work to other chimps and threw a tantrum when his pencil was taken away. For human artists, the ultimate proof of success is a one-man show, but Congo and Betsy were honored by a two-chimp show of their paintings in 1957 at London's Institute of Contemporary Art. The following year, Congo had a one-chimp show at London's Royal Festival Hall. What's more, al-most all of the paintings on exhibit at those chimp shows sold (to human buyers); plenty of human artists can't make that boast. Still other ape paintings were surreptitiously entered into exhibits by human artists and were enthusiastically acclaimed by unsuspecting art critics for their dynamism, rhythm, and sense of balance.

Equally unsuspecting were child psychologists who were given paintings by chimps from the Baltimore Zoo and were asked to diagnose the painters' problems. The psychologists guessed that a painting by a three-year-old male chimp was instead by an aggressive seven- or eight-year-old boy with paranoid tendencies. Two paintings by the same one-year-old female chimp were attributed to different ten-year-old girls, one painting indicating a belligerent girl of the schizoid type, the other a paranoid girl with strong father identification. It's a tribute to the psychologists' insight that they intuited the artists' sex correctly in each case; they were only wrong about the artists' species.

These paintings by our closest relatives do start to blur the distinction between human art and animal activities. Like human paintings, the ape paintings served no narrow utilitarian function of transmitting genes, and were instead just produced for satisfaction. One could object that the ape artists, like the elephant Siri, made their pictures just for their own satisfaction, while most human artists aim to communicate to other humans. The apes didn't even keep their paintings to enjoy but just discarded them. But that objection doesn't strike me as compelling, since the simplest human art (doodling) is also regularly discarded, and since one of the best pieces of art I own is a wood statue carved by a New Guinea villager who discarded it under his house after carving it. Even some human art that later became famous was created by artists for their private satisfaction: the composer Charles Ives published little of his music, and Franz Kafka not only didn't publish his three great novels but even forbade his executor to do so. (Fortunately, the executor disobeyed, thereby forcing Kafka's novels to take on a communicative function posthumously.)

However, there's a more serious objection against claiming a parallel between ape art and human art. Ape painting is just an unnatural activity of captive animals. One might insist that, since it's not a natural behavior, it couldn't illuminate the animal origins of art. Hence let's turn now to an undeniably natural and illuminating behavior: bowerbirds' building of bowers, the most elaborate structures built and decorated by any animal species other than humans.

* * *

IF I HADN'T already heard of bowers, I'd have mistaken the first one I saw for something man-made, as did nineteenth-century explorers in New Guinea. I had set out that morning from a New Guinea village, with its circular huts, neat rows of flowers, people wearing decorative beads, and little bows and arrows carried by children in imitation of their fathers' larger ones. Suddenly, in the jungle, I came across a beautifully woven circular hut eight feet in diameter and four feet high, with a doorway large enough for a child to enter and sit inside. In front of the hut was a lawn of green moss, clean of debris except for hundreds of natural objects of various colors that had obviously been placed there intentionally as decorations. They mainly consisted of flowers and fruits and leaves, but also some butterfly wings and fungi. Objects of similar color were grouped together, such as red fruits next to a group of red leaves. The largest decorations were a tall pile of black fungi facing the door, with another pile of orange fungi a few yards further from the door. All blue objects were grouped inside the hut, red ones outside, and yellow, purple, black, and a few green ones in other locations.

That hut was not a child's playground. It had instead been built and decorated by an otherwise unimpressive jay-size bird called a bowerbird, a member of a family of eighteen species confined to New Guinea and Australia. Bowers are erected by males for the sole purpose of seducing females, who then bear the sole responsibility for building the nest and rearing the young. Males are polygamous, try to mate with as many females as possible, and provide the female with nothing except sperm. Females, often in groups, cruise around the bowers and inspect all those in the vicinity before selecting one at which to mate. Human equivalents of such scenes are played out every night on Sunset Strip, a few miles from my home in Los Angeles.

Female bowerbirds select their bedmate by the quality of his bower, its number of decorations, and its conformity to local rules, which vary among species and populations of bowerbirds. Some populations prefer blue decorations, others red or green or gray, while some replace the hut with one or two towers, or a two-walled avenue, or a four-walled box. There are populations that paint their bowers with crushed leaves or else with oils that they excrete. These local differences in rules appear not to be hard-wired into the birds' genes. Instead, they are learned through younger birds' observing older birds during the many years that it takes a bowerbird to reach adulthood. Males learn the locally correct way to decorate, while females learn those same rules for the purpose of choosing a male.

At first, this system strikes us as absurd. After all, what a female bowerbird is trying to do is to pick a good mate. The evolutionary winner in such a mate-selection contest is that female bowerbird who picks that male bowerbird who makes it possible for her to leave the largest number of surviving offspring. What good does it do her to pick the guy with the blue fruits?

All animals, including us, face similar problems of mate selection. Consider those species (such as most European and North American songbirds) whose males carve out mutually exclusive territories that each male will share with his mate. The territory contains the nest site and food resources for the female to use in rearing her young. Hence a part of the female's task is to assess the quality of each male's territory. Or suppose that the male himself will assist in feeding and protecting the young, and in hunting cooperatively with the female. Then the female and male must assess each other's parenting and hunting skills and the quality of their relationship. All these things are hard enough to assess, but it's even harder for the female to assess a male when he provides nothing but sperm and genes, as is the case with male bowerbirds. How on earth is an animal to assess a prospective mate's genes, and what have blue fruits to do with good genes?

Animals don't have the time to produce ten offspring with each of many prospective mates, and to compare the outcomes (the eventual number of surviving offspring). Instead, they have to resort to shortcuts by relying on mating signals such as songs or ritualized displays. It's now a hotly contested problem in animal behavior to understand why, or even whether, those mating signals serve as veiled indicators of good genes. We have only to reflect on our own difficulties in selecting mates and in assessing the true wealth, parenting skills, and genetic quality of our various prospective partners.

In this light, reflect what it means when a female bowerbird finds a male with a good bower. She knows at once that that male is strong, since the bower he assembled weighs hundreds of times his own weight, and since he had to drag some individual decorations half his weight from dozens of yards distant. She knows that the male has the mechanical dexterity needed to weave hundreds of sticks into a hut, tower, or walls. He must have a good brain, to carry out the complex design correctly. He must have good vision and memory to search out the required hundreds of decorations in the jungle. He must be good at coping with life, to have survived to the age of perfecting all those skills. And he must be dominant over other males: since males spend much of their leisure time trying to wreck and steal from each other's bowers, only the best males end up with intact bowers and many decorations.

Thus, bower building provides a comprehensive test of male genes. It's as if women put each of their suitors in sequence through a weight-lifting contest, sewing contest, chess tournament, eye test, and boxing tournament, and finally went to bed with the winner. By comparison with bowerbirds, our efforts to identify mates with good genes are pathetic. We grasp at external bagatelles like facial features and earlobe lengths, or sex appeal and Porsche ownership, which tell nothing about intrinsic genetic worth. Think of all the human suffering caused by the sad truth that beautiful, sexy women or handsome, Porsche-owning men often prove to have miserable genes for other traits. It's no wonder that so many marriages end in divorce, as we belatedly realize how badly we chose and how flimsy our criteria were.

How did bowerbirds evolve to use art so cleverly for such important purposes? Most male birds woo females by advertising their colorful bodies, songs, displays, or offerings of food as dim indicators of good genes. Males of two groups of birds of paradise in New Guinea go one step further by clearing areas on the jungle floor, as bowerbirds do, to enhance their displays and show off their fancy plumage. Males of one of those birds of paradise have gone still further by decorating their cleared areas with objects useful to a nesting female: pieces of snakeskin to line her nest, pieces of chalk or mammal feces to eat for their minerals, and fruits to eat for their calories. Finally, bowerbirds have learned that decorative objects useless in themselves may nevertheless be useful indicators of good genes, if the objects are ones that were difficult to acquire and keep.

We can easily relate to that concept. Just think of all those ads showing handsome men presenting diamond rings to seemingly fertile young women. You can't eat a diamond ring, but a woman knows that the gift of such a ring tells far more about the resources that her suitor commands (and might devote to her offspring and herself) than a gift of a box of chocolates would tell. Yes, chocolates provide a few useful calories, but they're quickly gone and any jerk can afford to buy them. In contrast, the man who can afford that inedible diamond ring has money to support the woman and her kids, and also has whatever genes (for intelligence, persistence, energy, etc.) that it took to acquire or hold on to the money.

Thus, in the course of bowerbird evolution the female's attention has been lured from ornaments that are permanent parts of the male's body to ornaments that the male gathers. Whereas sexual selection in most species has produced differences between males and females in their bodily ornaments, in bowerbirds it has shifted toward causing males to emphasize collected ornaments separate from their bodies. From this perspective, bowerbirds are rather human. We, too, rarely court (or at least rarely initiate courtship) by displaying the beauties of our unadorned naked bodies. Instead, we swathe ourselves in colored cloths, spray or daub ourselves with perfumes and paints and powders, and augment our beauty with decorations ranging from jewels to sports cars. The parallel between bowerbirds and humans may be even closer if, as friends of mine who are into sports cars assure me, duller young men tend to decorate themselves with fancier sports cars.

Now LET'S REEXAMINE, in the light of bowerbirds, those three criteria supposedly separating human art from any animal production. Both bower styles and our art styles are learned rather than inherited, so there's no difference by the third criterion. As for the second criterion (doing it for aesthetic pleasure), it's unanswerable. We can't ask bowerbirds whether they get pleasure out of their art, and I suspect that many humans who claim to do so are just putting on cultural affectations. That leaves only the first criterion: Oscar Wilde's assertion that art is useless, in a narrow biological sense. His statement is definitely untrue of bower art, which serves a sexual function. But it's absurd to pretend any longer that our own art lacks biological functions. Instead, there are several ways in which art helps us to survive and to pass on our genes.

First, art often brings direct sexual benefits to its owner. It's not just a joke that a man bent on seduction invites a woman to view his etchings. In real life, dance and music and poetry are common preludes to sex.

Second and much more important, art brings indirect benefits to its owner. Art is a quick indicator of status, which—in human as in animal societies—is a key to acquiring food, land, and sex partners. Yes, bowerbirds get the credit for discovering the principle that ornaments separate from one's body are more flexible status symbols than ornaments that one has to grow. But we still get credit for running away with that principle. Cro-Magnons decorated their bodies with bracelets, pendants, and ocher; New Guinea villagers today decorate theirs with shells, fur, and bird-of-paradise plumes. In addition to these art forms for bodily adornment, both Cro-Magnons and New Guinea villagers produced larger art (carvings and paintings) of world quality. We know that New Guinea art signals superiority and wealth, because birds of paradise are hard to hunt, beautiful statues take talent to make, and both are very expensive to buy. These badges of distinction are essential for marital sex in New Guinea: brides are bought, and part of the price consists of luxury art. Elsewhere as well, art is often viewed as a signal of talent, money, or both.

In a world where art is a coin of sex, it's only a small further step for some artists to be able to convert art into food. There are whole societies that support themselves by making art for trade to food-producing groups. For example, the Siassi islanders, who lived on tiny islets with little room for gardens, survived by carving beautiful bowls that other tribes coveted for bride payments and paid for in food.

The same principles hold even more strongly in the modern world. Where we once signaled our status with bird feathers on our bodies and giant clam shells in our huts, we now do it with diamonds on our bodies and Picassos on our walls. Where Siassi islanders sold a carved bowl for the equivalent of twenty dollars, Richard Strauss built himself a villa with the proceeds from his opera *Salome* and earned a fortune from *Der Rosenkavalier*. Nowadays we read increasingly often of art sold at auction for tens of millions of dollars, and of art theft. In short, precisely because it serves as a signal of good genes and ample resources, art can be cashed in for still more genes and resources.

So far, I've considered only the benefits that art brings to individuals. But art also helps define human groups. Humans have always formed competing groups whose survival is essential if the individuals in that group are to pass on their genes. Human history largely consists of the details of groups' killing, enslaving, or expelling other groups. The winner takes the loser's land, sometimes also the loser's women, and thus the loser's opportunity to perpetuate genes. But group cohesion depends on the group's distinctive culture—especially its language, religion, and art (including stories and dances). Hence art is a significant force behind group survival. Even if you have better genes than most of your fellow tribesmen, that will do you no good should your whole tribe (including you) get annihilated by some other tribe.

By now, you're probably protesting that I've gone completely overboard in ascribing utility to art. What about all of us who just enjoy art, without converting it to status or sex? What about all the artists who remain celibate? Aren't there easier ways to seduce a sex partner than to take piano lessons for ten years? Isn't private satisfaction a (the?) main reason for our art, just as for Siri and Congo?

Of course. Such expansion of behaviors far beyond their original role is typical of animal species whose foraging efficiency gives them much leisure time, and who have brought their survival problems under control. Bowerbirds and birds of paradise have much leisure time, because they're big and feed on wild fruit trees that they can kick smaller birds out of. We have much leisure time because we use tools to obtain food. Animals with leisure time can channel it into more lavish signals to outdo the next guy. Those behaviors may then come to serve other purposes, such as representing information (a suggested function of Cro-Magnon cave paintings of hunted animals), relieving boredom (a real problem for captive apes and elephants), channeling neurotic energy (a problem for us as well as for them), and just providing pleasure. To maintain that art is useful isn't to deny that art provides pleasure. Indeed, if we weren't programmed to enjoy art, it couldn't serve most of its useful functions for us.

Perhaps we can now answer the question why art as we know it characterizes us but no other animal. Since chimps paint in captivity, why don't they do so in the wild? As an answer, I suggest that wild chimps still have their day filled with problems of finding food, surviving, and fending off rival chimp groups. If wild chimps had more leisure time plus the means to manufacture paints, they would be painting. The proof of my theory is that it actually happened: we're still 98 percent chimps in our genes.

CHAPTER 10

Agriculture's
Mixed Blessings

T O SCIENCE WE OWE DRAMATIC CHANGES IN OUR SMUG SELF-IMAGE.
Astronomy taught us that our Earth is not the center of the universe but merely one of nine planets circling one of billions of stars.
From biology we learned that humans were not specially created by
God but evolved along with tens of millions of other species. Now
archaeology is demolishing another sacred belief: that human history over the last million years has been a long tale of progress.

In particular, recent discoveries suggest that the adoption of agriculture (plus animal husbandry), supposedly our most decisive step
toward a better life, was actually a milestone for the worse as well as
for the better. With agriculture came not only greatly increased food
production and food storage, but also the gross social and sexual
inequality, the disease and despotism, that curse modern human
existence. Thus, among the human cultural hallmarks being discussed in Part Three of this book, agriculture represents in its mixed
blessings a halfway station between our noble traits already discussed
(art and language) and our unmitigated vices still to be discussed
(drug abuse, genocide, and environmental destructiveness).

At first, the evidence for progress and against this revisionist interpretation will strike twentieth-century Americans and Europeans as irrefutable. We are better off in almost every respect than people of the Middle Ages, who in turn had it easier than Ice Age cavemen, who were still better off than apes. If you're inclined to be cynical, just count our advantages. We enjoy the most abundant and varied food, the best tools and material goods, the longest and healthiest lives in human history. Most of us are safe from starvation and predators. We obtain most of our energy from oil and machines, not just from our sweat. What neo-Luddite among us would really trade today's life for that of a medieval peasant, caveman, or ape?

For most of our history, all humans had to practice a primitive life-style termed "hunting and gathering": they hunted wild animals and gathered wild plant food. That hunter-gatherer life-style is often characterized by anthropologists as "nasty, brutish, and short." Since no food is grown and little is stored, there is (according to this view) no respite from the time-consuming struggle that starts anew each day to find wild foods and avoid starving. Our escape from this misery was launched only after the end of the last Ice Age, when people began independently in different parts of the world to domesticate plants and animals. The agricultural revolution gradually spread until today it is nearly universal and few tribes of hunter-gatherers survive.

From the progressivist perspective on which I was brought up, the question "Why did almost all our hunter-gatherer ancestors adopt agriculture?" is silly. Of course they adopted it because agriculture is an efficient way to get more food for less work. Our planted crops yield far more tons per acre than do wild roots and berries. Just imagine savage hunters, exhausted from searching for nuts and chasing wild animals, suddenly gazing for the first time at a fruit-laden orchard or a pasture full of sheep. How many milliseconds do you think it took those hunters to appreciate the advantages of agriculture?

The progressivist party line goes further and credits agriculture with giving rise to art, the noblest flowering of the human spirit. Since crops can be stored, and since it takes less time to grow food in gardens than to find it in the jungle, agriculture gave us free time that hunter-gatherers never had. But free time is essential for creating art and enjoying it. Thus ultimately it was agriculture that, as its greatest gift, enabled us to build the Parthenon and compose the *B Minor Mass*.

AMONG OUR MAJOR CULTURAL HALLMARKS, agriculture is especially recent, having begun to emerge only ten thousand years ago. None of our primate relatives practices anything remotely resembling agriculture. For the most similar animal precedents, we must turn to ants, which invented not only plant domestication but also animal domestication.

Plant domestication is practiced by a group of several dozen related species of New World ants. All those ants cultivate specialized species of yeasts or fungi in gardens within the ants' nest. Rather than relying on natural soil, each gardener-ant species gathers its own particular type of compost: some ants grow their crop on caterpillar feces, others on insect corpses or dead plant material, and still others (the so-called leaf-cutter ants) on fresh leaves, stems, and flowers. For example, leaf-cutter ants clip off leaves, slice them into pieces, scrape off foreign fungi and bacteria, and take the pieces into underground nests. There the leaf fragments are crushed into moist pellets of a pastelike consistency, manured with ant saliva and feces, and seeded with the ants' preferred species of fungus, which serves as the ants' main or sole food. In an operation the equivalent of weeding a garden, the ants continually remove any spores or threads of other fungus species that they may find growing on their leaf paste. When a queen ant goes off to found a new colony, she carries with her a starting culture of the precious fungus, just as human pioneers take along seeds to plant.

As for animal domestication, ants obtain a concentrated sugary secretion termed honeydew from diverse insects, ranging from aphids, mealybugs, and scale insects to caterpillars, treehoppers, and spittle insects. In return for the honeydew, the ants protect their "cows" from predators and parasites. Some aphids have evolved into virtually the insect equivalent of domestic cattle: they lack offensive structures of their own, excrete honeydew from their anuses, and have a specialized anal anatomy designed to hold the droplet in place while an ant drinks it. To milk their cows and stimulate honeydew flow, ants stroke the aphids with their antennae. Some ants care for their aphids in the ants' nest during the cold winter, then in the spring carry the aphids at the correct stage of development to the correct part of the correct food plant. When aphids eventually develop wings and disperse in search of new habitat, some lucky ones are discovered by ants and "adopted."

Obviously, we didn't inherit plant and animal domestication directly from ants but reinvented it. Actually, "reevolved" is a better term than "reinvented," since our early steps toward agriculture did not consist of conscious experimentation toward an articulated goal. Instead, agriculture grew from human behaviors, and from responses or changes in plants and animals, leading without plan toward domestication. For example, animal domestication arose partly from people's keeping captive wild animals as pets, partly from wild animals' learning to profit from the proximity of people (e.g., wolves following human hunters to catch crippled prey). Similarly, early stages of plant domestication included people's harvesting wild plants and discarding seeds, which were thereby accidentally "planted." The inevitable result was unconscious selection of those plant and animal species and individuals most useful to humans. Eventually, conscious selection and care followed.

Now LET'S RETURN to the progressivist view of this agricultural revolution of ours. As I explained at the outset of this chapter, we're accustomed to assuming that the transition from the hunter-gatherer life-style to agriculture brought us health, longevity, security, leisure, and great art. While the case for this view *seems* overwhelming, it is hard to prove. How do you actually show that lives of people ten thousand years ago got better when they abandoned hunting for farming? Until recently, archaeologists couldn't test this question directly. Instead, they had to resort to indirect tests, whose results (surprisingly) failed to support the view of agriculture as an unmixed blessing.

Here is one example of such an indirect test. If agriculture had been visibly such a great idea, you'd expect it to have spread quickly, once it arose in some source area. In fact, the archaeological record shows that agriculture advanced across Europe at a snail's pace: barely one thousand yards per year! From its origins in the Near East around 8000 B.C., agriculture crept northwestward to reach Greece around 6000 B.C., Britain and Scandinavia only 2,500 years later.

That's hardly what you can call a wave of enthusiasm. As recently as the nineteenth century, all the Indians of California, now the fruit basket of America, remained hunter-gatherers, even though they knew of agriculture through trade with farming Indians in Arizona. Were California Indians really blind to their self-interest? Or could it instead be that they were smart enough to see, hidden beyond agriculture's glittering façade, the drawbacks that ensnared the rest of us?

Another indirect test of the progressivist view is to study whether surviving twentieth-century hunter-gatherers really are worse off than farmers. Scattered throughout the world, mainly in areas unsuitable for agriculture, several dozen groups of so-called "primitive people," like the Kalahari Desert Bushmen, continued to live as hunter-gatherers in recent years. Astonishingly, it turns out that these hunters generally have leisure time, sleep a lot, and work no harder than their farming neighbors. For instance, the average time devoted each week to obtaining food has been reported to be only twelve to nineteen hours for Bushmen; how many readers of this book can boast of such a short work week? As one Bushman replied when asked why he had not emulated neighboring tribes by adopting agriculture, "Why should we plant, when there are so many mongongo nuts in the world?"

Of course, one's belly isn't filled just by finding food; the food also has to be processed for eating, and that can take a lot of time for things like mongongo nuts. Hence it would be a mistake to swing to the opposite extreme from the progressivist view and to regard hunter-gatherers as living the life of leisure, as some anthropologists have done. However, it would also be a mistake to view them as working much harder than farmers. Compared to my physician and lawyer friends today, and to my shopkeeper grandparents in the early twentieth century, hunter-gatherers really do have more free time.

While farmers concentrate on high-carbohydrate crops like rice and potatoes, the mixture of wild plants and animals in the diets of surviving hunter-gatherers provides more protein and a better balance of other nutrients. The Bushmen's average daily food intake is 2,140 calories and 93 grams of protein, considerably greater than the RDA (Recommended Daily Allowance) for people of their small size but vigorous activity. Hunter-gatherers are healthy, suffer from little disease, enjoy a very diverse diet, and do not experience the periodic famines that befall farmers, dependent on few crops. It is almost inconceivable for Bushmen, who utilize eighty-five edible wild plants, to die of starvation, as did about a million Irish farmers and their families during the 1840s when a blight attacked potatoes, their staple crop.

Thus, the lives of at least the surviving modern hunter-gatherers aren't "nasty, brutish, and short," even though farmers have pushed them into the world's worst real estate. Hunters of the past, who still occupied fertile lands, could hardly have been worse off than modern hunters. But all those modern hunter societies have been affected by farming societies for thousands of years and don't tell us about the condition of hunters before the agricultural revolution. The progressivist view is really making a claim about the distant past: that the lives of people in each part of the world got better when they switched from hunting to farming. Archaeologists can date that switch by distinguishing remains of wild plants and animals from remains of domestic ones in prehistoric garbage dumps. How can one deduce the health of the prehistoric garbage makers, and thereby test directly for agriculture's supposed blessings?

THAT QUESTION has become answerable only in recent years, through the newly emerging science of "paleopathology": looking for signs of disease (the science of pathology) in remains of ancient peoples (from the Greek root *paleo* = ancient, as in paleontology). In some lucky situations, the paleopathologist has almost as much material to study as does a pathologist. For example, archaeologists in the deserts of Chile found well-preserved mummies whose medical condition at time of death could be determined by an autopsy, just as one would do on a fresh corpse in a hospital today. Feces of long-dead Indians who lived in dry caves in Nevada remained sufficiently well preserved to be examined for hookworm and other parasites.

Usually, though, the only human remains available for paleopathologists to study are skeletons, but they still permit a surprising number of deductions about health. To begin with, a skeleton identifies its owner's sex, and his/her weight and approximate age at time of death. Thus, with enough skeletons, one can construct mortality tables like those used by life-insurance companies to calculate expected life span and risk of death at any given age. Paleopathologists can also calculate growth rates by measuring bones of people of different ages, can examine teeth for cavities (signs of a high-carbohydrate diet) or enamel defects (signs of a poor diet in childhood), and can recognize scars that many diseases such as anemia, tuberculosis, leprosy, and osteoarthritis leave on bones.

One straightforward example of what paleopathologists have learned from skeletons concerns historical changes in height. Many modern cases illustrate how improved childhood nutrition leads to taller adults: for instance, we stoop to pass through doorways of medieval castles built for a shorter, malnourished population. Paleopathologists studying ancient skeletons from Greece and Turkey found a striking parallel. The average height of hunter-gatherers in that region toward the end of the Ice Age was a generous five feet ten inches for men, five feet six inches for women. With the adoption of agriculture, height crashed, reaching by 4000 B.C. a low value of only five feet three for men, five feet one for women. By classical times, heights were very slowly on the rise again, but modern Greeks and Turks have still not regained the heights of their healthy hunter-gatherer ancestors.

Another example of paleopathologists at work is the study of thousands of American Indian skeletons excavated from burial mounds in the Illinois and Ohio river valleys. Corn, first domesticated in Central America thousands of years ago, became the basis of intensive farming in those valleys around A.D. 1000. Until then, Indian hunter-gatherers had skeletons "so healthy it is somewhat discouraging to work with them," as one paleopathologist complained. With the arrival of corn, Indian skeletons suddenly became interesting to study. The number of cavities in an average adult's mouth jumped from fewer than one to nearly seven, and tooth loss and abscesses became rampant. Enamel defects in children's milk teeth imply that pregnant and nursing mothers were severely undernourished. Anemia quadrupled in frequency; tuberculosis became established as an epidemic disease; half the population suffered from yaws or syphilis; and two-thirds suffered from osteoarthritis and other degenerative diseases. Mortality rates at every age increased, with the result that only 1 percent of the population survived past age fifty, as compared to 5 percent in the golden days before corn. Almost one-fifth of the whole population died between the ages of one and four, probably because weaned toddlers succumbed to malnutrition and infectious diseases. Thus corn, usually considered among the New World's blessings, actually proved to be a public-health disaster. Similar conclusions about the transition from hunting to farming emerge from studies of skeletons elsewhere in the world.

There are at least three sets of reasons to explain these findings that agriculture was bad for health. First, hunter-gatherers enjoyed a varied diet with adequate amounts of protein, vitamins, and minerals, while farmers obtained most of their food from starchy crops. In effect, the farmers gained cheap calories at the cost of poor nutrition. Today just three high-carbohydrate plants—wheat, rice, and corn—provide more than 50 percent of the calories consumed by the human species.

Second, because of that dependence on one or a few crops, farmers ran a greater risk of starvation if one food crop failed than did hunters. The Irish potato famine is merely one of many examples.

Finally, most of today's leading infectious diseases and parasites of mankind could not become established until after the transition to agriculture. These killers persist only in societies of crowded, malnourished, sedentary people constantly reinfected by each other and by their own sewage. The cholera bacterium, for example, does not survive for long outside the human body. It spreads from one victim to the next through contamination of drinking water with feces of cholera patients. Measles dies out in small populations once it has either killed or immunized most potential hosts; only in populations numbering at least a few hundred thousand people can it maintain itself indefinitely. Such crowd epidemics could not persist in small, scattered bands of hunters who often shifted camp. Tuberculosis, leprosy, and cholera had to await the rise of farming, while smallpox, bubonic plague, and measles appeared only in the past few thousand years with the rise of even denser populations in cities.

Besides malnutrition, starvation, and epidemic diseases, farming brought another curse to humanity: class divisions. Hunter-gatherers have little or no stored food, and no concentrated food sources like orchards or herds of cows. Instead, they live off the wild plants and animals that they obtain each day. Everybody except for infants, the sick, and the old join in the search for food. Thus there can be no kings, no full-time professionals, no class of social parasites who grow fat on food seized from others.

Only in a farming population could contrasts between the disease-ridden masses and a healthy, nonproducing elite develop. Skeletons from Greek tombs at Mycenae around 1500 B.C. suggest that royals enjoyed a better diet than commoners, since the royal skeletons were two or three inches taller and had better teeth (on the average, 1 instead of 6 cavities or missing teeth). Among mummies from Chilean cemeteries around A.D. 1000, the elite were distinguished not only by ornaments and gold hair clips, but also by a fourfold lower rate of bone lesions stemming from infectious diseases.

These signs of health differentials within local communities of farmers in the past appear on a global scale in the modern world. To most American and European readers, the argument that humanity could on the average be better off as hunter-gatherers than we are today sounds ridiculous, because most people in industrial societies today enjoy better health than most hunter-gatherers. However, Americans and Europeans are an elite in today's world, dependent on oil and other materials imported from countries with large peasant populations and much lower health standards. If you could choose between being a middle-class American, a Bushman hunter, and a peasant farmer in Ethiopia, the first would undoubtedly be the healthiest choice, but the third might be the least healthy.

While giving rise to class divisions for the first time, farming may also have exacerbated sexual inequality already in existence. With the advent of agriculture, women often became beasts of burden, were drained by more frequent pregnancies (see below), and thus suffered poorer health. For example, among the Chilean mummies from A.D. 1000, women exceeded men in osteoarthritis and in bone lesions from infectious disease. In New Guinea farming communities today I often see women staggering under loads of vegetables and firewood while the men walk empty-handed. In one case I offered to pay some villagers to carry supplies from an airstrip to my mountain camp, and a group of men, women, and children volunteered. The heaviest item was a 110-pound bag of rice, which I lashed to a pole and assigned to a team of four men to shoulder the poles together. When I eventually caught up with the villagers, the men were carrying light loads, while one small woman weighing less than the bag of rice was bent under it, supporting its weight by a cord across her temples.

As for the claim that agriculture laid the foundations of art by providing us with leisure time, modern hunter-gatherers have on the average at least as much free time as do farmers. I grant that some people in industrial and farming societies enjoy more leisure than do hunter-gatherers, at the expense of many others who support them and have far less leisure. Farming undoubtedly made it possible to sustain full-time craftsmen and artists, without whom we would not have such large-scale art projects as the Sistine Chapel and Cologne Cathedral. However, the whole emphasis on leisure time as a critical factor in explaining artistic differences among human societies seems to me misguided. It's not lack of time that prevents us today from surpassing the beauty of the Parthenon. While postagricultural technological advances did make new art forms possible and art preservation easier, great paintings and sculptures on a smaller scale than that of Cologne Cathedral were already being produced by Cro-Magnon hunter-gatherers fifteen thousand years ago. Great art was still being produced in modern times by hunter-gatherers such as Eskimos and Pacific Northwest Indians. In addition, when we count up the specialists whom society became able to support after the advent of agriculture, we should recall not only Michelangelo and Shakespeare but also standing armies of professional killers.

WITH THE ADVENT OF AGRICULTURE an elite became healthier, but many people became worse off. Instead of the progressivist party line that we chose agriculture because it was good for us, a cynic might ask how we got trapped by agriculture despite its being such a mixed blessing.

The answer boils down to the adage "Might makes right." Farming could support far more people than hunting, whether or not it also brought on the average more food per mouth. (Population densities of hunter-gatherers are typically one person or less per square mile, while densities of farmers average at least ten times higher.) Partly, this is because an acre of field planted entirely in edible crops produces far more tons of food, hence lets one feed far more mouths, than an acre of forest with scattered edible wild plants. Partly, too, it's because no-madic hunter-gatherers have to keep their children spaced at four-year intervals by infanticide and other means, since a mother must carry her toddler until it's old enough to keep up with the adults. Because sedentary farmers don't have that problem, a woman can and does bear a child every two years. Perhaps the main reason we find it so hard to shake off the traditional view that farming was unequivocally good for us is that there's no doubt that it meant more tons of food per acre. We forget that it also resulted in more mouths to feed, and that health and quality of life depend on the amount of food per mouth.

As population densities of hunter-gatherers slowly rose at the end of the Ice Age, bands had to "choose," whether consciously or unconsciously, between feeding more mouths by taking the first steps toward agriculture, or else finding ways to limit growth. Some bands adopted the former solution, unable to anticipate the evils of farming, and seduced by the transient abundance they enjoyed until population growth caught up with increased food production. Such bands outbred and then drove off or killed the bands that chose to remain hunter-gatherers, because ten malnourished farmers can still outfight one healthy hunter. It's not that hunter-gatherers abandoned their lifestyle, but that those sensible enough not to abandon it were forced out of all areas except ones that farmers didn't want. Modern hunter-gatherers persist mainly in scattered areas useless for agriculture, such as the Arctic and deserts.

At this point it's ironic to recall the common complaint that archaeology is an expensive luxury, concerned with the remote past, and offering no lessons of present relevance. Archaeologists studying the rise of farming have reconstructed for us a stage at which we made one of the most crucial decisions in human history. Forced to choose between limiting population growth and trying to increase food production, we opted for the latter and ended up with starvation, warfare, and tyranny. The same choice faces us today, with the difference that we now can learn from the past.

HUNTER-GATHERERS PRACTICED the most successful and long-persistent life-style in the career of our species. In contrast, we are still struggling with the problems into which we descended with agriculture, and it is unclear whether we can solve them. Suppose that an archaeologist who had visited us from Outer Space were trying to explain human history to his fellow spacelings. The visitor might illustrate the results of his digs by a twenty-four-hour clock on which one hour of clock time represents a hundred thousand years of real past time. If the history of the human race began at midnight, then we would now be almost at the end of our first day. We lived as hunter-gatherers for nearly the whole of that day, from midnight through dawn, noon, and sunset. Finally, at 11:54 P.M. we adopted agriculture. In retrospect, the decision was inevitable, and there is now no question of turning back. But as our second midnight approaches, will the present plight of African peasants gradually spread to engulf all of us? Or will we somehow achieve those seductive blessings that we imagine behind agriculture's glittering façade, and that have so far eluded us except in mixed form?

CHAPTER 11

Why Do We Smoke, Drink, and Use Dangerous Drugs?

CHERNOBYL—FORMALDEHYDE IN DRYWALL—LEAD POISONING—smog—the *Valdez* oil spill—Love Canal—asbestos—Agent Orange ... Hardly a month goes by without our learning of yet another way in which we and our children have been exposed to toxic chemicals through the negligence of others. The public's outrage, sense of helplessness, and demand for change are growing. Why, then, do we do to ourselves what we cannot stand for others to do to us? How do we explain the paradox that many people intentionally consume, inject, or inhale toxic chemicals, such as alcohol, cocaine, and the chemicals in tobacco smoke? Why are various forms of this willful self-damage native to many contemporary societies, from primitive tribes to high-tech urbanites, and extending back into the past as far as we have written records? How did drug abuse become a hallmark virtually unique to the human species?

The problem isn't so much in understanding why we continue to take toxic chemicals once we've started. In part, that's because our drugs of abuse are addictive. Instead, the greater mystery is what impels us to start at all. Evidence for the damaging or lethal effects of alcohol, cocaine, and tobacco is by now overwhelming and famil-iar. Only the existence of some strong countervailing motives could explain why people consume these poisons voluntarily, even eagerly. It's as if unconscious programs were driving us to do something we know to be dangerous. What could those programs be?

Naturally, there is no single explanation: different motives carry different weight with different people and in different societies. For instance, some people drink to overcome their inhibitions or to join friends, others to deaden their feelings or drown their sorrows, still others because they like the taste of alcoholic beverages. Naturally, too, differences among human populations and social classes in their options for achieving satisfying lives largely account for geographic and class differences in chemical abuse. It's not surprising that self-destructive alcoholism is a bigger problem in high-unemployment areas of Ireland than in southeast England, or that cocaine and heroin addiction is commoner in Harlem than in affluent suburbs. One could be tempted to dismiss drug abuse as a human hallmark with obvious social and cultural causes, and in no need of a search for animal precedents.

However, none of the motives that I've just mentioned goes to the heart of the paradox of our actively seeking what we know to be harmful. In this chapter I'll propose one other con-tributing motive, which does address that paradox. It relates our chemical self-assaults to a wide range of seemingly self-destructive traits in animals, and to a general theory of animal signaling. It unifies a wide range of phenomena in our culture, from smoking and alcoholism to drug abuse. It has potential cross-cultural valid-ity, for it may explain not just phenomena of the western world but also some otherwise mystifying customs elsewhere, such as kerosene drinking by Indonesian kung fu experts. I'll also reach into the past and apply the theory to the seemingly bizarre practice of ceremo-nial enemas in ancient Mayan civilization.

LET ME BEGIN by relating how I arrived at this idea. One day, I was abruptly struck by the puzzle that companies manufacturing toxic chemicals for human use advertise their use explicitly. This business practice would seem a sure route to bankruptcy. Yet, while we don't tolerate ads for cocaine, ads for tobacco and alcohol are so widespread that we cease to regard their existence as puzzling. It hit me only after I had been living with New Guinea hunters in the jungle for many months, far from any advertising.

Day after day, my New Guinea friends had been asking me about western customs, and I had come to realize through their astonished responses how senseless many of our customs are. Then the months of fieldwork ended with one of those sudden transitions that modern transportation has made possible. On June 25 I was still in the jungle, watching a brilliant-colored male bird of paradise flap awkwardly across a clearing, dragging its three-foot-long tail behind it. On June 26 I was sitting in a Boeing 747 jet, reading the magazines and catching up on the wonders of western civilization.

I leafed through the first magazine. It fell open to a page with a photo of a tough-looking man on horseback chasing cows, and the name of a brand of cigarette in large letters below. The American in me knew what the photo was about. But part of me was still in the jungle, looking at that photo naïvely. Perhaps my reaction won't seem so strange to you if you try to imagine yourself completely unfamiliar with western society, seeing the ad for the first time, and trying to fathom the connection between chasing cows and smoking (or not smoking) cigarettes.

The naïve part of me, fresh out of the jungle, thought: such a brilliant antismoking ad! It's well known that smoking impairs athletic ability and causes cancer and early death. Cowboys are widely regarded as athletic and admirable. This ad must be a devastating new appeal by the antismoking forces, telling us that if we smoke that particular brand of cigarette, we won't be fit to be cowboys. What an effective message to our youth!

But then it became obvious that the ad had been put there by the cigarette company itself, which somehow hoped that readers would draw exactly the opposite message from the ad. How on earth did the company let its public-relations department talk it into such a disastrous miscalculation? Surely that ad would dissuade any person concerned about his/her strength and self-image from starting to smoke.

Still half immersed in the jungle, I turned to another page. There I saw a photo of a whiskey bottle on a table, a man sipping presumably the bottle's contents from a glass, and an obviously fertile young woman gazing at him admiringly as if she were on the verge of sexual surrender. How can that be? I asked myself. Everyone knows that alcohol interferes with sexual function, tends to make men impotent, makes one likely to stumble, impairs judgment, and predisposes to cirrhosis of the liver and other debilitating conditions. In the immortal words of the porter in Shakespeare's *Macbeth,* "It [alcohol] provokes the desire, but it takes away the performance." A man with such performance handicaps should conceal them at all costs from a woman he aims to seduce. Why is the man in the photo intentionally displaying those handicaps? Do whiskey manufacturers think that pictures of this impaired individual will help sell their product? One could expect that Mothers Against Drunk Driving would be the ones producing such ads, and that the whiskey companies would be suing to prevent publication.

Page after page of ads flaunted the use of cigarettes or strong alcohol, and hinted at their benefits. There were even pictures of young people smoking in the presence of attractive members of the opposite sex, as if to imply that smoking too brought sexual opportunities. Yet any nonsmoker who has ever been kissed by (or tried to kiss) a smoker knows how severely the smoker's bad breath compromises his or her sex appeal. The ads paradoxically implied not just sexual benefits but also platonic friendships, business opportunities, vigor, health, and happiness, when the direct conclusion to be drawn from the ads was actually the reverse.

As the days passed and I reimmersed myself in western civilization, I gradually stopped noticing its apparently self-defeating ads. I retreated into analyzing my field data and wondering instead about an entirely different paradox, involving bird evolution. But that paradox was what led me finally to understand one rationale behind cigarette and whiskey ads.

THE NEW PARADOX concerned why that male bird of paradise I had been watching on June 25 had evolved the impediment of a tail three feet long. Males of other bird of paradise species evolved other bizarre impediments, such as long plumes growing out of their eyebrows, the habit of hanging upside-down, and brilliant colors and loud calls likely to attract hawks. All those features must impair male survival, yet they also serve as the advertisements by which male birds of paradise woo female birds of paradise. Like many other biologists, I found myself wondering why male birds of paradise use such handicaps as advertisements, and why females find the handicaps attractive.

At that point I recalled a remarkable paper published in 1975 by an Israeli biologist, Amotz Zahavi. In that paper Zahavi proposed a novel general theory, still hotly debated by biologists, about the role of costly or self-destructive signals in animal behavior. For example, he attempted to explain how deleterious male traits might attract a female precisely because they constitute handicaps. On reflection, I decided that Zahavi's hypothesis might apply to the birds of paradise I studied. Suddenly I realized, with growing excitement, that his theory perhaps could also be extended to explain the paradox of our use of toxic chemicals, and our touting it in ads.

Zahavi's theory as he proposed it concerned the broad problem of animal communication. All animals need to devise quick, easily understood signals for conveying messages to their mates, potential mates, offspring, parents, rivals, and would-be predators. For example, consider a gazelle that notices a lion stalking it. It would be in the gazelle's interests to give a signal that the lion would interpret to mean, "I am a superior fast gazelle! You'll never succeed in catching me, so don't waste your time and energy on trying." Even if that gazelle really is able to outrun a lion, giving a signal that dissuades the lion from trying would save time and energy for the gazelle too.

But what signal will unequivocally tell the lion that it's hopeless? The gazelle can't take the time to run a demonstration hundred-yard dash in front of every lion that shows up. Perhaps gazelles could agree on some quick arbitrary signal that lions learn to understand: e.g., pawing the ground with the left hind foot means, "I claim that I'm fast!" However, such a purely arbitrary signal opens the door to cheating: any gazelle can easily give the signal regardless of its speed. Lions will then catch on that many slow gazelles giving the signal are lying, and lions will learn to ignore the signal. It's in the interests both of lions and of fast gazelles that the signal be believable. What type of signal could convince a lion of the gazelle's honesty?

The same dilemma arises in the problem of sexual selection and mate choice that I discussed in earlier chapters. This is especially a problem of how females pick males, since females invest more in reproduction, have more to lose, and have to be choosier. Ideally, a female should pick a male for his good genes to pass on to her offspring. Since genes themselves are hard to assess, a female should look for quick indicators of good genes in a male, and a superior male should provide such indicators. In practice, male traits such as plumage, songs, and displays usually serve as indicators. Why do males "choose" to advertise with those particular indicators, why should females trust a male's honesty and find those indicators attractive, and why do they imply good genes?

I've described the problem as if a gazelle or courting male voluntarily picks out some indicator from among many possible ones, and as if a lion or a female decides on reflection whether it's really a valid indicator of speed or good genes. In practice, of course, those "choices" are the result of evolution and become specified by genes. Those females who select males on the basis of indicators that really denote good male genes, and those males that use unambiguous indicators of good genes for self-advertisement, tend to leave the most offspring, as do those gazelles and lions that spare themselves unnecessary chases.

As it turns out, many of the advertising signals evolved by animals pose a paradox similar to that posed by cigarette ads. The indicators often seem not to suggest speed or good genes but instead to constitute handicaps, expenses, or sources of risk. For example, a gazelle's signal to a lion that it sees approaching consists of a peculiar behavior termed "stotting." Instead of running away as fast as possible, the gazelle runs slowly while repeatedly jumping high into the air with stiff-legged leaps. Why on earth should the gazelle indulge in this seemingly self-destructive display, which wastes time and energy and gives the lion a chance to catch up? Or think of the males of many animal species that sport large structures, such as a peacock's tail or a bird of paradise's plumes, that make movement difficult. Males of many more species have bright colors, loud songs, or conspicuous displays that attract predators. Why should a male advertise such an impediment, and why should a female like it? These paradoxes remain an important unsolved problem in animal behavior today.

Zahavi's theory goes to the heart of this paradox. According to his theory, those deleterious structures and behaviors constitute valid indicators that the signaling animal is being honest in its claim of superiority, precisely *because* those traits themselves impose handicaps. A signal that entails no cost lends itself to cheating, since even a slow or inferior animal can afford to give the signal. Only costly or deleterious signals are guarantees of honesty. For example, a slow gazelle that stotted at an approaching lion would seal its fate, whereas a fast gazelle could still outrun the lion after stotting. By stotting, the gazelle boasts to the lion, "I'm so fast that I can escape you even after giving you this head start." The lion thereby has grounds for believing in the gazelle's honesty, and both the lion and the gazelle profit by not wasting time and energy on a chase whose outcome is certain.

Similarly, as applied to males displaying toward females, Zahavi's theory reasons that any male that has managed to survive despite the handicap of a big tail or conspicuous song must have terrific genes in other respects. He has proved that he must be *especially* good at escaping predators, finding food, and resisting disease. The bigger the handicap, the more rigorous the test that he has passed. The female who selects such a male is like the medieval damsel testing her knight suitors by watching them slay dragons. When she sees a one-armed knight who can still slay a dragon, she knows that she has finally found a knight with great genes. And that knight, by flaunting his handicap, is actually flaunting his superiority.

It seems to me that Zahavi's theory applies to many costly or dangerous human behaviors aimed at achieving status in general or at sexual benefits in particular. For instance, men who woo women with costly gifts and other displays of wealth are in effect saying, "I have plenty of money to support you and children, and you can believe my boast because you see how much money I'm spending now without blanching." People who show off expensive jewels, sports cars, or works of art gain status because the signal can't be faked; everyone else knows what those ostentatious objects cost. American Indians of the Pacific Northwest used to seek status by competing to give away as much wealth as possible in ceremonies known as potlatch rituals. In the days before modern medicine, tattooing was not only painful but dangerous because of the risk of infection; hence tattooed people in effect were advertising two facets of their strength, resistance to disease plus tolerance of pain. Men on the Pacific island of Malekula have traditionally showed off by the insanely dangerous practice, now imitated elsewhere by bungee jumpers, of building a high tower and jumping off it headfirst, after tying one end of some stout vines to each ankle and the other end to the top of the tower. The length of the vines is calculated to stop the braggart's plunge while his head is still a few feet above the ground.

Survival guarantees that the jumper is courageous, carefully calculating, and a good builder.

Zahavi's theory can also be extended to human abuse of chemicals. Especially in adolescence and early adulthood, the age when drug abuse is most likely to begin, we are devoting much energy to asserting our status. I suggest that we share the same unconscious instinct that leads birds to indulge in dangerous displays. Ten thousand years ago, we "displayed" by challenging a lion or a tribal enemy. Today, we do it in other ways, such as by fast driving or by consuming dangerous drugs.

The messages of our old and new displays nevertheless remain the same: I'm strong and superior. Even to take drugs only once or twice, I must be strong enough to get past the burning, choking sensation of my first puff on a cigarette, or to get past the misery of my first hangover. To do it chronically and remain alive and healthy, I must be superior (so I imagine). It's a message to our rivals, our peers, our prospective mates—and to ourselves. The smoker's kiss may taste awful, and the drinker may be impotent in bed, but he or she still hopes to impress peers or attract mates by the implicit message of superiority.

Alas, the message may be valid for birds, but for us it's a false one. Like so many animal instincts in us, this one has become maladaptive in modern human society. If you can still walk after drinking a bottle of whiskey, it may prove that you have high levels of liver alcohol dehydrogenase, but it implies no superiority in other respects. If you haven't developed lung cancer after chronically smoking several packs of cigarettes daily, you may have a gene for resistance to lung cancer, but that gene doesn't convey intelligence, business acumen, or the ability to create happiness for your spouse and children.

It's true that animals with only brief lives and courtships have no alternative except to develop quick indicators, since prospective mates don't have enough time to measure each other's real quality. But we, with our long lives and courtships and business associations, have ample time to scrutinize each other's worth. We needn't rely on superficial, misleading indicators. Drug abuse is a classic instance of a once-useful instinct—the reliance on handicap signals—that has turned foul in us. It's that old instinct to which the tobacco and whiskey companies are directing their clever, obscene ads. If we legalized cocaine, the drug lords too would soon have ads appealing to the same instinct. You can easily picture it: the photo of the cowboy on his horse, or the suave man and the attractive maiden, above the tastefully displayed packet of white powder.

Now, LET'S TEST MY THEORY by jumping from western industrialized society to the other side of the world. Drug abuse did not begin with the industrial revolution. Tobacco was a native American Indian crop, native alcoholic beverages are widespread in the world, and cocaine and opium came to us from other societies. The oldest preserved code of laws, that of the Babylonian king Hammurabi (1792–50 B.C.), already contained a section regulating drinking houses. Hence my theory, if it's valid, should apply to other societies as well. As an instance of its cross-cultural explanatory power, I'll cite a practice you may not have heard of: kung fu kerosene drinking.

I learned of this practice when I was working in Indonesia with a wonderful young biologist named Ardy Irwanto. Ardy and I had come to like and admire each other, and to look out for each other's well-being. At one point, when we reached a troubled area and I expressed concern about dangerous people we might encounter, Ardy assured me, "No problem, Jared. I have kung fu grade eight." He explained that he practiced the Oriental martial art of kung fu and had reached a high level of proficiency, such that he could single-handedly fight off a group of eight attackers. To illustrate, Ardy showed me a scar in his back stemming from an attack by eight ruffians. One had knifed him, whereupon Ardy broke the arms of two and the skull of a third and the remainder fled. I had nothing to fear in Ardy's company, he told me.

One evening at our campsite, Ardy walked with his drinking cup up to our jerrycans. As usual, we had two cans: a blue one for water, and a red one for kerosene for our pressure lamp. To my horror, I watched Ardy pour from the red jerrycan and raise the cup to his lips. Remembering an awful moment during a mountaineering expedition when I had taken a sip of kerosene by mistake and spent all the next day coughing it back up, I screamed to Ardy to stop. But he raised his hand and said calmly, "No problem, Jared. I have kung fu grade eight."

Ardy explained that kung fu gave him strength, which he and his fellow kung fu masters tested each month by drinking a cup of kerosene. Without kung fu, of course, kerosene would make a weaker person sick: heaven forbid that I, Jared, for instance, should try it. But it did him, Ardy, no harm, because he had kung fu. He calmly retired to his tent to sip his kerosene and emerged the next morning, happy and healthy as usual.

I can't believe that kerosene did Ardy no harm. I wish that he could have found a less damaging way to make periodic tests of his preparedness. But for him and his kung fu associates, it served as an indicator of their strength and their advanced level of kung fu. Only a really robust person could get through that test. Kerosene drinking illustrates the handicap theory of toxic chemical use, in a form as startlingly repellent to us as our cigarettes and alcohol were to a horrified Ardy.

As my last example, I'll generalize my theory further by extending its applications to the past—in this case, to the civilization of Mayan Indians that flourished in Central America one or two thousand years ago. Archaeologists have been fascinated by Mayan success at creating an advanced society in the middle of tropical rain forest. Many Mayan achievements, such as their calendar, writing, astronomical knowledge, and agricultural practices, are now understood to varying degrees. But archaeologists were long puzzled by slender tubes of unknown purpose that they kept finding in Mayan excavations.

The tubes' function finally became clear with the discovery of painted vases showing scenes of the tubes' use: to administer intoxicating enemas. The vases depict a high-status figure, evidently a priest or a prince, receiving a ceremonial enema in the presence of other people. The enema tube is shown as connected to a bag of a frothy, beerlike beverage—probably containing either alcohol or hallucinogens or both, as suggested by practices of other Indian groups. Many Central and South American Indian tribes formerly practiced similar ritual enemas when first encountered by European explorers, and some still do so today. The substances known to be administered range from alcohol (made by fermenting agave sap or a tree bark) to tobacco, peyote, LSD derivatives, and mushroom-derived hallucinogens. Thus, the ritual enema is similar to our consumption of intoxicants by mouth, but there are four reasons why an enema constitutes a more effective and valid indicator of strength than does drinking.

First, it is possible to relapse into solitary drinking and thus to lose all opportunity for signaling one's high status to others. However, it is more difficult for a solitary person to administer the same beverage to himself or herself unassisted as an enema. An enema encourages one to enlist associates, and thereby automatically creates an occasion for self-advertisement. Second, more strength is required to handle alcohol as an enema than as a drink, since the alcohol goes directly into the intestine and thence to the bloodstream, and it isn't first diluted with food in the stomach. Third, drugs absorbed from the small intestine after ingestion by mouth pass first to the liver, where many drugs are detoxified before they can reach the brain and other sensitive organs. But drugs absorbed from the rectum after an enema bypass the liver. Finally, nausea may limit one's intake of drinks but not of enemas. Hence an enema seems to me a more convincing advertisement of superiority than are our whiskey ads. I recommend this concept to an ambitious public-relations firm competing for the account of one of the large distilleries.

LET'S NOW STEP BACK and summarize the perspective on chemical abuse that I've suggested. Although frequent self-destruction by chemicals may be unique to humans, I see it as fitting into a broad pattern of animal behavior and thus as having innumerable animal precedents. All animals have had to evolve signals for quickly communicating messages to other animals. If the signals were ones that any individual animal could master or acquire, they would lend themselves to rampant cheating and hence to disbelief. To be valid and believable, a signal must be one that guarantees the honesty of the signaler, by entailing a cost, risk, or burden that only superior individuals can afford. Many animal signals that would otherwise strike us as counterproductive—such as stotting by gazelles, or costly structures and risky displays with which males court females—can be understood in this light.

It seems to me that this perspective has contributed to the evolution not only of human art but also of human chemical abuse. Both art and chemical abuse are widespread human hallmarks characteristic of most known human societies. Both beg explanation, since it's not immediately obvious why they promote our survival through natural selection, or why they help us acquire mates through sexual selection. I argued earlier that art often serves as a valid indicator of an individual's superiority or status, since art requires skill to create and requires status or wealth to acquire. But those individuals perceived by their fellows as enjoying status thereby acquire enhanced access to resources and mates. I'm arguing now that humans seek status through many other costly displays besides art, and that some of those displays (like jumping from towers, fast driving, and chemical abuse) are surprisingly dangerous. The former costly displays advertise status or wealth; the latter dangerous ones advertise that the displaying individual can master even such risks and hence must be superior.

I don't claim, though, that this perspective affords a total understanding of art or chemical abuse. As I mentioned in connection with art, complex behaviors acquire a life of their own, go far beyond their original purpose (if there ever was just a single purpose), and may even originally have served multiple functions. Just as art is now motivated far more by pleasure than by need for advertisement, chemical abuse too is now clearly much more than an advertisement. It's also a way to get past inhibitions, drown sorrows, or just enjoy a good-tasting drink.

I also don't deny that, even from an evolutionary perspective, there remains a basic difference between human abuse of chemicals and its animal precedents. Stotting, long tails, and all the animal precedents that I described involve costs, but those behaviors persist because the costs are outweighed by the benefits. A stotting gazelle loses a possible head start in a chase, but gains by decreasing the likelihood that a lion will embark on a serious chase at all. A long-tailed male bird is encumbered in finding food or escaping predators, but those survival disadvantages imposed by natural selection are more than compensated by mating advantages gained through sexual selection. The net balance is more rather than fewer offspring to pass on the male's genes. Hence these animal traits only appear to be self-destructive; they are actually self-promoting.

In the case of our chemical abuse, though, the costs outweigh the benefits. Drug addicts and drunkards not only lead shorter lives, but they lose rather than gain attractiveness in the eyes of potential mates and lose the ability to care for children. These traits don't persist because of hidden advantages outweighing costs; they persist mainly because they are chemically addicting. Overall, they are self-

destructive, not self-promoting, behaviors. While gazelles may occasionally miscalculate in stotting, they don't commit suicide through
addiction to the excitement of stotting. In that respect, our self-
destructive abuse of chemicals diverged from its animal precursors to
become truly a human hallmark.

CHAPTER 12

Alone
in a Crowded
Universe

THE NEXT TIME YOU'RE OUTDOORS ON A CLEAR NIGHT AWAY FROM CITY lights, look up at the sky and get a sense of the myriads of stars. Next, find a pair of binoculars, train them on the Milky Way, and appreciate how many more stars escaped your naked eye. Then look at a photo of the Andromeda nebula as seen through a powerful telescope to realize how enormous is the number of stars that escaped your binoculars as well.

Once all those numbers have sunk in, you'll finally be ready to ask: How could humans possibly be unique in the universe? How many civilizations of intelligent beings like ourselves must be out there, looking back at us? How long before we are in communication with them, before we visit them, or before we are visited?

On Earth, we certainly are unique. No other species possesses language, art, or agriculture of a complexity remotely approaching ours. No other species abuses drugs. But we've seen in the last four chapters that, for each of those human hallmarks, there are many animal precedents or even precursors. Similarly, human intelligence arose directly from chimpanzee intelligence, which is impressive by the standards of other animals though still far below ours. Isn't it likely that some other species on some other planets have also developed such widespread animal precursors to the level of our own art, language, and intelligence?

Alas, most human hallmarks lack effects detectable at a distance of many light-years. If there were creatures enjoying art or addicted to drugs on planets orbiting even the nearest stars, we'd never know it. But fortunately there are two signs of intelligent beings elsewhere that might be detectable on Earth: space probes and radio signals. We ourselves are already becoming effective at sending out both, so surely other intelligent creatures have mastered the necessary skills. Where, then, are the expected flying saucers?

This seems to me one of the greatest puzzles in all of science. Given the billions of stars, and given the abilities that we know did develop in our own species, we ought to be detecting flying saucers or at least radio signals. There's no question about there being billions of stars. What is there about the human species, then, that could explain the missing saucers? Could we really be unique not only on Earth, but also in the accessible universe? In this chapter I'll argue that we can obtain a fresh perspective on our uniqueness by looking carefully at some other unique creatures here on Earth.

FOR A LONG TIME, people have asked themselves such questions. Already around 400 B.C. the philosopher Metrodorus wrote, "To consider the Earth the only populated world in an infinite space is as absurd as to assert that in an entire field sown with millet only one grain will grow." Not until 1960, however, did scientists make a serious first attempt to find the answer, by listening (unsuccessfully) for radio transmissions from two nearby stars. In 1974 astronomers at the giant Arecibo radio telescope tried to establish an interstellar dialogue, by beaming a powerful radio signal to the star cluster M13 in the constellation Hercules. The signal described to Hercules denizens what we earthlings look like, how many of us there are, and where the Earth is located in our solar system. Two years later the search for extraterrestrial life provided the main motivation behind the Viking missions to Mars, whose cost of about a billion dollars dwarfed all the U.S. National Science Foundation's expenditures (since its inception) for classifying the life known to exist on Earth.

More recently the U.S. government has decided to spend a further hundred million dollars to detect radio signals from any intelligent beings who might exist outside our solar system. Several spacecraft that we launched are now heading out of our solar system, carrying sound tapes and photographic records of our civilization to inform spacelings who might be encountered.

It's easy to understand why lay people as well as biologists would consider the detection of extraterrestrial life as possibly the most exciting scientific discovery ever made. Just imagine how it would affect our self-image to find that the universe holds other intelligent creatures, with complex societies, languages, and learned cultural traditions, and capable of communicating with us. Among those of us who believe in an afterlife and an ethically concerned deity, most would agree that an afterlife awaits humans but not beetles (or even chimpanzees). Creationists believe that our species had a separate origin through divine creation. Suppose, though, that we should detect on another planet a society of seven-legged creatures more intelligent and ethical than we are, and able to converse with us, but having radio receivers and transmitters in place of eyes and mouths. Shall we believe that those creatures (but still not chimps) share the afterlife with us, and that they too were divinely created?

Many scientists have tried to calculate the odds of there being intelligent creatures out there somewhere. Those calculations have spawned a whole new field of science termed exobiology—the sole scientific field whose subject matter has not yet been shown to exist. Let's now consider the numbers that encourage exobiologists to believe in their subject matter.

Exobiologists calculate the number of advanced technical civilizations in the universe by an equation known as the Green Bank formula, which multiplies a string of estimated numbers. Some of those numbers can be estimated with considerable confidence. There are billions of galaxies, each with billions of stars. Astronomers conclude that many stars probably have one or more planets each, and that many of those planets probably have an environment suitable for life. Biologists conclude that, where conditions suitable for life exist, life will probably evolve eventually. Multiplying all of those probabilities or numbers together, we conclude that there are likely to be billions of billions of planets supporting living creatures.

Now let's estimate what fraction of those planetary biotas include intelligent beings with advanced technical civilizations, which we'll define operationally as civilizations capable of interstellar radio communication. (This is a less demanding definition than flying-saucer capability, since our own development suggests that interstellar radio communication will precede interstellar probes.) Two arguments suggest that that fraction may be considerable. First, the sole planet where we are certain that life evolved—our own—did evolve an advanced technical civilization. We have already launched interplanetary probes. We have made progress with techniques for freezing and thawing life and for making life from DNA—techniques relevant to preserving life as we know it for the long duration of an interstellar trip. Technical progress in recent decades has been so rapid that manned interstellar probes surely will be feasible within a few centuries at the very most, since some of our unmanned interplanetary probes are already on their way out of our solar system.

However, this first argument suggesting that many other planetary biotas have evolved advanced technical civilizations isn't a compelling one. To use the language of statisticians, it suffers from the obvious flaw of very small sample size (how can you generalize from one case?) and very high ascertainment bias (we picked out that one case precisely because it evolved our own advanced technical civilization).

A second, stronger argument is that life on Earth is characterized by what biologists term convergent evolution. That is, seemingly whatever ecological niche or physiological adaptation you consider, many groups of creatures have converged by evolving independently to exploit that niche, or to acquire that adaptation. An obvious example is the independent evolution of flight by birds, bats, pterodactyls, and insects. Other spectacular cases are the independent evolution of eyes, and even of devices for electrocuting prey, by many animals. Within the past two decades, biochemists have recognized convergent evolution at the molecular level, such as the repeated evolution of similar protein-splitting enzymes. So common is convergent evolution of anatomy, physiology, biochemistry, and behavior that whenever biologists observe two species to be similar in some respect, one of the first questions they now ask is: did that similarity result from common ancestry or from convergence?

There's nothing surprising about the seeming ubiquity of convergent evolution. If you expose millions of species for millions of years to similar selective forces, of course you can expect similar solutions to emerge time and time again. We know that there has been much convergence among species on Earth, but by the same reasoning there should also be much convergence between Earth's species and those elsewhere. Hence, although radio communication is one of those things that happens to have evolved here only once so far, considerations of convergent evolution lead us to expect its evolution on some other planets as well. As the *Encyclopedia Britannica* puts it, "It is difficult to imagine life evolving on another planet without progressing towards intelligence."

But that conclusion brings us back to the puzzle I mentioned earlier. If many or most stars have planetary systems, and if many of those systems include at least one planet with conditions suitable for life, and if life is likely eventually to evolve where suitable conditions exist, and if about one percent of planets with life include an advanced technical civilization—then one estimates that our own galaxy alone contains about a million planets supporting advanced civilizations. But within only a few dozen light-years of us are several hundred stars, some (most?) of which surely have planets like ours, supporting life. Then where are all the flying saucers that we would expect? Where are the intelligent beings that should be visiting us, or at least directing radio signals at us? The silence is deafening.

Something must be wrong with the astronomers' calculations. They know what they're talking about when they estimate the number of planetary systems, and the fraction of those likely to be supporting life. I find these estimates plausible. Instead, the problem is likely to lie in the argument, based on convergent evolution, that a significant fraction of biotas will evolve advanced technical civilizations. Hence let's scrutinize more closely the inevitability of convergent evolution.

WOODPECKERS PROVIDE a good test case, because woodpecking is a terrific life-style that offers much more food than do flying saucers or radios. The "woodpecker niche" is based on digging holes in live wood and on prying off pieces of bark. That means dependable food sources all year round in the form of sap, insects living under bark, and insects burrowing into wood. It also means an excellent place for a nest, since a hole in a tree affords protection from wind, rain, predators, and temperature fluctuations. Other bird species besides woodpeckers can pull off the easier feat of digging nest holes in dead wood, but there are many fewer dead trees than live trees available.

These considerations mean that if we're counting on convergent evolution of radio communication, we can surely count on convergent evolution among many species to exploit the woodpecker niche. Not surprisingly, woodpeckers are very successful birds. There are nearly two hundred species, many of them common. They come in all sizes, from tiny birds the size of kinglets up to crow-sized. They are widespread over most of the world, except on oceanic islands too remote for them to reach by flying.

How hard is it to evolve to become a woodpecker? Two considerations might seem to suggest "Not very hard." Woodpeckers are not an extremely distinctive old group without close relatives, like egg-laying mammals. Instead, ornithologists have agreed for a long time that their closest relatives are honey guides, toucans, and barbets, to which woodpeckers are fairly similar except in their special adaptations for woodpecking. Woodpeckers have numerous such adaptations, but none is remotely as extraordinary as building radios, and all are readily seen as extensions of adaptations possessed by other birds. The adaptations fall into four groups.

First and most obvious are the adaptations for drilling in live wood. These include a chisel-like bill, nostrils protected with feathers to keep out sawdust, a thick skull, strong head and neck muscles, and a hinge between the base of the bill and the front of the skull to help spread the shock of pounding. These features for drilling in live wood can be traced to features of other birds much more easily than our radios can be traced to any primitive radios of chimpanzees. Many other birds, such as parrots, peck or bite holes in dead wood. Within the woodpecker family there is a gradation of drilling ability—from wrynecks, which can't excavate at all, to the many woodpeckers that drill in softer wood, to hardwood specialists like sapsuckers.

Another set of adaptations are those for perching vertically on bark, such as a stiff tail to press against bark as a brace, strong muscles for manipulating the tail, short legs, and long, curved toes. The evolution of these adaptations can be traced even more easily than can the adaptations for woodpecking. Even within the woodpecker family, wrynecks and piculets do not have stiff tails for use as braces. Many birds outside the woodpecker family, including creepers and pygmy parrots, do have stiff tails that they evolved to prop themselves on bark.

The third adaptation is an extremely long and extensible tongue, fully as long as our own tongues in some woodpeckers. Once a woodpecker has broken into the tunnel system of wood-dwelling insects at one point, the bird uses its tongue to lick out many branches of the system without having to drill a new hole for each branch. Woodpeckers' tongues have many animal precedents, including the similarly long insect-catching tongues of frogs, anteaters, and aardvarks.

Finally, woodpeckers have tough skins to withstand insect bites plus the stresses from pounding and from strong muscles. Anyone who has skinned and stuffed birds knows that some birds have much tougher skins than others. Taxidermists groan when given a pigeon, whose paper-thin skin tears almost as soon as you look at it, but smile when given a woodpecker, hawk, or parrot.

Thus, while woodpeckers have many adaptations for woodpecking, most of those adaptations have also evolved convergently in other birds or animals, and the unique skull adaptations can at least be traced to precursors. You might therefore expect the whole package of woodpecking to have evolved repeatedly, with the result that there would now be many groups of large animals capable of excavating into live wood for food or nest sites. But all modern woodpeckers are more closely related to each other than to any nonwoodpecker, proving that woodpecking evolved only once. Even on remote landmasses that woodpeckers never reached, like Australia, New Guinea, New Zealand, nothing else has evolved to exploit the splendid opportunities made available by the woodpecker life-style. Some birds and mammals on those landmasses do excavate dead wood or bark, but they are only feeble excuses for woodpeckers, and none can excavate in live wood. If woodpeckers hadn't evolved that one time in the Americas or Old World, a terrific niche would be flagrantly vacant over the whole Earth.

I HAVE DWELT on woodpeckers to illustrate that convergence is not universal, and that not all splendid opportunities are seized. I could have illustrated the same point with other, equally flagrant examples. The most ubiquitous opportunity available to animals is to consume plants, much of whose mass consists of cellulose. Yet no higher animal has managed to evolve a cellulose-digesting enzyme. Those animal herbivores that digest cellulose (such as cows) instead have to rely on microbes housed within their intestines. To take another example that I discussed in an earlier chapter, growing your own food would seem to offer obvious advantages for animals, but the only animals to master the trick before the dawn of human agriculture ten thousand years ago were leaf-cutter ants and a few other insects, which cultivate fungi or domesticate aphid "cows."

Thus, it has proved extraordinarily difficult to evolve even such obviously valuable adaptations as woodpecking, digesting cellulose efficiently, or growing one's own food. Radios do much less for one's food needs and would seem far less likely to evolve. Are our radios a fluke, unlikely to have been duplicated on any other planet?

Consider what biology might have taught us about the inevitability of radio evolution on Earth. If radio building were like woodpecking, some species might have evolved certain elements of the package or evolved them in inefficient form, although only one species managed to evolve the complete package. For instance, we might have found today that turkeys build radio transmitters but no receivers, while kangaroos build receivers but no transmitters. The fossil record might have shown dozens of now-extinct animals experimenting over the last half-billion years with metallurgy and increasingly complex electronic circuits, leading to electric toasters in the Triassic, battery-operated rat traps in the Oligocene, and finally radios in the Holocene. Fossils might have revealed five-watt transmitters built by trilobites, two-hundred-watt transmitters amidst bones of the last dinosaurs, and five-hundred-watt transmitters in use by sabertooths, until humans finally upped the power output enough to be the first to broadcast into space.

But none of that happened. Neither fossils nor living animals—not even our closest living relatives, the common and pygmy chimpanzees—had even the most remote precursors of radios. It's instructive to consider the experience of the human line itself. Neither australopithecines nor early *Homo sapiens* developed radios. As recently as 150 years ago, modern *Homo sapiens* didn't even have the concepts that would lead to radios. The first practical experiments didn't begin until around 1888; it's still less than one hundred years since Marconi built the first transmitter capable of broadcasting one mere mile; and we still aren't sending signals targeted at other stars, though the 1974 Arecibo experiment was our first attempt.

I mentioned early in this chapter that the existence of radios on the one planet known to us seemed at first to suggest a high probability of radios' evolving on other planets. In fact, closer scrutiny of Earth's history supports exactly the opposite conclusion: radios had a vanishingly low probability of evolving here. Only one of the billions of species that have existed on Earth showed any proclivities toward radios, and even it failed to do so for the first 69,999/70,000ths of its seven-million-year history. A visitor from Outer Space who had come to Earth as recently as the year 1800 would have written off any prospects of radios' being built here.

You might object that I'm being too stringent in looking for early precursors of radios themselves, when I should instead look just for the two qualities necessary to make radios: intelligence and mechanical dexterity. But the situation there is little more encouraging. Based on the very recent evolutionary experience of our own species, we arrogantly assume intelligence and dexterity to be the best way of taking over the world, and to have evolved inevitably. Think again about that quote I cited earlier from the *Encyclopedia Britannica*: "It is difficult to imagine life evolving on another planet without progressing towards intelligence." Earth history again supports exactly the opposite conclusion. In reality, vanishingly few animals on Earth have bothered with much of either intelligence or dexterity. No animal has acquired remotely as much of either as have we; those that have acquired a little of one (smart dolphins, dexterous spiders) have acquired none of the other; and the only other species to acquire a little of both (common and pygmy chimpanzees) have been rather unsuccessful. Earth's really successful species have instead been dumb and clumsy rats and beetles, which found better routes to their current dominance.

WE HAVE ONLY STILL to consider the last missing variable in the Green Bank formula for calculating the likely number of civilizations capable of interstellar radio communication. That variable is the lifetime of such a civilization. The intelligence and dexterity required to build radios are useful for other purposes that have been our species' hallmarks for much longer than have radios: purposes such as mass killing devices and means of environmental destruction. We have become so potent at both that we are gradually stewing in our civilization's juices. We may not enjoy the luxury of an end by slow stewing. Half-a-dozen countries now possess the means for bringing us all to a quick end, and still other countries are eagerly seeking to acquire those means. The wisdom of some past leaders of bomb-possessing nations, or of some present leaders of bomb-seeking nations, doesn't encourage us to believe that there will be radios on Earth for much longer.

It was an extremely unlikely fluke that we developed radios at all, and more of a fluke that we developed them before we developed the technology that could end us in a slow stew or fast bang. While Earth's history thus offers little hope that radio civilizations exist elsewhere, it also suggests that any that might exist are short-lived. Other intelligent civilizations that rose elsewhere probably reversed their own progress overnight, just as we now risk doing.

We're very lucky that that's so. I find it mind-boggling that the astronomers now eager to spend a hundred million dollars on the search for extraterrestrial life have never thought seriously about the most obvious question: what would happen if we found it, or if it found us. The astronomers tacitly assume that we and the little green monsters would welcome each other and settle down to fascinating conversations. Here again, our own experience on Earth offers useful guidance. We've already discovered two species that are very intelligent but technically less advanced than we are—the common chimpanzee and pygmy chimpanzee. Has our response been to sit down and try to communicate with them? Of course not. Instead we shoot them, dissect them, cut off their hands for trophies, put them on exhibit in cages, inject them with AIDS virus as a medical experiment, and destroy or take over their habitats. That response was predictable, because human explorers who discovered technically less advanced humans also regularly responded by shooting them, decimating their populations with new diseases, and destroying or taking over their habitats.

Any advanced extraterrestrials who discovered us would surely treat us in the same way. Think again of those astronomers who beamed radio signals into Space from Arecibo, describing Earth's location and its inhabitants. In its suicidal folly that act rivaled the folly of the last Inca emperor, Atahualpa, who described to his gold-crazy Spanish captors the wealth of his capital and provided them with guides for the journey. If there really are any radio civilizations within listening distance of us, then for heaven's sake let's turn off our own transmitters and try to escape detection, or we're doomed.

Fortunately for us, the silence from Outer Space is deafening. Yes, out there are billions of galaxies with billions of stars. Out there must be some transmitters as well, but not many, and they won't last long. Probably there are no others in our galaxy, and surely none within hundreds of light-years of us. What woodpeckers teach us about flying saucers is that we're unlikely ever to see one. For practical purposes, we're unique and alone in a crowded universe. Thank God!

PART FOUR

WORLD
CONQUERORS

Part Three discussed some of our cultural hallmarks and their animal precedents or precursors. Those cultural hallmarks—especially language, agriculture, and advanced technology—have been the causes of our rise. They are what permitted us to expand over the globe and become world conquerors.

That expansion, though, didn't just consist of our conquering areas previously unoccupied by the human species. It also involved the expansion of particular human populations that conquered, expelled, or killed other populations. We became conquerors of each other, as well as of the world. Thus, our expansion has been marked by yet another human hallmark that has animal precursors and that we've taken far beyond its animal limits—namely, our propensity to kill other members of our species en masse. Along with our environmental destructiveness, it now poses one of the two potential reasons that we may fall.

To appreciate our rise to the status of world conquerors, recall that most animal species are distributed over only a small part of the Earth's surface. For example, Hamilton's frog is confined to one forest patch of 37 acres plus one rock pile covering 720 square yards in New Zealand. The most widespread wild land mammal other than humans used to be the lion, which as of ten thousand years ago occupied most of Africa, much of Eurasia, and North plus northern South America. Even at that time of its greatest extent, though, the lion didn't reach Southeast Asia, Australia, southern South America, polar regions, or islands.

Humans used to have a typically mammalian restricted distribution, in warm, nonforested areas of Africa. As recently as fifty thousand years ago, we were still confined to tropical and mild-temperature areas of Africa and Eurasia. Then we expanded in turn to Australia and New Guinea (around fifty thousand years ago), cold parts of Europe (by thirty thousand years ago), Siberia (by twenty thousand years ago), North and South America (around eleven thousand years ago), and Polynesia (between thirty-six hundred and one thousand years ago). Today we occupy or at least visit not only all lands but also the surface of all the oceans, and we are starting to probe into Space and the oceans' abysses.

In the process of this world conquest, our species underwent a basic change in the relation among its populations. Most animal species with sufficiently wide geographic ranges fall into populations in contact with neighboring populations but not with distant ones. In this respect, too, humans used to be just another species of big mammal. Until relatively recently, most people spent their entire lives within a few dozen miles of their birthplaces, and had no way of learning even of the existence of people living at much greater distances. Relations between neighboring tribes were marked by an uneasy shifting balance between trade and xenophobic hostility.

This fragmentation promoted, and was reinforced by, the tendency for each human population to develop its own language and culture. Initially, the massive expansion of our species' geographic range involved a massive increase in our linguistic and cultural diversity. Among the "new" parts of our range occupied only within the last fifty thousand years, New Guinea and North and South America alone came to account for about half of the modern world's languages. But much of that long heritage of cultural diversity has been erased in the last five thousand years by the expansion of centralized political states. Freedom of travel—a modern invention—is now accelerating that homogenization of our language and culture. However, in a few areas of the world, notably New Guinea, Stone Age technology and our traditional xenophobic outlook persisted into the twentieth century, giving us a last glimpse of what the rest of the world used to be like.

The outcome of conflicts between expanding human groups has been heavily influenced by group differences in our cultural hallmarks. Especially decisive have been differences in military and maritime technology, in political organization, and in agriculture. Groups with more advanced agriculture thereby acquired the military advantage of larger population numbers, ability to support a permanent military caste, and resistance to infectious diseases against which sparser populations had evolved no defense.

All those cultural differences used to be ascribed to genetic superiority of conquering "advanced" peoples over conquered "primitive" ones. However, no evidence of such genetic superiority has been forthcoming. The likelihood of genetics' playing such a role is refuted by the ease with which the most dissimilar human groups have mastered each other's cultural techniques, given adequate learning opportunities. New Guineans born of Stone Age parents now pilot airplanes, while Amundsen and his Norwegian crew mastered Eskimo dog-sledding methods to reach the South Pole.

Instead, one has to ask why some people acquired the cultural advantages that let them conquer other people, despite lack of any evident genetic advantages. For example, was it purely by chance that Bantu peoples originating from equatorial Africa displaced Khoisan people over most of southern Africa, rather than vice versa? While we can't expect to identify ultimate environmental factors behind small-scale conquests, chance is likely to play less of a role and ultimate factors to be more compelling if we focus on large-scale population shifts over long times. Hence two chapters will examine two of the largest-scale shifts in recent history: the modern expansion of Europeans over the New World and Australia; and the perennial puzzle of how Indo-European languages managed earlier to overrun so much of Eurasia from an initially restricted homeland. We'll see clearly in the former case, and more speculatively in the latter, how each human society's culture and competitive position have been shaped by its biological and geographical heritage, especially by the plant and animal species available to it for domestication.

Competition among members of the same species isn't unique to humans. Among all animal species as well, the closest competitors are inevitably members of the same species, because they share the closest ecological similarity. What varies greatly among species is the form that competitive strife takes. In the most inconspicuous form, rival animals compete merely by consuming food potentially available to each other and exhibit no overt aggression. Mild escalation involves ritualized displays, or chasing. As a last resort, now documented in many species, rival animals kill each other.

The competing units also vary greatly among animal species. In most songbirds, such as American or European robins, individual males or else male-female pairs face off. Among lions and common chimpanzees, small groups of males who may be brothers fight, sometimes unto death. Packs of wolves or hyenas do battle, while ant colonies engage in large-scale wars with other colonies. Although for some species these contests may end in deaths, there is no animal species whose survival as a species is even remotely threatened by such deaths.

Humans compete with each other for territory, as do members of most animal species. Because we live in groups, much of our competition has taken the form of wars between adjacent groups, on the model of the wars between ant colonies rather than the small-scale contests between robins. As with adjacent groups of wolves and common chimps, relations of adjacent human tribes were traditionally marked by xenophobic hostility, intermittently relaxed to permit exchanges of mates (and, in our species, of goods as well). Xenophobia comes especially naturally to our species, because so much of our behavior is culturally rather than genetically specified, and because cultural differences among human populations are so marked. Those features make it easy for us, unlike wolves and chimps, to recognize members of other groups at a glance by their clothes or hair style.

What makes human xenophobia much more lethal than chimp xenophobia is of course our recent development of weapons for mass killing at a distance. While Jane Goodall described males of one group of common chimps gradually killing off individuals of the neighboring group and usurping their territory, those chimps had no means to kill chimps of a remote group, or to exterminate all chimps (including themselves). Thus, xenophobic murder has innumerable animal precursors, but only we have developed it to the point of threatening to bring about our fall as a species. Threatening our own existence has now joined art and language as a human hallmark. This section of the book will conclude by surveying the history of human genocide, to make clear the ugly tradition from which Dachau's ovens and modern nuclear warfare spring.

CHAPTER 13

The Last
First Contacts

On August 4, 1938, a biological exploring expedition from the American Museum of Natural History made a discovery that hastened toward its end a long phase of human history. That was the date on which the advance patrol of the Third Archbold Expedition (named after its leader, Richard Archbold) became the first outsiders to enter the Grand Valley of the Balim River, in the supposedly uninhabited interior of west New Guinea. To everyone's astonishment, the Grand Valley proved to be densely populated—by fifty thousand Papuans, living in the Stone Age, previously unknown to the rest of humanity and themselves unaware of others' existence. In search of undiscovered birds and mammals, Archbold had found an undiscovered human society.

To appreciate the significance of Archbold's finding, we need to understand the phenomenon of "first contact." As I mentioned earlier, most animal species occupy a geographic range confined to a small fraction of the Earth's surface. Of those species (like lions and grizzly bears) occurring on several continents, it's not the case that individuals from one continent visit one another. Instead, each continent, and usually each small part of a continent, has its own distinctive population, in contact with close neighbors but not with distant members of the same species. (Migratory songbirds constitute only apparently a glaring exception. Yes, they do commute seasonally between continents, but along a traditional path, and both the summer breeding range and the winter nonbreeding range of a given population tend to be quite circumscribed).

This geographic fidelity of animals is reflected in their geographic variability: populations of the same species in different geographic areas tend to evolve into different-looking subspecies, because most breeding remains within the same population. For example, no gorilla of the East African lowland species has ever turned up in West Africa or vice versa, though the eastern and western subspecies look sufficiently different for biologists to recognize a wanderer if there were any.

In these respects, we humans have been typical animals throughout most of our evolutionary history. Like other animals, each human population is genetically molded to its area's climate and diseases. But human populations are also impeded from freely mixing by linguistic and cultural barriers far stronger than in other animals. An anthropologist can identify from a person's naked appearance roughly where that person originated, and a linguist or student of dress styles can pinpoint origins much more closely. That's testimony to how sedentary human populations have been.

While we think of ourselves as travelers, we were quite the opposite throughout several million years of human evolution. Every human group was ignorant of the world beyond its own lands and those of its immediate neighbors. Only in recent millennia did changes in political organization and technology permit some people routinely to travel afar, to encounter distant peoples, and to learn firsthand about places and peoples that they had not personally visited. This process accelerated with Columbus's voyage of 1492, until today there remain only a few tribes in New Guinea and South America still awaiting first contact with remote outsiders. The Archbold Expedition's entry into the Grand Valley will be remembered as one of the last first contacts of a large human population. It was thus a landmark in the process by which humanity became transformed from thousands of tiny societies, collectively occupying only a fraction of the globe, to world conquerors with world knowledge.

How could such a numerous people as the Grand Valley's fifty thousand Papuans remain completely unknown to outsiders until 1938? How could those Papuans in turn remain completely ignorant of the outside world? How did first contact change human societies? I'll argue that this world before first contact—a world that is finally ending within our own generation—holds a key to the origins of human cultural diversity. As world conquerors, our species now numbers over five billion, compared to the mere ten million people who existed before the advent of agriculture. Ironically, though, our cultural diversity has plunged even as our numbers have soared.

To anyone who has not been to New Guinea, the long concealment of fifty thousand people there seems incomprehensible. After all, the Grand Valley lies only 115 miles from either New Guinea's north coast or south coast. Europeans discovered New Guinea in 1526, Dutch missionaries took up residence in 1852, and European colonial governments were established in 1884. Why did it take another fifty-four years longer to find the Grand Valley?

The answers—terrain, food, and porters—become obvious as soon as one sets foot in New Guinea and tries to walk away from an established trail. Swamps in the lowlands, endless series of knife-edge ridges in the mountains, and jungle that covers everything reduce one's progress to a few miles per day under the best conditions. On my 1983 expedition into the Kumawa Mountains, it took me and a team of twelve New Guineans two weeks to penetrate seven miles inland. But we had it easy, compared to the British Ornithologists' Union Jubilee Expedition. On January 4, 1910, they landed on New Guinea's coast and set off for the snow-capped mountains that they could see only a hundred miles inland. On February 12, 1911, they finally gave up and turned back, having covered less than half the distance (forty-five miles) in those thirteen months.

Compounding those terrain problems is the impossibility of living off the land, because of New Guinea's lack of big game animals. In lowland jungle the staple food plant of New Guineans is a tree called the sago palm, whose pith yields a substance with the consistency of rubber and the flavor of vomit. However, not even New Guineans can find enough wild foods to survive in the mountains. This problem was illustrated by a horrible sight on which the British explorer

Alexander Wollaston stumbled while descending a New Guinea jungle trail: the bodies of thirty recently dead New Guineans and two dying children, who had starved while trying to return from the lowlands to their mountain gardens without carrying enough provisions.

The paucity of wild foods in the jungle compels explorers going through uninhabited areas, or unable to count on obtaining food from native gardens, to bring their own rations. A porter can carry forty pounds, the weight of the food necessary to feed himself for about fourteen days. Thus, until the advent of planes made airdrops possible, all New Guinea expeditions that penetrated more than seven days' walk from the coast (fourteen days' round trip) did so by having teams of porters going back and forth, building up food depots inland. Here's a typical plan: fifty porters start from the coast with seven hundred man-days of food, deposit two hundred man-days' food five days inland, and return in another five days to the coast, having consumed the remaining five hundred man-days' food (fifty men times ten days) in the process. Then fifteen porters march to that first depot, pick up the cached two hundred man-days' food, deposit fifty man-days' food a further five days' march inland, and return to the first depot (reprovisioned in the meantime), having consumed the remaining hundred fifty man-days' food in the process. Then . . .

The expedition that came closest to discovering the Grand Valley before Archbold, the 1921–22 Kremer Expedition, used eight hundred porters, two hundred tons of food, and ten months of relaying to get four explorers inland to just beyond the Grand Valley. Unfortunately for Kremer, his route happened to pass a few miles west of the valley, whose existence he did not suspect because of intervening ridges and jungle.

Apart from these physical difficulties, the interior of New Guinea seemed to hold no attractions for missionaries or colonial governments, because it was believed to be virtually uninhabited. European explorers landing on the coast or rivers discovered many tribes in the lowlands living off sago and fish, but few people eking out an existence in the steep foothills. From either the north or south coast, the snow-capped Central Cordillera that forms New Guinea's backbone presents steep faces. It was assumed that the northern and southern faces met in a ridge. What remained invisible from the coasts was the existence of broad intermontane valleys, hidden behind those faces and suitable for agriculture.

For east New Guinea, the myth of an empty interior was shattered on May 26, 1930, when two Australian miners, Michael Leahy and Michael Dwyer, crossed a ridge of the Bismarck Mountains in search of gold, looked down at night on the valley beyond, and were alarmed to see countless dots of light: the cooking fires of thousands of people. For west New Guinea, the myth ended with Archbold's second survey flight on June 23, 1938. After hours of flying over jungle with few signs of humans, Archbold was astonished to spot the Grand Valley, looking like Holland: a cleared landscape devoid of jungle, neatly divided into small fields outlined by irrigation ditches, and with scattered hamlets. It took six more weeks before Archbold could establish camps at the nearest lake and river where his seaplane could land, and before patrols from those camps could reach the Grand Valley to make first contact with its inhabitants.

THAT'S WHY THE OUTSIDE WORLD didn't know of the Grand Valley till 1938. Why didn't the valley's inhabitants, now referred to as the Dani people, know of the outside world?

Part of the reason, of course, is the same logistic problems that faced the Kremer Expedition on its march inland, but in reverse. Yet those problems would be minor in areas of the world with gentler terrain and more wild foods than New Guinea, and thus they don't explain why all other human societies in the world also used to live in relative isolation. Instead, at this point we have to remind ourselves of a modern perspective that we take for granted. Our perspective didn't apply to New Guinea until very recently, and it didn't apply anywhere in the world ten thousand years ago.

Recall that the whole globe is now divided into political states, whose citizens enjoy more or less freedom to travel within the boundaries of their state and to visit other states. Anyone with the time, money, and desire can visit almost any country except for a few xenophobic holdouts, like North Korea. As a result, people and goods have diffused around the globe, and many items such as Coca-Cola are now available on every continent. I recall with embarrassment my visit in 1976 to a Pacific island called Rennell, whose isolated location, vertical sea cliffs without beaches, and fissured coral landscape had preserved its Polynesian culture unchanged until recently. Setting out at dawn from the coast, I plodded through jungle with not a trace of humans. When in the late afternoon I finally heard a woman's voice ahead and glimpsed a small hut, my head whirled with fantasies of the beautiful, unspoilt, grass-skirted, bare-breasted Polynesian maiden who awaited me at this remote site on this remote island. It was bad enough that the lady proved to be fat and with her husband. What humiliated my self-image as intrepid explorer was the University of Wisconsin sweatshirt that she wore.

In contrast, for all but the last ten thousand years of human history, unfettered travel was impossible, and diffusion of sweatshirts was very limited. Each village or band constituted a political unit, living in a perpetually shifting state of wars, truces, alliances, and trade with neighboring groups. Hence New Guinea highlanders spent their entire lives within ten miles of their birthplaces. They might occasionally enter lands bordering their village lands by stealth during a war raid, or by permission during a truce, but they had no social framework for travel beyond immediately neighboring lands. The notion of tolerating unrelated strangers was as unthinkable as the notion that any such stranger would dare appear.

Even today, the legacy of this no-trespassing mentality persists in many parts of the world. Whenever I go bird-watching in New Guinea, I take pains to stop at the nearest village to request permission to bird-watch on that village's land or rivers. On two occasions when I neglected that precaution (or asked permission at the wrong village) and proceeded to boat up a river, I found the river barred on my return by canoes of stone-throwing villagers, furious that I had violated their territory. When I was living among Elopi tribespeople in west New Guinea and wanted to cross the territory of the neighboring Fayu tribe to reach a nearby mountain, the Elopis explained to me matter-of-factly that the Fayus would kill me if I tried. From a New Guinea perspective, it seemed so perfectly natural and self-explanatory. Of course the Fayus will kill any trespasser; you surely don't think they're so stupid that they'd admit strangers to their territory? Strangers would just hunt their game animals, molest their women, introduce diseases, and reconnoiter the terrain in order to stage a raid later.

While most precontact peoples had trade relations with their neighbors, many thought they were the only humans in existence.

Perhaps the smoke of fires on the horizon, or an empty canoe floating past down a river did prove the existence of other people. But to venture out of one's territory to meet those humans, even if they lived only a few miles away, was equivalent to suicide. As one New Guinea highlander recalled his life before the first arrival of whites in 1930, "We had not seen far places. We knew only this side of the mountains. And we thought that we were the only living people."

Such isolation bred great genetic diversity. Each valley in New Guinea has not only its own language and culture, but also its own genetic abnormalities and local diseases. The first valley where I worked was the home of the Foré people, famous to science for their unique affliction with a fatal viral disease called "kuru," or laughing sickness, which accounted for over half of all deaths (especially among women) and left men outnumbering women three to one in some Foré villages. At Karimui, sixty miles to the west of the Foré area, kuru is completely unknown, and the people are instead afflicted with the world's highest incidence of leprosy. Still other tribes are unique in their high frequency of deaf mutes, or of male pseudo-hermaphrodites lacking penises, or of premature aging, or of delayed puberty.

Today we can picture areas of the globe that we haven't visited, from films and TV. We can read about them in books. English dictionaries exist for all the world's major languages, and most villages speaking minor languages still contain individuals who understand one of the world's major languages. For example, missionary linguists have studied literally hundreds of New Guinea and South American Indian languages in recent decades, and I have found some inhabitant speaking either Indonesian or Neo-Melanesian in every New Guinea village that I have visited, no matter how remote. Hence linguistic barriers no longer impede the worldwide flow of information. Almost every village in the world today has thereby obtained fairly direct accounts of the outside world and has yielded fairly direct accounts of itself.

In contrast, pre-contact peoples had no way to picture the outside world, or to learn about it directly. Information instead arrived via long chains of languages, with accuracy lost at each step—as in the children's game called "telephone," in which one child in a circle whispers a message to the next child, who in turn whispers it to his/her neighbor, until by the time the message is whispered back to the first child its meaning has become changed beyond recognition. As a result, New Guinea highlanders had no concept of the ocean a hundred miles distant, and knew nothing about the white men who had been prowling their coasts for several centuries. When highlanders tried to figure out why the first arriving white men wore trousers and belts, one theory was that the clothes served to conceal an enormously long penis coiled around the waist. Some Dani believed that a neighboring group of New Guineans munched grass and had their hands joined behind their back.

First-contact patrols had a traumatic effect that is difficult for those of us living in the modern world to imagine. Highlanders "discovered" by Michael Leahy in the 1930s, and interviewed fifty years later, still recalled perfectly where they were and what they were doing at that moment of first contact. Perhaps the closest parallel, to modern Americans and Europeans, is our recollection of one or two of the most important political events of our lives. Most Americans of my age recall that moment on December 7, 1941, when they heard of the Japanese attack on Pearl Harbor. We knew at once that our lives would be very different for years to come, as a result of the news. Yet even the impact of Pearl Harbor and of the resulting war on American society was minor, compared to the impact of a first-contact patrol on New Guinea highlanders. On that day, their world changed forever.

The patrols revolutionized the highlanders' material culture by bringing steel axes and matches, whose superiority over stone axes and fire drills was immediately obvious. The missionaries and government administrators who followed the patrols suppressed ingrained cultural practices like cannibalism, polygyny, homosexuality, and war. Other practices were discarded spontaneously by tribespeople themselves, in favor of new practices that they saw. But there was also a more profoundly unsettling revolution, in the highlanders' view of what comprised the universe. They and their neighbors were no longer the sole humans, with the sole way of life.

A book by Bob Connolly and Robin Anderson entitled *First Contact* poignantly relates that moment in the eastern highlands, as recalled in their old age by New Guineans and whites who met there as young adults or children in the 1930s. Terrified highlanders took the whites for returning ghosts, until the New Guineans dug up and scrutinized the whites' buried feces, sent terrified young girls to have sex with the intruders, and discovered that whites defecated and were men like themselves. Leahy wrote in his diaries that highlanders smelled bad, while at the same time the highlanders were finding the whites' smell strange and frightening. Leahy's obsession with gold was as bizarre to the highlanders as their obsession with their own form of wealth and currency—cowry shells—was to him. For the survivors of those Grand Valley Dani and Archbold Expedition members who met in 1938, such an account of first contact has yet to be written.

I SAID AT THE OUTSET that Archbold's entry into the Grand Valley was not only a watershed for the Dani, but also part of a watershed in human history. What difference did it make that all human groups used to live in relative isolation, awaiting first contact, while only a few such groups remain today? We can infer the answer by comparing those areas of the world where isolation ended long ago with those other areas where it persisted into modern times. We can also study the rapid changes that followed historical first contacts. These comparisons suggest that contact between distant peoples gradually obliterated much of the human cultural diversity that had arisen during millennia of isolation.

Take artistic diversity as one obvious example. Styles of sculpture, music, and dance used to vary greatly from village to village within New Guinea. Some villagers along the Sepik River and in the Asmat swamps produced carvings that are now world-famous because of their quality. But New Guinea villagers have been increasingly co-erced or seduced into abandoning their artistic traditions. When I visited an isolated tribelet of 578 people at Bomai in 1965, the missionary controlling the only store had just manipulated the people into burning all their art. Centuries of unique cultural development ("heathen artifacts," as the missionary put it) had thus been destroyed in one morning. On my first visit to remote New Guinea villages in 1964, I heard log drums and traditional songs; on my visits in the 1980s, I heard guitars, rock music, and battery-operated boom boxes. Anyone who has seen the Asmat carvings at New York's Metropolitan Museum of Art, or heard log drums played in antiphonal duet at breathtaking speed, can appreciate the enormous tragedy of post-contact loss of art.

232 JARED DIAMOND

There has been massive loss of languages as well. For example, Europe today has only about fifty languages, most of them belonging to a single language family (Indo-European). In contrast, New Guinea, with less than one-tenth of Europe's area and less than one-hundredth of its population, has about a thousand languages, many of them unrelated to any other known language in New Guinea or elsewhere! The average New Guinea language is spoken by a few thousand people living within a radius of ten miles. When I traveled sixty miles from Okapa to Karimui in New Guinea's eastern highlands, I passed through six languages, starting with Foré (a language with postpositions, like Finnish) and ending with Tudawhe (a language with alternative tones and nasalized vowels, like Chinese).

New Guinea shows linguists what the world used to be like, with each isolated tribe having its own language, until agriculture's rise permitted a few groups to expand and spread their tongue over large areas. It was only about six thousand years ago that the Indo-European expansion began, leading to the extermination of all prior western European languages except Basque. The Bantu expansion within the last few millennia similarly exterminated most other languages of tropical and sub-Saharan Africa, just as the Austronesian expansion did in Indonesia and the Philippines. In the New World alone, hundreds of American Indian languages have become extinct in recent centuries.

Isn't language loss a good thing, because fewer languages mean easier communication among the world's people? Perhaps, but it's a bad thing in other respects. Languages differ in structure and vocabulary, in how they express causation and feelings and personal responsibility, hence in how they shape our thoughts. There's no single-purpose "best" language: instead, different languages are better suited for different purposes. For instance, it may not have been an accident that Plato and Aristotle wrote in Greek, while Kant wrote in German. The grammatical particles of those two languages, plus their ease in forming compound words, may have helped make them the preeminent languages of western philosophy. Another example, familiar to all of us who studied Latin, is that highly inflected languages (ones in which word endings suffice to indicate sentence structure) can use variations of word order to convey nuances impossible with English. Our English word order is severely constrained by having to serve as the main clue to sentence structure. If English becomes a world language, that won't be because English was necessarily the best language for diplomacy.

The range of cultural practices in New Guinea also eclipses that within equivalent areas elsewhere in the modern world, because isolated tribes were able to live out social experiments that others would find utterly unacceptable. Forms of self-mutilation and cannibalism varied from tribe to tribe. At the time of first contact, some tribes went naked, others concealed their genitals and practiced extreme sexual prudery, and still others (including the Grand Valley Dani) flagrantly advertised the penis and testes with various props. Child-rearing practices ranged from extreme permissiveness (including freedom for Foré babies to grab hot objects and burn themselves), through punishment of misbehavior by rubbing a Baham child's face with stinging nettles, to extreme repression resulting in Kukukuku child suicide. Barua men pursued institutionalized bisexuality by living with the young boys in a large communal homosexual house, while each man had a separate small heterosexual house for his wife and daughters and infant sons. Tudawhes instead had two-story houses in which women, infants, unmarried girls, and pigs lived in the lower story, while men and unmarried boys lived in the upper story accessed by a separate ladder from the ground.

We wouldn't mourn the shrinking cultural diversity of the modern world if it only meant the end of self-mutilation and child suicide. But the societies whose cultural practices have now become dominant were selected just for economic and military success. Those qualities aren't necessarily the ones that foster happiness or promote long-term human survival. Our consumerism and our environmental exploitation serve us well at present but bode ill for the future. Features of American society that already rate as disasters in anyone's book include our treatment of old people, adolescent turmoil, abuse of psychotropic chemicals, and gross inequality. For each of these problem areas, there are (or were before first contact) many New Guinea societies that found far better solutions to the same issue.

UNFORTUNATELY, ALTERNATIVE MODELS of human society are rapidly disappearing, and the time has passed when humans could try out new models in isolation. Surely there are no remaining uncontacted populations anywhere as large as the one encountered by Archbold's patrol on that August day of 1938. When I worked on New Guinea's Rouffaer River in 1979, missionaries nearby had just found a tribe of four hundred nomads, who reported another uncontacted band five days' travel upstream. Small bands have also been turning up in remote parts of Peru and Brazil. But at some point within this last decade of the twentieth century, we can expect the last first contact, and the end of the last separate experiment at designing human society.

While that last first contact won't mean the end of human cultural diversity, much of which is proving capable of surviving television and travel, it certainly does mean a drastic reduction. That loss is to be mourned, for the reasons that I've just been discussing. But our xenophobia was tolerable only as long as our means to kill each other were too limited to bring about our fall as a species. When I try to think of reasons why nuclear weapons won't inexorably combine with our genocidal tendencies to break the records we've already set for genocide in the first half of the twentieth century, our accelerating cultural homogenization is one of the chief grounds for hope that I can identify. Loss of cultural diversity may be the price that we have to pay for survival.

CHAPTER 14

Accidental Conquerors

SOME OF THE MOST OBVIOUS FEATURES OF OUR DAILY LIVES POSE THE hardest questions for scientists. If you look around you in most locations in the United States or Australia, most of the people you see will be of European ancestry. At the same locations five hundred years ago, everyone without exception would have been an American Indian in the United States, a native (aboriginal) Australian in Australia. Why is it that Europeans came to replace most of the native population of North America and Australia, instead of Indians or native Australians coming to replace most of the original population of Europe?

This question can be rephrased to ask: Why was the ancient rate of technological and political development fastest in Eurasia, slower in the Americas (and in Africa south of the Sahara), and slowest in Australia? For example, in 1492 much of the population of Eurasia used iron tools, had writing and agriculture, had large centralized states with oceangoing ships, and was on the verge of industrialization. The Americas had agriculture, only a few large centralized states, writing in only one area, and no oceangoing ships or iron tools, and they were technologically and politically a few thousand years behind Eurasia. Australia lacked agriculture, writing, states, and ships, was still in a pre-first-contact condition, and used stone tools comparable to ones made over ten thousand years earlier in Eurasia. It was those technological and political differences—not the biological differences determining the outcome of competition among animal populations—that permitted Europeans to expand to other continents.

Nineteenth-century Europeans had a simple, racist answer to such questions. They concluded that they acquired their cultural head start through being inherently more intelligent, and that they therefore had a manifest destiny to conquer, displace, or kill "inferior" peoples. The trouble with this answer is that it is not just loathsome and arrogant, but also wrong. It's obvious that people differ enormously in the knowledge they acquire, depending on their circumstances as they grow up. But no convincing evidence of genetic differences in mental ability among peoples has been found, despite much effort.

Because of this legacy of racist explanations, the whole subject of human differences in level of civilization still reeks of racism. Yet there are obvious reasons why the subject begs to be properly explained. Those technological differences led to great tragedies in the past five hundred years, and their legacies of colonialism and conquest still powerfully shape our world today. Until we can come up with a convincing alternative explanation, the suspicion that racist genetic theories might be true will linger.

In this chapter I'll argue that continental differences in level of civilization arose from geography's effect on the development of our cultural hallmarks, not from human genetics. Continents differed in the resources on which civilization depended—especially in the wild animal and plant species that proved useful for domestication. Continents also differed in the ease with which domesticated species could spread from one area to another. Even today, Americans and Europeans are painfully aware how distant geographical features, like the Persian Gulf or the Isthmus of Panama, affect our lives. But geography and biogeography have been molding human lives even more profoundly for hundreds of thousands of years.

Why do I emphasize plant and animal species? As the biologist J. B. S. Haldane remarked, "Civilization is based, not only on men, but on plants and animals." Agriculture and herding, though they also brought the disadvantages discussed in Chapter 10, still made it possible to feed far more people per square mile of land than could live on the wild foods available in that same area. Storable food surpluses grown by some individuals permitted other individuals to devote themselves to metallurgy, manufacturing, writing—and to serving in full-time professional armies. Domestic animals provided not only meat and milk to feed people, but also wool and hides to clothe people, and power to transport people and goods. Animals also provided power to pull plows and carts, and thus to increase agricultural productivity greatly over that previously attainable by human muscle power alone.

As a result, the world's human population rose from about ten million around 10,000 B.C., when we were all still hunter-gatherers, to over five billion today. Dense populations were prerequisite to the rise of centralized states. Dense populations also promoted the evolution of infectious diseases, to which exposed populations then evolved some resistance but other populations didn't. All these factors determined who colonized and conquered whom. Europeans' conquest of America and Australia was due not to their better genes but to their worse germs (especially smallpox), more advanced technology (including weapons and ships), information storage through writing, and political organization—all stemming ultimately from continental differences in geography.

LET'S START WITH THE DIFFERENCES in domestic animals. By around 4000 B.C. west Eurasia already had its "Big Five" domestic livestock that continue to dominate today: sheep, goats, pigs, cows, and horses. East Asians domesticated four other cattle species that locally replace cows: yaks, water buffalo, gaur, and banteng. As already mentioned, these animals provided food, power, and clothing, while the horse was also of incalculable military value. (It was the tank, the truck, and the jeep of warfare until the nineteenth century.) Why didn't American Indians reap similar benefits by domesticating the corresponding native American mammal species: mountain sheep, mountain goats, peccaries, bison, and tapirs? Why didn't Indians mounted on tapirs, and native Australians mounted on kangaroos, invade and terrorize Eurasia?

The answer is that, even today, it has proved possible to domesticate only a tiny fraction of the world's wild mammal species. This becomes clear when one considers all the attempts that failed. Innumerable species reached the necessary first step of being kept captive as tame pets. In New Guinea villages I routinely find tamed possums and kangaroos, while I saw tamed monkeys and weasels in Amazonian Indian villages. Ancient Egyptians tamed gazelles, antelopes, cranes, and even hyenas and possibly giraffes. Romans were terrorized by the tamed African elephants with which Hannibal crossed the Alps (*not* Asian elephants, the tame elephant species in circuses today).

But all these incipient efforts at domestication failed. Domestication requires not just capturing individual wild animals and taming them, but getting them to breed in captivity and modifying them through selective breeding so as to be more useful to us. Since the domestication of horses around 4000 B.C. and reindeer a few thousand years later, no large European mammal has been added to our repertoire of successful domesticates. Thus, our few modern species of domestic mammals were quickly winnowed from hundreds of others that had been tried and abandoned.

Why have efforts at domesticating most animal species failed? It turns out that a wild animal must possess a whole suite of unusual characteristics for domestication to succeed. First, in most cases it must be a social species living in herds. A herd's subordinate individuals have instinctive submissive behaviors that they display toward dominant individuals, and that they can transfer toward humans. Asian mouflon sheep (the ancestors of domestic sheep) have such behaviors but North American bighorn sheep do not—a crucial difference that prevented Indians from domesticating the latter. Except for cats and ferrets, solitary territorial species have not been domesticated.

Second, species such as gazelles and many deer and antelopes, which instantly take flight at signs of danger instead of standing their ground, prove too nervous to manage. Our failure to domesticate deer is especially striking, since there are few other wild animals with which humans have been so closely associated for tens of thousands of years. Although deer have always been intensively hunted and often tamed, reindeer alone among the world's forty-one deer species were successfully domesticated. Territorial behavior, flight reflexes, or both eliminated the other forty species as candidates. Only reindeer had the necessary tolerance of intruders and gregarious, nonterritorial behavior.

Finally, as zoos often discover to their dismay, captive animals that are docile and healthy may nevertheless refuse to breed in cages. You yourself wouldn't want to carry out a lengthy courtship and copulate under the watchful eyes of others; many animals don't want to either. This problem of getting captive animals to breed has derailed persistent attempts to domesticate some potentially very valuable animals. For example, the finest wool in the world comes from the vicuña, a small camel species native to the Andes. But neither the Incas nor modern ranchers have ever been able to domesticate it, and wool must still be obtained by capturing wild vicuñas. Princes from ancient Assyrian kings to nineteenth-century Indian maharajahs have tamed cheetahs, the world's swiftest land mammals, for hunting. But every prince's cheetah had to be captured from the wild, and not even zoos were able to breed them until 1960.

Collectively, these reasons help explain why Eurasians succeeded in domesticating the Big Five but not other closely related species, and why American Indians did not domesticate bison, peccaries, tapirs, and mountain sheep or goats. The military value of the horse is especially interesting in illustrating what seemingly slight differences make one species uniquely prized, another useless. Horses belong to the order of mammals termed Perissodactyla, which consists of the hoofed mammals with an odd number of toes: horses, tapirs, and rhinoceroses. Of the seventeen living species of Perissodactyla, all four tapirs and all five rhinos, plus five of the eight wild horse species, have never been domesticated. Africans or Indians mounted on rhinos or tapirs would have trampled any European invaders, but it never happened.

A sixth wild horse relative, the wild ass of Africa, gave rise to domestic donkeys, which proved splendid as pack animals but useless as military chargers. The seventh wild horse relative, the onager of western Asia, may have been used to pull wagons for some centuries after 3000 B.C. But all accounts of the onager blast its vile disposition with adjectives like "bad-tempered," "irascible," "unapproachable," "unchangeable," and "inherently intractable." The vicious beasts had to be kept muzzled to prevent them from biting their attendants. When domesticated horses reached the Middle East around 2300 B.C., onagers were finally kicked onto the scrap heap of failed domesticates.

Horses revolutionized warfare in a way that no other animal, not even elephants or camels, ever rivaled. Soon after their domestication, they may have enabled herdsmen speaking the first Indo-European languages to begin the expansion that would eventually stamp their languages on much of the world. A few millennia later, hitched to battle chariots, horses became the unstoppable Sherman tanks of ancient war. After the invention of saddles and stirrups, they enabled Attila the Hun to devastate the Roman Empire, Genghis Khan to conquer an empire from Russia to China, and military kingdoms to arise in West Africa. A few dozen horses helped Cortés and Pizarro, leading only a few hundred Spaniards each, to overthrow the two most populous and advanced New World states, the Aztec and Inca empires. With futile Polish cavalry charges against Hitler's invading armies in September 1939, the military importance of this most universally prized of all domestic animals finally came to an end after six thousand years.

Ironically, relatives of the horses that Cortés and Pizarro rode had formerly been native to the New World. Had those horses survived, Montezuma and Atahualpa might have shattered the conquistadores with cavalry charges of their own. But, in a cruel twist of fate, America's horses had become extinct long before that, along with 80 or 90 percent of the other large animal species of the Americas and Australia. It happened around the time that the first human settlers— ancestors of modern Indians and native Australians—reached those continents. The Americas lost not only their horses but also other potentially domesticable species like large camels, ground sloths, and elephants. Australia and North America ended up with no domesticable mammal species at all, unless Indian dogs were derived from North American wolves. South America was left with only the guinea pig (used for food), alpaca (used for wool), and llama (used as a pack animal, but too small to carry a rider).

As a result, domestic mammals made no contribution to the protein needs of native Australians and Americans except in the Andes, where their contribution was still much slighter than in the Old World. No native American or Australian mammal ever pulled a plough, cart, or war chariot, gave milk, or bore a rider. The civilizations of the New World limped forward on human muscle power alone, while those of the Old World ran on the power of animal muscle, wind, and water.

Scientists still debate whether the prehistoric extinctions of most large American and Australian mammals were due to climatic factors or were caused by the first human settlers themselves. Whichever was the case, the extinctions may have virtually ensured that the descendants of those first settlers would be conquered over ten thousand years later by people from Eurasia and Africa, the continents that retained most of their large mammal species.

Do similar arguments apply to plants? Some parallels jump out immediately. As true of animals, only a tiny fraction of all wild plant species have proved suitable for domestication. For example, plant species in which a single hermaphroditic individual can pollinate itself (like wheat) were domesticated earlier and more easily than cross-pollinated species (like rye). The reason is that self-pollinating varieties are easier to select and then maintain as true strains, since they're not continually mixing with their wild relatives. As another example, although acorns of many oak species were a major food source in prehistoric Europe and North America, no oak has ever been domesticated, perhaps because squirrels remained much better than humans at selecting and planting acorns. For every domesticated plant that we still use today, many others were tried in the past and discarded. (What living American has eaten sumpweed, which Indians in the eastern United States domesticated for its seeds by around 2000 B.C.?).

Such considerations help explain the slow rate of human technological development in Australia. That continent's relative poverty in wild plants appropriate for domestication, as in appropriate wild animals, undoubtedly contributed to the failure of aboriginal Australians to develop agriculture. But it's not so obvious why agriculture in the Americas lagged behind that in the Old World. After all, many food plants now of worldwide importance were domesticated in the New World: corn, potatoes, tomatoes, and squash, to name just a few. The answer to this puzzle requires closer scrutiny of corn, the New World's most important crop.

Corn is a cereal—i.e., a grass with edible starchy seeds, like barley kernels or wheat grains. Cereals still provide most of the calories consumed by the human race. While all civilizations have depended on cereals, different native cereals have been domesticated by different civilizations: e.g., wheat, barley, oats, and rye in the Near East and Europe; rice, foxtail millet, and broomcorn millet in China and southeast Asia; sorghum, pearl millet, and finger millet in sub-Saharan Africa; but only corn in the New World. Soon after Columbus discovered America, corn was taken back to Europe by early explorers and spread around the globe, so that it now exceeds all other crops except wheat in world acreage planted. Why, then, didn't corn enable American Indian civilizations to develop as fast as the Old World civilizations fed by wheat and other cereals?

It turns out that corn was a much bigger pain in the neck to domesticate and grow, and gave an inferior product. Those will be fighting words to all of you who, like me, love hot buttered corn-on-the-cob. Throughout my childhood, I looked forward to late summer as the season to stop at roadside stands and pick out the best-looking fresh ears. Corn is the most important crop in the United States today, worth $22 billion to us and $50 billion to the world. But before you charge me with slander, please hear me out on the differences between corn and other cereals.

The Old World had over a dozen wild grasses that were easy to domesticate and grow. Their large seeds, favored by the Near East's highly seasonal climate, made their value obvious to incipient farmers. They were easy to harvest en masse with a sickle, easy to grind, easy to prepare for cooking, and easy to sow. Another subtle advantage was first recognized by University of Wisconsin botanist Hugh Iltis: we didn't have to figure out for ourselves that they could be stored, since wild rodents in the Near East already made caches of up to sixty pounds of those wild grass seeds.

The Old World grains were already productive in the wild: one can still harvest up to seven hundred pounds of grain per acre from wild wheat growing naturally on hillsides in the Near East. In a few weeks a family could harvest enough to feed itself for a year. Hence even before wheat and barley were domesticated, there were sedentary villages in Palestine that had already invented sickles, mortars and pestles, and storage pits, and that were supporting themselves on wild grains.

Domestication of wheat and barley wasn't a conscious act. It wasn't the case that several hunter-gatherers sat down one day, mourned the extinction of big game animals, discussed which particular wheat plants were best, planted the seeds of those plants, and thereby became farmers the next year. Instead, the process we call plant domestication—the changes in wild plants under cultivation—was an unintended by-product of people's preferring some wild plants over others, and hence accidentally spreading seeds of the preferred plants. In the case of wild cereals, people naturally preferred to harvest those with big seeds, those whose seeds were easy to remove from the seed coverings, and those with firm nonshattering stalks that held all the seeds together. It took only a few mutations, favored by this unconscious human selection, to produce the large-seeded, nonshattering cereal varieties that we refer to as domesticated rather than wild.

By around 8000 B.C., wheat and barley remains from archaeological digs at ancient Near Eastern village sites are beginning to show these changes. The development of bread wheats, other domestic varieties, and intentional sowing soon followed. Gradually, fewer remains of wild foods are found at the sites. By 6000 B.C., crop cultivation had been integrated with animal herding into a complete food-production system in the Near East. For better or worse, people were no longer hunter-gatherers but farmers and herders, en route to being civilized.

Now contrast these relatively straightforward Old World developments with what happened in the New World. Because the parts of the Americas where farming began lacked the Near East's highly seasonal climate, they lacked large-seeded grasses that were already productive in the wild. North American and Mexican Indians did start to domesticate three small-seeded wild grasses—maygrass, little barley, and a wild millet—but these were displaced by the arrival of corn and then of European cereals. Instead, the ancestor of corn was a Mexican wild grass that did have the advantage of big seeds but in other respects hardly seemed like a promising food plant: annual teosinte.

Teosinte ears look so different from corn ears that scientists argued about teosinte's precise role in corn's ancestry till recently, and even now some scientists remain unconvinced. No other crop underwent such drastic changes on domestication as did teosinte. It has only six to twelve kernels per ear, and they are inedible, because they're enclosed in stone-hard cases. One can chew teosinte stalks like sugar cane, as Mexican farmers still do. But no one uses its seeds today, and there is no indication that anyone did prehistorically either.

Hugh Iltis identified the key step in teosinte's becoming useful: a permanent sex change! In teosinte the side branches end in tassels composed of male flowers; in corn they end in female structures, the ears. Although that sounds like a drastic difference, it's really a simple hormonally controlled change that could have been started by a fungus, virus, or change in climate. Once some flowers on the tassel had changed sex to female, they would have produced edible naked grains likely to catch the attention of hungry hunter-gatherers. The tassel's central branch would then have been the beginning of a corncob. Early Mexican archaeological sites have yielded remains of tiny ears, barely an inch and a half long and much like the tiny ears of our Tom Thumb corn variety.

With that abrupt sex change, teosinte (alias corn) was now finally on the road to domestication. However, in contrast to the case with Near Eastern cereals, thousands of years of development still lay ahead before high-yield corns capable of sustaining villages or cities resulted. The final product was still much more difficult for Indian farmers to manage than were the cereals of Old World farmers. Corn ears had to be harvested individually by hand, rather than en masse with a sickle; the cobs had to be shucked; the kernels didn't fall off but had to be scraped or bitten off; and sowing the seeds involved planting them individually, rather than scattering them en masse. And the result was still poorer nutritionally than Old World cereals: lower protein content, deficiencies of nutritionally important amino acids, deficiency of the vitamin niacin (tending to cause the disease pellagra), and need for alkali treatment of the grain to partially overcome these deficiencies.

In short, characteristics of the New World's staple food crop made its potential value much harder to discern in the wild plant, harder to develop by domestication, and harder to extract even after domestication. Much of the lag between New World and Old World civilization may have been due to those peculiarities of one plant.

So FAR, I've discussed geography's biogeographic role in providing the local wild animal and plant species suitable for domestication. But there's another major role of geography that deserves mention. Each civilization has depended not only on its own food plants domesticated locally, but also on other food plants that arrived after having been first domesticated elsewhere. The predominantly north-south axis of the New World made such diffusion of food plants difficult; the predominantly east-west axis of the Old World made it easy (see Figure 6).

Today, we take plant diffusion so much for granted that we seldom stop to think where our foods originated. A typical American or European meal might consist of chicken (of Southeast Asian origin) with corn (from Mexico) or potatoes (from the southern Andes), seasoned with pepper (from India), accompanied by a piece of bread (from Near Eastern wheat) and butter (from Near Eastern cattle), and washed down by a cup of coffee (from Ethiopia). But this diffusion of valued plants and animals didn't begin just in modern times: it has been happening for thousands of years.

Plants and animals spread quickly and easily within a climate zone to which they're already adapted. To spread out of this zone, they have to develop new varieties with different climate tolerances. A glance at the map of the Old World in Figure 6 shows how species could shift long distances without encountering a change of climate. Many of these shifts proved enormously important in launching farming or herding in new areas, or enriching it in old areas. Species

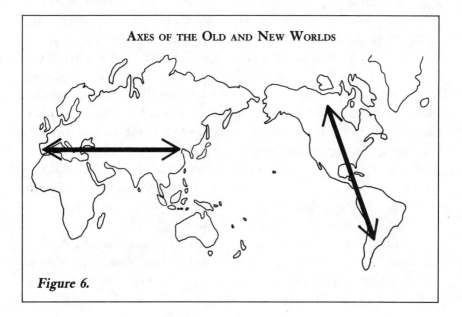

AXES OF THE OLD AND NEW WORLDS

Figure 6.

moved between China, India, the Near East, and Europe without ever leaving temperate latitudes of the northern hemisphere. Ironically, the U.S. patriotic song "America the Beautiful" invokes America's own spacious skies, its amber waves of grain. In reality, the most spacious skies of the northern hemisphere are in the Old World, where amber waves of related grains came to stretch for seven thousand miles from the English Channel to the China Sea.

The ancient Romans were already growing wheat and barley from the Near East, peaches and citrus fruits from China, cucumbers and sesame from India, and hemp and onions from central Asia, along with oats and poppies originating locally in Europe. Horses that spread from the Near East to West Africa revolutionized military tactics there, while sheep and cattle spread down from the highlands of East Africa to launch herding in southern Africa among the Hottentots, who lacked locally domesticated animals of their own. African sorghum and cotton reached India by around 2000 B.C., while bananas and yams from tropical Southeast Asia crossed the Indian Ocean to enrich agriculture in tropical Africa.

In the New World, however, the temperate zone of North America is isolated from the temperate zone of the Andes and southern South America by thousands of miles of tropics, in which temperate-zone species can't survive. As a result, the llama, alpaca, and guinea pig of the Andes never spread in prehistoric times to North America or even to Mexico, which consequently remained without any domestic mammals to carry packs or to produce wool or meat (except for corn-fed edible dogs). Potatoes as well failed to spread from the Andes to Mexico or North America, while sunflowers never spread from North America to the Andes. Many crops that were apparently shared prehistorically between North and South America actually occurred as different varieties or even species in the two continents, suggesting that they were domesticated independently in both areas. This seems true, for instance, of cotton, beans, lima beans, chili peppers, and tobacco. Corn did spread from Mexico to both North and South America, but it evidently wasn't easy, perhaps because of the time it took to develop varieties suited to other latitudes. Not until around A.D. 900—thousands of years after corn had emerged in Mexico—did corn become a staple food in the Mississippi Valley, thereby triggering the belated rise of the mysterious mound-building civilization of the American Midwest.

If the Old and New Worlds had each been rotated ninety degrees about their axes, the spread of crops and domestic animals would have been slower in the Old World, faster in the New World. The rates of rise of civilization would have been correspondingly different. Who knows whether that difference would have sufficed to let Montezuma or Atahualpa invade Europe, despite their lack of horses?

I'VE ARGUED, then, that continental differences in the rates of rise of civilization weren't an accident caused by a few individual geniuses. They weren't produced by the biological differences determining the outcome of competition among animal populations—e.g., some populations being able to run faster or digest food more efficiently than others. They also weren't the result of average differences among whole peoples in inventiveness; there is no evidence for such differences anyway. Instead, they were determined by biogeography's effect on cultural development. If Europe and Australia had exchanged their human populations twelve thousand years ago, it would have been the former native Australians, transplanted to Europe, who eventually invaded America and Australia from Europe.

Geography sets ground rules for the evolution, both biological and cultural, of all species, including our own. Geography's role in determining our modern political history is even more obvious than its role in determining the rate at which we domesticate plants and animals. From this perspective, it's almost funny to read that half of all American schoolchildren don't know where Panama is, but not at all funny when politicians display comparable ignorance. Among the many notorious examples of disasters brought on by politicians ignorant of geography, two must suffice: the unnatural boundaries drawn on the map of Africa by nineteenth-century European colonial powers, thereby undermining the stability of some modern African states that inherited those borders; and the borders of Eastern Europe drawn at the Treaty of Versailles in 1919 by politicians who knew little of that region, thereby helping fuel World War II.

Geography used to be a required subject in schools and colleges until a few decades ago, when it began to be dropped from many curricula. The mistaken belief arose then that geography consisted of little more than memorizing the names of capital cities. But twenty weeks of geography in the seventh grade isn't enough to teach our future politicians about the effects that maps really have on us. The fax machines and satellite communications that span the globe can't erase the differences among us bred by differences in location. In the long run, and on a broad scale, where we live has contributed heavily to making us who we are.

CHAPTER 15

Horses, Hittites,
and History

Y KSI, KAKSI, KOLME, NELJÄ, VIISI."

I watched the little girl counting out five marbles, one by one. Her act was familiar, but her words were strange. Almost anywhere else in Europe, I would have heard words like our English "one two three": "uno due tre" in Italy, "ein zwei drei" in Germany, "odin dva tri" in Russia. But I was vacationing in Finland, and Finnish is one of Europe's few non-Indo-European languages.

Today, most European languages and many Asian languages as far east as India are very similar to each other (see table of vocabulary on page 250). No matter how we complain while memorizing French word lists in school, these so-called "Indo-European" languages resemble English and each other, and differ from all the world's other languages, in vocabulary and grammar. Only 140 of the modern world's 5,000 tongues belong to this language family, but their importance is far out of proportion to their numbers. Thanks to the global expansion of Europeans since 1492—especially of people from England, Spain, Portugal, France, and Russia—nearly half the

Indo-European vs. non-Indo-European vocabulary

INDO-EUROPEAN LANGUAGES

English	one	two	three	mother	brother	sister
German	ein	zwei	drei	Mutter	Bruder	Schwester
French	un	deux	trois	mère	frère	soeur
Latin	unus	duo	tres	mater	frater	soror
Russian	odin	dva	tri	mat'	brat	sestra
Old Irish	oen	do	tri	mathir	brathir	siur
Tocharian	sas	wu	trey	macer	procer	ser
Lithuanian	vienas	du	trys	motina	brolis	seser
Sanskrit	eka	duva	trayas	matar	bhratar	svasar
PIE*	oynos	dwo	treyes	mater	bhrater	suesor

NON-INDO-EUROPEAN LANGUAGES

Finnish	yksi	kaksi	kolme	äiti	veli	sisar
Foré*	ka	tara	kakaga	nano	naganto	nanona

* PIE stands for Proto-Indo-European, the reconstructed mother tongue of the first Indo-Europeans. Foré is a language of the New Guinea Highlands. Note that most words are very similar among the Indo-European languages and totally different among the non-Indo-European languages.

world's present population of five billion now speak an Indo-European language as their native tongue.

To us it may seem perfectly natural, and in no need of further explanation, that most European languages resemble each other. Not until we go to parts of the world with great linguistic diversity do we realize how weird Europe's homogeneity is, and how it cries out for explanation. For example, in areas of the New Guinea highlands where I work and where first contact with the outside world began only in the twentieth century, languages as different as Chinese is from English replace each other over short distances. Eurasia as well must have been diverse in its pre-first-contact condition, and gradually became less so until finally some people speaking the mother tongue of the Indo-European language family steamrollered almost all other European languages out of existence.

Of all the processes by which the modern world lost its earlier linguistic diversity, the Indo-European expansion has been the most important. Its first stage, which long ago carried Indo-European languages over Europe and much of Asia, was followed by a second stage that began in 1492 and carried them to all other continents.

When and where did the steamroller start, and what gave it its power? Why wasn't Europe overrun instead by speakers of a language related to, say, Finnish or Assyrian?

While the Indo-European problem is the most famous problem of historical linguistics, it's a problem of archaeology and history as well. In the case of those Europeans who carried out the second stage of the Indo-European expansion, beginning in 1492, we know not only their vocabularies and grammars but also the ports from which they set out, the dates of their sailings, the names of their leaders, and why they succeeded in conquering. But the quest to understand the first stage is a search for an elusive people whose language and society lie veiled in the preliterate past, even though they became world conquerors and founded today's dominant societies. That quest is also a great detective story, whose solution depends on a language discovered behind a secret wall in a Buddhist monastery, and on an Italian language inexplicably preserved on the linen wrappings of an Egyptian mummy.

When you first think about it, you might be excused for dismissing the Indo-European problem as obviously insoluble. Since the Indo-European mother tongue arose before the origin of writing, isn't it almost by definition impossible to study? Even if we found the skeletons or pottery of the first Indo-Europeans, how would we recognize them? The skeletons and pottery of modern Hungarians, living in the center of Europe, are as typically European as goulash is typically Hungarian. A future archaeologist excavating a Hungarian city would never guess that Hungarians speak a non-Indo-European language, if no examples of writing itself were recovered. Even if we could somehow locate the place and time of the first Indo-Europeans, how could we hope to deduce what advantage let their language triumph?

Remarkably, it turns out that linguists have been able to extract answers to these questions from the languages themselves. I'll first explain why we are so confident that language distributions today reflect a steamroller in the past. Then I'll try to figure out when and where the mother tongue was spoken, and how it managed to take over so much of the world.

How can we infer that the modern Indo-European languages replaced other, now-vanished languages? I'm not talking about the observed second-stage replacements of the past five hundred years, which saw English and Spanish dislodge most native tongues of the Americas and Australia. Those modern expansions were obviously due to the advantages Europeans gained from guns, germs, iron, and political organization. Instead, I'm talking about the inferred first-stage replacement that saw Indo-European dislodge older languages of Europe and western Asia, and that must have happened before writing reached those areas.

The map in Figure 7 shows the distribution of Indo-European language branches surviving in 1492, just before Spanish began to leap across the Atlantic with Columbus. Three branches are especially familiar to most Europeans and Americans: Germanic (including English and German), Italic (including French and Spanish), and Slavic (including Russian), each branch with 12 to 16 surviving languages and 300 to 500 million speakers. The largest branch, however, is Indo-Iranian, with 90 languages and nearly 700 million speakers from Iran to India (including Romany, the language of Gypsies). Relatively tiny surviving branches are Greek, Albanian, Armenian, Baltic (consisting of Lithuanian and Latvian), and Celtic (including Welsh and Gaelic), each with only 2 to 10 million speakers. In addition, at least two Indo-European branches, Anatolian and Tocharian, vanished long ago but are known from extensive preserved writings, while others disappeared with fewer traces.

What proves that all these tongues are related to each other and distinct from other language stocks? One obvious clue is shared vocabulary, as illustrated by the word table on page 250 and thousands of other examples. A second clue is similar word endings (so-called inflectional endings) used to form verb conjugations and noun declensions. These endings are illustrated by part of the conjugation of "to be" on page 254. It becomes easier to recognize such similarities when you realize that word roots and endings shared between related languages are generally not shared identically. Instead, a particular sound in one language is often replaced by another sound in the other language. Familiar examples are the frequent equivalence of English "th" and German "d" (English "thing" = German "ding," "thank" = "danke"), or of English "s" and Spanish "es" (English "school" = "escuela," "stupid" = "estupido").

Those resemblances among the Indo-European languages are detailed, but much grosser features of sounds and word formation set

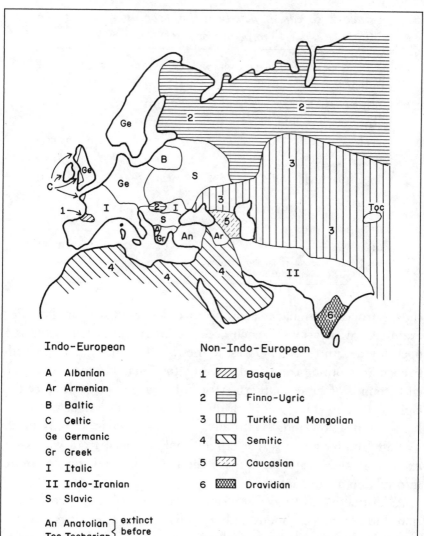

Figure 7. Language map of Europe and western Asia around 1492, just before the European discovery of the New World. There must have been other Indo-European language branches that had become extinct before then. However, the only ones for which we have long written texts are the Anatolian branch (including Hittite) and the Tocharian branch, whose homelands became occupied by speakers of Turkic and Mongolian languages before 1492.

Indo-European vs. non-Indo-European verb endings:
to be or not to be

INDO-EUROPEAN LANGUAGES

English	(I) am	(he) is
Gothic	im	ist
Latin	sum	est
Greek	eimi	esti
Sanskrit	asmi	asti
Old Church Slavonic	jesmi	jesti

NON-INDO-EUROPEAN LANGUAGES

Finnish	olen	on
Foré	miyuwe	miye

NOTE: Not just vocabulary but also verb and noun endings connect Indo-European languages and set them apart from other languages.

Indo-European languages apart from other language families. For example, my atrocious French accent embarrasses me as soon as I open my mouth to ask, "Où est le métro?" But my difficulties with French are nothing compared with my total inability to produce the click sounds of some southern African languages, or to produce the eight gradations of vowel pitch in the Lakes Plain languages of the New Guinea lowlands. Naturally, my Lakes Plain friends loved teaching me bird names that differed only in pitch from words for excrement, then watching me ask the next villager I met for more information about that "bird."

As distinctive to Indo-European as its sounds is its word formation. Indo-European nouns and verbs have various endings that we memorize assiduously when we learn a new language. (How many of you ex-scholars of Latin can still chant "amo amas amat amamus amatis amant"?) Each such ending conveys several types of information. For example, the "o" of "amo" specifies first person singular present active: the lover is I not my rival, one of me not two of me, I am giving not receiving love, and I am giving it now not yesterday. Heaven help the serenading lover who gets even a single one of those details wrong! But other languages, like Turkish, use a separate syllable or phoneme for each such type of information, while still other languages, like Vietnamese, virtually dispense with such variations of word form.

Given all these resemblances among Indo-European languages, how could the differences among them have arisen? A clue is that any language whose written documents span many centuries can be seen to change with time. For example, modern English-speakers find eighteenth-century English quaint but completely understandable; we can read Shakespeare (1564–1616), though we need notes to explain many of his words; but Old English texts, such as the poem *Beowulf* (around 700–750), are virtually a foreign language to us. (See example of the 23rd Psalm on page 275.) Hence, as speakers of one original language spread into different areas with limited contact, the independent changes of words and pronunciation in each area inevitably led to different dialects, such as those that have arisen in different parts of the U.S. in the few centuries since permanent English settlement began in 1607. With the passing of more centuries, dialects diverge to the point where their speakers can no longer understand each other and they now rank as distinct languages. One of the best-documented examples of this process is the development of the Romance languages from Latin. Surviving written texts from the eighth century onward show us how the languages of France, Italy, Spain, Portugal, and Rumania gradually diverged from Latin— and from each other.

The derivation of the modern Romance languages from Latin thus illustrates how groups of related languages develop from a shared ancestral tongue. Even if we had no surviving Latin texts, we could still reconstruct much of the Latin mother tongue by comparing traits in its daughter languages today. In the same way, one can reconstruct a family tree of all the Indo-European language branches, based partly on ancient texts and partly on inferences. Hence language evolution proceeds by descent and divergence, just as Darwin demonstrated for biological evolution. In their languages as well as their skeletons, modern Englishmen and Australians, who began to diverge with the colonization of Australia in 1788, are much more similar to each other than either are to the Chinese, from whom they diverged tens of thousands of years ago.

Given time, the languages within any part of the world will keep on diverging, held back only by contacts between adjacent peoples. An example of the end product is New Guinea, which had never been unified politically before European colonization, and where nearly one thousand mutually unintelligible languages—including dozens with no known relation to each other or to any other language in the world—are now spoken in an area the size of Texas. Thus, wherever you find the same language or related languages spoken over a wide area, you know that the clock of language evolution must have been restarted recently. That is, one language must have recently spread, eliminated other languages, and then started to differentiate all over again. Such a process accounts for the close similarities among southern Africa's Bantu languages, and among Austronesian languages of southeast Asia and the Pacific.

The Romance languages again provide our best-documented example. As of 500 B.C., Latin was confined to a small area around Rome and shared Italy with many other languages. The expansion of Latin-speaking Romans eradicated all those other languages of Italy, then eradicated entire branches of the Indo-European family elsewhere in Europe, like the continental Celtic languages. These sister branches were so thoroughly replaced by Latin that we know each of them only by scattered words, names, and inscriptions. With the subsequent overseas expansion of Spanish and Portuguese after 1492, the language spoken initially by a few hundred thousand Romans trampled hundreds of other languages out of existence, as it gave rise to the Romance languages spoken by half a billion people today.

If the Indo-European language family as a whole constituted a similar steamroller, we might expect to find trampled debris in the form of older non-Indo-European languages surviving here and there. The sole such vestige surviving in western Europe today is the Basque language of Spain, without known relations to any other language in the world. (The remaining non-Indo-European languages of modern Europe—Hungarian, Finnish, Estonian, and possibly Lapp—are relatively recent invaders of Europe from the east.) However, there were other languages spoken in Europe until Roman times, of which enough words or inscriptions have been preserved to identify them as non-Indo-European. The most extensively preserved of these vanished tongues is the mysterious Etruscan language of northwest Italy, for which we have a 281-line text written on a roll of linen that somehow ended up in Egypt as wrapping for a mummy. All such vanished non-Indo-European languages were part of the debris left from the Indo-European expansion.

Still more linguistic debris was swept up into the surviving Indo-

European languages themselves. To understand how linguists can recognize such debris, imagine that you, as a freshly arrived visitor from Outer Space, were given three books, one written in English by an Englishman, one by an American, and one by an Australian, about his or her country.

The language and most of the words in all three books would be the same. But if you compared the American book with the one about England, the American book would contain many place names that were obviously foreign to the basic language of the books—names like Massachusetts, Winnipesaukee, and Mississippi. The Australian book would contain more place names equally foreign to the language but unlike the American names—such as Woonarra, Goondiwindi, and Murrumbidgee. You might guess that English immigrants coming to America and Australia encountered natives who spoke different languages, and from whom the immigrants picked up names for local places and things. You'd even be able to infer something about the words and sounds of those unknown native languages. But we actually know the native American and Australian languages from which those borrowings took place, and we can confirm that your indirect inferences from the borrowed words alone would have been correct.

Linguists studying several Indo-European languages have similarly detected words borrowed from vanished, apparently non-Indo-European languages. For example, about one-sixth of Greek words whose derivations can be traced appear to be non-Indo-European. These words are just the sort that one might expect to have been borrowed by invading Greeks from the natives they encountered: place names like Corinth and Olympus, words for Greek crops like olive and vine, and names of gods or heroes like Athene and Odysseus. These words may be the linguistic legacy of Greece's pre-Indo-European population to the Greek speakers who overran them.

Thus, at least four types of evidence indicate that Indo-European languages are the products of an ancient steamroller. The evidence includes: the family-tree relationship of surviving Indo-European languages; the much greater linguistic diversity of areas like New Guinea that have not been recently overrun; the non-Indo-European languages that survived in Europe into Roman times or later; and the non-Indo-European legacy in several Indo-European languages.

* * *

GIVEN THIS EVIDENCE for an Indo-European mother tongue in the distant past, can one reconstruct something of this tongue? At first, the notion of learning how to write a vanished unwritten language seems absurd. In fact, linguists have been able to reconstruct much of the mother tongue by examining word roots shared among its daughter languages.

To take an example, if the word meaning "sheep" were totally different in each modern Indo-European language branch, we could conclude nothing about the word for "sheep" in the mother tongue. But if the word were similar in several branches, especially in ones as geographically distant as Indo-Iranian and Celtic, we might infer that the various branches had inherited the same root from the mother tongue. By knowing what sound shifts have taken place among the various daughter tongues, we could even reconstruct the form of the word root in the mother tongue.

As Figure 8 shows, the words for "sheep" in many Indo-European languages from India to Ireland really are very similar: "avis," "hawis," "ovis," "ois," "oi," etc. The modern English "sheep" is obviously from a different root, but English retains the original root in the word "ewe." Consideration of the sound shifts that the various Indo-European languages have undergone suggests that the original form was "owis."

Naturally, the same word root shared among several daughter languages doesn't automatically prove shared inheritance from the mother tongue. The word could also have spread later from one daughter language to another. Archaeologists skeptical of linguists' attempts to reconstruct mother tongues love to cite words like "coca-cola," shared among many modern European languages. The archaeologists claim that linguists would absurdly attribute "coca-cola" to the mother tongue of thousands of years ago. In fact, "coca-cola" illustrates how linguists distinguish recent borrowings from old inheritances: the word is obviously foreign ("coca" is actually from a Peruvian Indian word, "cola" West African); and it does not exhibit the same sound shifts among languages as do old Indo-European roots (in German it's still "Coca-Cola," not "Köcherköhler").

By such methods, linguists have been able to reconstruct much of the grammar and nearly two thousand word roots of the mother

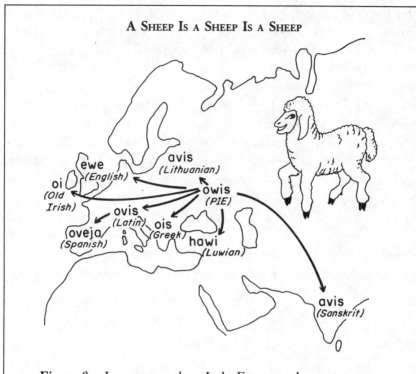

A SHEEP IS A SHEEP IS A SHEEP

Figure 8. In many modern Indo-European languages, as well as in some ancient ones that we know from preserved writings, the words meaning "sheep" are quite similar. These words must have been derived from an ancestral form that is inferred to have been "owis" and that was used in Proto-Indo-European (PIE), the unwritten mother tongue.

tongue, termed Proto-Indo-European but usually abbreviated as PIE. That's not to say that all words in modern Indo-European languages are descended from PIE: most are not, because there have been so many new inventions or borrowings (like the root "sheep" replacing the old PIE root "owis" in English). Our inherited PIE roots tend to be words for human universals that people surely were already naming thousands of years ago: words for the numbers and human relationships (as in the table on page 250); words for body parts and functions; and ubiquitous objects or concepts like "sky," "night," "summer," and "cold." Among the human universals thus reconstructed are such homely acts as "to break wind," with two distinct roots in PIE depending on whether one does it loudly or softly. The root for doing it loudly (PIE "perd") gave rise to a series of similar words in modern Indo-European languages ("perdet'," "pardate," etc.)—including English "fart" (see Figure 9).

So FAR, we've seen how linguists have been able to extract, from written languages, evidence of a preliterate mother tongue and steamroller. The obvious next questions are: when was PIE spoken, where was it spoken, and how was it able to overwhelm so many other languages? Let's begin with the matter of "when," another seemingly impossible question. It's bad enough that we have to infer the words of an unwritten language; how on earth do we determine when it was spoken?

HONORABLE ROOT, DISHONORABLE WORD

Figure 9. Just as in the case of words for "sheep," the words that mean "to fart loudly" are similar among many written Indo-European languages. This suggests an ancestral form inferred to have been "perd" and used in Proto-Indo-European (PIE), the unwritten mother tongue.

We can at least start to narrow down the possibilities by examining the oldest written samples of Indo-European languages. For a long time, the oldest samples that scholars could identify were Iranian texts of around 1000–800 B.C., and Sanskrit texts probably composed around 1200–1000 B.C. but written down later. Texts of a Mesopotamian kingdom called Mitanni, written in a non-Indo-European language but containing some words obviously borrowed from a language related to Sanskrit, push the proven existence of Sanskrit-like languages back to nearly 1500 B.C.

The next breakthrough was the late-nineteenth-century discovery of a mass of ancient Egyptian diplomatic correspondence. Most of it was written in a Semitic language, but two letters in an unknown language remained a mystery until excavations in Turkey uncovered thousands of tablets in the same tongue. The tablets proved to be the archives of a kingdom that thrived between 1650 and 1200 B.C. and that we now refer to by the biblical name "Hittite."

In 1917 scholars were astonished by the announcement that the Hittite language proved on deciphering to belong to a previously unknown, very distinctive and archaic, now-vanished branch of the Indo-European family, termed Anatolian. Some obviously Hittite-like names mentioned in earlier letters of Assyrian merchants at a trading post near the Hittite capital's future site push the detective trail back to nearly 1900 B.C. This remains our first direct evidence for the existence of any Indo-European language.

Thus, as of 1917, two Indo-European branches—Anatolian and Indo-Iranian—had been shown to exist by around 1900 and 1500 B.C., respectively. A third early branch was established in 1952, when the young British cryptographer Michael Ventris showed that ancient Crete's and Greece's so-called Linear B writing, which had resisted deciphering since its rediscovery around 1900, was an early form of the Greek language. Those Linear B tablets date to around 1300 B.C. But Hittite, Sanskrit, and early Greek are very different from each other, certainly more so than modern French and Spanish, which diverged by one thousand years ago. That suggests that the Hittite, Sanskrit, and Greek branches must have split off from PIE by 2500 B.C. or earlier.

How much earlier do the differences between those branches imply? How can we obtain a calibration factor that converts "percentage difference between languages" into "time since the languages began to diverge"? Some linguists use the rate of word change in historically documented written languages, like the changes from Anglo-Saxon to Chaucer's English to Modern English. These calculations, which belong to a science called glottochronology (= chronology of languages), yield the rule of thumb that languages replace about 20 percent of their basic vocabulary every one thousand years.

Most scholars reject glottochronology calculations, on the grounds that word-replacement rates must vary with social circumstances and with the particular words themselves. However, the same scholars are generally still willing to make a seat-of-the-pants estimate. The usual conclusion from either glottochronology or pants' seats is that the PIE language community may have started to break up into several daughter language communities by 3000 B.C., surely by 2500 B.C. and not before 5000 B.C.

There's still another, completely independent approach to the dating problem: the science termed linguistic paleontology. Just as paleontologists try to discover what the past was like by looking for relics buried in the ground, linguistic paleontologists do it by looking for relics buried in languages.

To understand how this works, recall that linguists have reconstructed nearly two thousand words of PIE vocabulary. It's not surprising that these include words like "brother" and "sky," which must have existed and been named since the dawn of human language. But PIE shouldn't have had a word for "gun," since guns weren't invented till around A.D. 1300, long after PIE speakers had already scattered to speak distinct languages in Turkey and India. In fact, the word for "gun" uses different roots in different Indo-European languages: "gun" in English, "fusil" in French, "ruzhyo" in Russian, and so on. The reason is obvious: different languages couldn't possibly have inherited the same root for "gun" from PIE, and they each had to invent or borrow their own word when guns were invented.

The gun example suggests that we should take a series of inventions whose dates we know and see which of those do and which don't have reconstructed names in PIE. Anything—like the gun—that was invented after PIE began to break up shouldn't have a reconstructed name. Anything—like brother—that was known as a concept or invented before the break-up might have a name. (It doesn't *have* to have a name, because plenty of PIE words have surely become lost. We know the PIE words for "eye" and "eyebrow" but not "eyelid," although PIE speakers must have had eyelids.)

Perhaps the earliest major developments *without* PIE names are battle chariots, which became widespread between 2000 and 1500 B.C., and iron, whose use became important between 1200 and 1000 B.C. The lack of PIE terms for these relatively late inventions doesn't surprise us, since the distinctness of Hittite had already convinced us that PIE broke up long before 2000 B.C. Among earlier developments that do have PIE names, there are words for "sheep" and "goat," first domesticated by around 8000 B.C.; cattle (including separate words for cow, steer, and ox), domesticated by 6400 B.C.; horses, domesticated by around 4000 B.C.; and plows, invented around the time that horses were domesticated. The latest datable invention with a PIE name is the wheel, invented around 3300 B.C.

By such reasoning linguistic paleontology, even in the absence of any other evidence, would date the break-up of PIE as before 2000 B.C. but after 3300 B.C. This conclusion agrees well with the one reached by extrapolating the differences between Hittite, Greek, and Sanskrit backward in time. If we wish to find traces of the first Indo-Europeans, we shall be safe to concentrate on the archaeological record between 2500 and 5000 B.C., and perhaps slightly before 3000 B.C.

HAVING REACHED FAIR AGREEMENT about the "when" question, let's now ask: *where* was PIE spoken? Linguists have disagreed about the PIE homeland ever since they first began to appreciate its significance. Almost every possible answer has been proposed, from the North Pole to India, and from the Atlantic to the Pacific shores of Eurasia. As the archaeologist J. P. Mallory puts it, the question is not "Where do scholars locate the Indo-European homeland?" but "Where do they put it *now?*"

To understand why this problem has proved so hard, let's first try to solve it quickly by looking at a map (Figure 7, page 253). As of 1492, most surviving Indo-European branches were virtually confined to western Europe, and only Indo-Iranian extended east of the Caspian Sea. Hence western Europe would be the most parsimonious solution to the search for the PIE homeland: the solution that required the fewest people to move long distances.

Unfortunately for that solution, in 1900 a "new" but long-extinct Indo-European language was discovered in a triply unlikely location. First, the language (Tocharian, as it is now called) turned up in a secret chamber behind a wall in a Buddhist cave monastery. The chamber contained a library of ancient documents in the strange language, written around A.D. 600–800 by Buddhist missionaries and traders. Second, the monastery lay in Chinese Turkestan, east of all extant Indo-European speakers and about a thousand miles removed from the nearest ones. Finally, Tocharian was not related to Indo-Iranian, the geographically closest branch of Indo-European, but possibly instead to branches used in Europe itself, thousands of miles to the west. It's as if we suddenly discovered that the early medieval inhabitants of Scotland spoke a language related to Chinese.

Obviously, the Tocharians didn't reach Chinese Turkestan by helicopter. They surely walked or rode there, and we have to assume that Central Asia formerly had many other Indo-European languages that disappeared without the good fortune to be preserved by documents in secret chambers. A modern linguistic map of Eurasia (Figure 7) makes it obvious what must have happened to Tocharian and all those other lost Indo-European languages of central Asia. That whole area today is occupied by people speaking Turkic or Mongolian languages, descendants of hordes that overran the area from the time of at least the Huns to Genghis Khan. Scholars debate whether Genghis Khan's armies slaughtered 2,400,000 or only 1,600,000 people when they captured Harat, but scholars agree that such activities transformed the linguistic map of Asia. In contrast, most Indo-European languages known to have disappeared in Europe—like the Celtic languages Caesar found spoken in Gaul—were replaced by other Indo-European languages. The apparently European center of gravity of Indo-European languages as of 1492 was an artifact of recent linguistic holocausts in Asia. If the PIE homeland really was centrally located within what by A.D. 600 became the Indo-European realm, stretching from Ireland to Chinese Turkestan, then that homeland would have been in the Russian steppes north of the Caucasus, rather than in western Europe.

Just as the languages themselves gave us some clues to the time of PIE's break-up, so too they contain clues to the location of the PIE homeland. One clue is that the language family to which Indo-European has the clearest connections is Finno-Ugric, the family that includes Finnish and other languages native to the forest zone of north Russia (see Figure 7). Now it's true that the links between Finno-Ugric and Indo-European languages are enormously weaker than those between German and English, which stem from the fact that the English language was brought to England from northwest Germany only fifteen hundred years ago. The links are also much weaker than those between the Germanic and Slavic language branches of Indo-European, which probably diverged a few thousand years ago. Instead, the links suggest a much older propinquity between the speakers of PIE and of Proto-Finno-Ugric. But since Finno-Ugric comes from the North Russian forests, that suggests a PIE homeland in the Russian steppe south of the forests. In contrast, if PIE had arisen much further south (say, in Turkey), the closest affinities of Indo-European might have been with the ancient Semitic languages of the Near East.

A second clue to the PIE homeland is the non-Indo-European vocabulary swept up as debris into quite a few Indo-European languages. I mentioned that this debris is especially noticeable in Greek, and it's also conspicuous in Hittite, Irish, and Sanskrit. That suggests that those areas used to be occupied by non-Indo-Europeans and were later invaded by Indo-Europeans. If so, the PIE homeland wasn't Ireland or India (which almost no one suggests today anyway), but it also wasn't Greece or Turkey (which some scholars still do suggest).

Conversely, the modern Indo-European language still most similar to PIE is Lithuanian. Our first preserved Lithuanian texts, from around A.D. 1500, contain as high a fraction of PIE word roots as do Sanskrit texts of nearly three thousand years earlier. The conservatism of Lithuanian suggests that it has been subject to few disturbing influences from non-Indo-European languages and may have remained near the PIE homeland. Formerly, Lithuanian and other Baltic languages were more widely distributed in Russia, until Goths and Slavs pushed the Balts back to their current shrunken domain of Lithuania and Latvia. Thus, this reasoning too suggests a PIE homeland in Russia.

A third clue comes from the reconstructed PIE vocabulary. We already saw how its inclusion of words for things familiar in 4000 B.C., but not for things unknown until 2000 B.C., helps date the time when PIE was spoken. Might it also pinpoint the place where PIE was spoken? PIE includes a word for snow ("snoighwos"), suggesting a temperate rather than tropical location and providing the root of our English word "snow." Of the many wild animals and plants with PIE names (like "mus" = mouse), most are widespread in the temperate zone of Eurasia and help to pin down the homeland's latitude but not its longitude.

To me, the strongest clue from the PIE vocabulary is what it lacked rather than included: words for many crops. PIE speakers surely did some farming, since they had words for plow and sickle. But only one word for an unspecified grain has survived. In contrast, the reconstructed proto-Bantu language of Africa, and the proto-Austronesian language of southeast Asia, have many crop names. Proto-Austronesian was spoken even longer ago than PIE, so that modern Austronesian languages have had more time to lose those old names for crops than have the modern Indo-European languages. Despite that, the modern Austronesian languages still contain far more old names of crops. Hence PIE speakers probably actually had few crops, and their descendants borrowed or invented crop names as they moved to more agricultural areas.

But that conclusion presents us with a double puzzle. First, by 3500 B.C. farming had become the dominant way of life in almost all of Europe and much of Asia. That severely narrows down the possible choices for the PIE homeland: It must have been an unusual area where farming was not so dominant. And second, it begs the question why PIE speakers were able to expand. A major cause of the Bantu and Austronesian expansions was that the first speakers of those language families were farmers, spreading into areas occupied by hunter-gatherers whom they could outnumber or dominate. For PIE speakers to have been rudimentary farmers invading a farming Europe turns historical experience on its head. Thus, we cannot solve the "where" of Indo-European origins until we have come to grips with the hardest question: why?

IN EUROPE JUST BEFORE THE AGE OF WRITING, there were not one but two economic revolutions so far-reaching in impact that they could have caused a linguistic steamroller. The first was the arrival of farming and herding, which originated in the Near East around 8000 B.C., leapt from Turkey to Greece around 6500 B.C., and then spread north and west to reach Britain and Scandinavia. Farming and herding permitted a large increase in human population numbers over those previously sustainable by hunting and gathering alone. Colin Renfrew, Professor of Archaeology at Cambridge

University in England, recently published a thought-provoking book arguing that those farmers from Turkey were the PIE speakers who brought Indo-European languages to Europe.

My first reaction to reading Renfrew's book was "Of course, he must be right!" Farming *had* to produce a linguistic upheaval in Europe, just as it did in Africa and southeast Asia. This is especially likely since, as geneticists have shown, those first farmers made the biggest contribution to the genes of modern Europeans.

But—Renfrew's theory ignores or dismisses all the linguistic evidence. Farmers reached Europe thousands of years before the estimated arrival of PIE. The first farmers lacked, and PIE speakers possessed, innovations like plows, wheels, and domesticated horses. PIE is strikingly deficient in words for the crops that defined the first farmers. Hittite, the oldest known Indo-European language of Turkey, isn't the Indo-European language closest to pure PIE, as one might expect from Renfrew's Turkey-based theory, but is instead the most deviant one. Renfrew's theory rests on nothing more than a syllogism: farming probably caused a steamroller, the PIE steamroller requires a cause, so farming is assumed to have been that cause. Everything else suggests that farming instead brought to Europe the older languages that PIE overran, like Etruscan and Basque.

But around 5000–3000 B.C.—at the right time for PIE origins—there was a second economic revolution in Eurasia. This later revolution coincided with the beginnings of metallurgy and involved a greatly expanded use of domestic animals—not just for meat and hides, as humans had been using wild animals for a million years, but for new purposes that included producing milk and wool, pulling plows, pulling wheeled vehicles, and riding. The revolution is richly reflected in the PIE vocabulary, through words for "yoke" and "plow," "milk" and "butter," "wool" and "weave," and a host of words associated with wheeled vehicles ("wheel," "axle," "shaft," "harness," "hub," and "lynchpin").

The economic significance of this revolution was to increase human population and power far beyond the levels made possible by farming and herding alone. For instance, through milk and its products one cow gradually yielded many more calories than did its meat alone. Plowing let a farmer plant much more acreage than he could with a hoe or digging stick. Animal-drawn vehicles let people exploit far more land and still bring its produce to their village for processing.

For some of these advances it's hard to say where they arose, because they spread so quickly. For example, wheeled vehicles were unknown before 3300 B.C., but within a few centuries of that date they were widely recorded throughout Europe and the Middle East. But there is one crucial advance whose origin can be identified: the domestication of horses. Just before their domestication, wild horses were absent from the Mideast and southern Europe, rare in northern Europe, and abundant only in the steppes of Russia eastward. The first evidence of horse domestication is for the Sredny Stog culture around 4000 B.C., in the steppes just north of the Black Sea, where archaeologist David Anthony has identified wear marks on horses' teeth that indicate use of a bit for riding.

Throughout the world, wherever and whenever domestic horses have been introduced, they have yielded enormous benefits for human societies. For the first time in human evolution, people could travel overland faster than their own legs could propel them. Speed helped hunters run down their prey and helped herders manage their sheep and cattle over large areas. Most important, speed helped warriors to launch quick surprise raids on distant enemies and to withdraw again before the enemies had time to organize a counterattack. Hence throughout the world the horse revolutionized warfare and enabled horse-owning peoples to terrorize their neighbors. The stereotype that Americans hold of Great Plains Indians as fearsome mounted warriors was actually created only recently, within a few generations from 1660 to 1770. Since European horses reached the U.S. West in advance of Europeans themselves and other European goods, we can be sure that the horse alone was what transformed Plains Indian society.

Archaeological evidence makes clear that domestic horses had similarly transformed human society on the Russian steppe much earlier, around 4000 B.C. The steppe habitat of open grassland was hard for people to exploit until they could use horses to solve the problems of distance and transport. Human occupation of the Russian steppe accelerated with horse domestication and then exploded with the invention of ox-drawn wheeled vehicles around 3300 B.C. The steppe economy came to be based on the combination of sheep and cattle for meat, milk, and wool, plus horses and wheeled vehicles for transport, and supplemented by a little farming.

There is no evidence for intensive agriculture and food storage at those early steppe sites, in marked contrast to the abundant evidence at other European and Mideast sites around the same time. Steppe peoples lacked large permanent settlements and were evidently highly mobile—again in contrast to the villages with rows of hundreds of two-story houses in southeast Europe at the time. What the horsemen lacked in architecture they made up for in military zeal, as attested by their lavish tombs (for men only!), filled with enormous numbers of daggers and other weapons, and sometimes even with wagons and horse skeletons.

Thus, Russia's Dnieper River (see Figure 10, below) marked an abrupt cultural boundary: to the east, the well-armed horsemen;

HOW INDO-EUROPEAN LANGUAGES MIGHT HAVE SPREAD

Figure 10. This map shows how surviving Indo-European languages might have spread. The inferred homeland where Proto-Indo-European (PIE), the mother tongue, was spoken lay in the Russian steppes north of the Black Sea and east of the Dnieper River.

to the west, the rich farming villages with their granaries. That proximity of wolves and sheep spelled T-R-O-U-B-L-E. Once the invention of the wheel completed the horsemen's economic package, their artifacts indicate a very rapid spread for thousands of miles eastward through the steppes of Central Asia (see map). From that movement, the ancestors of the Tocharians may have arisen. The steppe peoples' spread westward is marked by the concentration of European farming villages nearest the steppes into huge defensive settlements, then the collapse of those societies, and the appearance of characteristic steppe graves in Europe as far west as Hungary.

Of the innovations that drove the steppe peoples' steamroller, the sole one for which they clearly get full credit is the domestication of the horse. They might also have developed wheeled vehicles, milking, and wool technology independently of the Mideast's civilizations, but they borrowed sheep, cattle, metallurgy, and probably the plow from the Mideast or Europe. Thus, there was no single "secret weapon" that alone explains the steppe expansion. Instead, with horse domestication the steppe peoples became the first to put together the economic-military package that came to dominate the world for the next five thousand years—especially after they added intensive agriculture upon invading southeast Europe. Hence their success, like that of the second-stage European expansion that began in 1492, was an accident of biogeography. They happened to be the peoples whose homeland combined abundant wild horses and open steppe with proximity to Mideastern and European centers of civilization.

As UCLA archaeologist Marija Gimbutas has argued, Russia's steppe peoples west of the Ural Mountains in the fourth millennium B.C. fit well to the postulated picture of Proto-Indo-Europeans that we derived. They lived at the right time. Their culture included the important economic elements reconstructed for PIE (like wheels and horses), and lacked the elements lacking from PIE (like battle chariots and many crop terms). They lived in the right place for PIE: the temperate zone, south of Finno-Ugric peoples, near the later homeland of Lithuanians and other Balts.

If the fit is so good, why does the steppe theory of Indo-European

origins remain so controversial? There would have been no controversy if archaeologists had been able to demonstrate a rapid expansion of steppe culture from south Russia all the way to Ireland around
3000 B.C. But that didn't happen: direct evidence of the steppe invaders themselves extends no further west than Hungary. Instead,
around and after 3000 B.C. one finds a bewildering array of other
cultures developing in Europe and named for their artifacts (e.g., the
Corded Ware and Battle-axe Culture). Those emerging western European cultures combine steppe elements like horses and militarism
with old western European elements, especially settled agriculture.
Such facts cause many archaeologists to discount the steppe hypothesis altogether, and to see the emerging western European cultures as
local developments.

But there's an obvious reason why the steppe culture couldn't
spread intact to Ireland. The steppe itself reaches its western limit in
the plains of Hungary. That's where all subsequent steppe invaders
of Europe, like the Mongols, stopped. To spread further, steppe
society had to adapt to the forested landscape of western Europe—by
adopting intensive agriculture or by taking over existing European
societies and hybridizing with their peoples. Most of the genes of the
resulting hybrid societies may have been the genes of Old Europe.

If steppe people imposed PIE, their mother tongue, on southeast
Europe as far as Hungary, then it was the resulting daughter Indo-
European culture, not the original steppe culture itself, that spread to
derived granddaughter cultures elsewhere in Europe. Archaeological
evidence of major cultural change suggests that such granddaughter
cultures may have arisen throughout Europe and east to India between 3000 and 1500 B.C. Many non-Indo-European languages held
out long enough to be preserved in writing (like Etruscan), and
Basque still survives today. Thus, the Indo-European steamroller
wasn't a single wave, but a long chain of events that has taken five
thousand years.

As an analogy, consider how Indo-European languages came to
dominate North and South America today. We have abundant written records to prove that they stem from invasions of Indo-European
speakers from Europe. But those European immigrants didn't overrun the Americas in one step, and archaeologists don't find remains
of unmodified European cultures throughout the sixteenth-century
New World. That culture was useless on the U.S. frontier. Instead,

the colonists' culture was a highly modified or hybrid one, that combined Indo-European languages and much of European technology (like guns and iron) with American Indian crops and (especially in Central and South America) Indian genes. Some areas of the New World have taken many centuries for Indo-European language and economy to master. The takeover didn't reach the Arctic until this century. It's reaching much of the Amazon only now, and the Andes of Peru and Bolivia promise to remain Indian for a long time yet.

Suppose that some future archaeologist should dig in Brazil, after written records have been destroyed and Indo-European languages have disappeared from Europe. The archaeologist will find European artifacts suddenly appearing on the coast of Brazil around 1530, but penetrating the Amazon only very slowly thereafter. The people whom the archaeologist finds living in the Brazilian Amazon will be a genetic mishmash of American Indians, African blacks, Europeans, and Japanese, speaking Portuguese. The archaeologist will be unlikely to realize that Portuguese was an intrusive language, contributed by invaders, to a hybrid local society.

EVEN AFTER THE PIE EXPANSION of the 4th millennium B.C., new interactions of horses, steppe peoples, and Indo-European languages continued to shape Eurasian history. PIE horse technology was primitive and probably involved little more than a rope bit and bareback rider. For thousands of years thereafter, the military value of horses continued to improve with inventions ranging from metal bits and horse-drawn battle chariots around 2000 B.C. to the horseshoes, stirrups, and saddles of later cavalry. While most of these advances didn't originate in the steppes, steppe peoples were still the ones who profited the most, because they always had more pasture and hence more horses.

As horse technology evolved, Europe was invaded by many more steppe peoples, among whom the Huns, Turks, and Mongols are best known. These peoples carved out a succession of huge, short-lived empires, stretching from the steppes to eastern Europe. But never again were steppe peoples able to impose their language on western Europe. They enjoyed their biggest advantage at the outset, when PIE bareback riders invaded a Europe entirely without domestic horses.

There was another difference between these later recorded invasions and the earlier unrecorded PIE invasion. The later invaders were no longer Indo-European speakers from the western steppes, but speakers of Turkic and Mongol languages from the eastern steppes. Ironically, horses were what enabled Turkish tribes from central Asia in the eleventh century A.D. to invade the land of the first written Indo-European language, Hittite. The most important innovation of the first Indo-Europeans was thus turned against their descendants. Turks are largely European in their genes, but non-Indo-European (Turkish) in their language. Similarly, an invasion from the east in A.D. 896 left modern Hungary largely European in its genes but Finno-Ugric in its language. By illustrating how a small invading force of steppe horsemen could impose their language on a European society, Turkey and Hungary provide models of how the rest of Europe came to speak Indo-European.

Eventually, steppe peoples in general, regardless of their language, ceased to win in the face of western Europe's advancing technology. When the end came, it was swift. In A.D. 1241 the Mongols achieved the largest steppe empire that ever existed, stretching from Hungary to China. But after about A.D. 1500 the Indo-European-speaking Russians began to encroach on the steppes from the west. It took only a few more centuries of tsarist imperialism to conquer the steppe horsemen who had terrorized Europe and China for over five thousand years. Today the steppes are divided between Russia and China, and only Mongolia remains as a vestige of steppe independence.

Much racist nonsense has been written about the supposed superiority of Indo-European peoples themselves. Nazi propaganda invoked a pure Aryan race. In fact, Indo-Europeans have never been unified since the PIE expansion of five thousand years ago, and even PIE speakers themselves may have been divided among related cultures. Some of the most bitter fighting and vilest deeds of recorded history pitted one Indo-European group against another. The Jews, Gypsies, and Slavs, whom the Nazis sought to exterminate, conversed in languages as Indo-European as that of their persecutors. Speakers of Proto-Indo-European merely happened to be in the right place at the right time to put together a useful package of technology. Through that stroke of luck, theirs was the mother tongue whose daughter languages came to be spoken by half the world today.

A PROTO-INDO-EUROPEAN FABLE

OWIS EKWOOSQUE

Gwrreei owis, quesyo wlhnaa ne eest, ekwoons espeket, oinom ghe gwrrum woghom weghontm, oinomque megam bhorom, oinomque ghmmenm ooku bherontm.

Owis nu ekwomos ewewquet: "Keer aghnutoi moi ekwoons agontm nerm widntei."

Ekwoos tu ewewquont: "Kludhi, owei, keer ghe aghnutoi nsmei widntmos: neer, potis, owioom r wlhnaam sebhi gwhermom westrom qurnneuti. Neghi owioom wlhnaa esti."

Tod kekluwoos owis agrom ebhuget.

(THE) SHEEP AND (THE) HORSES

On (a) hill, (a) sheep that had no wool saw horses, one (of them) pulling (a) heavy wagon, one carrying (a) big load, and one carrying (a) man quickly.

(The) sheep said to (the) horses: "My heart pains me, seeing (a) man driving horses."

(The) horses said: "Listen, sheep, our hearts pain us when we see (this): (a) man, the master, makes (the) wool of (the) sheep into (a) warm garment for himself. And (the) sheep has no wool."

Having heard this, (the) sheep fled into (the) plain.

To PROVIDE SOME SENSE of how Proto-Indo-European (PIE) might have sounded, I give a made-up fable in reconstructed PIE, together with an English translation. The fable was invented over a century ago by the linguist August Schleicher. The revised version that I give is based on one published by W. P. Lehmann and L. Zgusta in 1979 and takes account of added understanding of PIE gained since Schleicher's time. The version reproduced here has been slightly altered from that of Lehmann and Zgusta to make it more "user friendly" for nonlinguists, with the advice of Jaan Puhvel.

While PIE initially looks strange, many words will prove familiar on scrutiny because of similar English or Latin roots derived from PIE. For instance, "owis" means "sheep" (cf. "ewe," "ovine"); "wlhnaa" means "wool"; "ekwoos" means "horses" (cf. "equestrian,"

Latin "equus"); "ghmmenm" means "man" (cf. "human," Latin "hominem"); "que" means "and," as in Latin; "megam" means "big" (cf. "megabucks"); "keer" means "heart" (cf. "core," "cardiology"); "moi" means "to me"; and "widntei" and "widntmos" mean "see" (cf. "video"). The PIE text lacks definite and indefinite articles ("the" and "a") and places the verb at the end of the clause or sentence.

While this sample text will show what some linguists think PIE was like, don't take it as an exact sample. Remember: PIE was never written; scholars differ on details of how to reconstruct PIE; and the fable itself is invented.

How English has changed over the last 1000 years: the 23rd Psalm

---

Modern (1989)
The Lord is my shepherd, I lack nothing.
He lets me lie down in green pastures.
He leads me to still waters.

King James Bible (1611)
The Lord is my shepherd, I shall not want.
He maketh me to lie down in green pastures.
He leadeth me beside the still waters.

Middle English (1100–1500)
Our Lord gouerneth me, and nothyng shal defailen to me.
In the sted of pastur he sett me ther.
He norissed me upon water of fyllyng.

Old English (800–1066)
Drihten me raet, ne byth me nanes godes wan.
And he me geset on swythe good feohland.
And fedde me be waetera stathum.

CHAPTER 16

In Black and White

WHILE THE ANNIVERSARY OF ANY NATION'S FOUNDING IS TAKEN AS cause for its inhabitants to celebrate, Australians had special cause in 1988, their bicentennial year. Few groups of colonists faced such obstacles as those who landed with the First Fleet at the future site of Sydney in 1788. Australia was still *terra incognita:* the colonists had no idea what to expect or how to survive. They were separated from their mother country by a sea voyage of fifteen thousand miles, lasting eight months. Two and a half years of near-starvation would pass until a further supply fleet arrived from England. Many of the settlers were convicts who had already been traumatized by the most brutal aspects of brutal eighteenth-century life. Despite those beginnings, the settlers survived, prospered, filled a continent, built a democracy, and established a distinctive national character. It's no wonder that Australians felt pride as they celebrated their nation's founding.

Nevertheless, one set of protests marred the celebrations. The white settlers were not the first Australians. Instead, Australia had been settled around fifty thousand years ago by the ancestors of the people now usually referred to as "Australian Aborigines" and also known in Australia as "blacks." In the course of English settlement, most of those original inhabitants were killed by the settlers or died of other causes, leading some modern descendants of the survivors to stage bicentenary protests instead of celebrations. The celebrations focused implicitly on how Australia became white. I shall begin this chapter by focusing instead on how Australia ceased to be black, and how courageous English settlers came to commit genocide.

Lest white Australians take offense, I should make clear that I am not accusing their forefathers of having done something uniquely horrendous. Instead, my reason for discussing the extermination of the Aborigines is precisely because it isn't unique: it's a well-documented example of a phenomenon whose frequency few people appreciate. While our first association to the world "genocide" is likely to be the killings in Nazi concentration camps, those were not even the largest-scale genocide of this century. The Tasmanians and hundreds of other peoples were modern targets of successful smaller extermination campaigns. Numerous peoples scattered throughout the world are potential targets in the near future. Yet genocide is such a painful subject that either we'd rather not think about it at all, or else we'd like to believe that nice people don't commit genocide, only Nazis do. But our refusal to think about it has consequences: we've done little to halt the numerous episodes of genocide since World War II, and we're not alert to where it may happen next. Together with our destruction of our own environmental resources, our genocidal tendencies coupled to nuclear weapons now constitute the two most likely means by which the human species may reverse all its progress virtually overnight.

Despite increasing interest in genocide on the part of psychologists and biologists as well as some lay people, basic questions about it remain disputed. Do any animals routinely kill members of their own species, or is that a human invention without animal precedents? Throughout human history, has genocide been a rare aberration, or has it been common enough to rank as a human hallmark along with art and language? Is its frequency now increasing, because modern weapons permit push-button genocide and thereby reduce our instinctive inhibitions about killing fellow humans? Why have so many cases attracted so little attention? Are genocidal killers abnormal individuals, or are they normal people placed in unusual situations?

To understand genocide, we cannot proceed narrowly but must draw on biology, ethics, and psychology. Hence our exploration of genocide will begin by tracing its biological history, from our animal ancestors to the twentieth century. After asking how killers have reconciled genocide with their ethical codes, we can examine its psychological effects on the perpetrators, surviving victims, and on-lookers. But before we search for answers to these questions, it is useful to start with the extermination of the Tasmanians, as a case study typical of a wide class of genocides.

TASMANIA IS A MOUNTAINOUS ISLAND similar in area to Ireland and lying two hundred miles off Australia's southeast coast. When dis-covered by Europeans in 1642, it supported about five thousand hunter-gatherers related to the Aborigines of the Australian main-land and with perhaps the simplest technology of any modern people. Tasmanians made only a few types of simple stone and wooden tools. Like the mainland Aborigines, they lacked metal tools, agriculture, livestock, pottery, and bows and arrows. Unlike the mainlanders, they also lacked boomerangs, dogs, nets, knowledge of sewing, and ability to start a fire.

Since the Tasmanians' sole boats were rafts capable of only short journeys, they had had no contact with any other humans since rising sea level cut off Tasmania from Australia ten thousand years ago. Confined to their private universe for hundreds of generations, they had survived the longest isolation in modern human history—an isolation otherwise depicted only in science fiction. When the white colonists of Australia finally ended that isolation, no two peoples on Earth were less equipped to understand each other than were Tas-manians and whites.

The tragic collision of these two peoples led to conflict almost as soon as British sealers and settlers arrived around 1800. Whites kid-napped Tasmanian children as laborers, kidnapped women as con-sorts, mutilated or killed men, trespassed on hunting grounds, and tried to clear Tasmanians off their land. Thus, the conflict quickly focused on lebensraum, which throughout human history has been among the commonest causes of genocide. As a result of the kidnap-pings, the native population of northeast Tasmania in November 1830 was reduced to seventy-two adult men, three adult women, and no children. One shepherd shot nineteen Tasmanians with a swivel gun loaded with nails. Four other shepherds ambushed a group of natives, killed thirty, and threw their bodies over a cliff remembered today as Victory Hill.

Naturally, Tasmanians retaliated, and whites counterretaliated in turn. To end the escalation, Governor Arthur in April 1828 ordered all Tasmanians to leave the part of their island already settled by Europeans. To enforce this order, government-sponsored groups called "roving parties," consisting of convicts led by police, hunted down and killed Tasmanians. With the declaration of martial law in November 1828, soldiers were authorized to kill on sight any Tasmanian in the settled areas. Next, a bounty was declared on the natives: five British pounds for each adult, two pounds for each child, caught alive. "Black catching," as it was called because of the Tasmanians' dark skins, became big business pursued by private as well as official roving parties. At the same time a commission headed by William Broughton, the Anglican archdeacon of Australia, was set up to recommend an overall policy toward the natives. After considering proposals to capture them for sale as slaves, poison or trap them, or hunt them with dogs, the commission settled on continued bounties and the use of mounted police.

In 1830 a remarkable missionary, George Augustus Robinson, was hired to round up the remaining Tasmanians and take them to Flinders Island, thirty miles away. Robinson was convinced that he was acting for the good of the Tasmanians. He was paid £300 in advance, £700 on completing the job. Undergoing real dangers and hardship, and aided by a courageous native woman named Truganini, he succeeded in bringing in the remaining natives—initially, by persuading them that a worse fate awaited them if they did not surrender, but later at gunpoint. Many of Robinson's captives died en route to Flinders, but about two hundred reached there, the last survivors of the former population of five thousand.

On Flinders Island Robinson was determined to civilize and christianize the survivors. His settlement was run like a jail, at a windy site with little fresh water. Children were separated from parents to facilitate the work of civilizing them. The regimented daily schedule included Bible reading, hymn singing, and inspection of beds and dishes for cleanness and neatness. However, the jail diet caused malnutrition, which combined with illness to make the natives die. Few infants survived more than a few weeks. The government reduced expenditures in the hope that the natives would die out. By 1869 only Truganini, one other woman, and one man remained alive.

William Lanner, the last Tasmanian man.
Photograph by Wooley, from the collection of the
Tasmanian Museum and Art Gallery.

These last three Tasmanians attracted the interest of scientists, who believed them to be a missing link between humans and apes. Hence, when the last man, one William Lanner, died in 1869, competing teams of physicians, led by Dr. George Stokell from the Royal

Society of Tasmania and Dr. W. L. Crowther from the Royal College of Surgeons, alternately dug up and reburied Lanner's body, cutting off parts of it and stealing them back and forth from each other. Dr. Crowther cut off the head, Dr. Stokell the hands and feet, and someone else the ears and nose, as souvenirs. Dr. Stokell made a tobacco pouch out of Lanner's skin.

Before Truganini, the last woman, died in 1876, she was terrified of similar post-mortem mutilation and asked in vain to be buried at sea. As she had feared, the Royal Society dug up her skeleton and put it on public display in the Tasmanian Museum, where it remained until 1947. In that year the Museum finally yielded to complaints of poor taste and transferred Truganini's skeleton to a room where only scientists could view it. That too stimulated complaints of poor taste. Finally, in 1976—the centenary year of Truganini's death—her skeleton was cremated over the museum's objections, and her ashes were scattered at sea as she had requested.

While the Tasmanians were few in number, their extermination was disproportionately influential in Australian history, because Tasmania was the first Australian colony to solve its native problem and achieved the most nearly final solution. It had done so by apparently succeeding in getting rid of all its natives. (Actually, some children of Tasmanian women by white sealers survived, and their descendants today constitute an embarrassment to the Tasmanian government, which has not figured out what to do about them.) Many whites on the Australian mainland envied the thoroughness of the Tasmanian solution and wanted to imitate it, but they also learned a lesson from it. The extermination of the Tasmanians had been carried out in settled areas in full view of the urban press, and had attracted some negative comment. Hence the extermination of the much more numerous mainland Aborigines was instead effected at or beyond the frontier, far from urban centers.

The mainland governments' instrument of this policy, modeled on the Tasmanian government's roving parties, was a branch of mounted police termed "Native Police," who used search-and-destroy tactics to kill or drive out Aborigines. A typical strategy was to surround a camp at night and to shoot the inhabitants in an attack at dawn. White settlers also made widespread use of poisoned food to kill Aborigines. Another common practice was roundups in which captured Aborigines were kept chained together at the neck while being

Truganini, the last Tasmanian woman.
Photograph by Wooley, from the collection of the
Tasmanian Museum and Art Gallery.

marched to jail and held there. The British novelist Anthony Trol-
lope expressed the prevailing nineteenth-century British attitude toward Aborigines when he wrote, "Of the Australian black man we
may certainly say that he has to go. That he should perish without
unnecessary suffering should be the aim of all who are concerned in
the matter."

These tactics continued in Australia long into the twentieth century. In an incident at Alice Springs in 1928, police massacred thirty-one Aborigines. The Australian Parliament refused to accept a report on the massacre, and two Aboriginal survivors (rather than the police) were put on trial for murder. Neck chains were still in use and defended as humane in 1958, when the Commissioner of Police for the state of Western Australia explained to the Melbourne *Herald* that Aboriginal prisoners preferred being chained.

The mainland Aborigines were too numerous to exterminate completely in the manner of the Tasmanians. However, from the arrival of British colonists in 1788 until the 1921 census, the Aboriginal population declined from about 300,000 to 60,000.

Today, the attitudes of white Australians toward their murderous history vary widely. While government policy and many whites' private views have become increasingly sympathetic to the Aborigines, other whites deny responsibility for genocide. For instance, in 1982 one of Australia's leading news magazines, *The Bulletin,* published a letter by a lady named Patricia Cobern, who denied indignantly that white settlers had exterminated the Tasmanians. In fact, wrote Ms. Cobern, the settlers were peace-loving and of high moral character, while Tasmanians were treacherous, murderous, warlike, filthy, gluttonous, vermin-infested, and disfigured by syphilis. Moreover, they took poor care of their infants, never bathed, and had repulsive marriage customs. They died out because of all those poor health practices, plus a death wish and lack of religious beliefs. It was just a coincidence that, after thousands of years of existence, they happened to die out during a conflict with the settlers. The only massacres were of settlers by Tasmanians, not vice versa. Besides, the settlers only armed themselves in self-defense, were unfamiliar with guns, and never shot more than forty-one Tasmanians at one time.

To PLACE THESE CASES of the Tasmanians and the Australian Aborigines in perspective, consider three maps of the world (Figures 11, 12, and 13), depicting for three different time periods some mass killings that have been labeled as genocides. These maps beg a question for which there is no simple answer: how to define genocide. Etymologically, it means "group killing": the Greek root "genos," meaning race, and the Latin root "-cide," meaning killing (as in suicide, in-

SOME GENOCIDES, 1492–1900

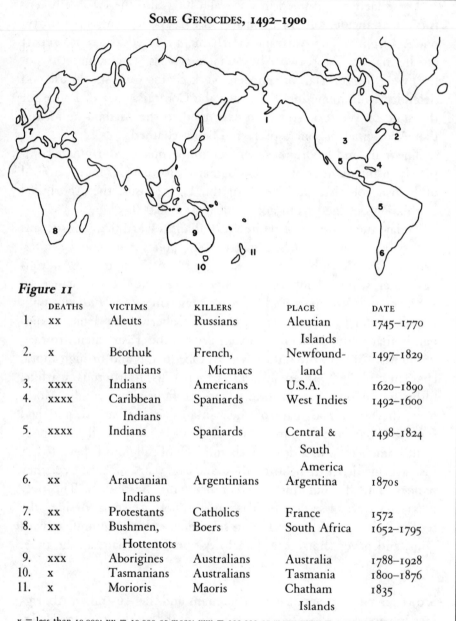

Figure 11

	DEATHS	VICTIMS	KILLERS	PLACE	DATE
1.	xx	Aleuts	Russians	Aleutian Islands	1745–1770
2.	x	Beothuk Indians	French, Micmacs	Newfound- land	1497–1829
3.	xxxx	Indians	Americans	U.S.A.	1620–1890
4.	xxxx	Caribbean Indians	Spaniards	West Indies	1492–1600
5.	xxxx	Indians	Spaniards	Central & South America	1498–1824
6.	xx	Araucanian Indians	Argentinians	Argentina	1870s
7.	xx	Protestants	Catholics	France	1572
8.	xx	Bushmen, Hottentots	Boers	South Africa	1652–1795
9.	xxx	Aborigines	Australians	Australia	1788–1928
10.	x	Tasmanians	Australians	Tasmania	1800–1876
11.	x	Morioris	Maoris	Chatham Islands	1835

x = less than 10,000; xx = 10,000 or more; xxx = 100,000 or more; xxxx = 1,000,000 or more

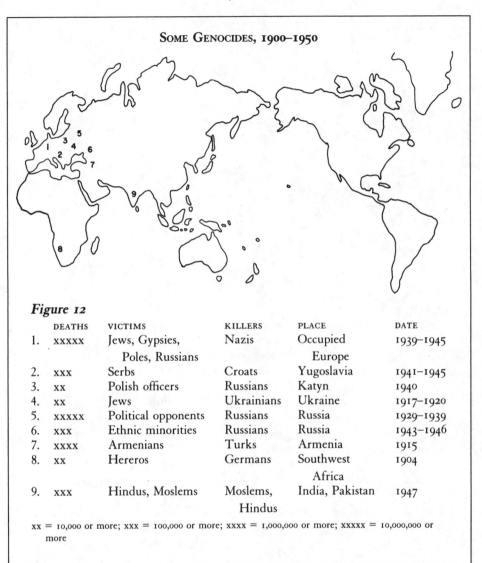

Figure 12

	DEATHS	VICTIMS	KILLERS	PLACE	DATE
1.	xxxxx	Jews, Gypsies, Poles, Russians	Nazis	Occupied Europe	1939–1945
2.	xxx	Serbs	Croats	Yugoslavia	1941–1945
3.	xx	Polish officers	Russians	Katyn	1940
4.	xx	Jews	Ukrainians	Ukraine	1917–1920
5.	xxxxx	Political opponents	Russians	Russia	1929–1939
6.	xxx	Ethnic minorities	Russians	Russia	1943–1946
7.	xxxx	Armenians	Turks	Armenia	1915
8.	xx	Hereros	Germans	Southwest Africa	1904
9.	xxx	Hindus, Moslems	Moslems, Hindus	India, Pakistan	1947

xx = 10,000 or more; xxx = 100,000 or more; xxxx = 1,000,000 or more; xxxxx = 10,000,000 or more

fanticide). The victims must be selected because they belong to a group, whether or not each victim as an individual has done something to provoke killing. As for the defining group characteristic, it may be racial (white Australians killing black Tasmanians), national (Russians killing fellow white Slavs, the Polish officers at Katyn in 1940), ethnic (the Hutu and Tutsi, two black African groups, killing each other in Rwanda and Burundi in the 1960s and 1970s), religious (Moslems and Christians killing each other in Lebanon in recent

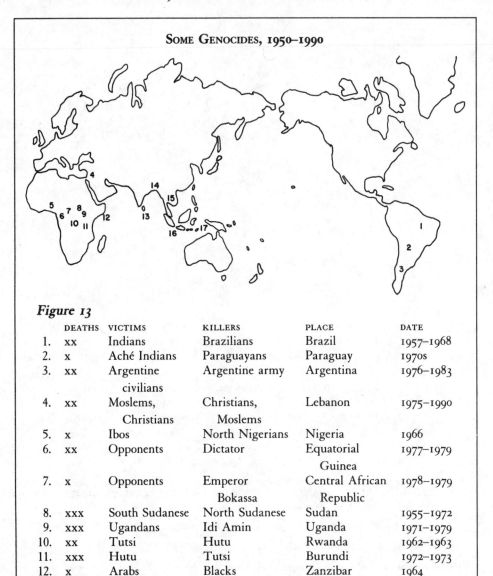

SOME GENOCIDES, 1950–1990

Figure 13

	DEATHS	VICTIMS	KILLERS	PLACE	DATE
1.	xx	Indians	Brazilians	Brazil	1957–1968
2.	x	Aché Indians	Paraguayans	Paraguay	1970s
3.	xx	Argentine civilians	Argentine army	Argentina	1976–1983
4.	xx	Moslems, Christians	Christians, Moslems	Lebanon	1975–1990
5.	x	Ibos	North Nigerians	Nigeria	1966
6.	xx	Opponents	Dictator	Equatorial Guinea	1977–1979
7.	x	Opponents	Emperor Bokassa	Central African Republic	1978–1979
8.	xxx	South Sudanese	North Sudanese	Sudan	1955–1972
9.	xxx	Ugandans	Idi Amin	Uganda	1971–1979
10.	xx	Tutsi	Hutu	Rwanda	1962–1963
11.	xxx	Hutu	Tutsi	Burundi	1972–1973
12.	x	Arabs	Blacks	Zanzibar	1964
13.	x	Tamils, Sinhalese	Sinhalese, Tamils	Sri Lanka	1985
14.	xxxx	Bengalis	Pakistani army	Bangladesh	1971
15.	xxxx	Cambodians	Khmer Rouge	Cambodia	1975–1979
16.	xxx	Communists and Chinese	Indonesians	Indonesia	1965–1967
17.	xx	Timorese	Indonesians	East Timor	1975–1976

x = less than 10,000; xx = 10,000 or more; xxx = 100,000 or more; xxxx = 1,000,000 or more decades), or political (the Khmer Rouge killing their fellow Cambodians from 1975 to 1979).

While collective killing is thus the essence of genocide, one can argue over how narrow a definition to adopt. The word "genocide" is often used so broadly that it loses meaning and we become tired of hearing it. Even if it is to be restricted to large-scale cases of collective killing, ambiguities remain. Here is a sample of the ambiguities:

How many deaths are needed for a killing to count as genocide rather than mere murder? This is a totally arbitrary question. Australians killed all five thousand Tasmanians, and American settlers killed the last twenty Susquehanna Indians in 1763. Does the small number of available victims disqualify these killings as genocidal, despite the completeness of extermination?

Must genocide be carried out by governments, or do private acts also count? The sociologist Irving Horowitz distinguished private acts as "assassination," and defined genocide as "a structural and systematic destruction of innocent people by a state bureaucratic apparatus." However, there is a complete continuum from "purely" governmental killings (Stalin's purges of his opponents) to "purely" private killings (Brazilian land-development companies hiring professional Indian killers). American Indians were killed by private citizens and the U.S. army alike, while the Ibos in Northern Nigeria were killed both by street mobs and by soldiers. In 1835 the Te Ati Awa tribe of New Zealand Maoris succeeded in a bold plan to capture a ship, load it with supplies, invade the Chatham Islands, kill three hundred of the occupants (another Polynesian group called the Morioris), enslave the remainder, and thereby take over the islands. By Horowitz's definition, this and many other equally well-planned exterminations of one tribal group by another do not constitute genocide, because the tribes lacked a state bureaucratic apparatus.

If people die en masse as a result of callous actions not specifically designed to kill them, does that count as genocide? Well-planned genocides include that of Tasmanians by Australians, that of Armenians by Turks during World War I, and (most notably) those committed by the Nazis during World War II. At the other extreme, when the Choctaw, Cherokee, and Creek Indians of southeastern U.S. states were forced to resettle west of the Mississippi River in the 1830s, it was not President Andrew Jackson's specific intent that many Indians should die en route, but he also did not take the measures that would have been necessary to keep them alive. Their numerous deaths were instead merely an inevitable result of forced marches in winter with little or no food or clothing.

An unusually candid statement about the role of intent in genocide emerged when the Paraguayan government was charged with complicity in the disappearance of the Guayaki Indians, who had been enslaved, tortured, deprived of food and medicine, and massacred. Paraguay's defense minister replied quite simply that there had been no intent to destroy the Guayaki: "Although there are victims and victimizers, there is not the third element necessary to establish the crime of genocide—that is, 'intent.' Therefore, as there is no intent, one cannot speak of 'genocide.' " Brazil's Permanent Representative to the UN similarly rebutted charges of Brazilian genocide against Amazonian Indians: ". . . there was lacking the special malice or motivation necessary to characterize the occurrence of genocide. The crimes in question were committed for exclusively economic reasons, the perpetrators having acted solely to take possession of the lands of their victims."

Some mass killings, such as those of Jews and Gypsies by Nazis, were unprovoked: the slaughter was not in retaliation for previous murders committed by the slaughtered. In many other cases, however, a mass killing culminates a series of murders and countermurders. When a provocation is followed by massive retaliation all out of proportion to the provocation, how do we decide when "mere" retaliation becomes genocide? At the Algerian town of Sétif in May 1945, celebrations of the end of World War II developed into a race riot in which Algerians killed 103 French. The savage French response consisted of planes' destroying forty-four villages, a cruiser bombarding coastal towns, civilian commandos organizing reprisal massacres, and troops killing indiscriminately. The Algerian dead numbered fifteen hundred according to the French, fifty thousand according to the Algerians. The interpretations of this event differ as do the estimates of the dead: to the French, it was suppression of a revolt; to the Algerians, it was a genocidal massacre.

GENOCIDES PROVE AS HARD TO PIGEONHOLE in their motivation as in their definition. While several motives may operate simultaneously, it is convenient to divide them into four types. In the first two types there is a real conflict of interest over land or power, whether or not the conflict is also disguised in ideology. In the other two types such conflict is minimal, and the motivation is more purely ideological or psychological.

Perhaps the commonest motive for genocide arises when a militarily stronger people attempts to occupy the land of a weaker people, who resist. Among the innumerable straightforward cases of this sort are not only the killing of Tasmanians and Australian Aborigines by white Australians, but also the killings of American Indians by white Americans, of Araucanian Indians by Argentinians, and of Bushmen and Hottentots by the Boer settlers of South Africa.

Another common motive involves a lengthy power struggle within a pluralistic society, leading to one group's seeking a final solution by killing the other. Cases involving two different ethnic groups are the killing of Tutsi in Rwanda by Hutu in 1962–63, of Hutu in Burundi by Tutsi in 1972–73, of Serbs by Croats in Yugoslavia during World War II, of Croats by Serbs at the end of that war, and of Arabs in Zanzibar by blacks in 1964. However, the killer and killed may belong to the same ethnic group and may differ only in political views. Such was the case in history's largest known genocide, claiming an estimated twenty million victims in the decade 1929–39 and sixty-six million between 1917 and 1959: that committed by the U.S.S.R. government against political opponents among its own citizens. Political killings lagging far behind this record are the Khmer Rouge purge of several million fellow Cambodians during the 1970s, and Indonesia's killing of hundreds of thousands of Communists in 1965–67.

In these two just-described motives for genocide, the victims could be viewed as a significant obstacle to the killers' control of land or power. At the opposite extreme are scapegoat killings of a helpless minority blamed for frustrations of their killers. Jews were killed by fourteenth-century Christians as scapegoats for the bubonic plague, by early twentieth-century Russians as scapegoats for Russia's political problems, by Ukrainians after World War I as scapegoats for the Bolshevist threat, and by Nazis during World War II as scapegoats for Germany's defeat in World War I. When the U.S. Seventh Cavalry slaughtered several hundred Sioux Indians at Wounded Knee in 1890, the soldiers were taking belated revenge for the Sioux's annihilating counterattack on Custer's Seventh Cavalry force at the Battle of the Little Big Horn fourteen years previously. In 1943–44, at the height of Russia's suffering from the Nazi invasion, Stalin ordered the killing or deportation of six ethnic minorities who served as scapegoats: the Balkars, Chechens, Crimean Tatars, Ingush, Kalmyks, and Karachai.

Racial and religious persecutions have served as the remaining class of motives. While I do not claim to understand the Nazi mentality, the Nazis' extermination of Gypsies may have stemmed from relatively "pure" racial motivation, while scapegoating joined religious and racial motives in the extermination of Jews. The list of religious massacres is almost infinitely long. It includes the First Crusaders' massacre of all Moslems and Jews in Jerusalem when that city was finally captured in 1099, and the St. Bartholomew's Day massacre of French Protestants by Catholics in 1572. Of course, racial and religious motives have contributed heavily to genocides provoked by land struggles, power struggles, and scapegoating.

EVEN IF ONE ALLOWS for disagreements over definitions and motives, plenty of cases of genocide remain. Let us now see how far back in and before our history as a species the record of genocide extends.

Is it true, as often claimed, that man is unique among animals in killing members of his own species? For example, the distinguished biologist Konrad Lorenz, in his book *On Aggression,* argued that animals' aggressive instincts are held in check by instinctive inhibitions against murder. But in human history this equilibrium supposedly became upset by the invention of weapons: our inherited inhibitions were no longer strong enough to restrain our newly acquired powers of killing. This view of man as the unique killer and evolutionary misfit has been accepted by Arthur Koestler and many other popular writers.

Actually, studies in recent decades have documented murder in many, though certainly not all, animal species. Massacre of a neighboring individual or troop may be beneficial to an animal, if it can thereby take over the neighbor's territory, food, or females. But attacks also involve some risk to the attacker. Many animal species lack the means to kill their fellows, and of those species with the means, some refrain from using them. It may sound utterly repugnant to do a cost/benefit analysis of murder, but such analyses nevertheless help one understand why murder appears to characterize only some animal species.

In nonsocial species, murders are necessarily just of one individual by another. However, in social carnivorous species, like lions, wolves, hyenas, and ants, murder may take the form of coordinated attacks by members of one troop on members of a neighboring troop—i.e., mass killings or "wars." The form of war varies among species. Males may spare and mate with neighboring females, kill the infants, and drive off (langur monkeys) or even kill (lions) neighboring males; or both males and females may be killed (wolves). As one example, here is Hans Kruuk's account of a battle between two hyena clans in Tanzania's Ngorongoro Crater:

"About a dozen of the Scratching Rock hyenas ... grabbed one of the Mungi males and bit him wherever they could—especially in the belly, the feet, and the ears. The victim was completely covered by his attackers, who proceeded to maul him for about ten minutes. . . . The Mungi male was literally pulled apart, and when I later studied the injuries more closely, it appeared that his ears were bitten off and so were his feet and testicles, he was paralyzed by a spinal injury, had large gashes in the hind legs and belly, and subcutaneous hemorrhages all over."

Of particular interest in understanding our genocidal origins is the behavior of two of our three closest relatives, gorillas and common chimpanzees. Two decades ago, any biologist would have assumed that our ability to wield tools and to lay concerted group plans made us far more murderous than apes—if indeed apes were murderous at all. Recent discoveries about apes suggest, however, that a gorilla or common chimp stands at least as good a chance of being murdered as does the average human. Among gorillas, for instance, males fight each other for ownership of harems of females, and the victor may kill the loser's infants as well as the loser himself. Such fighting is a major cause of death for infant and adult male gorillas. The typical gorilla mother loses at least one infant to infanticidal males in the course of her life. Conversely, 38 percent of infant gorilla deaths are due to infanticide.

Especially instructive, because it could be documented in detail, was the extermination of one of the common chimpanzee bands that Jane Goodall studied, carried out between 1974 and 1977 by another band. As of the end of 1973 the two bands were fairly evenly matched: the Kasakela band to the north, with eight mature males and occupying fifteen square kilometers; and the Kahama band to the south, with six mature males and occupying ten square kilometers. The first fatal incident occurred in January 1974, when six of the Kasakela adult males, one adolescent male, and one adult female left behind the young Kasakela chimps, traveled south, then moved silently and more quickly south when they heard chimp calls from that direction, until they surprised a Kahama male referred to as Godi. One Kasakela male pulled the fleeing Godi to the ground, sat on his head, and held down his legs while the others spent ten minutes hitting and biting him. Finally, one attacker threw a large rock at Godi, and the attackers then left. Although able to stand up, Godi was badly wounded, bleeding, and had puncture marks. He was never seen again and presumably died of his injuries.

The next month, three Kasakela males and one female again traveled south and attacked the Kahama male Dé, who was already weak from a previous attack or illness. The attackers pulled Dé out of a tree, stamped on him, bit and hit him, and tore off pieces of his skin. A Kahama estrus female with Dé was forced to return northward with the attackers. Two months later Dé was seen still alive but emaciated, with his spine and pelvis protruding, some fingernails and part of a toe torn off, and his scrotum shrunk to one-fifth of normal size. He was not seen thereafter.

In February 1975 five adult and one adolescent Kasakela males tracked down and attacked Goliath, an old Kahama male. For eighteen minutes they hit, bit, and kicked him, stamped on him, lifted and dropped him, dragged him over the ground, and twisted his leg. At the end of the attack Goliath was unable to sit up and was not seen again.

While the above attacks were aimed at Kahama males, in September 1975 the Kahama female Madam Bee was fatally injured after at least four nonfatal attacks over the course of the preceding year. The attack was carried out by four Kasakela adult males, while one adolescent male and four Kasakela females (including Madam Bee's kidnapped daughter) watched. The attackers hit, slapped, and dragged Madam Bee, stamped and pounded on her, threw her to the ground, picked her up and slammed her down, and rolled her downhill. She died five days later.

In May 1977 five Kasakela males killed the Kahama male Charlie, but details of the fight were not observed. In November 1977 six Kasakela males caught the Kahama male Sniff and hit, bit, and pulled him, dragged him by the legs, and broke his left leg. He was still alive the next day but was not seen again.

Of the remaining Kahama chimps, two adult males and two adult females disappeared from unknown causes, while two young females transferred to the Kasakela band, which proceeded to occupy the former Kahama territory. However, in 1979 the next band to the south, the larger Kalande band with at least nine adult males, began to encroach on Kasakela territory and may have accounted for several vanished or wounded Kasakela chimps. Similar intergroup assaults have been observed in the sole other long-term field study of common chimps, but not in long-term studies of pygmy chimps.

If one judges these murderous common chimps by the standards of human killers, it is hard not to be struck by their inefficiency. Even though groups of three to six attackers assaulted single victims, quickly rendered him or her defenseless, and continued the assault for ten to twenty minutes or more, the victim was always still alive at the end of that time. However, the attackers did succeed in immobilizing the victim and often causing eventual death. The pattern was that the victim initially crouched and may have tried to protect his head but then gave up any attempt at defense, and the attack continued beyond the point where the victim ceased moving. In this respect the interband attacks differ from the milder fights that often occur within a band. Chimps' inefficiency as killers reflects their lack of weapons, but it remains surprising that they have not learned to kill by strangling, although that would be within their capabilities.

Not only is each individual killing inefficient by our standards, but so is the whole course of chimp genocide. It took three years and ten months from the first killing of a Kahama chimp to the band's end, and all killings were of individuals, never of several Kahama chimps at once. In contrast, Australia's settlers often succeeded in eliminating a band of Aborigines in a single dawn attack. Partly, this inefficiency again reflects chimps' lack of weapons. Since all chimps are equally unarmed, killings can succeed only by several attackers' overpowering a single victim, whereas Australia's settlers had the advantage of guns over unarmed Aborigines and could shoot many at once. Partly, too, genocidal chimps are much inferior to humans in brainpower and hence in strategic planning. Chimps apparently cannot plan a night attack or a coordinated ambush by a split assault team.

However, genocidal chimps do seem to evince intent and unsophisticated planning. The Kahama killings resulted from Kasakela groups' proceeding directly, quickly, silently, and nervously toward or into Kahama territory, sitting in trees and listening for nearly an hour, and finally running to Kahama chimps that they detected. Chimps also share xenophobia with us: they clearly recognize members of other bands as different from members of their own band, and treat them very differently.

In short, of all our human hallmarks—art, spoken language, drugs, and the others—the one that has been derived most straightforwardly from animal precursors is genocide. Common chimps already carried out planned killings, extermination of neighboring bands, wars of territorial conquest, and abduction of young nubile females. If chimps were given spears and some instruction in their use, their killings would undoubtedly begin to approach ours in efficiency. Chimpanzee behavior suggests that a major reason for our human hallmark of group living was defense against other human groups, especially once we acquired weapons and a large enough brain to plan ambushes. If this reasoning is correct, then anthropologists' traditional emphasis on "man the hunter" as a driving force of human evolution might be valid after all—with the difference that we ourselves were our own prey as well as the predator that forced us into group living.

THUS, OF THE TWO PATTERNS of genocide commonest among humans, both have animal precedents: killing both men and women fits the common chimpanzee and wolf pattern, while killing men and sparing women fits the gorilla and lion pattern. Unprecedented even among animals, however, is a procedure adopted from 1976 to 1983 by the Argentine military, in the course of killing over 10,000 political opponents and their families, the *desaparecidos*. Victims included the usual men, nonpregnant women, and children down to the age of three or four years, who were often tortured before being killed. But Argentina's soldiers made a unique contribution to animal behavior when they arrested pregnant women: the women were kept alive until they delivered, and only then were they shot in the head, so that the newborn infant could be adopted by childless military parents.

Liliana Carmen Pereyra Azzarri (age twenty-one),
case 195 among the Argentine *desaparecidos* whom
human rights groups have sought to trace. In 1977
Liliana was abducted when she was five months
pregnant. She was kept alive in a torture center
(ESMA Military Academy) until she gave birth to
a boy in February 1978, whereupon she was killed
by a shotgun blast to the head from close quarters.
Her skeleton, found in a Mar de Plata cemetery where
other *desaparecidos* were buried, was identified in 1985.
Her son has not been found and may have been
taken by a military couple. Liliana's treatment exemplifies the concept of honor often invoked by the
former Argentine junta to justify its actions. I thank
the Abuelas de Plaza de Mayo for permission to reproduce Liliana's photograph.

If we are not unique among animals in our own propensity for murder, might our propensities nevertheless be a pathological fruit of modern civilization? Modern writers, disgusted by destruction of "primitive" societies by "advanced" societies, tend to idealize the former as noble savages who supposedly are peace-loving, or who commit only isolated murders rather than massacres. Erich Fromm believed the warfare of hunter-gatherer societies to be "characteristically unbloody." Certainly some preliterate peoples (Pygmies, Eskimos) seem less warlike than some others (New Guineans, Great Plains and Amazonian Indians). Even the warlike peoples—so it is claimed—practice war in a ritualized fashion and stop when only a few adversaries have been killed. But this idealization does not match my experience of the New Guinea highlanders, who are often cited as practicing limited or ritualized war. While most fighting in New Guinea consisted of skirmishes leaving no or few dead, groups sometimes did succeed in massacring their neighbors. Like other peoples, New Guineans tried to drive off or kill their neighbors on occasions when they found it advantageous, safe, or a matter of survival to do so.

When we consider early literate civilizations, written records testify to the frequency of genocide. The wars of the Greeks and Trojans, of Rome and Carthage, and of the Assyrians and Babylonians and Persians proceeded to a common end: the slaughter of the defeated irrespective of sex, or else the killing of the men and enslavement of the women. We all know the biblical account of how the walls of Jericho came tumbling down at the sound of Joshua's trumpets. Less often quoted is the sequel: Joshua obeyed the Lord's command to slaughter the inhabitants of Jericho as well as of Ai, Makkedah, Libnah, Hebron, Debir, and many other cities. This was considered so ordinary that the Book of Joshua devotes only a phrase to each slaughter, as if to say: of course he killed all the inhabitants, what else would you expect? The sole account requiring elaboration is of the slaughter at Jericho itself, where Joshua did something really unusual: he spared the lives of one family (because they had helped his messengers).

We find similar episodes in accounts of the wars of the Crusaders, Pacific islanders, and many other groups. Obviously, I'm not saying that slaughter of the defeated irrespective of sex has always followed crushing defeat in war. But either that outcome, or else milder versions like the killing of men and enslavement of women, happened often enough so that they must be considered more than a rare aberration in our view of human nature. Since 1950 there have been nearly twenty episodes of genocide, including two claiming over a million victims each (Bangladesh in 1971, Cambodia in the late 1970s) and four more with over a hundred thousand victims each (the Sudan and Indonesia in the 1960s, Burundi and Uganda in the 1970s) (see map on page 286).

Evidently, genocide has been part of our human and prehuman heritage for millions of years. In light of this long history, what about our impression that the genocides of the twentieth century are unique? There is little doubt that Stalin and Hitler set new records for number of victims, because they enjoyed three advantages over killers of earlier centuries: denser populations of victims, improved communications for rounding up victims, and improved technology for mass killing. As another example of how technology can expedite genocide, the Solomon Islanders of Roviana Lagoon in the Southwest Pacific were famous for their head-hunting raids, which depopulated neighboring islands. However, as my Roviana friends explained to me, these raids did not blossom until steel axes reached the Solomon Islands in the nineteenth century. Beheading a man with a stone axe is difficult, and the axe blade quickly loses its sharp edge and is tedious to resharpen.

A much more controversial question is whether technology also makes genocide psychologically easier today, as Konrad Lorenz has argued. His reasoning goes as follows. As humans evolved from apes, we depended increasingly for our food on killing animals. However, we also lived in societies of more and more individuals, between whom cooperation was essential. Such societies could not maintain themselves unless we developed strong inhibitions about killing fellow humans. Throughout most of our evolutionary history, our weapons operated only at close quarters, hence it was enough that we be inhibited from looking another person in the face and killing him/her. Modern push-button weapons bypassed these inhibitions by enabling us to kill without even seeing our victims' faces. Technology thus created the psychological prerequisites for the white-collar genocides of Auschwitz and Treblinka, of Hiroshima and Dresden.

I am uncertain whether this psychological argument really contributed significantly to the modern ease of genocide. The past frequency of genocide seems to have been at least as high as today's, though practical considerations limited the number of victims. To understand genocide further, we must leave dates and numbers and inquire about the ethics of killing.

THAT OUR URGE TO KILL is restrained by our ethics almost all the time is obvious. The puzzle is: what unleashes it?

Today, while we may divide the world's people into "us" and "them," we know that there are thousands of types of "them," all differing from each other as well as from us in language, appearance, and habits. To waste words on pointing this out seems silly: we all know it from books and television, and most of us also know it from firsthand experience of travel. It is hard to transfer ourselves back into the frame of mind prevailing throughout much of human history and already described in Chapter 13. Like chimpanzees, gorillas, and social carnivores, we lived in band territories. The known world was much smaller and simpler than it is today: there were only a few known types of "them," one's immediate neighbors.

For example, in New Guinea until recently, each tribe maintained a shifting pattern of warfare and alliance with each of its neighbors. A person might enter the next valley on a friendly visit (never quite without danger) or on a war raid, but the chances of being able to traverse a sequence of several valleys in friendship were negligible. The powerful rules about treatment of one's fellow "us" did not apply to "them," those dimly understood, neighboring enemies. As I walked between New Guinea valleys, people who themselves practiced cannibalism and were only a decade out of the Stone Age routinely warned me about the unspeakably primitive, vile, and cannibalistic habits of the people whom I would encounter in the next valley. Even Al Capone's gangs in twentieth-century Chicago made a policy of hiring out-of-town killers, so that the assassin could feel that he was killing one of "them" rather than of "us."

The writings of classical Greece reveal an extension of this tribal territorialism. The known world was larger and more diverse, but "us" Greeks were still distinguished from "them" barbarians. Our word "barbarian" is derived from the Greek *barbaroi*, which simply means non-Greek foreigners. Egyptians and Persians, whose level of civilization was like that of the Greeks, were nevertheless *barbaroi*.

The ideal of conduct was not to treat all men equally, but instead to reward one's friends and to punish one's enemies. When the Athenian author Xenophon wanted to express the highest praise for his admired leader Cyrus, Xenophon related how Cyrus always repaid his friends' good turns more generously, and how Cyrus retaliated on his enemies' misdeeds more severely (e.g., by gouging out their eyes or cutting off their hands).

Like the Mungi and Scratching Rocks hyena clans, humans practiced a dual standard of behavior: strong inhibitions about killing one of "us," but a green light to kill "them" when it was safe to do so. Genocide was acceptable under this dichotomy, whether one considers the dichotomy as an inherited animal instinct or as a uniquely human ethical code. We all still acquire in childhood our own arbitrary dichotomous criteria for respecting or scorning other humans. I recall a scene at Goroka airport in the New Guinea highlands, when my Tudawhe field assistants were standing awkwardly in torn shirts and bare feet, and an unshaven, unbathed white man with a strong Australian accent and hat crumpled over his eyes approached. Even before he had begun to sneer at the Tudawhes as "black bums, they won't be fit to run this country for a century," I had begun to think to myself, "Dumb Aussie redneck, why doesn't he go home to his goddamn sheep dip." There it was, a blueprint for genocide: I scorning the Australian, and he scorning the Tudawhes, based on collective characteristics taken in at a glance.

With time, this ancient dichotomizing has become increasingly unacceptable as a basis for an ethical code. Instead, there has been some tendency toward paying at least lip service to a universal code—i.e., one stipulating similar rules for treating different peoples. Genocide conflicts directly with a universal code.

Despite this ethical conflict, numerous modern genocidists have managed to take unabashed pride in their accomplishment. When Argentina's General Julio Argentino Roca opened the pampas for white settlement by ruthlessly exterminating the Araucanian Indians, a delighted and grateful Argentinian nation elected him president in 1880. How do today's genocidists wriggle out of the conflict between their actions and a universal code of ethics? They resort to one of three types of rationalizations, all of which are variations on a simple psychological theme: "Blame the victim!"

First, most believers in a universal code still consider self-defense justified. This is a usefully elastic rationalization, because "they" can invariably be provoked into some behavior adequate to justify self-defense. For instance, the Tasmanians delivered an excuse to genocidal white colonists by killing an estimated total of 183 colonists over 34 years, after being provoked by a far greater number of mutilations, kidnappings, rapes, and murders. Even Hitler claimed self-defense in starting World War II: he went to the trouble of faking a Polish attack on a German border post.

Possessing the "right" religion or race or political belief, or claiming to represent progress or a higher level of civilization, is a second traditional justification for doing anything, including genocide, to those possessing the wrong principle. When I was a student in Munich in 1962, unrepentant Nazis still explained to me matter-of-factly that the Germans had had to invade Russia, because the Russian people had adopted communism. My fifteen field assistants in New Guinea's Fakfak Mountains all looked pretty similar to me, but eventually they began explaining to me which of them were Moslems and who were Christians, and why the former (or the latter) were irredeemably lower humans. There is an almost universal hierarchy of scorn, according to which literate peoples with advanced metallurgy (e.g., white colonialists in Africa) look down on herders (e.g., Tutsi, Hottentots), who look down on farmers (e.g., Hutu), who look down on nomads or hunter-gatherers (e.g., Pygmies, Bushmen).

Finally, our ethical codes regard animals and humans differently. Thus, modern genocidists routinely compare their victims to animals in order to justify the killings. Nazis considered Jews to be subhuman lice; the French settlers of Algeria referred to local Moslems as *ratons* (rats); "civilized" Paraguayans described the Aché hunter-gatherers as rabid rats; Boers called Africans *bobbejaan* (baboons); and educated northern Nigerians viewed Ibos as subhuman vermin. The English language is rich with animal names used as pejoratives: you pig (ape, bitch, cur, dog, ox, rat, swine).

All three types of ethical rationalizations were employed by Australian colonists to justify exterminating Tasmanians. However, my fellow Americans and I can get better insight into the rationalization process by focusing on the case that we have been trained from childhood to rationalize: our not-quite-complete extermination of American Indians. A set of attitudes that we absorb goes roughly as follows:

To begin with, we don't discuss the Indian tragedy much—not nearly as much as the genocides of World War II in Europe, for instance. Our great national tragedy is instead viewed as the Civil War. Insofar as we stop to think about white-vs.-Indian conflict, we consider it as belonging to the distant past, and we describe it in military language: the Pequod War, Great Swamp Fight, Battle of Wounded Knee, Conquest of the West, etc. Indians, in our view, were warlike and violent even toward other Indian tribes, masters of ambush and treachery. They were famous for their barbarity, notably for the distinctively Indian practices of torturing captives and scalping enemies. They were few in number and lived as nomadic hunters, especially bison hunters. The Indian population of the United States as of 1492 is traditionally estimated at 1 million. This figure is so trivial, compared to the present U.S. population of 250 million, that the inevitability of whites' occupying this virtually empty continent becomes immediately apparent. Many Indians died from smallpox and other diseases. The aforementioned attitudes guided the Indian policy of the most admired U.S. presidents and leaders from George Washington onward (see quotations in "Indian Policies of Some Famous Americans," page 308).

These rationalizations rest on a transformation of historical facts. Military language implies declared warfare waged by adult male combatants. Actually, common white tactics were sneak attacks (often by civilians) on villages or encampments to kill Indians of any age and either sex. Within the first century of white settlement, governments were paying scalp bounties to semiprofessional killers of Indians. Contemporary European societies were at least as warlike and violent as Indian societies, when one considers the European frequency of rebellions, class wars, drunken violence, legalized violence against criminals, and total war, including destruction of food and property. Torture was exquisitely refined in Europe: think of drawing and quartering, burning at the stake, and the rack. While the precontact Indian population of North America is the subject of widely varying opinions, plausible recent estimates are about eighteen million, a population not reached by white settlers of the U.S. till around 1840. Although some Indians in the U.S. were seminomadic hunters without agriculture, most Indians in the U.S. were settled farmers living in villages. Disease may well have been the biggest killer of Indians, but some of the diseases were intentionally transmitted by whites, and the diseases still left plenty of Indians to kill by more direct means. It was only in 1916 that the last "wild" Indian in the United States (the Yahi Indian known as Ishi) died, and frank and unapologetic memoirs by the white killers of his tribe were still being published as recently as 1923.

In short, Americans romanticize the white versus Indian conflict as battles of grown men on horseback, fought by U.S. cavalry and cowboys against fierce nomadic bison hunters able to offer strong resistance. The conflict is more accurately described as one race of civilian peasant farmers exterminating another. We Americans remember with outrage our own losses at the Alamo (around 200 dead), on the battleship U.S.S. *Maine* (260 dead), and at Pearl Harbor (about 2,200 dead), the incidents that galvanized our support for the Mexican War, Spanish-American War, and World War II respectively. Yet these numbers of dead are dwarfed by the forgotten losses that we inflicted on the Indians. Introspection shows us how, in rewriting our great national tragedy, we like so many modern peoples reconciled genocide with a universal code of ethics. The solution was to plead self-defense and overriding principle, and to view the victims as savage animals.

OUR REWRITING OF AMERICAN HISTORY stems from the aspect of genocide that is of greatest practical importance in preventing it: its psychological effects on killers, victims, and third parties. The most puzzling question involves the effect, or rather the apparent noneffect, on third parties. On first thought, one might expect that no horror could grip public attention as much as the intentional, collective, and savage killing of many people. In reality, genocides rarely grip the public's attention in other countries, and even more rarely are interrupted by foreign intervention. Who among us paid much attention to the slaughter of Zanzibar's Arabs in 1964, or of Paraguay's Aché Indians in the 1970s?

Contrast our nonresponse to these and all the other genocides of recent decades with our strong reaction to the sole two cases of modern genocide that remain vivid in our imagination: that of the Nazis against the Jews, and (much less vivid for most people) that of the Turks against the Armenians. These cases differ in three crucial respects from the genocides we ignore: the victims were whites, with

Ishi, the last surviving Indian of the Yahi tribe of northern California. This photograph shows him starving and terrified on August 29, 1911, the day that he emerged from forty-one years of hiding in a remote canyon. Most of his tribe was massacred by white settlers between 1853 and 1870. In 1870 the sixteen survivors of the final massacre went into concealment in the Mount Lassen wilderness and continued to live as hunter-gatherers. In November 1908, when the survivors had dwindled to four, surveyors stumbled upon their camp and took all their tools, clothes, and winter food supply, with the result that three of the Yahis (Ishi's mother, his sister, and an old man) died. Ishi remained alone for three more years until he could stand it no longer and walked out to white civilization, expecting to be lynched there. In fact, he was employed by the University of California Museum at San Francisco and died of tuberculosis in 1916. The photo is from the archives of the Lowie Museum of Anthropology, University of California, Berkeley.

whom other whites identify; the perpetrators were our war enemies, whom we were encouraged to hate as evil (especially the Nazis); and there are articulate survivors in the United States who go to much effort to force us to remember. Thus, it takes a rather special constellation of circumstances to get third parties to focus on genocide.

The strange passivity of third parties is exemplified by that of governments, whose actions reflect collective human psychology. While the United Nations in 1948 adopted a Convention on Genocide that declared it a crime, the UN has never taken serious steps to prevent, halt, or punish it, despite complaints lodged before the UN against ongoing genocides in Bangladesh, Burundi, Cambodia, Paraguay, and Uganda. To a complaint lodged against Uganda at the height of Idi Amin's terror, the UN Secretary-General responded only by asking Amin himself to investigate. The United States is not even among the nations that ratified the UN Convention on Genocide.

Is our puzzling nonresponse because we did not know, or could not find out, about ongoing genocides? Certainly not: many genocides of the 1960s and 1970s received detailed publicity at the time, including those in Bangladesh, Brazil, Burundi, Cambodia, East Timor, Equatorial Guinea, Indonesia, Lebanon, Paraguay, Rwanda, Sudan, Uganda, and Zanzibar. (The casualties in Bangladesh and Cambodia each topped a million.) For example, in 1968 the Brazilian government filed criminal charges against 134 of the 700 employees of its Indian Protection Service for their acts in exterminating Amazonian Indian tribes. Among the acts detailed in the 5,115-page Figueiredo report by Brazil's attorney general, and announced at a press conference by Brazil's minister of the interior, were the following: killing of Indians by dynamite, machine guns, arsenic-laced sugar, and intentionally introduced smallpox, influenza, tuberculosis, and measles; kidnapping of Indian children as slaves; and the hiring of professional killers of Indians by land-development companies. Accounts of the Figueiredo report appeared in the American and British press, but failed to stimulate much reaction.

One might thus conclude that most people simply do not care about injustice done to other people, or regard it as none of their business. This is undoubtedly part of the explanation, but not all of it. Many people care passionately about some injustices, such as apartheid in South Africa; why not also about genocide? This question was addressed poignantly to the Organization of African States by Hutu victims of the Tutsi in Burundi, where somewhere between 80,000 and 200,000 Hutu were killed in 1972: "Tutsi apartheid is established more ferociously than the apartheid of Vorster, more inhumanly than Portuguese colonialism. Outside of Hitler's Nazi movement, there is nothing to compete with it in world history. And the peoples of Africa say nothing. African heads of state receive the executioner Micombero [president of Burundi, a Tutsi] and clasp his hand in fraternal greeting. Sirs, heads of state, if you wish to help the African peoples of Namibia, Zimbabwe, Angola, Mozambique, and Guinea-Bissau to liberate themselves from their white oppressors, you have no right to let Africans murder other Africans.... Are you waiting until the entire Hutu ethnic group of Burundi is exterminated before raising your voices?"

To understand this nonreaction of third parties, we need to appreciate the reaction of surviving victims. Psychiatrists who have studied witnesses of genocide, such as Auschwitz survivors, describe the effects on them as "psychological numbing." Most of us have experienced the intense and lasting pain that comes when a loved friend or relative dies a natural death, out of sight. It is virtually impossible for us to imagine the multiplied intensity of pain when one is forced to watch at close hand many loved friends and relatives being killed with extreme savagery. For the survivors, there is a shattering of the implicit belief system under which such savagery was forbidden; a sense of stigma that one must indeed be worthless to have been singled out for such cruelty; and a sense of guilt at surviving, when one's companions died. Just as intense physical pain numbs us, so does intense psychological pain: there is no other way to survive and remain sane. For me, these reactions were personified in a relative who survived two years in Auschwitz, and who remained practically unable to cry for decades afterward.

As for the reactions of the killers, those killers whose ethical code distinguishes between "us" and "them" may be able to feel pride, but those reared under a universal ethical code may share the numbing of their victims, exacerbated by the guilt of perpetration. Hundreds of thousands of Americans who fought in Vietnam suffered this numbing. Even the descendants of genocidists—descendants who have no individual responsibility—may feel a collective guilt, the mirror image of the collective labeling of victims that defines genocide. To reduce the pain of guilt, the descendants often rewrite history: witness the response of modern Americans, or that of Ms. Cobern and many other modern Australians.

We can now begin to understand better the nonreaction of third parties to genocide. Genocide inflicts crippling and lasting psychological damage on the victims and killers who experience it firsthand. But it also may leave deep scars on those who hear about it only secondhand, such as the children of Auschwitz survivors, or the psychotherapists who treat the survivors and Vietnam veterans. Therapists who have trained professionally to be able to listen to human misery often cannot bear to hear the sickening recollections of those involved in genocide. If paid professionals cannot stand it, who can blame the lay public for refusing to listen?

Consider the reactions of Robert Jay Lifton, an American psychiatrist who had already had much experience with survivors of extreme situations before he interviewed survivors of the Hiroshima A-bomb: "... now, instead of dealing with 'the atomic bomb problem,' I was confronted with the brutal details of actual experiences of human beings who sat before me. I found that the completion of each of these early interviews left me profoundly shocked and emotionally spent. But very soon—within a few days, in fact—I noticed that my reactions were changing. I was listening to descriptions of the same horrors, but their effect upon me had lessened. The experience was an unforgettable demonstration of the 'psychic closing off' we shall see to be characteristic of all aspects of atomic bomb exposure...."

WHAT GENOCIDES can we expect from *Homo sapiens* in the future? There are plenty of obvious reasons for pessimism. The world abounds with trouble spots that seem ripe for genocide: South Africa, Northern Ireland, Yugoslavia, Sri Lanka, New Caledonia, and the Middle East, to name just a few. Totalitarian governments bent on genocide seem unstoppable. Modern weaponry permits one to kill ever larger numbers of victims, to be a killer while wearing a coat and tie, and even to effect a universal genocide of the human race.

At the same time, I see grounds for cautious optimism that the future need not be as murderous as the past. In many countries today, people of different races or religions or ethnic groups live together, with varying degrees of social justice but at least without open mass murder: for instance, Switzerland, Belgium, Papua New Guinea, Fiji, even the post-Ishi U.S.A. Some genocides have been successfully interrupted, reduced, or prevented by the efforts or anticipated reactions of third parties. Even the Nazi extermination of Jews, which we view as the most efficient and unstoppable of genocides, was thwarted in Denmark, Bulgaria, and every other occupied state where the head of the dominant church publicly denounced deportation of Jews before or as soon as it began. A further hopeful sign is that modern travel, TV, and photography enable us to see other people living ten thousand miles away as human, like us. Much as we damn twentieth-century technology, it is blurring the distinction between "us" and "them" that makes genocide possible. While genocide was considered socially acceptable or even admirable in the pre-first-contact world, the modern spread of international culture and knowledge of distant peoples has been making it increasingly hard to justify.

Still, the risk of genocide will be with us as long as we cannot bear to understand it, and as long as we delude ourselves with the belief that only rare perverts could commit it. Granted, it's hard not to go numb while reading about genocide. It's hard to imagine how we, and other nice ordinary people that we know, could bring ourselves to look helpless people in the face while killing them. I came closest to being able to imagine it when a friend whom I had long known told me of a genocidal massacre at which he had been a killer:

Kariniga is a gentle Tudawhe tribesman who worked with me in New Guinea. We shared life-threatening situations, fears, and triumphs, and I like and admire him. One evening after I had known Kariniga for five years, he told me of an episode from his youth. There had been a long history of conflict between the Tudawhes and a neighboring village of Daribi tribesmen. Tudawhes and Daribis seem quite similar to me, but Kariniga had come to view Daribis as inexpressibly vile. In a series of ambushes the Daribis finally succeeded in picking off many Tudawhes, including Kariniga's father, until the surviving Tudawhes became desperate. All the remaining Tudawhe men surrounded the Daribi village at night and set fire to the huts at dawn. As the sleepy Daribis stumbled down the steps of their burning huts, they were speared. Some Daribis succeeded in escaping to hide in the forest, where Tudawhes tracked down and killed most of them during the following weeks. But the establish-

ment of Australian government control ended the hunt before Kariniga could catch his father's killer.

Since that evening, I've often found myself shuddering as I recalled details of it—the glow in Kariniga's eyes as he told me of the
dawn massacre; those intensely satisfying moments when he finally
drove his spear into some of his people's murderers; and his tears of
rage and frustration at the escape of his father's killer, whom he still
hoped to kill someday with poison. That evening, I thought I understood how at least one nice person had brought himself to kill.
The potential for genocide that circumstances thrust on Kariniga lies
within all of us. As the growth of world population sharpens conflicts
between and within societies, humans will have more urge to kill
each other, and more effective weapons with which to do it. To listen
to first-person accounts of genocide is unbearably painful. But if we
continue to turn away and not understand it, when will it be our own
turn to become the killers, or the victims?

INDIAN POLICIES OF SOME FAMOUS AMERICANS

President George Washington. "The immediate objectives are the total
destruction and devastation of their settlements. It will be essential to
ruin their crops in the ground and prevent their planting more."

Benjamin Franklin. "If it be the Design of Providence to Extirpate
these Savages in order to make room for Cultivators of the Earth, it
seems not improbable that Rum may be the appointed means."

President Thomas Jefferson. "This unfortunate race, whom we had
been taking so much pains to save and to civilize, have by their
unexpected desertion and ferocious barbarities justified extermination and now await our decision on their fate."

President John Quincy Adams. "What is the right of the huntsman to
the forest of a thousand miles over which he has accidentally ranged
in quest of prey?"

President James Monroe. "The hunter or savage state requires a greater extent of territory to sustain it, than is compatible with the progress and just claims of civilized life ... and must yield to it."

President Andrew Jackson. "They have neither the intelligence, the industry, the moral habits, nor the desire of improvement which are essential to any favorable change in their condition. Established in the midst of another and a superior race, and without appreciating the causes of their inferiority or seeking to control them, they must necessarily yield to the force of circumstances and ere long disappear."

Chief Justice John Marshall. "The tribes of Indians inhabiting this country were savages, whose occupation was war, and whose subsistence was drawn from the forest.... That law which regulates, and ought to regulate in general, the relations between the conqueror and conquered was incapable of application to a people under such circumstances. Discovery [of America by Europeans] gave an exclusive right to extinguish the Indian title of occupancy, either by purchase or by conquest."

President William Henry Harrison. "Is one of the fairest portions of the globe to remain in a state of nature, the haunt of a few wretched savages, when it seems destined by the Creator to give support to a large population and to be the seat of civilization?"

President Theodore Roosevelt. "The settler and pioneer have at bottom had justice on their side; this great continent could not have been kept as nothing but a game preserve for squalid savages."

General Philip Sheridan. "The only good Indians I ever saw were dead."

PART FIVE

REVERSING
OUR PROGRESS
OVERNIGHT

Our species is now at the pinnacle of its numbers, its geographic extent, its power, and the fraction of the Earth's productivity that it commands. That's the good news. The bad news is that we are also in the process of reversing all that progress much more rapidly than we created it. Our power threatens our own existence. We don't know whether we shall suddenly blow ourselves up before we would otherwise expire in a slow stew caused by global warming, pollution, habitat destruction, more mouths to feed, less food to feed those mouths, and extermination of other species that form our resource base. Are these dangers really new ones that have arisen since the Industrial Revolution, as widely assumed?

It's a common belief that species in a state of Nature live in balance with each other and with their environment. Predators don't exterminate their prey, nor do herbivores overgraze their plants. According to this view, humans are the unique misfit. If this were true, Nature would hold no lessons for us.

There is something to this view, insofar as species don't go extinct under natural conditions as rapidly as we are exterminating them now, except under rare circumstances. Such a rare event was the mass die-off sixty-five million years ago, possibly due to an asteroidal impact, that finished the dinosaurs. Since evolutionary multiplications of species are very slow, natural extinctions obviously must also be slow, otherwise we would have been left with no species long ago. Expressed alternatively, the vulnerable species get eliminated quickly, and what we see persisting in Nature are the robust species.

However, that broad conclusion still leaves us with many instructive examples of species' exterminating other species. Almost all known cases prove to combine two elements. First, the cases involve species reaching environments where they did not occur before, and where they encounter prey populations naïve to those invading predators. By the time that the ecological dust settles and a new equilibrium is reached, some of the newfound prey may have been exterminated. Second, the perpetrators of such exterminations prove to be so-called switching predators, which are not specialized to eat only a single prey species but can feed on many different ones. Although the predator exterminates some prey species, it survives by switching to others.

Such exterminations often occur when humans intentionally or accidentally transfer a species from one part of the globe to another. Rats, cats, goats, pigs, ants, and even snakes are among these transferred killers. For instance, during World War II a tree snake native to the Australian region was accidentally transported on ships or planes to the previously snake-free Pacific island of Guam. This predator has already exterminated or brought to the brink of extinction most of Guam's native forest-bird species, which had had no opportunity to evolve behavioral defenses against snakes. However, the snake is in no danger itself despite having virtually eliminated its bird prey, because it can switch to rats, mice, shrews, and lizards as victims. As another example, cats and foxes introduced into Australia by humans have been eating their way through Australia's small native marsupials and rats without endangering themselves, because there remain abundant rabbits and other prey species on which to feed.

We humans furnish the prime example of a switching predator. We eat everything from snails and seaweed to whales, mushrooms, and strawberries. We can overharvest some species to the point of extinction, and then just switch to other food. Hence a wave of extinctions has ensued every time that humans have reached a previously unoccupied part of the globe. The dodo, whose name has become synonymous with extinction, formerly lived on the island of Mauritius, half of whose land and freshwater bird species became extinct following the island's discovery in 1507. Dodos in particular were big, edible, flightless, and easily caught by hungry sailors. Hawaiian bird species similarly died out en masse following Hawaii's discovery by Polynesians fifteen hundred years ago, as did America's large mammal species after ancestral Indians arrived eleven thousand years ago. Extinction waves have also accompanied major improvements of hunting technology in lands long occupied by humans. For example, wild populations of the Arabian oryx, a beautiful antelope of the Near East, survived one million years of human hunting, only to succumb to high-powered rifles in 1972.

There are numerous animal precedents for our propensity to exterminate individual prey species but to sustain ourselves by switching to others. Is there any precedent for an animal population's destroying its entire resource base and eating its way into extinction? This outcome is uncommon, because animal numbers are regulated by many factors that tend automatically to lower birth rates or increase death rates when the animal is too numerous for its food supply, and vice versa when it is rare. For example, mortality due to external factors like predators, diseases, parasites, and starvation tends to increase at high population densities. High densities also trigger responses of the animal itself, such as infanticide, postponed breeding, and increased aggression. These responses and external factors generally reduce the animal's population and relieve its pressure on its resources before they can be exhausted.

Nevertheless, some animal populations actually have eaten themselves into extinction. One example involves the progeny of twenty-nine reindeer that were introduced in 1944 to St. Matthew Island in the Bering Sea. By 1963 they had multiplied to six thousand. But reindeer depend for food on slow-growing lichens, which on St. Matthew had no chance to recover from reindeer grazing, since the animals had nowhere to migrate. When a harsh winter struck in 1963–64, all the animals except forty-one females and one sterile male starved to death, leaving a doomed population on an island littered with thousands of skeletons. A similar example was the introduction of rabbits to Lisianski Island west of Hawaii in the first decade of this century. Within a decade the rabbits had eaten themselves into oblivion by consuming every plant on the island except two morning glories and a tobacco patch.

These and other similar examples of ecological suicide all involve populations that suddenly became free of the usual factors regulating their numbers. Rabbits and reindeer are normally subject to predators, and reindeer on continents use migration as a safety valve to leave an area and allow its vegetation to recover. But Lisianski and St. Matthew Islands lacked predators, and emigration was impossible, so that the animals bred and ate unchecked.

On reflection, it is clear that the entire human species has been equally successful in recently escaping from the former controls on our numbers. We eliminated predation on us long ago; twentieth-century medicine has greatly reduced our mortality from infectious disease; and some of our leading behavioral techniques of population control, such as infanticide, chronic war, and sexual abstinence, have become socially unacceptable. Our population is now doubling about every thirty-five years. Granted, that's not as fast as the St. Matthew reindeer. Island Earth is bigger than St. Matthew Island, and some of our resources are more elastic than lichens (though other resources, like oil, are less elastic). But the qualitative conclusion remains the same: no population can grow indefinitely.

Thus, our present ecological predicament has familiar animal precursors. Like many switching predators, we exterminate some prey species when we colonize a new environment or acquire new destructive power. Like some animal populations that suddenly escaped their former limits on growth, we risk destroying ourselves by destroying our resource base. What about the view that we were in a state of relative ecological equilibrium until the Industrial Revolution, and that only since then have we begun seriously to exterminate species and overexploit our environment? That Rousseauan fantasy will be taken up in the remaining three chapters of this book.

We'll first examine the widespread belief in a former Golden

Age, when we supposedly lived as noble savages practicing a conservation ethic and in harmony with Nature. In reality, mass extinctions have coincided with each major extension of human lebensraum during the last ten thousand years and possibly much longer. Our direct responsibility for the extinctions is clearest in the case of the most recent expansions, for which the evidence is still fresh: Europeans' expansion over the globe since 1492, and the somewhat earlier colonization of oceanic islands by Polynesians and the Malagasy. Older expansions such as the first human occupation of the Americas and Australia were also accompanied by mass extinctions, though the trail of evidence has had much more time to fade and hence conclusions about cause-and-effect are necessarily weaker.

It's not just that the Golden Age was blackened by mass extinctions. While no large human population has eaten itself out of existence, some populations on small islands have done so, and many large populations have damaged their resources to the point of economic collapse. The clearest examples come from isolated cultures, such as the Easter Island and Anasazi civilizations. But environmental factors also drove the major shifts in western civilization, including the successive collapses of Middle Eastern, then Greek, then Roman hegemony. Hence self-destructive abuse of our environment, far from being a modern invention, has long been a prime mover of human history.

We'll then look more closely at the biggest, most dramatic, and most controversial of these "Golden Age mass extinctions." Around eleven thousand years ago most of the large mammals of two entire continents, North America and South America, became extinct. Around the same time appears the first unequivocal evidence for human occupation of the Americas, by the ancestors of American Indians. It was the biggest expansion of human territory since *Homo erectus* spread out of Africa to colonize Europe and Asia a million years ago. The temporal coincidence between the first Americans and the last big American mammals, the lack of mass extinctions elsewhere in the world at that same time, and proofs that some of the now-extinct beasts were hunted have suggested what is termed the New World blitzkrieg hypothesis. According to this interpretation, as the first wave of human hunters multiplied and spread from Canada to Patagonia, they encoun-

tered big animals that had never seen humans before, and they exterminated as they marched. While this theory's critics are at least
as numerous as its backers, we'll try to make sense of the debate.

Finally, we'll seek to put approximate numbers on the count of
species that we have already driven into extinction. We shall start
with the firmest numbers: the species whose extinctions occurred
in modern times and were well documented, and for which the
search for survivors has been so thorough as to leave no doubt that
there are no survivors. Next come estimates of three less certain
numbers: the modern species that haven't been seen alive for some
time and that became extinct before anyone was aware of it; the
modern species that haven't even been "discovered" and named;
and the species that humans exterminated before the rise of modern science. That background will let us appraise the main mechanisms by which we exterminate, and the number of species that
we are likely to exterminate within my sons' lifetime—if we proceed at our current rate.

CHAPTER 17

The Golden Age That Never Was

> *Every part of the earth is sacred to
> my people. Every shining pine need-
> le, every sandy shore, every mist in the
> dark woods, every clearing and hum-
> ming insect is holy in the memory and
> experience of my people.... The white
> man ... is a stranger who comes in the
> night and takes from the land what-
> ever he needs. The earth is not his
> brother but his enemy.... Continue
> to contaminate your bed, and you will
> one night suffocate in your own waste.*

> —From a letter written in 1855 to President Franklin
> Pierce by Chief Seattle of the Duwanish tribe
> of American Indians.

ENVIRONMENTALISTS SICKENED BY THE DAMAGE THAT INDUSTRIAL
societies are wreaking on the world often look to the past as a Golden
Age. When Europeans began to settle America, the air and rivers
were pure, the landscape green, the Great Plains teeming with bison.
Today we breathe smog, worry about toxic chemicals in our drinking
water, pave over the landscape, and rarely see any large wild animal.
Worse is surely to come. By the time my infant sons reach retirement

age, half of the world's species will be extinct, the air radioactive, and the seas polluted with oil.

Undoubtedly, two simple reasons go a long way toward explaining our worsening mess: modern technology has far more power to cause havoc than did the stone axes of the past, and far more people are alive now than ever before. But a third factor may also have contributed: a change in attitudes. Unlike modern city dwellers, at least some preindustrial peoples—like the Duwanish, whose chief I quoted—depend on and revere their local environment. Stories abound of how such peoples are in effect practicing conservationists. As a New Guinea tribesman once explained to me, "It's our custom that if a hunter one day kills a pigeon in one direction from the village, he waits a week before hunting for pigeons again, and then goes in the opposite direction." We're only beginning to realize how sophisticated the conservationist policies of so-called primitive peoples actually are. For instance, well-intentioned foreign experts have made deserts out of large areas of Africa. In those same areas, local herders had thrived for uncounted millennia by making annual nomadic migrations, which ensured that land never became overgrazed.

The nostalgic outlook shared till recently by most of my environmentalist colleagues and me is part of a human tendency to view the past as a Golden Age in many other respects. A famous exponent of this outlook was the eighteenth-century French philosopher Jean-Jacques Rousseau, whose *Discourse on the Origin of Inequality* traced our degeneration from the Golden Age to the human misery that Rousseau saw around him. When eighteenth-century European explorers encountered preindustrial peoples like Polynesians and American Indians, those peoples became idealized in European salons as "noble savages" living in a continued Golden Age, untouched by such curses of civilization as religious intolerance, political tyranny, and social inequality.

Even now, the days of classical Greece and Rome are widely considered to be the Golden Age of western civilization. Ironically, the Greeks and Romans also saw themselves as degenerates from a past Golden Age. I can still recite half-conscious those lines of the Roman poet Ovid that I memorized in tenth-grade Latin, "Aurea prima sata est aetas, quae vindice nullo....": "First came the Golden Age, when men were honest and righteous of their own free will." Ovid went on to contrast those virtues with the rampant treachery and warfare of his own times. I have no doubt that any humans still alive in the radioactive soup of the twenty-second century will write equally nostalgically about our own era, which will then seem untroubled by comparison.

Given this widespread belief in a Golden Age, some recent discoveries by archaeologists and paleontologists have come as a shock. It's now clear that preindustrial societies have been exterminating species, destroying habitats and undermining their own existence for thousands of years. Some of the best-documented examples involve Polynesians and American Indians, the very peoples most often cited as exemplars of environmentalism. Needless to say, this revisionist view is hotly contested, not only in the halls of academia but also among lay people in Hawaii, New Zealand, and other areas with large Polynesian or Indian minorities. Are the new "discoveries" just one more piece of racist pseudo-science by which white settlers seek to justify dispossessing indigenous peoples? How can the discoveries be reconciled with all the evidence for conservationist practices by modern preindustrial peoples? If the discoveries are correct, can we use them as case histories to help us predict the fate that our own environmental policies may bring upon us? Can the recent findings explain some otherwise mysterious collapses of ancient civilizations, like those of Easter Island or the Maya Indians?

Before we can answer these controversial questions, we need to understand the new evidence belying the assumed past Golden Age of environmentalism. Let's first consider evidence for past waves of exterminations, then evidence for past destruction of habitats.

WHEN BRITISH COLONISTS began to settle New Zealand in the 1800s, they found no native land mammals except bats. That wasn't surprising: New Zealand is a remote island lying much too far from the continents for flightless mammals to reach. However, the colonists' plows uncovered the bones and eggshells of large birds that were then already extinct but that the Maori (the earlier Polynesian settlers of New Zealand) remembered by the name "moa." From complete skeletons, some of them evidently recent and still retaining skin and feathers, we have a good idea how moas must have looked alive: ostrichlike birds comprising a dozen species, and ranging from little ones "only" three feet high and forty pounds in weight up to giants of five hundred pounds and ten feet tall. Their food habits can be inferred from preserved gizzards containing twigs and leaves of dozens of plant species, showing them to have been herbivores. They used to be New Zealand's equivalents of big mammalian herbivores like deer and antelope.

While the moas are New Zealand's most famous extinct birds, many others have been described from fossil bones, totaling at least twenty-eight species that disappeared before Europeans arrived. Quite a few besides the moas were big and flightless, including a big duck, a giant coot, and an enormous goose. These flightless birds were descended from normal birds that had flown to New Zealand and that had then evolved to lose their expensive wing muscles in a land free of mammalian predators. Others of the vanished birds, such as a pelican, a swan, a giant raven, and a colossal eagle, were perfectly capable of flight.

Weighing up to thirty pounds, the eagle was by far the biggest and most powerful bird of prey in the world when it was alive. It dwarfed even the largest hawk now in existence, tropical America's harpy eagle. The New Zealand eagle would have been the sole predator capable of attacking adult moas. Although some moas were nearly twenty times heavier than the eagle, it still could have killed them by taking advantage of the moas' erect two-legged posture, crippling them with an attack on the long legs, then killing them with an attack on the head and long neck, and finally remaining for many days to consume the carcasses, just as lions take their time at consuming a giraffe. The eagle's habits may explain the many headless moa skeletons that have been found.

Up to this point I've discussed New Zealand's big extinct animals. But fossil hunters have also discovered the bones of small animals the size of mice and rats. Scampering or crawling on the ground were at least three species of flightless or weak-flying songbirds, several frogs, giant snails, many giant cricketlike insects up to double the weight of a mouse, and strange mouselike bats that rolled up their wings and ran. Some of these little animals were completely extinct by the time that Europeans arrived. Others still survived on small offshore islands near New Zealand, but their fossil bones show that they were formerly abundant on the New Zealand mainland. Collectively, all these now-extinct species that had evolved in isolation would have provided New Zealand with the ecological equivalents of the continents' flightless mammals that had never arrived: moas instead of deer, flightless geese and coots instead of rabbits, big crickets and little songbirds and bats instead of mice, and colossal eagles instead of leopards.

Fossils and biochemical evidence indicate that the moas' ancestors had reached New Zealand millions of years ago. When and why, after surviving for so long, did the moas finally become extinct? What disaster could have struck so many species as different as crickets, eagles, ducks, and moas? Specifically, were all these strange creatures still alive when the ancestors of the Maoris arrived around A.D. 1000?

At the time that I first visited New Zealand in 1966, the received wisdom was that moas had died out because of a change in climate, and that any moa species surviving to greet the Maoris were on their figurative last legs. New Zealanders took it as dogma that Maoris were conservationists and didn't exterminate the moas. There is still no doubt that Maoris, like other Polynesians, used stone tools, lived mainly by farming and fishing, and lacked the destructive power of modern industrial societies. At most, it was assumed, Maoris might have given the coup de grace to populations already on the verge of extinction. But three sets of discoveries have demolished this conviction.

First, much of New Zealand was covered with glaciers or cold tundra during the last Ice Age, ending about ten thousand years ago. Since then, the New Zealand climate has become much more favorable, with warmer temperatures and the spread of magnificent forests. The last moas died with their gizzards full of food, and enjoying the best climate that they had seen for tens of thousands of years.

Second, radiocarbon-dated bird bones from dated Maori archaeological sites prove that all known moa species were still present in abundance when the first Maoris stepped ashore. So were the extinct geese, ducks, swan, eagle, and other birds now known only from fossil bones. Within a few centuries, the moas and most of those other birds were extinct. It would have been an incredible coincidence if individuals of dozens of species that had occupied New Zealand for millions of years selected the precise geological moment of human arrival as the occasion to expire in synchrony.

Finally, more than a hundred large archaeological sites are

known—some of them covering dozens of acres—where Maoris cut up prodigious numbers of moas, cooked them in earth ovens, and discarded the remains. They ate the meat, used the skins for clothing, fashioned bones into fishhooks and jewelry, and blew out the eggs for use as water containers. During the nineteenth century moa bones were carted away from these sites by the wagonload. The number of moa skeletons in known Maori moa-hunter sites is estimated to be between 100,000 and 500,000, about ten times the number of moas likely to have been alive in New Zealand at any instant. Maoris must have been slaughtering moas for many generations.

Hence it is now clear that Maoris exterminated moas, at least partly by killing them, partly by robbing their nests of eggs, and probably partly as well by clearing some of the forests in which moas lived. Anyone who has hiked in New Zealand's rugged mountains will initially be incredulous at this thought. Just picture those travel posters of New Zealand's Fiordland, with its steep-walled gorges ten thousand feet deep, its four hundred inches of annual rainfall, and its cold winters. Even today, full-time professional hunters armed with telescopic rifles and operating from helicopters can't control the numbers of deer in those mountains. How could the few thousand Maoris living on New Zealand's South Island and Stewart Island, armed only with stone axes and clubs and operating on foot, have hunted down the last moas?

But there would have been a crucial difference between deer and moas. Deer have been selected for tens of thousands of generations to flee from human hunters, while moas had never seen humans until Maoris arrived. Like the naïve animals of the Galápagos Islands today, moas were probably tame enough for a hunter to walk up to one and club it. Unlike deer, moas may have had sufficiently low reproductive rates for a few hunters visiting a valley only once every couple of years to kill moas faster than they could breed. That's precisely what's happening today to New Guinea's largest surviving native mammal, a tree kangaroo in the remote Bewani Mountains. In areas settled by people, tree kangaroos are nocturnal, incredibly shy, live in trees, and are thus far harder to hunt than moas would have been. Despite all that, and despite the very small human population of the Bewanis, the cumulative effects of occasional hunting parties—literally one visit per valley per several years—have sufficed to bring this kangaroo to the verge of extinction. Having seen it happen to tree kangaroos, I now have no difficulty understanding how it happened to moas.

Not just moas but also all of New Zealand's other extinct bird species were still alive when Maoris landed. Most were gone a few centuries later. The larger ones—the swan and pelican, the flightless goose and coot—were surely hunted for food. The giant eagle, however, may have been killed by Maoris in self-defense. What do *you* think happened when that eagle, specialized at crippling and killing two-legged prey between three and ten feet tall, did when it saw its first six-foot-tall Maoris? Even today, Manchurian eagles trained for hunting occasionally kill their human handlers, but the Manchurian birds were mere dwarfs beside New Zealand's giant, which was preadapted to become a man killer.

Surely, though, neither self-defense nor hunting for food explains the rapid disappearance of New Zealand's peculiar crickets, snails, wrens, and bats. Why were so many of those species exterminated, either throughout their range or else everywhere except on some offshore islands? Deforestation may be part of the answer, but the major reason was the other hunters that Maoris intentionally or accidentally brought with them: rats! Just as moas that evolved in the absence of humans were defenseless against humans, so, too, small insular animals that evolved in the absence of rats were defenseless against rats. We know that the rat species spread by Europeans played a major role in modern exterminations of many bird species on Hawaii and other previously rat-free oceanic islands. For example, when rats finally reached Big South Cape Island off New Zealand in 1962, within three years they exterminated or decimated the populations of eight bird species and a bat. That's why so many New Zealand species are restricted today to rat-free islands, the sole places where they could survive when the rat tide accompanying the Maoris swept over the New Zealand mainland.

Thus, when the Maoris landed, they found an intact New Zealand biota of creatures so strange that we would dismiss them as science-fiction fantasies if we did not have their fossilized bones to convince us of their former existence. The scene was as close as we shall ever get to what we might see if we could reach another fertile planet on which life had evolved. Within a short time, much of that community had collapsed in a biological holocaust, and some of the remaining community collapsed in a second holocaust following the arrival of

Europeans. The end result is that New Zealand today has about half of the bird species that greeted the Maoris, and many of the survivors are either now at risk of extinction or else confined to islands with few introduced mammalian pests. A few centuries of hunting had sufficed to end millions of years of moa history.

NOT ONLY ON NEW ZEALAND but on all other remote Pacific islands where archaeologists have looked recently, bones of many now-extinct bird species have been found at sites of the first settlers, proving there too that the bird extinctions and human colonizations were somehow related. From all the main islands of Hawaii, paleontologists Storrs Olson and Helen James of the Smithsonian Institution have identified fossil bird species that disappeared during the Polynesian settlement that began around A.D. 500. The fossils include not only small honey creepers related to species still present but also bizarre flightless geese and ibises with no living close relatives at all. While Hawaii is notorious for its bird extinctions following European settlement, this earlier extinction wave had been unknown until Olson and James began publishing their discoveries in 1982. The known extinctions of Hawaiian birds before Captain Cook's arrival now total the incredible number of at least fifty species, nearly one-tenth the number of bird species breeding on mainland North America.

That's not to say that all these Hawaiian birds were hunted out of existence. Although geese probably were indeed exterminated by overhunting, like the moas, small songbirds are more likely to have been eliminated by rats that arrived with the first Hawaiians, or else by destruction of forests that Hawaiians cleared for agriculture. Similar discoveries of extinct birds at archaeological sites of early Polynesians have also been made on Tahiti, Fiji, Tonga, New Caledonia, the Marquesas Islands, Chatham Islands, Cook Islands, Solomon Islands, and Bismarck Archipelago.

An especially intriguing collision of birds and Polynesians took place on Henderson Island, an extremely remote speck of land lying in the tropical Pacific Ocean 125 miles east of Pitcairn Island, which is famous for its own isolation. (Recall that Pitcairn is so remote that the mutineers who wrested the H.M.S. *Bounty* from Captain Bligh lived undetected on Pitcairn for eighteen years until the island was rediscovered.) Henderson consists of jungle-covered coral riddled with crevices and totally unsuited for agriculture. Naturally, the island is now uninhabited and has been ever since Europeans first saw it in 1606. Henderson has often been cited as one of the world's most pristine habitats, totally unaffected by humans.

It was therefore a big surprise when Olson and fellow paleontologist David Steadman recently identified bones of two large species of pigeons, one smaller pigeon, and three seabirds that had gone extinct on Henderson some time between five hundred and eight hundred years ago. The same six species or close relatives had already been found in archaeological sites on several inhabited Polynesian islands, where it was clear how they could have been exterminated by people. The apparent contradiction of birds' also being exterminated by humans on uninhabited, seemingly uninhabitable Henderson was solved by the discovery there of former Polynesian sites with hundreds of cultural artifacts, proving that the island had actually been occupied by Polynesians for several centuries. At those same sites, along with the bones of the six bird species that were exterminated on Henderson, were the bones of other bird species that survived, plus many fish.

Thus, those early Polynesian colonists of Henderson evidently subsisted mainly on pigeons, seabirds, and fish until they had decimated the bird populations, at which point they had destroyed their food supply and either starved or else abandoned the island. The Pacific contains at least eleven other "mystery" islands besides Henderson, islands that were uninhabited on European discovery but that showed archaeological evidence of former occupation by Polynesians. Some of those islands had been settled for hundreds of years before their human population finally died out or left. All were small or in other respects marginally suitable for agriculture, leaving human settlers heavily dependent on birds and other animals for food. Given the widespread evidence for overexploitation of wild animals by early Polynesians, not only Henderson but the other mystery islands as well may represent the graveyards of human populations that ruined their own resource base.

LEST I LEAVE the impression that Polynesians were in any way unique as preindustrial exterminators, let's now jump nearly halfway around the globe to the world's fourth-largest island, Madagascar, lying in the Indian Ocean off the coast of Africa. When Portuguese explorers arrived around 1500, they found Madagascar already occupied by people now called the Malagasy. On geographic grounds, you might have expected their language to be related to African languages spoken a mere two hundred miles to the west, on the coast of Mozambique. Astonishingly, though, it actually proved to belong to a group of languages spoken on the Indonesian island of Borneo, on the opposite side of the Indian Ocean thousands of miles to the northeast. Physically, the Malagasy range in appearance from typical Indonesians to typical blacks of East Africa. These paradoxes are due to the Malagasy's having arrived between one thousand and two thousand years ago, as a result of Indonesian traders' voyaging around the Indian Ocean coastline to India and eventually to East Africa. In Madagascar they proceeded to build a society based on herding cattle, goats, and pigs, farming, and fishing, and linked to the East African coast by Muslim traders.

As interesting as Madagascar's people are the wild animals that it has—and those that it lacks. Living in enormous abundance on the nearby African mainland are many species of large and conspicuous beasts that run on the ground and are active by day—the antelopes, ostriches, zebras, baboons, and lions that draw modern tourists to East Africa. None of these animals, and no animals remotely equivalent to them, have occurred on Madagascar in modern times. They were kept out by the two hundred miles of sea separating Madagascar from Africa, just as the sea also kept Australia's marsupials from reaching New Zealand. Instead, Madagascar supports two dozen species of small, monkeylike primates called lemurs, weighing only up to twenty pounds and mostly active at night and living in trees. Various species of rodents, bats, insectivores, and relatives of mongooses also occur, yet the largest still weighs only about twenty-five pounds.

However, littering Madagascar's beaches are proofs of vanished giant birds, in the form of countless eggshells the size of a soccer ball. Eventually, bones turned up not only of the birds that laid those eggs but also of a remarkable suite of vanished large mammals and reptiles. The egg makers were half-a-dozen species of flightless birds up to ten feet tall and weighing up to one thousand pounds, like moas and ostriches but more massively built and hence now termed elephant birds. The reptiles were two species of giant land tortoises with shells about a yard long, and formerly very common, as indicated by the abundance of their bones. More diverse than either these large birds or reptiles were a dozen species of lemurs up to the size of a gorilla, and all larger than or at least as large as the largest surviving lemur species. To judge from the small size of the eye orbits in their skulls, all or most of the extinct lemurs were probably diurnal rather than nocturnal. Some of them evidently lived on the ground like baboons, while others climbed in trees like orangutans and koala bears.

As if all this were not enough, Madagascar also yielded the bones of an extinct "pygmy" hippopotamus ("only" the size of a cow), an aardvark, and a big mongoose-related carnivore built like a short-legged puma. Taken together, these extinct large animals formerly gave Madagascar the functional equivalents of the surviving large beasts for which tourists still flock to African game parks—just as did New Zealand's moas and other strange birds. The tortoises, elephant birds, and pygmy hippos would have been the herbivores in place of antelope and zebras; the lemurs would have replaced the baboons and great apes; and the mongoose-related carnivore made do for a leopard or scaled-down lion.

What happened to all these big extinct mammals, reptiles, and birds? We can be confident that at least some of them were alive to delight the eyes of the first arriving Malagasy, who used elephant-bird eggshells as water containers and discarded butchered bones of the pygmy hippo and some of the other species in their garbage heaps. In addition, the bones of all the other extinct species are known from fossil sites only a few thousand years old. Since they must have evolved and survived for millions of years until then, it is unlikely that all those animals had the foresight to give up the ghost just in those last few moments before hungry humans showed up. In fact, a few may still have been holding out in remote parts of Madagascar when Europeans arrived, since the seventeenth-century French governor Flacourt was given descriptions of an animal suggestive of the gorilla-sized lemur. The elephant birds may have survived long enough to become known to Arab traders in the Indian Ocean, and to give rise to the account of the rok (a giant bird) in the tale of Sindbad the Sailor.

Certainly some and probably all of Madagascar's vanished giants were somehow exterminated by the activities of the early Malagasy. It's not hard to understand why the elephant birds went extinct, since their eggshells made such convenient two-gallon jerrycans. While the Malagasy were herders and fishermen rather than big-game hunters, the other big animals would have been as easy prey as New Zealand's moas, since they had never seen humans before. That's presumably why the easy-to-see, easy-to-catch lemurs big enough to be worth the effort of butchering them—the large, diurnal, terrestrial species—all went extinct, while the small, nocturnal, tree-living ones all survived.

However, unintended by-products of Malagasy activities probably killed more big animals than did hunting. Fires lit to clear forest for pasture and to stimulate growth of new grass each year would have destroyed habitats on which the beasts depended. Grazing cattle and goats also transformed habitats, as well as competing directly with grazing tortoises and elephant birds for food. Introduced dogs and pigs would have preyed on ground-dwelling animals, their young, and their eggs. By the time the Portuguese arrived, Madagascar's once-abundant elephant birds had all been reduced to eggshells covering the beaches, skeletons in the ground, and vague memories of roks.

MADAGASCAR AND POLYNESIA merely provide well-documented examples of the extinction waves that probably unfolded on all large oceanic islands colonized by people before the European expansion of the last five hundred years. All such islands where life had evolved in the absence of humans used to have unique species of big animals that modern zoologists never saw alive. Mediterranean islands like Crete and Cyprus had pygmy hippos and giant tortoises (just as did Madagascar), as well as dwarf elephants and dwarf deer. The West Indies lost monkeys, ground sloths, a bear-sized rodent, and owls of several sizes: normal, giant, colossal, and titanic. It seems likely that these big birds, mammals, and tortoises too somehow succumbed to the first Mediterranean peoples or American Indians to reach their islands. Nor were birds, mammals, and tortoises the only victims: lizards, frogs, snails, and even large insects disappeared as well, comprising thousands of species when one adds up all oceanic islands. Olson describes these insular extinctions as "one of the swiftest and most profound biological catastrophes in the history of the world." However, we won't be sure that humans were responsible until the bones of the last animals and the remains of the first people have been dated more exactly for other islands, as has already been done for Polynesia and Madagascar.

In addition to these preindustrial extermination waves on islands, other species may have fallen victim to extermination waves on continents in the more distant past. About eleven thousand years ago, around the probable time that the first ancestors of American Indians reached the New World, most large species of mammals became extinct throughout all of North and South America. A long-standing debate has raged over whether these big mammals were done in by Indian hunters, or whether they just happened to succumb to climate changes around the same time. I'll explain in the next chapter why I personally think that hunters did it. However, it's much harder to pinpoint dates and causes of events that happened around eleven thousand years ago than it is for recent events like the Maori versus moa collision within the past one thousand years. Similarly, within the past fifty thousand years Australia was colonized by the ancestors of today's Aboriginal Australians *and* lost most of its species of big animals. Those animals included giant kangaroos, the "marsupial lion," and "marsupial rhinos" (known as diprotodonts), plus giant lizards, snakes, crocodiles, and birds. However, we still don't know whether the arrival of Australia's humans somehow caused the disappearance of Australia's big animals. Although it's now reasonably certain that the first preindustrial peoples to reach islands wrought havoc among island species, the jury is still out on the question whether this also happened on continents.

From all this evidence that the Golden Age was tarnished by exterminations of species, let's now turn to evidence for destruction of habitats. Three dramatic examples involve famous archaeological puzzles: the giant stone statues of Easter Island, the abandoned pueblos of the U.S. Southwest, and the ruins of Petra.

An aura of mystery has clung to Easter Island ever since it and its Polynesian inhabitants were "discovered" by the Dutch explorer Jakob Roggeveen in 1722. Lying in the Pacific Ocean 2,300 miles west of Chile, Easter surpasses even Henderson as one of the world's most isolated scraps of land. Hundreds of statues, weighing up to eighty-five tons and up to thirty-seven feet tall, were carved from volcanic quarries, somehow transported several miles, and raised to an upright position on platforms by people without metal or wheels and with no power source other than human muscle. Even more statues remain unfinished in the quarries, or lie finished but abandoned between the quarries and platforms. The scene today is as if the carvers and movers had suddenly walked off the job, leaving an eerily silent landscape.

When Roggeveen arrived, many statues were still standing, though new ones were no longer being carved. By 1840 all the erected statues had been deliberately toppled by the Easter Islanders themselves. How were such huge statues transported and erected, why were they eventually toppled, and why had carving ceased?

The first of those questions was answered when living Easter Islanders showed Thor Heyerdahl how their ancestors had used logs as rollers to transport the statues and then as levers to erect them. The other questions were solved by subsequent archaeological and pale-ontological studies that revealed Easter's gruesome history. When Polynesians settled Easter around A.D. 400, the island was covered by forest that they gradually proceeded to clear, in order to plant gardens and to obtain logs for canoes and for erecting statues. By around 1500 the human population had built up to about 7,000 (over 150 per square mile), about 1,000 statues had been carved, and at least 324 of those statues had been erected. But—the forest had been destroyed so thoroughly that not a single tree survived.

An immediate result of this self-inflicted ecological disaster was that the islanders no longer had the logs needed to transport and erect statues, so carving ceased. But deforestation also had two indirect consequences that brought starvation: soil erosion, hence lower crop yields, plus lack of timber to build canoes, hence less protein available from fishing. As a result, the population was now greater than Easter could support, and island society collapsed in a holocaust of internecine warfare and cannibalism. A warrior class took over; spear points manufactured in huge quantities came to litter the landscape; the defeated were eaten or enslaved; rival clans pulled down each other's statues; and people took to living in caves for self-protection. What had once been a lush island supporting one of the world's most remarkable civilizations deteriorated into the Easter Island of today:

a barren grassland littered with fallen statues, and supporting less than one-third of its former population.

OUR SECOND CASE STUDY of preindustrial habitat destruction involves the collapse of one of the most advanced Indian civilizations of North America. When Spanish explorers reached the U.S. Southwest, they found gigantic multistory dwellings (pueblos) standing uninhabited in the middle of treeless desert. For example, the 650-room dwelling at Chaco Canyon National Monument in New Mexico was 5 stories high, 670 feet long, and 315 feet wide, making it the largest building ever erected in North America until topped by steel skyscrapers in the late nineteenth century. Navajo Indians in the region knew of the vanished builders only as "Anasazi," meaning "the Ancient Ones."

Archaeologists subsequently established that construction of the Chaco pueblos began shortly after A.D. 900, and that occupation ceased in the twelfth century. Why did the Anasazi erect a city in a barren wasteland, of all unpromising places? Where did they obtain their firewood, or the sixteen-foot-long wooden beams (200,000 of them!), that supported the roofs? Why did they then abandon the city that they had built at such enormous effort?

The conventional view, analogous to the claim that Madagascar's elephant birds and New Zealand's moas died out from natural changes in climate, attributes the abandonment of Chaco Canyon to a drought. However, a different interpretation emerges from the work of paleobotanists Julio Betancourt, Thomas Van Devender, and their colleagues, who used an ingenious technique to decipher changes in Chaco vegetation through time. Their method relied on the little rodents called packrats, which gather plants and other materials into shelters (termed middens) that they eventually abandon after fifty to one hundred years but that remain well preserved under desert conditions. The plants can be identified centuries later, and the midden can be dated by radiocarbon techniques. Thus, each midden is virtually a time capsule of the local vegetation.

By this method, Betancourt and Van Devender were able to reconstruct the following course of events. At the time that the Chaco pueblos were erected, they were not surrounded by barren desert but by pinyon-juniper woodland, with ponderosa pine forest nearby. This discovery at once solves the mystery of where the firewood and timber came from, and disposes of the apparent paradox of an advanced civilization rising from barren desert. As occupation continued at Chaco, however, the woodland and forest were cleared until the environment became the treeless wasteland that it remains today. The Indians were then having to go over ten miles to get firewood, and over twenty-five miles to get pine logs. When the pine forest had been felled, they built an elaborate road system to haul spruce and fir logs from mountain slopes over fifty miles away, relying on nothing more than their own muscle power. In addition, the Anasazi had solved the problems of agriculture in a dry environment by building irrigation systems to concentrate available water into valley bottoms. As deforestation caused progressively increasing erosion and water runoff, and as irrigation channels gradually dug gullies into the ground, the water table may finally have dropped below the level of the Anasazi fields, making irrigation without pumps impossible. Thus, while drought may have made some contribution to the Anasazi abandonment of Chaco Canyon, a self-inflicted ecological disaster was also a major factor.

OUR REMAINING EXAMPLE of preindustrial habitat destruction illuminates the gradual geographic shift in the power center of ancient western civilizations. Recall that the first center of power and innovation was the Mideast, where so many crucial developments arose—agriculture, animal domestication, writing, imperial states, battle chariots, and others. Ascendancy shifted between Assyria, Babylon, Persia, and occasionally Egypt or Turkey, but remained in or near the Mideast. With the overthrow of the Persian Empire by Alexander the Great, ascendancy moved finally westward, at first to Greece, then to Rome, and later to western and northern Europe. Why did the Mideast, Greece, and Rome in turn lose their primacy? (The transient current importance of the Mideast, resting as it does on the single resource of oil, merely emphasizes by contrast the region's modern weakness in other respects.) Why do modern superpowers include the United States and the USSR, Germany and England, Japan and China, but no longer Greece and Persia?

This geographic shift in power is too big and lasting a pattern to have arisen by accident. A plausible hypothesis attributes it to each ancient center of civilization in turn ruining its resource base. The Mideast and Mediterranean were not always the degraded landscape that they appear today. In ancient times much of this area was a lush mosaic of wooded hills and fertile valleys. Thousands of years of deforestation, overgrazing, erosion, and valley siltation converted this heartland of western civilization into the relatively dry, barren, infertile landscape that predominates today. Archaeological surveys of ancient Greece have revealed several cycles of population growth alternating with population crashes and local abandonment of human settlement. In the growth phases, terracing and dams initially protected the landscape until felling of forests, clearing of steep slopes for agriculture, overgrazing by too many livestock, and planting of crops at too short intervals overwhelmed the system. The result each time was massive erosion of the hills, flooding of the valleys, and the collapse of local human society. One such event coincided with (and may have caused) the otherwise mysterious collapse of Greece's glorious Mycenean civilization, after which Greece fell back for several centuries into a dark age of illiteracy.

The support for this view of ancient environmental destruction comes from sources such as contemporary accounts and archaeological evidence. Yet a few sequences of photographs would constitute more decisive tests than all that anecdotal evidence combined. If we had snapshots of the same Greek hillside taken at thousand-year intervals, we could identify the plants, measure the ground cover, and calculate the shift from forest to goat-proof shrubs. We could thereby put numbers on the extent of environmental degradation.

Enter middens to the rescue again. While the Mideast doesn't have packrats, it does have rabbit-sized, marmotlike animals called hyraxes that build packrat-like middens. (Surprisingly, the closest living relatives of hyraxes may be elephants.) Three Arizona scientists—Patricia Fall, Cynthia Lindquist, and Steven Falconer—studied hyrax middens at Jordan's famous lost city of Petra, which typifies the paradox of ancient western civilization. Petra is now especially familiar to moviegoing aficionados of Steven Spielberg and George Lucas, whose film *Indiana Jones and the Last Crusade* shows Sean Connery and Harrison Ford searching for the Holy Grail in Petra's magnificent rock tombs and temples amidst the desert sand. Anyone who sees those scenes of Petra must wonder how such a wealthy city could have arisen and supported itself in such a bleak landscape. In fact, there was already a Neolithic village near the site of Petra before 7000 B.C., and farming and herding appeared there soon after. Under the Nabataean kingdom, of which it was the capital, Petra thrived as a commercial center controlling trade between Europe, Arabia, and the Orient. The city grew ever larger and richer under Roman, then Byzantine, control. But it was subsequently abandoned and so completely forgotten that its ruins were not rediscovered until 1812. What caused Petra's collapse?

Each hyrax midden at Petra yielded remains of up to one hundred plant species, and the habitat prevailing when each midden's owner was alive could be calibrated by comparing pollen proportions in the midden with those in modern habitats. From the middens, the following trajectory was reconstructed for the degradation of Petra's environment:

Petra lies in an area of dry Mediterranean climate not unlike that of the wooded mountains behind my home in Los Angeles. The original vegetation would have been a woodland dominated by oak and pistachio trees. By Roman and Byzantine times, most of the trees had been felled, and the surroundings had been degraded to an open steppe, as expressed in the fact that only 18 percent of midden pollen came from trees, the rest from low plants. (For comparison, trees contribute 40–85 percent of the pollen in modern Mediterranean forests, 18 percent in forest-steppe.) By A.D. 900, a few centuries after Byzantine control of the Petra area ended, two-thirds of the remaining trees had disappeared. Even shrubs, herbs, and grasses had declined, converting the environment into the desert that we see now. Surviving trees today have their lower branches pruned off by goats and are scattered on goat-proof cliffs or in groves protected from goats.

Juxtaposing these data from hyrax middens with archaeological and literary data yields the following interpretation. Deforestation from Neolithic to imperial times was driven by the clearing of land for agriculture, browsing by sheep and goats, gathering of firewood, and wood needs for house construction. Even Neolithic houses not only were supported by massive timbers but also consumed up to thirteen tons of firewood per house to make the plaster for the walls and floor. The imperial population explosion quickened the pace of forest destruction and overgrazing. Elaborate systems of channels, pipes, and cisterns were needed to collect and store water for the orchards and city.

After Byzantine authority collapsed, orchards were abandoned and the population crashed, but land degradation continued as the remaining inhabitants became dependent on intensive grazing. The insatiable goats began to eat their way through the shrubs, herbs, and grasses. The Ottoman government decimated surviving woodlands before the First World War, to obtain the wood needed for the Hejaz Railway. I and many other moviegoers thrilled at the sight of Arab guerrillas led by Lawrence of Arabia (a.k.a. Peter O'Toole) blowing up that railway in wide-screen Technicolor, without realizing that we were watching the last act in the destruction of Petra's forests.

Petra's ravaged landscape today is a metaphor for what happened to the rest of the cradle of western civilization. The modern surrounds of Petra could no more feed a city that commanded the world's main trade routes than the modern surrounds of Persepolis could feed the capital of a superpower such as the Persian Empire once was. The ruins of those cities, and of Athens and Rome, are monuments to states that destroyed their means of survival. Nor are Mediterranean civilizations the only literate societies that committed ecological suicide. The collapse of Classic Maya civilization in Central America, and of Harappan civilization in India's Indus Valley, are other obvious candidates for ecodisasters due to an expanding human population overwhelming its environment. While courses in the history of civilization often dwell on kings and barbarian invasions, deforestation and erosion may in the long run have been more important shapers of human history.

THESE ARE SOME of the recent discoveries making the supposed past Golden Age of environmentalism look increasingly mythical. Let's now go back to the larger issues I raised at the outset. First, how can these discoveries of past environmental damage be reconciled with accounts of conservationist practices by so many modern preindustrial peoples? Obviously, not all species have been exterminated, and not all habitats have been destroyed, so the Golden Age couldn't have been all black.

I suggest the following answer to this paradox. It's still true that small, long-established, egalitarian societies tend to evolve conservationist practices, because they've had plenty of time to get to know their local environment and to perceive their own self-interest. Instead, damage is likely to occur when people suddenly colonize an unfamiliar environment (like the first Maoris and Easter Islanders); or when people advance along a new frontier (like the first Indians to reach America), so that they can just move beyond the frontier when they've damaged the region behind; or when people acquire a new technology whose destructive power they haven't had time to appreciate (like modern New Guineans, now devastating pigeon populations with shotguns). Damage is also likely in centralized states that concentrate wealth in the hands of rulers, who are out of touch with their environment. And some species and habitats are more susceptible to damage than others—such as flightless birds that never had seen humans (like moas and elephant birds), or the dry, fragile, unforgiving environments in which both Mediterranean civilization and Anasazi civilization arose.

Second, are there any practical lessons that we can learn from these recent archaeological discoveries? Archaeology is often viewed as a socially irrelevant academic discipline that becomes a prime target for budget cuts whenever money gets tight. In fact, archaeological research is one of the best bargains available to government planners. All over the world, we're launching developments that have great potential for doing irreversible damage, and that are really just more powerful versions of ideas put into operation by past societies. We can't afford the experiment of developing five counties in five different ways and seeing which four counties get ruined. Instead, it will cost us much less in the long run if we hire archaeologists to find out what happened the last time than if we go making the same mistakes again.

Here's just one example. The American Southwest has over 100,000 square miles of pinyon-juniper woodland that we are exploiting more and more for firewood. Unfortunately, the U.S. Forest Service has little data available to help it calculate sustainable yields and recovery rates in that woodland. Yet the Anasazi already tried the experiment and miscalculated, with the result that the woodland still hasn't recovered in Chaco Canyon after over eight hundred years. Paying some archaeologists to reconstruct Anasazi firewood consumption would be cheaper than committing the same mistake and ruining 100,000 square miles of the United States, as we may now be doing.

Finally, let's face the touchiest question. Today, environmentalists view people who exterminate species and destroy habitats as morally bad. Industrial societies have jumped at any excuse to denigrate preindustrial peoples, in order to justify killing them and appropriating their land. Are the purported new finds about moas and Chaco Canyon vegetation just pseudo-scientific racism that in effect is saying, Maoris and Indians don't deserve fair treatment because they were bad?

What has to be remembered is that it's always been hard for humans to know the rate at which they can safely harvest biological resources indefinitely, without depleting them. A significant decline in resources may not be easy to distinguish from a normal year-to-year fluctuation. It's even harder to assess the rate at which new resources are being produced. By the time that the signs of decline are clear enough to convince everybody, it may be too late to save the species or habitat. Thus, preindustrial peoples who couldn't sustain their resources were guilty not of moral sins, but of failures to solve a really difficult ecological problem. Those failures were tragic, because they caused a collapse in life-style for the people themselves.

Tragic failures become moral sins only if one should have known better from the outset. In that regard there are two big differences between us and eleventh-century Anasazi Indians: scientific understanding, and literacy. We know, and they didn't know, how to draw graphs that plot sustainable resource population size as a function of resource harvesting rate. We can read about all the ecological disasters of the past; the Anasazi couldn't. Yet our generation continues to hunt whales and clear tropical rain forest as if no one had ever hunted moas or cleared pinyon-juniper woodland. The past was still a Golden Age, of ignorance, while the present is an Iron Age of willful blindness.

From this point of view it's beyond understanding to see modern societies repeating the past's suicidal ecological mismanagement, with much more powerful tools of destruction in the hands of far more people. It's as if we hadn't already run that particular film many times before in human history, and as if we didn't know the inevitable outcome. Shelley's sonnet "Ozymandias" evokes Persepolis, Tikal, and Easter Island equally well; perhaps it will someday evoke to others the ruins of our own civilization:

I met a traveller from an antique land
Who said: "Two vast and trunkless legs of stone
Stand in the desert. Near them, on the sand,
Half sunk, a shattered visage lies, whose frown,
And wrinkled lip, and sneer of cold command,
Tell that its sculptor well those passions read
Which yet survive, stamped on these lifeless things,
The hand that mocked them and the heart that fed;
And on the pedestal these words appear—
'My name is Ozymandias, king of kings:
Look on my works, ye Mighty, and despair!'
Nothing beside remains. Round the decay
Of that colossal wreck, boundless and bare
The lone and level sands stretch far away."

CHAPTER 18

Blitzkrieg and Thanksgiving in the New World

THE UNITED STATES DEVOTES TWO NATIONAL HOLIDAYS, COLUMBUS Day and Thanksgiving Day, to celebrating dramatic moments in the European "discovery" of the New World. No holidays commemorate the much earlier discovery by Indians. Yet archaeological excavations suggest that, in drama, that earlier discovery dwarfs the adventures of Christopher Columbus and of the Plymouth Pilgrims. Within perhaps as little as a thousand years of finding a way through an Arctic ice sheet to cross the present Canada-U.S. border, Indians had swept down to the tip of Patagonia and populated two productive and unexplored continents. The Indians' march southward was the greatest range expansion in the history of *Homo sapiens*. Nothing remotely like it can ever happen again on our planet.

The sweep southward was marked by another drama. When Indian hunters arrived, they found the Americas teeming with big mammals that are now extinct: elephantlike mammoths and mastodonts, ground sloths weighing up to three tons, armadillolike glyptodonts weighing up to one ton, bear-sized beavers, and sabertooth cats, plus American lions, cheetahs, camels, horses, and many others.

Had those beasts survived, today's tourists in Yellowstone National Park would be watching mammoths and lions along with the bears and bison. The question of what happened at that moment of hunters-meet-beasts is still highly controversial among archaeologists and paleontologists. According to the interpretation that seems most plausible to me, the outcome was a "blitzkrieg" in which the beasts were quickly exterminated—possibly within a mere ten years at any given site. If that view is correct, it would have been the most concentrated extinction of big animals since an asteroid collision knocked off the dinosaurs sixty-five million years ago. It would also have been the first of the series of blitzkriegs that marred our supposed Golden Age of environmental innocence, and that have remained a human hallmark ever since.

THAT DRAMATIC CONFRONTATION came as the finale to a long epic in which humans, spreading out of their center of origins in Africa, occupied all the other habitable continents. Our African ancestors expanded to Asia and Europe around a million years ago, and from Asia to Australia around fifty thousand years ago, leaving North and South America as the last habitable continents still without *Homo sapiens*.

From Canada to Tierra del Fuego, American Indians today are physically more homogeneous than the inhabitants of any other continent, implying that they arrived too recently to have become very diverse genetically. Even before archaeology uncovered evidence of the first Indians, it was clear that they must have originated from Asia, because modern Indians look similar to Asiatic Mongoloids. Much recent evidence from genetics and anthropology has made that conclusion certain. A glance at a map shows that by far the easiest route from Asia to America is across the Bering Strait separating Siberia from Alaska. The last land bridge across the strait existed (with a few brief interruptions) from about twenty-five thousand to ten thousand years ago.

However, colonization of the New World required more than a land bridge: there had to be people living at the Siberian end of the bridge. Because of its harsh climate the Siberian Arctic, too, was not colonized until late in human history. Those colonists must have come from the cold temperate zones of Asia or eastern Europe, as exemplified by Stone Age hunters who lived in what is now the Ukraine and who built their houses out of neatly stacked bones of mammoths. By at least twenty thousand years ago there were mammoth hunters in the Siberian Arctic as well, and by around twelve thousand years ago stone tools similar to those of the Siberian hunters appear in Alaska's archaeological record.

After traversing Siberia and the Bering Strait, the Ice Age hunters were still separated by one more barrier from their future hunting grounds in the U.S.: a broad ice cap like that covering Greenland today, but stretching coast-to-coast across Canada. At intervals during the Ice Ages a narrow, ice-free, north-south corridor opened through this ice cap, just east of the Rocky Mountains. One such corridor closed around twenty thousand years ago, but there had apparently as yet been no human in Alaska waiting to cross it. However, when the corridor next opened around twelve thousand years ago, the hunters must have been ready, for their telltale stone tools soon thereafter appear not only at the south end of the corridor near Edmonton (Alberta) but also elsewhere south of the ice cap. At that point, hunters met America's elephants and other great beasts, and the drama began.

Archaeologists term these pioneering ancestral Indians the Clovis people, since their stone tools were first recognized at an excavation near the town of Clovis, ten miles inside New Mexico from the Texas border. However, Clovis tools or ones similar to them have been found in all forty-eight contiguous states of the U.S., and from Edmonton in the north to Mexico. Vance Haynes, a University of Arizona archaeologist, has emphasized that the tools are much like those of the earlier eastern European and Siberian mammoth hunters, with one conspicuous exception: the flattish, two-faced stone spear points were "fluted" on each face as a result of a longitudinal groove having been chipped out to make it easier to bind the stone point to the shaft. It isn't clear whether the fluted points were mounted on spears to throw by hand, on darts to hurl by a throwing stick, or on lances to thrust. Somehow, though, the points were propelled into big mammals with enough force for the points sometimes to snap in half, or else to penetrate bone. Archaeologists have dug up skeletons of mammoths and bison with Clovis points inside the rib cages, including a mammoth from southern Arizona containing a total of eight points. At excavated Clovis sites, mammoths are by far the commonest prey (to judge from their bones), but other victims include bison, mastodont, tapir, camel, horse, and bear.

Among the startling discoveries about Clovis people is the speed of their spread. All Clovis sites in the U.S. dated by the most advanced radiocarbon techniques were occupied for only a few centuries, in the period just before 11,000 years ago. A human site even at the southern tip of Patagonia is dated at about 10,500 years. Thus, within about a millennium of emerging from the ice-free corridor at Edmonton, humans had spread from coast to coast and over the entire length of the New World.

Equally startling is the rapid transformation of Clovis culture. Around 11,000 years ago Clovis points are abruptly replaced by a smaller, more finely made model now known as Folsom points (after a site near Folsom, New Mexico, where they were first identified). The Folsom points are often found associated with bones of an extinct wide-horned bison, never with the mammoths preferred by Clovis hunters.

There may be a simple reason why Folsom hunters switched from mammoths to bison: there weren't any mammoths left. There also weren't any more mastodonts, camels, horses, giant ground sloths, and several dozen other types of big mammals. In all, North America lost an astonishing 73 percent, South America 80 percent, of their genera of big mammals around this time. Many paleontologists don't blame this American extinction spasm on Clovis hunters, since there is no surviving evidence of mass slaughter—only the fossilized bones of a few butchered carcasses here and there. Instead, those paleontologists attribute the extinctions to changes of climate and habitats at the end of the Ice Ages, just around the time that Clovis hunters arrived. That reasoning puzzles me for several reasons: ice-free habitats for mammals expanded rather than contracted as glaciers yielded to grass and forest; big American mammals had already survived the ends of at least twenty-two previous Ice Ages without such an extinction spasm; and there were far fewer extinctions in Europe and Asia when the glaciers of those continents melted around the same time.

If changing climate had been the cause, one might have expected opposite effects on species preferring hot and cold climates. Instead, radiocarbon-dated fossils from the Grand Canyon show that the Shasta ground sloth and Harrington's mountain goat, derived from areas of hot and cold climates respectively, both died out within a century or two of each other, around 11,100 years ago. The sloths were common until just before their sudden extinction. In their softball-sized dung balls, still well-preserved in some southwestern U.S. caves, botanists identified remains of plants on which the last sloths chomped: Mormon tea and globe mallow, which still occur around those caves today. It is highly suspicious that both those well-fed sloths and the goats of the Grand Canyon disappeared just after Clovis hunters reached Arizona. Juries have convicted murderers on the grounds of less compelling circumstantial evidence. If climate really was what did in the sloths, we would have to credit those supposedly stupid beasts with unsuspected intelligence, since they all chose to drop dead simultaneously at just the right instant to deceive some twentieth-century scientists into blaming Clovis hunters.

A more plausible explanation of this "coincidence" is that it really was a case of cause and effect. It was Paul Martin, a geoscientist at the University of Arizona, who described the dramatic outcome of hunter-meets-elephant as a "blitzkrieg." According to his view, the first hunters to emerge from the ice-free corridor at Edmonton thrived and multiplied, because they found an abundance of tame, easy-to-hunt big mammals. As the mammals were killed off in one area, the hunters and their offspring kept fanning out into new areas that still had abundant mammals, and kept exterminating the mammal populations at the front of their advance. By the time the hunters' front finally reached the south tip of South America, most of the big mammal species of the New World had been exterminated.

MARTIN'S THEORY has attracted lots of vigorous criticism, most of it centering on four doubts: Could a band of a hundred hunters arriving at Edmonton breed fast enough to populate a hemisphere in a thousand years? Could they spread fast enough to cover the nearly eight thousand miles from Edmonton to Patagonia in that time? Were Clovis hunters really the first people in the New World? And could Stone Age hunters really have pursued hundreds of millions of big mammals so efficiently that not a single individual survived, while nevertheless leaving little fossil evidence of their hunts?

Take first the question of breeding rates. Populations of modern hunter-gatherers on even their best hunting grounds number only about one per square mile. Hence, once the whole western hemisphere had been settled, its population of hunter-gatherers would have been at most ten million, since the New World's area outside of Canada and other areas covered by glaciers in Clovis times is about ten million square miles. In modern instances when colonists have arrived at an uninhabited land (e.g., when the H.M.S. *Bounty* mutineers reached Pitcairn Island), their population growth has been as rapid as 3.4 percent per year. That growth rate, which corresponds to each couple's having four surviving children and a mean generation time of 20 years, would multiply 100 hunters into 10 million in only 340 years. Thus, Clovis hunters should easily have been able to multiply to 10 million within a millennium.

Could the descendants of the Edmonton pioneers have reached the southern tip of South America in 1,000 years? The overland straight-line distance is slightly under 8,000 miles, so that they would have had to average 8 miles a year. That's a trivial task: any fit hunter or huntress could have fulfilled the year's quota in a day and not moved for another 364 days. The quarry from which a Clovis tool was made can often be identified by its local type of stone, and we know in that way that individual tools traveled up to 200 miles. Some of the nineteenth-century Zulu migrations in southern Africa are known to have covered nearly 3,000 miles in a mere 50 years.

Were Clovis hunters the first humans to spread south of the Canadian ice sheet? That's a harder question, and it's extremely controversial among archaeologists. Primacy claims for Clovis are inevitably based on negative evidence: there are no unequivocal human remains or artifacts with universally accepted pre-Clovis dates anywhere in the New World south of the former Canadian ice sheet. Mind you, there are dozens of *claims* of sites with pre-Clovis human evidence, but all or almost all of them are marred by serious questions about whether the material used for radiocarbon dating was contaminated by older carbon, or whether the dated material was really associated with the human remains, or whether the tools supposedly made by humans were just naturally shaped rocks. The two most nearly convincing of those claimed pre-Clovis sites are Meadowcroft Rock Shelter in Pennsylvania, dated to about sixteen thousand years ago, and the Monte Verde site in Chile, dated to at least thirteen thousand years ago. Monte Verde is described as having amazingly good preservation of many types of human artifacts, but those results haven't yet been published in detail, so they can't yet be properly evaluated. At Meadowcroft there has been an unresolved debate about whether the radiocarbon dates are in error, especially because the plant and animal species from the site are ones expected to have been living there only much more recently than sixteen thousand years ago.

In contrast, the evidence for Clovis people is undeniable, is to be found in all forty-eight contiguous states, and is accepted by all archaeologists. Evidence for the still earlier settlement of the other habitable continents by more primitive humans is also unequivocal and universally accepted. At one Clovis site after another, you can see a level with Clovis artifacts and bones of numerous large extinct mammal species; immediately above (i.e., younger than) the Clovis level, a level with Folsom artifacts but with the bones of not a single large extinct mammal except for bison; and immediately below the Clovis level, levels spanning thousands of years before Clovis times, reflecting benign environmental conditions, and full of the bones of large extinct mammals, but with not a single human artifact. How could people possibly have settled the New World in pre-Clovis times and *not* left behind the usual trail of abundant evidence that convinces archaeologists, like stone tools, hearths, occupied caves, and occasionally skeletons, with unequivocal radiocarbon dates? How could there have been pre-Clovis people who left no trace of their presence at Clovis sites, despite such favorable living conditions? How could people have gotten from Alaska to Pennsylvania or Chile, as if by helicopter, without leaving good evidence of their presence in all the intervening territory? For these reasons, I find it more plausible that the dates given for Meadowcroft and Monte Verde are somehow wrong than that they are correct. The Clovis-first interpretation makes good sense; the pre-Clovis interpretation just doesn't make sense to me.

THE OTHER HOTLY CONTESTED ARGUMENT over Martin's blitzkrieg theory concerns the supposed overhunting and extermination of big mammals. It seems hard to imagine how Stone Age hunters could kill a mammoth at all, much less hunt all mammoths to extinction.

Even if the hunters *could* slaughter mammoths, why would they *want* to? And where are all the skeletons now?

Certainly, when we stand under a mammoth skeleton in a museum, the thought of using a stone-tipped spear to attack such a gigantic tusked beast feels utterly suicidal. Yet modern Africans and Asians with equally simple weapons do succeed in killing elephants, often hunting as a group relying on ambush or fire, but sometimes stalking an elephant as a single hunter armed with a spear or poisoned arrow. These modern elephant hunters still rate as amateur dabblers, compared to the mammoth hunters of Clovis times, heirs to hundreds of thousands of years of hunting experience with stone tools. Museum artists like to depict late Stone Age hunters as naked brutes risking their lives to hurl boulders at an enraged charging mammoth, with one or two hunters already lying trampled to death on the ground. That's absurd. If any hunters had died in a typical mammoth hunt, mammoths would have exterminated hunters, rather than vice versa. Instead, a more realistic picture is of warmly clad professionals safely spearing a terrified mammoth ambushed in a narrow streambed.

Recall also that the big mammals of the New World had probably never seen humans before Clovis hunters, if the hunters indeed were the first people to reach the New World. We know from Antarctica and the Galápagos how tame and unafraid are animals that evolved in the absence of humans. When I visited New Guinea's isolated Foja Mountains, which lack any human population, I found the large tree kangaroos so tame that I could approach within a few yards of them. Probably the New World's large mammals were equally naïve and were killed off before they could have time to evolve a fear of man.

Could Clovis hunters have killed mammoths fast enough to exterminate them? Assume again that an average square mile supports one hunter-gatherer and (by comparison with elephants in Africa today) one mammoth, and that one-quarter of the Clovis population consisted of adult male hunters who each killed a mammoth every two months. That means six mammoths killed per four square miles per year, so the mammoths would have had to reproduce their numbers in less than a year to keep up with the killing. Yet modern elephants are slow breeders that take about twenty years to reproduce their numbers, and few other large mammal species breed fast enough to reproduce their numbers in less than three years. Thus, it could plausibly have taken Clovis hunters only a few years to exterminate the large mammals locally and to move on to the next area. Archaeologists trying to document the slaughter today are searching for needles in a fossil haystack: a few years' worth of butchered mammoth bones among the bones of all the mammoths that died naturally over hundreds of thousands of years. It's no wonder that so few mammoth carcasses with Clovis points among the ribs have been found.

Why would a Clovis hunter even want to kill a mammoth every two months, when a five-thousand-pound mammoth yielding twenty-five hundred pounds of meat would provide ten pounds of meat per day per person for two months for the hunter, his wife, and two children? Ten pounds may sound like gross gluttony, but it actually approaches the daily meat ration per person on the U.S. frontier in the last century. That's assuming that Clovis hunters really ate all twenty-five hundred pounds of mammoth meat. But to keep the meat for two months would require drying it: would you go to the work of drying a ton of meat, when you could instead just go kill a fresh mammoth? As Vance Haynes noted, Clovis mammoth kills prove to have been only partly butchered, suggesting very wasteful and selective utilization of meat by people living amidst an abundance of game. Some hunting probably wasn't for meat at all but for ivory, hides, or just machismo. Seals and whales have similarly been hunted in modern times for oil or fur, leaving the meat to rot. In New Guinea fishing villages I often see the discarded carcasses of large sharks, killed only for their fins to make the delicacy shark's fin soup.

We are all too familiar with the blitzkriegs by which modern European hunters nearly exterminated bison, whales, seals, and many other large animals. Recent archaeological discoveries on many oceanic islands have shown that such blitzkriegs were an outcome whenever earlier hunters reached a land with animals naïve to humans. Since the collision between humans and large naïve animals has always ended in an extermination spasm, how could it have been otherwise when Clovis hunters entered a naïve New World?

*   *   *

THIS END, though, would hardly have been foreseen by the first hunters to arrive at Edmonton. It must have been a dramatic moment when, after entering the ice-free corridor from an overpopulated, overhunted Alaska, they emerged to see herds of tame mammoths, camels, and other beasts. In front of them stretched the Great Plains to the horizon. As they began to explore, they must soon have realized (unlike Christopher Columbus and the Plymouth Pilgrims) that there were no people at all in front of them, and that they had truly arrived first in a fertile land. Those Edmonton Pilgrims, too, had cause to celebrate a Thanksgiving Day.

CHAPTER 19

The Second Cloud

Until our own generation, no one had grounds to worry whether the next human generation would survive or enjoy a planet worth living on. Ours is the first generation to be confronted with these questions about its children's future. We devote much of our lives to training our children to support themselves and to get along with other people. Increasingly, we're asking ourselves whether all those efforts of ours might be wasted.

These concerns arise because of two clouds hanging over us— clouds that would have similar consequences but that we view very differently. One, the risk of a nuclear holocaust, first revealed itself in the cloud over Hiroshima. Everyone agrees that the risk is real, since there are huge stockpiles of nuclear weapons and since politicians throughout history have occasionally made dumb miscalculations. Everyone agrees that, if a nuclear holocaust does happen, it will be bad for us and might even kill us all. This risk shapes much of current world diplomacy. The only thing about which we disagree is how best to handle it—e.g., whether we should aim for complete or partial nuclear disarmament, nuclear balance, or nuclear superiority.

The other cloud is the risk of an environmental holocaust, of which one often-discussed potential cause is the gradual extinction of most of the world's species. In contrast to the case with nuclear holocaust, there is almost complete disagreement about whether the risk of a mass extinction is real and about whether it would really do us much harm if it happened. For instance, one of the most frequently cited estimates is that humans have caused about 1 percent of the world's bird species to go extinct within the last few centuries. At one extreme, many thoughtful people—especially economists and industrial leaders, but also some biologists and many lay people— think that that loss of 1 percent would be inconsequential, even if it really happened. In fact, such people reason that 1 percent is a gross *over*estimate, that most species are superfluous to us, and that it would do us no harm to lose ten times more species. At the opposite extreme, many other thoughtful people—especially conservation biologists and a growing number of lay people belonging to environmentalist movements—think that the 1 percent figure is a gross *under*estimate, and that mass extinction would undermine the quality or possibility of human life. Obviously, it will make a big difference to our children which of these two extreme views is closer to the truth.

The risks of a nuclear holocaust and of an environmental holocaust constitute the two really pressing questions facing the human race today. Compared to these two clouds, our usual obsessions with cancer, AIDS, and diet pale into insignificance, because those problems don't threaten the survival of the human species. If the nuclear and environmental risks should not materialize, we'll have plenty of leisure time to solve bagatelles like cancer. If we fail to avert those two risks, solving cancer won't have helped us anyway.

How many species have humans really driven into extinction already? How many more are likely to go extinct within our kids' lifetimes? If more do go extinct, so what? How much do wrens contribute to our gross national product? Aren't all species destined to go extinct sooner or later? Is the claimed mass-extinction crisis a hysterical fantasy, a real risk for the future, or a proven event that's already well underway?

We need to go through three steps if we are to arrive at realistic estimates of the numbers involved in the mass-extinction debate. First, let's see how many species have gone extinct in modern times (i.e., since 1600). Second, let's estimate how many more extinctions had already occurred before 1600. As the third step, let's try to predict how many further ones are likely to happen within the life spans of ourselves, our children, and our grandchildren. Finally, let's ask what difference it all makes to us anyway.

THE FIRST STEP, that of calculating the number of species that have gone extinct in modern times, seems easy when one initially thinks about it. Just take some group of plants or animals, count up in a catalog the total number of species, mark off the ones known to have become extinct since 1600, and add them up. As a group on which to try this exercise, birds have the advantage that they're easy to see and identify, and hordes of bird-watchers watch them. As a result, more is known about them than about any other group of animals.

Approximately 9,000 species of birds exist today. Only one or two previously unknown species are still being discovered each year, so virtually all living birds have already been named. The leading agency concerned with the status of the world's birds—the International Council for Bird Preservation (ICBP)—lists 108 species of birds, plus many additional subspecies, as having become extinct since 1600. Virtually all of these extinctions were caused in one way or another by humans—more of that later. One hundred eight is about 1 percent of that total number of bird species, 9,000. That's where the 1 percent figure I mentioned earlier comes from.

Before we take that as the final word on the number of modern bird extinctions, let's understand how the number of 108 was arrived at. The ICBP decides to list a species as extinct only after that bird has been specifically looked for in areas where it was previously known to occur or might have turned up, and after it has not been found for many years. In many cases, birders have watched a population dwindle down to a few individuals and have followed the fates of those last individuals. For example, the most recent subspecies of bird to have gone extinct in the United States was the dusky seaside sparrow that lived in marshes near Titusville, Florida. As its population shrank owing to destruction of the marshes where it lived, wildlife agencies put identification bands on the few remaining sparrows so that they could be individually recognized. When only six remained, they were brought into captivity in order to protect and breed them.

Unfortunately, one after another died. The last individual, and with it the subspecies itself, died on June 16, 1987.

Thus, there is no doubt that the dusky seaside sparrow is extinct. Equally little doubt attaches to the many other subspecies and the 108 full species of birds listed as extinct. The full species listed as having vanished in North America since European settlement, and the years in which the last individual of each died, are: the great auk (1844), spectacled cormorant (1852), Labrador duck (1875), passenger pigeon (1914), and Carolina parakeet (1918). The great auk also formerly occurred in Europe, but no other European bird species is listed as having gone extinct since 1600, though some species have disappeared within Europe while surviving on other continents.

What about all those remaining bird species that did not fulfill the ICBP's rigorous criteria for extinction? Can we be certain that they still exist? For most North American and European birds the answer is "yes." Hundreds of thousands of fanatical bird-watchers monitor all bird species on these continents every year. The rarer the species, the more fanatical is the annual search for it. No North American or European bird species could possibly drift into extinction unnoticed. There is only one North American bird species whose current existence is uncertain: Bachman's warbler, last definitely recorded in 1977; but the ICBP hasn't given up hope for it because of more recent unconfirmed records. (The ivory-billed woodpecker may also be extinct, but the North American population is "only" a subspecies; a few individuals of the other subspecies of this woodpecker survive in Cuba.) Thus, the number of extinctions of North American bird species since 1600 is surely not fewer than five nor more than six. Every species but Bachman's warbler can be assigned to one of two categories: "definitely extinct" or "definitely in existence." Similarly, the number of European bird species extinct since 1600 is surely one—not two, not zero, but one.

Hence we have an exact, unequivocal answer to the question how many North American and European bird species have gone extinct since 1600. If we could be equally definite for other groups of species, our first step in assessing the mass-extinction debate would be complete. Unfortunately, this cut-and-dried situation does not apply to plants and other groups of animals, nor does it apply elsewhere in the world—least of all in the tropics, where the overwhelming majority of species lives. Most tropical countries have few or no bird-watchers, and no annual monitoring of birds. Many tropical areas have never again been monitored since they were first explored biologically many years ago. The status of many tropical species is unknown, because no one has seen them again or specifically looked for them since they were discovered. For instance, among the New Guinea birds that I study, Brass's friarbird is known only from eighteen specimens shot at one lagoon on the Idenburg River between March 22 and April 29, 1939. No scientist has revisited that lagoon, so we know nothing about the current status of Brass's friarbird.

At least we know where to look for that friarbird. Many other species have been described from specimens collected by nineteenth-century expeditions that provided only vague indications of the collecting site—e.g., "South America." Try resolving the status of some rare species when you have only that broad hint of where to look! The songs, behavior, and habitat preferences of such species are unknown. Hence we don't know where to seek them, or how to identify them if we glimpse or hear them.

Thus, the status of many tropical species cannot be classified either as "definitely extinct" or "definitely in existence," but just as "unknown." Instead, it becomes a matter of chance which species happens to attract the attention of some ornithologist, becomes the object of a specific search, and hence may be recognized as possibly extinct.

Here's an example. The Solomon Islands are another of my favorite birding areas in the tropical Pacific Ocean, and will be recalled by older Americans and Japanese as the site of some of the fiercest fighting in World War II. (Remember Guadalcanal, Henderson Field, President Kennedy's PT boat, the Tokyo Express?) The ICBP lists one Solomon bird species, Meek's crowned pigeon, as extinct. But when I tabulated all recent observations of all 164 known Solomon bird species, I noticed that 12 of those 164 species hadn't been encountered since 1953. Some of those 12 species are surely extinct, because they were formerly abundant and conspicuous, or because Solomon Islanders told me that those birds had been exterminated by cats.

Twelve species possibly extinct out of 164 still may not sound like much to worry about. However, the Solomons are in much better shape environmentally than most of the remaining tropical world, because they have relatively few people, few bird species, little economic development, and much natural forest. More typical of the tropics is Malaysia, which is rich in species and has had most of its lowland forest cut down. Biological explorers had identified 266 fish species dependent on fresh water in Malaysia's forest rivers. A recent search that lasted four years was able to find only 122 of those 266 species—fewer than half. The other 144 Malaysian freshwater fish species must either be extinct, rare, or very local. They reached that status before anyone noticed it.

Malaysia is typical of the tropics in the pressure it faces from humans. Fish are typical of all species other than birds, in that they attract only patchy scientific attention. The estimate that Malaysia has already lost (or nearly lost) half of its freshwater fish is therefore a reasonable ballpark figure for the status of plants, invertebrates, and vertebrates other than birds in much of the rest of the tropics.

That's one complication in trying to pinpoint the number of extinctions since 1600: the status of many or most named species is unknown. But there's a further complication. So far, we have been trying to assess extinctions only of those species that had already been discovered and described (named). Could any species have gone extinct before they were even described?

Of course there could, since sampling procedures suggest that the actual number of the world's species is near thirty million, but fewer than two million species have been described. Two examples illustrate the certainty of additional extinctions before description. Botanist Alwyn Gentry surveyed the plants of an isolated ridge in Ecuador called Centinela, where he found thirty-eight new species confined to that ridge. Shortly afterward, the ridge was logged and those plants were exterminated. On Grand Cayman Island in the Caribbean, zoologist Fred Thompson discovered two new species of land snails confined to forest on a limestone ridge that was completely cleared a few years later for a housing development.

The accident that Gentry and Thompson visited those ridges before rather than after they were cleared means that we have names for those extinct species. But most tropical areas that are being developed aren't first surveyed by biologists. There must have been land snails on Centinela, and plants and snails on innumerable other tropical ridges, that we exterminated before we discovered them.

In short, the problem of determining the number of modern extinctions seems at first to be simple and to lead to modest estimates— e.g., just five or six extinct bird species in all of North America plus

Europe. On reflection, though, we appreciate two reasons why published lists of species known to be extinct must be gross underestimates of the actual number of extinctions. First, by definition the published lists consider only named species, whereas the great majority of species (except in well-studied groups like birds) haven't even been named. Second, outside of North America and Europe and except for birds, the published lists consist only of those few named species that some biologist happened to get interested in for one or another reason and found to be extinct. Among all those remaining species of unknown status, many are likely to be extinct or nearly so: e.g., about half in the case of Malaysian freshwater fishes.

Now LET'S MOVE ON to the second step in evaluating the mass-extinction debate. Our estimates up to this point have concerned only those species exterminated since A.D. 1600, when scientific classification of species was beginning. These exterminations have taken place because the world's human population has grown in numbers, reached previously uninhabited areas, and invented increasingly destructive technologies. Did these factors spring up suddenly in 1600, after several million years of human history? Were there no exterminations before 1600?

Of course not. Until fifty thousand years ago, humans were confined to Africa plus the warmer areas of Europe and Asia. Between then and A.D. 1600 our species underwent a massive geographic expansion that took us to Australia and New Guinea around fifty thousand years ago, then to Siberia and most of North and South America, and finally to most of the world's remote oceanic islands only around 2000 B.C. We also underwent a massive expansion in numbers, from perhaps a few million people fifty thousand years ago to about half a billion in 1600. And our destructiveness also increased with the development of improved hunting skills in the last fifty thousand years, polished stone tools and agriculture in the last ten thousand years, and metal tools in the last six thousand years.

In every area of the world that paleontologists have studied and that humans first reached within the last fifty thousand years, human arrival approximately coincided with massive prehistoric extinctions. For Madagascar, New Zealand, Polynesia, Australia, the West Indies, the Americas, and Mediterranean islands, I've described those extinctions in the preceding two chapters. Ever since scientists became aware of these prehistoric extinction waves associated with human arrival, they've argued over whether people were the cause or just happened to arrive while animals were succumbing to climate changes. In the case of the extinction waves on Polynesian islands, there is now no reasonable doubt that Polynesian arrival in one way or another caused the extinctions. Bird extinctions and Polynesian arrival coincided within a few centuries at a time when no big climate change was happening, and bones of thousands of roasted moas have been found in Polynesian ovens. The coincidence of timing is equally convincing for Madagascar. But the causes of the earlier extinctions, especially those in Australia and the Americas, are still being debated.

As I explained for America's extinctions in the previous chapter, the evidence seems to me overwhelming that humans also played a role in those prehistoric extinctions outside Polynesia and Madagascar. In each part of the world an extinction wave occurred after the first arrival of humans, but didn't occur simultaneously in other areas undergoing similar climate swings, and didn't occur in the same area whenever similar climate swings had occurred previously.

So I doubt that climate did it. Instead, all of you who have visited Antarctica or the Galápagos know how tame the animals there are, being unaccustomed to humans until recently. Photographers can still walk up to those naïve animals as easily as hunters used to. I assume that the first arriving hunters similarly walked up to naïve mammoths and moas elsewhere in the world, while rats that came with the first hunters walked up to naïve little birds of Hawaii and other islands.

It's not just in those areas of the world previously unoccupied by humans that prehistoric humans probably exterminated species. Within the last twenty thousand years there were also extinctions in the areas long occupied by humans—in Eurasia, where woolly rhinos, mammoths, and giant deer ("Irish elk") died out, and in Africa, which lost its giant buffalo, giant hartebeest, and giant horse. These big beasts may also have been among the victims of prehistoric humans who had already been hunting them for a long time but who now were able to hunt them with better weapons than ever before. Eurasia's and Africa's big mammals weren't naïve toward humans, but they disappeared for the same two simple reasons that California's grizzly bear and Britain's bears, wolves, and beavers succumbed only in recent times, after thousands of years of human persecution. Those reasons were more people and better weaponry.

Can we at least estimate how many species were involved in these prehistoric extinctions? No one has ever tried to guess the number of plants, invertebrates, and lizards exterminated by prehistoric habitat destruction. But virtually all oceanic islands explored by paleontologists have yielded remains of recently extinct bird species. Extrapolation to those islands not yet paleontologically explored suggests that about two thousand bird species—one-fifth of all the birds that existed a few thousand years ago—were island species already exterminated prehistorically. That doesn't count birds that may have been exterminated prehistorically on the continents. Among genera of large mammals, about 73, 80, and 86 percent respectively became extinct in North America, South America, and Australia at the time of or after human arrival.

THE REMAINING STEP in evaluating the mass-extinction debate is to predict the future. Is the peak of the extinction wave that we've caused already past, or is most still to come? There are a couple of ways to assess this question.

A simple way is to reason that tomorrow's extinct species will be drawn from today's endangered species. How many species that still exist have populations already reduced to dangerously low levels? The ICBP estimates that at least 1,666 bird species are either endangered or at imminent risk of extinction—almost 20 percent of the world's surviving birds. I said "at least 1,666," because this number is an underestimate for the same reason I mentioned that the ICBP's estimate of extinct species was an underestimate. Both numbers are based just on those species whose status caught a scientist's attention, rather than on a reappraisal of the status of all bird species.

The alternative way of predicting what's to come is to understand the mechanisms by which we exterminate species. Human-caused extinctions may continue accelerating until human population and technology reach a plateau, but neither shows any signs of plateauing. Our population, which grew tenfold from half a billion in 1600 to over five billion now, is still growing at close to 2 percent per year. Every day brings new technological advances for changing the earth and its denizens. There are four main mechanisms by which our growing population exterminates species: by overhunting, species introduction, habitat destruction, and ripple effects. Let's see if these four mechanisms have plateaued.

Overhunting—killing animals faster than they can breed—is the main mechanism by which we've exterminated big animals, from mammoths to California grizzly bears. (The latter appears on the flag of California, the state in which I live, but many of my fellow Californians don't recall that we exterminated our state's symbol long ago). Have we already killed off all big animals that we might kill off? Obviously not. While the low numbers of whales led to an international ban on whaling for commercial purposes, Japan thereupon announced its decision to triple the rate at which it killed whales "for scientific reasons." We've all seen photos of the accelerating slaughter of Africa's elephants and rhinos for their ivory and horns respectively. At current rates of change, not just elephants and rhinos but most populations of most other large mammals of Africa and Southeast Asia will be extinct outside game parks and zoos in a decade or two.

The second mechanism by which we exterminate is through intentionally or accidentally introducing certain species to parts of the world where they didn't previously occur. Familiar examples of introduced species now firmly established in the U.S. are Norway rats, European starlings, boll weevils, and the fungi causing Dutch elm disease and chestnut blight. Europe too has acquired introduced species, of which the misnamed Norway rat is an example (it originated in Asia, not Norway). When species are introduced from one region to another, they often proceed to exterminate some of the native species they encounter, by eating them or causing diseases. The victims evolved in the absence of the introduced pests and never developed defenses against them. American chestnut trees have been virtually exterminated in this way by chestnut blight, an Asian fungus to which Asian chestnut trees are resistant. Similarly, goats and rats have exterminated many plants and birds on oceanic islands.

Have we already spread all possible pests all around the world? Obviously not: there are many islands still free of goats and Norway rats, and many insects and diseases to try to keep out of many countries by quarantines. The U.S. Department of Agriculture has been trying at great expense, but apparently without success, to forestall the arrival of killer bees and Mediterranean fruit flies. In fact, what will probably prove to be the biggest extinction wave caused by an introduced predator in modern times has just started in Africa's Lake Victoria, home to hundreds of species of remarkable fishes found nowhere else in the world. A large predatory fish called the Nile perch, intentionally introduced in a misguided effort to establish a new fishery, is now eating its way through the lake's unique fishes.

Habitat destruction is the third means by which we exterminate. Most species occur in just a certain type of habitat: marsh warblers live in marshes, while pine warblers live in pine forests. If one drains marshes or cuts forests, one eliminates the species dependent on those habitats just as certainly as if one were to shoot every individual of the species. For example, when all the forest on Cebu Island in the Philippines was logged, nine of the ten birds unique to Cebu became extinct.

In the case of habitat destruction, the worst is still to come because we are just starting in earnest to destroy tropical rain forests, the world's most species-rich habitats. The rain forests' biological richness is legendary: e.g., over fifteen hundred beetle species living in a single rain-forest tree species in Panama. Rain forests cover only 6 percent of the Earth's surface but harbor about half of its species. Each area of rain forest has large numbers of species unique to that area. To mention only some exceptionally rich rain forests now being destroyed, the felling of Brazil's Atlantic forest and Malaysia's lowland forest is already almost complete, and those of Borneo and the Philippines will be mostly logged within the next two decades. By the middle of the next century, the only large tracts of tropical rain forest likely to be still surviving will be in parts of Zaire and the Amazon Basin.

Every species depends on other species for food and for providing its habitat. Thus, species are connected to each other like branching rows of dominoes. Just as toppling one domino in a row will topple some others, so too the extermination of one species may lead to the loss of others, which may in turn push still others over the brink. This fourth mechanism of extinction may be described as a ripple effect. Nature consists of so many species, connected to each other in such complex ways, that it's virtually impossible to foresee where the ripple effects from the extinction of any particular species may lead.

For example, fifty years ago no one anticipated that the extinction of big predators (jaguars, pumas, and harpy eagles) on Panama's Barro Colorado Island would lead to the extinction there of little antbirds, and to massive changes in the tree-species composition of the island's forest. But it did, because the big predators used to eat medium-sized predators like peccaries, monkeys, and coatimundis, and medium-sized seedeaters like agoutis and pacas. With the disappearance of the big predators, there was a population explosion of the medium-sized predators, which proceeded to eat up the antbirds and their eggs. The medium-sized seedeaters also exploded in abundance and ate large seeds that had fallen on the ground, thereby suppressing the propagation of tree species producing large seeds and favoring instead the spread of competing tree species with small seeds. That shift in forest tree composition is expected in turn to cause an explosion of mice and rats feeding on small seeds, and hence to an explosion in hawks, owls, and ocelots preying on those small rodents. Thus, the extinction of three uncommon species of big predators will have triggered a rippling series of changes in the whole plant and animal community, including the extinction of many other species.

Through these four mechanisms—overhunting, species introductions, habitat destruction, and ripple effects—probably over half of existing species will be extinct or endangered by the middle of the next century, when this year's crop of human babies reaches age sixty. Like many fathers today, I often wonder how I'll describe to my twin sons the world that I grew up in and that they will never see. By the time they are old enough to come with me to New Guinea, one of the world's biological treasure houses, where I've worked for the past twenty-five years, most of New Guinea's eastern highlands will be deforested.

When one adds these extinctions we've already caused to those that we're about to cause, it's clear that the current extinction wave is surpassing the asteroid collision that wiped out the dinosaurs. Mammals, plants, and many other types of species survived that collision nearly unscathed, while the current wave is impacting everything from leeches and lilies to lions. Thus, the claimed extinction crisis is neither a hysterical fantasy nor just a serious risk for the future. Instead, it's an event that has already been accelerating for fifty thousand years and will start to approach completion in our children's lifetimes.

LET'S FINALLY CONSIDER two arguments that accept the reality of the extinction crisis but dismiss its significance. First, isn't extinction a natural process anyway? If so, why make a big deal about the extinctions happening now?

The answer to this first argument is that the current human-caused extinction rate is far higher than the natural rate. If the estimate that half the world's total of 30 million species will go extinct in the next century is correct, then species are now going extinct at a rate of about 150,000 per year, or 17 per hour. The world's 9,000 bird species are going extinct at a rate of at least 2 per year. But bird extinctions under natural conditions were at a rate of less than 1 per century, so the present rate is at least 200 times normal. Dismissing the extinction crisis on the grounds that extinction is natural would be just like dismissing genocide on the grounds that death is the natural fate of all humans.

The second argument is a simple one: So what? We care about our children, not about beetles and snail darters; who cares if ten million beetle species go extinct? The answer to this argument is equally simple. Like all species, we depend on other species for our existence, in many ways. Some of the most obvious ways are that other species produce the oxygen we breathe, absorb the carbon dioxide we exhale, decompose our sewage, provide our food, maintain the fertility of our soil, and provide our wood and paper.

Then couldn't we just preserve those particular species that we need, and let other species go extinct? Of course not, because the species we need also depend on other species. Just as Panama's ant-birds couldn't have anticipated their need for jaguars, the ecological row of dominoes is much too complex for us to have figured out which dominoes we can dispense with. For instance, could anyone please answer these three questions: Which ten tree species produce most of the world's paper pulp? For each of those ten tree species, which are the ten bird species that eat most of its insect pests, the ten insect species that pollinate most of its flowers, and the ten animal species that spread most of its seeds? Which other species do these ten birds, insects, and animals depend on? You'd have to be able to answer those three impossible questions if you were the president of a timber company trying to figure out which species you could afford to let go extinct.

If you're trying to evaluate some proposed development project that would bring in a million dollars but might exterminate a few species, it's still tempting to prefer the certain profit over the uncertain risk. Then consider the following analogy. Suppose someone offers you a million dollars in return for the privilege of painlessly cutting out two ounces of your valuable flesh. You figure that two ounces is only one thousandth of your body weight, so you'll still have nine-hundred-ninety-nine thousandths of your body left, which is plenty. That's fine if the two ounces come from your spare body fat and if they'll be removed by a skilled surgeon. But what if the surgeon just hacks two ounces from any conveniently accessible part of your body, or doesn't know which parts are essential? You might then find that the two ounces came from your urethra. And if you plan to sell off most of your body, as we now plan to sell off most of our planet's natural habitats, you're certain eventually to lose your urethra.

To CONCLUDE, let's place matters in perspective by comparing the two clouds I mentioned at the outset as hanging over our future. A nuclear holocaust is certain to prove disastrous, but it isn't happening now, and it may or may not happen in the future. An environmental holocaust is equally certain to prove disastrous, but it differs in that it's already well underway. It started tens of thousands of years ago, is now causing more damage than ever before, is in fact accelerating, and will climax within about a century if unchecked. The only uncertainties are whether the resulting disaster would strike our children or our grandchildren, and whether we choose to adopt now the many obvious countermeasures.

Epilogue:
Nothing Learned,
and Everything Forgotten?

Let's now draw together the themes of this book by tracing our rise over the last three million years, as well as our incipient reversal of all our progress more recently.

The first indications that our ancestors were in any respect unusual among animals were our extremely crude stone tools that began to appear in Africa by around two and a half million years ago. The quantities of tools suggest that they were beginning to play a regular, significant role in our livelihood. Among our closest relatives, in contrast, the pygmy chimpanzee and gorilla don't use tools, while the common chimpanzee occasionally makes some rudimentary ones but hardly depends on them for its existence.

Nevertheless, those crude tools of ours did not trigger any quantum jump in our success as a species. For another million and a half years, we remained confined to Africa. Around a million years ago we did manage to spread to warm areas of Europe and Asia, thereby becoming the most widespread of the three chimpanzee species but still much less widespread than lions. Our tools progressed only at an infinitely slow rate, from extremely crude to very crude. By a hundred thousand years ago, at least the human populations of Europe and western Asia, the Neanderthals, were regularly using fire. Yet in other respects we continued to rate as just another species of big mammal. We had developed not a trace of art, agriculture, or high technology. It's unknown whether we had developed language, drug addictions, or our strange modern sexual habits and life cycle, but Neanderthals rarely lived beyond age forty and hence may not yet have evolved female menopause.

Clear evidence of a Great Leap Forward in our behavior appears suddenly in Europe around forty thousand years ago, coincident with the arrival of anatomically modern *Homo sapiens* from Africa via the Near East. At that point, we began displaying art, technology based on specialized tools, cultural differences from place to place, and cultural innovation with time. This leap in behavior had undoubtedly been developing outside Europe, but the development must have been rapid, since the anatomically modern *Homo sapiens* populations living in southern Africa 100,000 years ago were still just glorified chimpanzees as judged by the debris in their cave sites. Whatever caused the leap, it must have involved only a tiny fraction of our genes, because we still differ from chimps in only 1.6 percent of our genes, and most of that difference had already developed long before our leap in behavior. The best guess I can make is that the leap was triggered by the perfection of our modern capacity for language.

Although we usually think of the Cro-Magnons as the first bearers of our noblest traits, they also bore the two traits that lie at the root of our current problems: our propensities to murder each other en masse and to destroy our environment. Even before Cro-Magnon times, fossil human skulls punctured by sharp objects and cracked to extract the brains bear witness to murder and cannibalism. The suddenness with which Neanderthals disappeared after Cro-Magnons arrived hints that genocide had now become efficient. Our efficiency at destroying our own resource base is suggested by extinctions of almost all large Australian animals following our colonization of Australia fifty thousand years ago, and of some large Eurasian and African mammals as our hunting technology improved. If the seeds of self-destruction have been so closely linked with the rise of advanced civilizations in other solar systems as well, it becomes easy to understand why we have not been visited by any flying saucers.

At the end of the last Ice Age around ten thousand years ago, the pace of our rise quickened. We occupied the Americas, coincident with a mass extinction of big mammals that we may have caused. Agriculture emerged soon thereafter. Some thousands of years later, the first written texts start to document the pace of our technical inventiveness. They also show that we were already addicted to drugs, and that genocide had become routine and admired. Habitat destruction began undermining many societies, and the first Polynesian and Malagasy settlers caused mass exterminations of species. From A.D. 1492 onward, the worldwide expansion of literate Europeans lets us trace our rise and fall in detail.

Within the last few decades we have developed the means to send radio signals to other stars, and also to blow ourselves up overnight. Even if we don't blunder into that quick end, our harnessing of much of the Earth's productivity, our exterminations of species, and our damage to our environment are accelerating at a rate that cannot be sustained for even another century. One might object that, if we look around us, we see no obvious sign that the climax of our history will come soon. In fact, the signs become obvious if one looks and then extrapolates. Starvation, pollution, and destructive technology are increasing; usable farmland, food stocks in the sea, other natural products, and environmental capacity to absorb wastes are decreasing. As more people with more power scramble for fewer resources, something has to give way.

So what is likely to happen?

There are many grounds for pessimism. Even if every human now alive were to die tomorrow, the damage that we have already inflicted on our environment would ensure that its degradation will continue for decades. Innumerable species already belong to the "living dead," with populations fallen to levels from which they cannot recover, even though not all individuals have died yet. Despite all our past self-destructive behavior from which we could have learned, many people who should know better dispute the need for limiting our population and continue to assault our environment. Others join that assault for selfish profit or out of ignorance. Even more people are too caught up in the desperate struggle for survival to be able to enjoy the luxury of weighing the consequences of their actions. All these facts suggest that the juggernaut of destruction has already reached unstoppable momentum, that we too are among the living dead, and that our future is as bleak as that of the other two chimpanzees.

This pessimistic view is captured by a cynical sentence that Arthur Wichmann, a Dutch explorer and professor, penned in another context in 1912. Wichmann had devoted a decade of his life to writing a monumental three-volume treatise on the history of New Guinea exploration. In 1,198 pages he evaluated every source of information about New Guinea that he could find, from the earliest reports filtering through Indonesia to the great expeditions of the nineteenth and early twentieth centuries. He grew disillusioned as he realized that successive explorers committed the same stupidities again and again: unwarranted pride in overstated accomplishments, refusal to acknowledge disastrous oversights, ignoring the experience of previous explorers, consequent repetition of previous errors, hence a long history of unnecessary sufferings and deaths. Looking back on this history, Wichmann predicted that future explorers would continue to repeat the same errors. The bitter last sentence that concluded Wichmann's last volume was: "Nothing learned, and everything forgotten!"

Despite all the grounds I've mentioned for being equally cynical about humanity's future, my view is that our situation isn't hopeless. We are the only ones creating our problems, so it's completely within our power to solve them. While our language and art and agriculture aren't quite unique, we really are unique among animals in our capacity to learn from the experience of others of our species living in distant places or in the distant past. Among the hopeful signs, there are many realistic, often-discussed policies by which we could avoid disaster, such as by limiting human population growth, preserving natural habitats, and adopting other environmental safeguards. Many governments are already doing some of these obvious things in some cases.

For example, awareness of environmental problems is spreading, and environmental movements are gaining political clout. Developers don't win all the battles, nor do shortsighted economic arguments always prevail. Many countries have lowered their rate of population growth in recent decades. While genocide hasn't vanished, the spread of communications technology has at least the potential for reducing our traditional xenophobia, and for making it harder to regard distant peoples as subhumans unlike ourselves. I was seven years old when the A-bombs were dropped on Hiroshima and Nagasaki, so I remember well the sense of an imminent risk of nuclear holocaust that prevailed for several decades thereafter. But nearly half a century has now passed without any further military use of nuclear weapons. The risk of a nuclear holocaust now seems more remote than at any other time since August 9, 1945.

My own outlook is conditioned by my experiences since 1979 as consultant to the Indonesian government, on setting up a nature reserve system in Indonesian New Guinea (called Irian Jaya province). On the face of it, Indonesia doesn't seem a promising place to hope for much success in preserving our shrinking natural habitats. Instead, Indonesia exemplifies the problems of tropical third-world countries in acute form. With over 180 million inhabitants, it is the world's fifth most populous country, as well as one of the poorer ones. The population is growing rapidly; nearly half of all Indonesians are under fifteen years old. Some provinces with inordinately high population density are exporting their population surpluses to the less populated provinces (such as Irian Jaya). There are no armies of bird-watchers, no broad-based indigenous environmental movements. The government is not a democracy in the western sense, and corruption is viewed as pervasive. Indonesia depends on logging of its virgin rain forests, second only to exploitation of oil and natural gas as a source of its foreign exchange.

For all these reasons, one might not expect preservation of species and habitats to be a national priority pursued seriously in Indonesia. When I first went to Irian Jaya, I was frankly doubtful that an effective conservation program would result. Fortunately, my Wichmann-like cynicism proved wrong. Thanks to the leadership of a core of Indonesians convinced of conservation's value, Irian Jaya now has the beginnings of a nature reserve system comprising 20 percent of the province's area. Nor do those reserves exist just on paper. As my work proceeded, I was pleasantly surprised to come across sawmills abandoned because they conflicted with nature reserves, park guards out on patrol, and management plans being drawn up. All these measures were adopted not out of idealism but out of cold-blooded, correct perception of Indonesia's natural self-interest. If Indonesia can do it, so can other countries with similar obstacles to environmentalism, as well as much richer countries with broad-based environmental movements.

We don't need novel, still-to-be invented technologies to solve our problems. We just need more governments to do many more of the same obvious things that some governments are already doing in some cases. Nor is it true that the average citizen is powerless. There are many causes of extinction that citizen groups have helped scale back in recent years—for instance, commercial whaling, hunting big cats for fur coats, and importing wild-caught chimpanzees, to mention just a few examples. In fact, this is one area where it's particularly easy for a modest donation by the average citizen to have a big impact, because all conservation organizations now have such modest budgets. For instance, the annual combined budget for *all* primate conservation projects that World Wildlife Fund supports throughout the world is only a few hundred thousand dollars. An extra thousand dollars means an extra project on some endangered monkey, ape, or lemur that might otherwise have been ignored. Pages 390–91 suggest some specific starting points for interested readers.

While I do see us facing serious problems with an uncertain prognosis, I'm cautiously optimistic. Even the cynical last sentence of Wichmann's book proved false: New Guinea explorers since Wichmann really have learned from the past and avoided the disastrous stupidities of their predecessors. A motto more appropriate for our future than Wichmann's motto comes from the memoirs of the statesman Otto von Bismarck. As he reflected on the world around him toward the end of his long life, he too had reasons to be cynical. Possessing a keen intellect and working at the center of European politics for decades, Bismarck had witnessed a history of unnecessarily repeated errors as gross as those pervading the early history of New Guinea exploration. But Bismarck still considered it worthwhile to write his memoirs, to draw lessons from history, and to dedicate his memoirs "to [my] children and grandchildren, towards an understanding of the past, and for guidance for the future."

This is also the spirit in which I dedicated this book to my young sons and their generation. If we will learn from our past that I have traced, our own future may yet prove brighter than that of the other two chimpanzees.

Acknowledgments

It's a pleasure for me to acknowledge the contributions of many people to this book. From my parents and from my teachers at Roxbury Latin School, I learned to pursue interests along many lines simultaneously. My debt to my many New Guinea friends will be obvious from the frequency with which I cite their experiences. I owe an equal debt to my many scientist friends and professional colleagues, who patiently explained the subtleties of their subjects and read my drafts. Earlier versions of most of the chapters appeared as articles in *Discover* magazine and in *Natural History* magazine. I've been fortunate to have John Brockman as my agent, and as my editors Leon Jaroff, Fred Golden, Gil Rogin, Paul Hoffman, and Marc Zabludoff at *Discover,* Alan Ternes and Ellen Goldensohn at *Natural History,* Thomas Miller at HarperCollins, Neil Belton at Hutchinson Radius Publishers, and my wife, Marie Cohen.

Further Readings

THESE SUGGESTIONS are for readers interested in reading further. In addition to key books and papers, I have also tended to favor recent references that provide comprehensive listings of the earlier literature. A journal title is followed by the volume number, followed after a colon by the first and last page number, and then the year of publication in parentheses.

CHAPTER 1. *A Tale of Three Chimps*

The literature on deducing relationships among humans and other primates by means of the DNA clock consists of technical articles in scientific journals. C. G. Sibley and J. E. Ahlquist present their studies in three papers: "The phylogeny of the hominoid primates, as indicated by DNA-DNA hybridization," *Journal of Molecular Evolution* 20: 2–15 (1984); "DNA hybridization evidence of hominoid phylogeny: results from an expanded data set," *Journal of Molecular Evolution* 26: 99–121 (1987); and C. G. Sibley, J. A. Comstock, and J. E. Ahlquist, "DNA hybridization evidence of hominoid phylogeny: a reanalysis of the data," *Journal of Molecular Evolution* 30: 202–236 (1990). Sibley's and Ahlquist's many studies of bird relationships by means of the same DNA methods are summarized in two books: C. G. Sibley and J. E. Ahlquist, *Phylogeny and Classification of Birds* (New Haven:

371

Yale University Press, 1990); and C. G. Sibley and B. L. Monroe, Jr., *Distribution and Taxonomy of the Birds of the World* (New Haven: Yale University Press, 1990).

Similar conclusions about human and primate relationships were obtained by DNA comparisons using a different method (termed the tetraethylammonium chloride method, rather than the hydroxyapatite method used by Sibley and Ahlquist). The results were described by A. Caccone and J. R. Powell, "DNA divergence among hominoids," *Evolution* 43: 925–942 (1989). A paper by the same authors explains how percentage similarity among DNAs can be calculated from DNA mixed melting points: A. Caccone, R. DeSalle, and J. R. Powell, "Calibration of the changing thermal stability of DNA duplexes and degree of base pair mismatch," *Journal of Molecular Evolution* 27: 212–216 (1988).

The above papers compare the entire genetic material (DNA) of two species by means of mixed melting points in order to obtain a single measure of overall similarity. Alternatively, a much more laborious method yielding much more detailed information about a tiny fraction of each species' DNA consists of determining the actual sequence of molecular units comprising that portion of DNA. Five studies stemming from a single laboratory and applying that method to human and primate relationships are: M. M. Miyamoto et al., "Phylogenetic relations of humans and African apes from DNA sequence in the Ψ-globin region," *Science* 238: 369–373 (1987); M. M. Miyamoto et al., "Molecular systematics of higher primates: genealogical relations and classification," *Proceedings of the National Academy of Sciences* 85: 7627–7631 (1988); M. Goodman et al., "Molecular phylogeny of the family of apes and humans," *Genome* 31: 316–335 (1989); M. M. Miyamoto and M. Goodman, "DNA systematics and evolution of primates," *Annual Reviews of Ecology and Systematics* 21: 197–220; and M. Goodman et al., "Primate evolution at the DNA level and a classification of hominoids," *Journal of Molecular Evolution* 30: 260–266 (1990). The same principle is applied to relationships among Lake Victoria's cichlid fishes by A. Meyer et al., "Monophyletic origin of Lake Victoria cichlid fishes suggested by mitochondrial DNA sequences," *Nature* 347: 550–553 (1990).

Two papers that vigorously criticize the DNA clock in general, and Sibley's and Ahlquist's application of it to human-primate relationships in particular, are: J. Marks, C. W. Schmidt, and V. M. Sarich, "DNA hybridization as a guide to phylogeny: relationships of the Hominoidea," *Journal of Human Evolution* 17: 769–786 (1988); and V. M. Sarich, C. W. Schmidt, and J. Marks, "DNA hybridization as a guide to phylogeny: a critical analysis," *Cladistics* 5: 3–32 (1989). In my view, the criticisms by Marks, Schmidt, and Sarich have been adequately answered. The good agreement between conclusions about human/primate relationships based on the DNA clock as measured by Sibley and Ahlquist, the DNA clock as measured by Caccone and Powell, and DNA sequencing further supports the correctness of these conclusions.

Other papers on the DNA clock are in two issues of the *Journal of Molecular Evolution* that also include some of the above-cited papers: volume 30, numbers 3 and 5 (1990).

CHAPTER 2. *The Great Leap Forward*

Among the many books providing detailed accounts of human evolution, the recent one that I found the most useful is by Richard Klein, *The Human Career* (Chicago: University of Chicago Press, 1989). Illustrated and less technical accounts are by Roger Lewin, *In the Age of Mankind* (Washington, D.C.: Smithsonian Books, 1988), and Brian Fagan, *The Journey from Eden* (New York: Thames and Hudson, 1990).

Two books presenting multiauthored technical accounts of recent human evolution are edited by Fred H. Smith and Frank Spencer, *The Origins of Modern Humans* (New York: Liss, 1984) and by Paul Mellars and Chris Stringer, *The Human Revolution: Behavioural and Biological Perspectives on the Origins of Modern Humans* (Edinburgh: Edinburgh University Press, 1989). Some recent articles on the dating and geography of human evolution are by C. B. Stringer and P. Andrews, "Genetic and fossil evidence for the origin of modern humans," *Science* 239: 1263–1268 (1988); H. Valladas et al., "Thermoluminescence dating of Mousterian 'proto-Cro-Magnon' remains from Israel and the origin of modern man" *Nature* 331: 614–616 (1988); C. B. Stringer et al., "ESR dates for the hominid burial site of Es Skhul in Israel," *Nature* 338: 756–758 (1989); J. L. Bischoff et al., "Abrupt Mousterian-Aurignacian boundaries at c. 40 ka bp: accelerator ^{14}C dates from l'Arbreda Cave (Catalunya, Spain)," *Journal of Archaeological Science* 16: 563–576 (1989); V. Cabrera-Valdes and J. Bischoff, "Accelerator ^{14}C dates for Early Upper Paleolithic (Basal Aurignacian) at El Castillo Cave (Spain)," *Journal of Archaeological Science* 16: 577–584 (1989); E. L. Simons, "Human origins," *Science* 245: 1343–1350 (1989); and R. Grün et al., "ESR dating evidence for early modern humans at Border Cave in South Africa," *Nature* 344: 537–539 (1990).

Three books with many beautiful illustrations of Ice Age art are by Randall White, *Dark Caves, Bright Visions* (New York: American Museum of Natural History, 1986); Mario Ruspoli, *Lascaux: The Final Photographs* (New York: Abrams, 1987); and Paul G. Bahn and Jean Vertut, *Images of the Ice Age* (New York: Facts on File, 1988).

Matthew H. Nitecki and Doris V. Nitecki, *The Evolution of Human Hunting* (New York: Plenum Press, 1986), provide a series of chapters by various authors on that subject.

The question whether Neanderthals really did bury their dead is debated in an article by R. H. Gargett, "Grave shortcomings: the evidence for Neanderthal burial," and in accompanying responses published in *Current Anthropology* 30: 157–190 (1989).

Three sources that will provide an entrance into the literature on the linked questions of human vocal-tract anatomy and whether Neanderthals could speak are: a book by Philip Lieberman, *The Biology and Evolution of Language* (Cambridge, Mass.: Harvard University Press, 1984); another book by E. S. Crelin, *The Human Vocal Tract* (New York: Vantage Press, 1987); and an article by B. Arensburg et al., "A Middle Palaeolithic human hyoid bone," *Nature* 338: 758–760 (1989).

CHAPTER 3. *The Evolution of Human Sexuality*

CHAPTER 4. *The Science of Adultery*

For anyone interested in an evolutionary approach to behavior in general (including reproductive behavior), two books are a must: E. O. Wilson, *Sociobiology* (Cambridge, Mass.: Harvard University Press, 1975), and John Alcock, *Animal Behavior,* 4th ed. (Sunderland: Sinauer, 1989).

Outstanding books that discuss the evolution of sexual behavior include Donald Symons, *The Evolution of Human Sexuality* (Oxford: Oxford University Press, 1979); R. D. Alexander, *Darwinism and Human Affairs* (Seattle: University of Washington Press, 1979); Napoleon A. Chagnon and William Irons, *Evolutionary Biology and Human Social Behavior* (North Scituate, Mass.: Duxbury, Press, 1979); Tim Halliday, *Sexual Strategies* (Chicago: University of Chicago Press, 1980); Glenn Hausfater and Sarah Hrdy, *Infanticide* (Hawthorne, N.Y.: Aldine, 1980); Sarah Hrdy, *The Woman That Never Evolved* (Cambridge, Mass.: Harvard University Press, 1981); Nancy Tanner, *On Becoming Human* (New York: Cambridge University Press, 1981); Frances Dahlberg, *Woman the Gatherer* (New Haven: Yale University Press, 1981); Martin Daly and Margo Wilson, *Sex, Evolution, and Behavior* (Boston: Willard Grant Press, 1983); Bettyann Kevles, *Females of the Species* (Cambridge, Mass.: Harvard University Press, 1986); and Hanny Lightfoot-Klein, *Prisoners of Ritual: An Odyssey into Female Genital Circumcision in Africa* (Binghamton: Harrington Park Press, 1989).

Books dealing specifically with primate reproductive biology include C. E. Graham, *Reproductive Biology of the Great Apes* (New York: Academic Press, 1981); B. B. Smuts et al., *Primate Societies* (Chicago: University of Chicago Press, 1986); Jane Goodall, *The Chimpanzees of Gombe* (Cambridge, Mass.: Harvard University Press, 1986); Toshisada Nishida, *The Chimpanzees of the Mahale Mountains, Sexual and Life History Strategies* (Tokyo: University of Tokyo Press, 1990); and Takayoshi Kano, *The Last Ape: Pygmy Chimpanzee Behavior and Ecology* (Stanford: Stanford University Press, 1991).

Articles on the evolution of sexual physiology and behavior include the following: R. V. Short, "The evolution of human reproduction," *Proceed-*

ings of the Royal Society (*London*), series B 195: 3–24 (1976); R. V. Short, "Sexual selection and its component parts, somatic and genetical selection, as illustrated by man and the great apes," *Advances in the Study of Behavior* 9: 131–158 (1979); N. Burley, "The evolution of concealed ovulation," *American Naturalist* 114: 835–858 (1979); A. H. Harcourt et al., "Testis weight, body weight, and breeding system in primates," *Nature* 293: 55–57 (1981); R. D. Martin and R. M. May, "Outward signs of breeding," *Nature* 293: 7–9 (1981); M. Daly and M. I. Wilson, "Whom are newborn babies said to resemble?," *Ethology and Sociobiology* 3: 69–78 (1982); M. Daly, M. Wilson, and S. J. Weghorst, "Male sexual jealousy," *Ethology and Sociobiology* 3: 11–27 (1982); A. F. Dixson, "Observations on the evolution and behavioral significance of 'sexual skin' in female primates," *Advances in the Study of Behavior* 13: 63–106 (1983); S. J. Andelman, "Evolution of concealed ovulation in vervet monkeys (*Cercopithecus aethiops*)," *American Naturalist* 129: 785–799 (1987); and P. H. Harvey and R. M. May, "Out for the sperm count," *Nature* 337: 508–509 (1989).

Chapter 4 discussed several examples illustrating how birds combine extramarital sex with apparent monogamy. Detailed examples of such studies are presented in papers by D. W. Mock, "Display repertoire shifts and extra-marital courtship in herons," *Behaviour* 69: 57–71 (1979); P. Mineau and F. Cooke, "Rape in the lesser snow goose," *Behaviour* 70: 280–291 (1979); D. F. Werschel, "Nesting ecology of the Little Blue Heron: promiscuous behavior," *Condor* 84: 381–384 (1982); M. A. Fitch and G. W. Shuart, "Requirements for a mixed reproductive strategy in avian species," *American Naturalist* 124: 116–126 (1984); and R. Alatalo et al., "Extra-pair copulations and mate guarding in the polyterritorial pied flycatcher, *Ficedula hypoleuca*," *Behavior* 101: 139–155 (1987).

CHAPTER 5. *How We Pick Our Mates and Sex Partners*

Not surprisingly, this topic has called forth much scientific study. Some papers exemplifying the literature on mate choice by humans are the following: E. Walster et al., "Importance of physical attractiveness in dating behavior," *Journal of Personality and Social Psychology* 4: 508–516 (1966); J. N. Spuhler, "Assortative mating with respect to physical characteristics," *Eugenics Quarterly* 15: 128–140 (1968); E. Berscheid and K. Dion, "Physical attractiveness and dating choice: a test of the matching hypothesis," *Journal of Experimental Social Psychology* 7: 173–189 (1971); S. G. Vandenberg, "Assortative mating, or who marries whom?," *Behavior Genetics* 2: 127–157 (1972); G. E. DeYoung and B. Fleischer, "Motivational and personality trait relationships in mate selection," *Behavior Genetics* 6: 1–6 (1976); E. Crognier, "Assortative mating for physical features in an African population from Chad," *Journal of Human Evolution* 6: 105–114 (1977); P. N. Bentler and M. D. Newcomb, "Longitudinal study of marital success and failure,"

Journal of Consulting and Clinical Psychology 46: 1053–1070 (1978); R. C. Johnson et al., "Secular change in degree of assortatative mating for ability?," *Behavior Genetics* 10: 1–8 (1980); W. E. Nance et al., "A model for the analysis of mate selection in the marriages of twins," *Acta Geneticae Medicae Gemellologiae* 29: 91–101 (1980); D. Thiessen and B. Gregg, "Human assortative mating and genetic equilibrium: an evolutionary perspective," *Ethology and Sociobiology* 1: 111–140 (1980); D. M. Buss, "Human mate selection," *American Scientist* 73: 47–51 (1985); A. C. Heath and L. J. Eaves, "Resolving the effects of phenotype and social background on mate selection," *Behavior Genetics* 15: 75–90 (1985); and A. C. Heath et al., "No decline in assortative mating for educational level," *Behavior Genetics* 15: 349–369 (1985). Also relevant is a book by B. I. Murstein, *Who Will Marry Whom? Theories and Research in Marital Choice* (New York: Springer, 1976).

The literature on mate choice by animals is at least as extensive as that for humans. A good starting point is a book edited by Patrick Bateson, *Mate Choice* (Cambridge, Mass.: Cambridge University Press, 1983). Bateson's own studies on Japanese quail are summarized in chapter 11 of that book, and also in his papers "Sexual imprinting and optimal outbreeding," *Nature* 273: 659–660 (1978) and "Preferences for cousins in Japanese quail," *Nature* 295: 236–237 (1982). Studies of mice and rats that grow up to prefer the perfumes of their mothers or fathers are described by T. J. Fillion and E. M. Blass, "Infantile experience with suckling odors determines adult sexual behavior in male rats," *Science* 231: 729–731 (1986), and by B. D'Udine and E. Alleva, "Early experience and sexual preferences in rodents," pages 311–327 in the above-cited book by Patrick Bateson.

Finally, some other relevant papers are cited under the further readings for chapters 3, 4, 6, and 11.

CHAPTER 6. *Sexual Selection, and the Origin of Human Races*

Darwin's own classic account is still a good introduction to natural selection: Charles Darwin, *On the Origin of Species by Means of Natural Selection, or the Preservation of Favored Races in the Struggle for Life* (London: John Murray, 1859). An outstanding modern account is that of Ernst Mayr, *Animal Species and Evolution* (Cambridge, Mass.: Harvard University Press, 1963).

Three books by Carleton S. Coon describe human geographic variation, compare it to geographic variation in climate, and attempt to account for human variation in terms of natural selection: *The Origin of Races* (New York: Knopf, 1962), *The Living Races of Man* (New York: Knopf, 1965), and *Racial Adaptations* (Chicago: Nelson-Hall, 1982). Three other relevant books are by Stanley M. Garn, *Human Races,* 2nd ed. (Springfield, Ill.: Thomas, 1965), especially its chapter 5; K. F. Dyer, *The Biology of Racial*

Integration (Bristol: Scientechnica, 1974), especially its chapters 2 and 3; and A. S. Boughey, *Man and the Environment,* 2nd ed. (New York: Macmillan, 1975).

Interpretations of geographic variation in human skin color in terms of natural selection are put forward by W. F. Loomis, "Skin-pigment regulation of vitamin-D biosynthesis in man," *Science* 157: 501–506 (1967); Vernon Riley, *Pigmentation* (New York: Appleton-Century-Crofts, 1972), especially its chapter 2; R. F. Branda and J. W. Eaton, "Skin color and nutrient photolysis: an evolutionary hypothesis," *Science* 201: 625–626 (1978); P. J. Byard, "Quantitative genetics of human skin color," *Yearbook of Physical Anthropology* 24: 123–137 (1981); and W. J. Hamilton III, *Life's Color Code* (New York: McGraw-Hill, 1983). Human geographic variation in response to cold is described by G. M. Brown and J. Page, "The effect of chronic exposure to cold on temperature and blood flow of the hand," *Journal of Applied Physiology* 5: 221–227 (1952), and T. Adams and B. G. Covino, "Racial variations to a standardized cold stress," *Journal of Applied Physiology* 12: 9–12 (1958).

Just as for natural selection, Darwin's own account remains a good introduction to sexual selection: Charles Darwin, *The Descent of Man, and Selection in Relation to Sex* (London: John Murray, 1871). The further readings listed under Chapter 5 for mate selection by animals are also relevant to this chapter. Malte Andersson describes his experiments on how female widowbirds responded to males with artificially shortened or lengthened tails in an article "Female choice selects for extreme tail length in a widowbird," *Nature* 299: 818–820 (1982). Three papers describing mate choice by white, blue, and pink snow geese are by F. Cooke and C. M. McNally, "Mate selection and colour preferences in Lesser Snow Geese," *Behaviour* 53: 151–170 (1975); F. Cooke et al., "Assortative mating in Lesser Snow Geese (*Anser caerulescens*)," *Behavior Genetics* 6: 127–140 (1976); and F. Cooke and J. C. Davies, "Assortative mating, mate choice, and reproductive fitness in Snow Geese," pages 279–295 in the already-cited book *Mate Choice* by Patrick Bateson.

CHAPTER 7. *Why Do We Grow Old and Die?*

The classic paper in which George Williams presented an evolutionary theory of aging is "Pleiotropy, natural selection, and the evolution of senescence," *Evolution* 11: 398–411 (1957). Other papers that have employed evolutionary approaches are by G. Bell, "Evolutionary and nonevolutionary theories of senescence," *American Naturalist* 124: 600–603 (1984); E. Beutler, "Planned obsolescence in humans and in other biosystems," *Perspectives in Biology and Medicine* 29: 175–179 (1986); R. J. Goss, "Why mammals don't regenerate—or do they?," *News in Physiological Sciences* 2: 112–115 (1987);

L. D. Mueller, "Evolution of accelerated senescence in laboratory populations of *Drosophila*," *Proceedings of the National Academy of Sciences* 84: 1974–1977 (1987); and T. B. Kirkwood, "The nature and causes of ageing," pages 193–206 in a book edited by D. Evered and J. Whelan, *Research and the Ageing Population* (Chichester: John Wiley, 1988).

Two books exemplifying the physiological (proximate-cause) approach to aging are by R. L. Walford, *The Immunologic Theory of Aging* (Copenhagen: Munksgaard, 1969), and MacFarlane Burnett, *Intrinsic Mutagenesis: A Genetic Approach to Ageing* (New York: John Wiley, 1974).

Some papers exemplifying the literature on biological repair and turnover are by R. W. Young, "Biological renewal: applications to the eye," *Transactions of the Ophthalmological Societies of the United Kingdom* 102: 42–75 (1982); A. Bernstein et al., "Genetic damage, mutation, and the evolution of sex," *Science* 229: 1277–1281 (1985); J. F. Dice, "Molecular determinants of protein half-lives in eukaryotic cells," *Federation of American Societies for Experimental Biology Journal* 1: 349–357 (1987); P. C. Hanawalt, "On the role of DNA damage and repair processes in aging: evidence for and against," pages 183–198 in a book edited by H. R. Warner et al., *Modern Biological Theories of Aging* (New York: Raven Press, 1987); and M. Radman and R. Wagner, "The high fidelity of DNA duplication," *Scientific American* 259, no. 2: 40–46 (August 1988).

While all readers will be aware of the changes in their own bodies with age, three papers describing the cruel facts for three different systems are: R. L. Doty et al., "Smell identification ability: changes with age," *Science* 226: 1441–1443 (1984); J. Menken et al., "Age and infertility," *Science* 233: 1389–1394 (1986); and R. Katzman, "Normal aging and the brain," *News in Physiological Sciences* 3: 197–200 (1988).

"The Adventure of the Creeping Man" will be found in Arthur Conan Doyle's *The Complete Sherlock Holmes* (New York: Doubleday, 1960). In case you think that attempts at self-rejuvenation by hormonal injections were only a fantasy of Doyle's, read about how it was actually attempted: David Hamilton, *The Monkey Gland Affair* (London: Chatto and Windus, 1986).

CHAPTER 8. *Bridges to Human Language*

How Monkeys See the World (Chicago: University of Chicago Press, 1990), by Dorothy Cheney and Robert Seyfarth, is not only a readable account of vervet vocal communications, but also a good introduction to studies of how animals in general communicate to each other and view the world.

Derek Bickerton has described his studies of creolization and his views on human language origins in two books and several papers. The books are *Roots of Language* (Ann Arbor: Karoma Press, 1981) and *Language and*

Species (Chicago: University of Chicago Press, 1990). The papers include "Creole languages," in *Scientific American* 249, no. 1: 116–122 (1983); "The language bioprogram hypothesis," in *Behavioral and Brain Sciences* 7: 173–221 (1984); and "Creole languages and the bioprogram," in *Linguistics: The Cambridge Survey,* vol. 2, pp. 267–284, edited by F. J. Newmeyer (Cambridge: Cambridge University Press, 1988). The second of those articles includes, and the third is immediately followed by, presentations by other authors whose views often diverge from Bickerton's.

Pidgin and Creole Languages, by Robert A. Hall, Jr. (Ithaca: Cornell University Press, 1966), is an older account of its subject. The best introduction to Neo-Melanesian is the book by F. Mihalic, *The Jacaranda Diary and Grammar of Melanesian Pidgin* (Milton, Queensland: Jacaranda Press, 1971). Roger Keesing's book *Melanesian Pidgin and the Oceanic Substrate* (Stanford: Stanford University Press, 1988) explores the history of Neo-Melanesian.

Among the many influential books on language by Noam Chomsky are *Language and Mind* (New York: Harcourt Brace, 1968) and *Knowledge of Language: Its Nature, Origin, and Use* (New York: Praeger, 1985).

References to some related fields that I mentioned only briefly in Chapter 8 will also be of interest. Susan Curtiss's book *Genie: a Psycholinguistic Study of a Modern-Day "Wild Child"* (New York: Academic Press, 1977) relates both a gut-wrenching human tragedy and a detailed study of a child whose parents' pathologies isolated her from normal human language and contact until age thirteen. Recent accounts of efforts to teach languagelike communication to captive apes include Carolyn Ristau and Donald Robbins's paper "Language and the great apes: a critical review," in *Advances in the Study of Behavior,* vol. 12, pp. 141–255, edited by J. S. Rosenblatt et al. (New York: Academic Press, 1982); E. S. Savage-Rumbaugh, *Ape Language: From Conditioned Response to Symbol* (New York: Columbia University Press, 1986); and "Symbols: their communicative use, comprehension, and combination by bonobos (*Pan paniscus*)," by E. S. Savage-Rumbaugh et al., in *Advances in Infancy Research,* vol. 6, pp. 221–278, edited by Carolyn Rovee-Collier and Lewis Lipsitt (Norwood, N.J.: Ablex Publishing Corporation, 1990). Some starting points in the large literature on early language learning by children include Melissa Bowerman's chapter "Language Development" in *Handbook of Cross-cultural Psychology: Developmental Psychology,* vol. 4, pp. 93–185, edited by Harvey Triandis and Alastair Heron (Boston: Allyn and Bacon, 1981); Eric Wanner and Lila Gleitman, *Language Acquisition: The State of the Art* (Cambridge, Mass.: Cambridge University Press, 1982); Dan Slobin, *The Crosslinguistic Study of Language Acquisition,* vols. 1 and 2 (Hillsdale, N.J.: Lawrence Erlbaum Associates, 1985); and Frank S. Kessel, *The Development of Language and Language Researchers: Essays in Honor of Roger Brown* (Hillsdale, N.J.: Lawrence Erlbaum Associates, 1988).

CHAPTER 9. *Animal Origins of Art*

The book that describes elephant art and illustrates it with photographs of the artist and of her drawings is by David Gucwa and James Ehmann, *To Whom It May Concern: An Investigation of the Art of Elephants* (New York: Norton, 1985). For a similar account of ape art, see Desmond Morris, *The Biology of Art* (New York: Knopf, 1962). Animal art is also treated by Thomas Sebeok, *The Play of Musement* (Bloomington: Indiana University Press, 1981).

There are two fine illustrated books on bowerbirds and birds of paradise, with pictures of their bowers: E. T. Gilliard, *Birds of Paradise and Bower Birds* (Garden City, N.Y.: Natural History Press, 1969), and W. T. Cooper and J. M. Forshaw, *The Birds of Paradise and Bower Birds* (Sydney: Collins, 1977). For a more recent technical account, see my article "Biology of birds of paradise and bowerbirds," *Annual Reviews of Ecology and Systematics* 17: 17–37 (1986). I published two accounts of the bowerbird species with the fanciest bower: "Bower building and decoration by the bowerbird *Amblyornis inornatus*," *Ethology* 74: 177–204 (1987); and "Experimental study of bower decoration by the bowerbird *Amblyornis inornatus*, using colored poker chips," *American Naturalist* 131: 631–653 (1988). Gerald Borgia proved by experiments that female bowerbirds really do care about males' bower decorations, in his paper, "Bower quality, number of decorations and mating success of male satin bowerbirds (*Ptilonorhynchus violaceus*): an experimental analysis," *Animal Behaviour* 33: 266–271 (1985). Birds of paradise with somewhat similar habits are described by S. G. and M. A. Pruett-Jones, "The use of court objects by Lawes' Parotia," *Condor* 90: 538–545 (1988).

CHAPTER 10. *Agriculture's Mixed Blessings*

The health consequences of giving up hunting for farming receive detailed treatment in a book edited by Mark Cohen and George Armelagos, *Paleopathology at the Origins of Agriculture* (Orlando: Academic Press, 1984), and in *The Paleolithic Prescription* (New York: Harper & Row, 1988) by S. Boyd Eaton, Marjorie Shostak, and Melvin Konner. The world's hunter-gatherers are summarized in a book edited by Richard B. Lee and Irven DeVore, *Man the Hunter* (Chicago: Aldine, 1968). References describing the work schedule of hunter-gatherers, and in some cases comparing it with that of farmers, include the same book, plus the book by Richard Lee *The !Kung San* (Cambridge, Mass.: Cambridge University Press, 1979), and the following articles: K. Hawkes et al., "Aché at the settlement: contrasts between farming and foraging," *Human Ecology* 15: 133–161 (1987); K. Hawkes et al., "Hardworking Hadza grandmothers," pages 341–366 in *Comparative Socioecology of Mammals and Man,* edited by V. Standen and R.

Foley (London: Blackwell, 1987); and K. Hill and A. M. Hurtado, "Hunter-gatherers of the New World," *American Scientist* 77: 437–443 (1989). The slow spread of ancient farmers across Europe is described by Albert J. Ammerman and L. L. Cavalli-Sforza, *The Neolithic Transition and the Genetics of Populations in Europe* (Princeton: Princeton University Press, 1984).

CHAPTER 11. *Why Do We Smoke, Drink, and Use Dangerous Drugs?*

Amotz Zahavi explains his handicap theory in two papers: "Mate selection—a selection for a handicap," *Journal of Theoretical Biology* 53: 205–214 (1975), and "The cost of honesty (further remarks on the handicap principle)," *Journal of Theoretical Biology* 67: 603–605 (1977). Two other well-known models of how animals evolve to choose their mates are the runaway selection model and the truth-in-advertising model. The former was developed in a book by R. A. Fisher, *The Genetical Theory of Natural Selection* (Oxford: Clarendon Press, 1930); the latter, in a paper by A. Kodric-Brown and J. H. Brown, "Truth in advertising: the kinds of traits favored by sexual selection," *American Naturalist* 14: 309–323 (1984). These various models are evaluated by Mark Kirkpatrick and Michael Ryan, "The evolution of mating preferences and the paradox of the lek," *Nature* 350: 33–38 (1991). Melvin Konner develops another perspective on risky human behaviors in a chapter "Why the reckless survive" from his book with the same title (New York: Viking, 1990). For discussions of American Indian enemas, see Peter Furst's and Michael Coe's account of the discovery of Maya enema vases in their article "Ritual enemas," *Natural History Magazine* 86: 88–91 (March 1977); Johannes Wilbert's book *Tobacco and Shamanism in South America* (New Haven: Yale University Press, 1987); and Justin Kerr's *The Maya Vase Book*, 2 vols. (New York: Kerr Associates, 1989 and 1990), illustrating Maya vases and analyzing one enema vase in detail on pages 349–361 of volume 2. Also relevant are the many further readings on sexual selection and mate choice already listed under Chapters 5 and 6.

CHAPTER 12. *Alone in a Crowded Universe*

Pioneering calculations arguing for the existence of intelligent extraterrestrial life were carried out by I. S. Shklovskii and Carl Sagan, *Intelligent Life in the Universe* (San Francisco: Holden-Day, 1966). Arguments for and against, and what it might mean for us if we do discover extraterrestrials out there, form the subject of the book *Extraterrestrials: Science and Alien Intelligence,* edited by E. Regis, Jr. (Cambridge, Mass.: Cambridge University Press, 1985).

CHAPTER 13. *The Last First Contacts*

Bob Connolly's and Robin Anderson's book *First Contact* (New York: Viking Penguin, 1987) describes first contact in the New Guinea highlands through the eyes of both the whites and the New Guineans who met there. The quotation on page 229 is taken from their book. Other gripping accounts of first contacts and of precontact conditions include Don Richardson's *Peace Child* (Ventura: Regal Books, 1974) for the Sawi people of southwest New Guinea, and Napoleon A. Chagnon's *Yanomamo, The Fierce People,* 3rd edition (New York: Holt, Rinehart and Winston, 1983) for the Yanomamo Indians of Venezuela and Brazil. A good history of the exploration of New Guinea is by Gavin Souter, *New Guinea: The Last Unknown* (London: Angus and Robertson, 1963). The leaders of the Third Archbold Expedition describe their entrance into the Grand Valley of the Balim River in the report by Richard Archbold et al., "Results of the Archbold Expedition," *Bulletin of the American Museum of Natural History* 79: 197–288 (1942). Two accounts by earlier explorers who attempted to penetrate the mountains of New Guinea are by A. F. R. Wollaston, *Pygmies and Papuans* (London: Smith Elder, 1912), and A. S. Meek, *A Naturalist in Cannibal Land* (London: Fisher Unwin, 1913).

CHAPTER 14. *Accidental Conquerors*

Books that discuss plant as well as animal domestication in relation to the development of civilization include C. D. Darlington, *The Evolution of Man and Society* (New York: Simon and Schuster, 1969); Peter J. Ucko and G. W. Dimbleby, *The Domestication and Exploitation of Plants and Animals* (Chicago: Aldine, 1969); Erich Isaac, *Geography of Domestication* (Englewood Cliffs, N.J.: Prentice-Hall, 1970); and David R. Harris and Gordon C. Hillman, *Foraging and Farming* (London: Unwin Hyman, 1989).

References on animal domestication include S. Bokonyi, *History of Domestic Mammals in Central and Eastern Europe* (Budapest: Akademiai, 1974); S. J. M. Davis and F. R. Valla, "Evidence for domestication of the dog 12,000 years ago in the Natufian of Israel," *Nature* 276: 608–610 (1978); Juliet Clutton-Brock, "Man-made dogs," *Science* 197: 1340–1342 (1977), and *Domesticated Animals from Early Times* (London: British Museum of Natural History, 1981); Andrew Sherratt, "Plough and pastoralism: aspects of the secondary products revolution," pages 261–305 in a book edited by Ian Hodder et al., *Pattern of the Past* (Cambridge: Cambridge University Press, 1981); Stanley J. Olsen, *Origins of the Domestic Dog* (Tucson: University of Arizona Press, 1985); E. S. Wing, "Domestication of Andean mammals," pages 246–264 in a book edited by F. Vuilleumier and M. Monasterio, *High Altitude Tropical Biogeography* (New York: Oxford University Press, 1986); Simon N. J. Davis, *The Archaeology of Animals* (New Haven: Yale University Press, 1987); Dennis C. Turner and Patrick Bateson, *The Domestic Cat: The Biology of Its Behavior* (Cambridge: Cambridge University Press, 1988); and Wolf Herre and Manfred Rohrs, *Haustiere—zoologisch gesehen,* 2nd ed. (Stuttgart: Fischer, 1990).

Domestication specifically of the horse, and its importance, are the subjects of books by Frank G. Row, *The Indian and the Horse* (Norman: University of Oklahoma Press, 1955); Robin Law, *The Horse in West African History* (Oxford: Oxford University Press, 1980); and Matthew J. Kust, *Man and Horse in History* (Alexandria, Va.: Plutarch Press, 1983). The development of wheeled vehicles, including war chariots, is treated in books by M. A. Littauer and J. H. Crouwel, *Wheeled Vehicles and Ridden Animals in the Ancient Near East* (Leiden: Brill, 1979), and by Stuart Piggott, *The Earliest Wheeled Transport* (London: Thames and Hudson, 1983). Edward Shaughnessy describes the arrival of the horse and chariot in China in an article "Historical perspectives on the introduction of the chariot into China," *Harvard Journal of Asiatic Studies* 48: 189–237 (1988).

For general accounts of plant domestication, see Kent V. Flannery, "The origins of agriculture," *Annual Review of Anthropology* 2: 271–310 (1973); Charles B. Heiser, Jr., *Seed to Civilization,* new edition (Cambridge, Mass.: Harvard University Press, 1990), and *Of Plants and Peoples* (Norman: University of Oklahoma Press, 1985); David Rindos, *The Origins of Agriculture: An Evolutionary Perspective* (New York: Academic Press, 1984); and Hugh H. Iltis, "Maize evolution and agricultural origins," pages 195–213 in a book edited by T. R. Soderstrom et al., *Grass Systematics and Evolution* (Washington, D.C.: Smithsonian Institution Press, 1987). This and other papers by Iltis are a stimulating source of ideas about the differing ease of cereal domestication in the Old and New World.

Plant domestication specifically in the Old World is treated by Jane Renfrew, *Palaeoethnobotany* (New York: Columbia University Press, 1973), and by Daniel Zohary and Maria Hopf, *Domestication of Plants in the Old World* (Oxford: Clarendon Press, 1988). Corresponding accounts for the New World include Richard S. MacNeish, "The food-gathering and incipient agricultural stage of prehistoric Middle America," pages 413–426 in a book edited by Robert Wauchope and Robert C. West, *Handbook of Middle American Indians,* Volume 1: *Natural Environment and Early Cultures* (Austin: University of Texas Press, 1964); P. C. Mangelsdorf et al., "Origins of agriculture in Middle America," pages 427–445 in the just-cited book by Wauchope and West; D. Ugent, "The potato," *Science* 170: 1161–1166 (1970); C. B. Heiser, Jr., "Origins of some cultivated New World plants," *Annual Reviews of Ecology and Systematics* 10: 309–326 (1979); H. H. Iltis, "From teosinte to maize: the catastrophic sexual dismutation," *Science* 222: 886–894 (1983); William F. Keegan, *Emergent Horticultural Economies of the Eastern Woodlands* (Carbondale: Southern Illinois University, 1987); and B. D. Smith, "Origins of agriculture in eastern North America," *Science* 246: 1566–1571 (1989). Three pioneering books point out the asymmetrical intercontinental spread of diseases, pests, and weeds: William H. McNeill, *Plagues and Peoples* (Garden City, N.Y.: Anchor Press, 1976); and Alfred W. Crosby, *The Columbian Exchange: Biological and Cultural Consequences of 1492* (Westport: Greenwood Press, 1972), and *Ecological Imperialism: The Biological Expansion of Europe, 900–1900* (Cambridge: Cambridge University Press, 1986).

CHAPTER 15. *Horses, Hittites, and History*

Two stimulating, knowledgeable recent books summarizing the Indo-European problem are by Colin Renfrew, *Archaeology and Language* (Cambridge: Cambridge University Press, 1987), and J. P. Mallory, *In Search of the Indo-Europeans* (London: Thames and Hudson, 1989). For the reasons explained in my chapter 15, I agree with Mallory's conclusions, and disagree with Renfrew's, concerning the approximate time and place of proto-Indo-European origins.

An older but still useful comprehensive multiauthored book is by George Cardona et al., *Indo-European and Indo-Europeans* (Philadelphia: University of Pennsylvania Press, 1970). A journal titled (what else?) *The Journal of Indo-European Studies* is the main outlet for technical publication in this field.

The view that both Mallory and I find persuasive is supported in the writings of Marija Gimbutas, who is the author of four books in this field: *The Balts* (New York: Praeger, 1963), *The Slavs* (London: Thames and Hudson, 1971), *The Goddesses and Gods of Old Europe* (London: Thames and Hudson, 1982), and *The Language of the Goddess* (New York: Harper & Row, 1989). Gimbutas also described her work in chapters in the book by Cardona et al. cited above, in the books by Polomé and by Bernhard and Kandler-Pálsson cited below, and in the *Journal of Indo-European Studies* 1: 1–20 and 163–214 (1973), 5: 277–338 (1977), 8: 273–315 (1980), and 13: 185–201 (1985).

Books or monographs dealing with early Indo-European peoples themselves are by Emile Benveniste, *Indo-European Language and Society* (London: Faber and Faber, 1973); Edgar Polomé, *The Indo-Europeans in the Fourth and Third Millennia* (Ann Arbor: Karoma, 1982); Wolfram Bernhard and Anneliese Kandler-Pálsson, *Ethnogenese europäischer Völker* (Stuttgart: Fischer, 1986); and Wolfram Nagel, "Indogermanen und Alter Orient: Rückblick und Ausblick auf den Stand des Indogermanenproblems," *Mitteilungen der Deutschen Orient-Gesellschaft zu Berlin* 119: 157–213 (1987). Books on the languages themselves include those by Henrik Birnbaum and Jaan Puhvel, *Ancient Indo-European Dialects* (Berkeley: University of California Press, 1966); W. B. Lockwood, *Indo-European Philology* (London: Hutchinson, 1969); Norman Bird, *The Distribution of Indo-European Root Morphemes* (Wiesbaden: Harrassowitz, 1982); and Philip

Baldi, *An Introduction to the Indo-European Languages* (Carbondale: Southern Illinois University Press, 1983). Paul Friedrich's book *Proto-Indo-European Trees* (Chicago: University of Chicago Press, 1970) uses the evidence of tree names in an attempt to deduce the Indo-European homeland.

W. P. Lehmann and L. Zgusta provide and discuss a sample of reconstructed Proto-Indo-European in their chapter "Schleicher's tale after a century," pages 455–466 in *Studies in Diachronic, Synchronic, and Topological Linguistics,* edited by Bela Brogyany (Amsterdam: Benjamins, 1979). For a slightly altered version of their sample, see page 274 of this book.

The references to the domestication and importance of horses cited under Chapter 14 are also relevant to the role of horses in Indo-European expansion. Papers specifically on this subject are by David Anthony, "The 'Kurgan culture,' Indo-European origins and the domestication of the horse: a reconsideration," *Current Anthropology* 27: 291–313 (1986); and by David Anthony and Dorcas Brown, "The origins of horseback riding," *Antiquity* 65: 22–38 (1991).

CHAPTER 16. *In Black and White*

Three books providing general surveys of genocide are by Irving Horowitz, *Genocide: State Power and Mass Murder* (New Brunswick: Transaction Books, 1976); Leo Kuper, *The Pity of It All* (London: Gerald Duckworth, 1977); and Leo Kuper, *Genocide: Its Political Use in the 20th Century* (New Haven, Yale University Press, 1981). A gifted psychiatrist, Robert J. Lifton, has published studies of the psychological effects of genocide on its perpetrators and survivors, including *Death in Life: Survivors of Hiroshima* (New York: Random House, 1967) and *The Broken Connection* (New York: Simon and Schuster, 1979).

Books that describe the extermination of the Tasmanians and other native Australian groups include: N. J. B. Plomley, *Friendly Mission: The Tasmanian Journals and Papers of George Augustus Robinson 1829–1834* (Hobart: Tasmanian Historical Research Association, 1966); C. D. Rowley, *The Destruction of Aboriginal Society,* vol. 1 (Canberra: Australian National University Press, 1970); and Lyndall Ryan, *The Aboriginal Tasmanians* (St. Lucia: University of Queensland Press, 1981). Patricia Cobern's letter indignantly denying that Australian whites exterminated the Tasmanians has been reprinted as an appendix to the book by J. Peter White and James F. O'Connell, *A Prehistory of Australia, New Guinea, and Sahul* (New York: Academic Press, 1982).

Among the many books and articles detailing the extermination of American Indians by white settlers are: Wilcomb E. Washburn, "The moral and legal justification for dispossessing the Indians," pages 15–32 in a book edited by James Morton Smith, *Seventeenth Century America* (Chapel Hill:

University of North Carolina Press, 1959); Alvin M. Josephy, Jr., *The American Heritage Book of Indians* (New York: Simon and Schuster, 1961); Howard Peckham and Charles Gibson, *Attitudes of Colonial Powers Towards the American Indian* (Salt Lake City: University of Utah Press, 1969); Francis Jennings, *The Invasion of America: Indians, Colonialism, and the Cant of Conquest* (Chapel Hill: University of North Carolina Press, 1975); Wilcomb E. Washburn, *The Indian in America* (New York: Harper & Row, 1975); Arrell Morgan Gibson, *The American Indian, Prehistory to the Present* (Lexington, Mass.: Heath, 1980); and Wilbur H. Jacobs, *Dispossessing the American Indian* (Norman: University of Oklahoma Press, 1985). The extermination of the Yahi Indians, and the survival of Ishi, are the subjects of Theodora Kroeber's classic book *Ishi in Two Worlds: A Biography of the Last Wild Indian in North America* (Berkeley: University of California Press, 1961). The extermination of Brazil's Indians is treated by Sheldon Davis, *Victims of the Miracle* (Cambridge: Cambridge University Press, 1977).

Genocide under Stalin is described in books by Robert Conquest, including *The Harvest of Sorrow* (New York: Oxford University Press, 1986).

Accounts of murder and mass murder of animals by other animals of the same species are given by E. O. Wilson, *Sociobiology* (Cambridge, Mass: Harvard University Press, 1975); Cynthia Moss, *Portraits in the Wild,* 2nd ed. (Chicago: University of Chicago Press, 1982); and Jane Goodall, *The Chimpanzees of Gombe* (Cambridge, Mass.: Harvard University Press, 1986). Hans Kruuk's account of hyena murder that I quote is from his book *The Spotted Hyena: a Study of Predation and Social Behavior* (Chicago: University of Chicago Press, 1972).

CHAPTER 17. *The Golden Age That Never Was*

Extinctions of animals in the Late Pleistocene and Early Recent era are described comprehensively in a book edited by Paul Martin and Richard Klein, *Quaternary Extinctions* (Tucson: University of Arizona Press, 1984). For the history of deforestation, see John Perlin's book *A Forest Journey* (New York: Norton, 1989).

Comprehensive accounts of New Zealand's plants, animals, geology, and climate will be found in a book edited by G. Kuschel, *Biogeography and Ecology in New Zealand* (Hague: Junk, V. T., 1975). New Zealand extinctions are summarized in chapters 32–34 of the above-cited book by Martin and Klein. Atholl Anderson summarized our knowledge of moas in his book *Prodigious Birds* (Cambridge: Cambridge University Press, 1989). Moas are also the subject of a supplement to the *New Zealand Journal of Ecology,* vol. 12 (1989); see especially the articles by Richard Holdaway on pages 11–25, and by Ian Atkinson and R. M. Greenwood on pages 67–96. Other key articles relevant to moas are by G. Caughley, "The colonization of New Zealand by the Polynesians," *Journal of the Royal Society of New*

Zealand 18: 245–270 (1988), and by A. Anderson, "Mechanics of overkill in the extinction of New Zealand moas," *Journal of Archaeological Science* 16: 137–151 (1989).

Extinctions in Madagascar and Hawaii are described in Chapters 26 and 35 respectively of the above-cited book by Martin and Klein. The Henderson Island story is told by David Steadman and Storrs Olson, "Bird remains from an archaeological site on Henderson Island, South Pacific: man-caused extinctions on an 'uninhabited' island," *Proceedings of the National Academy of Sciences* 82: 6191–6195 (1985). See under suggested readings for Chapter 18 for accounts of extinctions in the Americas.

The grisly end of Easter Island civilization is recounted by Patrick V. Kirch in his book *The Evolution of the Polynesian Chiefdoms* (Cambridge: Cambridge University Press, 1984). Easter's deforestation was reconstructed by J. Flenley, "Stratigraphic evidence of environmental change on Easter Island," *Asian Perspectives* 22: 33–40 (1979), and by J. Flenley and S. King, "Late Quaternary pollen records from Easter Island," *Nature* 307: 47–50 (1984).

Some accounts of the rise and fall of Anasazi settlement at Chaco Canyon are: J. L. Betancourt and T. R. Van Devender, "Holocene vegetation in Chaco Canyon, New Mexico," *Science* 214: 656–658 (1981); M. L. Samuels and J. L. Betancourt, "Modeling the long-term effects of fuelwood harvests on pinyon-juniper woodlands," *Environmental Management* 6: 505–515 (1982); J. L. Betancourt et al., "Prehistoric long-distance transport of construction beams, Chaco Canyon, New Mexico," *American Antiquity* 51: 370–375 (1986); Kendrick Frazier, *People of Chaco: A Canyon and Its Culture* (New York: Norton, 1986); and Alden C. Hayes et al., *Archaeological Surveys of Chaco Canyon* (Albuquerque: University of New Mexico Press, 1987).

Everything that anyone would want to know about *Packrat Middens* is described in a book with that title by Julio Betancourt, Thomas Van Devender, and Paul Martin (Tucson: University of Arizona Press, 1990). In particular, Chapter 19 of that book analyzes the hyrax middens from Petra.

The possible link between environmental damage and the decline of Greek civilization is explored by K. O. Pope and T. H. van Andel, "Late Quaternary civilization and soil formation in the southern Argolid: its history, causes and archaeological implications," *Journal of Archaeological Science* 11: 281–306 (1984); T. H. van Andel et al., "Five thousand years of land use and abuse in the southern Argolid," *Hesperia* 55: 103–128 (1986); and C. Runnels and T. H. van Andel, "The evolution of settlement in the southern Argolid, Greece: an economic explanation," *Hesperia* 56: 303–334 (1987).

Books on the rise and fall of Maya civilization include those by T. Patrick Culbert, *The Classic Maya Collapse* (Albuquerque: University of New Mexico Press, 1973); Michael D. Coe, *The Maya*, 3rd. ed. (London: Thames and Hudson, 1984); Sylvanus G. Morley et al., *The Ancient Maya*, 4th ed. (Stanford: Stanford University Press, 1983); Charles Gallenkamp, *Maya: The*

Riddle and Rediscovery of a Lost Civilization, 3rd rev. ed. (New York: Viking Penguin, 1985); and Linda Schele and David Freidel, *A Forest of Kings* (New York: William Morrow, 1990).

For a comparative account of collapses of civilizations, see the book edited by Norman Yoffee and George L. Cowgill, *The Collapse of Ancient States and Civilizations* (Tucson: University of Arizona Press, 1988).

CHAPTER 18. *Blitzkrieg and Thanksgiving in the New World*

Three books provide good starting points and many references to the large, contentious literature on human settlement and extinctions of large animals in the New World. They are: the book by Paul Martin and Richard Klein cited under Chapter 17; Brian Fagan, *The Great Journey* (New York: Thames and Hudson, 1987); and Ronald C. Carlisle (editor), *Americans Before Columbus: Ice-Age Origins* (Ethnology Monograph No. 12, Department of Anthropology, University of Pittsburgh, 1988).

The blitzkrieg hypothesis was outlined by Paul Martin in his article "The discovery of America," *Science* 179: 969–974 (1973), and modeled mathematically by J. E. Mosimann and Martin in "Simulating overkill by Paleoindians," *American Scientist* 63: 304–313 (1975).

The series of articles that C. Vance Haynes, Jr., has published on Clovis culture and its origins include a chapter (pages 345–353) of the book by Martin and Klein (above), plus the following selected articles: "Fluted projectile points: their age and dispersion," *Science* 145: 1408–1413 (1961); "The Clovis culture," *Canadian Journal of Anthropology* 1: 115–121 (1980); and "Clovis origin update," *The Kiva* 52: 83–93 (1987).

For the simultaneous extinction of the Shasta ground sloth and Harrington's mountain goat, see J. I. Mead et al., "Extinction of Harrington's mountain goat," *Proceedings of the National Academy of Sciences* 83: 836–839 (1986). Critiques of pre-Clovis claims are provided by Roger Owen in a chapter "The Americas: the case against an Ice-Age human population," pages 517–563 in a book edited by Fred H. Smith and Frank Spencer, *The Origins of Modern Humans* (New York: Liss, 1984); by Dena Dincauze, "An archaeo-logical evaluation of the case for pre-Clovis occupations," in *Advances in World Archaeology* 3: 275–323 (1984); and by Thomas Lynch, "Glacial-age man in South America? A critical review," in *American Antiquity* 55: 12–36 (1990). Arguments in support of a pre-Clovis date for human occupation levels at Meadowcroft Rockshelter are summarized by James Adovasio in "Meadowcroft Rockshelter, 1973–1977: a synopsis," pages 97–131 in J. E. Ericson et al., *Peopling of the New World* (Los Altos, Calif.: Ballena Press, 1982), and in "Who are those guys?: some biased thoughts on the initial peopling of the New World," pages 45–61 in the above-cited *Americans Before Columbus: Ice-Age Origins,* edited by Ronald C. Carlisle. The first of several projected volumes with a detailed description of the Monte Verde site is by T. D. Dillehay, *Monte Verde: A Late Pleistocene Settlement in Chile,* Volume I: *Palaeoenvironment and Site Contexts* (Washington, D.C.: Smithsonian Institution Press, 1989).

Readers interested in keeping up on the story of the first Americans and the last mammoths will enjoy subscribing to a quarterly newspaper, *Mammoth Trumpet,* obtainable from the Center for the Study of the First Americans, Anthropology Department, Oregon State University, Corvallis, Ore., 97331.

CHAPTER 19. *The Second Cloud*

Species-by-species accounts of extinct and endangered species are contained in the Red Data Books published by the International Union for Conservation of Nature and Natural Resources (abbreviated IUCN). There are separate books for various groups of plants and animals, and separate books are also now appearing for different continents. Corresponding books for birds have been prepared by the International Council for Bird Preservation, abbreviated ICBP: Warren B. King, editor, *Endangered Birds of the World: The ICBP Red Data Book* (Washington, D.C.: Smithsonian Institution Press, 1981); and N. J. Collar and P. Andrew, *Birds to Watch: The ICBP World Checklist of Threatened Birds* (Cambridge: ICBP, 1988).

A summary and analysis of modern and Ice Age extinctions and their mechanisms are provided by my article "Historic extinctions: a Rosetta Stone for understanding prehistoric extinctions," pages 824–862 in the book *Quaternary Extinctions* by Martin and Klein, cited under Chapter 17. The problem of overlooked extinctions is discussed in my article "Extant unless proven extinct? Or extinct unless proven extant?" in *Conservation Biology* 1: 77–79 (1987). Terry Erwin estimates the total number of living species in a paper "Tropical forests: their richness in Coleoptera and other arthropod species," *The Coleopterists' Bulletin* 36: 74–75 (1982).

Further readings on Pleistocene and Early Recent extinctions are given under Chapters 17 and 18. In addition, Storrs Olson reviews extinctions of island birds in an article "Extinction on islands: man as a catastrophe," pages 50–53 of a book edited by David Western and Mary Pearl, *Conservation for the Twenty-first Century* (New York: Oxford University Press, 1989). Ian Atkinson's article on pages 54–75 of the same book, "Introduced animals and extinctions," summarizes the havoc wrought by rats and other pests.

EPILOGUE: *Nothing Learned, and Everything Forgotten?*

Many excellent books discuss the present and future of the extinction crisis and the other crises now facing humanity, their causes, and what to do about them. Among them are the following:

John J. Berger, *Restoring the Earth: How Americans are Working to Renew Our Damaged Environment* (New York: Knopf, 1985).

————, editor, *Environmental Restoration: Science and Strategies for Restoring the Earth* (Washington, D.C.: Island Press, 1990).

John Cairns, Jr., *Rehabilitating Damaged Ecosystems* (Boca Raton, Fl.: CRC Press, 1988).

John Cairns, Jr., K. L. Dickson, and E. E. Herricks, *Recovery and Restoration of Damaged Ecosystems* (Charlottesville: University Press of Virginia, 1977).

Anne and Paul Ehrlich, *Earth* (New York: Franklin Watts, 1987).

Paul and Anne Ehrlich, *Extinction* (New York: Random House, 1981).

————, *The Population Explosion* (New York: Simon and Schuster, 1990).

————, *Healing Earth* (New York: Addison Wesley, 1991).

Paul Ehrlich et al., *The Cold and the Dark* (New York: Norton, 1984).

D. Furguson and N. Furguson, *Sacred Cows at the Public Trough* (Bend, Ore.: Maverick Publications, 1983).

Suzanne Head and Robert Heinzman, editors, *Lessons of the Rainforest* (San Francisco: Sierra Club Books, 1990).

Jeffrey A. McNeely, *Economics and Biological Diversity* (Gland: International Union for the Conservation of Nature, 1988).

Jeffrey A. McNeeley et al., *Conserving the World's Biological Diversity* (Gland: International Union for the Conservation of Nature, 1990).

Norman Myers, *Conversion of Tropical Moist Forests* (Washington, D.C.: National Academy of Sciences, 1980).

————, *Gaia: An Atlas of Planet Management* (New York: Doubleday, 1984).

————, *The Primary Source* (New York: Norton, 1985).

Michael Oppenheimer and Robert Boyle, *Dead Heat: The Race against the Greenhouse Effect* (New York: Basic Books, 1990).

Walter V. Reid and Kenton R. Miller, *Keeping Options Alive: The Scientific Basis for Conserving Biodiversity* (Washington, D.C.: World Resources Institute, 1989).

Sharon L. Roan, *Ozone Crisis: The Fifteen-Year Evolution of a Sudden Global Emergency* (New York: Wiley, 1989).

Robin Russell Jones and Tom Wigley, editors, *Ozone Depletion: Health and Environmental Consequences* (New York: Wiley, 1989).

Steven H. Schneider, *Global Warming: Are We Entering the Greenhouse Century?* 2nd ed. (San Francisco: Sierra Club Books, 1990).

Michael E. Soulé, editor, *Conservation Biology: The Science of Scarcity and Diversity* (Sunderland, Mass.: Sinauer, 1986).

John Terborgh, *Where Have All the Birds Gone?* (Princeton: Princeton University Press, 1990).

E. O. Wilson, *Biophilia* (Cambridge, Mass.: Harvard University Press, 1984).

————, editor, *Biodiversity* (Washington, D.C.: National Academy Press, 1988).

Finally, readers interested enough to want to pursue further readings may also want suggestions about what to do to reduce the risk that our children's generation will be the one to go extinct. As I explained in the text, the average citizen can do a good deal, both by being active politically and by giving even modest amounts of money to conservation organizations. Here are the names, addresses, and telephone numbers of a few of the best-known and largest such organizations, among the many that are worthy of support:

Conservation International, 1015 Eighteenth Street NW, Suite 1000, Washington, D.C. 20036 (202-429-5660).

Defenders of Wildlife, 1244 Nineteenth Street NW, Washington, D.C. 20036 (202-659-9510).

Ducks Unlimited, 1 Waterfowl Way, Long Grove, IL 60047 (708-438-4300).

Environmental Defense Fund, 257 Park Avenue South, New York, NY 10010 (212-505-2100).

Friends of the Earth, 218 D Street SE, Washington, D.C. 20002 (202-544-2600).

Greenpeace, 436 U Street NW, Box 3720, Washington, D.C. 20007 (202-462-8817).

League of Conservation Voters, 1150 Connecticut Avenue NW, Washington, D.C. 20036 (202-785-8683).

National Audubon Society, 950 Third Avenue, New York, NY 10022 (212-546-9100).

National Resources Defense Council, 40 West Twentieth Street, New York, NY 10011 (212-727-2700).

Nature Conservancy, 1815 Lynn Street, Arlington, VA 22209 (703-841-5300).

Rainforest Action Network, 301 Broadway, Suite A, San Francisco, CA 94133 (415-398-4404).

Sierra Club, 730 Polk Street, San Francisco, CA 94109 (415-776-2211).

Trout Unlimited, 501 Church Street NE, Vienna, VA 22180 (703-281-1100).

Wilderness Society, 900 Seventeenth Street NW, Washington, D.C. 20006-2596 (202-833-2300).

World Wildlife Fund, National Headquarters, 1250 Twenty-Fourth Street NW, Suite 500, Washington, D.C. 20037 (202-223-8210).

Zero Population Growth, 1400 Sixteenth Street NW, Suite 320, Washington, D.C. 20036 (202-332-2200).

Index